The Housing Act 1996

AUSTRALIA
LBC Information Services
Brisbane • Sydney • Melbourne • Perth

CANADA
Carswell
Ottawa • Toronto • Calgary • Montreal • Vancouver

AGENTS:
Steimatzky's Agency Ltd., Tel Aviv;
N. M. Tripathi (Private) Ltd., Bombay;
Eastern Law House (Private) Ltd., Calcutta;
M.P.P. House, Bangalore;
Universal Book Traders, Delhi;
Aditya Books, Delhi;
MacMillan Shuppan KK, Tokyo;
Pakistan Law House, Karachi

The Housing Act 1996

with annotations by

Andrew Arden Q.C.
LL.B., Barrister

and

Caroline Hunter
B.A., Barrister,
Lecturer in Law,
University of Nottingham

LONDON
SWEET & MAXWELL
1996

Published in 1996 by
Sweet & Maxwell Limited of
100 Avenue Road
London NW3 3PF
Typeset by MFK Information Services Ltd,
Hitchin, Herts
Printed and bound in Great Britain by
Butler & Tanner Ltd, Frome and London

A CIP catalogue record for this book is available
from The British Library

ISBN 0–421–58670–2

CONTENTS

Preface to 1996 Housing Acts

Since 1979, housing law has undergone a revolution. The principal changes were, first, the introduction of security of tenure, right to buy and other "tenants' charter" provisions of the Housing Act 1980, as extended by the Housing and Building Control Act 1984, and secondly the substitution of assured protection for Rent Act protection in the private sector by the Housing Act 1988, and—in the same Act—the transfer to assured protection from secure for the tenants of registered housing associations, as well as measures for transferring stock from public to private ownership.

Other changes included the introduction of a new housing subsidy system in the 1980 Act, replaced by the Local Government and Housing Act 1989 at the same time as the introduction of the ring-fenced Housing Revenue Account (itself backed by new local government capital finance controls of general application), the "shorthold" concept in the private sector, initially as an exemption from Rent Act protection (1980) Act, subsequently from assured protection (1989 Act), and the growth of rights for long leaseholders (Landlord and Tenant Act 1987, Leasehold Reform, Housing and Urban Renewal Act 1993). Along the way, in 1985 the Housing Acts were consolidated, housing association funding was re-shaped by the 1988 Act, and grant aid for unfit and unsatisfactory housing—as it had evolved between 1964 and 1974—was reformed by the 1989 Act.

The two 1996 Acts touch most of these—and a number of other—areas. In broad outline, Pt. I of the Housing Act 1996 re-casts the so-called "quasi-public sector" from (principally) registered housing associations into a body of registered social landlords (designed to encourage local housing companies, but including existing registered associations). Part II strengthens the existing law on Houses in Multiple Occupation. Part III governs the private sector: its Chaps. I and III extend the rights of long leaseholders, by reference back to both the 1987 and the 1993 Acts (and to the Leasehold Reform Act 1967); Chap. II changes the emphasis of assured protection to make shortholds the presumptive norm (which accords with practice in the fully private sector, but alters it where landlords are registered associated). Part IV is concerned with housing benefit (and is of minor effect).

Part V represents a new direction in public housing, under the general heading of "Conduct of Tenants". Chapter I creates the "introductory" (originally, probationary) tenancy, as an adoptive exemption from full security, and is not dissimilar in kind from shorthold in that it permits the recovery of possession without any need for specific grounds. Chapter II extensively broadens the traditional "nuisance and annoyance" ground so as to include activity on and around estates and to make it easier to use, and introduces a new ground to enable possession to be recovered when one partner has left the home on account of the violence of the other. (Analogous changes are made to assured protection.) Chapter III facilitates injunctive relief, also designed to tackle anti-social behaviour on and around public sector estates.

Parts VI and VII should be read together. Part VI introduces a national allocation regime, designed (a) to eliminate access to public housing by categories of immigrant, and (b) to prevent the dominance of allocation to the homeless. Part VII restates the law of homelessness, with a number of changes, including (i) the exclusion of categories of immigrant, and (ii) the reduction of rights from the allocation of a permanent (or indefinite) home to accommodation which will be of limited duration (pending allocation under Pt. VI. Ironically, intervening case-law means that this may have served to have increased rather than, as intended, to have reduced the rights of the homeless).

Part I of the Housing Grants, Construction and Regeneration Act 1996 is designed to eliminate—in all but a small, residual category—entitlement to mandatory grant-aid; in addition, it introduces the "deferred action notice" to slow down the use of the unfitness and disrepair provisions of the Housing Act 1985. Part II comprises a statutory re-writing of construction law; Pt. III introduces the Architects' Registration Council in place of a number of boards and committees under the Architects (Registration) Act 1931; and, Pt. IV puts on a statutory basis the Single Regeneration Budget, which in recent years had come to replace such schemes as Estate Action and City Challenge. It also provides for relocation grants which may become available where clearance area action is taken under the Housing Act 1985.

Because the changes contained in these two Acts reflect such a wide range of housing policies, each Part has its own—in some cases extensive—Introduction (though both sets of annotations share this Preface). The above is a cursory identification of principal issues; readers' attention is invited to the individual Part Introductions for more (and more accurate) detail. We would like to take this opportunity, however, to express our thanks to a number of people who have helped, directly or indirectly, in the preparation of these annotations.

Our colleagues at Arden Chambers have commonly found themselves dragged into impromptu debate on the meaning of one or another clause (unusually at an extremely inconvenient time) and, in particular, Christopher Baker and Jonathan Manning made substantive contributions in relation to Pt. VII of the Housing Act. The Current Law team at Sweet & Maxwell provided swift and efficient support. We could not produce material (especially of such bulk) and keep abreast of the (large number of) changes as the Bills passed through Parliament, without the technical aid with which Sweet & Maxwell provides us over the range of our publications for them (including the Housing Encyclopedia and the Housing Law Reports).

Finally, we pay tribute to Emma (aged 4), and Thomas (aged 7) and Sophie (aged 4), who could probably have made more sense of the material than we have done and to whom it—and much else—is dedicated.

The law was stated as at July 31, 1996, although it was possible to add some subsequent cases, and we have scheduled at p. xxxv the commencement orders which were available by proof-stage.

Andrew Arden Q.C.
Arden Chambers,
59 Fleet Street,
London, EC4Y 1JU.

Caroline Hunter
Nottingham University
and
Arden Chambers.

September 30, 1996.

TABLE OF CASES

References are to the Introduction or the General Note to the specified section, Part or Schedule.

ix

Table of Cases

Table of Cases

Table of Cases

Table of Cases

Table of Cases

Table of Cases

Table of Cases

Table of Cases

TABLE OF STATUTES

References are to the Introduction of the General Note to the specified section, Part or Schedule.

TABLE OF STATUTORY INSTRUMENTS

References are to the Introduction of the General Note to the specified section, Part or Schedule.

TABLE OF SECTIONS IN FORCE

The following provisions of the Housing Act 1996 have been brought into force by commencement orders up to and including S.I. 1996 No. 2658 (C.76):

Provision	Date of Commencement	S.I.
s.1	01.10.96	1996 No. 2402
s.2(7), (8)	01.08.96	1996 No. 2048
s.2 (insofar as not already in force)	01.10.96	1996 No. 2402
s.3(2) (partially)	01.08.96	1996 No. 2048
s.3 (insofar as not already in force)	01.10.96	1996 No. 2048
s.4 (insofar as not already in force)	01.10.96	1996 No. 2048
s.5	01.08.96	1996 No. 2048
s.6 (insofar as not already in force)	01.10.96	1996 No. 2402
s.7 (partially)	01.08.96	1996 No. 2048
s.7 (insofar as not already in force)	01.10.96	1996 No. 2402
s.8	01.10.96	1996 No. 2402
s.9(3)	01.08.96	1996 No. 2048
s.9 (insofar as not already in force)	01.10.96	1996 No. 2402
s.10–15	01.10.96	1996 No. 2402
s.17	01.08.96	1996 No. 2048
s.18(2) and (7) (partially)	01.10.96	1996 No. 2402
s.20(3) (partially)	01.10.96	1996 No. 2402
s.21(3) (partially)	01.10.96	1996 No. 2402
ss.22 and 23	01.10.96	1996 No. 2048
s.24 (partially)	01.08.96	1996 No. 2048
s.25 (partially)	01.10.96	1996 No. 2402
s.27 (partially)	01.10.96	1996 No. 2402
s.28(3) (partially)	01.10.96	1996 No. 2402
s.28(4)	01.08.96	1996 No. 2048
s.29 (partially)	01.08.96	1996 No. 2048
ss.30–34	01.10.96	1996 No. 2402
s.36(1)–(6)	01.08.96	1996 No. 2048
s.36(7)	01.10.96	1996 No. 2402
ss.37–50	01.10.96	1996 No. 2402
s.51 (partially)	01.08.96	1996 No. 2048
ss.52–54	01.08.96	1996 No. 2048
s.55(1) (partially)	01.08.96	1996 No. 2048
s.55(1) (partially)	01.10.96	1996 No. 2402
s.55(2) and (3)	01.08.96	1996 No. 2048
ss.56–64	01.08.96	1996 No. 2048
s.65 (partially)	01.10.96	1996 No. 2402

Provision	Date of Commencement	S.I.
s.66 (partially)	01.10.96	1996 No. 2402
s.72 (partially)	01.10.96	1996 No. 2402
s.75 (partially)	01.10.96	1996 No. 2402
s.76	01.10.96	1996 No. 2402
s.77	01.10.96	1996 No. 2402
s.80(3)	01.10.96	1996 No. 2402
s.83(3) (partially)	23.08.96	1996 No. 2212
s.84	23.08.96	1996 No. 2212
s.86(4) and (5) (partially)	23.08.96	1996 No. 2212
s.88–91	23.08.96	1996 No. 2212
s.92 (partially)	23.08.96	1996 No. 2212
s.92 (insofar as not yet in force)	01.10.96	1996 No. 2212
s.93	23.08.96	1996 No. 2212
s.96 (partially)	23.08.96	1996 No. 2212
s.105	23.08.96	1996 No. 2212
s.106 (partially)	23.08.96	1996 No. 2212
ss.107–109	23.08.96	1996 No. 2212
ss.111–117	23.08.96	1996 No. 2212
s.119 (partially)	23.08.96	1996 No. 2212
s.129(3) and (4)	01.10.96	1996 No. 2402
s.135	01.10.96	1996 No. 2402
s.138(4) and (6)	01.10.96	1996 No. 2402
s.139	01.10.96	1996 No. 2402
s.140	01.10.96	1996 No. 2402
s.141(2) and (3)	01.10.96	1996 No. 2402
s.142	01.10.96	1996 No. 2402
s.143	01.10.96	1996 No. 2402
s.147 (partially)	01.10.96	1996 No. 2402
s.160(4) and (5)	01.10.96	1996 No. 2402
s.161(2) and (3) (partially)	01.10.96	1996 No. 2402
s.162(4) (partially)	01.10.96	1996 No. 2402
s.163(7) (partially)	01.10.96	1996 No. 2402
s.165(1), (2) and (5)	01.10.96	1996 No. 2402
s.167(3)–(5)	01.10.96	1996 No. 2402
s.167 (partially)	23.10.96	1996 No. 2658
s.169	01.10.96	1996 No. 2402
s.172	01.10.96	1996 No. 2402
s.174	01.10.96	1996 No. 2402
s.177(3)	01.10.96	1996 No. 2402
s.182	01.10.96	1996 No. 2402
s.183(2)	01.10.96	1996 No. 2402
s.185(2) and (3) (partially)	01.10.96	1996 No. 2402
s.189(2)–(4)	01.10.96	1996 No. 2402
s.194(6) (partially)	01.10.96	1996 No. 2402
s.198(4)–(7) (partially)	01.10.96	1996 No. 2402
s.199(5)	01.10.96	1996 No. 2402

Table of Sections in Force

Provision	Date of Commencement	S.I.
s.203(1), (2) and (7)	01.10.96	1996 No. 2402
s.207(4)–(6) (partially)	01.10.96	1996 No. 2402
s.210(2)	01.10.96	1996 No. 2402
s.215	01.10.96	1996 No. 2402
s.217	01.10.96	1996 No. 2402
s.218	01.10.96	1996 No. 2402
s.219	24.09.96	1996 No. 2402
s.220	24.09.96	1996 No. 2402
s.222 (partially)	24.09.96	1996 No. 2402
s.222 (partially)	01.10.96	1996 No. 2402
s.227 (partially)	24.09.96	1996 No. 2402
s.227 (partially)	01.10.96	1996 No. 2402

HOUSING ACT 1996*

(1996 c. 52)

Arrangement of Sections

Part I

Social rented sector

Chapter I

Registered social landlords

Chapter II

Disposal of land and related matters

Chapter III

Grants and other financial matters

---

* Annotations by Andrew Arden, Q.C., LL.B., Barrister, Caroline Hunter, B.A., Barrister, Lecturer in Law, University of Nottingham.

CHAPTER IV

GENERAL POWERS OF THE CORPORATION

CHAPTER V

MISCELLANEOUS AND GENERAL PROVISIONS

PART II

HOUSES IN MULTIPLE OCCUPATION

Registration schemes

Other amendments of Part XI of the Housing Act 1985

Common lodging houses

PART III

LANDLORD AND TENANT

CHAPTER I

TENANTS' RIGHTS

Forfeiture

Service charges

Appointment of manager

Right of first refusal

General legal advice

Part V

Conduct of tenants

Chapter I

Introductory tenancies

Chapter II

Repossession, &c.: secure and assured tenancies

Chapter III

Injunctions against anti-social behaviour

PART VI

ALLOCATION OF HOUSING ACCOMMODATION

Introductory

The housing register

The allocation scheme

Supplementary

PART VII

HOMELESSNESS

Homelessness and threatened homelessness

General functions in relation to homelessness or threatened homelessness

Application for assistance in case of homelessness or threatened homelessness

Eligibility for assistance

Interim duty to accommodate

PART VIII

MISCELLANEOUS AND GENERAL PROVISIONS

Miscellaneous

Final provisions

An Act to make provision about housing, including provision about the social rented sector, houses in multiple occupation, landlord and tenant matters, the administration of housing benefit, the conduct of tenants, the allocation of housing accommodation by local housing authorities and homelessness; and for connected purposes. [24th July 1996]

PARLIAMENTARY DEBATES
Hansard, H.C. Vol. 269, col. 902; Vol. 270, col. 647; Vol. 276, cols. 770, 913; Vol. 282, col. 33. H.L. Vol. 571, col. 1752; Vol. 572, cols. 560, 735, 1367, 1434, 1577, 1654, 1839, 1908; Vol. 573, cols.165, 256, 319, 390, 767, 802, 849, 1216; Vol. 574, cols. 12, 83, 298, 368, 446, 507, 837, 1289.

PART I

SOCIAL RENTED SECTOR

INTRODUCTION AND GENERAL NOTE TO PART I

One of the central planks of the drive to demunicipalise social housing is the extension of the range of bodies who build and manage social rented housing, including new and local, non-profit making "housing companies", with local authority and tenant involvement—but not control—to take on social housing (primarily by large-scale voluntary transfers of stock): see generally, Our Future Homes (White Paper, 1995), Chap. 4, and the linked D.O.E. Consultation Paper, More Choice in the Social Rented Sector (July 1995). The intention is to open up social rented housing to new types of landlord, and to allow companies and other bodies to compete with housing associations for funds for the provision of new social housing.

Such landlords will—along with housing associations—be termed "social landlords", and will be supervised by "the Corporation": see ss.2 *et seq*. The Corporation means—in England—the Housing Corporation, and in Wales, Housing for Wales: see s.56. The Corporation, accordingly, continues to expand.

The Corporation. The Corporation was originally the Housing Corporation, established by the Housing Act 1964 (c. 56) to promote and assist the development of "housing societies", to administer a scheme for the provision of housing by way of cost rent and co-ownership: the basis of the scheme was the power to make loans, intended to "pump prime" loans from the private sector, rather than grant or subsidy. Housing societies were non-profit making bodies, registered under the Industrial and Provident Societies Act 1893 (c. 39). The loan powers of the Housing Corporation were extended to housing associations by the Housing Finance Act 1972 (c. 47), s.77, meaning, for this purpose, that registration under what was by then the Industrial and Provident Societies Act 1965 (c. 12) was no longer a prerequisite.

The scheme was an extension of arrangements introduced under powers in the Housing Act 1961 (c. 65), which were designed to fill "the gap left between private enterprise providing houses largely for sale and local authorities erecting houses for letting with the aid of Exchequer subsidies" (National Federation of Housing Societies, Annual Report, 1961) and administered by the National Federation (later to become the National Federation of Housing Associations): see also Housing, Cmnd. 2050, 1963. The scheme as extended was considered too large for the National Federation, and the Housing Corporation was created to administer it instead.

The scheme as enlarged was not, however, a success (see, *e.g.* Voluntary Housing, Autumn 1973—"consensus of opinion ... that co-ownership, as it is known today, was no longer viable or administratively acceptable due mainly to the high level of interest rates ... "). Over the same period, there had been a rapid expansion in the activities of low cost, general family or special needs housing associations, much of it promoted and supported by local authorities (see now, below, s.22). Such associations had a long and honourable history: before 1919, when powers originating in the Housing of the Working Classes Acts 1885 and 1890 were still voluntary, and were not widely adopted by local authorities, they were the prime suppliers of "social housing" as that term has come to be—and continues to be—used. Their origins were to be found in the charitable trusts, founded and endowed by philanthropists and industrialists (and many of which remain active to the present day).

This growth was not without its problems. Even though by the end of the 1960s local authority loans to housing associations had grown to an excess of £26m, the only controls on their activities were those limited supervisory powers enjoyed by the Registrar of Friendly Societies and the Charity Commissioners, and such additional powers as local authority lenders might introduce under mortgage deed or other loan agreement (including for rate fund contribution by way of continuing, revenue subsidy where needed). Amongst the problems was the growth of the "fee-earning" associations, in which a group of building professionals and tradesmen, *e.g.* architect, surveyor, contractor, together with other professionals, including lawyers and accountants, would form the committee of an association and undertake all of its development activities, using these public funds to pay themselves for doing so.

This inevitably created a dangerous development arrangement, insofar as no individual or group had a client role, *i.e.* an interest in overseeing, or duty to oversee the development work of the association (whether new-build or improvement and/or conversion). Other abuses included failure to develop, which meant that public assets (land and/or finance) were too commonly left in disuse, and practices the effect of which was to use public assets in order to produce a development which could be passed quickly into the private sector and re-sold at a profit. (See, generally, Housing Associations, A Working Paper of the Central Housing Advisory Group, 1971; see also, Report on Housing Associations to the Greater London Council, 1983.)

In 1968, the Central Housing Advisory Committee (appointed under the Housing Act 1957 (c. 56), s.143, repealed by Housing Rents and Subsidies Act 1975 (c. 6), s.13 and Sched. 6) appointed the Cohen (Sub-)Committee to conduct a review which, *inter alia*, concluded that there was a need for an expansion of the role of the Corporation to include "the job of listing associations to qualify for public support", so as "to obviate the risk of the exploitation of assets brought into being with the aid of public funds" (see Cohen, Chap. 7, Summary).

In April, 1973, the White Paper, *Widening the Choice: The Next Steps in Housing* (Cmnd. 5280), declared the government's intentions: "The government believes that the trend towards a municipal monopoly of rented accommodation is unhealthy in itself ... The government therefore proposes to widen the range and choice of rented accommodation by the expansion of the voluntary housing movement ... The Corporation's new remit will in particular help housing associations to be active where housing conditions are worst and housing needs are greatest. It will seek out housing land and support housing associations in its purchase. It will promote similar opportunities for housing associations to purchase existing houses and to convert and improve them to a decent standard".

Against this background, the Housing Act 1974 (c. 44) contained provisions conferring on the Housing Corporation powers to register housing associations, and to monitor and regulate their activities, extending the power to investigate associations and to intervene in their affairs by the removal and appointment of committee members and otherwise. Only associations registered with the Housing Corporation would qualify for public funds, whether from central government or from local authorities. At that stage, while the Housing Corporation did not directly award grants, it approved development programmes for associations, which unlocked the award of funds; it also enjoyed powers of compulsory purchase, and extended powers of borrowing, lending to housing associations and guaranteeing their own borrowings.

By the Housing Act 1988 (c. 50), the award of central government funding was transferred—from April 1, 1989—to the Housing Corporation and to the new body (also created by the 1988 Act), Housing for Wales. (The term "the Corporation"—is statutorily used [see s.56, below]—and is used here—to mean both the Housing Corporation and Housing for Wales). "... In relation to housing associations" it has been said "it acts ... as promoter, banker, policeman, judge and executioner rolled into one" (Alder & Handy, *Housing Association Law* (2nd ed.), p. 214).

The 1988 Act also saw an expansion of the role of the Corporation, in a different direction. This Act (Pt. IV) conferred on "approved landlords" the right to acquire the freehold interest in dwellings owned by public landlords, pursuant to the "Tenants' Choice" scheme, and therefore subject to the overriding requirement of support from the tenants. (See now, below, Sched.18, para. 1, repealing Pt. IV in its entirety). An "approved landlord" is one who is approved by the Corporation: 1988, s.94. (While this has generally meant registered housing associations in practice, it is not a statutory requirement that approved landlords should be registered housing associations.)

In addition to the Tenants' Choice scheme, the term "approved landlord", meaning a landlord approved by the Corporation, also applies to that class of landlord to whom property transferred (likewise, subject to support from the tenants) from a local authority to a Housing Action Trust, under 1988, Pt. III, may subsequently be transferred, *i.e.* at the end of the life of the H.A.T. or at the end of a relevant phase of its activities: see 1988, s.79. (A landlord who was approved for Pt. IV purposes is automatically deemed to be approved for Pt. III purposes: *ibid.*).

Note

Although, therefore, there is much that is familiar, if not identical, to earlier housing association law, and although as such it is certain that some if not many of the earlier subordinate instruments filling out much of the detail of how this Part will operate in practice will be restated under this Part, the temptation to use such materials—and guidance under the previous law—in explanation or elaboration of this Part has been resisted, as (until the new details are available) these notes will quickly be not merely out of date in that respect but may actively tend to mislead (and, in the *interregnum*, may subsequently prove guilty of having raised false expectations). With very few exceptions (where earlier guidance or instrument is the only practicable way to explain an otherwise elliptical statutory expression), these notes (as those under Pt. VII, below, and those in the Housing Grants, Construction and Regeneration Act 1996 (c. 53)) are accordingly confined to the policy statements or publications already available, and the statutory provisions themselves.

CHAPTER I

REGISTERED SOCIAL LANDLORDS

Registration

The register of social landlords

1.—(1) The Corporation shall maintain a register of social landlords which shall be open to inspection at all reasonable times at the head office of the Corporation.

(2) On the commencement of this section every housing association which immediately before commencement was registered in the register kept by the Corporation under Part I of the Housing Associations Act 1985 shall be registered as a social landlord.

DEFINITIONS
"Corporation": s.56.
"housing association": s.230.

GENERAL NOTE
See Introduction to Pt. I, above.

In some cases (see s.6, below, see also Sched. 1, paras. 4, 23, 24), decisions of the Corporation may be appealed to the High Court. In such cases, the Court's jurisdiction is appellate, by way of rehearing: see notes to s.6, below. In other cases, however, and when what is in issue is a general or policy decision of the Corporation, while there is no appeal the Corporation will—as a statutory corporation—still be subject to the control of the High Court by way of judicial review, under R.S.C. Ord. 53, if it offends against principles of public or administrative law.

The linchpin of modern judicial review is the decision in *Associated Provincial Picture Houses v. Wednesbury Corporation* [1948] 1 K.B. 223, C.A., from which many of what remain the best-known propositions of administrative law still derive, *e.g.* the need to take all relevant considerations into account and to disregard the irrelevant, the obligation to act in good faith, the requirement that a body properly direct itself in law, and the "catch-all" or "fail-safe" restriction that a body must not reach a decision so perverse or absurd that no reasonable body—exercising the relevant function—could reach it.

The most recent revision of the principles was that rendered by Lord Diplock in *Council of Civil Services Unions v. Minister for the Civil Service* [1985] 1 A.C. 374, H.L., described by Lord Scarman in *Nottinghamshire C.C. v. Secretary of State for the Environment* [1986] 1 A.C. 249, H.L. as "classical", albeit not exhaustive, in which Lord Diplock classified grounds for intervention under the headings "illegality", "irrationality", and "procedural impropriety", the former importing proper direction of law, the second cross-referring to *Wednesbury* unreasonable, and the third embracing procedural requirements, whether statutory, or implied, and so incorporating the requirement to act fairly or, as it may be termed, in accordance with natural justice.

Of course, it is the Corporation which has been entrusted with decisions under this Part and, therefore, not only will the burden lie on anyone who seeks to challenge its decision (*Cannock Chase v. Kelly* [1978] 1 W.L.R. 1, C.A.) but it will be a difficult burden, to upset the very foundation of—or approach to—a decision as distinct from the issues of judgment and opinion, based on experience, which Parliament has entrusted to the Corporation: see, *e.g. In Re Puhlhofer* [1986] A.C. 484, H.L. If, however, a decision is shown to have been based on a particular state of affairs, then while their evaluation will be for the Corporation, whether or not they existed will be a matter into which the court can enquire: *Secretary of State for Education and Science v. Tameside M.B.C.* [1977] A.C. 1014, H.L.

The Corporation must act so as to promote and not to defeat the purposes of the legislation: *Padfield v. Minister of Agriculture, Fisheries & Food* [1968] A.C. 997, H.L., *Meade v. L.B. Haringey* [1979] 1 W.L.R. 637, C.A., *R. v. Tower Hamlets L.B.C., ex p. Chetnik Developments Ltd.* [1988] A.C. 858, H.L., *Crédit Suisse v. Allerdale M.B.C., Crédit Suisse v. L.B. Waltham Forest, The Times,* May 20, 1996, C.A. The Corporation must reach its own decision, rather than blindly adopt—or allow itself to be fettered by—the decision of another, *e.g.* a local authority, the Secretary of State, and must reach its own decision on each application, rather than reaching a blanket decision about a particular category of cases: *Stringer v. Minister of Housing and Local Government* [1970] 1 W.L.R. 1281, C.A., *British Oxygen Co. v. Minister of Technology* [1971] A.C. 610, H.L., *R. v. Eastleigh B.C., ex p. Betts* [1983] A.C. 610, H.L., *A.G., ex rel. Tilley v. Wandsworth L.B.C.* [1981] 1 W.L.R. 854, C.A.

The otherwise onerous obligation to consider each case on its own merits is leavened by the proposition—to be found in these cases—that a body discharging public duties, or reaching a decision subject to public law, may adopt a policy or a guideline as to how categories of decisions will be reached, provided there is room for exceptions to be made, or—put another way—they consider in each case whether or not it is appropriate to apply the policy.

The general principles may be found in a growing body of legal literature, ranging from the authoritative *Administrative Law*, Wade & Forsyth, 7th. ed., through the discursive *Judicial Review of Administrative Action*, de Smith, Woolf & Jowell, 5th. ed., to some excellent and readable brief summaries in works such as *Judicial Review Proceedings*, Manning, and *Judicial Review: Law and Procedure*, Gordon, 2nd. ed. See also Fordham's *Judicial Review Handbook* (1994, and accompanying loose-leaf update). Almost all of the substantial number of cases cited in the notes to Pt. VII, below, have been decisions in the judicial review jurisdiction; the notes to s.204, below, contain a further—and much fuller—statement of the principles on which judicial review may be available.

Subs. (1)

The Corporation is obliged to maintain a register of housing associations under s.3 of the Housing Associations Act 1985 (c. 69), which obligation is now replaced by the register of social landlords. The requirement that it is open to inspection is not new.

There is no explicit definition of "social landlord": references throughout the Act are to registered social landlords, meaning those which have been registered pursuant to Pt. I, Chap. I.

Subs. (2)

All housing associations registered immediately before the commencement of this Part are automatically to be registered as social landlords. As at the introduction of the Housing Bill, some 2,200 housing associations were so registered (*Hansard* (H.C.), Standing Committee G, First Sitting, February 6, 1996, col. 31, Minister for Local Government, Housing and Urban Regeneration [Mr Curry]), compared with some 2,400 registered by the end of March 1977 (by which time the initial task of registration was substantially completed: see 1977 Annual Report of the Housing Corporation) and 3,068 by the time of the Annual Report for 1980/81; by 1981/82, however, there had been a small decline to 3,020, and by 1982/83, a substantial decline to 2,721.

Housing Association. This has (ss.63, 230) the meaning given by the Housing Associations Act 1985, s.1 (which dates back to Housing Act 1935 (c. 40) in substantially the same form), as follows:

"(1) ... a society, body of trustees or company-
(a) which is established for the purpose of, or amongst whose objects or powers are included those of, providing, constructing, improving or managing, or facilitating or encouraging the construction or improvement of, housing accommodation, and
(b) which does not trade for profit or whose constitution or rules prohibit the issue of capital with interest or dividend exceeding such rate as may be prescribed by the Treasury, whether with or without differentiation as between share and loan capital."

See further, notes to s.2(2), below.

Eligibility for registration

2.—(1) A body is eligible for registration as a social landlord if it is—
(a) a registered charity which is a housing association,
(b) a society registered under the Industrial and Provident Societies Act 1965 which satisfies the conditions in subsection (2), or
(c) a company registered under the Companies Act 1985 which satisfies those conditions.

(2) The conditions are that the body is non-profit-making and is established for the purpose of, or has among its objects or powers, the provision, construction, improvement or management of—
(a) houses to be kept available for letting,
(b) houses for occupation by members of the body, where the rules of the body restrict membership to persons entitled or prospectively entitled (as tenants or otherwise) to occupy a house provided or managed by the body, or

(c) hostels,

and that any additional purposes or objects are among those specified in sub-section (4).

(3) For the purposes of this section a body is non-profit-making if—

(a) it does not trade for profit, or

(b) its constitution or rules prohibit the issue of capital with interest or dividend exceeding the rate prescribed by the Treasury for the purposes of section 1(1)(b) of the Housing Associations Act 1985.

(4) The permissible additional purposes or objects are—

(a) providing land, amenities or services, or providing, constructing, repairing or improving buildings, for its residents, either exclusively or together with other persons;

(b) acquiring, or repairing and improving, or creating by the conversion of houses or other property, houses to be disposed of on sale, on lease or on shared ownership terms;

(c) constructing houses to be disposed of on shared ownership terms;

(d) managing houses held on leases or other lettings (not being houses within subsection (2)(a) or (b)) or blocks of flats;

(e) providing services of any description for owners or occupiers of houses in arranging or carrying out works of maintenance, repair or improvement, or encouraging or facilitating the carrying out of such works;

(f) encouraging and giving advice on the forming of housing associations or providing services for, and giving advice on the running of, such associations and other voluntary organisations concerned with housing, or matters connected with housing.

(5) A body is not ineligible for registration as a social landlord by reason only that its powers include power—

(a) to acquire commercial premises or businesses as an incidental part of a project or series of projects undertaken for purposes or objects falling within subsection (2) or (4);

(b) to repair, improve or convert commercial premises acquired as mentioned in paragraph (a) or to carry on for a limited period any business so acquired;

(c) to repair or improve houses, or buildings in which houses are situated, after a disposal of the houses by the body by way of sale or lease or on shared ownership terms.

(6) In this section—

"block of flats" means a building containing two or more flats which are held on leases or other lettings and which are occupied or intended to be occupied wholly or mainly for residential purposes;

"disposed of on shared ownership terms" means disposed of on a lease—

(a) granted on a payment of a premium calculated by reference to a percentage of the value of the house or of the cost of providing it, or

(b) under which the tenant (or his personal representatives) will or may be entitled to a sum calculated by reference directly or indirectly to the value of the house;

"letting" includes the grant of a licence to occupy;

"residents", in relation to a body, means persons occupying a house or hostel provided or managed by the body; and

"voluntary organisation" means an organisation whose activities are not carried on for profit.

(7) The Secretary of State may by order specify permissible purposes, objects or powers additional to those specified in subsections (4) and (5).

The order may (without prejudice to the inclusion of other incidental or supplementary provisions) contain such provision as the Secretary of State thinks fit with respect to the priority of mortgages entered into in pursuance of any additional purposes, objects or powers.

(8) An order under subsection (7) shall be made by statutory instrument which shall be subject to annulment in pursuance of a resolution of either House of Parliament.

DEFINITIONS
"block of flats": subs. (6).
"hostel": s.63.
"house": s.63.
"housing association": s.230.
"letting": subs. (6).
"provision": s.63(2).
"registered charity": s.58.
"registration": s.1.
"resident": subs. (6).
"shared ownership terms": subs. (6).
"society": s.57.
"tenant": s.229.

GENERAL NOTE
It has long been (see, *e.g.* Cohen, 1971, Report to Greater London Council, 1983, Introduction to Pt. I, above) a matter for critical comment that the types of bodies qualifying as "housing associations" as the term is generally or statutorily used (see Housing Associations Act 1985, s.1, see note to s.1(2), above, see further notes to subs. (2), below) are so many and so varied—they can be societies registered under the Industrial and Provident Societies Act 1965, companies registered under the Companies Act 1985, and/or bodies (whether or not a society, company or trust) which qualify as a registered charity. The term housing association is defined, rather, by its purpose and objects (see notes to subs. (2), below).

This diversity is—in its application to the new, broader category of "social landlord"—unchanged: a social landlord may be a charity, an industrial and provident society or a company. In the case of a charity, it must also be a housing association (as defined in s.1, Housing Associations Act 1985), which imports similar conditions to those applied by subs. (2) below to the other two classes of landlord.

An individual cannot be a social landlord; nor can a partnership.

What all the bodies will necessarily have in common is that they are non-profit making: charities, because that is imported by s.1, Housing Associations Act 1985; societies and companies, because of the conditions of subs. (2). (See also subs. (3).)

Subs. (1)
This subsection replicates Housing Associations Act 1985, s.4(1), extended to include companies.

Registered charity. This means (s.58) a charity which is registered under s.3, Charities Act 1993, not being an exempt charity within the meaning of that Act.

"Charity" means any institution—corporate or not—established for charitable purposes, and which is subject to the control of the High Court (in the exercise of its jurisdiction over charities); Charities Act 1993, s.96(1). Of the four principal categories of charity (*Income Tax Special Purposes Commissioners v. Pemsel* [1891] A.C. 531, H.L.)—for the relief of poverty, for the advancement of education, for the advancement of religion, and for other purposes beneficial to the community—it is the last, and in some circumstances the first, which will be relevant (if at all) under this Act.

"Exempt charities" are (Charities Act 1993 (c. 10), s.96) those comprised in *ibid.*, Sched. 2, meaning—in general terms—most university and schools charities and certain national bodies, *e.g.* Victoria and Albert Museum, National Gallery, British Library, Church Commissioners. A society registered under the Industrial and Provident Societies Act 1965 is also exempt (Sched. 2(y)).

Society registered under the Industrial and Provident Societies Act 1965. Registration under the Industrial and Provident Societies Act 1965 requires (s.1(1)): (a) compliance with the formal and constitutional requirements of *ibid.*, Sched. 1, (b) location of the registered office pursuant to the rules of the society in Great Britain or the Channel Islands, and (c) compliance, to the satisfaction of the registrar, with one of two conditions, either that the society is a bona fide co-operative society, or that there are special reasons, in view of the fact that the society's business is being or will be conducted for the benefit of the community, why it should be registered under the 1965 Act rather than under the Companies Act 1985 (c. 6). A registered society is a body corporate, with limited liability: 1965, s.3.

Company registered under the Companies Act 1985, i.e. an incorporated body, with or without limited liability—1985, s.1(1). Note, however, that references in this Act to such a company which is also a registered charity, are *not* included save where expressly so provided, *i.e.* they are treated as registered charities, rather than registered companies: below, s.55(2). This is immediately relevant, as the additional requirements of subs. (2), below, need only be fulfilled on the part of 1965 Act societies and registered companies.

Subss. (2), (3)

This subsection is in the same terms as Housing Associations Act 1985, s.4(2).

This subsection contains the principal conditions which must be satisfied by societies registered under the Industrial and Provident Societies Act 1965 and companies registered under the Companies Act 1985 wishing to register as social landlords, but *not* by registered charities. Accordingly, the latter may have whatever purposes, objects and powers.

The *first*—and fundamental—requirement is that the body in question does not "trade for profit". This means that it must not trade for a profit for use and enjoyment, as distinct from raising profits on particular activities (or over a particular period) which have to be retained and re-employed for the purposes of the business or activity; the latter class of profit does not, accordingly, preclude qualification within this definition—see *Goodman v. Dolphin Square Trust* (1979) 38 P.&C.R. 257, C.A. A co-ownership housing association does not trade for profit when it makes equity share payments to its members: *R. v. Birmingham Housing Benefit Review Board, ex p. Ellery* (1989) 21 H.L.R. 398, Q.B.D.

A body is also to be considered non-profit making if, under its constitution, it cannot issue capital with interest or dividend exceeding the rate for the time being prescribed by the Treasury for the purposes of s.1(1)(b), Housing Associations Act 1985 (subs. (3)). This extension of the basic principle is designed "to provide cover for any existing registered association that may have the power to pay interest or dividend at the rate prescribed by the Treasury": (*Hansard* (H.C.), April 29, 1996, Report Stage, Minister for Local Government, Housing and Urban Regeneration [Mr Curry], col. 811).

The *second* requirement is that the body was *either* established for the purpose of, *or* has amongst its objects or powers the provision, construction, improvement or management of:

(a) houses to be kept available for letting, or
(b) houses for occupation by members of the body, or
(c) hostels.

(In all cases, "houses" includes flats or parts of other buildings occupied or intended to be occupied as a separate dwelling: see below, s.63(1). See *ibid.* for the definition of hostel.)

The second category—houses for occupation by members of the body—is only applicable if the rules of the body restrict membership to persons actually or prospectively entitled—whether as tenants or otherwise, *e.g.* long leaseholders, or else licensees—to occupy a house provided by the body. This incorporates the long-standing (see, *e.g.*, Housing Act 1964, s.1) definition covering co-operatives and co-ownerships—which can mean anything from a new-build co-ownership scheme, to a short-life arrangement in stock scheduled for demolition or redevelopment—although is not quite co-extensive with the definition in Housing Associations Act 1985, s.1(2) (and in Housing Act 1985, s.5(2)) of "fully mutual" housing association, as there is no requirement for the rules of the body to preclude the grant or assignment of tenancies to non-members: s.63(1). Thus, all members must be actual or prospective tenants, but not all tenants or other occupiers need be members.

The *third* requirement is that if there are any purposes or objects outside of those specified in subs. (2), they must fall within subs. (3).

This would seem to mean *express* purposes or objects, for all corporate bodies will have power to do those things which are reasonably incidental to the attainment or pursuit of their objects: see, *e.g. Rolled Steel v. British Steel Corporation* [1986] Ch. 246, C.A. See also *Halifax Building Society v. Chamberlain Martin Spurgeon, Halifax Building Society v. Meridian Housing Association* (1995) 27 H.L.R. 123, Ch.D.

Subs. (4)

This subsection is modelled on Housing Associations Act 1985, s.4(3), as amended by Housing Act 1988, s.48(1).

The permissible additional purposes or objects which may be pursued by a landlord wishing to register as a social landlord are those specified in this subsection:

(a) Providing land, amenities or services, for the occupiers of its houses or hostels, or providing, constructing, repairing or improving buildings for them: this permits the provision of all manner of resources or facilities to—even to the point of building new houses for—residents, whether exclusively for residents or whether also available to others (*e.g.* facilities for children or for the elderly, etc., which might mean recreational or care, and which might mean confined to the residents of its own stock, or might be available to others in the locality). So far as repairs and improvements are concerned, however, such services may be provided even to non-residents, under subs. (3)(e).

(b) Acquiring, repairing or improving, or converting, houses for outright sale, or for disposal by way of lease, *i.e.* long lease, or on shared ownership lease. The latter term is familiar to the housing association movement, and was familiar (if not much used) in relation to right to buy under Pt. V, Housing Act 1985, until replaced by the "rent to mortgage scheme" under Leasehold Reform, Housing and Urban Development Act 1993 (c. 28).

The definition of shared ownership lease (subs. (6)) is the same as under Housing Associations Act 1985, s.106.

(c) Houses may be specifically constructed for shared ownership disposal.

(d) Managing property, *i.e.* additional property, not already being managed by them pursuant to the body's principal purpose under subs. (2), whether other houses, flats or blocks of flats (see subs. (5)). This could include housing management put out to the private sector following competitive tendering under Local Government Act 1988, Pt. I.

(e) A body may carry on the business as repairs and maintenance (and improvement) contractors or facilitators, not merely for their own residents (see subs. (3)(a)) but for any owners or occupiers of housing. This could include building works put out to the private sector following competitive tendering under Local Government, Planning and Land Act 1980, Pt. III.

(f) A body may also carry on secondary housing association activities, *i.e.* promoting the formation of, or providing support to, associations, *e.g.* embryonic associations, or associations which are and will remain small, perhaps too small to merit employing their own full-time staff.

Subs. (5)

This subsection is modelled on Housing Associations Act 1985, s.4(4).

Provided that they are no more than *powers*, rather than *purposes*, a body is not precluded from registering as a social landlord because it has power to acquire commercial premises *incidental* to a principal activity (*e.g.* in the course of acquiring land for redevelopment) and then to repair, improve or convert premises so acquired or even to carry on the business for a limited time, or to repair or improve houses, or buildings with houses in them, which have been disposed of by way of sale, lease or on shared ownership (which may mean sale to previous tenants, or even directly to prospective tenants).

Subs. (7)

The permissible purposes, objects or powers may be extended by the Secretary of State, but not reduced.

Registration

3.—(1) The Corporation may register as a social landlord any body which is eligible for such registration.

(2) An application for registration shall be made in such manner, and shall be accompanied by such fee (if any), as the Corporation may determine.

(3) As soon as may be after registering a body as a social landlord the Corporation shall give notice of the registration—

    (a) in the case of a registered charity, to the Charity Commissioners,

    (b) in the case of an industrial and provident society, to the appropriate registrar, and

    (c) in the case of a company registered under the Companies Act 1985 (including such a company which is also a registered charity), to the registrar of companies,

who shall record the registration.

(4) A body which at any time is, or was, registered as a social landlord shall, for all purposes other than rectification of the register, be conclusively presumed to be, or to have been, at that time a body eligible for registration as a social landlord.

DEFINITIONS

    "appropriate registrar": s.57.

    "Corporation": s.56.

"register": s.1.
"registered charity": s.58.
"registration": s.1.

GENERAL NOTE

On the face of it, this section gives the Corporation absolute discretion whether or not to register a social landlord. Under s.5, below, however, it must establish registration criteria, which it must publish (and which it may vary), and to which it must have regard when deciding whether to register a landlord. Thus, if a body appears to qualify according to the criteria, and no explanation is available for a refusal to register, there will undoubtedly be a *prima facie* case for appeal against the decision under s.6, below.

Subs. (3)

The Charity Commissioners, the Registrar of Friendly Societies or the Registrar of Companies as the case may be, are to be notified of registration of a social landlord by the Corporation.

Removal from the register

4.—(1) A body which has been registered as a social landlord shall not be removed from the register except in accordance with this section.

(2) If it appears to the Corporation that a body which is on the register of social landlords—

(a) is no longer a body eligible for such registration, or

(b) has ceased to exist or does not operate,

the Corporation shall, after giving the body at least 14 days' notice, remove it from the register.

(3) In the case of a body which appears to the Corporation to have ceased to exist or not to operate, notice under subsection (2) shall be deemed to be given to the body if it is served at the address last known to the Corporation to be the principal place of business of the body.

(4) A body which is registered as a social landlord may request the Corporation to remove it from the register and the Corporation may do so, subject to the following provisions.

(5) Before removing a body from the register of social landlords under subsection (4) the Corporation shall consult the local authorities in whose area the body operates; and the Corporation shall also inform those authorities of its decision.

(6) As soon as may be after removing a body from the register of social landlords the Corporation shall give notice of the removal—

(a) in the case of a registered charity, to the Charity Commissioners,

(b) in the case of an industrial and provident society, to the appropriate registrar, and

(c) in the case of a company registered under the Companies Act 1985 (including such a company which is also a registered charity), to the registrar of companies,

who shall record the removal.

DEFINITIONS

"appropriate registrar": s.57.
"Corporation": s.56.
"register": s.1.
"registered charity": s.58.

GENERAL NOTE

This section permits the Corporation to remove a body from the register of social landlords in one of two circumstances: (a) it is no longer eligible for registration; or, (b) it has ceased to exist or does not operate. The Corporation must give the body a minimum of 14 days notice, in the latter case by serving the notice at the last address known to the Corporation as the principal place of business of the body. The power is based on Housing Associations Act 1985, s.6.

A registered social landlord may also ask to be removed from the register, but the Corporation has power to establish criteria to be satisfied where a body seeks to be removed, to which it must have regard when deciding whether or not to remove the body from the register: see notes to s.5, below. A decision to remove, or not to remove, under this section is appealable to the High Court, under s.6, below.

Subs. (2)
Loss of eligibility refers to the requirements of s.2, including the requirements, where applicable, as to purposes, objects and powers. De-registration may follow the use of the Corporation's extensive powers of inquiry under s.7 and Sched. 1, below. As to appeal against de-registration, see below, s.6.

Subs. (5)
Consultation: see notes to s.5, below.

Subs. (6)
On de-registration, the Corporation must notify the same persons as it was obliged to notify on registration: see notes to s.3(3), above.

Criteria for registration or removal from register

5.—(1) The Corporation shall establish (and may from time to time vary) criteria which should be satisfied by a body seeking registration as a social landlord; and in deciding whether to register a body the Corporation shall have regard to whether those criteria are met.

(2) The Corporation shall establish (and may from time to time vary) criteria which should be satisfied where such a body seeks to be removed from the register of social landlords; and in deciding whether to remove a body from the register the Corporation shall have regard to whether those criteria are met.

(3) Before establishing or varying any such criteria the Corporation shall consult such bodies representative of registered social landlords, and such bodies representative of local authorities, as it thinks fit.

(4) The Corporation shall publish the criteria for registration and the criteria for removal from the register in such manner as the Corporation considers appropriate for bringing the criteria to the notice of bodies representative of registered social landlords and bodies representative of local authorities.

DEFINITION
"Corporation": s.56.

GENERAL NOTE
The Corporation's discretion to register a landlord—and to comply with a request to remove a social landlord from the register—is governed by this section, which requires it to establish (and vary) criteria, to which the Corporation must have regard.

The current criteria, under Housing Associations Act 1985, s.5, are to be found in HAR/12, and impose requirements as to proper control by the managing body of an association, sound financial basis, adequate standards of development and housing management skills, and the intended role of the association in relation to needs in the area where it proposes to operate.

These, however, will need to be revised to take account of the changes, in particular the Housing Corporation may be expected to introduce criteria to ensure that local housing companies (see above, Introduction to Pt. I) do not—and cannot—fall within the categories of local authority controlled, and local authority influenced, companies, within the meaning of Local Government and Housing Act 1989 (c. 42), Pt. V and regulations thereunder: see More Choice in the Social Rented Sector, D.O.E. Consultation Paper, July 1995.

Subs. (1)
Although there is no obligation to give reasons for a refusal to register, where a landlord appears to fall within the criteria it may be that such a duty will be implied by law. In *R. v. Secretary of State for the Home Department, ex p. Doody et al.* [1994] 1 A.C. 531, H.L., the House of Lords confirmed that there is no general duty to give reasons for administrative decisions. This was, however, somewhat qualified by Lord Mustill's statement that "nevertheless it is broadly beyond question that such a duty may in appropriate circumstances be implied," endorsing the analysis of the factors material to the implication of such a duty to be found in *R. v. Civil Service Appeal Board, ex p. Cunningham* [1991] 4 All E.R. 310, *i.e.* where there is some-

thing in a decision which "cries out for some explanation", and where the absence of any explanation will support the inference that the reasoning is flawed or aberrant (see also *R. v. Higher Education Funding Council, ex p. Institute of Dental Surgery* [1994] 1 W.L.R. 242, Q.B.D.).

See further *R. v. R.B. Kensington and Chelsea, ex p. Grillo* (1995) 28 H.L.R. 94, C.A., in which it was said that while there is no general obligation on administrative authorities to give reasons for their decisions, such a duty may be implied in appropriate circumstances; including the nature of the adjudicating process and the facts of the particular case; the law needed to develop on a case by case basis and it was too early to formulate any general principle. Thus, in *R. v. Corporation of the City of London, ex p. Matson, The Times*, October 20, 1995, C.A., fairness and justice required the Court of Aldermen of the City of London to give reasons when deciding not to ratify the election of an alderman. See further notes to ss.203, 204, below.

Subs. (2)
"The terms of ... withdrawal must safeguard or recoup the public investment in the housing concerned and protect the interests of tenants ..." (More Choice in the Social Rented Sector, D.O.E. Consultation Paper, July 1995, para. 5.80).

Subs. (3)
Consultation. The obligation to consult is mandatory.
"... [T]he essence of consultation is the communication of a genuine invitation to give advice and a genuine consideration of that advice ... To achieve consultation sufficient information must be supplied by the consulting to the consulted party to enable it to tender helpful advice. Sufficient time must be given by the consulting to the consulted party. Sufficient, in that context, does not mean ample, but at least enough to enable the relevant purpose to be fulfilled. By helpful advice, in this context, I mean sufficiently informed and considered information or advice about aspects of the form or substance of the proposals, or their implications for the consulted party, being aspects material to the implementation of the proposal as to which the party consulted might have relevant information nor advice to offer" (*per* Webster J., *R. v. Secretary of State for Social Services, ex p. Association of Metropolitan Authorities* [1986] 1 W.L.R. 1 at p.4).

See also *R. v. Brent L.B.C., ex p. Gunning* (1985) 84 L.G.R. 168, *R. v. Warwickshire D.C., ex p. Bailey* [1991] C.O.D. 284.

Appeal against decision on removal

6.—(1) A body which is aggrieved by a decision of the Corporation—
(a) not to register it as a social landlord, or
(b) to remove or not to remove it from the register of social landlords,
may appeal against the decision to the High Court.

(2) If an appeal is brought against a decision relating to the removal of a body from the register, the Corporation shall not remove the body from the register until the appeal has been finally determined or is withdrawn.

(3) As soon as may be after an appeal is brought against a decision relating to the removal of a body from the register, the Corporation shall give notice of the appeal—
(a) in the case of a registered charity, to the Charity Commissioners,
(b) in the case of an industrial and provident society, to the appropriate registrar, and
(c) in the case of a company registered under the Companies Act 1985 (including such a company which is also a registered charity), to the registrar of companies.

DEFINITIONS
"appropriate registrar": s.57.
"Corporation": s.56.
"register": s.1.
"registered charity": s.58.

GENERAL NOTE
There is a right of appeal to the High Court against refusal to register, or against de-registration. In the latter case, the social landlord may remain on the register pending final determination of the appeal. As soon as an appeal has been brought, the Corporation must notify those (commissioners/registrars) who it is bound to notify on registration under s.3(3), and on de-

registration under s.4(6): see notes to s.3(3), above.

Appeal will lie under R.S.C. Ord. 55. As the grounds are *not* limited to points of law (*cf.* below, s.204), then full powers of rehearing are available to the High Court, which has extensive powers to receive new evidence, and reach any such decision as could have been reached by the Corporation: see Ord. 55, r. 7. The grounds, therefore, are not confined to those available on judicial review (see above, notes to s.1, see below, notes to s.204). While the Corporation is bound to be served with the Notice of Motion, it is not, on the face of the order, entitled to be heard. There is, however, ample power for the court to permit the Corporation to be heard, and indeed to be joined as a respondent: see *Dolphin Packaging Material v. Pensions Ombudsman*, High Court, November 10, 1993, Transcript; see also *S (A Minor) v. Special Educational Needs Tribunal* [1995] 1 W.L.R. 1627).

Regulation of registered social landlords

Regulation of registered social landlords

7. Schedule 1 has effect for the regulation of registered social landlords.
Part I relates to the control of payments to members and similar matters.
Part II relates to the constitution, change of rules, amalgamation or dissolution of a registered social landlord.
Part III relates to accounts and audit.
Part IV relates to inquiries into the affairs of a registered social landlord.

DEFINITION
"registered social landlord": s.1.

GENERAL NOTE
Schedule 1 contains a substantial body of control on registered social landlords, in terms of payments and benefits to committee members and officers (Pt. I), the Corporation's powers to replace committee members, directors and trustees, to petition for winding up (Pt. II), the audit and accounting requirements which are applicable (Pt. III), and the Corporation's powers of inquiry into the affairs of a registered social landlord, and related powers (Pt. IV).

For all of these purposes, "officer" means any trustee, secretary or treasurer of a charity, any treasurer, secretary, committee member, manager or servant of an industrial and provident society (see s.74, Industrial and Provident Societies Act 1965), or any director, manager or secretary of a company (see s.744, Companies Act 1985): see s.59, below.

The powers are modelled on, and largely analogous to, those to be found in Housing Associations Act 1985, ss.13–32.

It needs to be borne in mind, however, that these powers—extensive as they are—are not exhaustive. *In addition*, the Corporation has "monitoring powers" (s.30), power to determine performance standards (s.34), and power to issue management guidance (s.36), compliance with which it can be investigated by the Corporation (s.37), and non-compliance with which may be taken into account when deciding for the purposes of this section or otherwise whether action needs to be taken to secure the proper management of the affairs of a registered social landlord or whether there has been mismanagement (see s.36(7)).

CHAPTER II

DISPOSAL OF LAND AND RELATED MATTERS

Power of registered social landlord to dispose of land

Power of registered social landlord to dispose of land

8.—(1) A registered social landlord has power by virtue of this section and not otherwise to dispose, in such manner as it thinks fit, of land held by it.

(2) Section 39 of the Settled Land Act 1925 (disposal of land by trustees) does not apply to the disposal of land by a registered social landlord; and accordingly the disposal need not be for the best consideration in money that can reasonably be obtained.

Nothing in this subsection shall be taken to authorise any action on the part of a charity which would conflict with the trusts of the charity.

(3) This section has effect subject to section 9 (control by Corporation of land transactions).

DEFINITIONS
"Corporation": s.56.
"registered social landlord": s.1.

GENERAL NOTE
Although phrased permissively, this section, which is modelled on s.8, Housing Associations Act 1985, contains a statutory inhibition on the powers of a registered social landlord. All of the bodies which may qualify as registered social landlord will normally have power—expressly or implied—to dispose of land which they hold. This section overrides and replaces such express or implied powers. It is an important element in the control of land disposal by the Corporation, to be found in s.9, below. No consent is needed, however, if the disposal is pursuant to the right to buy under Housing Act 1985, or the preserved right to buy under Housing Act 1985, and to those enjoy the right to acquire under s.16 (see General Note to s.16, below): see s.10(3), below.

Subs. (1)
"Land" includes "buildings and other structures, land covered with water, and any estate, interest, easement, servitude or right in or over land": Interpretation Act 1978 (c. 30), Sched. 1.

Subs. (2)
Section 39, Settled Land Act 1925 (c. 18), governs the powers of a tenant for life and the trustees of a settlement so far as concerns land qualifying as settled land, and identifies the conditions on which settled land can be sold. By *ibid.*, s.29, s.39 is applicable to the trustees of a charity of a public trust. The conditions include a requirement to obtain the best consideration in money that can reasonably be obtained. The removal of the condition does not, however, authorise any action which would otherwise conflict with the trusts of a charity.

Without this section, registered social landlords which are charities would be unable to dispose of properties at a discount, even if otherwise so empowered by the Housing Corporation and even if the trusts of the charity so permit (as in *Joseph Rowntree Memorial Trust Housing Association v. Attorney-General* [1983] Ch. 159 leasehold dwellings for the elderly were held to fall within charitable objects even though in some circumstances leases might be assigned to people who were not elderly and so were outwith the purposes of the trust; the provision of housing by means other than rent is not *per se* non-charitable—the test is the relief of a socially worthy need).

Control by Corporation of land transactions

Consent required for disposal of land by registered social landlord

9.—(1) The consent of the Corporation, given by order under the seal of the Corporation, is required for any disposal of land by a registered social landlord under section 8.

(2) The consent of the Corporation may be so given—
  (a) generally to all registered social landlords or to a particular landlord or description of landlords;
  (b) in relation to particular land or in relation to a particular description of land,
and may be given subject to conditions.

(3) Before giving any consent other than a consent in relation to a particular landlord or particular land, the Corporation shall consult such bodies representative of registered social landlords as it thinks fit.

(4) A disposal of a house by a registered social landlord made without the consent required by this section is void unless—
  (a) the disposal is to an individual (or to two or more individuals),
  (b) the disposal does not extend to any other house, and
  (c) the landlord reasonably believes that the individual or individuals intend to use the house as their principal dwelling.

(5) Any other disposal by a registered social landlord which requires consent under this section is valid in favour of a person claiming under the landlord notwithstanding that that consent has not been given; and a person dealing with a registered social landlord, or with a person claiming under

such a landlord, shall not be concerned to see or inquire whether any such consent has been given.

(6) Where at the time of its removal from the register of social landlords a body owns land, this section continues to apply to that land after the removal as if the body concerned continued to be a registered social landlord.

(7) For the purposes of this section "disposal" means sale, lease, mortgage, charge or any other disposition.

(8) This section has effect subject to section 10 (lettings and other disposals not requiring consent of Corporation).

DEFINITIONS
"Corporation": s.56.
"house": s.63.
"registered social landlord": s.1.

GENERAL NOTE
This section is modelled on ss.9, 12 of the Housing Associations Act 1985.

The starting point is the requirement for the consent of the Corporation, under seal, for any disposal of land by a registered social landlord. Consent may be general or specific, whether in terms of landlords or land, and may be subject to conditions (subs. (2)). However, no consent is needed if the disposal falls within s.10, below, which includes disposals under the right to buy or right to acquire: see notes to s.8, above, s.16, below—s.10(3).

A disposal *of a house* is void, unless it falls within the category defined by subs. (4). In *Rosemary Simmons Memorial Housing Association v. United Dominions Trust* [1986] 1 W.L.R. 1440, 19 H.L.R. 108, Ch.D., a development including a house, staff flat, 40 self-contained units, gardener's bungalow, and a garage block, was held (unsurprisingly) not to be saved by the analogous, earlier provisions. The purpose of the provisions is to prevent any wholesale disposal being used as a device to escape controls (see also subs. (6)), so that, in substance, public monies have been used to pump-prime a private profit (*cf.* Introduction to Pt. I, above). Accordingly, *all* house disposals are void unless

(a) to one or more individuals, as distinct from corporations;
(b) only one house is involved in the disposal; and
(c) the landlord reasonably believes that the intention is for the purchaser or purchasers to use the property as his or their principal dwelling.

There is no definition of principal dwelling, but reliance may be placed on the (extensive) case law developed under corresponding security legislation, *i.e.* Leasehold Reform Act 1967 (c. 88), Housing Act 1985 (c. 68), Housing Act 1988 (c. 50), where the terms "only or main home" and "only or principal home" are used, as distinct from under the Rent Act 1977 (c. 42) where the criterion is use as "his residence" has long been construed to mean, in effect, use as "a" residence (There is, for these purposes, no distinction to be drawn between occupation as a home and as a residence: see *Crawley B.C. v. Sawyer* (1987) 20 H.L.R. 98, C.A.).

Any *other* disposal, *i.e.* of land which does not comprise the "disposal of a house" within subs. (4), is not invalidated by want of consent: subs. (5). Purchasers are accordingly protected.

Subs. (1)
"Land" includes "buildings and other structures, land covered with water, and any estate, interest, easement, servitude or right in or over land": Interpretation Act 1978, Sched. 1.

Subs. (3)
General consents require prior consultation: see notes to s.5, above.

Subs. (4)
Were it not for the statutory provisions of this and the previous sections, an *ultra vires* disposal by a registered social landlord would not necessarily be void. The position of such bodies is not to be equated to the position of local housing authorities, whose disposals contrary to their powers would be void (see *e.g. Rhyl U.D.C. v. Rhyl Amusements* [1959] 1 W.L.R. 465, see also *Crédit Suisse v. Allerdale B.C., Crédit Suisse v. L.B. Waltham Forest, The Times*, May 20, 1996, C.A.) but for any statutory saving (see Housing Act 1985, s.44, in largely the same terms as subs. (4) of this section). Where a private body (which term includes all of the bodies who are eligible to register as social landlord, *cf. Peabody Housing Association v. Green* (1978) 38 P.&C.R. 644, C.A.) is involved, then the questions which arise concern:

(a) whether the disposal is *intra vires* the powers of the body in question, even if incorrectly exercised, in which case the body will be bound by it (see *Rolled Steel Products v. British*

Steel Corporation [1986] 1 Ch. 246, C.A.—"... If a particular act ... is of a category which, on the true construction of the company's memorandum is *capable* of being performed as reasonably incidental to the attainment or pursuit of its objects, it will not be rendered *ultra vires* the company merely because in a particular instance its directors, in performing the act in its name, are in truth doing so for purposes other than those set out in its memorandum ..." *per* Slade L.J. at p.295/C–D); and

(b) what kind of body it is, for the purpose of considering whether s.9, European Communities Act 1972 (c. 68) (see Companies Act 1985, ss.35, 35A, 35B) applies so as to save the disposal in any event to (see also *Rosemary Simmons v. United Dominion Trust* [1986] 1 W.L.R. 1440, 19 H.L.R. 108, Ch.D. in which it was held that a society registered under the Industrial and Provident Societies Act 1965 did *not* so qualify).

Subs. (6)
Constraints continue to apply to land owned by a registered social landlord at the time of de-registration even after de-registration.

Subs. (7)
By s.14, an option to call for a disposal is treated as a disposal, if the disposal is a "relevant disposal" which is not an "exempted disposal": see notes to s.15, below.

Lettings and other disposals not requiring consent of Corporation

10.—(1) A letting by a registered social landlord does not require consent under section 9 if it is—

(a) a letting of land under an assured tenancy or an assured agricultural occupancy, or what would be an assured tenancy or an assured agricultural occupancy but for any of paragraphs 4 to 8, or paragraph 12(1)(h), of Schedule 1 to the Housing Act 1988, or

(b) a letting of land under a secure tenancy or what would be a secure tenancy but for any of paragraphs 2 to 12 of Schedule 1 to the Housing Act 1985.

(2) Consent under section 9 is not required in the case of a disposal to which section 81 or 133 of the Housing Act 1988 applies (certain disposals for which the consent of the Secretary of State is required).

(3) Consent under section 9 is not required for a disposal under Part V of the Housing Act 1985 (the right to buy) or under the right conferred by section 16 below (the right to acquire).

DEFINITIONS
"assured agricultural occupancy": s.230.
"assured tenancy": s.230.
"registered social landlord": s.1.
"secure tenancy": s.230.

GENERAL NOTE
There are, broadly, three classes of disposal under s.9, above, which do not require consent:
(a) Categories of Letting (subs. (1));
(b) Transferred Property (subs. (2)); and
(c) Right to buy/to acquire.

Subs. (1)

Categories of Letting
Assured Tenancies and Occupancies. Since the coming into force of the Housing Act 1988 (January 15, 1989) assured tenancies have been the usual form of letting in the wholly private sector, and by housing associations, replacing (i) Rent Act security for most private tenants, and (ii) Housing Act 1985 security for most housing association tenants (and in each case, Rent Act control of rents). There are exceptions (see Housing Act 1988, ss.34, 35), but these are confined to (transitional) cases where there is what might be called some "prior element", *e.g.* grants of new tenancies to tenants within the previous regime, in the same or other property: see next note. In the case of works in agriculture, living in tied accommodation, the prior regime of the Rent (Agriculture) Act 1976 (c. 80) was replaced by that of the "assured agricultural occupancy" under the 1988 Act (see, now, Pt. III, Chap. II, below).

There is a number of exceptions to status as an assured tenant or assured agricultural occupancy: see Sched. 1, Housing Act 1988. Assured *shorthold* tenancies do not, however, form an exception: while there are special provisions which govern them, they are none the less assured tenancies as it were in their own right (see 1988 Act, s.20(1): "... an assured shorthold tenancy is an assured tenancy which ..." complies with stated conditions. See, now, Pt. III, Chap. II, below). Accordingly, a letting of an assured shorthold tenancy is a letting of an assured tenancy, and within the general dispensation conferred by this section.

The *non*-assured lettings which are also within the dispensation are those within 1988 Act, Sched. 1, paras. 4–8 and 12(1)(h):

(a) Business lettings;
(b) Licensed premises;
(c) Tenancies of agricultural land;
(d) Tenancies of agricultural holdings;
(e) Student lettings; and
(f) Lettings by fully mutual housing associations (see notes to s.63, below).

Secure Tenancies. This is the regime applicable to—primarily—local authority lettings. It remains applicable to housing associations, however, in a small number of circumstances, to be found in 1988 Act, s.35, where:

(i) The contract for the tenancy preceded January 15, 1989 (which, evidently, is now unlikely to arise, although it is not *theoretically* impossible);
(ii) The tenancy is granted to a person who, alone or jointly with others, immediately before it was granted, was a secure tenant (which would import one of joint secure tenants), and it is granted by the same landlord;
(iii) The tenancy was granted as a result of proceedings for possession in relation to which the provision of suitable alternative accommodation was an element of the ground, and the court orders that the new tenancy is to be secure;
(iv) The tenancy is granted under the provisions of Housing Act 1985, Pt. XVI (repurchase of defective system-built housing).

There is no analogous provision, permitting a registered social landlord to grant a protected (Rent Act) tenancy, in those (few) circumstances analogous to s.35, 1988 Act, to be found in its s.34: this omission can be dealt with by a General Consent under s.8(2).

The *non*-secure lettings which are also within the dispensation are those within 1985 Act, Sched. 1, paras. 2–12:

(A) Categories of tied accommodation;
(B) Land acquired for development;
(C) Accommodation for homeless persons (but see now below, Sched. 17);
(D) Job mobility schemes;
(E) Sub-leasing schemes;
(F) Temporary relocation of tenants during major works;
(G) Agricultural holdings;
(H) Licensed premises;
(I) Student lettings;
(J) Business lettings;
(K) Almshouses.

Subs. (2)

Transferred Property

There is no requirement for consent when consent is *already* required for the disposal, pursuant to ss.81, 133, Housing Act 1988. The consent needed is that of the Secretary of State.

The first of these arises when a Housing Action Trust under 1988, Pt. III, which has taken over property from a local authority, then disposes of land (towards the end of its life or a particular stage of its activities) which is subject to a secure tenancy, to an "approved person" (see Introduction to Pt. I, above), which may well have been a housing association, which has now become a registered social landlord. In such a case, the conveyance to the approved person will have applied a requirement of consent from the Secretary of State before any further disposal (with certain exceptions, including those to be found in subs. (1), above). If such consent is obtained, there is no additional requirement for the consent of the Corporation under this section (or Act).

The second arises when the disposal *to* the registered social landlord was by a local authority, which will have needed the consent of the Secretary of State under either s.32 or s.43, Housing Act 1985. Unless that consent otherwise provides, then, by s.133, Housing Act 1988, it contains a similar restraint on further disposal without the consent of the Secretary of State (subject to the same exceptions to be found in s.81). Before giving that consent, the Secretary of State is bound to consult the Corporation if the Corporation's consent would otherwise be needed (see also below, Sched. 18, para. 8). If the Secretary of State's consent is given, then there is no need additionally to obtain the consent of the Corporation under this section.

Subs. (3)
Consent is not needed for disposals pursuant to right to buy under Housing Act 1985, Pt. V, or the right to acquire under s.16, below: see notes thereto.

Covenant for repayment of discount on disposal

11.—(1) Where on a disposal of a house by a registered social landlord, in accordance with a consent given by the Corporation under section 9, a discount has been given to the purchaser, and the consent does not provide otherwise, the conveyance, grant or assignment shall contain a covenant binding on the purchaser and his successors in title to the following effect.

(2) The covenant shall be to pay to the landlord on demand, if within a period of three years there is a relevant disposal which is not an exempted disposal (but if there is more than one such disposal then only on the first of them), an amount equal to the discount reduced by one-third for each complete year which has elapsed after the conveyance, grant or assignment and before the further disposal.

(3) The liability that may arise under the covenant is a charge on the house, taking effect as if it had been created by deed expressed to be by way of legal mortgage.

(4) A charge taking effect by virtue of this section is a land charge for the purposes of section 59 of the Land Registration Act 1925 notwithstanding subsection (5) of that section (exclusion of mortgages), and subsection (2) of that section applies accordingly with respect to its protection and realisation.

(5) Where there is a relevant disposal which is an exempted disposal by virtue of section 15(4)(d) or (e) (compulsory disposal or disposal of yard, garden, &c.)—

(a) the covenant required by this section is not binding on the person to whom the disposal is made or any successor in title of his, and

(b) the covenant and the charge taking effect by virtue of this section ceases to apply in relation to the property disposed of.

DEFINITIONS
"Corporation": s.56.
"disposal": s.9(7).
"exempted disposal": s.15.
"house": s.63.
"registered social landlord": s.1.
"relevant disposal": s.15.

GENERAL NOTE
This is the first of a number of sections modelled on the right to buy provisions of Housing Act 1985, Pt. V. For the background, see D.O.E. Consultation Paper, Proposals for a Purchase Grant Scheme for Housing Association Tenants, linked to the White Paper "Our Future Homes".

Secure tenants generally enjoy the right to buy under Pt. V, Housing Act 1985. Although tenants of housing associations with tenancies which pre-dated January 15, 1989 (or within the small category of lettings with a prior element—see notes to s.8(1), above) are secure, those whose landlords are or were charitable housing associations and trusts (see notes to s.2(2), above) have at all times been excluded from the right to buy (now, by 1985 Act, Sched. 5, para. 1).

Assured tenants—which is what the majority of the tenants of registered social landlords other than those whose tenancies began before January 15, 1989 (see notes to s.8(1), above) will be—do not have the right to buy under Pt. V, 1985 Act *unless* they are the former secure tenants of local authorities (or some other bodies within Pt. V); these assured tenants have a "preserved right to buy" (added to 1985 Act by Housing and Planning Act 1986 (c. 63)), but of course again this does not include the tenants of charitable housing associations and trusts who have at all times been excluded from the right to buy.

Assured tenants without the right to buy, or the preserved right to buy, who are housing association tenants, may none the less have been able to take advantage of the voluntary Tenants' Incentive Scheme to obtain a "portable discount" in order to buy in the private sector, and free up their rented dwelling; alternatively, Housing Corporation consent has been available for voluntary sales (by associations) to tenants, at a discount.

This Act introduces a new right to buy, distinguished from the right to buy and from the preserved right to buy by the designation "right to acquire" (see s.16, below). There are also the right to enfranchise under Leasehold Reform Act 1967, and the right to collective enfranchisement under Leasehold Reform, Housing and Urban Development Act 1993. (See further, Pt. III, Chap. III, below.)

Subs. (1)

This section is modelled on Housing Act 1985, s.155. It only applies where there has been:
(a) A disposal by a registered social landlord,
(b) Under a consent from the Corporation, and
(c) Subject to a discount.

"Discount" is not defined, but is not the discount which is applicable to the new right to acquire under s.16, below (see s.17) as such disposals are not subject to Corporation consent. This section is accordingly concerned with voluntary disposals, and does not apply if the consent in question otherwise provides.

Subs. (2)

The covenant requires repayment of discount, less one-third of it for each complete year following the disposal. The covenant is triggered by a disposal which is:
(a) A relevant disposal, which
(b) Is not an exempted disposal.

The covenant is, however, only triggered on the first disposal: once the discount (or appropriate proportion of it) has been repaid, there is no entitlement (on a further disposal) to a further recoupment.

The covenant is an incumbrance on the property, to be taken into account when valuing the property for tax purposes, *e.g.* in connection with inheritance tax: see *Alexander v. Commissioners of Inland Revenue* (1991) 23 H.L.R. 236, C.A.

Subss. (3), (4)

Liability under the covenant takes effect as a legal charge, and is a land charge within s.59, Land Registration Act 1925 (c. 21). It will accordingly bind successors in title, although once it is effected by a disposal (*i.e.* a relevant disposal which is not an exempted disposal), it ceases to bite (see subs. (2)).

Subs. (5)

If there is a relevant disposal which is an exempted disposal, the covenant is not effected and accordingly will continue to bind successors in title to the original covenantor. Where there is a relevant disposal which is an exempted disposal which falls within s.15(4)(d) or (e), the covenant does not bind the successor. Section 15(4)(d) is a compulsory purchase; s.15(4)(e) is the sale of a yard, garden, outhouse or appurtenance belonging to a house or usually enjoyed with it, within the definition of "house" by s.63, below.

Priority of charge for repayment of discount

12.—(1) The charge taking effect by virtue of section 11 (charge for repayment of discount) has priority immediately after any legal charge securing an amount—
(a) left outstanding by the purchaser, or
(b) advanced to him by an approved lending institution for the purpose of enabling him to acquire the interest disposed of on the first disposal, subject to the following provisions.

(2) An advance which is made for a purpose other than that mentioned in subsection (1)(b) and which is secured by a legal charge having priority to the charge taking effect by virtue of section 11, and any further advance which is so secured, shall rank in priority to that charge if, and only if, the registered social landlord by notice served on the institution concerned gives consent.

The landlord shall give consent if the purpose of the advance or further advance is an approved purpose.

(3) The registered social landlord may at any time by notice served on an

approved lending institution postpone the charge taking effect by virtue of section 11 to an advance or further advance which—

(a) is made to the purchaser by that institution, and

(b) is secured by a legal charge not having priority to that charge;

and the landlord shall serve such a notice if the purpose of the advance or further advance is an approved purpose.

(4) The covenant required by section 11 does not, by virtue of its binding successors in title of the purchaser, bind a person exercising rights under a charge having priority over the charge taking effect by virtue of that section, or a person deriving title under him.

A provision of the conveyance, grant or assignment, or of a collateral agreement, is void in so far as it purports to authorise a forfeiture, or to impose a penalty or disability, in the event of any such person failing to comply with that covenant.

(5) In this section "approved lending institution" means—

(a) a building society, bank, insurance company or friendly society,

(b) the Corporation, or

(c) any body specified, or of a class or description specified, in an order made under section 156 of the Housing Act 1985 (which makes corresponding provision in relation to disposals in pursuance of the right to buy).

(6) The following are "approved purposes" for the purposes of this section—

(a) to enable the purchaser to defray, or to defray on his behalf, any of the following—

(i) the cost of any works to the house,

(ii) any service charge payable in respect of the house for works, whether or not to the house, and

(iii) any service charge or other amount payable in respect of the house for insurance, whether or not of the house, and

(b) to enable the purchaser to discharge, or to discharge on his behalf, any of the following—

(i) so much as is still outstanding of any advance or further advance which ranks in priority to the charge taking effect by virtue of section 11,

(ii) any arrears of interest on such an advance or further advance, and

(iii) any costs and expenses incurred in enforcing payment of any such interest, or repayment (in whole or in part) of any such advance or further advance.

In this subsection "service charge" has the meaning given by section 621A of the Housing Act 1985.

(7) Where different parts of an advance or further advance are made for different purposes, each of those parts shall be regarded as a separate advance or further advance for the purposes of this section.

DEFINITIONS

"approved lending institution": subs. (5).

"approved purpose": subs. (6).

"Corporation": s.56.

"registered social landlord": s.1.

GENERAL NOTE

This section governs the priority of the repayment covenant defined by s.11, above. It is modelled on s.156, Housing Act 1985. The provisions of this section apply only to disposals subject to a Corporation consent, *i.e.* a voluntary scheme.

Despite the length of the section, the provisions are relatively straightforward. The repayment covenant has priority behind any charge securing the purchase itself, *i.e.* left outstanding by the purchaser or advanced by "an approved lending institution" (subs. (1)). Any other charge, even if otherwise in priority, only takes priority if the registered social landlord consents, which it is bound to do if the charge is to secure an advance for "an approved purpose" (subs. (2)): the effect of this formulation is to add (approved purposes) to the category taking priority. Likewise, the landlord must postpone its charge to an advance or further advance from an approved lending institution if for an approved purpose, and may do so if not for an approved purpose (subs. (3)).

Where the covenant takes priority behind another charge, it does not bind the beneficiary of the charge, or a person claiming under him, *i.e.* a purchaser, and any provision purporting to authorise a forfeiture or impose a penalty for non-compliance with the covenant in such circumstances is *per se* void (subs. (4)).

Subss. (2), (3)

Subsection (2) deals with charges which *precede* the repayment covenant, which lose their priority without the consent of the landlord, which consent must be given if for an approved purpose; subs. (3) deals with charges which *follow* the repayment covenant, but which may take priority over it with the consent of the landlord, which consent must be given if for an approved purpose. While the subs. (2) preservation of priority can apply to any lending institution, the subs. (3) grant of priority is only available to an approved lending institution.

Subs. (5)

Although building society, bank, insurance company and friendly society are all defined under the Housing Act 1985, s.622, by reference to, respectively, the Building Societies Act 1986 (c. 53), the Banking Act 1987 (c. 16) (and the former Protection of Depositors Act 1963 (c. 22)), the Insurance Companies Act 1982 (c. 50), and the Friendly Societies Act 1974 (c. 46) (and earlier legislation) (and see now the Friendly Societies Act 1992 (c. 40)), there is neither express definition nor statutory incorporation in this Act: none the less, there can be little doubt that the same definitions will apply. See also Pt. III of the Banking Act 1987 prohibiting the use of the term "bank", except by an authorised institution under that Act and the Insurance Companies Act 1982 prohibiting the carrying on of insurance business except as authorised by that Act.

In addition to these bodies, the Corporation itself is an approved lending institution, and so is any body approved for the purposes of s.156, Housing Act 1985.

Subs. (6)

The approved purposes relate to (a) works to the property, (b) service charges, (c) insurance costs in respect of the house—even if not of the house, (d) discharge of an existing priority charge, (e) arrears of interest on an existing priority charge, and (f) costs incurred in respect of enforcement of existing priority charges. The latter group is designed to permit the substitution of a new mortgage; the former, to meet outgoings on the property, not least those resulting from service charges. This reflects the major problem of high service charges on blocks of flats which caused significant concern in the early 1990s, sometimes leading to charges which exceeded the (not uncommonly *falling*) value of the dwellings themselves.

Service Charge: this means (Housing Act 1985, s.621A(1), added by Housing and Planning Act 1986, Sched. 5, para. 9)

"an amount payable by a purchaser or lessee of premises—

(a) which is payable, directly or indirectly, for services, repairs, maintenance or insurance or the vendor's or lessor's costs of management, and

(b) the whole or part of which varies or may vary according to the relevant costs".

Relevant costs are those incurred or to be incurred by or on behalf of the person who pays for them, *i.e.* landlord or vendor, or a superior landlord, in connection with the items specified in s.621A(1), whether or not in the period for which they are incurred, including overheads. See also Landlord and Tenant Act 1985 (c. 70), s.18. The costs are exactly that, costs without any element of profit "markup": *Regis Property Co. v. Dudley* [1959] A.C. 370, H.L. The practical effect, however, is overcome by the express inclusion of "overheads" and "management". See also *Russell v. Laimond Properties* (1983) 269 E.G. 49, treating costs as money laid out, as distinct from lost revenue or income.

Service charges only include repairs and maintenance, not improvements: *Sutton (Hastoe) Housing Association v. Williams* (1988) 20 H.L.R. 321, C.A. However, "works" in subs. (6)(a)(i) is clearly wide enough to include improvements, although probably not, in context, wide enough to cover a fixed charge (for services) which is *not* variable and, as such, not within the definition of service charge (see *Coventry C.C. v. Cole* (1993) 25 H.L.R. 555, C.A.).

Restriction on disposal of houses in National Parks, &c.

13.—(1) On the disposal by a registered social landlord, in accordance with a consent given by the Corporation under section 9, of a house situated in—

    (a) a National Park,

    (b) an area designated under section 87 of the National Parks and Access to the Countryside Act 1949 as an area of outstanding natural beauty, or

    (c) an area designated as a rural area by order under section 157 of the Housing Act 1985,

the conveyance, grant or assignment may (unless it contains a condition of a kind mentioned in section 33(2)(b) or (c) of the Housing Act 1985 (right of pre-emption or restriction on assignment)) contain a covenant to the following effect limiting the freedom of the purchaser (including any successor in title of his and any person deriving title under him or such a successor) to dispose of the house.

(2) The limitation is that until such time (if any) as may be notified in writing by the registered social landlord to the purchaser or a successor in title of his, there will be no relevant disposal which is not an exempted disposal without the written consent of the landlord.

(3) That consent shall not be withheld if the person to whom the disposal is made (or, if it is made to more than one person, at least one of them) has, throughout the period of three years immediately preceding the application for consent—

    (a) had his place of work in a region designated by order under section 157(3) of the Housing Act 1985 which, or part of which, is comprised in the National Park or area concerned, or

    (b) had his only or principal home in such a region,

or if he has had the one in part or parts of that period and the other in the remainder.

The region need not have been the same throughout the period.

(4) A disposal in breach of such a covenant as is mentioned above is void.

(5) The limitation imposed by such a covenant is a local land charge and, if the land is registered under the Land Registration Act 1925, the Chief Land Registrar shall enter the appropriate restriction on the register of title as if an application to that effect had been made under section 58 of that Act.

(6) In this section "purchaser" means the person acquiring the interest disposed of by the first disposal.

(7) Where there is a relevant disposal which is an exempted disposal by virtue of section 15(4)(d) or (e) (compulsory disposal or disposal of yard, garden, &c.), any such covenant as is mentioned in this section ceases to apply in relation to the property disposed of.

DEFINITIONS

    "exempted disposal": s.15.

    "house": s.63.

    "registered social landlord": s.1.

    "relevant disposal": s.15.

GENERAL NOTE

This section is modelled on Housing Act 1985, s.157. The section applies only to disposals subject to a Corporation consent, *i.e.* a voluntary scheme.

It permits the inclusion of a covenant restricting the category of purchaser to whom a property in a National Park, area of outstanding natural beauty or Housing Act 1985 designated rural area may be conveyed, assigned or sub-let by the grant of a lease or tenancy. Such a covenant is an alternative to a pre-emption condition or an outright prohibition on assignment or sub-letting; pre-emption for this purpose means a condition that before any sale, assignment or grant the owner offers to sell or lease the land to the vendor, and allows the vendor one month to refuse or accept the offer (see Housing Act 1985, s.33).

The covenant is that there will be no relevant disposal which is not an exempted disposal without the consent of the landlord, which consent is not to be withheld if the person to whom the disposal is to be made (or if more than one, at least one of them) qualifies under subs. (3), *i.e.* has lived (as to "only or principal home", see notes to s.9(3), above) or worked in or around the area in question for the previous three years (or has partly so lived and partly so worked. The region in which he has lived and/or worked must be a region which or part of which is comprised in the area in which the house is situated, but if there is more than one such region applicable to the area in question, it need not have been the same region throughout).

The intention is to prevent acquisitions from registered social landlords finding their way into use as second homes. The covenant binds any successor or person claiming under the purchaser, *i.e.* who qualifies on the basis of work or residence, or who takes under an exempted disposal, or to the disposal to whom the landlord voluntarily consents (subs. (1)). Any other disposal will be void: subs. (4).

Subs. (4)
A disposal in breach of the covenant is void. For this purpose, disposal includes the grant of an option allowing the grantee to call for a relevant disposal which is not an exempted disposal (as to which, see s.15, below): s.14(1). However, consent to the grant of such an option would be treated as consent to the disposal itself (s.14(2)).

Subs. (5)
The covenant is to be protected under Land Registration Act 1925, s.58, which means that the landlord will receive notification prior to any transfer. This follows the precedent set by 1985 Act, s.157, as local land charges are not normally protected on the register, and never by restriction under 1925 Act, s.58.

Subs. (7)
If there is a relevant disposal which is an exempted disposal, the covenant will continue to bind successors in title to the original covenantor. Where there is a relevant disposal which is an exempted disposal which falls within s.15(4)(d) or (e), however, the covenant ceases to apply in relation to the property disposed of. Section 15(4)(d) is a compulsory purchase; s.15(4)(e) is the sale of a yard, garden, outhouse or appurtenance belonging to a house or usually enjoyed with it, within the definition of "house" by s.62, below.

Treatment of options

14.—(1) For the purposes of sections 9 to 13 the grant of an option enabling a person to call for a relevant disposal which is not an exempted disposal shall be treated as such a disposal made to him.

(2) For the purposes of section 13(2) (requirement of consent to disposal of house in National Park, &c.) consent to such a grant shall be treated as consent to a disposal made in pursuance of the option.

GENERAL NOTE
See notes to ss.9–13, above.

Relevant and exempted disposals

15.—(1) In sections 11 to 14 the expression "relevant disposal which is not an exempted disposal" shall be construed as follows.

(2) A disposal, whether of the whole or part of the house, is a relevant disposal if it is—
(a) a conveyance of the freehold or an assignment of the lease, or
(b) the grant of a lease or sub-lease (other than a mortgage term) for a term of more than 21 years otherwise than at a rack-rent.
(3) For the purposes of subsection (2)(b) it shall be assumed—
(a) that any option to renew or extend a lease or sub-lease, whether or not forming part of a series of options, is exercised, and
(b) that any option to terminate a lease or sub-lease is not exercised.
(4) A disposal is an exempted disposal if—
(a) it is a disposal of the whole of the house and a conveyance of the freehold or an assignment of the lease and the person or each of the persons to whom it is made is a qualifying person (as defined in subsection (5));
(b) it is a vesting of the whole of the house in a person taking under a will or on an intestacy;

(c) it is a disposal of the whole of the house in pursuance of any such order as is mentioned in subsection (6);

(d) it is a compulsory disposal (as defined in subsection (7));

(e) the property disposed of is a yard, garden, outhouses or appurtenances belonging to a house or usually enjoyed with it.

(5) For the purposes of subsection (4)(a) a person is a qualifying person in relation to a disposal if—

(a) he is the person or one of the persons by whom the disposal is made,

(b) he is the spouse or a former spouse of that person or one of those persons, or

(c) he is a member of the family of that person or one of those persons and has resided with him throughout the period of twelve months ending with the disposal.

(6) The orders referred to in subsection (4)(c) are orders under—

(a) section 24 or 24A of the Matrimonial Causes Act 1973 (property adjustment orders or orders for the sale of property in connection with matrimonial proceedings);

(b) section 2 of the Inheritance (Provision for Family and Dependants) Act 1975 (orders as to financial provision to be made from estate);

(c) section 17 of the Matrimonial and Family Proceedings Act 1984 (property adjustment orders or orders for the sale of property after overseas divorce, &c.); or

(d) paragraph 1 of Schedule 1 to the Children Act 1989 (orders for financial relief against parents).

(7) For the purposes of subsection (4)(d) a compulsory disposal is a disposal of property which is acquired compulsorily, or is acquired by a person who has made or would have made, or for whom another person has made or would have made, a compulsory purchase order authorising its compulsory purchase for the purposes for which it is acquired.

DEFINITIONS

"disposal": subs. (2).

"house": s.63.

"lease": s.229.

"member of the family": s.62.

GENERAL NOTE

This section is modelled on the Housing Act 1985, ss.159, 160.

This section defines the disposals which will, *prima facie*, attract repayment of discount under s.11, above, or which will vitiate a disposal in contravention of a restrictive covenant under s.13, above, *unless* the relevant disposal is also an exempted disposal.

The provisions of this section apply only to disposals subject to a Corporation consent, *i.e.* a voluntary scheme.

Subss. (2), (3)

A conveyance of the freehold is a relevant disposal, as is the assignment of the lease which has been acquired; so also is the grant of a lease (by a freeholder) or sub-lease (by a lessee)—excluding a lease or sub-lease by way of mortgage—for a term of more than 21 years otherwise than at a rack-rent, *i.e.* otherwise than at its full rental value. Conventional tenancies, accordingly, are not relevant disposals; it is *sales*—in the sense of some value being paid other than by way of rent—which it is intended to catch.

A sub-tenancy for the whole of the unexpired period of a lease will take effect as an assignment at law, and is likely, therefore, to attract repayment: *Milmo v. Carrerras* [1946] K.B. 306. A right of re-entry or to forfeit will not prevent the lease being for more than 21 years: *Quinlan v. Avis* (1933) 149 L.T. 214. The term "rack-rent" means a rent of, or near, the full annual value of a property (*Re Sawyer and Wilhall* [1919] 2 Ch. 333) determined as at the date of the grant (*London Corporation v. Cusack-Smith* [1955] A.C. 337). It has been defined as "the full amount which a landlord can reasonably be expected to get from a tenant", so that if property is subject to some category of control, *e.g.* the limited controls on rents under Housing Act 1988, the maximum permitted rent is the rack-rent: *Rawlance v. Croydon Corporation* [1952] 2 Q.B. 803, C.A.

"Conveyance" itself means "an instrument that transfers property from one person to another" (*Eastbourne Corporation v. A.G.* [1904] A.C. 155, H.L.). The somewhat broader definition in Law of Property Act 1925, s.205(1)(ii) is not imported into this Act. An instrument which does not pass a legal estate will not qualify as a conveyance even if sufficient to amount to an enforceable contract for the conveyance and so pass an equitable interest in the property under the rule in *Walsh v. Lonsdale* [1882] 21 Ch.D. 9, *Rodger v. Harrison* (1893) 1 Q.B. 161, *I.R.C. v. Angus* (1889) 23 Q.B.D. 579.

Subss. (4)–(7)
Qualifying Persons. Excepted from the repayment provisions of s.11—and the provisions vitiating a disposal to a non-qualifying person under s.13—are disposals between joint tenants, *i.e.* if the person *to* whom the disposal is made if he is the person (*e.g.* vesting in oneself as beneficial owner) or one of the persons *by* whom it is made, or such a person's spouse or member of the family (see notes to s.62, below) who has resided with him throughout the period of 12 months ending with the disposal. See notes to s.131, below.

Death. A vesting of the whole house (*i.e.* as opposed to inheritance of a share in it) on death is an exempted disposal.

Matrimonial Breakdown. A disposal in pursuance of an order under any of the provisions in subs. (6) is an exempted disposal. This now includes a sale of the property resulting from an order under Matrimonial Causes Act 1973 (c. 18), s.24A, *cf. R. v. Rushmore B.C., ex p. Barrett* (1988) 20 H.L.R. 366, C.A. under the right to buy provisions of Housing Act 1985.

Compulsory Disposal. If the property is bought by a body enjoying compulsory purchase powers, for the purposes for which the powers are enjoyed, whether by order or by agreement, the disposal is exempted.

Yard, Garden, etc. The definition of "house" under s.63 includes the "usual" extension to yard, garden, outhouses and appurtenances belonging to or usually enjoyed with the house, and a disposal of them is exempted.

Right of tenant to acquire dwelling

Right of tenant to acquire dwelling

16.—(1) A tenant of a registered social landlord has the right to acquire the dwelling of which he is a tenant if—
   (a) he is a tenant under an assured tenancy, other than an assured short-hold tenancy or a long tenancy, or under a secure tenancy,
   (b) the dwelling was provided with public money and has remained in the social rented sector, and
   (c) he satisfies any further qualifying conditions applicable under Part V of the Housing Act 1985 (the right to buy) as it applies in relation to the right conferred by this section.
   (2) For this purpose a dwelling shall be regarded as provided with public money if—
   (a) it was provided or acquired wholly or in part by means of a grant under section 18 (social housing grant),
   (b) it was provided or acquired wholly or in part by applying or appropriating sums standing in the disposal proceeds fund of a registered social landlord (see section 25), or
   (c) it was acquired by a registered social landlord after the commencement of this paragraph on a disposal by a public sector landlord at a time when it was capable of being let as a separate dwelling.
   (3) A dwelling shall be regarded for the purposes of this section as having remained within the social rented sector if, since it was so provided or acquired—
   (a) the person holding the freehold interest in the dwelling has been either a registered social landlord or a public sector landlord; and
   (b) any person holding an interest as lessee (otherwise than as mortgagee) in the dwelling has been—
      (i) an individual holding otherwise than under a long tenancy; or
      (ii) a registered social landlord or a public sector landlord.

(4) A dwelling shall be regarded for the purposes of this section as provided by means of a grant under section 18 (social housing grant) if, and only if, the Corporation when making the grant notified the recipient that the dwelling was to be so regarded.

The Corporation shall before making the grant inform the applicant that it proposes to give such a notice and allow him an opportunity to withdraw his application within a specified time.

DEFINITIONS
　　"assured shorthold tenancy": s.230.
　　"assured tenancy": s.230.
　　"long tenancy": s.63.
　　"provided": s.63(2).
　　"provided with public money": subs. (2).
　　"public sector landlord": s.63.
　　"registered social landlord": s.1.
　　"secure tenancy": s.230.
　　"social rented sector": subs. (3).
　　"tenant": s.229.

GENERAL NOTE
　　It is this section, brief as it is, which in substance reinstates the right to buy, *sub nom.* right to acquire, to the tenants of housing associations, and extends it to other tenants of registered social landlords: see General Note to s.11, above. The right, however, applies only to publicly-funded dwellings acquired under the provisions of this Act, *i.e.* after its commencement. Existing stock, it was said in Committee (*Hansard*, (H.C.), Standing Committee G, Third Sitting, February 13, 1996, col. 76, Minister for Local Government, Housing and Urban Regeneration [Mr Curry]), would be dealt with under a voluntary scheme, from April 1996, presumably under a Corporation consent, and subject to the provisions of ss.11–15, above.
　　This section, however, does no more than set out the *pre*-conditions to acquisition in terms of persons qualifying to exercise it (subs. (1)), and property (subss. (2)–(4)). The conditions for, and terms of, exercise of the right to acquire are to be the same as under Pt. V, Housing Act 1985, save so far as may be prescribed by regulations made under s.17, below, predominantly by adaptation of Pt. V, Housing Act 1985.
　　Due to the introduction of private sector funding that this legislation hopes for, it is an important part of the qualifications to this scheme that—where Corporation grant is the basis for its application—notice prior to the grant is given that the dwelling will fall within it, to allow a landlord to withdraw the application and rely wholly on private funds.
　　In addition to the provisions of this section, which may take a dwelling out of the right to acquire, the Secretary of State may designate rural areas which are outwith it, under s.17(1)(b), below.

Subs. (1)
Assured tenancy. This has been the standard form of letting since January 15, 1989 (commencement of Housing Act 1988, Pt. I), where the landlord has been either a housing association or a (wholly) private landlord: see notes to s.10(1), above. Exceptions to assured security are to be found in Housing Act 1988, Sched. 1.
　　Although a (very) few tenants of registered social landlords may be Rent Act protected, there is no provision which will confer on them the right to acquire. As, however, a landlord will have to register, it may be that the Corporation will set a criterion for registration under s.5, above, which secures an assurance that such tenants would likewise be able to acquire on analogous terms to the right conferred by this section. As all registered social landlords are non-profit making, it is likely that this would not be contentious.
　　Some assured tenants will already have the preserved right to buy, added to Housing Act 1985, Pt. V, by Housing and Planning Act 1986, *i.e.* where their properties have been transferred from public sector ownership to a housing association. However, some assured tenants who were previously secure tenants will not enjoy even the preserved right to buy because, *e.g.* their landlords were charities, and these may now be permitted to benefit from the right to acquire— see s.17(3)(b), below.

Secure tenancy. This was the standard form of letting between the commencement of the Housing Act 1980 (c. 51) (October 3, 1980), which conferred security of tenure on public sector tenants and—until replaced by assured tenancies under the Housing Act 1988—housing association tenants. Exceptions to security are to be found (now) in Housing Act 1985, Sched. 1. Tenants of registered social landlords may be secure tenants by reason of the transitional, "prior element" provisions of the 1988 Act—see notes to s.10(1), above.

Secure tenants will already enjoy the right to buy, unless excluded from it by 1985, Sched. 5. As with assured tenants, those who do not enjoy it may now be permitted to benefit from the right to acquire—see s.17(3)(b), below.

Some assured and secure tenants are excluded from the right to acquire:

(a) *Assured shorthold tenancy*. As noted (above, notes to s.10(1)), these are assured tenancies which fulfil certain conditions, including a minimum six month period and the service on them of a notice, against whom, in addition to the grounds for possession available against an "ordinary" assured tenant, possession can be sought by following a set procedure. See now, below, Pt. III, Chap. II.

(b) *Long tenancy*. This primarily means (Housing Act 1985, ss.187, 115) a tenancy granted for a term certain of at least 21 years (whether or not previously terminable by re-entry or forfeiture), including those granted under 1985 Act, Pt. V, *i.e.* right to buy (even if, in those few circumstances when this can arise, it is for 21 years or less—see 1985 Act, Sched. 6, para. 12, where the property is a house and the landlord had a lease of less than 21 years and five days *as at the date when the grant is made—cf.* below, note on 1985 Act, Sched. 5, para. 4, or where the purchase is less than 21 years and five days before the expiry of another right to buy lease in the same building).

Also within the definition is a tenancy for a term fixed by law (Law of Property Act 1922 (c. 16), s.145, Sched. 15, Law of Property Act 1925 (c. 20), s.202) under a grant with a covenant or obligation for permanent renewal, unless a sub-lease under a tenancy which is not itself a long tenancy.

Provision is also made to bring within the definition certain shared ownership leases granted by housing associations: see 1985 Act, s.115(2).

Part V, Housing Act 1985. The right to buy is not enjoyed by every secure tenant. There is a number of additional qualifying conditions (although these may be excepted, adapted or modified by regulations under s.16(2)(b), below):

(i) *Minimum period*. Housing Act 1985, Sched. 4 governs the calculation of periods of time for the purposes (a) of the residential qualification, and (b) of the amount of discount available; the minimum residential qualification must be at least two years—*ibid.*, s.119.

(ii) *Exceptions: ibid.*, Sched. 5 contains a number of exceptions to the right to buy:

Para. 1 Charities;

Para. 2 Co-operative housing associations (see notes to s.7 and Sched. 1, para. 2, above);

Para. 3 Housing associations which have at no time received funding under specified enactments (being the principal housing association grants and grants from local authorities, under the 1974–1988 legislation);

Para. 4 Where the property is a house and the landlord has an insufficient interest to grant a lease for a term of 21 years *as at the date when the tenant serves notice claiming the right to buy*—which may mean that there is still an effective right to buy, albeit on a shorter term, as at the date of the grant—*cf.* above, note on Long Tenancy; or, where the property is a flat and the landlord has a lease of less than 50 years (at the date of notice claiming right);

Para. 5 Specified lettings in connection with employment;

Para. 7 Dwellings adapted for the disabled within a sheltered group;

Para. 9 Dwellings in sheltered accommodation for people suffering from a mental disorder;

Para. 10 Sheltered accommodation for the elderly;

Para. 11 Adapted accommodation for the elderly;

Para. 12 Crown property.

The restriction on *exercise* of the right to buy (1985, s.121, *i.e.* possession order pending, insolvency) would not seem to amount to a "qualifying condition" for this purpose.

Subs. (2)

It was said in Committee (*Hansard* (H.C.), Standing Committee G, Third Sitting, February 13, 1996, col. 76, Minister for Local Government, Housing and Urban Regeneration [Mr Curry]) that properties within the right to acquire were properties "exclusively ... yet to be built". Yet the wording does not suggest that property "provided or acquired under section 18" is confined to new-build, even if that may well be the policy intention: indeed, s.63(2) states that the provision of a house or dwelling includes both new-build and conversion, and alteration, enlargement, repair or improvement of an existing dwelling or house. Furthermore, property acquired by a registered social landlord from a public sector landlord would not seem to be likely to be newly built after the commencement of this Act, given its underlying policy.

The first property qualification is that it was provided with public money, which is defined to mean provided or acquired—wholly or in part—with grant aid under s.18, below, or by application of the "disposals proceeds funds" (ss.24, 18—thereby allowing registered social landlords to replace stock sold under the right to acquire), or acquired by transfer from a public sector landlord, *i.e.* voluntarily, or pursuant to Pts. III or IV of the Housing Act 1988 (see Introduction to Pt. I, above).

Public sector landlord. This means any of the landlords whose tenants are secure, under s.80(1), Housing Act 1985 Act:

(a) Local authorities;

(b) New town corporations;

(c) Housing action trusts (*cf.* Introduction to Pt. I, above, referring to Pt. III, 1988 Act);

(d) Urban Development Corporation (see Local Government, Planning and Land Act 1980, Pt. XVI—see 1985 Act, s.4);

(e) Development Board for Rural Wales;

(f) Housing co-operatives within the meaning of 1985 Act, s.80(1), *i.e.* of an authority's own stock, under now superseded provisions—see s.27B, 1985 Act; *cf.* below, s.19).

Let as a separate dwelling. The property must have been capable of being let as a separate dwelling at the time of acquisition. The primary restraint imposed by this qualification is that the property must already have been constructed or converted to use as self-contained housing accommodation, which would exclude hostels, or buildings not yet made suitable as housing.

The phrase "let as a separate dwelling" has been in widespread use in security statutes throughout the century (see Increase of Rent and Mortgage Interest (War Restrictions) Act 1915 (c. 97), s.2(2), and subsequent Rent Acts, and the Housing Acts from 1980 onwards; see currently, Housing Act 1985, s.79 and Housing Act 1988, s.1), and a considerable body of case law has built up around it. It follows, however, that the property will also have to be let as a separate dwelling when the tenant wishes to acquire it, as this is a condition of being an assured or secure tenancy.

Much of the law which has built up around the phrase concerns whether or not there has been a *letting, i.e.* a tenancy as distinct from a licence. As what is in issue here is *capability*, this does not arise. Likewise the case law on the word "as", considers the *purpose* of a letting, and will not be relevant.

Nor, indeed, will the fact that an acquisition may have been of more than one dwelling at a time, *e.g.* a block of flats, disqualify the property, for it is the qualities of each unit that will determine whether or not *it* is capable of being let as a separate dwelling, rather than whether or not the acquisition was of "a" separate dwelling. The only part of the case law that is imported is that which concerns the expression "separate dwelling": even if the premises contain no more than a single room (see *e.g. Curl v. Angelo* [1948] 2 All E.R. 189, C.A.), it must be capable of being used in a way that involves no sharing of living accommodation with another. It is what is meant by living accommodation, therefore, that is important.

It has been held that "living accommodation" does not include a bathroom or lavatory, being rooms which one visits for a specific purpose rather than in a broader sense for the primary purposes of living, or in which a significant amount of time is spent (*Cole v. Harris* [1945] K.B. 474, C.A., *Curl, Goodrich v. Paisner* [1957] A.C. 65, H.L., *March v. Cooper* [1969] 1 W.L.R. 803, C.A.). The primary living purposes are sleeping, cooking and feeding—*Wright v. Howell* (1947) 92 S.J. 26, C.A., *Curl*). A kitchen is accordingly living accommodation (*Neale v. del Soto* [1945] K.B. 144, C.A., *Sharpe v. Nicholls* (1945) 147 E.G. 177, C.A.), even a kitchenette too small to eat in (*Winters v. Dance* [1949] L.J.R. 165, C.A.), so that if premises do not contain their own cooking facilities, they cannot be said to be capable of being let as a separate dwelling.

What is crucial is the *terms* of the letting, or the rights which have been conferred: where a kitchen was shared with the landlord, so that there was no letting as a separate dwelling, and the landlord's interest passed to another (his mortgagee), a limited company, the tenant remained without a letting as a separate dwelling, even if (which did not need to be decided) the company could not exercise such a sharing right (*sed dubitante*—why should a company landlord not share a kitchen with a residential tenant, *e.g.* for the use of staff, or indeed of directors or visitors?), the tenant's only *entitlement* was to shared use and at any time in the future a non-corporate landlord could take over the landlord's interest: *The Mortgage Corporation v. Ubah, The Times,* March 21, 1996, 28 H.L.R. forthcoming, C.A. (see also *Stanley v. Compton* [1951] 1 All E.R. 859, C.A.).

All of these cases must, however, be considered with some caution, as the *context* will always be relevant, and this provision is concerned with a right to acquire. Leaving aside whether anyone would *wish* to purchase somewhere without a sufficient degree of separateness, the courts are likely to construe the section so as to avoid absurd consequences.

Subs. (3)

The second property qualification is that the dwelling is still within the social rented sector, which means that—since the property was acquired within subs. (2)—*both*:

(a) The freeholder has been either a registered social landlord or a public sector landlord (see notes to subs. (2), above); and,

(b) Anyone else with an interest in the property (other than as a mortgagee) has been either an individual holding on something less than a long tenancy (see notes to subs. (1), above), or a registered social landlord or public sector landlord.

In substance, then, ownership of and interest in the property must be confined (mortgagees excepted) to these landlords and their tenants, commonly so-called, to the exclusion of a long-leaseholder.

Subs. (4)

This provision allows a registered landlord to opt to provide a dwelling that will not be subject to the right to acquire, by relying entirely on private funds. (The landlord will not, however, be able to rely on its s.24 reserves from prior disposals in order to avoid the right.) The obligation on the Corporation is a positive obligation: silence, or omission, will leave the property outside the scheme.

Right of tenant to acquire dwelling: supplementary provisions

17.—(1) The Secretary of State may by order—

(a) specify the amount or rate of discount to be given on the exercise of the right conferred by section 16; and

(b) designate rural areas in relation to dwellings in which the right conferred by that section does not arise.

(2) The provisions of Part V of the Housing Act 1985 apply in relation to the right to acquire under section 16—

(a) subject to any order under subsection (1) above, and

(b) subject to such other exceptions, adaptations and other modifications as may be specified by regulations made by the Secretary of State.

(3) The regulations may provide—

(a) that the powers of the Secretary of State under sections 164 to 170 of that Act (powers to intervene, give directions or assist) do not apply,

(b) that paragraphs 1 and 3 (exceptions for charities and certain housing associations), and paragraph 11 (right of appeal to Secretary of State), of Schedule 5 to that Act do not apply,

(c) that the provisions of Part V of that Act relating to the right to acquire on rent to mortgage terms do not apply,

(d) that the provisions of that Part relating to restrictions on disposals in National Parks, &c. do not apply, and

(e) that the provisions of that Part relating to the preserved right to buy do not apply.

Nothing in this subsection affects the generality of the power conferred by subsection (2).

(4) The specified exceptions, adaptations and other modifications shall take the form of textual amendments of the provisions of Part V of that Act as they apply in relation to the right to buy under that Part; and the first regulations, and any subsequent consolidating regulations, shall set out the provisions of Part V as they so apply.

(5) An order or regulations under this section—

(a) may make different provision for different cases or classes of case including different areas, and

(b) may contain such incidental, supplementary and transitional provisions as the Secretary of State considers appropriate.

(6) Before making an order which would have the effect that an area ceased to be designated under subsection (1)(b), the Secretary of State shall consult—

(a) the local housing authority or authorities in whose district the area or any part of it is situated or, if the order is general in its effect, local housing authorities in general, and

(b) such bodies appearing to him to be representative of registered social landlords as he considers appropriate.

(7) An order or regulations under this section shall be made by statutory instrument which shall be subject to annulment in pursuance of a resolution

of either House of Parliament.

GENERAL NOTE

This section empowers the Secretary of State, by order or regulation (pursuant to the negative Parliamentary procedure: see subs. (6)), to provide for discounts on the exercise of the right to acquire, and to designate rural areas where it is not to apply, and otherwise to adapt Pt. V, Housing Act 1985 for the purposes of the right to acquire.

Subs. (1)
Discount. Where the right to acquire is exercised, the discount will be the subject of a grant under s.20, below.
Rural Areas. The intention is to designate "settlements with populations of fewer than 3,000 people", although does not necessarily "exclude the possibility that some settlements with populations marginally over the 3,000 level could have special reasons for wanting to be included ... I do not intend to take the line of biblical certainty": *Hansard*, (H.C.), Standing Committee G, Third Sitting, February 13, 1996, col. 88, Minister for Local Government, Housing and Urban Regeneration (Mr Curry). In Wales, however, a different approach may be anticipated, based rather on population density, starting at areas with a population density of fewer than 150 person per square kilometre (the O.E.C.D. definition of rurality): *ibid.*, Parliamentary Under-Secretary of State for Wales (Mr Gwilym Jones), at col. 89.

Subs. (2)
The Secretary of State may except, adapt or otherwise modify Pt. V, 1985 Act. This power would not seem to extend to the qualifying conditions governed by s.16(1)(c): *generalibus specialia derogant, i.e.* where Parliament has specifically dealt with something, it overrides general provisions.

Subs. (3)
The powers to disapply the Secretary of State's regulatory functions in relation to right to buy—including the power to intervene in an authority's discharge of their duties under Pt. V—reflect the powers of the Corporation under this Act. Those to disapply restrictions on disposals in National Parks, etc. (*cf.* above, s.13) reflect the power to designate rural areas under subs. (1)(b). Those to disapply the preserved right to buy reflect the availability of the right to acquire under s.16 to dwellings acquired from public sector landlords, under *ibid.*, s.16(2)(c).

Subs. (4)
The first regulations are to set out the provisions of Pt. V as adapted or modified.

CHAPTER III

GRANTS AND OTHER FINANCIAL MATTERS

Grants and other financial assistance

Social housing grants

18.—(1) The Corporation may make grants to registered social landlords in respect of expenditure incurred or to be incurred by them in connection with their housing activities.

(2) The Corporation, acting in accordance with such principles as it may from time to time determine, shall specify in relation to grants under this section—

(a) the procedure to be followed in relation to applications for grant,

(b) the circumstances in which grant is or is not to be payable,

(c) the method for calculating, and any limitations on, the amount of grant, and

(d) the manner in which, and time or times at which, grant is to be paid.

(3) In making a grant under this section, the Corporation may provide that the grant is conditional on compliance by the landlord with such conditions as the Corporation may specify.

(4) The Corporation may, with the agreement of a local housing authority, appoint the authority to act as its agent in connection with the assessment and

payment of grant under this section.

(5) The appointment shall be on such terms as the Corporation may, with the approval of the Secretary of State given with the consent of the Treasury, specify; and the authority shall act in accordance with those terms.

(6) Where—

(a) a grant under this section is payable to a registered social landlord, and

(b) at any time property to which the grant relates becomes vested in, or is leased for a term of years to, or reverts to, another registered social landlord, or trustees for another such landlord,

this section (including this subsection) shall have effect after that time as if the grant, or such proportion of it as is specified or determined under subsection (7), were payable to the other landlord.

(7) The proportion mentioned in subsection (6) is that which, in the circumstances of the particular case—

(a) the Corporation, acting in accordance with such principles as it may from time to time determine, may specify as being appropriate, or

(b) the Corporation may determine to be appropriate.

(8) Where one of the landlords mentioned in subsection (6) is registered by the Housing Corporation and another is registered by Housing for Wales, the determination mentioned in subsection (7) shall be such as shall be agreed between the two Corporations.

DEFINITIONS

"Corporation": s.56.
"housing activities": s.63.
"local housing authority": s.230.
"provision": s.63(2).
"registered social landlord": s.1.

GENERAL NOTE

Replacing (*cf.* below, s.28) housing association grant and revenue deficit grant under Housing Act 1988, ss.50, 51) is the "social housing grant", the substantive details of which—procedures, circumstances in which payable, amounts, payment—will be determined by the Corporation: subs. (2). Grants may be subject to conditions: subs. (3). Payment of grant is at the discretion of the Corporation ("may make", *cf.* s.20, below—"shall make").

Grants are, however, only payable to registered social landlords "in respect of expenditure incurred or to be incurred by them in connection with the provision of social housing and other housing activities" (subs. (1)). Again (*cf.* above, notes to s.16) "provision" is not confined to new-build provision of houses, and in any case would be extended by "other housing activities" (see also s.19, below): see s.63(2) defining provision to include both new-build and conversion, and alteration, enlargement, repair or, improvement of existing property. The D.O.E. Consultation Paper, *More Choice In The Rented Sector*, July 1995, linked to the White Paper, *Our Future Homes*, describes—as the "package" landlords will be expected to deliver—a "social housing 'product' which Government is 'buying' either with grants to subsidise new-build or rehabilitation ...".

Grants paid in error, of law or fact, will be recoverable by the Corporation on the principle of restitution (unjust enrichment), whether by deduction from a subsequent grant payment or otherwise (*Auckland Harbour Board v. R.* [1924] A.C. 318, P.C.), although the defence of "change of position" may be available: *Lipkin Gorman v. Karpnale* [1991] 2 A.C. 548, H.L. See also *R. v. Secretary of State for the Environment, ex p. L.B. Camden* (1995) 28 H.L.R. 321, Q.B.D.

Expenditure incurred or to be incurred. Identical wording is to be found in Housing Act 1985, s.621A(1) and s.18, Landlord and Tenant Act 1985, on service charges (see notes to s.12, above; see also below, Pt. III, Chap. I), although words must always be read in their individual context.

Expenditure is incurred when the payer comes under a liability to make a payment, rather than when the payment itself is made, but not a loss or expenditure which is no more than impending, threatened or anticipated: see, *e.g.*, *Capital and Counties Freehold Equity Trust v. B.L. Plc* [1987] 2 E.G.L.R. 49, *West Ham Corporation v. Grant* (1888) 40 Ch.D. 331, *Law v. Coburn* [1972] 1 W.L.R. 1238; see also *New Zealand Flax Investments v. Federal Commissioner* (1938) 61 C.L.R. 179 at p.207, *Federal Commissioner for Taxation v. James Flood Pty.*

(1953) 88 C.L.R. 492, *King v. Commissioner of Inland Revenue* [1974] 2 N.Z.L.R. 190.

Subs. (2)
 Determinations may make different provision for different classes of landlord or of housing activity or areas: see s.53, below.

Subss. (4), (5)
 Local housing authorities continue (see most recently s.50, Housing Act 1988) to have a role as agents for the Corporation in the administration of grants (assessment and payment). See also for their historical and current *direct* role, s.22 and notes thereto, below. This is one of the means by which a local housing authority can merge their local policies, both under s.22, below, and under their own direct powers, with those of the Corporation. Appointment of authorities is to be on the terms that the Corporation specify, with the approval of the Secretary of State given with the consent of the Treasury.
 Local housing authorities are district councils, London borough councils, the Common Council of the City of London and the Council of the Isles of Scilly and in Wales, county or county boroughs: Housing Act 1985, s.1.
 This provision is the source of the power for local housing authorities to undertake the agency activity, as the Corporation is not a public body on whose behalf authorities are empowered under Local Authorities (Goods and Services) Act 1970 (c. 39), s.1, to undertake "administrative, professional or technical services" (although registered housing associations are identified as "public bodies" on whose behalf authorities may so act, by Local Authorities (Goods and Services) (Public Bodies) Order 1975 (S.I. 1975 No. 193).
 Conduct by the authority outwith the terms specified by the Corporation, *e.g.* payment of more grant than a landlord is entitled to, will—as a question of the powers of a public body—be *ultra vires,* void and recoverable (by the authority from the landlord): see, *e.g. Crédit Suisse v. Allerdale B.C., Crédit Suisse v. L.B. Waltham Forest, The Times,* May 20, 1996, C.A., *Westdeutsche Landesbank Girozentrale v. L.B. Islington* [1996] 2 All E.R. 961, H.L., *Kleinwort Benson v. South Tyneside M.B.C.* [1994] 4 All E.R. 972, *South Tyneside M.B.C. v. Svenska International Plc* [1995] 1 All E.R. 545.
 As such, it does not seem that the normal law of agency could apply so as to fix the Corporation with liability; in any event, as the terms of the agency will be those for which the Corporation itself—also a public body—needs the approval of the Secretary of State, *its* powers (to act through the agency of a local housing authority) are substantively likewise statutorily fettered, for which reason even on the law of agency, the authority as agent cannot enjoy more powers than those of the principal—see, generally, Bowstead & Reynolds on Agency, 16th ed, sp. Arts. 22, 23, 73-25.

Subss. (6)–(8)
 The purpose of these provisions is to ensure that the grant follows the property to which it relates.

Land subject to housing management agreement

 19. A registered social landlord is not entitled to a grant under section 18 (social housing grant) in respect of land comprised in a management agreement within the meaning of the Housing Act 1985 (see sections 27(2) and 27B(4) of that Act: delegation of housing management functions by certain authorities).

DEFINITION
 "registered social landlord": s.1.

GENERAL NOTE
 Local authority housing may—with the approval of the Secretary of State—be made the subject of a management agreement, whereby someone other than the authority may undertake management tasks as agent for the authority (contrary to the normal rule that where Parliament confers a power on a body, that body must exercise it for itself and cannot delegate it save so far as it is expressly empowered to, which in the case of a local authority means under the terms of s.101, Local Government Act 1972 (c. 70), *i.e.* to a committee, sub-committee or officer of the authority, or to another local authority, or to a joint committee together with another authority; see now, however, the Deregulation and Contracting Out Act 1994 (c. 40), s.70 and orders thereunder. The extension of compulsory competitive tendering to housing management [under Local Government Act 1988] has also served to dilute the practical effect of the normal rule).
 A local authority cannot, of course, be a registered social landlord (see s.2, above). This sec-

tion prevents a registered social landlord—who may well be amongst those to whom local authority management is transferred by agreement or as a result of competitive tendering—applying for social housing grant in relation to local authority housing. Housing co-operatives under superseded provisions of the Housing Acts (see also notes to s.16(2), above) are likewise not able to apply for social housing grant for property within their agreements.

Purchase grant where right to acquire exercised

20.—(1) The Corporation shall make grants to registered social landlords in respect of discounts given by them to persons exercising the right to acquire conferred by section 16.

(2) The amount of the grant for any year shall be the aggregate value of the discounts given in that year.

(3) The Corporation, acting in accordance with such principles as it may from time to time determine, shall specify in relation to grants under this section—

(a) the procedure to be followed in relation to applications for grant,

(b) the manner in which, and time or times at which, grant is to be paid.

(4) In making a grant the Corporation may provide that the grant is conditional on compliance by the registered social landlord with such conditions as the Corporation may specify.

DEFINITIONS

"Corporation": s.56.

"registered social landlord": s.1.

GENERAL NOTE

Registered social landlords who have to allow a discount on the right to acquire under s.16, above (see also s.17) are to be reimbursed annually by way of grant representing the aggregate value of those discounts, determined as the Corporation specifies, and potentially subject to conditions (*e.g.* for repayment to the Corporation of grant in the event of claw-back of discount from the former tenant).

See the following section for grants for discounts on voluntary disposals.

Subs. (3)

A determination may make different provision for different classes of landlord or areas: see s.53, below.

Purchase grant in respect of other disposals

21.—(1) The Corporation may make grants to registered social landlords in respect of discounts on disposals by them of dwellings to tenants otherwise than in pursuance of the right conferred by section 16.

(2) The Corporation shall make such a grant if the tenant was entitled to exercise the right conferred by section 16 in relation to another dwelling of the landlord's.

The amount of the grant in such a case shall not exceed the amount of the discount to which the tenant would have been entitled in respect of the other dwelling.

(3) The Corporation, acting in accordance with such principles as it may from time to time determine, shall specify in relation to grants under this section—

(a) the procedure to be followed in relation to applications for grant;

(b) the circumstances in which grant is or is not to be payable;

(c) the method for calculating, and any limitations on, the amount of grant; and

(d) the manner in which, and time or times at which, grant is to be paid.

(4) In making a grant under this section, the Corporation may provide that

the grant is conditional on compliance by the registered social landlord with such conditions as the Corporation may specify.

GENERAL NOTE
    Disposals need not only be pursuant to the right to acquire under s.16, above, but may also be voluntary under a general consent (s.9, above), and pursuant to the terms of ss.11–15). Voluntary sales may likewise be subject to discount provisions: see in particular s.11 and notes thereto, above. If the disposal is not of the property let to the tenant, but to another property belonging to the landlord, then the Corporation *must* pay a grant in respect of the discount (not exceeding the amount which would have been payable had the purchase been pursuant to the right to acquire and, therefore, the grant pursuant to s.19, above); in any other case, the grant will be discretionary.

Subss. (3), (4)
    The grants are as determined by the Corporation, and may be subject to conditions (*e.g.* for repayment to the Corporation of grant in the event of claw-back of discount from the former tenant). A determination may make different provision for different classes of landlord or areas: see s.53, below.

Assistance from local authorities

22.—(1) A local authority may promote—
    (a) the formation of bodies to act as registered social landlords, and
    (b) the extension of the objects or activities of registered social landlords.
    (2) A local authority may for the assistance of any registered social landlord subscribe for share or loan capital of the landlord.
    (3) A local authority may for the assistance of a registered social landlord—
    (a) make grants or loans to the landlord, or
    (b) guarantee or join in guaranteeing the payment of the principal of, and interest on, money borrowed by the landlord (including money borrowed by the issue of loan capital) or of interest on share capital issued by the landlord.
    (4) A local housing authority may sell or supply under a hire-purchase agreement furniture to the occupants of houses provided by a registered social landlord, and may buy furniture for that purpose.
    In this subsection "hire-purchase agreement" means a hire-purchase agreement or conditional sale agreement within the meaning of the Consumer Credit Act 1974.

GENERAL NOTE
    This is a provision with honourable historical antecedents, dating back to s.18, Housing, Town Planning, etc. Act 1919 (c. 35), pursuant to which "a local authority ... may promote the formation or extension of or ... assist a public utility society whose objects include the erection, improvement or management of houses for the working classes ...," to assist which societies the authority could "make grants or loans to the society ... subscribe for any share or loan capital of the society ... guarantee or join in guaranteeing the payment of interest on money borrowed by the society or of any share or loan capital issued by the society".
    The provision was replicated in Housing Act 1925, s.70, and the reference to public utility society replaced with a reference to housing associations by Housing Act 1935 (c. 40), s.26. The provision was further replicated, as thus altered to refer to housing associations, in Housing Act 1936 (c. 51), s.93 and in Housing Act 1957 (c. 56), s.119. By amendment under the Housing Act 1974 (c. 44), s.17, the powers were confined to *registered* housing associations, and thus were they

replicated in Housing Associations Act 1985 (c. 69), ss.58–60. The powers are now transferred, in substantively the same form as they have existed since 1919, for use in relation to registered social landlords.

It is under this power that local authorities may be expected to form local housing companies: see notes to s.2, above.

Local authorities also enjoy powers to provide financial assistance to other landlords, by way of grant or loan, guarantee, indemnity or acquisition of share or loan capital, in relation to property which is to be privately let, under Pt. III, Local Government Act 1988, which power, however, may not be exercised without the consent of the Secretary of State.

The existence of these express powers means that local authorities cannot guarantee housing activities in other circumstances, or to other bodies, using the general incidental powers in s.111, Local Government Act 1972: see *Crédit Suisse v. Allerdale M.B.C., Crédit Suisse v. L.B. Waltham Forest, The Times*, May 20, 1996, C.A.

Loans by Public Works Loans Commissioners

23.—(1) The Public Works Loans Commissioners may lend money to a registered social landlord—

(a) for the purpose of constructing or improving, or facilitating or encouraging the construction or improvement, of dwellings,

(b) for the purchase of dwellings which the landlord desires to purchase with a view to their improvement, and

(c) for the purchase and development of land.

(2) A loan for any of those purposes, and interest on the loan, shall be secured by a mortgage of—

(a) the land in respect of which that purpose is to be carried out, and

(b) such other lands (if any) as may be offered as security for the loan;

and the money lent shall not exceed three-quarters (or, if the payment of the principal of, and interest on, the loan is guaranteed by a local authority, nine-tenths) of the value, to be ascertained to the satisfaction of the Public Works Commissioners, of the estate or interest in the land proposed to be so mortgaged.

(3) Loans may be made by instalments as the building of dwellings or other work on the land mortgaged under subsection (2) progresses (so, however, that the total amount lent does not at any time exceed the amount specified in that subsection); and a mortgage may accordingly be made to secure such loans to be so made.

(4) If the loan exceeds two-thirds of the value referred to in subsection (2), and is not guaranteed as to principal and interest by a local authority, the Public Works Loans Commissioners shall require, in addition to such a mortgage as is mentioned in that subsection, such further security as they think fit.

(5) Subject to subsection (6), the period for repayment of a loan under this section shall not exceed 40 years, and no money shall be lent on mortgage of any land unless the estate proposed to be mortgaged is either an estate in fee simple absolute in possession or an estate for a term of years absolute of which not less than 50 years are unexpired at the date of the loan.

(6) Where a loan under this section is made for the purpose of carrying out a scheme for the provision of houses approved by the Secretary of State, the maximum period for the repayment of the loan is 50 instead of 40 years, and money may be lent on the mortgage of an estate for a term of years absolute of which a period of not less than ten years in excess of the period fixed for the repayment of the sums advanced remains unexpired at the date of the loan.

DEFINITION
"registered social landlord": s.1.

GENERAL NOTE
As with assistance from local authorities under provisions preceding s.22, above, there has long been power for public utilities, and later housing associations (and yet later, registered housing associations), to borrow from the Public Works Loans Commissioners, both for new-build and acquisition of existing housing to improve it, see Housing, Town Planning, etc., Act

1919, s.19, Housing Act 1925, s.90, Housing Act 1936, s.92, Housing (Financial Provisions) Act 1958, s.47, Housing Associations Act 1985, s.67.

This facility is now available to all registered social landlords, for the full range of purposes identified—new-build, and acquisition and improvement—to be secured by mortgage, but not exceeding three-quarters of the value of the security for the loan unless the loan is guaranteed by a local authority, in which case the maximum is 90% (subs. (2)). The security must have 50 years unexpired (subs. (5)), and the loan must be for a maximum of 40 years; however, if the loan is for the purposes of the provision of houses within a scheme approved by the Secretary of State, the maximum term may be 50 years, and the minimum security is either freehold or a leasehold which has more than 10 further years unexpired (subs. (6)).

Treatment of disposal proceeds

The disposal proceeds fund

24.—(1) A registered social landlord shall show separately in its accounts for any period ending after the coming into force of this section its net disposal proceeds.

(2) The net disposal proceeds of a registered social landlord are—

(a) the net proceeds of sale received by it in respect of any disposal of land to a tenant—

(i) in pursuance of the right conferred by section 16 (right of tenant to acquire dwelling), or

(ii) in respect of which a grant was made under section 21 (purchase grant in respect of other disposals);

(b) payments of grant received by it under section 20 or 21 (purchase grant);

(c) where any such grant has been paid to it, any repayments of discount in respect of which the grant was given; and

(d) such other proceeds of sale or payments of grant (if any) as the Corporation may from time to time determine.

(3) The net proceeds of sale means the proceeds of sale less an amount calculated in accordance with a determination by the Corporation.

(4) The disposal proceeds shall be shown in a fund to be known as a disposal proceeds fund.

(5) The method of constituting the fund and showing it in the landlord's accounts shall be as required by determination of the Corporation under paragraph 16 of Schedule 1 (general requirements as to accounts).

(6) Interest shall be added to the fund in accordance with a determination made by the Corporation.

(7) Where this section applies in relation to the proceeds of sale arising on a disposal, section 27 below (recovery, &c. of social housing grants) and section 52 of the Housing Act 1988 (recovery, &c. of grants under that Act and earlier enactments) do not apply.

DEFINITIONS
"Corporation": s.56.
"registered social landlord": s.1.
"tenant": s.229.

GENERAL NOTE

The purpose of this section is to ensure that the proceeds of disposal of publicly-funded housing are only used in an approved manner: see following section. To effect this, s.24 requires all registered social landlords to maintain its accounts so as to identify separately its "net disposal proceeds" (as defined), to be shown in a fund to be called the "disposals proceeds fund" (subs. (4)).

The determinations which the Corporation make under this section may make different provision for different classes of landlord or areas: see s.53, below.

Subs. (1)

The provisions are applicable to the accounts for a registered social landlord for any period *ending* (not commencing) after the commencement of the section.

Subs. (2)
The proceeds at issue are:
(a) sale pursuant to the right to acquire (s.16, above) or voluntary disposals (qualifying for discount grant under s.21);
(b) the discount grants (ss.20, 21) themselves;
(c) discounts repaid (see ss.11, 16, above);
(d) such other proceeds of sale or payments of grant as the Corporation determine "from time to time", *i.e.* by general determination.

Subs. (3)
The Corporation determines how sale proceeds are calculated, so that, *e.g.* administrative costs of sale may be deducted (*cf.* Local Government and Housing Act 1989 (c. 42), s.59(9)).

Subs. (5)
The Corporation likewise determines (under Sched. 1, para. 16) how the fund is to be constituted and shown in the accounts.

Subs. (6)
Constitution as a fund, as distinct from a mere account, facilitates the accretion of interest, according to a determination of the Corporation.

Subs. (7)
Provisions governing the recovery of grant under both this Act and Housing Act 1988, s.52, are not applicable to a disposal to which this section applies.

Application or appropriation of disposal proceeds

25.—(1) The sums standing in the disposal proceeds account of a registered social landlord ("disposal proceeds") may only be applied or appropriated by it for such purposes and in such manner as the Corporation may determine.

(2) If any disposal proceeds are not applied or appropriated as mentioned in subsection (1) within such time as is specified by determination of the Corporation, the Corporation may direct that the whole or part of them shall be paid to it.

DEFINITIONS
"Corporation": s.56.
"registered social landlord": s.1.

GENERAL NOTE
It is this section which empowers the Corporation to determine how the disposals proceeds fund may be applied or the uses to which it may be appropriated (which it is presumably to be anticipated, will include by the provision of new housing: see s.16(2)(b), above); the Corporation may also direct the payment to it of all or part of any such amount not applied or appropriated in accordance with a determination. A determination may make different provision for different classes of landlord or of housing activity or areas: see s.53, below.

Disposal proceeds: power to require information

26.—(1) The Corporation may give notice—
(a) to all registered social landlords,
(b) to registered social landlords of a particular description, or
(c) to particular registered social landlords,
requiring them to furnish it with such information as it may reasonably require in connection with the exercise of its functions under sections 24 and 25 (treatment of disposal proceeds).

(2) A notice under subsection (1)(a) or (b) may be given by publication in such manner as the Corporation considers appropriate for bringing it to the attention of the landlords concerned.

DEFINITIONS
"Corporation": s.56.
"registered social landlord": s.1.

GENERAL NOTE
This section is ancillary to ss.24, 25, and empowers the Corporation to require the provision of information from registered social landlords: it is a general power, analogous to the performance standards information powers in s.35, below, although not backed by criminal sanctions for non-compliance nor subject to controls on further disclosure. It is additional to the more specific, "monitoring" powers of s.29, below.

Recovery, &c. of social housing grants

Recovery, &c. of social housing grants

27.—(1) Where a registered social landlord has received a grant under section 18 (social housing grant), the following powers are exercisable in such events as the Corporation may from time to time determine.

(2) The Corporation may, acting in accordance with such principles as it has determined—

   (a) reduce any grant payable by it, or suspend or cancel any instalment of any such grant, or

   (b) direct the registered social landlord to apply or appropriate for such purposes as the Corporation may specify, or to pay to the Corporation, such amount as the Corporation may specify.

(3) A direction by the Corporation under subsection (2)(b) may require the application, appropriation or payment of an amount with interest.

(4) Any such direction shall specify—

   (a) the rate or rates of interest (whether fixed or variable) which is or are applicable,

   (b) the date from which interest is payable, and

   (c) any provision for suspended or reduced interest which is applicable.

The date from which interest is payable must not be earlier than the date of the event giving rise to the exercise of the Corporation's powers under this section.

(5) In subsection (4)(c)—

   (a) provision for suspended interest means provision to the effect that if the principal amount is applied, appropriated or paid before a date specified in the direction, no interest will be payable for any period after the date of the direction; and

   (b) provision for reduced interest means provision to the effect that if the principal amount is so applied, appropriated or paid, any interest payable will be payable at a rate or rates lower than the rate or rates which would otherwise be applicable.

(6) Where—

   (a) a registered social landlord has received a payment in respect of a grant under section 18, and

   (b) at any time property to which the grant relates becomes vested in, or is leased for a term of years to, or reverts to, some other registered social landlord, this section (including this subsection) shall have effect in relation to periods after that time as if the grant, or such proportion of it as may be determined by the Corporation to be appropriate, had been made to that other registered social landlord.

(7) The matters specified in a direction under subsection (4)(a) to (c), and the proportion mentioned in subsection (6), shall be—

   (a) such as the Corporation, acting in accordance with such principles as it may from time to time determine, may specify as being appropriate, or

   (b) such as the Corporation may determine to be appropriate in the particular case.

DEFINITIONS
   "Corporation": s.56.
   "registered social landlord": s.1.

GENERAL NOTE

This section is modelled on Housing Act 1988, s.52.

It permits the Corporation to reduce, or to suspend or cancel any instalment of, social housing grant under s.18, or to redirect or pay to the Corporation "any amount" that the Corporation may specify. There is a distinction in the wording, which means that it cannot effectively be argued that "amount" here means "amount of social housing grant" (see also "pay to the Corporation" rather than "repay"): once grant monies have been paid, they will normally have been "used" (to select a neutral term) in one way or another (proper or not); if the correct interpretation was "amount of social housing grant", it could mean that this power was unavailable once spent; accordingly, the only precondition is that the landlord has received a grant under s.18.

If the land to which the grant relates is transferred to another registered social landlord, then by subs. (6) these provisions are applicable to the new landlord, in such proportions as the Corporation may determine, from which it follows that what is in mind under this section is what is still, or was once, a specific social housing grant, rather than a general power applicable to any registered social landlord which has at any time received a social housing grant.

The powers are, however, only exercisable on the basis of "principles" determined by the Corporation (subs. (1)). A determination may make different provision for different classes of landlord or of housing activity or areas: see s.52, below.

Subs. (3)

Interest may be added to the amount ordered to be applied, appropriated or repaid.

Subss. (4), (5)

If the Corporation requires the addition of interest, it must specify the rate or rates applicable, the date from when interest is payable, and "any provision for suspended or reduced interest" which is applicable, meaning incentives for early or part payment.

Subs. (7)

Both the interest provisions of subs. (4), and the apportionment provisions of subs. (6), may be exercised either according to principles determined by the Corporation—in which case, the determination may make different provision for different classes of landlord or of housing activity or areas (see s.52, below)—or in respect of an individual case.

Grants, &c. under earlier enactments

Grants under ss.50 to 55 of the Housing Act 1988

28.—(1) No application for a grant under section 50 of the Housing Act 1988 (housing association grant) may be made after the commencement of this subsection.

(2) No application for a grant under section 51 of that Act (revenue deficit grant) may be made after the commencement of this subsection except by an association which had such a deficit as is mentioned in that section for any of the years beginning 1st April 1994, 1st April 1995 or 1st April 1996.

(3) Section 52 of that Act (recovery, &c. of grants) is amended as follows—

(a) in subsection (2)(c), for "to pay to it" substitute "to apply or appropriate for such purposes as the Corporation may specify, or to pay to the Corporation,";

(b) in the closing words of subsection (2), for the words from "requiring" to "interest on that amount" substitute "may require the application, appropriation or payment of an amount with interest";

(c) in subsection (7), for the words from "requiring" to "to the Corporation" substitute "requiring the application, appropriation or payment of an amount with interest";

(d) in subsection (8)(a), for the words from "the amount" to "is paid" substitute "the principal amount is applied, appropriated or paid";

(e) in subsection (8)(b), for "that amount is so paid" substitute "the principal amount is so applied, appropriated or paid".

(4) In section 53 of that Act (determinations by Corporation), for subsection (2) (requirement of approval of Secretary of State and, in the case of a

general determination, consent of the Treasury) substitute—

"(2) The Corporation shall not make a general determination under the foregoing provisions of this Part except with the approval of the Secretary of State.".

(5) In section 55(1) of that Act (surplus rental income: cases in which section applies), omit paragraph (a).

(6) Any reference in sections 50 to 55 of that Act to registration as a housing association shall be construed after the commencement of section 1 of this Act (the register of social landlords) as a reference to registration as a social landlord.

DEFINITION
"registration": s.1.

GENERAL NOTE
This section comprises the transitional provisions pursuant to which housing association grants under Housing Act 1988, s.50 are phased out by the exclusion of new applications. Existing applications will continue, although general determinations as to their payment will (in future) be subject only to the approval of the Secretary of State (rather than, as hitherto, the approval of the Secretary of State with the consent of the Treasury)—see subs. (4).

The position so far as it concerns revenue deficit grants under *ibid.*, s.51, is a little more complex. Such grants are, as their name implies, applied for periodically, *i.e.* when, and if, needed. By subs. (2), such grants will in the future only be available to a registered housing association in receipt of revenue deficit grant immediately before commencement, or which had such a deficit in the three financial years identified.

Commutation of payments of special residual subsidy

29.—(1) The Secretary of State may, after consultation with a housing association, determine to commute any payments of special residual subsidy payable to the association under paragraph 2 of Part I of Schedule 5 to the Housing Associations Act 1985 for the financial year 1998–99 and subsequent years.

(2) Where the Secretary of State makes such a determination the payments of special residual subsidy payable to a housing association shall be commuted into a single sum calculated in such manner, and payable on such date, as the Secretary of State may consider appropriate.

(3) If after a commuted payment has been made to a housing association it appears to the Secretary of State that the payment was smaller or greater than it should have been, the Secretary of State may make a further payment to the association or require the association to repay to him such sum as he may direct.

(4) The Secretary of State may delegate to the Housing Corporation, to such extent and subject to such conditions as he may specify, any of his functions under this section and, where he does so, references to him in this section shall be construed accordingly.

GENERAL NOTE
This section mirrors s.157, Local Government and Housing Act 1989, and provides for the commutation to a single sum of periodic payments of "special residual subsidy" under Housing Associations Act 1985, Sched. 5, Pt. I, para. 2: this deals with subsidies completed no later than the financial year 1974/75, approved under the Housing Subsidies Act 1967 (c. 29) but payable under Housing Finance Act 1972 (c. 47).

CHAPTER IV

GENERAL POWERS OF THE CORPORATION

Information

General power to obtain information

30.—(1) The Corporation may for any purpose connected with the discharge of any of its functions in relation to registered social landlords serve a notice on a person requiring him—

    (a) to give to the Corporation, at a time and place and in the form and manner specified in the notice, such information relating to the affairs of a registered social landlord as may be specified or described in the notice, or

    (b) to produce to the Corporation or a person authorised by the Corporation, at a time and place specified in the notice, any documents relating to the affairs of the registered social landlord which are specified or described in the notice and are in his custody or under his control.

(2) A notice under this section may be served on—

    (a) a registered social landlord,

    (b) any person who is, or has been, an officer, member, employee or agent of a registered social landlord,

    (c) a subsidiary or associate of a registered social landlord,

    (d) any person who is, or has been, an officer, member, employee or agent of a subsidiary or associate of a registered social landlord, or

    (e) any other person whom the Corporation has reason to believe is or may be in possession of relevant information.

In this section "agent" includes banker, solicitor and auditor.

(3) No notice shall be served on a person within paragraphs (b) to (e) of subsection (2) unless—

    (a) a notice has been served on the registered social landlord and has not been complied with, or

    (b) the Corporation believes that the information or documents in question are not in the possession of the landlord.

(4) Nothing in this section authorises the Corporation to require—

    (a) the disclosure of anything which a person would be entitled to refuse to disclose on grounds of legal professional privilege in proceedings in the High Court, or

    (b) the disclosure by a banker of anything in breach of any duty of confidentiality owed by him to a person other than a registered social landlord or a subsidiary or associate of a registered social landlord.

(5) A notice under this section shall be given under the seal of the Corporation.

(6) References in this section to a document are to anything in which information of any description is recorded; and in relation to a document in which information is recorded otherwise than in legible form, references to producing it are to producing it in legible form.

(7) Where by virtue of this section documents are produced to any person, he may take copies of or make extracts from them.

DEFINITIONS

    "agent": subs. (2).
    "associate": s.61.
    "Corporation": s.56.
    "officer": s.59.
    "registered social landlord": s.1.
    "subsidiary": s.60.

GENERAL NOTE

    This section is modelled on the Housing Associations Act 1985, s.27A, expanded to mirror the investigative powers formerly only available during an inquiry under *ibid.*, s.28 (see now, Sched. 1, Pt. IV). It is the Corporation's principal power of "monitoring" registered social landlords: *cf.* above, Introduction to Pt. I. The powers are available "for any purpose connected with the discharge of any of [the Corporation's] functions in relation to registered social landlords", which is so widely cast that it permits the Corporation to seek information for any legitimate purpose.

    Those on whom the notice may be served are the landlord, any one who is, or has been, an officer, member, employee or agent of the landlord, a subsidiary or associate of the landlord, or any current or former such officers, members, employees or agents, or anyone else whom the Corporation or appointed person has reason to believe is or may be in possession of relevant information. No notice can be served on any other than the landlord unless one of the conditions in subs. (3) has been fulfilled.

For these purposes, "agent" specifically includes banker, solicitor or auditor. However, no information or documentation can be required under these provisions which is privileged information given to a solicitor (acting as such), or that would require a banker to disclose information about the affairs of any of its other customers (other than a registered social landlord, subsidiary or associate of a registered social landlord).

Express protection of privilege is necessary, in view of the recent trend to allow statutory inquiries to override it: see, *e.g. British and Commonwealth Holdings Plc v. Spicer & Oppenheim* [1993] A.C. 425, H.L., and *Bishopsgate Investment Management v. Maxwell* [1993] Ch. 1, C.A., under the Insolvency Act 1986, s.236, *Re London United Investments Plc* [1992] Ch. 578, C.A. under the Companies Act 1985, s.434, and *Bank of England v. Riley* [1992] Ch. 475, C.A. under the Banking Act 1987, s.42.

Officer. This means any trustee, secretary or treasurer of a charity, any treasurer, secretary, committee member, manager or servant of an industrial and provident society (see s.74, Industrial and Provident Societies Act 1965), or any director, manager or secretary of a company (see s.744, Companies Act 1985): see s.59, below.

Subsidiary. This means a company in respect to whom one of the following conditions is applicable—
(a) The registered social landlord is a member of the company and controls the composition of the board of directors;
(b) The registered social landlord holds more than half of the company's nominal equity share capital;
(c) The company is a subsidiary within the meaning of the Companies Act 1985 or the Friendly and Industrial and Provident Societies Act 1968 of another company, in respect of which (a) or (b) is fulfilled.
See further notes to s.60, below.

Associate. This means a company of which the registered social landlord is a subsidiary, and any other subsidiary of that company—see further notes to ss.60, 61, below.

Enforcement of notice to provide information, &c.

31.—(1) A person who without reasonable excuse fails to do anything required of him by a notice under section 30 commits an offence and is liable on summary conviction to a fine not exceeding level 5 on the standard scale.

(2) A person who intentionally alters, suppresses or destroys a document which he has been required by a notice under section 30 to produce commits an offence and is liable—

(a) on summary conviction, to a fine not exceeding the statutory maximum,

(b) on conviction on indictment, to a fine.

(3) Proceedings for an offence under subsection (1) or (2) may be brought only by or with the consent of the Corporation or the Director of Public Prosecutions.

(4) If a person makes default in complying with a notice under section 30, the High Court may, on the application of the Corporation, make such order as the court thinks fit for requiring the default to be made good.

Any such order may provide that all the costs or expenses of and incidental to the application shall be borne by the person in default or by any officers of a body who are responsible for its default.

DEFINITION
"Corporation": s.56.

GENERAL NOTE
Non-compliance with a notice under s.30, and interference with a document required thereunder, are criminal offences, prosecution of which may be authorised either by the Corporation or by the Director of Public Prosecutions. See also s.223, below, as to the concurrent liability of a director, manager, secretary or other similar officer of a corporate body with whose consent or

connivance an offence is proved to have been committed.

In addition, the Corporation may seek an order requiring compliance from the High Court. This overturns the effect of *Ashby v. Ebdon* (1984) 17 H.L.R. 1, Ch.D., under s.19, Housing Act 1974, in which it was held that the only means by which a person could enforce an analogous, earlier obligation was by way of relator action (by the Attorney-General), or by asking the Attorney-General to take action in his own name. This limitation would seem to continue to apply to a person appointed to conduct an investigation under s.7 and Sched. 1 (see para. 21), to whom the powers of this section are otherwise generally available. This is not necessarily an anomaly: it is one thing to confer this power (of enforcement of the criminal law) on the Corporation, but quite another to extend it to anyone who the Corporation may happen to appoint to conduct an investigation.

Disclosure of information to the Corporation

32.—(1) A body or person to whom this section applies may, subject to the following provisions, disclose to the Corporation, for the purpose of enabling the Corporation to discharge any of its functions relating to registered social landlords, any information received by that body or person under or for the purposes of any enactment.

(2) This section applies to the following bodies and persons—
(a) any government department (including a Northern Ireland department);
(b) any local authority;
(c) any constable; and
(d) any other body or person discharging functions of a public nature (including a body or person discharging regulatory functions in relation to any description of activities).

(3) This section has effect subject to any express restriction on disclosure imposed by or under any other enactment.

(4) Nothing in this section shall be construed as affecting any power of disclosure exercisable apart from this section.

DEFINITIONS
"Corporation": s.56.
"registered social landlord": s.1.

GENERAL NOTE
This section enables those identified by it to provide the Corporation with any information which has come into possession under or for the purposes of any enactment (including subordinate legislation), provided that the purpose of giving it to the Corporation is to enable the Corporation to discharge any of its functions in relation to registered social landlords.

A provision in the original Bill would have confined the information which the Commissioners of Customs and Excise, or the Commissioners of Inland Revenue, could pass on to the Corporation, but this was withdrawn by the government in Committee to put them on the same footing as everyone else: see *Hansard* (H.C.), Standing Committee G, Fifth Sitting, February 15, 1996, cols. 160–162, Parliamentary Under-Secretary of State for the Environment (Mr Clappison).

The issues are "confidentiality" and defamation. There is a general principle that confidences should be preserved and protected by law, although the "public interest may be outweighed by some other countervailing public interest which favours disclosure ..." (*per* Lord Goff of Chieveley, *A.G. v. Guardian Newspapers (No. 2)* [1990] 1 A.C. 109, H.L.).

"Three elements are normally required if, apart from contract, a case of breach of confidence is to succeed. First, the information itself ... must 'have the necessary quality of confidence about it' [*per* Lord Greene M.R. in *Saltman Engineering Co. v. Campbell Engineering Co. Ltd.* (1948) 65 R.P.C. 203, C.A.]. Secondly, that information must have been imparted in circumstances importing an obligation of confidence. Thirdly, there must be an unauthorised use of that information to the detriment of the party communicating it" (*per* Megarry J., in *Coco v. A.N. Clark (Engineers)* (1969) R.P.C. 41, cited by Lord Griffiths in *Guardian (No. 2)* at p.268/B–C).

"The courts have, however, always refused to uphold the right to confidence when to do so would be to cover up wrongdoing," Lord Griffiths added (at p.268/G–H). See also *R. v. Secretary of State for the Environment, ex p. L.B. Tower Hamlets* [1993] Q.B. 632, (1993) 25 H.L.R. 524, C.A.

See further *Marcel v. Commissioner of Police* [1992] 1 Ch. 225, C.A., particularly at p.261/ A–B, *per* Nolan L.J.:

"The statutory powers given to the police are plainly coupled with a public law duty. The precise extent of the duty is, I think, difficult to define in general terms and with due regard to the rights of individuals. In the context of the seizure and retention of documents, I would hold that the public law duty is combined with a private law duty of confidentiality towards the owner of the documents ... of the same character as that which formed the basis of the House of Lords decision in ... [*Guardian (No. 2)*]. It arises from the relationship between the parties."

See also at p.262/C, *per* Sir Christopher Slade:

"In my judgment, documents seized by a public authority from a private citizen in exercise of a statutory power can properly be used only for those purposes for which the relevant legislation contemplated that they might be used ..."

See further *R. v. Birmingham C.C., ex p. O* [1983] 1 A.C. 578, H.L.

If there is any doubt about whether or not the duty of confidentiality is applicable, then there arises a fear about the disclosure of information, *i.e.* that the person who discloses it may be vulnerable to litigation, either for defamation or for breach of confidence. Where powers, duties and obligations such as those which are to be found in this Part are concerned, which are or may be unfamiliar to, *e.g.* the police or some other public body, it is that much more difficult to reach a decision to disclose information; and, where a decision is difficult to reach, then officials—probably hard-pressed in any event—may understandably be less inclined to take them than otherwise, or understandably more inclined to the stance of least exposure.

Where there is a statutory power of disclosure, however, then not only will there be no risk of action for breach of confidence but also, absent malice, no risk of being sued in defamation; a (qualified) privilege will attach.

It follows that the purpose of this section—and of the next—is to encourage the mutual exchange of information between public bodies, to enable them all the better to discharge their duties. Disclosure to the Corporation may, however, be subject to express restriction on further disclosure, in which case disclosure by the Corporation under the next section is itself subject to the same restriction: see notes to s.33(3), below.

Subs. (3)

The section does not repeal or override any express statutory restriction on disclosure.

Subs. (4)

Conversely, the section does not serve to limit any existing power of disclosure (*cf.* General Note, above), *i.e.* as a matter of statutory implication.

Disclosure of information by the Corporation

33.—(1) The Corporation may disclose to a body or person to whom this section applies any information received by it relating to a registered social landlord—

(a) for any purpose connected with the discharge of the functions of the Corporation in relation to such landlords, or

(b) for the purpose of enabling or assisting that body or person to discharge any of its or his functions.

(2) This section applies to the following bodies and persons—

(a) any government department (including a Northern Ireland department);

(b) any local authority;

(c) any constable; and

(d) any other body or person discharging functions of a public nature (including a body or person discharging regulatory functions in relation to any description of activities).

Paragraph (d) extends to any such body or person in a country or territory outside the United Kingdom.

(3) Where any information disclosed to the Corporation under section 32 is so disclosed subject to any express restriction on the further disclosure of the information, the Corporation's power of disclosure under this section is exercisable subject to that restriction.

A person who discloses information in contravention of any such restriction commits an offence and is liable on summary conviction to a fine not exceeding level 3 on the standard scale.

(4) Any information disclosed by the Corporation under this section may be subject by the Corporation to any express restriction on the further disclosure of the information.

(5) A person who discloses information in contravention of any such restriction commits an offence and is liable on summary conviction to a fine not exceeding level 3 on the standard scale.

Proceedings for such an offence may be brought only by or with the consent of the Corporation or the Director of Public Prosecutions.

(6) Nothing in this section shall be construed as affecting any power of disclosure exercisable apart from this section.

DEFINITIONS
   "Corporation": s.56.
   "registered social landlord": s.1.

GENERAL NOTE
   This section is in some ways the mirror image of the last, empowering the Corporation to disclose information to other statutory officials or bodies, in the same way that they are empowered to disclose to the Corporation under the last section—see General Note, thereto, for the general principles of confidentiality at issue.

Subs. (3)
   If the disclosure to the Corporation by another statutory official or body is subject to an express restriction on further disclosure, this section takes subject to it: see subs. (3). The first sentence in subs. (3) is not free from ambiguity. On its face, it would suggest that the express restriction against further disclosure imposed on the Corporation would operate so as to override or fetter this section; however, the penal provision of the second sentence strongly suggests that the subsection serves to carry the express restriction through to the Corporation's "disclosee" rather than to prevent the Corporation engaging in the further disclosure itself.

Subs. (4)
   This is "the Raynsford memorial amendment" (Opposition Spokesman on Housing), adopted, recommended and so described by the Minister for Local Government, Housing and Urban Regeneration (Mr Curry) in Committee, _Hansard_ (H.C.), Standing Committee G, Fifth Sitting, February 15, 1996, col. 162, the self-evident purpose of which is to permit the Corporation to introduce its own restrictions on further disclosure, instead of being confined to those which its original informant had imposed (and which continue to bind by subs. (3), above).

Subs. (6)
   The section does not serve to limit any existing power of disclosure (_cf._ General Note to s.35, above), _i.e._ as a matter of statutory implication.

Standards of performance

Standards of performance

34. The Corporation may, after consultation with persons or bodies appearing to it to be representative of registered social landlords, from time to time—
   (a) determine such standards of performance in connection with the provision of housing as, in its opinion, ought to be achieved by such landlords, and
   (b) arrange for the publication, in such form and in such manner as it considers appropriate, of the standards so determined.

DEFINITION
   "registered social landlord": s.1.

GENERAL NOTE
   The Corporation enjoys power to set "performance standards", relating to the _provision_ of

housing (and, therefore, distinct from the housing management guidance which it may issue under s.36, below) as ought to be achieved by registered social landlords, which standards it may publish in such form and manner as it considers appropriate. For the purpose of monitoring and publicising levels of compliance, the Corporation has power to collect information under s.35, below. A determination may make different provision for different classes of landlord or of housing activity or areas: see s.53 below.

"Provision" of housing in context (and read together with s.35(5) below) seems wide enough to govern, *e.g.* void turn-around time, or allocation, as well as new-build activity. See also s.36(2)(a). It is envisaged that there will be discernibly separate standards: see s.35(2) ("each standard determined under section 34").

The Corporation must, however, before reaching its opinion on performance standards, consult with "persons or bodies appearing to it to be representative of social landlords", one of which will be the National Federation of Housing Associations (see Introduction to Pt. I, above; see s.33, Housing Associations Act 1985).

As to consultation, see notes to s.5, above. The issue of performance standards without consultation will be *ultra vires* and the standards as issued will not enjoy any validity, in particular— bearing the criminal sanctions of s.35(3) in mind—in relation to the collection of information under s.35.

Information as to levels of performance

35.—(1) The Corporation shall from time to time collect information as to the levels of performance achieved by registered social landlords in connection with the provision of housing.

(2) On or before such date in each year as may be specified in a direction given by the Corporation, each registered social landlord shall provide the Corporation, as respects each standard determined under section 34, with such information as to the level of performance achieved by him as may be so specified.

(3) A registered social landlord who without reasonable excuse fails to do anything required of him by a direction under subsection (2) commits an offence and is liable on summary conviction to a fine not exceeding level 5 on the standard scale.

Proceedings for such an offence may be brought only by or with the consent of the Corporation or the Director of Public Prosecutions.

(4) The Corporation shall at least once in every year arrange for the publication, in such form and in such manner as it considers appropriate, of such of the information collected by or provided to it under this section as appears to it expedient to give to tenants or potential tenants of registered social landlords.

(5) In arranging for the publication of any such information the Corporation shall have regard to the need for excluding, so far as that is practicable—

    (a) any matter which relates to the affairs of an individual, where publication of that matter would or might, in the opinion of the Corporation, seriously and prejudicially affect the interests of that individual; and

    (b) any matter which relates specifically to the affairs of a particular body of persons, whether corporate or unincorporate, where publication of that matter would or might, in the opinion of the Corporation, seriously and prejudicially affect the interests of that body.

DEFINITIONS
"Corporation": s.56.
"registered social landlord": s.1.
"tenancy": s.229.
"tenant": s.229.

GENERAL NOTE
The performance information must be provided to the Corporation, in accordance with its direction, non-compliance with which without reasonable excuse constitutes an offence punishable by a fine not exceeding level 5 on the standard scale, consent to prosecute which may be

obtained from the Corporation or from the Director of Public Prosecutions.

Subs. (2)

The information may be collected "from time to time", but it is clearly anticipated that returns will be provided annually.

Subs. (4)

The Corporation is under a duty at least once a year to arrange for publication of performance information, in such form and manner as it considers appropriate, of such information "as appears to it expedient" to give to tenants and to potential tenants, presumably meaning such information as assists a tenant (or, perhaps, a group of local authority tenants consulted under Housing Act 1985, Sched. 3A on a L.S.V.T. [see Introduction to Pt. I, above]) to select landlords or else to make other choices to which the performance of a landlord may be relevant. "Expedient", *i.e.* advantageous, or fit, proper or suitable to the circumstances (O.E.D.).

Subs. (5)

A further provision restricting the information which the Corporation may disclose (*cf.* above, ss.32, 33), although cast in more general, and subjective terms, *i.e.* the Corporation need only "have regard to" the exclusion of material "seriously and prejudicially" affecting the interests of an individual or body, *cf. de Falco v. Crawley B.C.* [1980] Q.B. 460, C.A.

Housing management

Issue of guidance by the Corporation

36.—(1) The Corporation may issue guidance with respect to the management of housing accommodation by registered social landlords.

(2) Guidance under this section may, in particular, be issued with respect to—

(a) the housing demands for which provision should be made and the means of meeting those demands;

(b) the allocation of housing accommodation between individuals;

(c) the terms of tenancies and the principles upon which levels of rent should be determined;

(d) standards of maintenance and repair and the means of achieving those standards;

(e) the services to be provided to tenants;

(f) the procedures to be adopted to deal with complaints by tenants against a landlord;

(g) consultation and communication with tenants;

(h) the devolution to tenants of decisions concerning the management of housing accommodation.

(3) Before issuing any guidance under this section the Corporation shall—

(a) consult such bodies appearing to it to be representative of registered social landlords as it considers appropriate, and

(b) submit a draft of the proposed guidance to the Secretary of State for his approval.

(4) If the Secretary of State gives his approval to the draft submitted to him, the Corporation shall issue the guidance in such manner as the Corporation considers appropriate for bringing it to the notice of the landlords concerned.

(5) Guidance issued under this section may be revised or withdrawn; and subsections (3) and (4) apply in relation to the revision of guidance as in relation to its issue.

(6) Guidance under this section may make different provision in relation to different cases and, in particular, in relation to different areas, different descriptions of housing accommodation and different descriptions of registered social landlord.

(7) In considering whether action needs to be taken to secure the proper management of the affairs of a registered social landlord or whether there has been mismanagement, the Corporation may have regard (among other

matters) to the extent to which any guidance under this section is being or has been followed.

DEFINITIONS
"Corporation": s.56.
"housing accommodation": s.63.
"registered social landlord": s.1.
"tenancy": s.229.
"tenant": s.229.

GENERAL NOTE
This section is based on the Housing Associations Act 1985, s.36A, added by Housing Act 1988, s.49, pursuant to which the Corporation has issued guidance under H.C. 36/94, "Guidance on the Management of Accommodation Let on Assured Tenancies by Registered Housing Associations". There is also guidance in Housing Management Practice in Shared Housing, Hostels and Special Needs Housing, Housing Management Practices for Fully Mutual Co-Operatives and Housing Management Practice for Long Leases and Shared Ownership.

The extent to which this guidance has been followed may be taken into account by the Corporation when determining (a) whether action needs to be taken to secure the proper management of the affairs of a registered social landlord, and (b) whether or not there has been mismanagement, for the purposes of the exercise of powers under Sched. 1 (see notes thereto, below) or otherwise.

The schedule of particular matters which may be the subject of guidance governs: the categories of tenant to be targeted; how allocation points are calculated or priority otherwise determined; terms of tenancies; rent levels; standards of maintenance and repair; services to tenants; complaints procedures (and see s.51, below); devolution of management control to tenants; and, consultation and communication with tenants. Accordingly, all of the principal aspects of housing management are expected to be covered. Related to guidance on maintenance and repair, the Corporation enjoys power of entry under s.37, below, backed by an offence of obstruction under s.38.

Subss. (3)–(4)
On "consultation", see General Note to s.5, above.

The wording of the relationship with the Secretary of State is interesting and unusual: instead of qualifying the power to issue guidance, the requirement (if it is) to obtain the approval of the Secretary of State is spread between the duty to submit the draft of proposed guidance (presumably, *after* it has been the subject of consultation with others, *n.b.* the use of the word "proposed" in subs. (3)(b), *cf.* its omission in the opening words of the subsection), and the obligation to issue the guidance "if the Secretary of State gives his approval to the draft" in subs. (4).

On the face of it, therefore, there would appear to be power (but not an obligation) to issue guidance which had *not* secured the approval of the Secretary of State.

Powers of entry

37.—(1) This section applies where it appears to the Corporation that a registered social landlord may be failing to maintain or repair any premises in accordance with guidance issued under section 36.

(2) A person authorised by the Corporation may at any reasonable time, on giving not less than 28 days' notice of his intention to the landlord concerned, enter any such premises for the purpose of survey and examination.

(3) Where such notice is given to the landlord, the landlord shall give the occupier or occupiers of the premises not less than seven days' notice of the proposed survey and examination.

A landlord who fails to do so commits an offence and is liable on summary conviction to a fine not exceeding level 3 on the standard scale.

(4) Proceedings for an offence under subsection (3) may be brought only by or with the consent of the Corporation or the Director of Public Prosecutions.

(5) An authorisation for the purposes of this section shall be in writing stating the particular purpose or purposes for which the entry is authorised and shall, if so required, be produced for inspection by the occupier or anyone acting on his behalf.

(6) The Corporation shall give a copy of any survey carried out in exercise

of the powers conferred by this section to the landlord concerned.

(7) The Corporation may require the landlord concerned to pay to it such amount as the Corporation may determine towards the costs of carrying out any survey under this section.

DEFINITIONS
"Corporation": s.56.
"registered social landlord": s.1.

GENERAL NOTE
On a minimum of 28 days' notice of intention to landlord, the Corporation can survey any premises, where it appears that guidance on maintenance and repair issued under s.36 *may* not be being complied with. This permits entry on a relatively low threshold (*cf.* notes to s.188, below). The landlord has to give not less than seven days' notice to the occupier, and if he fails to do so is liable to a penalty of not more than scale 3 on the standard scale, which may be prosecuted with the consent of either the Corporation or the Director of Public Prosecutions.

Subs. (4)
There is no requirement to give the subs. (2) notice in writing, but entry is only available to an authorised person, and that authority must be in writing, must state the purpose of the entry, and must be produced on demand for the inspection of the occupier. This is a mandatory condition to the power of entry, and no offence will be committed under s.38, below, if it is not complied with: see *Stroud v. Bradbury* [1952] 2 All E.R. 76, D.C.
"Authorised person" is not confined to an employee of the Corporation.

Subs. (5)
Any survey carried out in exercise of the power must be copied to the landlord but *not* to the occupier. There seems to be no over-riding reason why it should attract any public interest immunity such as to protect it from production in court on the instigation of the occupier, as such disclosure would not seem to be capable of hampering the Corporation's use of the power or impede the carrying out of the statutory purpose for which the powers were conferred: see, *e.g.*, *Bookbinder v. Tebbitt (No. 2)* [1992] 1 W.L.R. 217, considering *Alfred Crompton Amusement Machines Ltd. v. Customs and Excise Commissioners (No. 2)* [1974] A.C. 405, H.L., and *Neilson v. Laugharne* [1981] Q.B. 736, C.A.
The most common reason why the occupier would seek the survey would be to establish notice of disrepair: see, *e.g.*, *O'Brien v. Robinson* [1973] A.C. 912, H.L., *Sheldon v. West Bromwich Corporation* (1973) 13 H.L.R. 23, C.A., *McGreal v. Wake* (1984) 13 H.L.R. 107, C.A. The fact that the notice was not from the tenant will not affect the matter, nor even that the inspection was not (necessarily) for that express purpose: see also *Dinefwr B.C. v. Jones* (1987) 19 H.L.R. 445, C.A., *Hall v. Howard* (1988) 20 H.L.R. 566, C.A. (An alternative reason may be—to the extent that it is applied by s.17, above, to the right to acquire under s.16, above—to show that the landlord failed to comply with the obligation in Housing Act 1985, s.125(4A), to disclose structural defects "known to the landlord").

Subs. (6)
The landlord may be required to pay the Corporation's costs of the survey and inspection.

Penalty for obstruction of person exercising power of entry

38.—(1) It is an offence for a registered social landlord or any of its officers or employees to obstruct a person authorised under section 37 (powers of entry) to enter premises in the performance of anything which he is authorised by that section to do.

(2) A person who commits such an offence is liable on summary conviction to a fine not exceeding level 3 on the standard scale.

(3) Proceedings for such an offence may be brought only by or with the consent of the Corporation or the Director of Public Prosecutions.

DEFINITIONS
"officer": s.59.
"registered social landlord": s.1.

GENERAL NOTE
This section makes a criminal offence of obstruction of a person authorised (provided prop-

erly so authorised: see notes to s.37(4), above) under s.37, punishable by a fine of up to level 3 on the standard scale, but only capable of being committed by the landlord, or any of its officers or employees, not an occupier or some other person (see also Minister for Local Government, Housing and Urban Regeneration [Mr Curry], *Hansard* (H.C.), Standing Committee G, Fifth Sitting, February 15, 1996, col. 177). The offence may be prosecuted with the consent of the Corporation or the Director of Public Prosecutions.

See also s.223, below, as to the concurrent liability of a director, manager, secretary or other similar officer of a corporate body with whose consent or connivance an offence is proved to have been committed.

Insolvency, &c. of registered social landlord

Insolvency, &c. of registered social landlord: scheme of provisions

39.—(1) The following sections make provision—
   (a) for notice to be given to the Corporation of any proposal to take certain steps in relation to a registered social landlord (section 40), and for further notice to be given when any such step is taken (section 41),
   (b) for a moratorium on the disposal of land, and certain other assets, held by the registered social landlord (sections 42 and 43),
   (c) for proposals by the Corporation as to the future ownership and management of the land held by the landlord (section 44), which are binding if agreed (section 45),
   (d) for the appointment of a manager to implement agreed proposals (section 46) and as to the powers of such a manager (sections 47 and 48),
   (e) for the giving of assistance by the Corporation (section 49), and
   (f) for application to the court to secure compliance with the agreed proposals (section 50).
(2) In those sections—
   "disposal" means sale, lease, mortgage, charge or any other disposition, and includes the grant of an option;
   "secured creditor" means a creditor who holds a mortgage or charge (including a floating charge) over land held by the landlord or any existing or future interest of the landlord in rents or other receipts from land; and
   "security" means any mortgage, charge or other security.
(3) The Secretary of State may make provision by order defining for the purposes of those sections what is meant by a step to enforce security over land.

Any such order shall be made by statutory instrument which shall be subject to annulment in pursuance of a resolution of either House of Parliament.

DEFINITIONS
   "Corporation": s.56.
   "registered social landlord": s.1.
   "steps": s.40.

GENERAL NOTE
This is the first in a new set of provisions, additional to the powers exercisable by the Corporation resulting from an investigation or audit under Sched. 1, Pt. IV (see notes thereto, below). The provisions permit the Corporation to enjoy the benefit of a moratorium (see s.42, below) during which it can make proposals (under s.44) as to the future ownership and management of the land of registered social landlords against whom steps are threatened (as identified in s.40, below), to enforce a mortgage, charge or other security.

The proposals replace the original ideas, which in substance were intended to empower the Corporation to make transfer orders in like circumstances, which it was considered (for good reason) would deter the private sector from investing in social housing, within the purpose and policy of this Part of the Act (see *Our Future Homes* (White Paper, 1995), Chap. 4). Instead, a framework for consensus has been put forward, and is (helpfully) introduced by this section.

The purpose remains to provide the Corporation with an early opportunity to deal with assets which have been funded by social (housing) money, in order to secure their continued use for social housing, and therefore to prevent their realisation in other ways.

Initial notice to the Corporation

40.—(1) Notice must be given to the Corporation before any of the steps mentioned below is taken in relation to a registered social landlord.

The person by whom the notice must be given is indicated in the second column.

(2) Where the registered social landlord is an industrial and provident society, the steps and the person by whom notice must be given are—

Any step to enforce any security over land held by the landlord.	The person proposing to take the step.
Presenting a petition for the winding up of the landlord.	The petitioner.
Passing a petition for the winding up of the landlord.	The landlord.

(3) Where the registered social landlord is a company registered under the Companies Act 1985 (including a registered charity), the steps and the person by whom notice must be given are—

Any step to enforce any security over land held by the landlord.	The person proposing to take the step.
Applying for an administration order.	The applicant.
Presenting a petition for the winding up of the landlord.	The petitioner.
Passing a resolution for the winding up of the landlord.	The landlord.

(4) Where the registered social landlord is a registered charity (other than a company registered under the Companies Act 1985), the steps and the person by whom notice must be given are—

Any step to enforce any security over land held by the landlord.	The person proposing to take the step.

(5) Notice need not be given under this section in relation to a resolution for voluntary winding up where the consent of the Corporation is required (see paragraphs 12(4) and 13(6) of Schedule 1).

(6) Any step purportedly taken without the requisite notice being given under this section is ineffective.

DEFINITIONS
"Corporation": s.56.
"registered social landlord": s.1.
"step to enforce any security": s.39(3).

GENERAL NOTE
This section identifies (a) the requirement to give notice to the Corporation before any of (b) the identified steps are taken in relation to a registered landlord, and (c) by whom the notice must be given. The requirement does not apply where the Corporation's consent is already required under Sched. 1, paras. 12, 13: see notes thereto, below. The requirement does not apply where the action is being taken by the Secretary of State, the Attorney-General or the Charity Commissioners.

The steps are those which involve enforcing any security over land held by the registered social landlord. The Secretary of State has power (s.39(3)) to define what is meant by a step to enforce security. The steps are also those which involve application for an administration order, voluntary winding up, a winding-up petition.

Administration Order. An administration order may be made under Pt. II, Insolvency Act 1986 when a court is satisfied that a company is or is likely to become unable to pay its debts, and considers that the making of an order would be likely to achieve:

the survival of the company as a going concern, or

the approval of a voluntary arrangement (composition with creditors by agreement), or

the sanctioning of a compromise or arrangement under s.425, Companies Act 1985, *i.e.* so as to bind a minority, or

a more advantageous realisation of assets than would follow a winding-up order (Insolvency Act 1986, s.8).

The procedure is by way of petition, of which notice has to be given to anyone who has appointed, or may be entitled to appoint, an administrative receiver (*ibid.*, s.9) and, now, to the Corporation.

Voluntary Arrangement. Likewise, no voluntary arrangement can be proposed by the directors of a company (Insolvency Act 1986, Pt. I) without prior notice to the Corporation. Nor can the court make an order under s.425 (or ss.427, 427A), Companies Act 1985, without such prior notification to the Corporation: s.50(4), below.

Winding Up. A winding up may be voluntary, by resolution of those who control the affairs of a society or company, *i.e.* members, shareholders or directors; it may also be procured by the creditors. A compulsory winding up is, in effect, by application to and order of the court. See Insolvency Act 1986, Pt. IV.

See, generally, Fletcher, *The Law of Insolvency*, 2nd. ed.

"Land" includes "buildings and other structures, land covered with water, and any estate, interest, easement, servitude or right in or over land": Interpretation Act 1978, Sched. 1.

Subs. (3)

A step without notice is simply without effect.

Further notice to be given to the Corporation

41.—(1) Notice must be given to the Corporation as soon as may be after any of the steps mentioned below is taken in relation to a registered social landlord.

The person by whom the notice must be given is indicated in the second column.

(2) Where the registered social landlord is an industrial and provident society, the steps and the person by whom notice must be given are—

The taking of a step to enforce any security over land held by the landlord.	The person taking the step.
The making of an order for the winding up of the landlord.	The petitioner.
The passing of a resolution for the winding up of the landlord.	The landlord.

(3) Where the registered social landlord is a company registered under the Companies Act 1985 (including a registered charity), the steps and the person by whom notice must be given are—

The taking of a step to enforce any security over land held by the landlord.	The person taking the step.
The making of an administration order.	The person who applied for the order.
The making of an order for the winding up of the landlord.	The petitioner.
The passing of a resolution for the winding up of the landlord.	The landlord.

(4) Where the registered social landlord is a registered charity (other than a company registered under the Companies Act 1985), the steps and the person by whom notice must be given are—

The taking of a step to enforce any security over land held by the landlord.	The person taking the step.

(5) Failure to give notice under this section does not affect the validity of any step taken; but the period of 28 days mentioned in section 43(1) (period after which moratorium on disposal of land, &c. ends) does not begin to run until any requisite notice has been given under this section.

DEFINITIONS
　　"Corporation": s.56.
　　"moratorium": s.42.
　　"registered social landlord": s.1.
　　"step to enforce any security": s.39(3).

GENERAL NOTE
　　This section is a second stage at which notice must be given, as a safety net (and will include cases where a first stage requirement does not bite because this Part has not yet been brought into force), and requires notice not of the intention to take a relevant step, but after it has been taken, or that a resolution has been passed or an order made. The failure does not invalidate the (preceding) action, which is presumably why the time for notice is the vague "as soon as may be", but the Corporation's protection is to be found instead in postponement of commencement of the period of "moratorium" during which the relevant land cannot be disposed of without the consent of the Corporation, so as to enable the Corporation to make its proposals (under s.44, below).

Moratorium on disposal of land, &c.

42.—(1) Where any of the steps mentioned in section 41 is taken in relation to a registered social landlord, there is a moratorium on the disposal of land held by the landlord.
　　(2) During the moratorium the consent of the Corporation under this section is required (except as mentioned below) for any disposal of land held by the landlord, whether by the landlord itself or any person having a power of disposal in relation to the land.
　　Consent under this section may be given in advance and may be given subject to conditions.
　　(3) Consent is not required under this section for any such disposal as is mentioned in section 10(1), (2) or (3) (lettings and other disposals not requiring consent under section 9).
　　(4) A disposal made without the consent required by this section is void.
　　(5) Nothing in this section prevents a liquidator from disclaiming any land held by the landlord as onerous property.
　　(6) The provisions of this section apply in relation to any existing or future interest of the landlord in rent or other receipts arising from land as they apply to an interest in land.

DEFINITIONS
　　"Corporation": s.56.
　　"registered social landlord": s.1.

GENERAL NOTE
　　The substance of the provisions is to be found in the moratorium (which lasts for the period identified by s.43 below).
　　The moratorium does not come into existence unless the triggering event defined by s.41 above, takes place, so that there is no consequence (save to give the Corporation time to prepare) which results from the notice of that event that is required by s.40. It does, however, encourage all parties to find their own solutions, in which it is likely to be the case that the Corporation will play an informal part, so as to put to the benefit of the circumstance its experience and contacts, and perhaps (and properly) so as to secure its preferred end without the need to go through the moratorium process: if it does so participate, the Corporation should, how-

ever, make clear at all times that it is without prejudice to its right to avail itself of the moratorium, should the period between notice and triggering event not prove fruitful.

Subs. (2)
    The effect of the moratorium is to prevent disposal of any land held by the registered social landlord, by landlord or liquidator, administrator, administrative receiver or receiver, without the consent of the Corporation, which may be given in advance and/or conditionally.

Subs. (3)
    No consent is needed for those disposals as are mentioned in s.10: see notes thereto, above.

Subs. (4)
    Disposal without consent (where needed) is void: see notes to s.9, above.

Subs. (5)
    This provision preserves the power of the liquidator to disclaim onerous property (Insolvency Act 1986, ss.178–182), the effect of which is not to destroy any asset which the Corporation might wish to see pass within the social rented sector, but to dissolve by disclaimer an interest that would positively diminish its value or inhibit such a transfer.

Period of moratorium

   43.—(1) The moratorium in consequence of the taking of any step as mentioned in section 41—
    (a) begins when the step is taken, and
    (b) ends at the end of the period of 28 days beginning with the day on
        which notice of its having been taken was given to the Corporation
        under that section,
subject to the following provisions.
    (2) The taking of any further step as mentioned in section 41 at a time when a moratorium is already in force does not start a further moratorium or affect the duration of the existing one.
    (3) A moratorium may be extended from time to time with the consent of all the landlord's secured creditors.
    Notice of any such extension shall be given by the Corporation to—
    (a) the landlord, and
    (b) any liquidator, administrative receiver, receiver or administrator
        appointed in respect of the landlord or any land held by it.
    (4) If during a moratorium the Corporation considers that the proper management of the landlord's land can be secured without making proposals under section 44 (proposals as to ownership and management of landlord's land), the Corporation may direct that the moratorium shall cease to have effect.
    Before making any such direction the Corporation shall consult the person who took the step which brought about the moratorium.
    (5) When a moratorium comes to an end, or ceases to have effect under subsection (4), the Corporation shall give notice of that fact to the landlord and the landlord's secured creditors.
    (6) When a moratorium comes to an end (but not when it ceases to have effect under subsection (4)), the following provisions of this section apply.
    The Corporation's notice shall, in such a case, inform the landlord and the landlord's secured creditors of the effect of those provisions.
    (7) If any further step as mentioned in section 41 is taken within the period of three years after the end of the original period of the moratorium, the moratorium may be renewed with the consent of all the landlord's secured creditors (which may be given before or after the step is taken).
    Notice of any such renewal shall be given by the Corporation to the persons to whom notice of an extension is required to be given under subsection (3).
    (8) If a moratorium ends without any proposals being agreed, then, for a

period of three years the taking of any further step as mentioned in section 41 does not start a further moratorium except with the consent of the landlord's secured creditors as mentioned in subsection (7) above.

General Note

This section defines the life of the moratorium: it begins on the day the triggering step in s.41 is taken, and ends 28 days after notice is given to the Corporation under that section. (Cases where no notice is required are those where a winding up petition is presented by the Secretary of State or the Corporation itself: s.41(4).) If there is a further triggering step taken during this period, there is neither a new moratorium, nor an extension of the existing moratorium: subs. (2). The moratorium can be extended with the consent of all the creditors holding a mortgage or charge over the registered social landlord's land or its interests in rents and receipts from land (see s.39(2)): subs. (3). The Corporation has to give notice of an extension to the persons identified in *ibid*.

The Corporation has power to direct that the moratorium should cease to have effect, if it considers that the proper management of the land can be achieved without proposals under the following section: subs. (4). Before using this power, it must consult with the person whose action brought about the moratorium: *ibid.* (As to consultation, see notes to s.5, above). It has to give notice of the ending or cessation of the moratorium to the landlord, and to the secured creditors: subs. (5).

If a further step is taken within three years of the end of the original moratorium (but not merely its cessation to have effect under subs. (4): see subs. (6)), then the moratorium can be renewed, or revived, with the consent of all the secured creditors: subs. (7). This clearly will only have effect from its renewal and cannot, *e.g.*, retrospectively invalidate intervening transactions. The Corporation has to give notice of renewal to the same persons as it has to notify of an extension: *ibid*.

Unless there is such consent, a further triggering step within the three years will mean that there will be no further moratorium: subs. (8). This does not obviate the need for notice under either s.40 or s.41 (because there will in each case still be some point to the notice, *i.e.* the opportunity to take voluntary steps, and/or to seek agreement to a renewed moratorium).

Proposals as to ownership and management of landlord's land

44.—(1) During the moratorium (see sections 42 and 43) the Corporation may make proposals as to the future ownership and management of the land held by the registered social landlord, designed to secure the continued proper management of the landlord's land by a registered social landlord.

(2) In drawing up its proposals the Corporation—

(a) shall consult the landlord and, so far as is practicable, its tenants, and

(b) shall have regard to the interests of all the landlord's creditors, both secured and unsecured.

(3) The Corporation shall also consult—

(a) where the landlord is an industrial and provident society, the appropriate registrar, and

(b) where the landlord is a registered charity, the Charity Commissioners.

(4) No proposals shall be made under which—

(a) a preferential debt of the landlord is to be paid otherwise than in priority to debts which are not preferential debts, or

(b) a preferential creditor is to be paid a smaller proportion of his preferential debt than another preferential creditor, except with the concurrence of the creditor concerned.

In this subsection references to preferential debts and preferential creditors have the same meaning as in the Insolvency Act 1986.

(5) So far as practicable no proposals shall be made which have the effect that unsecured creditors of the landlord are in a worse position than they would otherwise be.

(6) Where the landlord is a charity the proposals shall not require the landlord to act outside the terms of its trusts, and any disposal of housing accom-

modation occupied under a tenancy or licence from the landlord must be to another charity whose objects appear to the Corporation to be, as nearly as practicable, akin to those of the landlord.

(7) The Corporation shall serve a copy of its proposals on—

(a) the landlord and its officers,

(b) the secured creditors of the landlord, and

(c) any liquidator, administrator, administrative receiver or receiver appointed in respect of the landlord or its land;

and it shall make such arrangements as it considers appropriate to see that the members, tenants and unsecured creditors of the landlord are informed of the proposals.

DEFINITIONS

"Corporation": s.56.

"registered social landlord": s.1.

"secured creditors": s.39.

GENERAL NOTE

The general purpose of the moratorium is to enable the Corporation to make proposals for future ownership and management of the land of the registered social landlord, designed to secure its continued proper management, which undoubtedly comprises transfer to another registered social landlord and in any event is a broad objective, not fettered in any way save generally by the purposes of the legislation (see above, notes to s.1) and by the express terms of this section, as to:

(a) the need to consult (see notes to s.5, above): subss. (2)(a), (3);

(b) the need to have regard to the interests of all the creditors, not merely the secured creditors: subs. (2)(b);

(c) the prohibition on alteration of preferences (see Insolvency Act 1986, s.239): subs. (4);

(d) the desirability of ensuring that no unsecured creditors of the landlord are worse off than otherwise: subs. (5);

(e) the need to ensure that a charitable landlord remains within the terms of its trusts, and that its occupied accommodation is transferred to a charity with objects as like as practicable to those of the landlord: subs. (6);

(f) the need to serve copies of proposals on all the principal persons identified in subs. (7), and otherwise to make arrangements for notifying the others so identified: *ibid.*

Effect of agreed proposals

45.—(1) The following provisions apply if proposals made by the Corporation under section 44 are agreed, with or without modifications, by all the secured creditors of the registered social landlord.

(2) Once agreed the proposals are binding on the Corporation, the landlord, all the landlord's creditors (whether secured or unsecured) and any liquidator, administrator, administrative receiver or receiver appointed in respect of the landlord or its land.

(3) It is the duty of—

(a) the members of the committee where the landlord is an industrial and provident society,

(b) the directors where the landlord is a company registered under the Companies Act 1985 (including a company which is a registered charity), and

(c) the trustees where the landlord is a charitable trust,

to co-operate in the implementation of the proposals.

This does not mean that they have to do anything contrary to any fiduciary or other duty owed by them.

(4) The Corporation shall serve a copy of the agreed proposals on—

(a) the landlord and its officers,

(b) the secured creditors of the landlord, and

(c) any liquidator, administrator, administrative receiver or receiver appointed in respect of the landlord or its land, and

(d) where the landlord is an industrial and provident society or registered charity, the appropriate registrar or the Charity Commissioners, as the case may be;

and it shall make such arrangements as it considers appropriate to see that the members, tenants and unsecured creditors of the landlord are informed of the proposals.

(5) The proposals may subsequently be amended with the consent of the Corporation and all the landlord's secured creditors.

Section 44(2) to (7) and subsections (2) to (4) above apply in relation to the amended proposals as in relation to the original proposals.

DEFINITIONS
"Corporation": s.56.
"registered social landlord": s.1.
"secured creditors": s.39.

GENERAL NOTE
If all the *secured* creditors agree with the Corporation's proposal—as modified if necessary—then the proposals will be binding on the registered social landlord and all its creditors (secured or not), and its liquidator, administrator, administrative receiver, or receiver appointed in respect of the landlord or of its land: subs. (2). Subject to their overriding fiduciary or other duties, the committee members, directors or trustees are obliged to co-operate in their implementation: subs. (3). The Corporation has to serve a copy of the agreed proposals, *i.e.* as modified, on the principal persons identified in subs. (4), and otherwise must make its arrangements for notifying the others so identified: *ibid.* There is power for the Corporation and the secured creditors (*en bloc*) to agree further modifications, although the Corporation must then re-consult under s.44: subs. (5).

Appointment of manager to implement agreed proposals

46.—(1) Where proposals agreed as mentioned in section 45 so provide, the Corporation may by order under its seal appoint a manager to implement the proposals or such of them as are specified in the order.

(2) If the landlord is a registered charity, the Corporation shall give notice to the Charity Commissioners of the appointment.

(3) Where proposals make provision for the appointment of a manager, they shall also provide for the payment of his reasonable remuneration and expenses.

(4) The Corporation may give the manager directions in relation to the carrying out of his functions.

(5) The manager may apply to the High Court for directions in relation to any particular matter arising in connection with the carrying out of his functions.

A direction of the court supersedes any direction of the Corporation in respect of the same matter.

(6) If a vacancy occurs by death, resignation or otherwise in the office of manager, the Corporation may by further order under its seal fill the vacancy.

DEFINITIONS
"Corporation": s.56.
"registered social landlord": s.1.
"secured creditors": s.39.

GENERAL NOTE
This section empowers the Corporation—by agreement with the secured creditors under s.45—to appoint a manager (with the powers identified in s.47, below) to implement the agreed proposals: subs. (1). The proposals must govern how the manager is to be remunerated (and see the power of the Corporation to assist, in s.48, below): subs. (2).

The Corporation can give the manager directions (subs. (4)), but, like a manager or receiver appointed by a court, the manager can apply to the High Court for directions in the exercise of his functions, *e.g.* where he is in any doubt about his powers, or to safeguard his position, or indeed in substance to overrule a direction of the Corporation: subs. (5).

Powers of the manager

47.—(1) An order under section 46(1) shall confer on the manager power generally to do all such things as are necessary for carrying out his functions.

(2) The order may include the following specific powers—

1. Power to take possession of the land held by the landlord and for that purpose to take any legal proceedings which seem to him expedient.
2. Power to sell or otherwise dispose of the land by public auction or private contract.
3. Power to raise or borrow money and for that purpose to grant security over the land.
4. Power to appoint a solicitor or accountant or other professionally qualified person to assist him in the performance of his functions.
5. Power to bring or defend legal proceedings relating to the land in the name and on behalf of the landlord.
6. Power to refer to arbitration any question affecting the land.
7. Power to effect and maintain insurance in respect of the land.
8. Power where the landlord is a body corporate to use the seal of the body corporate for purposes relating to the land.
9. Power to do all acts and to execute in the name and on behalf of the landlord any deed, receipt or other document relating to the land.
10. Power to appoint an agent to do anything which he is unable to do for himself or which can more conveniently be done by an agent, and power to employ and dismiss any employees.
11. Power to do all such things (including the carrying out of works) as may be necessary in connection with the management or transfer of the land.
12. Power to make any payment which is necessary or incidental to the performance of his functions.
13. Power to carry on the business of the landlord so far as relating to the management or transfer of the land.
14. Power to grant or accept a surrender of a lease or tenancy of any of the land, and to take a lease or tenancy of any property required or convenient for the landlord's housing activities.
15. Power to make any arrangement or compromise on behalf of the landlord in relation to the management or transfer of the land.
16. Power to do all other things incidental to the exercise of any of the above powers.

(3) In carrying out his functions the manager acts as the landlord's agent and he is not personally liable on a contract which he enters into as manager.

(4) A person dealing with the manager in good faith and for value is not concerned to inquire whether the manager is acting within his powers.

(5) The manager shall, so far as practicable, consult the landlord's tenants about any exercise of his powers which is likely to affect them and inform them about any such exercise of his powers.

DEFINITION
"housing activities": s.63.

GENERAL NOTE
The manager can enjoy—if the order appointing him so directs—a wide range of powers, modelled on those conferred on an administrator or administrative receiver under Insolvency Act 1986, Sched. 1 (but, noticeably, *not* including power to present or defend a winding-up petition). Further powers may be conferred by s.48, below.

In general, the position of the manager is closer to that of an administrative receiver, whose powers under *ibid.*, Sched. 1 are confined to the property of which he is the receiver or manager, rather than the assets of the company as a whole with which the administrator will be concerned—see *ibid.*, s.43(2)(b)).

The powers are:

to take possession, to sell the land, to raise or borrow money including using the land as security, to appoint professionals to assist him, to take or defend legal proceedings in the landlord's name or to refer any matter to arbitration, to insure, to use the landlord's corporate seal (if applicable), to execute deeds, receipts and other documents, to appoint agents or employ and dismiss employees, to do anything necessary to the management and transfer of the land, to make payments, to carry on the landlord's business as it relates to the management and transfer of the land, to grant leases or tenancies or accept a surrender of such, or take a lease of property for the purpose of carrying on the landlord's housing activities, to make any arrangement or compromise on behalf of the landlord relating to the management and transfer, and to do anything else which is incidental to any of the foregoing.

Subs. (3)

The manager is in the same position as an administrator or administrative receiver under Insolvency Act 1986, ss.14(5), 44(1), so far as his status as agent is concerned, but does not incur personal liability on his contracts (which puts his position on the same footing as an administrator, but not an administrative receiver—see *ibid.* s.44(1)(b), expressly so providing for personal liability in the latter case). The landlord is, accordingly, bound by his actions.

This general accretion of liability to the landlord by way of agency, however, is only effective so far as the manager is exercising his powers, *i.e.* powers which he actually has. This matches the common law position, in which an agent is entitled to be indemnified against all losses and liabilities incurred "in the execution of his authority" (see Reynolds & Bowstead on Agency, 16th ed., Art. 64; *cf.* Art. 65, not entitled, *inter alia*, where not authorised, or where resulting from own negligence, default, or breach of duty).

Subs. (4)

This subsection, which is based on Insolvency Act 1986, s.14(6), protects third parties from an attempt by the landlord or the manager to raise *vires* by way of defence to a claim.

Subs. (5)

As to consultation, see notes to s.5, above.

Powers of the manager: transfer of engagements

48.—(1) An order under section 46(1) may, where the landlord is an industrial and provident society, give the manager power to make and execute on behalf of the society an instrument transferring the engagements of the society.

(2) Any such instrument has the same effect as a transfer of engagements under section 51 or 52 of the Industrial and Provident Societies Act 1965 (transfer of engagements by special resolution to another society or a company).

In particular, its effect is subject to section 54 of that Act (saving for rights of creditors).

(3) A copy of the instrument, signed by the manager, shall be sent to the appropriate registrar and registered by him; and until that copy is so registered the instrument shall not take effect.

(4) It is the duty of the manager to send a copy for registration within 14 days from the day on which the instrument is executed; but this does not invalidate registration after that time.

GENERAL NOTE

This section applies to industrial and provident societies only. If empowered to do so by an order made under s.46, the manager can transfer the engagements of one society to another, in which case it is treated as a transfer by special resolution under the Industrial and Provident Societies Act 1965, which is without prejudice to the rights of creditors under *ibid.*, s.54.

Assistance by the Corporation

49.—(1) The Corporation may give such assistance as it thinks fit—
(a) to the landlord, for the purpose of preserving the position pending the

making of and agreement to proposals;
- (b) to the landlord or a manager appointed under section 46, for the purpose of carrying out any agreed proposals.

(2) The Corporation may, in particular—
- (a) lend staff;
- (b) pay or secure payment of the manager's reasonable remuneration and expenses;
- (c) give such financial assistance as appears to the Corporation to be appropriate.

(3) The following forms of assistance require the consent of the Secretary of State—
- (a) making grants or loans;
- (b) agreeing to indemnify the manager in respect of liabilities incurred or loss or damage sustained by him in connection with his functions;
- (c) paying or guaranteeing the repayment of the principal of, the payment of interest on and the discharge of any other financial obligation in connection with any sum borrowed (before or after the making of the order) and secured on any land disposed of.

DEFINITION
"Corporation": s.56.

GENERAL NOTE
If a registered social landlord is sufficiently in financial difficulties for a security to be enforced, the Corporation may well have to provide the financial resources—and other resources, such as staff—to effect the transfer, which this section gives it power to do, subject to the consent of the Secretary of State so far as concerns the specific forms of assistance identified in subs. (3). A prospective manager, too, is likely to be unwilling to accept the transfer task if the primary source from which he will derive his protection—the landlord as principal (see s.47(4), above)—is not solid.

Application to court to secure compliance with agreed proposals

50.—(1) The landlord or any creditor of the landlord may apply to the High Court on the ground that an action of the manager appointed under section 46 is not in accordance with the agreed proposals.

On such an application the court may confirm, reverse or modify any act or decision of the manager, give him directions or make such other order as it thinks fit.

(2) The Corporation or any other person bound by agreed proposals may apply to the High Court on the ground that any action, or proposed action, by another person bound by the proposals is not in accordance with those proposals.

On such an application the court may—
- (a) declare any such action to be ineffective, and
- (b) grant such relief by way of injunction, damages or otherwise as appears to the court appropriate.

DEFINITIONS
"Corporation": s.56.
"registered social landlord": s.1.
"secured creditor": s.39.

GENERAL NOTE
This section enables the landlord, a creditor, and the Corporation, or any other person bound by the proposals, to apply to the High Court on the ground that an action (or a proposed action: see subs. (2)) of the manager is not in accordance with the agreed proposals: subs. (1). The court's powers on such an application are extremely wide: see subss. (1), (2).

CHAPTER V

MISCELLANEOUS AND GENERAL PROVISIONS

Housing complaints

Schemes for investigation of complaints

51.—(1) The provisions of Schedule 2 have effect for the purpose of enabling tenants and other individuals to have complaints against social landlords investigated by a housing ombudsman in accordance with a scheme approved by the Secretary of State.

(2) For the purposes of that Schedule a "social landlord" means—

(a) a registered social landlord;

(b) a transferee of housing pursuant to a qualifying disposal under section 135 of the Leasehold Reform, Housing and Urban Development Act 1993;

(c) a body which has acquired dwellings under Part IV of the Housing Act 1988 (change of landlord: secure tenants); or

(d) any other body which was at any time registered with the Corporation and which owns or manages publicly-funded dwellings.

(3) In subsection (2)(d) a "publicly-funded dwelling" means a dwelling which was—

(a) provided by means of a grant under—

section 18 of this Act (social housing grant), or

section 50 of the Housing Act 1988, section 41 of the Housing Associations Act 1985, or section 29 or 29A of the Housing Act 1974 (housing association grant); or

(b) acquired on a disposal by a public sector landlord.

(4) The Secretary of State may by order add to or amend the descriptions of landlords who are to be treated as social landlords for the purposes of Schedule 2.

(5) Before making any such order the Secretary of State shall consult such persons as he considers appropriate.

(6) Any such order shall be made by statutory instrument which shall be subject to annulment in pursuance of a resolution of either House of Parliament.

DEFINITIONS

"Corporation": s.56.
"publicly funded dwelling": subs. (3).
"public sector landlord": s.63.
"registered social landlord": s.1.
"tenant": s.229.

GENERAL NOTE

This section puts on a statutory footing the work hitherto being done on the basis of a scheme established by the Housing Corporation in 1993, the Housing Associations Tenants Ombudsman Service. The intention in the White Paper, *Our Future Homes*, was that all of what are now called registered social landlords would be "subject to the Ombudsman's oversight" (p.41), with other landlords such as the operators of private retirement housing able to join the scheme on a voluntary basis.

These proposals were elaborated in the D.O.E. Consultation Paper, More Choice in the Social Rented Sector (July 1995). There is no intention to change the functions of the Service of investigating and helping to resolve tenants' complaints. However, by this stage the proposals had shifted, to adopt the model to be found in Building Societies Act 1986 (c. 53), Sched. 12, whereby landlords (identified by the Secretary of State) are obliged to belong to an Ombudsman scheme, approved by the Secretary of State, which deals with those matters specified by legislation. It follows that, although at the outset it is likely that the present scheme is the one that will be adopted, under the current Ombudsman, groups of landlords, *e.g.* in a particular geographical area, or according to a particular area of housing activity, could decide to establish their own, discrete scheme.

Though modelled on the Building Societies Act 1986, however, the mandatory elements of this Act are—on its face—somewhat weaker. The mandatory elements of a 1986 Act scheme are to be found in its Sched. 12, Pt. III, in some detail; here, while the sorts of matters to be covered by the scheme are identified in Sched. 2, para. 2, and there are some minimum powers conferred on the Housing Ombudsman under Sched. 2, para. 7, the principal details of the Ombudsman's range of responsibilities, and any strengthening of his powers on an adverse determination, are left to be controlled, ultimately, only by the grant or withholding of approval by the Secretary of State.

By way of example, there is nothing on the face of this Act:

(a) to require that a scheme covers maladministration (see 1986, Sched. 12, Pt. III, para. 1)—the closest this Act comes is merely the requirement that a determination is to be made by reference to what the Housing Ombudsman considers "fair in all the circumstances of the case" (see Sched. 2, para. 7(1), below); or

(b) limiting the grounds on which a complaint can be excluded (Building Societies Act 1986, Sched. 12, Pt. III, para. 2)—here, Sched. 2, para. 2/5 identifies court proceedings as being amongst those which will lead to exclusion; or

(c) empowering "the adjudicator" (widely known—but not statutorily—as the Building Societies Ombudsman) to extend the scope of his investigation of his own motion (Building Societies Act 1986, Sched. 12, Pt. III, para. 3); or

(d) to have regard to any particular information published by the body (*ibid.*, para. 4).

Subs. (1)

It is tenants "and other individuals" who may complain, which permits complaints by people living with tenants, as well as people whose complaint is the refusal of a tenancy: but see Sched. 2, para. 2/6, and notes thereto, below.

Subs. (2)

All "social landlords" must be a member of the scheme: Sched. 2, para. 1. This term is wider than, but includes, "registered social landlord", and extends to cover any transferee of public housing under a large scale voluntary transfer (disposals programme) under s.135, Leasehold Reform, Housing and Urban Development Act 1993.

It also covers bodies which *have* at some time been registered with the Corporation, which means de-registered social landlords, or—as the wording seems wide enough to include—a housing association de-registered before the commencement of this Act and accordingly only ever registered with the Corporation under the Housing Act 1974 and/or the Housing Associations Act 1985. However, these bodies are only within the definition (and the requirement) if they own or manage "publicly-funded dwellings".

Subs. (3)

This defines the publicly-funded dwellings, ownership or management of which will oblige a landlord to belong to an approved scheme, because the dwelling was funded by social housing grant under s.18, above, or by housing association grant under the provisions of the Housing Acts 1974–1988, or which were acquired on a disposal by a public sector landlord (as to which, see notes to s.16(2), above).

There is no inclusion of property which is merely funded by disposal proceeds under s.25, above. Once a landlord is bound to belong to a scheme, however, the obligation extends to all its housing activities.

Subs. (4)

The Secretary of State retains control over the landlords which must belong to an approved scheme.

Subs. (5)

"Consultation": see notes to s.5, above.

Orders and determinations

General provisions as to orders

52.—(1) The following provisions apply to any power of the Secretary of State under this Part to make an order.

(2) An order may make different provision for different cases or descriptions of case.

This includes power to make different provision for different bodies or descriptions of body, different provision for different housing activities and different provision for different areas.

(3) An order may contain such supplementary, incidental, consequential or transitional provisions and savings as the Secretary of State considers appropriate.

DEFINITION
"housing activities": s.63.

General provisions as to determinations

53.—(1) The following provisions apply to determinations of the Corporation or the Secretary of State under this Part.

(2) A determination may make different provision for different cases or descriptions of case.

This includes power to make—

(a) different provision for different registered social landlords or descriptions of registered social landlord, and

(b) different provision for different housing activities and different provision for different areas;

and for the purposes of paragraph (b) descriptions may be framed by reference to any matters whatever, including in particular, in the case of housing activities, the manner in which they are financed.

(3) In this Part a general determination means a determination which does not relate solely to a particular case.

(4) Before making a general determination, the Corporation or the Secretary of State shall consult such bodies appearing to them to be representative of registered social landlords as they consider appropriate.

(5) After making a general determination, the Corporation or the Secretary of State shall publish the determination in such manner as they consider appropriate for bringing the determination to the notice of the landlords concerned.

DEFINITIONS
"Corporation": s.56.
"housing activities": s.63.
"registered social landlord": s.1.

GENERAL NOTE
On consultation, see General Note to s.5, above.

The reference to ways in which housing activities have been financed reflects the intention that an increasing part of the funding of social housing will come from the private finance sector, see White Paper, *Our Future Homes*, Chap. Four.

Determinations of the Corporation requiring approval

54. The Corporation shall not make—

(a) a general determination under paragraph 16 of Schedule 1 (accounting and audit requirements for registered social landlords) or section 18 (social housing grant), or

(b) any determination under section 27 (recovery, &c. of social housing grants),

except with the approval of the Secretary of State.

DEFINITIONS
"Corporation": s.56.
"registered social landlord": s.1.

GENERAL NOTE
The Corporation must have the consent of the Secretary of State before making a general determination as to accounting and audit requirements, and *any* determination—general or specific—under s.27, to recover social housing grant.

Minor and consequential amendments

Minor and consequential amendments: Part I

55.—(1) The enactments mentioned in Schedule 3 have effect with the minor amendments specified there.

(2) The Secretary of State may by order make such amendments or repeals of any enactment as appear to him necessary or expedient in consequence of the provisions of this Part.

(3) Any such order shall be made by statutory instrument which shall be subject to annulment in pursuance of a resolution of either House of Parliament.

GENERAL NOTE

Attention may be drawn to the extended powers of the Audit Commission.

The Corporation and the Audit Commission can agree programmes of comparative study allowing the latter to make recommendations for improving the "economy, efficiency and effectiveness of registered social landlord". If such a programme cannot be agreed, a programme proposed by either of them can be referred to the Secretary of State, who can direct it to be carried out with or without modifications. The Commission are to determine the studies to be carried out to give effect to the programme. The Corporation must reimburse the Commission. The Commission must publish its reports, and before doing so must show a draft to the Corporation and consider whether to revise it in the light of the Corporation's comments. The Commission is given added powers (subject to the consent of the Corporation) to obtain information from a registered social landlord, and may disclose it to the Corporation.

In addition, the Commission may provide the Corporation with consultancy services, relating to the audit of accounts, *i.e.* may assist the Corporation to determine audit requirements (under Sched. 1, Pt. III).

Interpretation

Meaning of "the Corporation"

56.—(1) In this Part "the Corporation" means the Housing Corporation or Housing for Wales, as follows.

(2) In relation to a registered social landlord, or a body applying for such registration, which is—

    (a) a registered charity which has its address for the purposes of registration by the Charity Commissioners in Wales,

    (b) an industrial and provident society which has its registered office for the purposes of the Industrial and Provident Societies Act 1965 in Wales, or

    (c) a company registered under the Companies Act 1985 which has its registered office for the purposes of that Act in Wales,

"the Corporation" means Housing for Wales.

(3) In relation to any other registered social landlord or body applying for such registration, "the Corporation" means the Housing Corporation.

(4) Nothing in this Part shall be construed as requiring the Housing Corporation and Housing for Wales to establish the same criteria for registration as a social landlord, or otherwise to act on the same principles in respect of any matter in relation to which they have functions under this Part.

Definitions relating to industrial and provident societies

57.—(1) In this Part, in relation to an industrial and provident society—

    "appropriate registrar" has the same meaning as in the Industrial and Provident Societies Act 1965 (where it is defined in section 73(1)(c) by reference to the situation of the society's registered office);

    "committee" means the committee of management or other directing body of the society; and

    "co-opted member", in relation to the committee, includes any person co-opted to serve on the committee, whether he is a member of the society or not.

(2) Any reference in this Part to a member of the committee of an industrial and provident society includes a co-opted member.

Appropriate Registrar. By s.73 of the Industrial and Provident Societies Act 1965, there is a Chief Registrar of Friendly Societies, and Assistant Registrars of Friendly Societies, who are the appropriate registrars for England, Wales or the Channel Islands, and an Assistant Registrar of Friendly Societies for Scotland.

Definitions relating to charities

58.—(1) In this Part—
(a) "charity" and "trusts", in relation to a charity, have the same meaning as in the Charities Act 1993, and "trustee" means a charitable trustee within the meaning of that Act; and
(b) "registered charity" means a charity which is registered under section 3 of that Act and is not an exempt charity within the meaning of that Act.

(2) References in this Part to a company registered under the Companies Act 1985 do not include a company which is a registered charity, except where otherwise provided.

GENERAL NOTE
See notes to s.2(1), above.

Meaning of "officer" of registered social landlord

59.—(1) References in this Part to an officer of a registered social landlord are—
(a) in the case of a registered charity which is not a company registered under the Companies Act 1985, to any trustee, secretary or treasurer of the charity;
(b) in the case of an industrial and provident society, to any officer of the society as defined in section 74 of the Industrial and Provident Societies Act 1965; and
(c) in the case of a company registered under the Companies Act 1985 (including such a company which is also a registered charity), to any director or other officer of the company within the meaning of that Act.

(2) Any such reference includes, in the case of an industrial and provident society, a co-opted member of the committee of the society.

GENERAL NOTE
See General Note to s.7, above.

Meaning of "subsidiary"

60.—(1) In this Part "subsidiary", in relation to a registered social landlord, means a company with respect to which one of the following conditions is fulfilled—
(a) the landlord is a member of the company and controls the composition of the board of directors;
(b) the landlord holds more than half in nominal value of the company's equity share capital; or
(c) the company is a subsidiary, within the meaning of the Companies Act 1985 or the Friendly and Industrial and Provident Societies Act 1968, of another company which, by virtue of paragraph (a) or paragraph (b), is itself a subsidiary of the landlord.

(2) For the purposes of subsection (1)(a), the composition of a company's board of directors shall be deemed to be controlled by a registered social landlord if, but only if, the landlord, by the exercise of some power exercisable by him without the consent or concurrence of any other person, can appoint or remove the holders of all or a majority of the directorships.

(3) In relation to a company which is an industrial and provident society—
(a) any reference in this section to the board of directors is a reference to the committee of management of the society; and
(b) the reference in subsection (2) to the holders of all or a majority of the directorships is a reference—

(i) to all or a majority of the members of the committee, or
(ii) if the landlord is himself a member of the committee, such number as together with him would constitute a majority.

(4) In the case of a registered social landlord which is a body of trustees, references in this section to the landlord are to the trustees acting as such.

GENERAL NOTE

Subsidiary. Companies Act 1985, s.736: "A company is a subsidiary of another company if that other company holds a majority of the voting rights in it, or is a member of it and has the right to appoint or remove a majority of its board of directors, or is a member of it and controls alone, pursuant to an agreement with other shareholders or members, a majority of the voting rights in it. A company is also a subsidiary of one company if it is the subsidiary of a subsidiary of it."

Voting rights, in the case of a company with share capital, means the voting rights conferred on shareholders; otherwise, it is the voting rights of those members who can vote on all, or substantially all, general meetings of the company: s.736A(1).

The right to appoint or remove a majority of the board is the right to appoint or remove directors holding a majority of the voting rights at meetings of the board (on all, or substantially all, matters): s.736A(2). A company has the right to appoint to a directorship of the putative subsidiary if the appointment follows necessarily from appointment as director of the putative holding company, or the directorship is held by the company itself: s.736A(3).

When rights are only exercisable in certain circumstances, they are only taken into account when those circumstances have arisen and continue to apply, or when the circumstances are within the control of the person having the right: s.736A(4). Rights held in a fiduciary capacity are ignored: s.736A(5). Rights held by nominees for another are treated as that other's (and rights are so treated when the nominee is bound to act on that other's instructions, or with his consent or concurrence): s.736A(6). Provision is also made for (i) rights attaching to securities, and (ii) rights held or exercisable by subsidiaries.

Friendly and Industrial and Provident Societies Act 1968, s.15: A company is a subsidiary of an industrial and provident society if the society either is a member of the company and controls the composition of its board of directors, or holds more than half the nominal value of the company's equity share capital, *i.e.* the same definition as in subs.(1)(a), (b), here.

There is control of the composition of the board if the society can—without the consent of anyone else—appoint or remove all or a majority of the directors: s.15(2). There is power to appoint a director if the directorship is held by the society, appointment as director follows from appointment as a member of the committee of the society, or the appointment requires the consent of the society: s.15(3).

When determining ownership of share capital, and when determining whether or not the society has powers, shares held and powers exercisable in a fiduciary capacity are not treated as belonging to the society, whereas shares held and powers exercisable by nominees for the society are treated as belonging to it; shares held and powers exercisable by virtue of a debenture, or a trust deed securing any issue of a debenture, are ignored; and, shares held and powers exercisable as security for the purposes of a loan executed in the ordinary business of a society (the business of which includes the lending of money) are not treated as held or exercisable by the society: s.15(4).

Meaning of "associate"

61.—(1) In this Part "associate", in relation to a registered social landlord, means—

(a) any body of which the landlord is a subsidiary, and
(b) any other subsidiary of such a body.

(2) In this section "subsidiary" has the same meaning as in the Companies Act 1985 or the Friendly and Industrial and Provident Societies Act 1968 or, in the case of a body which is itself a registered social landlord, has the meaning given by section 60.

GENERAL NOTE

Subsidiary. See General Note to s.60, above.

Members of a person's family

62.—(1) A person is a member of another's family within the meaning of this Part if—

(a) he is the spouse of that person, or he and that person live together as husband and wife, or
(b) he is that person's parent, grandparent, child, grandchild, brother, sister, uncle, aunt, nephew or niece.

(2) For the purpose of subsection (1)(b)—
(a) a relationship by marriage shall be treated as a relationship by blood,
(b) a relationship of the half-blood shall be treated as a relationship of the whole blood, and
(c) the stepchild of a person shall be treated as his child.

GENERAL NOTE

This section restates Housing Act 1985, s.113 (adapted in the light of Family Law Reform Act 1987 (c. 42) to remove now otiose references to illegitimacy): see also s.140, below. It is applicable to clawback of discount under s.14, above, and to the prohibition on payments to be found in Sched. 1, para. 1—see notes to s.7, above.

Cohabitation. It is self-evident that cohabitants can be living together as husband and wife, but that does not mean that every cohabitation so qualifies (nor does homosexual cohabitation so qualify: see *Harrogate B.C. v. Simpson* (1984) 17 H.L.R. 205, C.A.).

Sexual relations are not determinative. In *Adeoso v. Adeoso* [1980] 1 W.L.R. 1535, C.A., it was held that a couple living in a two-room flat (*i.e.* one bedroom and a living room) had to be considered to be living in the same household "as husband and wife", albeit that for months they had not spoken, had communicated only by notes, that each slept in one of the rooms and kept the doors locked, but shared the rent and electricity charge. (This was for the purposes of Domestic Violence and Matrimonial Proceedings Act 1976 (c. 50), s.1(2) and, as such, should be treated with some caution insofar as words must always be read in context).

Whether or not persons are living together as husband and wife is in part a question of intention: in *City of Westminster v. Peart* (1991) 24 H.L.R. 389, C.A., a couple who had reconciled were held not to be living together as husband and wife, on the particular facts of the case including particularly that the defendant had retained another flat.

Under the Rent Acts, it was initially held that a cohabitant could not succeed as a member of the family of a deceased tenant: see *Brock v. Wollams* [1949] 2 K.B. 388, C.A., *Gammans v. Ekins* [1950] 2 K.B. 328, C.A. In *Hawes v. Evenden* [1953] 1 W.L.R. 1169, C.A., however, a woman who had lived with a man for 12 years without taking his name, and who had two children by him, was held to be a member of his family. In *Dyson Holdings v. Fox* [1976] 1 Q.B. 503, C.A., a stable, 20-year period of cohabitation without marriage, but in which the woman had taken the man's name, was held to be a family relationship, having regard to the changing popular meaning of the word "family".

This last approach was rejected in *Helby v. Rafferty* [1979] 1 W.L.R. 13, C.A., wherein it was held that the word "family" should have the meaning applicable when first used by Parliament; a man, accordingly, was unable to succeed to the tenancy of a woman with whom he had lived for approximately five years, as her lover, sharing expenses, caring for her while she was dying, but neither having taken the other's name. In *Watson v. Lucas* [1980] 1 W.L.R. 1493, C.A., conversely, and considering themselves bound by *Dyson*, the Court of Appeal held that a man who had lived with a woman for nearly 20 years, even although he had never divorced his lawful wife, was a member of her family.

Children. It is unclear whether a *de facto*—but not *de jure*—adopted child can fall within the definition: see *Brock v. Wollams* (above), where this was allowed under the Rent Acts, even though by the time the question arose the child had achieved his majority. As there can be no *de jure* adoption between adults, there can accordingly be no *de facto* such adoption: see *Carega Properties S.C. v. Sharratt* [1979] 1 W.L.R. 928, H.L.

Minor definitions

63.—(1) In this Part—
"dwelling" means a building or part of a building occupied or intended to be occupied as a separate dwelling, together with any yard, garden, outhouses and appurtenances belonging to it or usually enjoyed with it;
"fully mutual", in relation to a housing association, and "co-operative housing association" have the same meaning as in the Housing Associations Act 1985 (see section 1(2) of that Act);
"hostel" means a building in which is provided for persons generally or for a class or classes of persons—
(a) residential accommodation otherwise than in separate and self-contained premises, and
(b) either board or facilities for the preparation of food

adequate to the needs of those persons, or both;
"house" includes—
>>(a) any part of a building occupied or intended to be occupied as a separate dwelling, and
>>(b) any yard, garden, outhouses and appurtenances belonging to it or usually enjoyed with it;

"housing accommodation" includes flats, lodging-houses and hostels;
"housing activities" means, in relation to a registered social landlord, all its activities in pursuance of the purposes, objects and powers mentioned in or specified under section 2;
"information" includes accounts, estimates and returns;
"local authority" has the same meaning as in the Housing Associations Act 1985;
"long tenancy" has the same meaning as in Part V of the Housing Act 1985;
"modifications" includes additions, alterations and omissions and cognate expressions shall be construed accordingly;
"notice" means notice in writing;
"public sector landlord" means any of the authorities or bodies within section 80(1) of the Housing Act 1985 (the landlord condition for secure tenancies);
"registrar of companies" has the same meaning as in the Companies Act 1985;
"statutory tenancy" has the same meaning as in the Housing Act 1985.

(2) References in this Part to the provision of a dwelling or house include the provision of a dwelling or house—
>>(a) by erecting the dwelling or house, or converting a building into dwellings or a house, or
>>(b) by altering, enlarging, repairing or improving an existing dwelling or house;

and references to a dwelling or house provided by means of a grant or other financial assistance are to its being so provided directly or indirectly.

GENERAL NOTE

Subs. (1)
Dwelling. Whether or not something can properly be called a dwelling is to be determined by asking whether occupation as a dwelling is intended as at the date the question arises: see *R. v. L.B. Camden, ex p. Comyn Ching & Co.* (1984) 47 P. & C.R. 417. A building formerly in occupation as an H.M.O., *e.g.* bedsitting rooms, vacated for conversion to self-contained flats, ceases to be an H.M.O. when it is emptied with the intention that it should not return to H.M.O. occupation: *R. v. Kerrier D.C., ex p. Guppy's (Bridport) Ltd. (No. 2)* (1985) 17 H.L.R. 426, C.A.

The intention must be that the dwelling is to be occupied as a separate dwelling: see notes to s.16(2), above.

"Yards, garden, outhouses and appurtenances": see note on *House*, below.

Fully Mutual. A fully mutual housing association is one the rules of which restrict membership to tenants or prospective tenants, and preclude the grant or assignment to non-members: Housing Associations Act 1985, s.1(2). A co-operative housing association is a fully mutual association registered under the Industrial and Provident Societies Act 1965.

Hostel. This is based on s.622, Housing Act 1985.

House. The word "house" has been the subject of considerable litigation, both under the Housing Acts and otherwise. Care must be taken when applying case law that is derived from other legislation, and even from other parts of the Housing Acts: see *Quillotex Co. Ltd. v. Minister of Housing and Local Government* [1966] 1 Q.B. 704, C.A., *Annicola Investments Ltd. v. Minister of Housing and Local Government* [1968] 1 Q.B. 631, C.A., *R. v. Cardiff C.C., ex p. Cross* (1981) 1 H.L.R. 54, Q.B.D. (upheld on appeal at (1982) 6 H.L.R. 1, C.A.).

Whether or not something is a house is a mixed question of law (involving construction of the Act in question) and fact (*In Re Butler, Camberwell (Wingfield Mews) No. 2 Clearance Order 1936* [1939] 1 K.B. 570, C.A.) to be left in the first instance to the decision-maker, with whose decision the courts can only interfere on conventional (administrative law) grounds (see notes to s.1, above, s.203, below): *Re South Shields (D'Arcy Street) Compulsory Purchase Order 1937* [1939] 1 All E.R. 419, C.A.; *Ashbridge Investments Ltd. v. Minister of Housing and Local Government* [1965] 1 W.L.R. 1320, C.A.

Nor does the word have a very precise meaning: *Quillotex* (above). It is a "building for human habitation": *Reed v. Hastings Corporation* (1964) 62 L.G.R. 588, C.A., or a "building constructed or adapted for use as or for the purposes of a dwelling" (*Ashbridge Investments*, above). A garage or workshop with a dwelling above was held to be a house in *In Re Butler* (above)—see also *Re Hammersmith (Bergham Mews) Clearance Order 1936* [1937] 3 All E.R. 539. Where a building is used partly for residential purposes, and partly for others, it has to be looked at as a whole to ascertain whether, as a question of degree, it can properly be described as a house: *Annicola* (above). It need not be shown that all the rooms in a building are in residential use: *Premier Garage Co. v. Ilkeston Corporation* (1933) 97 J.P. 786.

Although original construction is important (*In Re Butler*, above), use at the time the question falls to be determined is also relevant (*ibid.*, see also *Grosvenor v. Hampstead Junction Railway* [1957] L.J. Ch. 731; an unfinished house may qualify as a house—*Alexander v. Crystal Palace Railway* (1862) 30 Beav. 556; a building constructed as a house but used for other purposes has been considered to remain a house—*Howard v. Minister of Housing and Local Government* (1967) 65 L.G.R. 257.

Although housing accommodation can include flats, a building subdivided into flats can remain a house, whether or not so constructed: *Annicola* (above), *Quillotex* (above), *Benabo v. Wood Green B.C.* [1946] 1 K.B. 38, *Critchell v. L.B. Lambeth* [1957] 2 Q.B. 535, C.A., *Okereke v. L.B. Brent* [1967] 1 Q.B. 42, C.A. The flat itself can, because of the statutory definition, be a house (overturning *R. v. L.B. Lambeth, ex p. Clayhope* (1987) 19 H.L.R. 426, C.A.).

Again, though housing accommodation can include lodging-houses and hostels, a hostel or building used for multiple occupation, or as a lodging-house, may yet qualify as a house in its own right: see *London County Council v. Rowton Houses Ltd.* (1897) 62 J.P. 68, *Re Ross and Leicester Corporation* (1932) 96 J.P. 459, *R. v. L.B. Southwark, ex p. Lewis Levy Ltd.* (1983) 8 H.L.R. 1, *R. v. L.B. Camden, ex p. Rowton (Camden Town) Ltd.* (1983) 10 H.L.R. 28.

In *Lake v. Bennett* [1970] 1 Q.B. 663, C.A., under Leasehold Reform Act 1967, Lord Denning M.R. doubted whether a tower block could *ever* reasonably be called a house, but Salmon L.J. emphasised that the decision did not necessarily affect the Housing Acts, and the wording of the 1967 Act does refer to a house "reasonably so-called".

"Appurtenances". This extended definition of house (and, now, of dwelling: see above) dates back to the Artizans and Labourers Dwellings Act 1868 (c. 130), and has been maintained since (see, *e.g.* Housing of the Working Classes Act 1890 (c. 70), s.29, Housing Act 1925, s.135, Housing Act 1936, s.188, Housing Act 1957, s.189, Housing Act 1985, s.56). In *Trim v. Sturminster R.D.C.* [1938] 2 K.B. 508, under the 1936 Act, 10 acres of grassland were let together with a cottage. On the question whether they were appurtenant to the cottage, it was held that the expression "appurtenances" meant only such matters as outhouses, yards and gardens, but not the land itself: how much of the land could be included in this definition depended on the facts, but would certainly be less than the whole of the 10 acres that had been thus let.

In *Clymo v. Shell-Mex & B.P. Ltd.* (1963) 10 R.R.C. 85, C.A., under Rating and Valuation Act 1925 (c. 90), it was held that open land surrounded by depot buildings was appurtenant to the buildings, on the basis that had there been a conveyance or demise the land would have passed without any need specifically to mention it. In *Methuen-Campbell v. Walters* [1979] Q.B. 525, under Leasehold Reform Act 1967 (c. 88), it was held that land cannot ordinarily be appurtenant to land, although the ordinary and strict meaning of the word appurtenant could yield to a wider meaning if the context so requires.

In *Hansford v. Jago* [1921] 1 Ch. 322, a right of way was held to come within the word "appurtenance". In *Sovmots Investments Ltd. v. Secretary of State for the Environment* [1979] A.C. 144, H.L., however, it was held that appurtenances could not include rights of way and other ancillary rights not yet defined or in some cases even in existence (though specifically overturned by Local Government (Miscellaneous Provisions) Act 1976 (c. 57), s.13, so far as concerns compulsory purchase by local authorities). In *R. v. L.B. Lambeth, ex p. Clayhope* at first instance ((1986) 18 H.L.R. 541), it was held that the common parts and the roof of a block of flats were not appurtenant to each and every flat. (This was not considered in the Court of Appeal—above—as it did not arise in the light of the finding that the flats were not houses.)

In *F.F.F. Estates v. Hackney L.B.C.* [1981] Q.B. 503, 3 H.L.R. 107, C.A., however, the court, considering the meaning of dwelling in connection with improvement notices under Pt. VII, Housing Act 1985, said that the case law on rights passing on a conveyance was not of "any real help".

Housing Accommodation. The term "flat" is not defined, although it is used in Housing Act 1985, s.118, to mean that which is not a house, *i.e.* that which overlaps or "underlaps" another part of the structure of the building of which it forms a part (*ibid.* s.183).

Long Tenancy. See notes to s.16(1), above.

Public sector landlord. See notes to s.16(2), above.

Statutory tenancy. This means (Housing Act 1985, s.622) a statutory tenancy under the Rent Act 1977 or the Rent (Agriculture) Act 1976, *i.e.* the right of irremovability conferred in the private sector, before Housing Act 1988, so long as premises continued to be used as a home.

Subs. (2)
This definition is based on Housing Act 1985, s.9, and includes new-build and conversion, alteration and enlargement, improvement and repair. Housing may be provided, even if it produces no net increase in the number of units available: see *Andreiser v. Minister of Housing and Local Government* (1965) 109 S.J. 594.

Index of defined expressions

64. The following Table shows provisions defining or otherwise explaining expressions used in this Part (other than provisions defining or explaining an expression used in the same section)—

appointed person (in relation to inquiry into affairs of registered social landlord)	paragraph 20 of Schedule 1
appropriate registrar (in relation to an industrial and provident society)	section 57(1)
associate (in relation to a registered social landlord)	section 61(1)
assured tenancy	section 230
assured agricultural occupancy	section 230
assured shorthold tenancy	section 230
charity	section 58(1)(a)
committee member (in relation to an industrial and provident society)	section 57(2)
company registered under the Companies Act 1985	section 58(2)
co-operative housing association	section 63
co-opted member (of committee of industrial and provident society)	section 57(1)
the Corporation	section 56
disposal proceeds fund	section 24
dwelling	section 63
enactment	section 230
fully mutual housing association	section 63
hostel	section 63
house	section 63
housing accommodation	section 63
housing activities	section 63
housing association	section 230
industrial and provident society	section 2(1)(b)
information	section 63
lease	section 229
local authority	section 63
long tenancy	section 63
member of family	section 62
modifications	section 63
notice	section 63
officer of registered social landlord	section 59
provision (in relation to dwelling or house)	section 63(2)
public sector landlord	section 63
register, registered and registration (in relation to social landlords)	section 1
registered charity	section 58(1)(b)
registrar of companies	section 63

relevant disposal which is not an exempted disposal (in sections 11 to 14)	section 15
secure tenancy	section 230
social housing grant	section 18(1)
statutory tenancy	section 63
subsidiary (in relation to a registered social landlord)	section 60(1)
trustee and trusts (in relation to a charity)	section 58(1)(a)

PART II

HOUSES IN MULTIPLE OCCUPATION

Registration schemes

INTRODUCTION

Controls over houses in multiple occupation (H.M.O.s) were first introduced in 1958, and the powers were extended on no fewer than three occasions during the 1960s. Further amendments were made in the 1980s. Since the first controls were introduced it has been recognised that H.M.O.s present a particular housing problem, and the further powers included in this Part of the Act are a recognition that the problem still continues. It is currently estimated that there are about 638,000 H.M.O.s in England and Wales. According to the English House Condition Survey in 1993, four out of 10 H.M.O.s were unfit for human habitation. A study for the Campaign for Bedsit Rights by G. Randall estimated that the chances of being killed or injured by fire in an H.M.O. are 28 times higher than for residents of other dwellings.

The provisions relating to H.M.O.s are now contained in Pt. XI of the Housing Act 1985 (c. 68), as amended by the Local Government and Housing Act 1989 (c. 42). Recognising that there was still a continuing problem, in November 1994 the government initiated a review of H.M.O.s by means of a consultation paper "*Houses in Multiple Occupation—Consultation Paper on the Case for Licensing*". Although 75 per cent of the responses to that paper were in favour of a mandatory licensing scheme, the government rejected this approach "because of the inherent danger that it would lead to excessive cost and bureaucracy by forcing every local authority to follow a standard licensing approach" (Improving Standards in Houses in Multiple Occupation, D.O.E. Consultation Paper, July 1995, para. 2.1).

Instead, the government has opted for giving authorities powers to adopt a scheme, which is far stronger than the existing registration scheme (to be found in s.346 of the 1985 Act). Only about one third of authorities have chosen to use the existing scheme. The majority of the provisions in this Part relate to this new registration scheme.

House in multiple occupation

The key definition for the application of these provisions is that of "house in multiple occupation". Despite opposition amendments the government resisted attempts to amend the definition during passage of the Bill. The definition is therefore to be found in Housing Act 1985, s.345 (as amended by Local Government and Housing Act 1989, Sched. 9, para. 44):

"(1) In this Part 'house in multiple occupation' means a house which is occupied by persons who do not form a single household.

(2) For the purposes of this section 'house' in the expression 'house in multiple occupation', includes any part of a building which—

(a) apart from this subsection would not be regarded as a house; and

(b) was originally constructed or subsequently adapted for occupation by a single household;

and any reference in this Part to a flat in multiple occupation is a reference to a part of a building which, whether by virtue of this subsection or without regard to it, constitutes a house in multiple occupation."

The definition therefore has three elements: "house", "occupied" and "by persons who do not form a single household".

House. The extended definition statutorily incorporates the decisions in *R. v. London Borough of Southwark, ex p. Lewis Levy* (1983) 8 H.L.R. 1; *R. v. London Borough of Camden, ex p. Rowton (Camden Town)* (1983) 10 H.L.R. 28, in which the term "house" was held—for the purposes of H.M.O. legislation—to apply to a hostel or building used for multiple-occupation or as a lodging-house. Similarly, a large house operating as a holiday home for children has been held to be a house: *Reed v. Hastings Corporation* [1964] L.G.R. 588. In that case Lord Harman said " 'house' means what it obviously is, namely, a place fitted and used and adapted for human habitation". The decision was followed in *R. v. London Borough of Hackney, ex p. Evenbray* (1987) 19 H.L.R. 557, where it was held that a part of a hotel occupied by homeless families was a house, since it was a building constructed and used for human habitation.

Occupied. In order to show that the house is occupied it is not necessary to show any particular legal arrangement: *Minford Properties v. London Borough of Hammersmith* [1978] 247 E.G. 561. The word broadly means "lived in": *Silbers v. Southwark London Borough Council* (1977) 76 L.G.R. 421. This is wide enough to cover a bed and breakfast hotel occupied by homeless families placed there by local authorities in pursuance of their duties to the homeless under Pt. III of the 1985 Act or Pt. VII of the Housing Act 1996: *Thrasyvoulou v. London Borough of Hackney* (1986) 18 H.L.R. 370.

Single household. There is no statutory definition of single household. It has been said that "both the expression 'household' and membership of it is a question of fact and degree, there being no certain indicia the presence or absence of which is by itself conclusive..." (*per* Lord Hailsham, *Simmons v. Pizzey* [1979] A.C. 37, H.L.). In that case, some 75 women were in occupation of a women's refuge. None of the occupants intended to live there indefinitely. No occupant had any special part of the house to herself, so that there was no concept of separate households. Rather, the women organised the business of the house collectively, eating and undertaking the arrangements of the house together. It was held that this could not, however, amount to occupation as a single household.

More recently, in *Barnes v. Sheffield City Council* (1995) 27 H.L.R. 719, the Court of Appeal considered whether a group of students living in a shared house were a single household. The Court said that although it would be wrong to suggest that there was a litmus test which could be applied to the question whether there were separate household, the following factors were helpful indicators:

(a) Whether the persons living in the house came to it as a single group or whether they were independently recruited;
(b) What facilities were shared;
(c) Whether the occupiers were responsible for the whole house or just their particular rooms;
(d) Whether individual tenants were able to, or did, lock other occupiers out of their rooms;
(e) Whose responsibility it was to recruit new occupiers when individuals left;
(f) Who allocated rooms;
(g) The size of the property;
(h) How stable the group composition was;
(i) Whether the mode of living was communal.

The decision of the county court judge that the house was not an H.M.O. because the group of students occupying it was a single household was upheld.

See also *Silbers v. Southwark London Borough Council*, above; *cf. London Borough of Hackney v. Ezedinma* [1981] 3 All E.R. 438.

Local Housing Authority
These are district councils, London borough councils, the Common Council of the City of London, Welsh county councils or county borough councils and the Council of the Isles of Scilly, and those unitary authorities on which housing has devolved under Local Government Act 1992: see s.1, Housing Act 1985.

Making and approval of registration schemes

65.—(1) In Part XI of the Housing Act 1985 (houses in multiple occupation), for section 346 (registration schemes) substitute—

"Registration schemes
346.—(1) A local housing authority may make a registration scheme authorising the authority to compile and maintain a register for their district of houses in multiple occupation.

(2) A registration scheme need not be for the whole of the authority's district and need not apply to every description of house in multiple occupation.

(3) A registration scheme may vary or revoke a previous registration scheme; and the local housing authority may at any time by order revoke a registration scheme.

Contents of registration scheme
346A.—(1) A registration scheme shall make it the duty of such person as may be specified by the scheme to register a house to which the

scheme applies and to renew the registration as and when required by the scheme.

(2) A registration scheme shall provide that registration under the scheme—

(a) shall be for a period of five years from the date of first registration, and

(b) may on application be renewed, subject to such conditions as are specified in the scheme, for further periods of five years at a time.

(3) A registration scheme may—

(a) specify the particulars to be inserted in the register,

(b) make it the duty of such persons as may be specified by the scheme to give the authority as regards a house all or any of the particulars specified in the scheme,

(c) make it the duty of such persons as may be specified by the scheme to notify the authority of any change which makes it necessary to alter the particulars inserted in the register as regards a house.

(4) A registration scheme shall, subject to subsection (5)—

(a) require the payment on first registration of a reasonable fee of an amount determined by the local housing authority, and

(b) require the payment on any renewal of registration of half the fee which would then have been payable on a first registration of the house.

(5) The Secretary of State may by order make provision as to the fee payable on registration—

(a) specifying the maximum permissible fee (whether by specifying an amount or a method for calculating an amount), and

(b) specifying cases in which no fee is payable.

(6) An order under subsection (5)—

(a) may make different provision with respect to different cases or descriptions of case (including different provision for different areas), and

(b) shall be made by statutory instrument which shall be subject to annulment in pursuance of a resolution of either House of Parliament.

Model schemes and confirmation of schemes

346B.—(1) The Secretary of State may prepare model registration schemes.

(2) Model registration schemes may be prepared with or without control provisions (see section 347) or special control provisions (see section 348B); and different model schemes may be prepared for different descriptions of authorities and for different areas.

(3) A registration scheme which conforms to a model scheme—

(a) does not require confirmation by the Secretary of State, and

(b) comes into force on such date (at least one month after the making of the scheme) as may be specified in the scheme.

(4) Any other registration scheme does not come into force unless and until confirmed by the Secretary of State.

(5) The Secretary of State may if he thinks fit confirm such a scheme with or without modifications.

(6) A scheme requiring confirmation shall not come into force before it has been confirmed but, subject to that, comes into force on such date as may be specified in the scheme or, if no date is specified, one month after it is confirmed.".

(2) In section 351(1) of the Housing Act 1985 (proof of matters relating to registration scheme), in paragraph (c) at the beginning insert "that the scheme did not require confirmation by the Secretary of State or".

DEFINITIONS

DEFINITIONS
"local housing authority": H.A. 1985, s.1.
"house in multiple occupation": H.A. 1985, s.345.

GENERAL NOTE
A new registration scheme for houses in multiple occupation, replacing that to be found in the Housing Act 1985 (c. 68), ss.346 to 349, is to be found in this and the following six sections.

S.346
Local housing authorities have a discretion to introduce a registration scheme for houses in multiple occupation in their areas (see Introduction, above), which schemes may cover the whole of an area or only part of it: subs. (2). Authorities may also limit the types of houses in multiple occupation to which the scheme will apply: *ibid.*

S.346A
This new section contains the basic elements of a registration scheme:
(i) The scheme must specify who is under the duty to register and renew registration of H.M.O.s (subs. (1));
(ii) Registration is for a period of five years, renewable for similar periods thereafter (subs. (2));
(iii) In order to obtain information about H.M.O.s the scheme may (subs. (3))
    (a) specify particulars to be included on the register,
    (b) include a duty on specified persons to provide the specified particulars relating to the H.M.O., and
    (c) require notification of changes in the particulars.
In the event of non-compliance with the duty to provide information, under s.350 of the 1985 Act local authorities have an ancillary power to require information to be provided by a person who has an estate or interest in, or who lives in, the house, for the purposes of establishing whether a property is registrable and for ascertaining relevant particulars. Failure to provide the information or knowingly making a misstatement is an offence: s.350(2).
As under the existing registration scheme, charges will be levied for registration, to a maximum set by the Secretary of State, with half this rate for re-registration (subss. (4), (5) and (6)). The government has indicated that it will carry out a review of the appropriate level of fees (see Standing Committee G, Housing Bill, Sixth Sitting, col. 205, Minister for Local Government, Housing and Urban Regeneration, Mr Curry). It seems likely that this will lead to an increase over the current level (£40 per house, or £30 per habitable room where control provisions apply, see S.I. 1991 No. 982) as "it is important that local authorities receive from registration the funds that they need for the work that they must undertake" (*ibid.*). The DoE consultation paper—*Improving Standards in Houses in Multiple Occupation*, July 1995, para. 3.9—suggests a fee for initial registration of up to £60 per habitable room and £30 per room for re-registration.
Breach of, or failure to comply with, the provisions of the registration scheme is a criminal offence (and a continuing offence, see *Camden London Borough Council v. Marshall*, *The Times*, July 11, 1996, 28 H.L.R. forthcoming, D.C.): see new s.348G (s.68), below.

S.346B
Under the existing registration system, and despite the existence of model schemes, the individual approval of the Secretary of State was required before a registration scheme could come into effect in any authority. Schemes which comply with model schemes prepared by the Secretary of State will now not require confirmation (subs. (4)). Any other scheme will not come into effect until it is specifically confirmed (subs. (5)).
As originally drafted, the Bill contained a number of exclusions from the requirement to register, *e.g.* properties containing only two households, or one household and up to four other persons, and all H.M.O.s which are divided entirely into self-contained flats. The specific exclusions were later removed from the Bill, but it is likely that a variety of model registration schemes will be prepared, some of which will allow these categories of H.M.O. to be excluded from the scheme. It is also envisaged that H.M.O.s which are subject to other regulatory schemes, *e.g.* under the Registered Homes Act 1984 (c. 23), the Children Act 1989 (c. 41) or the Probation Service Act 1993 (c. 47) will be excluded from the model registration schemes: see *per* Mr Clappison (Parliamentary Under-Secretary for the Environment), *Hansard* (H.C.), Report, April 29, 1996, cols. 873–874.

Registration schemes: control provisions

66. In Part XI of the Housing Act 1985 (houses in multiple occupation), for sections 347 and 348 (registration schemes: control provisions) substitute—

"Control provisions
347.—(1) A registration scheme may contain control provisions, that is to say, provisions for preventing multiple occupation of a house unless—
(a) the house is registered, and
(b) the number of households or persons occupying it does not exceed the number registered for it.

(2) Control provisions may prohibit persons from permitting others to take up residence in a house or part of a house but shall not prohibit a person from taking up or remaining in residence in the house.

(3) Control provisions shall not prevent the occupation of a house by a greater number of households or persons than the number registered for it if all of those households or persons have been in occupation of the house without interruption since before the number was first registered.

Control provisions: decisions on applications and appeals
348.—(1) Control provisions may enable the local housing authority, on an application for first registration of a house or a renewal or variation of registration—
(a) to refuse the application on the ground that the house is unsuitable and incapable of being made suitable for such occupation as would be permitted if the application were granted;
(b) to refuse the application on the ground that the person having control of the house or the person intended to be the person managing the house is not a fit and proper person;
(c) to require as a condition of granting the application that such works as will make the house suitable for such occupation as would be permitted if the application were granted are executed within such time as the authority may determine;
(d) to impose such conditions relating to the management of the house during the period of registration as the authority may determine.

(2) Control provisions shall provide that the local housing authority shall give an applicant a written statement of their reasons where they—
(a) refuse to grant his application for first registration or for a renewal or variation of registration,
(b) require the execution of works as a condition of granting such an application, or
(c) impose conditions relating to the management of the house.

(3) Where the local housing authority—
(a) notify an applicant that they refuse to grant his application for first registration or for the renewal or variation of a registration,
(b) notify an applicant that they require the execution of works as a condition of granting such an application,
(c) notify an applicant that they intend to impose conditions relating to the management of the house, or
(d) do not within five weeks of receiving the application, or such longer period as may be agreed in writing between the authority and the applicant, register the house or vary or renew the registration in accordance with the application,
the applicant may, within 21 days of being so notified or of the end of the period mentioned in paragraph (d), or such longer period as the authority may in writing allow, appeal to the county court.

(4) On appeal the court may confirm, reverse or vary the decision of the authority.

(5) Where the decision of the authority was a refusal—

(a) to grant an application for first registration of a house, or

(b) for the renewal or variation of the registration,

the court may direct the authority to grant the application as made or as varied in such manner as the court may direct.

(6) For the purposes of subsections (4)and (5) an appeal under subsection (3)(d) shall be treated as an appeal against a decision of the authority to refuse the application.

(7) Where the decision of the authority was to impose conditions relating to the management of the house, the court may direct the authority to grant the application without imposing the conditions or to impose the conditions as varied in such manner as the court may direct.

Control provisions: other decisions and appeals

348A.—(1) Control provisions may enable the local housing authority at any time during a period of registration (whether or not an application has been made—

(a) to alter the number of households or persons for which a house is registered or revoke the registration on the ground that the house is unsuitable and incapable of being made suitable for such occupation as is permitted by virtue of the registration; or

(b) to alter the number of households or persons for which a house is registered or revoke the registration unless such works are executed within a specified time as will make the house in question suitable for such occupation as is permitted by virtue of the registration.

(2) Control provisions which confer on a local housing authority any such power as is mentioned in subsection (1) shall provide that the authority shall, in deciding whether to exercise the power, apply the same standards in relation to the circumstances existing at the time of the decision as were applied at the beginning of the period of registration.

(3) Control provisions may enable the local housing authority to revoke a registration if they consider that—

(a) the person having control of the house or the person managing it is not a fit and proper person, or

(b) there has been a breach of conditions relating to the management of the house.

(4) Control provisions shall also provide that the local housing authority shall—

(a) notify the person having control of a house and the person managing it of any decision by the authority to exercise a power mentioned in subsection (1) or (3) in relation to the house, and

(b) at the same time give them a written statement of the authority's reasons.

(5) A person who has been so notified may within 21 days of being so notified, or such longer period as the authority may in writing allow, appeal to the county court.

(6) On appeal the court may confirm, reverse or vary the decision of the authority.".

DEFINITIONS

"house in multiple occupation": H.A. 1985, s.345.

"local housing authority": H.A. 1985, s.1.

"person having control": H.A. 1985, s.398(5).

"person managing": s.79: H.A. 1985, s.398(6).

"registration scheme": s.65: H.A. 1985, s.346.

GENERAL NOTE

This and the next section provide for two further layers to be added to a registration scheme: "control provisions" and "special control provisions".

S.347

As under the previous s.347, which this replaces, control provisions may be contained in a registration scheme. These provisions can be used as an alternative to information requirements under s.346A(3)(b) and (c), although as registration remains an essential under this section, some particulars will presumably still have to be provided under s.346A(3)(a).

The essential difference is that while s.346A requires only that information be provided, this section permits the authority to impose limits on households or persons in occupation: subs. (1). The limit must be related to specific numbers (subs. (1)(b)), which would appear to mean by "type" of property, or by specific application to individual properties, and may prohibit people from permitting others to take up residence in the house, or even part of it: subs. (2). However, control provisions cannot prohibit people from taking up residence (*ibid.*) (*i.e.* they cannot be addressed to individual occupiers), nor can they require someone to leave the property (*ibid.*). Where all the households or persons living in the house have been in occupation since before the house was first registered, the control provisions cannot prevent occupation by that number of households or persons, even when it exceeds the number for which the house is registered: subs. (3).

As a "prohibition or restriction on the use of land binding on successive owners" the scheme must be registered as a local land charge under the Local Land Charges Act 1975 (c. 76), s.1(1).

Breach of, or failure to comply with, the provisions of the registration scheme is a criminal offence (and a continuing offence, see *Camden London Borough Council v. Marshall, The Times*, July 11, 1996, 28 H.L.R. forthcoming, D.C.): see new s.348G (s.68), below.

S.348

Where the authority adopts control provisions within s.347, it is given the power to refuse registration on the grounds set out in subs. (1)(a) and (b): house unsuitable and incapable of being made suitable; or, person having control or intended manager not a fit and proper person. "Person having control" is defined by s.398(5) of the 1985 Act as:

"the person who receives the rack-rent of the premises, whether on his own account or as agent or trustee of another person, or who would so receive it if the premises were let at a rack-rent (and for this purpose a 'rack-rent' means a rent which is not less than 2/3 of the full net annual value of the premises)."

This definition has received considerable judicial attention when used in other statutes, and elsewhere in the 1985 Act: see *Kensington Borough Council v. Allen* [1926] 1 K.B. 576; *Truman, Hanbury, Buxton & Co. v. Kerslake* [1894] 2 Q.B. 774; *London Corporation v. Cusack-Smith* [1955] A.C. 337; *Pollway Nominees v. London Borough of Croydon* [1987] A.C. 79; *White v. Barnet London Borough Council* (1989) 21 H.L.R. 346. The last two cases concerned application of the definition to flats and buildings containing flats. The person having control of a flat which is let on a long lease will normally be the leaseholder, as the rent will usually fall below the two-thirds criterion: *Pollway*. The fact that statute may constrain the recoverable rent will not affect the issue: that which is a statutory will limit what can reasonably be expected (*Rawlance v. Croydon Corporation* [1952] 2 Q.B. 803, C.A.).

The definition of "person managing" is amended by s.79 below, see notes thereto.

As an alternative to refusal of registration, control provisions may permit the authority to require that works be carried out to render the house suitable for as many as will occupy under the registration, or that certain management requirements be imposed: subs. (1)(c) and (d).

Where an application for registration (variation or renewal) is refused, works are required, or management conditions are imposed, the authority will have to provide the applicant for registration with a written statement of reasons (subs. (2)) which may be used as the basis of an appeal to the county court: subs. (3). There can also be an appeal if the authority does not reply to the application within five weeks, or such longer period as the applicant agrees in writing (*ibid.*); in such a case, failure to reply is treated as a refusal of the application: subs. (6). Appeals must be brought within 21 days of notification, or 21 days of the five-week (or that period as extended) failure to respond, unless the authority agrees a longer period in writing: subs. (3). On appeal, the court may confirm, reverse or vary the decision of the authority and can issue directions or lift or impose conditions: subss. (4), (5) and (7).

Breach of, or failure to comply with, the provisions of the registration scheme is a criminal offence (and a continuing offence, see *Camden London Borough Council v. Marshall, The Times*, July 11, 1996, 28 H.L.R. forthcoming, D.C.): see new s.348G (s.68), below.

S.348A

This is a new power in relation to control schemes which permits the authority, at any time during the period of registration (see new s.346(2), above), and whether or not any application has been made:

(a) to alter the number of households or persons for which the house is registered, or revoke registration altogether, either because it is unsuitable or incapable of being made suitable, or because works have not been carried out to make the house suitable; or

(b) to revoke registration because works have not been carried out (subs. (1)).

In deciding whether to exercise this power, the authority must apply the same standards in relation to the circumstances existing at the time of the decision as were applied at the beginning of the registration period (subs. (2)). Authorities may not, therefore, decide to apply more stringent standards part-way through the registration period. Registration may also be revoked if the authority considers the person having control or managing to be not a fit and proper person, *e.g.* where ownership has changed during the registration period or there has been a breach of management conditions imposed under new s.348(2)(c).

If the authority exercises its powers under this section, there are similar notification and appeal provisions as under new s.348: subs. (4), (5) and (6). Breach of, or failure to comply with, the provisions of the registration scheme is a criminal offence (and a continuing offence, see *Camden London Borough Council v. Marshall, The Times,* July 11, 1996, 28 H.L.R. forthcoming, D.C.): see new s.348G (s.68), below.

Registration schemes: special control provisions

67.—(1) In Part XI of the Housing Act 1985 (houses in multiple occupation), after section 348A (as inserted by section 66 above) insert—

"Special control provisions

348B.—(1) A registration scheme which contains control provisions may also contain special control provisions, that is, provisions for preventing houses in multiple occupation, by reason of their existence or the behaviour of their residents, from adversely affecting the amenity or character of the area in which they are situated.

(2) Special control provisions may provide for the refusal or revocation of registration, for reducing the number of households or persons for which a house is registered and for imposing conditions of registration.

(3) The conditions of registration may include conditions relating to the management of the house or the behaviour of its occupants.

(4) Special control provisions may authorise the revocation of registration in the case of—

(a) occupation of the house by more households or persons than the registration permits, or

(b) a breach of any condition imposed in pursuance of the special control provisions,

which is due to a relevant management failure.

(5) Special control provisions shall not authorise the refusal of—

(a) an application for first registration of a house which has been in operation as a house in multiple occupation since before the introduction by the local housing authority of a registration scheme with special control provisions, or

(b) any application for renewal of registration of a house previously registered under such a scheme,

unless there has been a relevant management failure.

(6) Special control provisions may provide that in any other case where an application is made for first registration of a house the local housing authority may take into account the number of houses in multiple occupation in the vicinity in deciding whether to permit or refuse registration.

Special control provisions: general provisions as to decisions and appeals

348C.—(1) Special control provisions shall provide that the local housing authority shall give a written statement of their reasons to the applicant where they refuse to grant his application for first registration, or for a renewal or variation of a registration, or impose conditions of registration on such an application.

(2) Special control provisions shall provide that the authority shall give written notice to the person having control of the house and the person managing it of any decision by the authority—

    (a) to vary the conditions of registration (otherwise than on an application to which subsection (1) applies), or

    (b) to revoke the registration of the house,

and at the same time give them a written statement of the authority's reasons.

(3) Where in accordance with special control provisions the local housing authority—

    (a) notify an applicant that they refuse to grant his application for first registration or for the renewal or variation of a registration,

    (b) notify such an applicant of the imposition of conditions of registration, or

    (c) give notice to the person having control or the person managing the house of any such decision as is mentioned in subsection (2),

that person may, within 21 days of being so notified, or such longer period as the authority may in writing allow, appeal to the county court.

(4) If on appeal it appears to the court—

    (a) that there has been any informality, defect or error in, or in connection with, the authority's decision, or

    (b) that the authority acted unreasonably,

the court may reverse or vary the decision of the authority.

(5) In so far as an appeal is based on the ground mentioned in subsection (4)(a), the court shall dismiss the appeal if it is satisfied that the informality, defect or error was not a material one.

(6) Where the decision of the authority was a refusal—

    (a) to grant an application for first registration of a house, or

    (b) for the renewal or variation of the registration,

the court may direct the authority to grant the application as made or as varied in such manner as the court may direct.

(7) Where the decision of the authority was to impose conditions of registration, the court may direct the authority to grant the application without imposing the conditions or to impose the conditions as varied in such manner as the court may direct.

Special control provisions: occupancy directions

348D.—(1) Special control provisions may provide that where the local housing authority decide that the registration of a house should be revoked the authority may direct that the level of occupation of the house be reduced, within such period of not less than 28 days as they may direct, to a level such that the registration scheme does not apply.

Such a direction is referred to in this Part as an "occupancy direction".

(2) Special control provisions shall provide that the authority shall only make an occupancy direction if it appears to the authority that there has been a relevant management failure resulting in a serious adverse effect on the amenity or character of the area in which the house is situated.

(3) In considering whether to make an occupancy direction the authority shall take into account the interests of the occupants of the house and the person having control of the house as well as the interests of local residents and businesses.

(4) Special control provisions may require the person having control of the house, and the person managing it, to take all reasonably practicable steps to comply with an occupancy direction.

(5) Nothing in Part I of the Housing Act 1988 prevents possession being obtained by any person in order to comply with an occupancy direction.

(6) Nothing in this section affects any liability in respect of any other contravention or failure to comply with control provisions or special control provisions.

Special control provisions: decisions and appeals relating to occupancy directions

348E.—(1) Special control provisions shall provide that where the local housing authority make an occupancy direction in respect of a house they shall give written notice of the direction to the person having control of the house and the person managing it and at the same time give them a written statement of the authority's reasons.

(2) A person aggrieved by an occupancy direction may, within 21 days after the date of the service of notice as mentioned in subsection (1), appeal to the county court.

(3) If on appeal it appears to the court—

(a) that there has been any informality, defect or error in, or in connection with, the authority's decision, or

(b) that the authority acted unreasonably,

the court may make such order either confirming, quashing or varying the notice as it thinks fit.

(4) In so far as an appeal is based on the ground mentioned in subsection (3)(a), the court shall dismiss the appeal if it is satisfied that the informality, defect or error was not a material one.

(5) If an appeal is brought the direction does not become operative until—

(a) a decision on the appeal confirming the direction (with or without variation) is given and the period within which an appeal to the Court of Appeal may be brought expires without any such appeal having been brought, or

(b) if a further appeal to the Court of Appeal is brought, a decision on that appeal is given confirming the direction (with or without variation).

(6) For this purpose the withdrawal of an appeal has the same effect as a decision confirming the direction or decision appealed against.

Special control provisions: "relevant management failure"

348F. A "relevant management failure" for the purposes of sections 348B to 348E (special control provisions) means a failure on the part of the person having control of, or the person managing, a house in multiple occupation to take such steps as are reasonably practicable to prevent the existence of the house or the behaviour of its residents from adversely affecting the amenity or character of the area in which the house is situated, or to reduce any such adverse effect.".

(2) In section 400 of the Housing Act 1985 (index of defined expressions: Part XI), at the appropriate places insert—

"occupancy direction (in connection with special control provisions)	section 348D
relevant management failure (for purposes of section 348B to 348E)	section 348F
special control provisions	section 348B".

DEFINITIONS
"house in multiple occupation": H.A. 1985, s.345.
"local housing authority": H.A. 1985, s.1.
"person having control": H.A. 1985, s.398(5).

"person managing": s.79: H.A. 1985, s.398(6).
"registration scheme": s.65: H.A. 1985, s.346.

GENERAL NOTE

This second level of control—"special control provisions"—adds a new layer to registration schemes to prevent H.M.O.s "by reason of their existence or the behaviour of their residents, ... adversely affecting the amenity or character of the area in which they are situated": new s.348B(1). (See further notes to new s.348F, below, as to meaning of "amenity or character of the area".) It may be perceived, therefore, as being in part an aspect of the broader policy of discouraging anti-social behaviour: see Pt. V, Chaps. II and III, below.

There are four main powers:

(a) refusal of registration where there has been a "management failure";

(b) refusal of registration if the authority believes there are already sufficient H.M.O.s in the area and that the presence of another will have an adverse effect;

(c) revocation of registration for breach of conditions, or over-occupation due to a management failure;

(d) imposition of an occupancy direction where registration is revoked, to enable authorities to speed up the reduction in residents.

In recognition of the particularly draconian nature of the powers (see in particular new s.348D below), the government has said that it will not provide model registration schemes which include special control provisions (*Hansard* (H.C.), Standing Committee G, Housing Bill, Eighth Sitting, col. 283, *per* Mr Curry [Minister for Local Government, Housing and Urban Regeneration], (although *cf.* the rather contradictory comment at *ibid.* col. 290, "the Department will offer model schemes for the special control powers,") which means that an individual application will have to be made to the Secretary of State should an authority wish to include them (see new s.346B, above).

S.348B

This section sets out the contents of special control provisions. They may provide for the refusal or revocation of registration, reduction of the numbers of households or persons for which a house is registered, or the imposition of conditions: subs. (2). Conditions may include ones which relate to the management of the house or the behaviour of its occupants: subs. (3). As (unlike other elements of registration schemes, which are principally directed at the owners and managers of H.M.O.s) the residents could be in breach of a condition relating to their behaviour, it is possible that they could commit a criminal offence under the new s.348G (s.68, below).

Registration may be revoked in two circumstances:

(a) where there is occupation in excess of that permitted by the registration; or,

(b) where there is breach of a condition and, in either case, this is due to a relevant management failure (subs. (4)). Relevant management failure is defined by new s.348F, see notes thereto, below.

H.M.O.s in occupation before the registration came into effect are protected from refusal of registration (or renewal) under the special control provisions, except in the case where there has been a relevant management failure: subs. (5). Except in the case of these existing H.M.O.s, the authority may refuse a first application for registration on the basis of the sufficiency of H.M.O.s in the vicinity (subs. (6)). There is no statutory definition of vicinity: "the natural and ordinary meaning of the word must, therefore, be used, but meaning must be construed in the context of legislation ... I cannot take it further" *per* Mr Curry (Minister for Local Government, Housing and Urban Regeneration, *Hansard* (H.C.), Standing Committee G, Eighth sitting, col. 290. In the context of the Official Secrets Act 1920 the natural meaning of vicinity was said to be "the state of being near in space": *Adler v. George* [1964] 1 All E.R. 628.

As a "prohibition or restriction on the use of land binding on successive owners", the scheme must be registered as a local land charge under the Local Land Charges Act 1975 (c. 76), s.1(1).

Breach of, or failure to comply with, the provisions of the registration scheme is a criminal offence (and a continuing offence, see *Camden London Borough Council v. Marshall, The Times*, July 11, 1996, 28 H.L.R. forthcoming, D.C.): see new s.348G (s.68), below.

S.348C

If the authority refuses registration (renewal or variation), or imposes conditions, it must give a written statement of reasons to the applicant: subs. (1). Written notice must also be given to the person having control and the person managing the house (see notes to new s.348, above as to the definition of these) if the authority varies the conditions applying or revokes the registration: subs. (2).

Appeal. Appeals must be brought within 21 days, or such longer period as the authority may, in writing allow: subs. (3). Appeal can be against refusal of registration, or its renewal or variation, imposition of condition, or refusal of a variation or revocation under subs. (2): *ibid.* There is no extensive list of grounds for appeal (*cf.* s.353(2) of the 1985 Act), the grounds being but two: informality, defect or error in, or in connection with, the authority's decision; or, that the authority acted unreasonably: subs. (4). The former ground is wide enough to permit an assertion that the local housing authority is acting *ultra vires, e.g.* because the conditions imposed do not fall within the scheme or there has been no relevant management failure: see *Nolan v. Leeds City Council* (1990) 23 H.L.R. 135. The court may dismiss an appeal on this ground, however, if the informality, defect or error is not a material one: subs. (5).

It is not clear under the second ground (acting unreasonably) how "unreasonable" the conduct must be but it does not seem to be limited to *Wednesbury* unreasonableness (see notes to s.204, below), *i.e.* a decision that no reasonable authority would make, as *Wednesbury* unreasonableness renders the decision void, which means that it would qualify on the first ground.

If either ground of appeal is made out, the court may reverse or vary the decision (subs. (4)) and, in the case of a refusal to register or renew or vary registration, direct the authority to grant the registration: subs. (6). Where conditions have been imposed, the court may lift or vary the conditions: subs. (7).

S.348D

Where the authority decides to revoke the registration (which it may do under new s.348B(4)), this section provides for an "occupancy direction" to accelerate reduction in the number of occupiers to below that at which registration is required. The period for the reduction may not be shorter than 28 days: subs. (1). An occupancy direction can only be made if there has been a serious management failure (see notes to new s.348F, below) which has resulted in a serious adverse effect on the amenity or character of the area: subs. (2).

The person having control of the house or the person managing (as to which see notes to new s.348, above) may be required under special control provisions to take all reasonably practicable steps to comply with the occupancy direction, *i.e.* to reduce the level of occupancy within the specified time-scale: subs. (4). Reasonably practicable steps will not encompass everything which might be possible (see *Jenkins v. Allied Ironfounders* [1970] 1 W.L.R. 304, H.L.), but rather will involve weighing up the ability to reduce to occupancy level against the costs, time and trouble involved (see *per* Asquith L.J. in *Edwards v. National Coal Board* [1949] 1 K.B. 704 at 712). It will accordingly not be reasonably practicable to reduce occupancy levels if occupiers are unwilling to leave voluntarily, and the landlord has only limited ability to gain possession through the courts.

In order to enable possession to be obtained, however, all assured and assured shorthold tenants lose their protection (subs. (5)), although not, it should be noted those who are protected under the Rent Act 1977 (c. 42). Subsection (5) is in similar terms to those found in s.276 of the 1985 Act in relation to closing and demolition orders, under which it has been held that the section does not serve to terminate the contractual tenancy, so that before a landlord can recover possession he must (if he can) determine the tenancy in the normal way: *Aslan v. Murphy* (1989) 21 H.L.R. 532, C.A. Where there are tenants on fixed term contracts, the landlord will have to wait the expiry of the fixed term before evicting, unless there is a basis for forfeiting the lease.

Given the potential loss of security for assured tenants the authority must, in deciding whether to make a direction, take into account the interests of the occupants and the person having control of the house, as well as those of local residents and businesses: subs. (3). "This is an important safeguard, which will ensure that the authority looks at both sides of the problem": *Hansard* (H.C.), Standing Committee G, Housing Bill, Eighth Sitting, col. 282, *per* Mr Curry (Minister for Local Government, Housing and Urban Regeneration).

New s.348E

Notice of the occupancy direction and reasons for it must be served on the person having control of the house and the person managing it (as to which, see notes to new s.348, above). No notice of the direction need be served on the occupiers, although if they do become aware of it within the 21-day period allowed for appeal, they could, as a "person aggrieved" by the notice, appeal under subs. (2). A person is aggrieved if deprived of a legal entitlement (see *ex p. Sidebotham* (1880) 14 Ch. D. 458 and *R. v. London Quarter Session, ex p. Westminster Corporation* [1951] 2 K.B. 508), and if occupiers lose their security of tenure due to the direction, they will certainly fall within this category.

Appeals may be brought on the same basis as under new s.348C (see notes thereto, above), and the county court has like power to confirm, quash or vary the direction: subss. (3) and (4). If an appeal is brought within the 21 days allowed, the direction does not become operative until confirmation by the county court, together with the passing of time to appeal to the Court of

Appeal (four weeks—R.S.C., Ord. 59, r. 19): subs. (5). If an appeal is brought to the Court of Appeal, then the notice does not become operative until the decision of that court; if an appeal is brought but withdrawn, the withdrawal has the effect of a decision dismissing the appeal, at whichever level—to or from the county court: *ibid.*, subs. (6).

New s.348F

This section defines the important concept of "relevant management failure", for the purposes of ss.346B(4), (5) and 348D(2). The failure must be by either the person having control of, or the person managing, the house (as to which see notes to new s.348, above) and encompasses failing to take all such steps as are reasonably practicable to prevent the existence of the house or the behaviour of the residents from adversely affecting the amenity or character of the area or to reduce any such adverse affect.

Reasonably practicable steps are not defined (*cf.* Control of Pollution Act 1974 (c. 40), s.72). They are likely to fall into two categories: first, maintaining the physical condition of the property; secondly, taking steps to ensure that agreements with occupiers require reasonable behaviour and enforcing such agreements, if needs be, through injunction or eviction. However, simply because a course of action is open to the person having control or managing, it does not mean that it is reasonably practicable. In the context of the Factories Acts, Asquith L.J. said (*Edwards v. National Coal Board* [1949] 1 K.B. 704 at 712):

"'Reasonably practicable' is a narrower term than 'physically possible' and seems to me to imply that a computation must be made by the owner, in which the quantum of risk is placed on one scale and the sacrifice involved in the measures necessary for averting the risk (whether in money, time or trouble) is placed in the other; and that if it be shown that there is a gross disproportion between them—the risk being insignificant in relation to the sacrifice—the defendants discharge the onus on them".

See also *Marshall v. Gotham* [1954] A.C. 360, H.L. and *Jenkins v. Allied Ironfounders* [1970] 1 W.L.R. 304, H.L.

In the end, however, too much reliance should not be placed on cases from different statutory contexts since "the word 'practicable' is an ordinary English work of great flexibility: it takes its meaning from its context" *per* Scarman L.J. in *Dedman v. British Building and Engineering Appliances* [1974] 1 W.L.R. 171 at 179. He continued: "whenever used, it is a call for the exercise of common sense, a warning that sound judgement will be impossible without compromise".

Another matter which will call for the exercise of common sense is the judgment as to when the amenity or character of an area is being adversely affected. In reaching this decision authorities will have to consider both the physical environment and more intangible matters, as amenity refers to the "visual appearance and the pleasure of ... enjoyment of land" (*per* Willis J. in *Cartwright v. Post Office* [1968] 2 Q.B. 439, Q.B.D.).

Offences in connection with registration schemes

68.—(1) In Part XI of the Housing Act 1985, after section 348F (as inserted by section 67 above) insert—

"Offences in connection with registration schemes

348G.—(1) A person who contravenes or fails to comply with a provision of a registration scheme commits an offence.

(2) A person who commits an offence under this section consisting of a contravention of so much of control provisions as relates—

　(a)　to occupation to a greater extent than permitted under those provisions of a house which is not registered, or

　(b)　to occupation of a house which is registered by more households or persons than the registration permits,

is liable on summary conviction to a fine not exceeding level 5 on the standard scale.

(3) A person who commits an offence under this section consisting of a contravention of so much of special control provisions as requires all reasonably practicable steps to be taken to comply with an occupancy direction is liable on summary conviction to a fine not exceeding level 5 on the standard scale.

(4) A person who commits any other offence under this section is liable on summary conviction to a fine not exceeding level 4 on the stan-

dard scale.".

(2) In section 395(2) of the Housing Act 1985 (power of entry to ascertain if offence being committed), for "section 346(6)" substitute "section 348G".

DEFINITIONS
"control provisions": s.66: H.A. 1985, s.347.
"registration scheme": s.65: H.A. 1985, s.346.
"special control provisions": s.67: H.A. 1985, s.348B.

GENERAL NOTE
The new s.348G, added by this section, creates summary offences in relation to contravention of, or failure to comply with, a registration scheme, generally punishable by a fine up to level 4 on the standard scale (currently £2,500, Criminal Justice Act 1982 (c. 48), as amended by the Criminal Justice Act 1991 (c. 53)): subss. (1) and (4). The offence of failure to comply is a continuing offence: *Camden London Borough Council v. Marshall, The Times,* July 11, 1996, 28 H.L.R. forthcoming, D.C. In two instances, a higher penalty up to level five (£5,000) may be levied:
   (a) contravention of control provisions (see new s.347, above) relating to occupation at higher levels than permitted (subs. (2));
   (b) contravention of special control provisions requiring all reasonably practicable steps to be taken to comply with an occupancy direction (see new s.348D, above): subs. (3).

Information requirements in connection with registration schemes

69.—(1) In Part XI of the Housing Act 1985 (houses in multiple occupation), for section 349 (steps required to inform public about registration schemes) substitute—

"Steps required to inform public about schemes

349.—(1) Where a local housing authority intend to make a registration scheme which does not require confirmation by the Secretary of State, they shall publish notice of their intention at least one month before the scheme is made.

As soon as the scheme is made, the local housing authority shall publish a notice stating—
   (a) that a registration scheme which does not require confirmation has been made, and
   (b) the date on which the scheme is to come into force.

(2) Where a local housing authority intend to submit to the Secretary of State a registration scheme which requires his confirmation, they shall publish notice of their intention at least one month before the scheme is submitted.

As soon as the scheme is confirmed, the local housing authority shall publish a notice stating—
   (a) that a registration scheme has been confirmed, and
   (b) the date on which the scheme is to come into force.

(3) A notice under subsection (1) or (2) of the authority's intention to make a scheme or submit a scheme for confirmation shall—
   (a) describe any steps which will have to be taken under the scheme by those concerned with registrable houses (other than steps which have only to be taken after a notice from the authority), and
   (b) name a place where a copy of the scheme may be seen at all reasonable hours.

(4) After publication of notice under subsection (1) or (2) that a registration scheme has been made or confirmed, and for as long as the scheme is in force, the local housing authority—
   (a) shall keep a copy of the scheme, and of the register, available for public inspection at the offices of the authority free of charge at all reasonable hours, and
   (b) on request, and on payment of such reasonable fee as the auth-

ority may require, shall supply a copy of the scheme or the register, or of any entry in the register, to any person.

(5) If the local housing authority revoke a registration scheme by order they shall publish notice of the order.

(6) In this section "publish" means publish in one or more newspapers circulating in the district of the local housing authority concerned.".

(2) In section 350(1) of the Housing Act 1985 (power to require information for purposes of scheme) for the words "a person" substitute "the person having control of the house or the person managing the house or any person".

DEFINITIONS
"local housing authority": H.A. 1985, s.1.
"person having control": H.A. 1985, s.398(5).
"person managing": s.79: H.A. 1985, s.398(6).
"registration scheme": s.65: H.A. 1985, s.346.

GENERAL NOTE
The new s.349, substituted by this section, contains the publicity duties imposed on local authorities in relation to registration schemes. The requirements vary depending on whether or not the scheme requires confirmation by the Secretary of State (as to which see new s.346B, above). In any event, the publicity must extend to describing the steps which have to be taken by those placed under duties by the scheme. The scheme and the register must also be available for inspection, free of charge, and a copy of them must be made available at a reasonable cost.

Existing registration schemes

70.—(1) The amendments made by sections 65 to 69 do not apply to registration schemes in force immediately before the coming into force of those sections.

(2) The unamended provisions of Part XI of the Housing Act 1985 continue to apply to such schemes, subject as follows.

(3) Any such scheme may be revoked—

(a) by a new scheme complying with the provisions of that Part as amended, or

(b) by order of the local housing authority.

(4) If not so revoked any such scheme shall cease to have effect at the end of the period of two years beginning with the date on which the amendments come into force.

DEFINITION
"local housing authority": H.A. 1985, s.1.

GENERAL NOTE
This section makes provision for existing registration schemes. Where an authority has an existing registration scheme, it will continue in force for a period of two years, under the Housing Act 1985 (c. 68) *as unamended* (by this Act), unless in the meantime the authority decides to revoke it or to introduce a new scheme.

Other amendments of Part XI of the Housing Act 1985

Restriction on notices requiring execution of works

71.—(1) In section 352 of the Housing Act 1985 (power to require execution of works to render premises fit for number of occupants), at end insert—

"(7) Where a local housing authority serve a notice under this section in respect of any of the requirements specified in subsection (1A), and the works specified in the notice are carried out, whether by the person on whom the notice was served or by the local housing authority under section 375, the authority shall not, within the period of five years from the service of the notice, serve another notice under this section in respect of the same requirement unless they consider that there has been a change of circumstances in relation to the premises.

(8) Such a change may, in particular, relate to the condition of the premises or the availability or use of the facilities mentioned in subsection (1A).".

(2) The above amendment does not apply in relation to a notice served under section 352 of the Housing Act 1985 before this section comes into force.

DEFINITION
"local housing authority": H.A. 1985, s.1.

GENERAL NOTE
Under the Housing Act 1985 (c. 68), s.352, where authorities are of the opinion that an H.M.O. is unfit for its current number of occupants, they may serve notice requiring works to the premises. An H.M.O. will be unfit when it fails to meet one or more of the criteria set out in s.352(1A) and, having regard to the number of individuals and households currently accommodated on the premises, the premises are, by reason of that failure, not reasonably suitable for occupation: s.352(1). The criteria an H.M.O. must meet are that (s.352(1A)):

"(a) there are satisfactory facilities for the storage, preparation and cooking of food including an adequate number of sinks with a satisfactory supply of hot and cold water;
(b) it has an adequate number of suitably located water-closets for the exclusive use of the occupants;
(c) it has, for the exclusive use of the occupants, an adequate number of suitably located fixed baths or showers and wash-hand basins each of which is provided with a satisfactory supply of hot and cold water;
(d) ... there are adequate means of escape from fire;
(e) there are adequate other fire precautions. "

The new subss. (7) and (8), added to s.352 by this section, prevent authorities from requiring works in relation to any of the criteria more frequently than every five years, unless there has been a change of circumstances in relation to the premises, particularly one relating to the condition of the premises or the availability or use of facilities set out in the criteria.

Recovery of expenses of notice requiring execution of works

72.—(1) After section 352 of the Housing Act 1985 insert—

"Recovery of expenses of notice under s.352

352A.—(1) A local housing authority may, as a means of recovering certain administrative and other expenses incurred by them in serving a notice under section 352, make such reasonable charge as they consider appropriate.

(2) The expenses are the expenses incurred in—
(a) determining whether to serve a notice under that section,
(b) identifying the works to be specified in the notice, and
(c) serving the notice.

(3) The amount of the charge shall not exceed such amount as is specified by order of the Secretary of State.

(4) A charge under this section may be recovered by the authority from any person on whom the notice under section 352 is served.

(5) The provisions of Schedule 10 apply to the recovery by the authority of a charge under this section as they apply to the recovery of expenses incurred by the authority under section 375 (expenses of carrying out works required by notice).

(6) An order under this section—
(a) may make different provision with respect to different cases or descriptions of case (including different provision for different areas), and
(b) shall be made by statutory instrument which shall be subject to annulment in pursuance of a resolution of either House of

Parliament.

(7) This section has effect subject to any order under section 353(6) (power of court on appeal against s.352 notice).".

(2) In section 353 of that Act (appeal against notice under section 352), after subsection (5) insert—

"(6) Where the court allows an appeal under this section or makes an order under subsection (5), it may make such order as it thinks fit reducing, quashing or requiring the repayment of any charge under section 352A made in respect of the notice to which the appeal relates.".

(3) The above amendments do not apply in relation to a notice served under section 352 of the Housing Act 1985 before this section comes into force.

DEFINITION
"local housing authority": H.A. 1985, s.1.

GENERAL NOTE
At present, if an authority carries out works following the service of a notice under s.352 of the 1985 Act (as to which see notes to s.71, above), it may recover its costs of doing the works. Recovery is governed by Sched. 10 to the 1985 Act, which provides, where necessary, for recovery through payment of rents from occupiers directly to the authority, or by placing a charging order on the property.

Under the new s.352A, added by this section, authorities may now also seek the expenses incurred in determining whether to serve a notice, identifying the works required and actual service of the notice. The charge is recoverable from the person served with the notice, which will be either the person having control of the house or the person managing it (as to which see notes to new s.348, above). Any charge is limited to a maximum set by the Secretary of State.

Duty to keep premises fit for number of occupants

73.—(1) After section 353 of the Housing Act 1985 insert—

"Duty to keep premises fit for number of occupants

353A.—(1) It is the duty of the person having control of a house in multiple occupation, and of the person managing it, to take such steps as are reasonably practicable to prevent the occurrence of a state of affairs calling for the service of a notice or further notice under section 352 (notice requiring execution of works to render house fit for number of occupants).

(2) A breach of that duty is actionable in damages at the suit of any tenant or other occupant of the premises, or any other person who suffers loss, damage or personal injury in consequence of the breach.

(3) A person who fails to comply with the duty imposed on him by subsection (1) commits a summary offence and is liable on conviction to a fine not exceeding level 5 on the standard scale.".

(2) In section 395(2) of the Housing Act 1985 (power of entry to ascertain whether offence being committed), after the entry for section 346(6) insert—

"section 353A (failure to keep premises fit for number of occupants),".

DEFINITIONS
"person having control": H.A. 1985, s.398(5).
"person managing": s.79: H.A. 1985, s.398(6).

GENERAL NOTE
Until now, the requirement to comply with legislation governing housing standards has been enforced through local authority action (civil or criminal prosecution). For the first time, the new s.353A, added by this section, provides a statutory duty which is enforceable by occupiers of substandard housing.

The duty is imposed on the person having control of the house (as to which see notes to new s.348, above) and on the person managing (see notes to s.76(2), below). The duty imposed on such persons is to take all reasonably practicable steps (see notes to new s.348F (s.67) above) to prevent the occurrence of a state of affairs calling for a notice under s.352 (as to which see notes to s.71, above).

Failure to take those practicable steps is made specifically actionable by tenants, other occupiers and others (*e.g.* visitors) who suffer loss, damage or personal injury in consequence of the breach. In addition, it is a summary offence to fail to comply with the duty, punishable by a fine not exceeding level 5 on the standard scale (currently £5,000).

Section 354 direction to be local land charge

74. In section 354 of the Housing Act 1985 (power to limit number of occupants of house), at the end insert—

"(8) A direction under this section is a local land charge.".

GENERAL NOTE

When an authority is of the opinion that an H.M.O. is unfit under s.352 of the 1985 Act (see notes to s.71, above), the authority may, in addition or as an alternative to serving a works notice, serve a direction limiting the number of occupants of the house. Such a direction is now to be a local land charge.

Means of escape from fire

75.—(1) Section 365 of the Housing Act 1985 (means of escape from fire: general provisions as to exercise of powers) is amended as follows.

(2) In subsection (1)(b) (ground for exercise of additional powers) after "paragraph (d)" insert "or (e)".

(3) For subsection (3) (consultation requirements) substitute—

"(3) The local housing authority shall consult with the fire authority concerned before exercising any of the powers mentioned in subsection (2)—
　　(a) where they are under a duty to exercise those powers, or
　　(b) where they are not under such a duty but may exercise those powers and the house is of such description or is occupied in such manner as the Secretary of State may specify by order for the purposes of this subsection.".

(4) In subsection (4) (orders) for "or (2A)" substitute ", (2A) or (3)".

(5) In subsection (5) (other powers unaffected) omit "and (e)".

DEFINITION

"local housing authority": H.A. 1985, s.1.

GENERAL NOTE

Under the Housing Act 1985 (c. 68), s.352, authorities may serve a notice requiring works to the premises where in their opinion an H.M.O. is unfit for its current number of occupants. An H.M.O. will be unfit where it fails to meet one or more of the criteria set out in s.352(1A) and, having regard to the number of individuals and households currently accommodated on the premises, by reason of that failure the premises are not reasonably suitable for occupation: s.352(1). See also notes to s.71, above.

Under s.352(1A) of the Housing Act 1985, two of the criteria are:

"(d) ... there are adequate means of escape from fire;

(e) there are adequate other fire precautions. "

Where a house is found unfit by reason of failure to meet the criterion in para. (d), the local housing authority has additional power (under s.365) either to accept an undertaking, or to make a closing order on part of the house, under s.368. The effect of the amendments to s.365 to be found in subss. (2) and (5) of this section is to extend that additional power to unfitness arising from para. (e).

The amendments made by subss. (3) and (4) slightly alter the consultation requirements with fire authorities. Currently, before serving a notice under s.352, accepting an undertaking, or making a closing order because of inadequate means of escape from fire, the local housing authority must consult the fire authority. The consultation duty will now also arise in relation to action regarding fire precautions, although only in those cases where the housing authority is under a duty to act and otherwise as specified by the Secretary of State. Action is only mandatory (currently) in cases falling under the Housing (Means of Escape from Fire in Houses in Multiple Occupation) Order 1981 (S.I. 1981 No. 1576), *i.e.* in houses of at least three storeys (excluding basements) and in which the combined floor area, including any staircases and basements, exceeds 500 square metres. It is currently estimated that this applies to some 20,000 H.M.O.s. The government has indicated that it proposes to increase the number of H.M.O.s to which the mandatory requirements apply by extending it to properties with more than two storeys and provision for six or more tenants: *Improving Standards in Houses in Multiple Occupation*, para. 3.2, DoE, July 1995.

Works notices: improvement of enforcement procedures

76. After section 377 of the Housing Act 1985 insert—

"Works notices: improvement of enforcement procedures

377A.—(1) The Secretary of State may by order provide that a local housing authority shall act as specified in the order before serving a works notice.

In this section a "works notice" means a notice under section 352 or 372 (notices requiring the execution of works).

(2) An order under this section may provide that the authority—

(a) shall as soon as practicable give to the person on whom the works notice is to be served a written notice which satisfies the requirements of subsection (3); and

(b) shall not serve the works notice until after the end of such period beginning with the giving of a notice which satisfies the requirements of subsection (3) as may be determined by or under the order.

(3) A notice satisfies the requirements of this subsection if it—

(a) states the works which in the authority's opinion should be undertaken, and explains why and within what period;

(b) explains the grounds on which it appears to the authority that the works notice might be served;

(c) states the type of works notice which is to be served, the consequences of serving it and whether there is a right to make representations before, or a right of appeal against, the serving of it.

(4) An order under this section may also provide that, before the authority serves the works notice on any person, they—

(a) shall give to that person a written notice stating—

(i) that they are considering serving the works notice and the reasons why they are considering serving the notice; and

(ii) that the person may, within a period specified in the written notice, make written representations to them or, if the person so requests, make oral representations to them in the presence of a person determined by or under the order; and

(b) shall consider any representations which are duly made and not withdrawn.

(5) An order under this section may in particular—

(a) make provision as to the consequences of any failure to comply with a provision made by the order;

(b) contain such consequential, incidental, supplementary or transitional provisions and savings as the Secretary of State considers appropriate (including provisions modifying enactments relating to the periods within which proceedings must be brought).

(6) An order under this section—

(a) may make different provision with respect to different cases or descriptions of case (including different provision for different areas), and

(b) shall be made by statutory instrument which shall be subject to annulment in pursuance of a resolution of either House of Parliament.

(7) Nothing in any order under this section shall—
(a) preclude a local housing authority from serving a works notice on any person, or from requiring any person to take immediate remedial action to avoid a works notice being served on him, in any case where it appears to them to be necessary to serve such a notice or impose such a requirement; or
(b) require such an authority to disclose any information the disclosure of which would be contrary to the public interest.".

DEFINITION
"local housing authority": H.A. 1985, s.1.

GENERAL NOTE
Local authorities can require works to be carried out to an H.M.O. either under s.352 of the 1985 Act to remedy unfitness (see notes to s.75, above), or under s.372 to remedy management neglect. The new s.377A, added by this section, permits the Secretary of State to provide greater procedural safeguards for those on whom notices can be served, to give them the opportunity to remedy any default without incurring criminal liability. The new section makes provision for the introduction of two notices which the Secretary of State may by order require to be served prior to works notices under ss.352 or 372.

Under subss. (2) and (3), authorities may be required to serve a notice which contains the details set out in subs. (3), as to what works are required, why they are required and within what period they should be carried out. The notice would be served on the person on whom the works notice is to be served. The notice would also state whether there is a right to make representations before service or a right to appeal after service. Such a notice would be required to be served as soon as practicable and would, once served, preclude service of a works notice for a period determined by the order.

The second type of notice, under subs. (4), may be served on any person, not just those on whom the works notice is to be served, and would inform the recipient that the authority is considering serving the works notice, the reasons why and that the person may make representations to the authority.

Where immediate action is deemed necessary by an authority, however, the authority will not be precluded from taking it: subs. (7)(a). Nor will authorities be required to reveal information the disclosure of which would be contrary to the public interest: subs. (7)(b).

Codes of practice

77. After section 395 of the Housing Act 1985 insert—

"Codes of practice
395A.—(1) The Secretary of State may by order—
(a) approve any code of practice (whether prepared by him or another person) which, in his opinion, gives suitable guidance to any person in relation to any matter arising under this Part;
(b) approve any modification of such a code; or
(c) withdraw such a code or modification.
(2) The Secretary of State shall only approve a code of practice or a modification of a code if he is satisfied that—
(a) the code or modification has been published (whether by him or by another person) in such manner as he considers appropriate for the purpose of bringing the code or modification to the notice of those likely to be affected by it; or
(b) arrangements have been made for the code or modification to be so published.
(3) The Secretary of State may approve—
(a) more than one code of practice in relation to the same matter;
(b) a code of practice which makes different provision with respect to different cases or descriptions of case (including different provision for different areas).
(4) A failure to comply with a code of practice for the time being approved under this section shall not of itself render a person liable to

any civil or criminal proceedings; but in any civil or criminal proceedings—

(a) any code of practice approved under this section shall be admissible in evidence, and

(b) any provision of any such code which appears to the court to be relevant to any question arising in the proceedings shall be taken into account in determining that question.

(5) An order under this section shall be made by statutory instrument which shall be subject to annulment in pursuance of a resolution of either House of Parliament.

(6) In this section references to a code of practice include references to a part of a code of practice.".

GENERAL NOTE

Extensive guidance to authorities is already issued by the DoE in the form of circulars (most recently Circular 12/90). It is now intended to strengthen this guidance by issuing it in the form of approved Codes of Practice, which will also have the effect of making it more widely available.

Failure to comply with a Code does not itself create any civil or criminal liability, but a Code will be admissible in evidence in proceedings and where relevant must be taken into account in determining questions arising in the proceedings: s.395A(4). This is a familiar formulation in relation to other Codes, see *e.g.* the Race Relations Act 1976 (c. 74), s.47(10) and the Sex Discrimination Act 1975 (c. 65), s.56A(10) for Codes issued respectively by the Commisssion for Racial Equality and the Equal Opportunities Commission. Given the enhanced liability of landlords and agents to comply with the duty under s.352 of the 1985 Act (see s.73 above), the Codes will be particularly important to landlords and their agents, and the Codes will include guidance on what facilities should be provided: see *Hansard* (H.C.), Standing Committee G, Housing Bill, Eighth Sitting, col. 313, *per* Mr. Clappison (Parliamentary Under-Secretary of State, DoE).

In addition, *Improving Standards in Houses in Multiple Occupation*, para. 3.18, DoE, July 1995 states: "It is likely that priority will be given to updating the standards set out in DoE Circular 12/92 to promote a more goal-based approach to fire safety and risk assessment, taking into account any nationally agreed standards on Fire Safety which may be developed in accordance with the Fire Safety Scrutiny recommendations".

Increase of fines, &c.

78.—(1) In section 350(2) of the Housing Act 1985 (information in relation to registration schemes)—

(a) in paragraph (a) (failure to give information) for "level 2" substitute "level 3", and

(b) in paragraph (b) (mis-statement) for "level 3" substitute "level 5".

(2) In section 355(2) of that Act (failure to comply with occupancy restrictions) for "level 4" substitute "level 5".

(3) In section 356(2) of that Act (information in relation to occupation of house) for "level 2" substitute "level 3".

(4) In section 364(2) of that Act (information in relation to overcrowding) for "level 2 on the standard scale" substitute ", in the case of such failure, level 3 on the standard scale and, in the case of furnishing such a statement, level 5 on the standard scale".

(5) In section 368(3) of that Act (use of house in contravention of undertaking) omit from "and if" to the end.

(6) In section 369(5) of that Act (failure to comply with management code) for "level 3" substitute "level 5".

(7) In section 376(1) and (2) of that Act (penalties for failures to execute works) for "level 4" substitute in each case "level 5".

(8) In section 377(3) of that Act (failure to permit execution of works) for the words from "level 3" to the end substitute "level 5 on the standard scale".

(9) In section 387(5) of that Act (failure to permit carrying out of works) for the words from "level 3" to the end substitute "level 5 on the standard scale".

(10) In section 396(2) of that Act (penalty for obstruction) for the words "level 3" substitute "level 4".

GENERAL NOTE
A number of criminal offences are created by Pt. XI of the Housing Act 1985 (c. 68). This section increases the maximum fines for offences, by either one or two levels. The levels are set out in the Criminal Justice Act 1982 (c. 48), s.37(2), as amended by the Criminal Justice Act 1991 (c. 53), s.17(1). The relevant levels are as follows:

Level 3—£1,000
Level 4—£2,500
Level 5—£5,000.

Minor amendments

79.—(1) In section 355(1) of the Housing Act 1985 (effect of direction limiting number of occupants) for the words from "the number" to the end substitute "any individual to take up residence in that house or part unless the number of individuals or households then occupying the house or part would not exceed the limit specified in the direction.".

(2) In section 398 of the Housing Act 1985 for subsection (6) (meaning of "person managing") substitute—

"(6) "Person managing"—

(a) means the person who, being an owner or lessee of the premises—

(i) receives, directly or through an agent or trustee, rents or other payments from persons who are tenants of parts of the premises, or who are lodgers, or

(ii) would so receive those rents or other payments but for having entered into an arrangement (whether in pursuance of a court order or otherwise) with another person who is not an owner or lessee of the premises by virtue of which that other person receives the rents or other payments, and

(b) includes, where those rents or other payments are received through another person as agent or trustee, that other person.".

(3) In Part IV of Schedule 13 to the Housing Act 1985 (control order followed by compulsory purchase order), in paragraph 22 (application of provisions where compulsory purchase order is made within 28 days of a control order), for "28 days" substitute "eight weeks".

GENERAL NOTE

Subs. (2)
Many of the duties in relation to houses in multiple occupation fall upon the "person managing" the H.M.O. The definition is amended by this subsection by the addition of a new subs. (6)(a)(ii) to s.398 of the 1985 Act, to overturn the effect of the decision in *London Borough of Wandsworth v. Sparling* (1987) 20 H.L.R. 169, Q.B.D., in which it was held that the owner of a property who was not receiving the rents (because they were being paid directly to the local authority to satisfy arrears of rates), was not the person managing.

Subs. (3)
The most draconian step which can be taken by a local housing authority in relation to an H.M.O. is the imposition of a control order under Housing Act 1985 (c. 68), s.379. Under a control order, the authority effectively displaces the owner of the H.M.O. and takes over management of it. Once a control order has been made, the authority must either prepare a management scheme for the property in accordance with Sched. 13 of the 1985 Act, or else make a compulsory purchase order. While the authority has eight weeks to make and serve the management scheme on the owner, a compulsory purchase order is required to be made within four weeks. The provisions of Sched. 13 are amended, by this subsection, to extend that time to eight weeks.

Common lodging houses

Repeal of Part XII of the Housing Act 1985

80.—(1) Part XII of the Housing Act 1985 (common lodging houses) is hereby repealed.

(2) In consequence of the above repeal—

(a) in section 619(2) of the Housing Act 1985, for "The other provisions of this Act" substitute "The provisions of Parts I to XI and XIII to XVIII of this Act"; and

(b) in section 65(2)(a) of the Housing Act 1988, for "XII" substitute "XI".

(3) The Secretary of State may by order make such consequential amendments or repeals in any local Act as he considers necessary or expedient.

Any such order shall be made by statutory instrument which shall be subject to annulment in pursuance of a resolution of either House of Parliament.

GENERAL NOTE

Provisions relating to the control of common lodging houses in the Housing Act 1985 (c. 68), Pt. XII derived most immediately from the Public Health Act 1936 (c. 49), and are the only remaining housing provisions which refer specifically to the "poor". The provisions have fallen into increasing disuse, as authorities have preferred to regulate hostel accommodation, which may fall within the definition of a common lodging house, through the H.M.O. provisions. Accordingly Pt. XII is now repealed.

PART III

LANDLORD AND TENANT

CHAPTER I

TENANTS' RIGHTS

Forfeiture

INTRODUCTION

This Part contains three quite separate Chapters. Chapter I is concerned with the rights of long leaseholders. The problems of bad management by freeholders and their agents of flats is most particularly a problem in London, where there is a large number of leasehold properties. Three particular problems are addressed in Chap. I: service charges, bad management by freeholders and the right of first refusal. In the case of each, the rights of leaseholders are extended.

Chapter II, while brief, brings about a fundamental change in security of tenure for private sector tenants. The Housing Act 1988 (c. 50) maintained long-term security of tenure through the assured tenancy. Landlords could, however, opt to grant "assured shorthold tenancies" by fulfilling specified notice requirements, which gave tenants a minimum of six months' security, at the end of which the landlord was guaranteed possession, provided two months' notice had been given to the tenant. The assured shorthold has proved popular with landlords. Over two thirds of the lettings by private landlords under the 1988 Act are shortholds: *The Legislative Framework for Private Renting*, Consultation Paper linked to the Housing White Paper *Our Future Homes*, para. 2.5.

Nonetheless, it appears that landlords still have problems ensuring that their tenancies fall within the assured shorthold regime: *ibid.* para. 2.7. Chapter II accordingly makes *all* new lettings under the Housing Act 1988 *automatically* shorthold, without any formalities, unless the landlord specifically creates a fully assured tenancy. The option to create a fully assured tenancy is unlikely to be taken by wholly private sector landlords, but will enable housing associations and other social landlords, who also fall within the 1988 Act regime, to grant greater security to their tenants.

Chapter III returns to the problems of long leaseholders. Leaseholders of houses have the right to enfranchise or extend their lease under the Leasehold Reform Act 1967 (c. 88), while leascholders of flats have a right to collective enfranchisement and lease extension under the Leasehold Reform, Housing and Urban Development Act 1993 (c. 28). These rights are also extended by Chap. III. In particular, the low rent test is lifted for most holders of leases over 50 years. Other minor amendments are made to both Acts.

Restriction on termination of tenancy for failure to pay service charge

81.—(1) A landlord may not, in relation to premises let as a dwelling, exercise a right of re-entry or forfeiture for failure to pay a service charge unless

the amount of the service charge—
    (a) is agreed or admitted by the tenant, or
    (b) has been the subject of determination by a court or by an arbitral
        tribunal in proceedings pursuant to an arbitration agreement (within
        the meaning of Part I of the Arbitration Act 1996).

(2) Where the amount is the subject of determination, the landlord may
not exercise any such right of re-entry or forfeiture until after the end of the
period of 14 days beginning with the day after that on which the decision of
the court or arbitral tribunal is given.

(3) For the purposes of this section the amount of a service charge shall be
taken to be determined when the decision of the court or arbitral tribunal is
given, notwithstanding the possibility of an appeal or other legal challenge to
the decision.

(4) The reference in subsection (1) to premises let as a dwelling does not
include premises let on—
    (a) a tenancy to which Part II of the Landlord and Tenant Act 1954
        applies (business tenancies),
    (b) a tenancy of an agricultural holding within the meaning of the Agricul-
        tural Holdings Act 1986 in relation to which that Act applies, or
    (c) a farm business tenancy within the meaning of the Agricultural
        Tenancies Act 1995.

(5) In this section "service charge" means a service charge within the
meaning of section 18(1) of the Landlord and Tenant Act 1985, other than
one excluded from that section by section 27 of that Act (rent of dwelling
registered and not entered as variable).

(6) Nothing in this section affects the exercise of a right of re-entry or forfeiture on other grounds.

GENERAL NOTE

Most long leases of dwellings (primarily flats) contain provision for the payment of service
charges to cover the management costs of the freeholder and repair and improvement of the
property. Failure to pay service charges is enforceable through action to forfeit the lease. This
can lead to the leaseholder losing a valuable asset because of failure to pay a relatively small sum
owing by way of service charges which are in dispute. The problem has become particularly
acute in London, where a number of landlords have "systematically exploited the scope of levying service charges" *per* Mr Clappison (Parliamentary Under-Secretary for the Environment),
Hansard (H.C.), March 28, 1996, Standing Committee G, col. 881. The intention of this section is
to prevent landlords being able to use forfeiture as the first means of enforcing payment of a
service charge: *ibid.* col. 882.

Forfeiture is effected by the lessor committing some act which affords clear evidence of his
intention to forfeit and determine the lease. Although at common law re-entry could be effected
by self-help, in residential lettings where someone is lawfully residing in the premises, or any
part of them, forfeiture can only be enforced by proceedings in court: Protection from Eviction
Act 1977 (c. 43), s.2. In the usual case, therefore, the issue and service of a writ claiming possession will operate as a re-entry in law and so bring about a forfeiture as soon as it is served on
the tenant: *Calabar Properties v. Seagull Autos* [1969] 1 Ch. 451.

In order to exercise the right of forfeiture, *i.e.* issue proceedings for possession or, where the
premises are empty, by physical re-entry, the landlord will now either have to have already
obtained the agreement of the tenant that the amount of service charge is owing, or secured a
court order or arbitration award to that effect: subs. (1). A court order may be sought only in the
county court and not the High Court: see s.95. Tenants will need to take care that they do not
inadvertently agree to or admit the amount of service charge, losing the protection of the section. The prohibition on forfeiture only applies to service charges (as defined, see below) in
respect of premises let as a dwelling, excluding dwellings which are let as part of a business or
farm lease: see subs. (4).

Where a court order or arbitration agreement has been obtained, the prohibition on re-entry
or forfeiture is lifted 14 days after the determination, notwithstanding the prospect of appeal:
subss. (2) and (3).

Service Charge. Service charge has the same meaning as in the Landlord and Tenant Act 1985 (c.
70), s.18(1) (see subs. (5)), which provides (as amended by the Landlord and Tenant Act 1987 (c.
31)):

"(1) ... 'service charge' means an amount payable by a tenant of a dwelling as part of or in addition to the rent—
    (a) which is payable, directly or indirectly, for services, repair, maintenance or insurance or the landlord's costs of management, and
    (b) the whole of part of which varies or may vary according to the relevant costs.
(2) The relevant costs are the costs or estimated costs incurred or to be incurred by or on behalf of the landlord, or a superior landlord, in connection with matters for which the service charge is payable.
(3) For this purpose—
    (a) 'costs' includes overheads, and
    (b) costs are relevant in relation to a service charge whether they are incurred, or to be incurred, in the period for which the service charge is payable or in an earlier or later period."

Section 27 of the 1985 Act excludes as service charges Rent Act 1977 rents registered under Pt. IV of the 1977 Act, unless they are registered as variable. The definition does not include some charges which may be levied by the landlord. It does not encompass charges which do not refer to "services, repairs, maintenance or insurance or the landlord's costs of management", *e.g.* improvements: *Sutton (Hastoe) Housing Association v. Williams* (1988) 20 H.L.R. 321, C.A. Nor will it apply to charges which are not variable according to relevant costs: *Coventry City Council v. Cole* (1993) 25 H.L.R. 555, C.A.

Notice under s.146 of the Law of Property Act 1925

82.—(1) Nothing in section 81 (restriction on termination of tenancy for failure to pay service charge) affects the power of a landlord to serve a notice under section 146(1) of the Law of Property Act 1925 (restrictions on and relief against forfeiture: notice of breach of covenant or condition).

(2) But such a notice in respect of premises let as a dwelling and failure to pay a service charge is ineffective unless it complies with the following requirements.

(3) It must state that section 81 applies and set out the effect of subsection (1) of that section.

The Secretary of State may by regulations prescribe a form of words to be used for that purpose.

(4) The information or words required must be in characters not less conspicuous than those used in the notice—
    (a)　to indicate that the tenancy may be forfeited, or
    (b)　to specify the breach complained of
whichever is the more conspicuous.

(5) In this section "premises let as a dwelling" and "service charge" have the same meaning as in section 81.

(6) Regulations under this section—
    (a)　shall be made by statutory instrument, and
    (b)　may make different provision for different cases or classes of case including different areas.

DEFINITIONS
"premises let as a dwelling": s.82.
"service charge": s.82.

GENERAL NOTE
Section 146 of the Law of Property Act 1925 (c. 20) contains the statutory jurisdiction to afford relief against forfeiture for breaches of covenant, *other than* non-payment of rent. The forfeiture will be void unless prior notice under s.146(1) is served on the tenant. To be valid, the statutory notice must specify the breach complained of, require it to be remedied (if possible), and require the tenant to make compensation in money for the breach (if the landlord so requires). If the notice is not complied with, the landlord may proceed to forfeit, although the tenant may apply to the court for relief at any time while the landlord is proceeding to enforce the forfeiture. Nothing in s.81 is to be taken to affect the power to serve notice under s.146, so that a landlord can still take this first step in the forfeiture process, even though he is not entitled to go ahead and execute the forfeiture unless and until the conditions in s.81 have been met. The s.146 notice will also have to comply with the requirements set out in subss. (2), (3) and (4), giving the tenant notice of his rights under s.81.

Service charges

Determination of reasonableness of service charges

83.—(1) In section 19 of the Landlord and Tenant Act 1985 (limitation of service charges: reasonableness), after subsection (2) insert—

"(2A) A tenant by whom, or a landlord to whom, a service charge is alleged to be payable may apply to a leasehold valuation tribunal for a determination—

(a) whether costs incurred for services, repairs, maintenance, insurance or management were reasonably incurred,

(b) whether services or works for which costs were incurred are of a reasonable standard, or

(c) whether an amount payable before costs are incurred is reasonable.

(2B) An application may also be made to a leasehold valuation tribunal by a tenant by whom, or landlord to whom, a service charge may be payable for a determination—

(a) whether if costs were incurred for services, repairs, maintenance, insurance or management of any specified description they would be reasonable,

(b) whether services provided or works carried out to a particular specification would be of a reasonable standard, or

(c) what amount payable before costs are incurred would be reasonable.

(2C) No application under subsection (2A) or (2B) may be made in respect of a matter which—

(a) has been agreed or admitted by the tenant,

(b) under an arbitration agreement to which the tenant is a party is to be referred to arbitration, or

(c) has been the subject of determination by a court or arbitral tribunal.".

(2) In the Schedule to the Landlord and Tenant Act 1985, for paragraph 8 (right to challenge landlord's choice of insurers) substitute—

"**8.**—(1) This paragraph applies where a tenancy of a dwelling requires the tenant to insure the dwelling with an insurer nominated by the landlord.

(2) The tenant or landlord may apply to a county court or leasehold valuation tribunal for a determination whether—

(a) the insurance which is available from the nominated insurer for insuring the tenant's dwelling is unsatisfactory in any respect, or

(b) the premiums payable in respect of any such insurance are excessive.

(3) No such application may be made in respect of a matter which—

(a) has been agreed or admitted by the tenant,

(b) under an arbitration agreement to which the tenant is a party is to be referred to arbitration, or

(c) has been the subject of determination by a court or arbitral tribunal.

(4) On an application under this paragraph the court or tribunal may make—

(a) an order requiring the landlord to nominate such other insurer as is specified in the order, or

(b) an order requiring him to nominate another insurer who satisfies such requirements in relation to the insurance of the dwelling as are specified in the order.

(5) Any such order of a leasehold valuation tribunal may, with the leave of the court, be enforced in the same way as an order of a county court to the same effect.

(6) An agreement by the tenant of a dwelling (other than an arbitration agreement) is void in so far as it purports to provide for a deter-

mination in a particular manner, or on particular evidence, of any question which may be the subject of an application under this paragraph.".

(3) In the Landlord and Tenant Act 1985 before section 32 under the heading "*Supplementary provisions*" insert—

"Jurisdiction of leasehold valuation tribunal

31A.—(1) The jurisdiction conferred by this Act on a leasehold valuation tribunal is exercisable by a rent assessment committee constituted in accordance with Schedule 10 to the Rent Act 1977 which when so constituted for the purposes of exercising any such jurisdiction shall be known as a leasehold valuation tribunal.

(2) The power to make regulations under section 74(1)(b) of the Rent Act 1977 (procedure of rent assessment committees) extends to prescribing the procedure to be followed in connection with any proceedings before a leasehold valuation tribunal under this Act.

(3) Such regulations may, in particular, make provision—

(a) for securing consistency where numerous applications under this Act are or may be brought in respect of the same or substantially the same matters; and

(b) empowering a leasehold valuation tribunal to dismiss an application, in whole or in part, on the ground that it is frivolous or vexatious or otherwise an abuse of the process of the tribunal.

(4) No costs incurred by a party in connection with proceedings under this Act before a leasehold valuation tribunal shall be recoverable by order of any court.

(5) Paragraphs 2, 3 and 7 of Schedule 22 to the Housing Act 1980 (supplementary provisions relating to leasehold valuation tribunals: appeals and provision of information) apply to a leasehold valuation tribunal constituted for the purposes of this section.

(6) No appeal shall lie to the Lands Tribunal from a decision of a leasehold valuation tribunal under this Act without the leave of the leasehold valuation tribunal concerned or the Lands Tribunal.

(7) On any such appeal—

(a) the Lands Tribunal may exercise any power available to the leasehold valuation tribunal in relation to the original matter, and

(b) an order of the Lands Tribunal may be enforced in the same way as an order of the leasehold valuation tribunal.

Leasehold valuation tribunal: applications and fees

31B.—(1) The Secretary of State may make provision by order as to the form of, or the particulars to be contained in, an application made to a leasehold valuation tribunal under this Act.

(2) The Secretary of State may make provision by order—

(a) requiring the payment of fees in respect of any such application, or in respect of any proceedings before, a leasehold valuation tribunal under this Act; and

(b) empowering a leasehold valuation tribunal to require a party to proceedings before it to reimburse any other party the whole or part of any fees paid by him.

(3) The fees payable shall be such as may be specified in or determined in accordance with the order subject to this limit, that the fees payable in respect of any one application or reference by the court together with any proceedings before the tribunal arising out of that application or reference shall not exceed £500 or such other amount as may be specified by order of the Secretary of State.

(4) An order under this section may make different provision for different cases or classes of case or for different areas.

(5) An order may in particular—

(a) make different provision in relation to proceedings transferred to the tribunal from that applicable where an application was made to the tribunal, and

(b) provide for the reduction or waiver of fees by reference to the financial resources of the party by whom they are to be paid or met.

(6) In the latter case the order may apply, subject to such modifications as may be specified in the order, any other statutory means-testing regime as it has effect from time to time.

(7) An order under this section shall be made by statutory instrument.

(8) No order altering the limit under subsection (3) shall be made unless a draft of the order has been laid before and approved by a resolution of each House of Parliament.

(9) Any other order under this section, unless it contains only such provision as is mentioned in subsection (1), shall be subject to annulment in pursuance of a resolution of either House of Parliament.

Transfer of cases from county court

31C.—(1) Where in any proceedings before a court there falls for determination a question falling within the jurisdiction of a leasehold valuation tribunal under this Act, the court—

(a) may by order transfer to such a tribunal so much of the proceedings as relate to the determination of that question, and

(b) may then dispose of all or any remaining proceedings, or adjourn the disposal of all or any of such proceedings, pending the determination of that question by the tribunal, as it thinks fit.

(2) When the tribunal has determined the question, the court may give effect to the determination in an order of the court.

(3) Any such order shall be treated as a determination by the court for the purposes of section 81 of the Housing Act 1996 (restriction on termination of tenancy for failure to pay service charge).

(4) Rules of court may prescribe the procedure to be followed in the court in connection with or in consequence of a transfer under this section."

(4) For section 20C of the Landlord and Tenant Act 1985 (limitation of service charges: costs of court proceedings) substitute—

"Limitation of service charges: costs of proceedings

20C.—(1) A tenant may make an application for an order that all or any of the costs incurred, or to be incurred, by the landlord in connection with proceedings before a court or leasehold valuation tribunal, or the Lands Tribunal, or in connection with arbitration proceedings, are not to be regarded as relevant costs to be taken into account in determining the amount of any service charge payable by the tenant or any other person or persons specified in the application.

(2) The application shall be made—

(a) in the case of court proceedings; to the court before which the proceedings are taking place or, if the application is made after the proceedings are concluded, to a county court;

(b) in the case of proceedings before a leasehold valuation tribunal, to the tribunal before which the proceedings are taking place or, if the application is made after the proceedings are concluded, to any leasehold valuation tribunal;

(c) in the case of proceedings before the Lands Tribunal, to the tribunal;

(d) in the case of arbitration proceedings, to the arbitral tribunal or, if the application is made after the proceedings are concluded, to a county court.

(3) The court or tribunal to which the application is made may make

such order on the application as it considers just and equitable in the circumstances.".

(5) In section 38 of the Landlord and Tenant Act 1985 (minor definitions), at the appropriate place insert—

" "arbitration agreement", "arbitration proceedings" and "arbitral tribunal" have the same meaning as in Part I of the Arbitration Act 1996;".

(6) In section 39 of that Act (index of defined expressions), at the appropriate place insert—

"arbitration agreement, arbitration pro-   section 38"
ceedings and arbitral tribunal

GENERAL NOTE

Subs. (1)

The Landlord and Tenant Act 1985 (c. 70), s.19, limits the recovery of service charges to charges which are reasonably incurred, and only so far as works or services are to a reasonable standard. Section 19(4) allowed a landlord or a tenant to seek a declaration in the county court on these issues, even though no other relief was being sought. In order to provide a cheaper forum for tenants, that jurisdiction is now to be transferred to the Leasehold Valuation Tribunal (LVT) (see notes to subs. (3), below and see also s.119 governing LVT pre-trial reviews). The application to the LVT may be made by either the landlord or the tenant once the service charge is alleged to be payable, *i.e.* once the landlord claims it is due in accordance with the lease: new subs. (2A). An application may also be made where a "service charge may be payable": new subs. (2B). Such an application could be made, *e.g.* where the landlord has produced estimates for works in accordance with s.20 of the 1985 Act and the tenant is of the view that these indicate that an unreasonable amount is going to be spent and therefore wants a determination of what is a reasonable amount before the costs are incurred. Application is not available in the circumstances set out in new subs. (2C) and, again, tenants will need to be careful that they have not inadvertently agreed or admitted any matter on which they could have sought a ruling from the LVT.

Subs. (2)

Paragraph 8 of the Schedule to the Landlord and Tenant Act 1985 (added by Landlord and Tenant Act 1987 (c. 31), s.43(2)) permits a challenge to the landlord's choice of an insurer, and to excessive demands for premiums. Jurisdiction in this matter was formerly exclusive to the county courts, but either landlord or tenant may now choose between county court and LVT.

Subs. (3)

Since 1980, Rent Assessment Committees have been given various valuation duties under the Leasehold Reform Act 1967 (c. 88), and later the Leasehold Reform, Housing and Urban Development Act 1993 (c. 28); when exercising these functions, they are known as Leasehold Valuation Tribunals. Appeal from the LVT is to the Lands Tribunal, under the provisions of Housing Act 1980 (c. 51), Sched. 22, para. 2; note, however, that for the purposes of the Landlord and Tenant Act 1985, leave to appeal must be obtained either from the LVT itself or from the Lands Tribunal: new s.31A(6). The Secretary of State has power to prescribe procedures for the LVT when exercising this new jurisdiction (subs. (2)). In particular, these will be available to deal with multiple applications in respect of the same or substantially the same matters, presumably by some form of test case mechanism, and also with frivolous, vexatious and abusive applications: subs. (3). Frivolous and vexatious means those cases "which are obviously frivolous or vexatious or obviously unsustainable": *per* Lindley L.J. in *A.G. of Duchy of Lancaster v. L. & N.W. Ry* [1892] 3 Ch. 274, p. 277.

The process of using the LVT is intended to be cheaper than that of the county court and applicants will not be deterred by the prospect of having to pay the other side's cost if they lose: see new s.31A(4). Nonetheless, applicants will have to pay a fee (new s.31B(2)), as prescribed by the Secretary of State, and the order prescribing the level of fees must be framed with a view to making the service self-funding (new s.31B(3)), although there will be an element of means-testing in the amount of the fee payable: new s.31B(5) and (6).

Many cases started by landlords in the county court for a determination under s.81, above, are likely to turn on the reasonableness of the service charges. The new s.31C provides for transfer from the county court to the LVT of matters which fall within LVT jurisdiction. Once determined by the LVT, the court may give effect to the determination by means of a court order and such an order is treated as a determination by the court for the purposes of s.81, entitling the landlord to proceed with forfeiture: new s.31C(2) and (3).

Subs. (4)

Many landlords engaged in litigation with their tenants seek to recover the cost of the litigation from their tenants under service charge provisions. Depending on the wording of the lease, this may be possible even where the tenants have been successful, *e.g.* in disputing a service charge demand, and the landlord is ordered to pay costs. Section 20C provides for application to the court that all or part of costs incurred by the landlord in any court proceedings are not to be regarded as relevant costs in determining the amount of the service charge. Section 20C is now extended to apply not only to court proceedings, but also to those before an LVT, the Lands Tribunal or in arbitration.

Subs. (6)

"An 'arbitration agreement' means an agreement to submit to arbitration present or future disputes": Arbitration Act 1996 (c. 23), s.6. "Arbitration proceedings" and "arbitral tribunal" are not defined specifically in that Act.

Right to appoint surveyor to advise on matters relating to service charges

84.—(1) A recognised tenants' association may appoint a surveyor for the purposes of this section to advise on any matters relating to, or which may give rise to, service charges payable to a landlord by one or more members of the association.

The provisions of Schedule 4 have effect for conferring on a surveyor so appointed rights of access to documents and premises.

(2) A person shall not be so appointed unless he is a qualified surveyor.

For this purpose "qualified surveyor" has the same meaning as in section 78(4)(a) of the Leasehold Reform, Housing and Urban Development Act 1993 (persons qualified for appointment to carry out management audit).

(3) The appointment shall take effect for the purposes of this section upon notice in writing being given to the landlord by the association stating the name and address of the surveyor, the duration of his appointment and the matters in respect of which he is appointed.

(4) An appointment shall cease to have effect for the purposes of this section if the association gives notice in writing to the landlord to that effect or if the association ceases to exist.

(5) A notice is duly given under this section to a landlord of any tenants if it is given to a person who receives on behalf of the landlord the rent payable by those tenants; and a person to whom such a notice is so given shall forward it as soon as may be to the landlord.

(6) In this section—

"recognised tenants' association" has the same meaning as in the provisions of the Landlord and Tenant Act 1985 relating to service charges (see section 29 of that Act); and

"service charge" means a service charge within the meaning of section 18(1) of that Act, other than one excluded from that section by section 27 of that Act (rent of dwelling registered and not entered as variable).

GENERAL NOTE

Tenants' associations may be recognised under the Landlord and Tenant Act 1985 (c. 70), s.29. Recognition requires either acknowledgement from the landlord given to the secretary of the association, or certification by one of the Lord Chancellor's appointees to the Rent Assessment Panel for the registration area in which the dwellings are situated: *ibid.* s.29(1) and (4). Once thus recognised, the association has a role under ss.20 to 23 of the 1985 Act and must be served with and consulted on estimates of costs of works (s.20), provided with summaries of relevant costs (s.21), permitted to inspect supporting accounts (s.22), and to obtain information held by a superior landlord (s.23). In order that the association may more effectively exercise these rights, they may appoint a qualified surveyor to advise on matters relating to, or which may give rise to, service charges payable by members of the association: subs. (1).

A qualified surveyor is "a fellow or professional associate of the Royal Institution of Chartered Surveyors or of the Incorporated Society of Valuers and Auctioneers" or an individual who fulfils any other requirement specified by the Secretary of State by regulation: Leasehold Reform, Housing and Urban Development Act 1993 (c. 28), s.78(4)(a) and (5). By regulations, members or fellows of the Architects and Surveyors Institute are also qualified: Collective Enfranchisement and Tenants' Audit (Qualified Surveyors) Regulations 1994 (S.I. 1994 No. 1263).

The landlord must be notified of the appointment of the surveyor, or cessation of appointment, in accordance with subss. (3), (4) and (5). While appointed, the surveyor has the rights to inspect documents and premises conferred by Sched. 4. Access to documents and premises must be given free of charge, although the costs of providing these may be recharged to the tenants as management costs: Sched. 4, paras. 3(5), 4(4). A reasonable charge may be made by the landlord for the cost of taking copies or extracts of documents: para. 3(6). Other persons may be required to give access to documents either where they are responsible for applying the proceeds of the service charge or they are under an obligation to a tenant who pays the service charge in respect of any matter to which the charge relates: para. 3(2).

The rights are exercised by service by the surveyor of a notice in writing on the landlord or other person (documents), or by making a request to the landlord (premises): paras. 3(3), 4(3). If co-operation is not forthcoming, the rights can be enforced through court order: para. 5. The county court has jurisdiction in this matter: see s.95.

Appointment of manager

Appointment of manager by the court

85.—(1) Section 24 of the Landlord and Tenant Act 1987 (appointment of manager by the court) is amended as follows.

(2) In subsection (2) (circumstances in which order may be made), in paragraph (a) (breach of obligation by landlord), omit sub-paragraph (ii) (requirement that circumstances likely to continue).

(3) In that subsection, after paragraph (a), and before the word "or" following that paragraph, insert—

"(ab) where the court is satisfied—

(i) that unreasonable service charges have been made, or are proposed or likely to be made, and

(ii) that it is just and convenient to make the order in all the circumstances of the case;

(ac) where the court is satisfied—

(i) that the landlord has failed to comply with any relevant provision of a code of practice approved by the Secretary of State under section 87 of the Leasehold Reform, Housing and Urban Development Act 1993 (codes of management practice), and

(ii) that it is just and convenient to make the order in all the circumstances of the case;".

(4) After that subsection insert—

"(2A) For the purposes of subsection (2)(ab) a service charge shall be taken to be unreasonable—

(a) if the amount is unreasonable having regard to the items for which it is payable,

(b) if the items for which it is payable are of an unnecessarily high standard, or

(c) if the items for which it is payable are of an insufficient standard with the result that additional service charges are or may be incurred.

In that provision and this subsection "service charge" means a service charge within the meaning of section 18(1) of the Landlord and Tenant Act 1985, other than one excluded from that section by section 27 of that Act (rent of dwelling registered and not entered as variable).".

(5) The above amendments apply to applications for an order under section 24 of the Landlord and Tenant Act 1987 which are made after this section comes into force.

In relation to any such application the reference in the inserted subsection (2)(ab) to service charges which have been made includes services charges made before that date.

(6) After subsection (9) insert—

"(9A) The court shall not vary or discharge an order under subsection (9) on a landlord's application unless it is satisfied—

(a) that the variation or discharge of the order will not result in a recurrence of the circumstances which led to the order being made, and

(b) that it is just and convenient in all the circumstances of the case to vary or discharge the order.".

GENERAL NOTE

Part II of the Landlord and Tenant Act 1987 (c. 31) deals with the appointment of managers by the court, to assume responsibility for the management of premises containing flats. Section 24(2) of that Act sets out the preconditions which must be satisfied before the court may make such an order. The amendments made to s.24 by this section alter those preconditions so as to make it easier to obtain the appointment of a manager. Note that in accordance with s.86, the jurisdiction to make such orders is to be transferred to the Leasehold Valuation Tribunal (LVT) (see notes to s.83(3), above).

One ground for making an order is that the landlord is in breach of an obligation to the tenant in respect of management of the premises. By subs. (2), the section is amended so that the court (LVT) no longer has to be satisfied that a breach is likely to continue. By subs. (3), two new grounds are added. The first relates to unreasonable service charges (see notes to s.83 above). The second relates to a failure to comply with codes of practice issued under Leasehold Reform, Housing and Urban Development Act 1993 (c. 28), s.87, which permits the Secretary of State to approve codes "designed to promote desirable practices in relation to any matter or matters directly or indirectly concerned with the management of residential property". Only one code has so far been approved, which relates to the management of leasehold sheltered housing: "*The Association of Retirement Housing Managers' Code of Practice for the Management of Leasehold Sheltered Housing*", approved by S.I. 1995 No. 3149.

Subs. (6)

Section 24(9) of the 1987 Act provides for applications to vary or discharge orders appointing a manager. When sought by a landlord, the power of the court (LVT) to make a variation or discharge is now to be more tightly circumscribed by the new subs. (9A).

Appointment of manager: transfer of jurisdiction to leasehold valuation tribunal

86.—(1) Part II of the Landlord and Tenant Act 1987 (appointment of managers by the court) is amended as follows for the purpose of transferring to a leasehold valuation tribunal the jurisdiction of the court under that Part.

(2) In the following contexts for "the court", in the first (or only) place where it occurs, substitute "a leasehold valuation tribunal": section 21(1), section 22(2)(b), section 22(3), section 23(1), section 24(1), (2), (9) and (10); and in every other context in those sections, except section 21(6), for "the court" substitute "the tribunal".

(3) In section 21(6) (exclusion of application under inherent jurisdiction of court) for "any jurisdiction existing apart from this Act" substitute "any jurisdiction".

(4) In section 23(2)—

(a) for "Rules of court" substitute "Procedure regulations", and

(b) in paragraph (a), for "rules" substitute "regulations".

(5) After section 24 insert—

"Jurisdiction of leasehold valuation tribunal

24A.—(1) The jurisdiction conferred by this Part on a leasehold valuation tribunal is exercisable by a rent assessment committee constituted in accordance with Schedule 10 to the Rent Act 1977 which when so constituted for the purposes of exercising any such jurisdiction shall be known as a leasehold valuation tribunal.

(2) The power to make regulations under section 74(1)(b) of the Rent Act 1977 (procedure of rent assessment committees) extends to prescribing the procedure to be followed in connection with any proceedings before a leasehold valuation tribunal under this Part.

Such regulations are referred to in this Part as "procedure regulations".

(3) Procedure regulations may, in particular, make provision—

(a) for securing consistency where numerous applications under this Part are or may be brought in respect of the same or substantially the same matters; and

(b) empowering a leasehold valuation tribunal to dismiss an application, in whole or in part, on the ground that it is frivolous or vexatious or otherwise an abuse of the process of the tribunal.

(4) Any order made by a leasehold valuation tribunal under this Part may, with the leave of the court, be enforced in the same way as an order of the county court.

(5) No costs incurred by a party in connection with proceedings under this Part before a leasehold valuation tribunal shall be recoverable by order of any court.

(6) Paragraphs 2, 3 and 7 of Schedule 22 to the Housing Act 1980 (supplementary provisions relating to leasehold valuation tribunals: appeals and provision of information) apply to a leasehold valuation tribunal constituted for the purposes of this section.

(7) No appeal shall lie to the Lands Tribunal from a decision of a leasehold valuation tribunal under this Part without the leave of the leasehold valuation tribunal concerned or the Lands Tribunal.

(8) On an appeal to the Lands Tribunal from a decision of a leasehold valuation tribunal under this Part—

(a) the Lands Tribunal may exercise any power available to the leasehold valuation tribunal in relation to the original matter, and

(b) an order of the Lands Tribunal may be enforced in the same way as an order of the leasehold valuation tribunal.

Leasehold valuation tribunal: applications and fees

24B.—(1) The Secretary of State may make provision by order as to the form of, or the particulars to be contained in, an application made to a leasehold valuation tribunal under this Part.

(2) The Secretary of State may make provision by order—

(a) requiring the payment of fees in respect of any such application, or in respect of any proceedings before, a leasehold valuation tribunal under this Part; and

(b) empowering a leasehold valuation tribunal to require a party to proceedings before it to reimburse any other party the whole or part of any fees paid by him.

(3) The fees payable shall be such as may be specified in or determined in accordance with the order subject to this limit, that the fees payable in respect of any one application or reference by the court together with any proceedings before the tribunal arising out of that application or reference shall not exceed £500 or such other amount as may be specified by order of the Secretary of State.

(4) An order under this section may make different provision for different cases or classes of case or for different areas.

(5) An order may, in particular, provide for the reduction or waiver of fees by reference to the financial resources of the party by whom they are to be paid or met.

Any such order may apply, subject to such modifications as may be specified in the order, any other statutory means-testing regime as it has effect from time to time.

(6) An order under this section shall be made by statutory instrument.

(7) No order altering the limit under subsection (3) shall be made unless a draft of the order has been laid before and approved by a resolution of each House of Parliament.

(8) Any other order under this section, unless it contains only such provision as is mentioned in subsection (1), shall be subject to annulment in pursuance of a resolution of either House of Parliament.".

(6) In section 52 of the Landlord and Tenant Act 1987 (jurisdiction of county courts), in subsection (2)(a) for "Parts I to IV" substitute "Parts I, III and IV".

GENERAL NOTE

Applications to appoint a manager under Pt. II of the Landlord and Tenant Act 1987 (c. 31) could be made to the county court, or in some circumstances to the High Court (see *ibid.* s.52). The jurisdiction is transferred by this section to the Leasehold Valuation Tribunal (LVT) and is in the same terms as the new Landlord and Tenant Act 1985 (c. 70), ss.31A and 31B (see notes to s.83(3), above), save that an order of the LVT may with the leave of the court be enforced as a county court order: new s.24A(4).

Text of Part II of the Landlord and Tenant Act 1987, as amended

87. The text of Part II of the Landlord and Tenant Act 1987 as amended by this Act is set out in Schedule 5.

Period after which acquisition order may be made

88. In Part III of the Landlord and Tenant Act 1987 (compulsory acquisition by tenants of their landlord's interest), in section 29(3) (conditions for making acquisition orders: period since appointment of manager under Part II) for "three years" substitute "two years".

GENERAL NOTE

Part III of the Landlord and Tenant Act 1987 (c. 31) provides for the compulsory acquisition of blocks of flats, where the landlord has failed to discharge his obligations relating to the repair, maintenance, insurance or management of the premises and

(i) either the appointment of a manager under Pt. II of the Act (see notes to s.85, above) would not be an adequate remedy, or

(ii) such a manager has been appointed for three years preceding the date of application.

The effect of the amendment in this section is to reduce that three-year period to two years.

Right of first refusal

Application of right of first refusal in relation to contracts

89.—(1) After section 4 of the Landlord and Tenant Act 1987 (relevant disposals) insert—

"Application of provisions to contracts

4A.—(1) The provisions of this Part apply to a contract to create or transfer an estate or interest in land, whether conditional or unconditional and whether or not enforceable by specific performance, as they apply in relation to a disposal consisting of the creation or transfer of such an estate or interest.

As they so apply—

(a) references to a disposal of any description shall be construed as references to a contract to make such a disposal;

(b) references to making a disposal of any description shall be construed as references to entering into a contract to make such a disposal; and

(c) references to the transferee under the disposal shall be construed as references to the other party to the contract and include a reference to any other person to whom an estate or interest is to be granted or transferred in pursuance of the contract.

(2) The provisions of this Part apply to an assignment of rights under such a contract as is mentioned in subsection (1) as they apply in relation to a disposal consisting of the transfer of an estate or interest in land.

As they so apply—

(a) references to a disposal of any description shall be construed as references to an assignment of rights under a contract to make such a disposal;

(b) references to making a disposal of any description shall be construed as references to making an assignment of rights under a contract to make such a disposal;

(c) references to the landlord shall be construed as references to the assignor; and

(d) references to the transferee under the disposal shall be construed as references to the assignee of such rights.

(3) The provisions of this Part apply to a contract to make such an assignment as is mentioned in subsection (2) as they apply (in accordance with subsection (1)) to a contract to create or transfer an estate or interest in land.

(4) Nothing in this section affects the operation of the provisions of this Part relating to options or rights of pre-emption.".

(2) In section 4(2) of the Landlord and Tenant Act 1987 (relevant disposals: excluded disposals), for paragraph (i) (certain disposals in pursuance of existing obligations) substitute—

"(i) a disposal in pursuance of a contract, option or right of pre-emption binding on the landlord (except as provided by section 3D (application of sections 11 to 17 to disposal in pursuance of option or right of pre-emption));".

(3) In section 20(1) (interpretation), in the definition of "disposal" for "has the meaning given by section 4(3)" substitute "shall be construed in accordance with section 4(3) and section 4A (application of provisions to contracts)".

GENERAL NOTE

Part I of the Landlord and Tenant Act 1987 (c. 31) gives certain tenants a right of first refusal on a relevant disposal affecting premises which contain two or more flats.The Act was described as "ill-drafted, complicated and confused" by Sir Nicholas Browne-Wilkinson in *Denetower v. Toop* (1991) 23 H.L.R. 362, and has been subject to numerous attempts by landlords to avoid its application. The amendments in this and the following three sections attempt to address some of the problems which have emerged.

Section 1 of the 1987 Act provides that a landlord shall not make a "relevant disposal" (defined in s.4) affecting any premises to which Pt. I applies unless he has first served a notice in accordance with s.5, offering the tenants the right of first refusal, or unless the disposal is pursuant to the provisions of Pt. I. By s.4(1), a relevant disposal arises on "the disposal by the landlord of any estate or interest (whether legal or equitable) in [the] premises". In *Mainwaring v. Trustees of Henry Smith's Charities* (1996) 28 H.L.R. 584, the Court of Appeal held, somewhat reluctantly, that a "relevant disposal" took place on the completion of a conveyance and not on exchange of contracts.The new s.4A added by this section reverses this decision and applies the right of first refusal to a contract to create or transfer an estate or interest in land.

Notice required to be given by landlord making disposal

90.—(1) In section 4(2) of the Landlord and Tenant Act 1987 (disposals which are not relevant disposals for the purposes of Part I of that Act), for paragraph (l) substitute—

"(l) a disposal by a body corporate to a company which has been an associated company of that body for at least two years.".

(2) The above amendment does not apply to a disposal made in pursuance of an obligation entered into before the commencement of this section.

GENERAL NOTE
At present, all disposals to associated companies of the landlord are exempt from the right of first refusal. A holding company, subsidiary company or subsidiary of a holding company is an associate company: Landlord and Tenant Act 1987 (c. 31), s.20(1). To prevent abuse, companies will now have to have been associated for at least two years before being able to claim exemption.

Offence of failure to comply with requirements of Part I

91.—(1) After section 10 of the Landlord and Tenant Act 1987 insert—

"Offence of failure to comply with requirements of Part I
10A.—(1) A landlord commits an offence if, without reasonable excuse, he makes a relevant disposal affecting premises to which this Part applies—
  (a) without having first complied with the requirements of section 5 as regards the service of notices on the qualifying tenants of flats contained in the premises, or
  (b) in contravention of any prohibition or restriction imposed by sections 6 to 10.

(2) A person guilty of an offence under this section is liable on summary conviction to a fine not exceeding level 5 on the standard scale.

(3) Where an offence under this section committed by a body corporate is proved—
  (a) to have been committed with the consent or connivance of a director, manager, secretary or other similar officer of the body corporate, or a person purporting to act in such a capacity, or
  (b) to be due to any neglect on the part of such an officer or person,
he, as well as the body corporate, is guilty of the offence and liable to be proceeded against and punished accordingly.

Where the affairs of a body corporate are managed by its members, the above provision applies in relation to the acts and defaults of a member in connection with his functions of management as if he were a director of the body corporate.

(4) Proceedings for an offence under this section may be brought by a local housing authority (within the meaning of section 1 of the Housing Act 1985).

(5) Nothing in this section affects the validity of the disposal.".

(2) The above amendment does not apply to a disposal made in pursuance of an obligation entered into before the commencement of this section.

GENERAL NOTE
One of the major problems with the Landlord and Tenant Act 1987 (c. 31) has been the lack of an adequate enforcement mechanism where the landlord has failed to inform the tenants of a sale but has simply proceeded with it, see the comments of Sir Thomas Bingham M.R. in *Belvedere Court Management v. Frogmore Developments* (1995) 28 H.L.R. 398 at 407. This is remedied by the creation of a criminal offence, which is committed by a landlord where, without reasonable excuse, he makes a sale without first serving the notices required by the 1987 Act, s.5, or otherwise contravenes the prohibitions or restrictions imposed by ss.6 to 10 of the Act. The offence will be summary and is punishable by a fine of up to level 5 on the standard scale (currently £5,000): subs. (2). Where the landlord is a corporate body, the offence can be committed not only by the body, but also by an individual working for it: see subs. (3). The principal prosecuting authorities are to be local housing authorities: subs. (4).

Procedure for exercise of rights of first refusal

92.—(1) Part I of the Landlord and Tenant Act 1987 (tenants' rights of first refusal) is amended in accordance with Schedule 6.

(2) The amendments restate the principal provisions of that Part so as to—
(a) simplify the procedures for the exercise of the rights conferred on tenants, and
(b) apply those procedures in relation to contracts and certain special cases.
(3) In Schedule 6—
Part I sets out provisions replacing sections 5 to 10 of the Act (rights of first refusal),
Part II sets out provisions replacing sections 11 to 15 of the Act (enforcement by tenants of rights against purchaser),
Part III sets out provisions replacing sections 16 and 17 of the Act (enforcement of rights against subsequent purchasers and termination of rights), and
Part IV contains consequential amendments.

GENERAL NOTE
The provisions of Pt. I of the Landlord and Tenant Act 1987 (c. 31) are further amended by Sched. 6.

Part I
A more detailed regime for service of an offer notice when the landlord is proposing to make a disposal—dealing with the different types of disposal—is introduced by the new ss.5A to 5D. Section 6, dealing with acceptance of the landlord's offer, has been simplified. Sections 7, 8 and 8A deal with subsequent stages of the process, failure to accept the offer and the landlord's obligations when the tenants accept the offer and nominate a purchaser.
A new principle of "advance or withdraw" has been introduced, with the effect that a failure by either side to act is treated as withdrawal. New ss.8B to 8D cover the landlord's obligation in the special cases of auctions, disposal for non-monetary consideration and options. One particular area that has been clarified is that of options and rights of pre-emption: the right of first refusal can be exercised not only on the grant of an option or right of pre-emption, but also on its exercise.
Apart from withdrawal (dealt with in new s.9B), the only way in which the landlord can avoid sale to the tenants is if the premises cease to be premises to which Part I of the 1987 Act applies. In those circumstances the offer lapses. The landlord can, however, only proceed to sell on the open market in such circumstances after having served a notice on the tenants; this cannot now be done if a binding contract has been entered into, and the landlord has no lawful basis to rescind the contract: new s.10.

Part II
The amendments in Pt. II of Sched. 6 concern ss.11 to 15 of the 1987 Act, which provide for enforcement of the right of first refusal after the landlord has disposed of his interest to a third party. These have had to be changed in the light of the fact that the relevant disposal now includes exchange of contracts (see s.89, above). New s.12A allows the tenants to take the benefit of the contract if they find out about it before completion. New s.12B, as the current provisions, deals with the position where sale is being compelled after completion to the third party. The other sections correspond to existing sections of the Act. Enforcement of these rights will be assisted by the new s.3A, added to the Landlord and Tenant Act 1985, by s.93, below, which requires new landlords to inform tenants of assignments *to* them, which fall within the 1987 Act.

Part III
Sections 16 and 17, which deal with the consequences when tenants exercise their rights against a third party purchaser but discover that the purchaser no longer has an interest in the premises, have been amended to fit in with the new procedures relating to enforcement against third parties, and to provide for deemed withdrawal where the tenants do not proceed.

Duty of new landlord to inform tenant of rights

93.—(1) In the Landlord and Tenant Act 1985, after section 3 (duty to inform tenant of assignment of landlord's interest) insert—

"Duty to inform tenant of possible right to acquire landlord's interest
3A.—(1) Where a new landlord is required by section 3(1) to give notice to a tenant of an assignment to him, then if—
(a) the tenant is a qualifying tenant within the meaning of Part I of the Landlord and Tenant Act 1987 (tenants' rights of first refusal), and

   (b) the assignment was a relevant disposal within the meaning of that Part affecting premises to which at the time of the disposal that Part applied,

the landlord shall give also notice in writing to the tenant to the following effect.

(2) The notice shall state—

   (a) that the disposal to the landlord was one to which Part I of the Landlord and Tenant Act 1987 applied;

   (b) that the tenant (together with other qualifying tenants) may have the right under that Part—

       (i) to obtain information about the disposal, and

       (ii) to acquire the landlord's interest in the whole or part of the premises in which the tenant's flat is situated; and

   (c) the time within which any such right must be exercised, and the fact that the time would run from the date of receipt of notice under this section by the requisite majority of qualifying tenants (within the meaning of that Part).

(3) A person who is required to give notice under this section and who fails, without reasonable excuse, to do so within the time allowed for giving notice under section 3(1) commits a summary offence and is liable on conviction to a fine not exceeding level 4 on the standard scale.".

(2) In section 32(1) of the Landlord and Tenant Act 1985 (provisions not applying to tenancies within Part II of the Landlord and Tenant Act 1954), for "sections 1 to 3" substitute "sections 1 to 3A".

GENERAL NOTE

This is a further attempt to improve the operation of the Landlord and Tenant Act 1987 (c. 31), Pt. I, by addition to the Landlord and Tenant Act 1985 (c. 70). Section 3 of the 1985 Act requires a new landlord to inform tenants of the assignment, of his name and of his address. Failure to comply with the requirement is a criminal offence. In addition, the new landlord is now to be under an obligation to inform tenants qualifying under Pt. I of the 1987 Act if there has been a relevant disposal, and of relevant rights under the 1987 Act. Failure to serve the notice within the period required by s.3(1) of the 1985 Act, *i.e.* by the next rent date or a period of two months (whichever is the later), will also be a criminal offence, punishable by a fine of up to level 4 on the standard scale, currently £2,500.

General legal advice

Provision of general legal advice about residential tenancies

94.—(1) The Secretary of State may give financial assistance to any person in relation to the provision by that person of general advice about—

   (a) any aspect of the law of landlord and tenant, so far as relating to residential tenancies, or

   (b) Chapter IV of Part I of the Leasehold Reform, Housing and Urban Development Act 1993 (estate management schemes in connection with enfranchisement).

(2) Financial assistance under this section may be given in such form and on such terms as the Secretary of State considers appropriate.

(3) The terms on which financial assistance under this section may be given may, in particular, include provision as to the circumstances in which the assistance must be repaid or otherwise made good to the Secretary of State and the manner in which that is to be done.

GENERAL NOTE

Following the coming into force of the Leasehold Reform, Housing and Urban Development Act 1993 (c. 28), the government established the Leasehold Enfranchisement Advisory Service, with joint public and private sector funding, to provide initial information to landlords and tenants on the legislative provisions relating to leasehold enfranchisement. Since its inception, it has dealt with approximately 8,000 inquiries (*per* Mr Clappison (Parliamentary Under-Secretary of State for the Environment), *Hansard* (H.C.), Third Reading, April 30, 1996, Vol. 276, col. 915).

Following the coming into force of the Leasehold Reform, Housing and Urban Development Act 1993 (c. 28), the government established the Leasehold Enfranchisement Advisory Service, with joint public and private sector funding, to provide initial information to landlords and tenants on the legislative provisions relating to leasehold enfranchisement. Since its inception, it has dealt with approximately 8,000 inquiries (*per* Mr Clappison (Parliamentary Under-Secretary of State for the Environment), *Hansard* (H.C.), Third Reading, April 30, 1996, Vol. 276, col. 915).

The government initially committed funding for three years, in the belief that growing familiarity with the provisions of the 1993 Act would mean that the demand for advice would decline.

That has now been reconsidered and, given the amendments to leaseholders' rights in this Act, the government formed the view that "there is further scope for an impartial advice service to help in that area": *ibid.*

The initial advice service was funded under the DoE's special grants programme, which is intended to be time limited. "The purpose of the new clause is ... to give the Secretary of State a specific power to provide financial support to an advice service dealing with landlord and tenant issues, on a more permanent footing": *ibid.*

Supplementary

Jurisdiction of county courts

95.—(1) Any jurisdiction expressed by a provision to which this section applies to be conferred on the court shall be exercised by a county court.

(2) There shall also be brought in a county court any proceedings for determining any question arising under or by virtue of any provision to which this section applies.

(3) Where, however, other proceedings are properly brought in the High Court, that court has jurisdiction to hear and determine proceedings to which subsection (1) or (2) applies which are joined with those proceedings.

(4) Where proceedings are brought in a county court by virtue of subsection (1) or (2), that court has jurisdiction to hear and determine other proceedings joined with those proceedings despite the fact that they would otherwise be outside its jurisdiction.

(5) The provisions to which this section applies are—
(a) section 81 (restriction on termination of tenancy for failure to pay service charge), and
(b) section 84 (right to appoint surveyor to advise on matters relating to service charges) and Schedule 4 (rights exercisable by surveyor appointed by tenants' association).

CHAPTER II

ASSURED TENANCIES

Assured shorthold tenancies

Tenancies which are assured shorthold tenancies

96.—(1) In Chapter II of Part I of the Housing Act 1988 (assured shorthold tenancies) there shall be inserted at the beginning—

"Assured shorthold tenancies: post-Housing Act 1996 tenancies
19A. An assured tenancy which—
(a) is entered into on or after the day on which section 96 of the Housing Act 1996 comes into force (otherwise than pursuant to a contract made before that day), or
(b) comes into being by virtue of section 5 above on the coming to an end of an assured tenancy within paragraph (a) above,
is an assured shorthold tenancy unless it falls within any paragraph in Schedule 2A to this Act.".

(2) After Schedule 2 to that Act there shall be inserted the Schedule set out in Schedule 7 to this Act.

GENERAL NOTE

The Housing Act 1988 (c. 50) introduced substantial deregulation of the private rented sector, through the assured and, more particularly, the assured shorthold, tenancy. An assured shorthold tenancy under the 1988 Act is one which, in addition to fulfilling the requirements for an assured tenancy, is granted for a fixed term of not less than six months (which contains no power for the landlord to determine the tenancy within that period, other than by way of forfeiture), and on whom, before the tenancy began, a notice in the prescribed form has been served by the person who is to be the landlord under the tenancy, on the person who is to be the tenant, stating that the tenancy is to be shorthold: 1988 Act, s.20.

The latter procedural requirement "can pose a trap for inexperienced landlords, and may deter owners of empty properties from putting them to use": *"Our Future Homes"*, D.O.E. White Paper, (Cm. 2901), June 1995, p. 22. This has been reflected to some extent by an increasing number of cases on the validity of the grant of an assured shorthold, see *e.g. Panayi v. Roberts* (1993) 25 H.L.R. 421, C.A.; *Bedding v. McCarthy* (1993) 27 H.L.R. 103, C.A.; *Lower Street Properties v. Jones* (1996) 28 H.L.R. forthcoming, C.A.

The principal difference between an assured and an assured shorthold tenancy is the security of tenure which tenants obtain. Possession of an assured tenancy can only be gained by serving notice of seeking possession, and obtaining a court order, on one of a number of (mandatory or discretionary) grounds for possession. By contrast, once the fixed term for an assured shorthold tenancy has expired, and provided the landlord has served the requisite notice under s.21 of the 1988 Act, possession is automatic, and may be obtained through an accelerated paper procedure in the county court (see C.C.R. Ord. 49, r. 6A).

This section reverses the current situation under which lettings in the private sector are assured unless the procedural requirement to serve notice is complied with. Instead, under the new s.19A to be added to the Housing Act 1988, all new assured tenancies will be assured shorthold, unless they fall within the list of exceptions in s.19A itself or in the new Sched. 2A. Landlords will not be required to serve any notice on the tenant, nor will there be any requirement that the tenancy is of a fixed term (although see notes to s.99, below as to the security that assured shorthold tenants will have). An assured statutory periodic tenancy arising under s.5 of the 1988 Act (on termination of a fixed term tenancy) will also be an assured shorthold, provided that the fixed term was granted after the coming into force of this provision and that it does not otherwise fall within any of the exceptions: new s.19A(1)(b).

Exceptions. A number of exceptions are provided for:

(i) Tenancies in pursuance of a contract entered into prior to Housing Act 1996, s.96 coming into force: new s.19A(a).

(ii) Tenancies excluded by notice: new Sched. 2A, paras. 1 and 2. The landlord can opt in to a fully assured tenancy at the outset by notice served on the tenant prior to the tenancy being entered into, stating that the assured tenancy is not a shorthold: para. 1. The option to grant the greater security can also be adopted by the landlord at a later date: para. 2. This opting into assured tenancies is most likely to be used by registered social landlords, who are also subject to the security regime of the Housing Act 1988 (c. 50). The use of assured shortholds is likely to be the subject of guidance from the Housing Corporation (see s.36, above), as it is currently through the "Guidance on the Management of Accommodation Let on Assured Tenancies by Registered Housing Associations" issued under s.36A of the Housing Associations Act 1985 (c. 69). When housing the homeless, however, registered social landlords will have to use assured shortholds, see s.209, below.

(iii) Tenancies containing exclusionary provision: new Sched. 2A, para. 3. In addition to serving a notice opting in, a landlord may do so by including a provision to that effect in the tenancy agreement.

(iv) Assured tenancies by succession: para. 4. Under the Housing Act 1988, s.39, the Rent Act 1977 (c. 42) was amended so that first successions to members of the family, and all second successions under the 1977 Act, became assured tenancies, rather than statutory. Such successions will continue to take effect as fully assured, rather than assured shorthold tenancies, save as already provided for in s.39(7) of the 1988 Act.

(v) Former secure tenancies: para. 5. Where property is transferred from local authorities to housing associations, *e.g.* under large scale voluntary transfer, or the private sector, *e.g.* on termination of a housing action trust, the tenants will move from being secure to being assured. In such circumstances, they will not become shorthold tenants.

(vi) Tenancies arising under Sched. 10 to the Local Government and Housing Act 1989 (c. 42): para. 6. Where a long tenancy at a low rent expires, security of tenure is governed either by the Landlord and Tenant Act 1954 (c. 56), Part I, in which case the tenancy becomes statutory under the Rent Act 1977, or by Sched. 10 to the 1989 Act, in which case it becomes assured. In the latter case, such tenancies will not become shortholds.

(vii) Tenancies replacing non-shortholds: paras. 7 and 8. Paragraph 7 contains an anti-avoidance provision to prevent a landlord switching an assured tenant to an assured shorthold, without notice, by the device of a new tenancy. The premises need not be the same, and it is sufficient if the tenant was only one of a number of joint tenants of the former tenancy. The provisions only apply, however, where the landlord (including one of joint landlords) is the same under both the former, and the new tenancies and where there is no *hiatus* between the former and new tenancies. The protection does not operate as a complete bar to the grant of assured shortholds to former assured tenants (*cf.* the Housing Act 1988, s.21(3)), but requires instead that the landlord should serve a notice in the prescribed form on the tenant stating that the new tenancy is to be a shorthold.

Where under s.5 of the 1988 Act a statutory periodic tenancy arises on the ending of a fixed term assured tenancy, the tenancy will not become a shorthold, unless the original fixed term was itself assured: para. 8.

(viii) Assured agricultural occupancies: para. 9. Occupiers of tied agricultural and forestry properties are given security of tenure by Pt. I, Chap. III of the Housing Act 1988, which affords such occupiers, whether tenants or licensees, security equivalent to that of an assured tenancy, and applies the assured tenancy regime to them (with appropriate modifications). Assured agricultural occupancies are not brought within the automatic shorthold regime, although landlords may opt into it by serving notice under para. 9(2) (subject to the protection in paras. 9(3) and (4) for those to whom an assured tenancy is granted initially).

Duty of landlord to provide statement of terms of assured shorthold tenancy

97. After section 20 of the Housing Act 1988 there shall be inserted—

"Post-Housing Act 1996 tenancies: duty of landlord to provide statement as to terms of tenancy

20A.—(1) Subject to subsection (3) below, a tenant under an assured shorthold tenancy to which section 19A above applies may, by notice in writing, require the landlord under that tenancy to provide him with a written statement of any term of the tenancy which—

(a) falls within subsection (2) below, and

(b) is not evidenced in writing.

(2) The following terms of a tenancy fall within this subsection, namely—

(a) the date on which the tenancy began or, if it is a statutory periodic tenancy or a tenancy to which section 39(7) below applies, the date on which the tenancy came into being,

(b) the rent payable under the tenancy and the dates on which that rent is payable,

(c) any term providing for a review of the rent payable under the tenancy, and

(d) in the case of a fixed term tenancy, the length of the fixed term.

(3) No notice may be given under subsection (1) above in relation to a term of the tenancy if—

(a) the landlord under the tenancy has provided a statement of that term in response to an earlier notice under that subsection given by the tenant under the tenancy, and

(b) the term has not been varied since the provision of the statement referred to in paragraph (a) above.

(4) A landlord who fails, without reasonable excuse, to comply with a notice under subsection (1) above within the period of 28 days beginning with the date on which he received the notice is liable on summary conviction to a fine not exceeding level 4 on the standard scale.

(5) A statement provided for the purposes of subsection (1) above shall not be regarded as conclusive evidence of what was agreed by the parties to the tenancy in question.

(6) Where—

(a) a term of a statutory periodic tenancy is one which has effect by virtue of section 5(3)(e) above, or

(b) a term of a tenancy to which subsection (7) of section 39 below applies is one which has effect by virtue of subsection (6)(e) of that section,

subsection (1) above shall have effect in relation to it as if paragraph (b) related to the term of the tenancy from which it derives.

(7) In subsections (1) and (3) above—

(a) references to the tenant under the tenancy shall, in the case of joint tenants, be taken to be references to any of the tenants, and

(b) references to the landlord under the tenancy shall, in the case of joint landlords, be taken to be references to any of the landlords."

GENERAL NOTE

Because all assured shorthold tenancies have had to be for a fixed term, and have required notice to be served in advance of the tenancy being entered into, nearly all assured shortholds were in the form of written tenancy agreements. With the changes being effected by s.96, above (no notice and no fixed term required), far less formality will be needed to create an assured shorthold. While the government resisted attempts by the Opposition to require landlords to provide a written tenancy agreement for all shortholds, they did concede that tenants should have the right to a written statement of certain terms of the tenancy when demanded by the tenant.

Under the new Housing Act 1988, s.20A added by this section, the tenant (or any one of joint tenants: subs. (7)) under an assured shorthold, who does not already have the terms in writing, may, by notice in writing, demand (subs. (1)) from the landlord (or any one of joint landlords: subs. (7)) that the following information be provided in a written statement (subs. (2)):

(i) the date on which the tenancy began, or if arising by statutory provision (ss. 5(7), 39(7)) the date on which it came into being;

(ii) the rent payable and the date it is due;

(iii) any term providing for review of the rent;

(iv) where the tenancy is a fixed term, the length of the fixed term.

The landlord does not have to provide notice of any other terms, *e.g.* as to repair (Landlord and Tenant Act 1985, s.11, *cf.* the rights of secure tenants under Housing Act 1985, s.104). The information need only be provided once, unless the terms have been varied.

Failure to provide the statement without reasonable excuse, is a summary offence punishable with a fine not exceeding level 4 on the standard scale (currently £2,500): subs. (4). Where the terms are in dispute, the statement is not to be regarded as conclusive evidence of what was agreed between the parties: subs. (5).

Form of notices under s.21 of the Housing Act 1988

98.—(1) Section 21 of the Housing Act 1988 (recovery of possession on expiry or termination of assured shorthold tenancy) shall be amended as follows.

(2) In subsection (1)(b) (which requires the landlord under a fixed term tenancy to give two months' notice to recover possession), after "notice" there shall be inserted "in writing".

(3) In subsection (4)(a) (corresponding provision for periodic tenancies), after "notice", where it first occurs, there shall be inserted "in writing".

GENERAL NOTE

Possession of an assured shorthold tenancy cannot be obtained unless the landlord has given the tenant not less than two months' notice stating that he requires possession of the dwelling-house: Housing Act 1988 (c. 50), s.21(1)(b), (4)(a). As originally enacted, there was no specific requirement that this notice be in writing, and in *Lower Street Properties v. Jones* (1996) 28 H.L.R. forthcoming, C.A., it was held that writing was not necessary and that the notice could be proved by agreement or in any other way considered to be appropriate. These amendments provide that notice must now be in writing.

Restriction on recovery of possession on expiry or termination

99. In section 21 of the Housing Act 1988 there shall be inserted at the end—

"(5) Where an order for possession under subsection (1) or (4) above is made in relation to a dwelling-house let on a tenancy to which section 19A above applies, the order may not be made so as to take effect earlier than—

(a) in the case of a tenancy which is not a replacement tenancy, six months after the beginning of the tenancy, and

(b) in the case of a replacement tenancy, six months after the beginning of the original tenancy.

(6) In subsection (5)(b) above, the reference to the original tenancy is—

(a) where the replacement tenancy came into being on the coming to an end of a tenancy which was not a replacement tenancy, to the immediately preceding tenancy, and

(b) where there have been successive replacement tenancies, to the tenancy immediately preceding the first in the succession of replacement tenancies.

(7) For the purposes of this section, a replacement tenancy is a tenancy—

(a) which comes into being on the coming to an end of an assured short-

hold tenancy, and
  (b) under which, on its coming into being—
        (i) the landlord and tenant are the same as under the earlier tenancy as at its coming to an end, and
        (ii) the premises let are the same or substantially the same as those let under the earlier tenancy as at that time.".

GENERAL NOTE
While there was a minimum requirement of a six-month fixed term for all assured shorthold tenancies, this also procured a minimum period of security of tenure (unless there was provision for forfeiture or re-entry, and one of the grounds for possession for an assured tenancy could be relied on), as the court could not make an order for possession of an assured shorthold tenancy unless the fixed term had come to an end: the Housing Act 1988 (c. 50), s.21(1)(a), (4). As there is now to be no requirement of a fixed term of six months (see notes to s.96, above), s.21 is amended to prevent possession being ordered until at least six months has elapsed from the grant of the tenancy. The six months runs from the grant of the first tenancy, and not the start of any replacement tenancy, whether the replacement tenancy arises by agreement with the landlord or as a statutory periodic tenancy under the 1988 Act, s.5: new subss. (5)(b), (6) and (7).

Applications for determination of rent: time limit

100.—(1) Section 22 of the Housing Act 1988 (reference of excessive rents to rent assessment committee) shall be amended as follows.

(2) In subsection (2) (circumstances in which no application under the section may be made) after paragraph (a) there shall be inserted—
    "(aa) the tenancy is one to which section 19A above applies and more than six months have elapsed since the beginning of the tenancy or, in the case of a replacement tenancy, since the beginning of the original tenancy; or".

(3) At the end there shall be inserted—
    "(6) In subsection (2)(aa) above, the references to the original tenancy and to a replacement tenancy shall be construed in accordance with subsections (6) and (7) respectively of section 21 above.".

GENERAL NOTE
The Housing Act 1988 (c. 50), s.22, provides for the reference of rents of assured shorthold properties to the Rent Assessment Committee. Applications can only be made during the initial fixed term of the tenancy: the 1988 Act, s.22(2)(b). That is now amended in relation to new shortholds (which do not have to comply with the requirement of a fixed term, see notes to s.96, above), so as to allow application during the first six months from the grant of the original tenancy. The Secretary of State has reserved the power to disapply the right to apply to the Rent Assessment Committee altogether, under the 1988 Act, s.23, and has indicated an intention so to do in *The Legislative Framework for Private Renting*, consultation paper linked to Housing White Paper, *Our Future Homes*, June 1995, para. 2.12.

Grounds for possession

Mandatory possession for non-payment of rent: reduction in arrears required

101. In Part I of Schedule 2 to the Housing Act 1988 (grounds on which court must order possession) in Ground 8 (rent unpaid for certain periods)—
  (a) in paragraph (a) (rent payable weekly or fortnightly) for "thirteen weeks" there shall be substituted "eight weeks", and
  (b) in paragraph (b) (rent payable monthly) for "three months" there shall be substituted "two months".

GENERAL NOTE
Where lettings are on the basis of a fully assured tenancy—as distinct from an assured short-hold—possession may be ordered under one of the mandatory and discretionary grounds to be found in the Housing Act 1988 (c. 50), Sched. 2. There are three grounds concerned with rent arrears, of which Ground 8 is a mandatory ground based on arrears of rent, where more than 13

weeks' (where payable weekly or fortnightly) or three months' (where payable monthly) rent is lawfully due from the tenant, both at the time of issuing a notice of seeking possession and at the date of the hearing. Those periods are reduced to eight weeks and two months respectively by this section.

Recovery of possession where grant induced by false statement

102. In Part II of Schedule 2 to the Housing Act 1988 (grounds on which court may order possession) there shall be inserted at the end—

"Ground 17

The tenant is the person, or one of the persons, to whom the tenancy was granted and the landlord was induced to grant the tenancy by a false statement made knowingly or recklessly by—
  (a) the tenant, or
  (b) a person acting at the tenant's instigation.".

GENERAL NOTE
  The new discretionary ground for possession to be added to Sched. 2 to the Housing Act 1988 (c. 50) by this section is modelled on Ground 5 of the Housing Act 1985 (c. 68), (as amended by s.145, below, so as to add a false statement given not by the tenant but by someone else at his instigation). Note that the landlord must be *induced* to grant the tenancy by the false statement, so that a statement which is patently false or which any reasonable landlord would have disregarded is unlikely to qualify. Clearly, an attempt to recover possession on this ground implies a most serious charge and, given the quasi-criminal language of the provision, a burden of proof analogous to that applicable in criminal proceedings was adopted by the county court judge in *Rushcliffe Borough Council v. Watson* (1991) 24 H.L.R. 124, C.A. The Court of Appeal upheld the judge's exercise of his discretion to grant possession against a tenant who had stated that she was a lodger in a property, of which in fact she was the tenant.

Assured agricultural occupancies

Assured agricultural occupancies: exclusion of tenancies of agricultural holdings and farm business tenancies

103.—(1) Section 24 of the Housing Act 1988 (assured agricultural occupancies) shall be amended as follows.
  (2) In subsection (2)(b) (under which a tenancy is an assured agricultural occupancy if it would be an assured tenancy, but for paragraph 7 of Schedule 1 to that Act) there shall be inserted at the end "and is not an excepted tenancy".
  (3) After subsection (2) there shall be inserted—
  "(2A) For the purposes of subsection (2)(b) above, a tenancy is an excepted tenancy if it is—
    (a) a tenancy of an agricultural holding within the meaning of the Agricultural Holdings Act 1986 in relation to which that Act applies, or
    (b) a farm business tenancy within the meaning of the Agricultural Tenancies Act 1995.".

GENERAL NOTE
  Occupiers of tied agricultural and forestry properties enjoy security of tenure under s.24 of the Housing Act 1988 (c. 50), which affords such occupiers, whether tenants or licensees, security equivalent to that available under an assured tenancy and applies the assured tenancy regime to them with appropriate modifications. Security of tenure is granted notwithstanding the fact that the occupancy may be under a licence or may be at a low or no rent: s.24(2).
  Where a farm is comprised in an agricultural holding or a farm business tenancy, the person responsible for the control of the farm, whether the farm tenant or employee of the tenant, is prevented from being an assured tenant under the Housing Act 1988, by Sched. 2A, para. 7, but re-included for the purposes of s.24. The effect of this is that a farmer may fall under both the security of tenure provisions for farms, *i.e.* the Agricultural Holdings Act 1986 (c. 5) or the

Agricultural Tenancies Act 1995 (c. 8), and s.24 of the 1988 Act. It was not intended that both regimes should apply, and this amendment clarifies the position, so it is only the employees of tenants of agricultural holdings or farm businesses who can claim the benefit of s.24.

Consequential amendments

Consequential amendments: assured tenancies

104. The enactments mentioned in Schedule 8 have effect with the amendments specified there which are consequential on the provisions of this Chapter.

CHAPTER III

LEASEHOLD REFORM

Scope of rights

Low rent test: nil rateable values

105.—(1) In section 4(1) of the Leasehold Reform Act 1967 (meaning of "low rent")—

(a) in paragraph (i) (cases where rent limit of two-thirds of rateable value on later of appropriate day and first day of term applies), for the words from "or (where" to "that date" there shall be substituted ", or on or after 1st April 1990 in pursuance of a contract made before that date, and the property had a rateable value other than nil at the date of the commencement of the tenancy or else at any time before 1st April 1990,",

(b) in paragraph (ii) (other cases), for the words from "is entered" to "1990)," there shall be substituted "does not fall within paragraph (i) above,", and

(c) in paragraph (a) (definition of "appropriate day" by reference to section 25(3) of the Rent Act 1977), there shall be inserted at the end "if the reference in paragraph (a) of that provision to a rateable value were to a rateable value other than nil".

(2) In section 4A of the Leasehold Reform Act 1967 (alternative rent limits for the purposes of section 1A(2) of that Act)—

(a) in subsection (1)(b) (cases where rent limit of two-thirds of rateable value on the relevant date applies), for sub-paragraph (ii) there shall be substituted—

"(ii) the property had a rateable value other than nil at the date of commencement of the tenancy or else at any time before 1st April 1990,", and

(b) in subsection (2), for paragraph (b) there shall be substituted—

"(b) "the relevant date" means the date of the commencement of the tenancy or, if the property did not have a rateable value, or had a rateable value of nil, on that date, the date on which it first had a rateable value other than nil;".

(3) In section 8 of the Leasehold Reform, Housing and Urban Development Act 1993 (leases at a low rent)—

(a) in subsection (1)(b) (cases where rent limit of two-thirds of rateable value on the appropriate date applies), for sub-paragraph (ii) there shall be substituted—

"(ii) the flat had a rateable value other than nil at the date of the commencement of the lease or else at any time before 1st April 1990,", and

(b) in subsection (2), for paragraph (b) there shall be substituted—

"(b) "the appropriate date" means the date of commencement of the lease or, if the flat in question did not have a rateable value, or had a rateable value of nil, on that date, the date on which the flat first had a rateable value other than nil;".

GENERAL NOTE

The Leasehold Reform Act 1967 (c. 88) enables tenants of houses held on long leases at low rents, who fulfil the necessary residential qualification, compulsorily to acquire the freehold of their houses, or an extension of 50 years to their leasehold term. The Leasehold Reform, Housing and Urban Development Act 1993 (c. 28), Part I gives a right to long leaseholders to "collective enfranchisement" of blocks of flats. Under both provisions, entitlement depends on a low rent test, *i.e.* enfranchisement is only available to those who are long leaseholders conventionally so-called, paying only a ground rent rather than a market rent. This section makes amendments to the definition of low rent for both Acts; see also s.106, below, lifting completely the requirement of a low rent in some circumstances.

Low rent has traditionally been defined by reference to the rateable value of the property. Rents which do not exceed two-thirds of the rateable value are at a low rent (the 1967 Act, ss.4(1)(i), 4A(1)(b); the 1993 Act, s.8(1)(b)), although, since the abolition of rates, other methods of assessing low rents have been added for new lettings (*post*-March 31, 1990), see s.4(1)(ii) added by the References to Rating (Housing) Regulations 1990 (S.I. 1990 No. 434). The amendments in this section address the problem of properties which had a nil rateable value at the date of letting, *e.g.* because the property was unfit for human habitation when let on an understanding that the lessee would restore the property, or leases were granted as conversions off the drawing-board. As currently drafted, such properties would not be let at a low rent. The effect of the amendments is to take the first subsequent date on which such a property has a rateable value before April 1, 1990, as the relevant date on which to assess whether the property is at a low rent.

Low rent test: extension of rights

106. Schedule 9 (which makes provision for conferring an additional right to enfranchisement in relation to tenancies which fail the low rent test and for introducing an alternative to the low rent test in the case of the right to collective enfranchisement and the right to a new lease) shall have effect.

GENERAL NOTE

As noted to s.105, above, the right to enfranchise under both the Leasehold Reform Act 1967 (c. 88) and the Leasehold Reform, Housing and Urban Development Act 1993 (c. 28), depends on a low rent test. A further requirement is that the tenancy is let on a long lease, *i.e.* a lease "granted for a term of certain years exceeding twenty one years": the 1967 Act, s.3(1); the 1993 Act, s.7. The right to enfranchise is extended (by amendments made in Sched. 9) to cases which do not fulfil the low rent requirement, but which are let on a fixed term exceeding 50 years in the case of the 1967 Act, or 35 years in the case of the 1993 Act.

In order to fulfil the requirement of a specific term certain, the tenant "must at some point of time be, or have been, in a position to say that, subject to options to determine, rights of re-entry and so forth, he is entitled to remain in tenant for the next 21 years, whether at law or in equity": *per* Russell L.J. in *Roberts v. Church Commissioners* [1972] 1 Q.B. 278, C.A., *i.e.* 21 years or whatever term is relevant to the legislation in question. In that case, the lease was originally of 10¼ years from March 25, 1950. The landlords agreed to extend this in 1952 to 21¼ years, to be backdated to the date of the original grant of the tenancy. This did not fulfil the requirement of a term certain exceeding 21 years as at no time was the tenant in a position to say that there was an entitlement to remain tenant for 21 years.

Collective enfranchisement: multiple freeholders

107.—(1) In section 3 of the Leasehold Reform, Housing and Urban Development Act 1993 (premises in respect of which the right to collective enfranchisement is exercisable), in subsection (1)(a), the words "and the freehold of the whole of the building or of that part of the building is owned by the same person" shall be omitted.

(2) In section 4 of that Act (premises excluded from the right to collective enfranchisement), after subsection (3) there shall be inserted—

"(3A) Where different persons own the freehold of different parts of premises within subsection (1) of section 3, this Chapter does not apply to the premises if any of those parts is a self-contained part of a building for the purposes of that section.".

(3) In section 1(3) of that Act (additional property which may be acquired by tenants exercising the right to collective enfranchisement), the words "the freehold of it is owned by the person who owns the freehold of the relevant premises and" shall be omitted.

(4) Schedule 10 (amendments consequential on this section) shall have effect.

GENERAL NOTE

The right to collective enfranchisement under the Leasehold Reform, Housing and Urban Development Act 1993 (c. 28) is not available where the freehold of the building is owned by more than one person: the 1993 Act, s.3(1)(a). This has led to an easy avoidance mechanism, which landlords have exploited by granting a flying freehold of one flat in a block, often to a company which they control. The restriction is lifted by the amendment in this section. However, if ownership is of a self-contained part of a building, *i.e.* one that is structurally detached or vertically divided from the remainder of the building, such that it could be redeveloped independently, without any overlapping of services (the 1993 Act, s.3(2)), it is to be excluded from the right of collective enfranchisement. A number of consequential amendments are made by Sched. 10.

Valuation

Collective enfranchisement: removal of need for professional valuation of interests to be acquired

108. In section 13 of the Leasehold Reform, Housing and Urban Development Act 1993 (notice by qualifying tenants of claim to exercise right to collective enfranchisement) subsection (6) (tenants to obtain professional valuation of interests proposed to be acquired before giving notice) shall cease to have effect.

GENERAL NOTE

The process of exercising the right to collective enfranchisement under the Leasehold Reform, Housing and Urban Development Act 1993 (c. 28) is commenced by service by the tenants of an initial notice under s.13 of the 1993 Act. Under s.13(6), before serving such a notice the tenants have to obtain a valuation of the freehold interest of the premises, so that the tenants are aware of the costs that will be involved, before they embark on the process. This has proved unnecessarily expensive and bureaucratic and is now to cease to have effect.

Collective enfranchisement: valuation principles

109.—(1) Schedule 6 to the Leasehold Reform, Housing and Urban Development Act 1993 (purchase price payable by nominee purchaser) shall be amended as follows.

(2) In paragraph 3(1) (freeholder's interest to be valued on the basis that neither the nominee purchaser nor any participating tenant is in the market) for "neither the nominee purchaser nor any participating tenant" there shall be substituted "no person who falls within sub-paragraph (1A)".

(3) After paragraph 3(1) there shall be inserted—

"(1A) A person falls within this sub-paragraph if he is—

(a) the nominee purchaser, or

(b) a tenant of premises contained in the specified premises, or

(c) an owner of an interest which the nominee purchaser is to acquire in pursuance of section 2(1)(b).".

(4) In paragraph 7 (value of intermediate leasehold interests) after sub-paragraph (1) there shall be inserted—

"(1A) In its application in accordance with sub-paragraph (1), paragraph 3(1A) shall have effect with the addition after paragraph (a) of—

"(aa) an owner of a freehold interest in the specified premises, or" ".

(5) In paragraph 11 (value of other interests) after sub-paragraph (3) there shall be inserted—

"(4) In its application in accordance with sub-paragraph (2) above,

paragraph 3(1A) shall have effect with the addition after paragraph (a) of—
　　"(aa)　an owner of a freehold interest in the specified premises, or" ".

GENERAL NOTE
　The price of collective enfranchisement under the Leasehold Reform, Housing and Urban Development Act 1993 (c. 28) is governed by its Sched. 6. There are three aspects of the calculation: the open market valuation of the freeholder's interest; the freeholder's share of the marriage value; and compensation for losses resulting from enfranchisement. The first element is currently calculated on the assumption that neither the nominee purchaser nor any participating tenant wishes to purchase the premises. This section makes a number of technical amendments to this valuation process.

New leases: valuation principles

110.—(1) Schedule 13 to the Leasehold Reform, Housing and Urban Development Act 1993 (premium and other amounts payable by tenant on grant of new lease) shall be amended as mentioned in subsections (2) to (4) below.

(2) In paragraph 3(2) (landlord's interest to be valued on the basis that the tenant is not buying or seeking to buy) for "the tenant not" there shall ɩe substituted "neither the tenant nor any owner of an intermediate leasehold interest".

(3) In paragraph 4(3) (calculation of marriage value) for paragraph (a) (value of tenant's interest) there shall be substituted—
　　"(a)　the value of the interest of the tenant under his existing lease shall be determined in accordance with paragraph 4A;
　　(aa)　the value of the interest to be held by the tenant under the new lease shall be determined in accordance with paragraph 4B;",
and, in paragraph (b), for "that sub-paragraph" there shall be substituted "sub-paragraph (2)".

(4) After paragraph 4 there shall be inserted—
　　"4A.—(1) Subject to the provisions of this paragraph, the value of the interest of the tenant under the existing lease is the amount which at the valuation date that interest might be expected to realise if sold on the open market by a willing seller (with neither the landlord nor any owner of an intermediate leasehold interest buying or seeking to buy) on the following assumptions—
　　　(a)　on the assumption that the vendor is selling such interest as is held by the tenant subject to any interest inferior to the interest of the tenant;
　　　(b)　on the assumption that Chapter I and this Chapter confer no right to acquire any interest in any premises containing the tenant's flat or to acquire any new lease;
　　　(c)　on the assumption that any increase in the value of the flat which is attributable to an improvement carried out at his own expense by the tenant or by any predecessor in title is to be disregarded; and
　　　(d)　on the assumption that (subject to paragraph (b)) the vendor is selling with and subject to the rights and burdens with and subject to which any interest inferior to the existing lease of the tenant has effect.

(2) It is hereby declared that the fact that sub-paragraph (1) requires assumptions to be made in relation to particular matters does not preclude the making of assumptions as to other matters where those assumptions are appropriate for determining the amount which at the valuation date the interest of the tenant under his existing lease might be expected to realise if sold as mentioned in that sub-paragraph.

(3) In determining any such amount there shall be made such deduc-

tion (if any) in respect of any defect in title as on a sale of that interest on the open market might be expected to be allowed between a willing seller and a willing buyer.

(4) Subject to sub-paragraph (5), the value of the interest of the tenant under his existing lease shall not be increased by reason of—

(a) any transaction which—

    (i) is entered into after 19th January 1996, and

    (ii) involves the creation or transfer of an interest inferior to the tenant's existing lease; or

(b) any alteration after that date of the terms on which any such inferior interest is held.

(5) Sub-paragraph (4) shall not apply to any transaction which falls within paragraph (a) of that sub-paragraph if—

(a) the transaction is entered into in pursuance of a contract entered into on or before the date mentioned in that paragraph; and

(b) the amount of the premium payable by the tenant in respect of the grant of the new lease was determined on or before that date either by agreement or by a leasehold valuation tribunal under this Chapter.

4B.—(1) Subject to the provisions of this paragraph, the value of the interest to be held by the tenant under the new lease is the amount which at the valuation date that interest (assuming it to have been granted to him at that date) might be expected to realise if sold on the open market by a willing seller (with the owner of any interest superior to the interest of the tenant not buying or seeking to buy) on the following assumptions—

(a) on the assumption that the vendor is selling such interest as is to be held by the tenant under the new lease subject to the inferior interests to which the tenant's existing lease is subject at the valuation date;

(b) on the assumption that Chapter I and this Chapter confer no right to acquire any interest in any premises containing the tenant's flat or to acquire any new lease;

(c) on the assumption that there is to be disregarded any increase in the value of the flat which would fall to be disregarded under paragraph (c) of sub-paragraph (1) of paragraph 4A in valuing in accordance with that sub-paragraph the interest of the tenant under his existing lease; and

(d) on the assumption that (subject to paragraph (b)) the vendor is selling with and subject to the rights and burdens with and subject to which any interest inferior to the tenant's existing lease at the valuation date then has effect.

(2) It is hereby declared that the fact that sub-paragraph (1) requires assumptions to be made in relation to particular matters does not preclude the making of assumptions as to other matters where those assumptions are appropriate for determining the amount which at the valuation date the interest to be held by the tenant under the new lease might be expected to realise if sold as mentioned in that sub-paragraph.

(3) In determining any such amount there shall be made such deduction (if any) in respect of any defect in title as on a sale of that interest on the open market might be expected to be allowed between a willing seller and a willing buyer.

(4) Subject to sub-paragraph (5), the value of the interest to be held by the tenant under the new lease shall not be decreased by reason of—

(a) any transaction which—

    (i) is entered into after 19th January 1996, and

    (ii) involves the creation or transfer of an interest inferior to the tenant's existing lease; or

(b) any alteration after that date of the terms on which any such inferior interest is held.

(5) Sub-paragraph (4) shall not apply to any transaction which falls within paragraph (a) of that sub-paragraph if—

(a) the transaction is entered into in pursuance of a contract entered into on or before the date mentioned in that paragraph; and

(b) the amount of the premium payable by the tenant in respect of the grant of the new lease was determined on or before that date either by agreement or by a leasehold valuation tribunal under this Chapter.".

(5) This section applies in relation to any claim made after 19th January 1996 by the giving of notice under section 42 of the Act of 1993 unless the amount of the premium payable in pursuance of the claim has been determined, either by agreement or by a leasehold valuation tribunal under Chapter II of the Act of 1993, before the day on which this Act is passed.

GENERAL NOTE

Under the Leasehold Reform, Housing and Urban Development Act 1993 (c. 28), tenants of long leases of flats have the right to extend their leases for a further 50 years. The price to be paid by the tenant is governed by Sched. 13 to the 1993 Act. The basis is similar to that under Sched. 6, see notes to s.109, above, save that the valuation is not of the freeholder's interest, but of the diminution in value of the landlord's reversionary interest in respect of which the extended lease is granted. This section contains technical amendments to the assumptions on which this valuation is achieved. In particular, the rights granted under the 1993 Act are themselves to be disregarded (new s.4A(1)(b)), as are tenant's improvements (new s.4A(1)(c)).

The section applies to claims made after January 19, 1996, unless the premium has been determined prior to the day on which the Act is passed: subs. (5).

Trusts

Satisfaction of residence condition: collective enfranchisement

111.—(1) In section 6 of the Leasehold Reform, Housing and Urban Development Act 1993 (which provides when a qualifying tenant of a flat satisfies the residence condition) for subsection (4) there shall be substituted—

"(4) Subsection (1) shall not apply where a lease is vested in trustees (other than a sole tenant for life within the meaning of the Settled Land Act 1925), and, in that case, a qualifying tenant of a flat shall, for the purposes of this Chapter, be treated as satisfying the residence condition at any time when the condition in subsection (5) is satisfied with respect to an individual having an interest under the trust (whether or not also a trustee).

(5) That condition is that the individual has occupied the flat as his only or principal home—

(a) for the last twelve months, or

(b) for periods amounting to three years in the last ten years, whether or not he has used the flat also for other purposes.

(6) For the purposes of subsection (5)—

(a) any reference to the flat includes a reference to part of it; and

(b) it is immaterial whether at any particular time the individual's occupation was in right of the lease by virtue of which the trustees are a qualifying tenant or in right of some other lease or otherwise."

(2) In section 13(3)(e)(iii) of that Act (particulars of satisfaction of residence condition to be included in the notice by which qualifying tenants exercise right to collective enfranchisement)—

(a) after "which he" there shall be inserted ", or, where the tenant's lease is vested as mentioned in section 6(4), the individual concerned,", and

(b) for "his", in the first place where it occurs, there shall be substituted "the".

GENERAL NOTE

In order to qualify for the right to collective enfranchisement under the Leasehold Reform, Housing and Urban Development Act 1993 (c. 28) tenants must fulfil the residential requirement to be found in s.6 of the 1993 Act. The amendments in this section clarify and extend the position where leases are vested in trustees. Where the lease is held under the Settled Land Act 1925 (c. 18), and the occupier is the sole tenant for life, then the tenancy would appear to fall within the existing conditions. The sole tenant for life will be the qualifying tenant, and if the relevant conditions are fulfilled will be able to participate in the collective enfranchisement. In relation to other leases held on trust, the residential requirement may now be fulfilled by someone having an interest under the trust, who also fulfils the residence requirements set out in new subss. (5) and (6) of s.6. If there is a person fulfilling the residence requirement, the trustees will be the qualifying tenant for the purposes of the Act: see further s.113.

Satisfaction of residence condition: new leases

112.—(1) Section 39 of the Leasehold Reform, Housing and Urban Development Act 1993 (right of qualifying tenant of flat to acquire new lease) shall be amended as mentioned in subsections (2) to (4) below.

(2) In subsection (2) (circumstances in which the right conferred) for paragraph (b) (residence condition) there shall be substituted—

"(b) the condition specified in subsection (2A) or, as the case may be, (2B) is satisfied.

(2A) Where the lease by virtue of which the tenant is a qualifying tenant is vested in trustees (other than a sole tenant for life within the meaning of the Settled Land Act 1925), the condition is that an individual having an interest under the trust (whether or not also a trustee) has occupied the flat as his only or principal home—

(a) for the last three years, or

(b) for periods amounting to three years in the last ten years, whether or not he has used it also for other purposes.

(2B) Where the lease by virtue of which the tenant is a qualifying tenant is not vested as mentioned in subsection (2A), the condition is that the tenant has occupied the flat as his only or principal home—

(a) for the last three years, or

(b) for periods amounting to three years in the last ten years, whether or not he has used it also for other purposes.".

(3) After subsection (4) there shall be inserted—

"(4A) For the purposes of subsection (2A)—

(a) any reference to the flat includes a reference to part of it; and

(b) it is immaterial whether at any particular time the individual's occupation was in right of the lease by virtue of which the trustees are a qualifying tenant or in right of some other lease or otherwise.".

(4) In subsection (5), for "(2)(b)" there shall be substituted "(2B)".

(5) In section 42 of that Act (notice by qualifying tenant of claim to exercise right) for subsection (4) there shall be substituted—

"(4) If the tenant's lease is vested as mentioned in section 39(2A), the reference to the tenant in subsection (3)(b)(iv) shall be read as a reference to any individual with respect to whom it is claimed the condition in section 39(2A) is satisfied.".

GENERAL NOTE

This section makes equivalent provision for trustees to exercise the right to extend a lease of a flat under the Leasehold Reform, Housing and Urban Development Act 1993 (c. 28), to that made for collective enfranchisement. See notes to s.111, above.

Powers of trustees

113. After section 93 of the Leasehold Reform, Housing and Urban Development Act 1993 there shall be inserted—

"Powers of trustees in relation to rights under Chapters I and II

93A.—(1) Where trustees are a qualifying tenant of a flat for the purposes of Chapter I or II, their powers under the instrument regulating the trusts shall include power to participate in the exercise of the right to collective enfranchisement under Chapter I or, as the case may be, to exercise the right to a new lease under Chapter II.

(2) Subsection (1) shall not apply where the instrument regulating the trusts—

    (a) is made on or after the day on which section 113 of the Housing Act 1996 comes into force, and

    (b) contains an explicit direction to the contrary.

(3) The powers conferred by subsection (1) shall be exercisable with the like consent or on the like direction (if any) as may be required for the exercise of the trustees' powers (or ordinary powers) of investment.

(4) The following purposes, namely—

    (a) those authorised for the application of capital money by section 73 of the Settled Land Act 1925, or by that section as applied by section 28 of the Law of Property Act 1925 in relation to trusts for sale, and

    (b) those authorised by section 71 of the Settled Land Act 1925, or by that section as so applied, as purposes for which moneys may be raised by mortgage,

shall include the payment of any expenses incurred by a tenant for life or statutory owners or by trustees for sale, as the case may be, in or in connection with participation in the exercise of the right to collective enfranchisement under Chapter I or in or in connection with the exercise of the right to a new lease under Chapter II.".

GENERAL NOTE

Given that trustees are now permitted to exercise rights under the Leasehold Reform, Housing and Urban Development Act 1993 (c. 28) (see ss.111 and 112), provision is made by this section for trustees to enjoy the trust power to do so. Such powers will automatically be given to trustees, except in the case of trusts established after the date on which the section comes into force, where the power is explicitly excluded in the trust instrument.

Miscellaneous

Minor amendment of section 1(1)(a) of Leasehold Reform Act 1967

114. In section 1 of the Leasehold Reform Act 1967 (tenants entitled to enfranchisement or extension), in subsection (1)(a)—

    (a) in sub-paragraph (i), for the words from "or (where" to "that date," there shall be substituted ", or on or after 1st April 1990 in pursuance of a contract made before that date, and the house and premises had a rateable value at the date of commencement of the tenancy or else at any time before 1st April 1990,", and

    (b) in sub-paragraph (ii), for the words from "is entered" to " 1990)," there shall be substituted "does not fall within sub-paragraph (i) above,".

GENERAL NOTE

Under the Leasehold Reform Act 1967 (c. 88) the right to enfranchise or extend the lease is not available for high-value properties, *i.e.* those over the rateable value limit in s.1. This section makes a minor amendment to Leasehold Reform Act 1967, s.1(1), to take into account properties which originally had a nil rateable value, but which are brought within the scheme by the amendments made by s.105, above.

Power for leasehold valuation tribunal to determine amount of costs payable under Leasehold Reform Act 1967

115. In section 21(1) of the Leasehold Reform Act 1967 (matters to be determined by leasehold valuation tribunal), after paragraph (b) there shall be inserted—

"(ba) the amount of any costs payable under section 9(4) or 14(2);".

GENERAL NOTE

Where a tenant seeks to exercise his right to enfranchise or extend his lease under the Leasehold Reform Act 1967 (c. 88), the tenant must pay the landlord's usual conveyancing and valuation costs, whether or not the purchase is in fact completed, save where the Act provides otherwise. Disputes as to the amounts of this compensation are now to fall within the jurisdiction of the leasehold valuation tribunal.

Compensation for postponement of termination in connection with ineffective claims

116. Schedule 11 (which makes, in relation to claims to enfranchisement or an extended lease under Part I of the Leasehold Reform Act 1967 and claims to collective enfranchisement or a new lease under Chapter I or II of Part I of the Leasehold Reform, Housing and Urban Development Act 1993, provision for compensation of the landlord where the claim has prolonged an existing tenancy, but is ineffective) shall have effect.

GENERAL NOTE

Under the Leasehold Reform Act 1967 (c. 88) and the Leasehold Reform, Housing and Urban Development Act 1993 (c. 28), applications for enfranchisement or extension of a long lease can be made at any time before the expiry of the lease. Where they are made in the few months before expiry of the lease, and the matter is not settled before the lease expires, the legislation provides for the lease to be continued during the currency of the claim and for three months afterwards. In most cases where a long lease expires and the tenant holds over, Part I of the Landlord and Tenant Act 1954 (c. 56) provides for continued security of tenure but the tenant has to pay a market rent. While a claim under the 1967 or 1993 Act is in progress, this increase in rent will not come into effect and the tenant continues to pay a ground rent only; even if the claim is unsuccessful, the landlord cannot claim an increased rent from the original expiry date.

The amendments in Sched. 11 tackle this issue under both Acts, so that when a claim under the 1967 or 1993 Acts is made within two years of the expiry of the long lease, and the claim is not effective, the tenant will now have to pay the landlord compensation amounting to the difference between the market rent and the ground rent actually paid, for the period between the earliest date when the lease could have terminated and when the claim ceases to have effect. Provision is also made for cases where there has been a change in the identity of the leaseholder's immediate landlord.

The provisions are not coming into effect immediately, but are timed to coincide with the coming into effect of Sched. 10 to the Local Government and Housing Act 1989 (c. 42), which is replacing Pt. I of the Landlord and Tenant Act 1954 as from January 15, 1999.

Priority of interests on grant of new lease

117. After section 58 of the Leasehold Reform, Housing and Urban Development Act 1993 there shall be inserted—

"Priority of interests on grant of new lease

58A.—(1) Where a lease granted under section 56 takes effect subject to two or more interests to which the existing lease was subject immediately before its surrender, the interests shall have the same priority in relation to one another on the grant of the new lease as they had immediately before the surrender of the existing lease.

(2) Subsection (1) is subject to agreement to the contrary.

(3) Where a person who is entitled on the grant of a lease under section 56 to rights of occupation in relation to the flat comprised in that lease was entitled immediately before the surrender of the existing lease to rights of occupation in relation to the flat comprised in that lease, the rights to which he is entitled on the grant of the new lease shall be treated as a continuation of the rights to which he was entitled immediately before the surrender of the existing lease.

(4) In this section—

"the existing lease", in relation to a lease granted under section 56, means the lease surrendered on the grant of the new lease, and

"rights of occupation" has the same meaning as in the Matrimonial Homes Act 1983.".

GENERAL NOTE

Where a tenant is entitled to extend a lease under the Leasehold Reform, Housing and Urban Development Act 1993 (c. 28), the extension is effected under s.56, requiring the landlord to grant and the tenant to accept a new lease in substitution for the existing lease. Section 58(4) provides that where the lease of a flat is extended in this way, any mortgage will take effect against the new extended lease in the same way as it applied to the old lease. The position where there is more than one third party interest in the lease is less clear. The new s.58A added to the 1993 Act by this section, is intended to deal with the problem. Interests which applied to the old lease apply to the new lease in the same priority as they applied to the old lease: new s.58A(1) (but subject to agreement to the contrary—new s.58A(2)).

New subs. (3) provides for rights of occupation under the Matrimonial Homes Act 1983 (c. 19) to be treated as a continuation of the rights to which the spouse was entitled immediately before the surrender of the old lease.

Estate management schemes in connection with enfranchisement by virtue of s.106

118.—(1) Chapter IV of Part I of the 1993 Act, except section 75(1), (estate management schemes in connection with enfranchisement by virtue of that Act) shall also have effect subject to the modifications mentioned in subsections (2) to (4) below.

(2) In section 69(1) (definition of estate management schemes), for paragraphs (a) and (b) there shall be substituted—

"(a) acquiring the landlord's interest in their house and premises ("the house") under Part I of the Leasehold Reform Act 1967 by virtue of the provisions of section 1AA of that Act (as inserted by paragraph 1 of Schedule 9 to the Housing Act 1996), or

(b) acquiring the landlord's interest in any premises ("the premises") in accordance with Chapter I of this Part of this Act by virtue of the amendments of that Chapter made by paragraph 3 of Schedule 9 to the Housing Act 1996,".

(3) In section 70 (time limit for applications for approval), for "two years beginning with the date of the coming into force of this section" there shall be substituted "two years beginning with the coming into force of section 118 of the Housing Act 1996".

(4) In section 74 (effect of application for approval on claim to acquire freehold), in subsection (1)—

(a) in paragraph (b), in sub-paragraph (i), the words from "being" to the end shall be omitted, and

(b) after that paragraph there shall be inserted "and

(c) in the case of an application for the approval of a scheme as an estate management scheme, the scheme would extend to the house or premises if acquired in pursuance of the notice.".

(5) Section 94(6) to (8) of the 1993 Act (estate management schemes relating to Crown land) shall also have effect with the substitution for any reference to a provision of Chapter IV of Part I of that Act of a reference to that provision as it has effect by virtue of subsection (1) above.

(6) In section 33 of the National Heritage Act 1983 (general functions of the Historic Buildings and Monuments Commission for England), after subsection (2B) there shall be inserted—

"(2C) In subsection (2B), references to provisions of the Leasehold Reform, Housing and Urban Development Act 1993 include references to those provisions as they have effect by virtue of section 118(1) of the Housing Act 1996.".

(7) In section 72 of the Planning (Listed Buildings and Conservation Areas) Act 1990 (general duty as respects conservation area in exercise of planning functions), at the end there shall be inserted—

"(3) In subsection (2), references to provisions of the Leasehold Reform, Housing and Urban Development Act 1993 include references to those provisions as they have effect by virtue of section 118(1) of the Housing Act 1996.".

(8) In this section, "the 1993 Act" means the Leasehold Reform, Housing and Urban Development Act 1993.

Where a right to enfranchise has been granted, provision has also been made for the former landlord to apply to have some continuing degree of control over property in the area, see s.19 of the Leasehold Reform Act 1967 (c. 88). Under the Leasehold Reform, Housing and Urban Development Act 1993 (c. 28), in relation to properties which may be enfranchised collectively under that Act and to properties falling under an extension of the 1967 Act (added by the 1993 Act), this is achieved through an estate management scheme: see the 1993 Act, s.69. Leasehold valuation tribunals may approve a scheme on the application of a landlord, if satisfied that a scheme is necessary to maintain adequate standards of appearance and amenity or to regulate development: see s.70. In general, such applications had to be made within two years of the Act coming into force, *i.e.* by October 31, 1995. Because new properties have become enfranchiseable under s.105 above, landlords affected are given a further two-year period to apply for a scheme.

Leasehold valuation tribunals: pre-trial review

119.—(1) Procedure regulations may make provision in relation to proceedings before a leasehold valuation tribunal—
   (a) for the holding of a pre-trial review, on the application of a party to the proceedings or of the tribunal's own motion; and
   (b) for the exercise of the functions of the tribunal in relation to, or at, a pre-trial review by a single member who is qualified to exercise them.

(2) In subsection (1) "procedure regulations" means regulations under section 74(1)(b) of the Rent Act 1977, as that section applies in relation to leasehold valuation tribunals.

(3) For the purposes of subsection (1)(b)—
   (a) a "member" means a member of the panel provided for in Schedule 10 to that Act, and
   (b) a member is qualified to exercise the functions referred to if he was appointed to that panel by the Lord Chancellor.

Given the extended jurisdiction of the Leasehold valuation tribunal (LVT) (see in particular ss.83 and 86 above), provision is made by this section for a pre-trial review. It is suggested that this would be held by a single member of the LVT and would "allow the parties to indicate to each other, and to the tribunal, the points on which they are agreed and the points on which they disagree, and to indicate broadly the evidence which they will be bringing forward. This will allow each of the parties to be better prepared, and to concentrate on the issues which are in dispute. This should save time and effort both before the main hearing and at the hearing itself. A pre-trial review would provide a better opportunity to identify the length and complexity of a case and to negotiate on the spot a firm date for the hearing to begin" *per* Lord Lucas (Government Whip), *Hansard* (H.L.), July 10, 1996, Report (2nd day), Vol. 574, col. 399.

PART IV

HOUSING BENEFIT AND RELATED MATTERS

INTRODUCTION

This part makes a number of minor amendments to the administration of housing benefit and council tax benefit. The principal changes relate to central government subsidy and "pre-tenancy determinations" of housing benefit by rent officers.

Payment of housing benefit to third parties

120.—(1) In section 5 of the Social Security Administration Act 1992 (regulations about claims for and payments of benefit), after subsection (5) insert—

"(6) As it has effect in relation to housing benefit subsection (1)(p) above authorises provision requiring the making of payments of benefit to another person, on behalf of the beneficiary, in such circumstances as may be prescribed.".

(2) The above amendment shall be deemed always to have had effect; and provision corresponding to that made by the amendment shall be deemed to have had effect at all material times in relation to corresponding earlier enactments.

GENERAL NOTE

Section 5 of the Social Security Administration Act 1992 (c. 5) provides for the making of regulations about claims and payments of benefit, including housing benefit. By s.5(1)(p) regulations may provide:

"for the circumstances and manner in which payments of such a benefit *may* be made to another person on behalf of the beneficiary for any purpose, which may be to discharge, in whole or in part, an obligation of the beneficiary or any other person" (emphasis added).

The Housing Benefit (General) Regulations 1987 (S.I. 1987 No. 1971) make provision for circumstances where housing benefit *must* be paid to the landlord (see reg. 93). As currently worded, s.5(1)(p) could be thought only to authorise permissive payments of benefit to another person, as distinct from mandatory payment to another. Subsection (6), to be added to s.5 by this section, clarifies the legal position, authorising such mandatory payments. The effect of the amendment is retrospective: subs. (2).

Administration of housing benefit, &c

121. Part VIII of the Social Security Administration Act 1992 (arrangements for housing benefit and council tax benefit and related subsidies) is amended in accordance with Schedule 12.

GENERAL NOTE

Attention may be drawn to the following amendments made to the Social Security Administration Act 1992 (c. 5), by Sched. 12:

Para. 1.

Section 134 of the 1992 Act provides for the housing benefit scheme to be in the form of rebates and allowances. The section has not been amended to take into account the replacement of rent rebates by community charge benefit, and subsequently council tax benefit, and the amendments to it in para. 1 belatedly reflect this change. They also make provision in subparas. (7) and (8) for the use of subsidiary limits on the permitted total which an authority may spend on discretionary payments of housing benefit.

Para. 3.

Provision for a subsidiary limit on the permitted total is also made for council tax.

Para. 4.

Subsidy for housing benefit and council tax benefit is currently governed by separate sections of the 1992 Act (ss.135 to 137 (housing benefit) and s.140 (council tax benefit)). These sections are repealed and replaced by the new ss.140A to 140G, which bring the two classes of benefit together. The changes made to the subsidy regime include: provision for a fixed amount or nil subsidy (s.140B(3)); provision for the imposition of conditions on the payment of subsidy and to recover overpaid subsidy or subsidy paid where there has been a breach of conditions (s.140C(3)); an end to the requirement for an annual order (s.140F); and, provision for payments where there are joint arrangements between authorities for the discharge of housing benefit or council tax benefit functions (s.140E). Section 140C(3) is in similar terms to the recovery provisions for Housing Revenue Account subsidy in Local Government and Housing Act 1989 (c. 42), s.86. This power is independent of the right of the Secretary of State to recoup any overpayment of subsidy on other grounds, *e.g.* error of law or mistake of fact: see *R. v. Secretary of State for the Environment, ex p. L.B. Camden* (1995) 28 H.L.R. 321, Q.B.D. In such a case, which will be based on the principle of restitution (unjust enrichment), the Secretary of State may deduct the amount from a subsequent payment of subsidy (*Auckland Harbour Board v. R.* [1924] A.C. 318, P.C.), although the defence of "change of position" may be available: *Lipkin Gorman v. Karpnale* [1991] 2 A.C. 548, H.L. If it is raised as a defence to a recoupment by way of deduction, it is a matter for the Secretary of State whether or not he accepts it; *he* is not obliged to refer it to a court to be tested, although the authority could still do so (see *Camden*).

Functions of rent officers in connection with housing benefit and rent allowance subsidy

122.—(1) The Secretary of State may by order require rent officers to carry out such functions as may be specified in the order in connection with housing benefit and rent allowance subsidy.

(2) Without prejudice to the generality of subsection (1), an order under this section may contain provision—

(a) enabling a prospective landlord to apply for a determination for the purposes of any application for housing benefit which may be made by a tenant of a dwelling which he proposes to let;

(b) as to the payment of a fee by the landlord for that determination;

(c) requiring the landlord to give a copy of the determination to the appropriate local authority; and

(d) enabling the appropriate local authority to seek a redetermination when a claim for housing benefit or rent allowance subsidy is made.

(3) Regulations under section 130(4) of the Social Security Contributions and Benefits Act 1992 (housing benefit: manner of determining appropriate maximum benefit) may provide for benefit to be limited by reference to determinations made by rent officers in exercise of functions conferred under this section.

(4) In relation to rent allowance subsidy, the Secretary of State may by order under section 140B of the Social Security Administration Act 1992—

(a) provide for any calculation under subsection (2) of that section to be made,

(b) specify any additions and deductions as are referred to in that subsection, and

(c) exercise his discretion as to what is unreasonable for the purposes of subsection (4) of that section,

by reference to determinations made by rent officers in exercise of functions conferred on them under this section.

(5) The Secretary of State may by any such regulations or order as are mentioned in subsection (3) or (4) require a local authority in any prescribed case—

(a) to apply to a rent officer for a determination to be made in pursuance of the functions conferred on them under this section, and

(b) to do so within such time as may be specified in the order or regulations.

(6) An order under this section—

(a) shall be made by statutory instrument which shall be subject to annulment in pursuance of a resolution of either House of Parliament;

(b) may make different provision for different cases or classes of case and

for different areas; and
(c) may contain such transitional, incidental and supplementary provisions as appear to the Secretary of State to be desirable.
(7) In this section "housing benefit" and "rent allowance subsidy" have the
same meaning as in Part VIII of the Social Security Administration Act 1992.

GENERAL NOTE
    The powers of the Secretary of State to prescribe a role for rent officers in relation to housing
benefit are currently to be found in the Housing Act 1988, s.121 and the Social Security Administration Act 1992, s.136. This section replaces those sections, and continues the process of limiting
the housing benefit subsidy payable by the government to local authorities (directly, by regulations under the Social Security Contributions and Benefits Act 1992 (c. 4), s.130(4), or less
directly under the Social Security Administration Act 1992 (c. 5), s.140B—see Sched. 12 below),
by determining whether rents are unreasonably high.

Subs. (2)
    Provision is made for pre-tenancy determinations, which may be sought by landlords. Such
determinations "will allow people who need benefit and their landlords to find out before sign-
ing a tenancy agreement how much of the rent is likely to be supported by benefit": *Our Future
Homes*, (White Paper, 1995), p. 37. Landlords may, however, have to pay a fee for the service.

Consequential amendments: Part IV

123. The enactments mentioned in Schedule 13 have effect with the
amendments specified there which are consequential on the provisions of
this Part.

PART V

CONDUCT OF TENANTS

CHAPTER I

INTRODUCTORY TENANCIES

General provisions

INTRODUCTION
    When the Housing Act 1980 came into force, it conferred security of tenure on the tenants
(and licensees: see now, s.126, below) of, *inter alia*, local housing authorities and housing associations: a number of other public bodies were included; on the creation of a new public body,
Housing Action Trusts under Pt. III, Housing Act 1988 (see General Note to s.1 above), they
were likewise brought within this code of security. The security was a condition *sine qua non* to
the right to buy: without security of tenure, many public landlords (of that era) could have been
expected to react to applications to buy with notices to quit. These tenants were known as
"secure tenants".
    The code was, accordingly, and subject to its specified exceptions, comprehensive. (Most
notable of its departures from the long-standing, well-known code of security under the Rent
Acts, dating from 1915, was the absence of any ground for possession that was the provision of
suitable alternative accommodation *simpliciter, i.e.* a pure management removal *per se*. While
there were grounds in relation to which such accommodation had and has still to be provided to a
secure tenant as an element in the claim for possession, it is only relevant when attached to
certain other grounds.)
    Meanwhile, as it were back on the private front, the traditional code of security under the
Rent Acts—known since 1965 as protected tenancy (formerly, controlled tenancy), and in each
case coupled to statutory tenancy (being the designation for security of tenure once the contract
of tenancy had ended)—was subject by Housing Act 1980 to an exception, the shorthold tenancy, designed to revive private renting by allowing landlords to recover possession without any of
the usual grounds—and without the provision of alternative accommodation—by (a) service of
a notice preceding the tenancy, and (b) compliance with notice procedures on termination.
    When Rent Act protection was replaced by Housing Act assured security of tenure by Hous-
ing Act 1988—assured tenancy—it likewise carried with it as an exception, a category of assured
shorthold tenancy modelled on the protected shorthold. At the same time, housing association

security was transferred from the 1980 Act code (by now, consolidated into Housing Act 1985) to the new private sector code, including the assured shorthold exception to full security.

This Act now introduces an optional exception to secure tenancy (and licence: see s.126, below), the "introductory tenancy" (and licence: *ibid.*). In some ways, it operates like the short-hold in the private sector, insofar as it provides (see below, s.128) for repossession by following a specified procedure, without more. The principal difference, however, is that—while shortholds enjoy a *minimum* period of contractual security before possession can be sought against them (see now, Pt. III, Chap. I, above)—the introductory tenancy enjoys a *maximum* life and if not brought to an end within it, will become secure: see s.125, below.

Introductory tenancies

124.—(1) A local housing authority or a housing action trust may elect to operate an introductory tenancy regime.

(2) When such an election is in force, every periodic tenancy of a dwelling-house entered into or adopted by the authority or trust shall, if it would otherwise be a secure tenancy, be an introductory tenancy, unless immediately before the tenancy was entered into or adopted the tenant or, in the case of joint tenants, one or more of them was—

(a) a secure tenant of the same or another dwelling-house, or

(b) an assured tenant of a registered social landlord (otherwise than under an assured shorthold tenancy) in respect of the same or another dwelling-house.

(3) Subsection (2) does not apply to a tenancy entered into or adopted in pursuance of a contract made before the election was made.

(4) For the purposes of this Chapter a periodic tenancy is adopted by a person if that person becomes the landlord under the tenancy, whether on a disposal or surrender of the interest of the former landlord.

(5) An election under this section may be revoked at any time, without prejudice to the making of a further election.

DEFINITIONS
"adopted": subs. (4).
"assured shorthold tenancy": s.230.
"assured tenancy": s.230.
"housing action trust": s.230.
"local housing authority": s.230.
"registered social landlord": s.1.
"secure tenancy": s.230.
"tenancy": s.229.

GENERAL NOTE
The purpose of this innovatory class of tenancy is not expressed: while the landlord has to give reasons for its decisions (see s.128, below), and those decisions may be subject to internal review (see s.129, below), for which again (if adverse) the landlord also has to give reasons, there is no limitation on what they may be; the only sense of intention is that which can be derived from the title of this Part (Conduct of Tenants) and the contents of its remaining Chapters (domestic violence, nuisance and annoyance, etc.—see generally below). The White Paper, *Our Future Homes*, described the scheme as one for "tenancies on a probationary basis", to allow landlords at any time during the probationary period to be able to terminate the tenancies of "the minority of tenants who do not behave responsibly" (Chap. 7).

What this Chapter does not make clear, then, is whether an introductory tenancy (or licence) can be terminated for reasons *other than* what may for brevity and convenience be categorised as "anti-social behaviour", *e.g.* changed allocation policies (see further Pt. VI, below) or demands, management removal, under-occupation. It is beyond question that termination that is *mala fide, e.g.* for racial or political reasons, would be unlawful (see the general discussion of principles of administrative law in the notes to s.1, above, and s.204, below), and equally clear that a decision to terminate is reviewable: see *Bristol D.C. v. Clark* [1975] 1 W.L.R. 1443, C.A., *Cannock Chase D.C. v. Kelly* [1978] 1 W.L.R. 1, C.A., *Sevenoaks D.C. v. Emmott* (1980) 130 New L.J. 139, C.A.

Although the burden will lie on the tenant or licensee to show that there has been a public law failure in this respect, and although it would not normally be sufficient to challenge an eviction merely to prove that the tenant has been what one might call "a good tenant" (*ibid.*), in the case of an introductory tenancy which it has been decided to terminate, there is an obligation to state reasons for the decision, and on the review: see ss.128, 129, below. Accordingly case law on the entitlement of a tenant or licensee to be treated fairly in terms of a decision to evict him, even where there is no statutory security (see, *e.g.*, *Sevenoaks v. Emmott*, above; see also *Hammersmith & Fulham L.B.C. v. Ruddock* [1980] C.L.Y. 134, C.A., *Hammersmith & Fulham L.B.C. v. Jimenez* (1980) 130 New L.J. 1011, C.A.) will not need to be relied on—the statutory procedure will, it is submitted, be sufficient.

What this does not answer, however, is the procedural issue, *i.e.* where or how to challenge the decision to evict. *In the first instance*, doubtless that will normally mean by utilising the "internal review" provisions of s.129, below. Internal review need not be resorted to, it would seem, where the defence is that the tenancy or licence is not (or is no longer) introductory: that could be challenged *either* by way of judicial review, *or* indeed—and a lot more easily—by resisting the proceedings in the county court.

The latter would seem the natural course, to the extent that it might be anticipated that the High Court would be disinclined to grant leave to pursue such a claim, although one answer to this may be that unless the issue is resolved before matters are taken further, the *benefits* of the internal review will have been lost. (This, however, is not a strong argument: the tenant or licensee can have recourse to internal review "without prejudice" to his contention that the tenancy or licence is not introductory.)

By and large, and without seeking to lay down an absolute proposition, the High Court on judicial review is not the most suitable forum for determining the statutory construction of security legislation: this is a task conferred by Parliament on county courts in the first instance, subject to appeal, see s.138, below giving jurisdiction to the county court "to determine questions arising under this Chapter". The county court itself has ample jurisdiction to entertain applications for a declaration relating to the use and occupation of land (see s.138, below, and C.C.R. Ord. 6), and could as easily as the High Court prevent the landlord from proceeding until the issue is resolved. If, therefore, the only basis for resisting the claim is that the tenancy or licence is not introductory, the preferable course—and perhaps the only course that will be permitted—will be in the county court, whether by awaiting and resisting the claim for possession, or pre-emptive declaratory proceedings, as advised.

This, however, deals only with a defence based on statutory construction. Where the defence is based on vitiation of the decision to evict on grounds such as reasonableness or rationality, the "normal" forum for the resolution of such issues *is* the High Court (Crown Office) by way of judicial review. There is little doubt but that the tenant or licensee seeking to challenge a decision to evict on such grounds *could* proceed by way of judicial review, but see s.138(3) below. Indeed, it would seem that he will be able to do so, without utilising the internal review machinery, if the basis of the challenge is that it is outwith the powers of the landlord to proceed because of improper purpose or an analogous deficiency, as this is in substance a challenge to the very jurisdiction of the internal review: see, *e.g. Roy v. Kensington & Chelsea & Westminster Family Practitioner Committee* [1992] 1 A.C. 624, H.L.

"An administrative appeal on the merits of a case is something quite different from judicial determination of the legality of the whole matter" (Wade & Forsyth, *Administrative Law*, 7th ed., p. 721). However, "Recently... It had been said that, where there is some right of appeal, judicial review will not be granted 'save in the most exceptional circumstances'; and that the normal rule is that the applicant 'should first exhaust whatever other rights he has by way of appeal'. This novel attitude, which does not appear to be based on authority, may be due to the increasing pressure of applications for judicial review..." (*ibid.*, p. 723. See, *e.g. R. v. Inland Revenue Commissioners, ex p. Preston* [1985] A.C. 835, H.L., although it still seems to have been accepted that judicial review—without prior appeal—would be available where what was in issue was abuse of power or unlawfulness). How these conflicting principles will work in the less rarefied atmosphere of introductory tenancies in the social housing sector remains to be seen.

More relevant is the question whether a challenge on public law grounds such as these will be open in the county court. In principle, it would seem to be open to an occupier to do so, by application of the reasoning in *Wandsworth L.B.C. v. Winder* [1985] A.C. 461, 17 H.L.R. 196, H.L., in which a tenant was held entitled to resist a claim for possession based on arrears of rent, where the challenge was to rent increases which he averred were unreasonable to the extent of being unlawful. Because he was defending the proceedings, and because he was defending a vested contractual right, his defence could be raised without a prior decision on judicial review quashing the rent increase.

In other cases, however, it has been held that there was no analogous (or perhaps any) vested right within *Winder*, and that proceedings for possession would have to be adjourned pending application for judicial review: see, *e.g.*, *West Glamorgan C.C. v. Rafferty* [1987] 1 W.L.R. 457, 18 H.L.R. 375, C.A., *Avon C.C. v. Buscott* [1988] Q.B. 656, 20 H.L.R. 395, C.A.; see also *L.B. Tower*

Hamlets v. Abdi (1992) 25 H.L.R. 90, C.A., *L.B. Hackney v. Lambourne* (1992) 26 H.L.R. 172, C.A.

It is submitted that *Winder* is wide enough to permit a public law challenge to be raised in the county court, especially if it is by way of defending proceedings (rather than initiating them, *cf.* above, on declaration in the county court), although the safest course is invariably the "belt-and-braces" approach of entering an internal appeal "without prejudice", entering a defence if matters proceed that far, *and* seeking leave.

Subs. (1)

Local housing authorities are district councils and London borough councils, the Common Council of the City of London and the Council of the Isles of Scilly, county or county borough councils in Wales: see s.1, Housing Act 1985.

Housing Action Trusts ("H.A.T.") are bodies established by order of the Secretary of State under Pt. III, Housing Act 1988, which take over some of an authority's stock—in order to secure its repair or improvement, its proper and effective management and use, to encourage diversity of landlords, or generally to secure or facilitate the improvement of living conditions, the social conditions and the general environment of an area (*ibid.*, s.63)—and in due course pass it on to other, "approved" landlords (see also Introduction to Pt. I, above).

These provisions are optional, in the sense that they do not automatically apply and the authority or H.A.T. must make a decision whether or not to operate the scheme ("introductory tenancy regime"): there is no reservation of the decision to a full Council or Trust, so that the decision could—if properly delegated—be taken by a committee or sub-committee or even by an officer (see Local Government Act 1972, s.101). The decision can be revoked: see subs. (5). For the effect of revocation on existing introductory tenancies, see s.125(5), below.

Subss. (2), (3)

Once the regime is in force, however, it automatically applies to every periodic tenancy (or licence: see s.126, below) granted by the authority or H.A.T. which would otherwise have been a secure tenancy, save as excepted. It follows that tenancies excluded from security by Housing Act 1985, s.79 and Sched. 1, are *not* introductory tenancies but, as now, mere contractual tenancies. The exclusions, in brief, are:

    1. Long leases (see notes to s.16(1));
    2. Categories of tied accommodation;
    3. Land acquired for development;
    4. Accommodation for homeless persons (see now Pt. VII, below);
    5. Job mobility schemes;
    6. Sub-leasing schemes;
    7. Temporary relocation of tenants during major works;
    8. Agricultural holdings;
    9. Licensed premises;
    10. Student lettings;
    11. Business lettings;
    12. Almshouses.

Periodic Tenancy. Although not defined, a periodic tenancy is one which is not for a fixed-term, *i.e.* one which requires (at common law) determination by the landlord by notice to quit, as distinct from a tenancy which will expire by effluxion of time (leaving aside issues of forfeiture, break clauses, etc.).

Exception. The introductory regime does not, however, apply if the grant is to someone who was, immediately before the grant, a secure tenant (in the same or another property), or the assured tenant of a registered social landlord (which will normally necessarily mean another property, save in the politically unlikely but legally not impossible event of the property of a registered social landlord passing into public ownership); if the tenancy is a joint tenancy, then if any one of the joint tenants so qualified, the exception will apply. It is less clear whether if the tenant was one of joint secure or assured tenants, the exception will likewise apply (*cf.* the wording of Housing Act 1988, s.20(3)(a), s.34(1)(b), (4)(b), s.35(1)(b)—"a" tenant under, etc.).

In *Dibbs v. Campbell* (1988) 20 H.L.R. 374, C.A., a failure to give up physical possession pursuant to a formal deed of surrender, which had been entered into specifically to create a gap between the two tenancies (so that the second could qualify as a shorthold protected tenancy under the Housing Act 1980, s.52), was not fatal to the arrangement, and the later tenancy was held not to follow immediately on the earlier. In this case, however, the earlier tenancy was one which it had been intended would be shorthold, but which had failed so to qualify because of the landlord's omission to register a rent within 28 days of the grant, *i.e.* the "merits" were in favour of upholding the arrangement.

The earlier tenancy does not qualify as an assured tenancy for the purposes of this exception if it was an assured shorthold tenancy (see notes to s.16(1), above), although such a tenancy may count towards the maximum period of introductory tenancy (see s.125(4), below). Shorthold tenants do not have anything that may be called "full security" to lose; see also the White Paper, *Our Future Homes*, at p. 44, referring to Corporation review of the use of assured shortholds "as an element in dealing with anti-social behaviour" (see also s.125(4), below).

Prior Contract. This means a legally enforceable contract. All contracts entered into since September 27, 1989, for the sale or other disposition of land—therefore, including grant of lease— must have been made in writing, and by including all of the terms in one document (or, where contracts are exchanged, in each of them): Law of Property (Miscellaneous Provisions) Act 1989, s.2. The terms need not be set out in the document, however: they can be incorporated by cross-reference to another document. The document must be signed by or on behalf of each of the parties, save in the case of exchange, where each document must be signed by at least one: *ibid.*, s.2(3).

These requirements do not apply to leases within s.54(2), Law of Property Act 1925 (*ibid.*, s.2(5)(a)), which means "the creation by parol of leases taking effect in possession for a term not exceeding three years ... at the best rent which can be reasonably obtained without taking a fine", which includes a periodic tenancy). It was *formerly* the case that a contract for a tenancy had to be in writing, even if the grant itself would not require to be in writing: Law of Property Act 1925, s.40 (and see *Botting v. Martin* (1808) Camp. 317, *Crago v. Julian* [1992] 1 W.L.R. 372, C.A.). Section 40 was, however, replaced by s.2, 1989 Act (*ibid.*, s.2(8)).

Subs. (4)

This subsection defines "adoption" (of tenancy—or licence, see s.126, below) for the purposes of this Chapter. It covers not only transfer of a landlord's interest to another (disposal), but also the surrender of a landlord's lease to a superior landlord or the freeholder: this preserves the common law position and applies whether the sub-tenancy is a lawful or an unlawful sub-tenancy—see *Parker v. Jones* [1910] 2 K.B. 32, see also *Pennell v. Payne* [1994] E.G.C.S. 196, C.A. overruling the proposition formerly understood to be correct (*Mellor v. Watkins* (1874) L.R. 9 Q.B. 400) that the same was true of a tenant's notice to quit. By inference, therefore, it does *not* include the expiry of a landlord's lease by effluxion of time, or the forfeiture of a landlord's lease, in neither of which eventualities would a sub-tenancy at common law come to be the (direct) tenancy of the holder of the superior interest (*cf.* Rent Act 1977, s.137, which—for the purposes of that Act alone—had that effect).

Subs. (5)

If the landlord revokes the election, the introductory tenancy will become secure: see below, s.125(5)(c).

Duration of introductory tenancy

125.—(1) A tenancy remains an introductory tenancy until the end of the trial period, unless one of the events mentioned in subsection (5) occurs before the end of that period.

(2) The "trial period" is the period of one year beginning with—

(a) in the case of a tenancy which was entered into by a local housing authority or housing action trust—

　(i) the date on which the tenancy was entered into, or

　(ii) if later, the date on which a tenant was first entitled to possession under the tenancy; or

(b) in the case of a tenancy which was adopted by a local housing authority or housing action trust, the date of adoption;

subject as follows.

(3) Where the tenant under an introductory tenancy was formerly a tenant under another introductory tenancy, or held an assured shorthold tenancy from a registered social landlord, any period or periods during which he was such a tenant shall count towards the trial period, provided—

(a) if there was one such period, it ended immediately before the date specified in subsection (2), and

(b) if there was more than one such period, the most recent period ended immediately before that date and each period succeeded the other without interruption.

(4) Where there are joint tenants under an introductory tenancy, the reference in subsection (3) to the tenant shall be construed as referring to the joint tenant in whose case the application of that subsection produces the earliest starting date for the trial period.

(5) A tenancy ceases to be an introductory tenancy if, before the end of the trial period—

    (a) the circumstances are such that the tenancy would not otherwise be a secure tenancy,

    (b) a person or body other than a local housing authority or housing action trust becomes the landlord under the tenancy,

    (c) the election in force when the tenancy was entered into or adopted is revoked, or

    (d) the tenancy ceases to be an introductory tenancy by virtue of section 133(3) (succession).

(6) A tenancy does not come to an end merely because it ceases to be an introductory tenancy, but a tenancy which has once ceased to be an introductory tenancy cannot subsequently become an introductory tenancy.

(7) This section has effect subject to section 130 (effect of beginning proceedings for possession).

DEFINITIONS
    "adopted": subs. (4).
    "assured shorthold tenancy": s.230.
    "assured tenancy": s.230.
    "housing action trust": s.230.
    "introductory tenancy": s.124.
    "local housing authority": s.230.
    "registered social landlord": s.1.
    "secure tenancy": s.230.
    "tenancy": s.229.
    "trial period": subs. (2).

GENERAL NOTE
This section defines the life of the introductory tenancy (or licence—see s.126, below), by reference both to its commencement and its conclusion. When an introductory tenancy comes to an end (see subs. (5)), the tenancy does not come to an end, but will become either secure (a tenancy being secure "at any time when" the landlord and tenant conditions are satisfied, and none of the exceptions applies—see Housing Act 1985, s.79(1)) or an ordinary contractual tenancy (subs. (6)). (But *cf.* below, s.130, where proceedings for possession have been commenced and are not finally determined before the time when the trial period would otherwise come to an end).

Subss. (2)–(4)
The life of the introductory tenancy is the "trial period". Its "basic" quality is a period of one year (subs. (2)), which runs from:

    (a) If a new introductory tenancy, the date when the tenancy was entered into by the local housing authority or H.A.T., or when the tenant was first entitled to take up possession under it; or,

    (b) If the introductory tenancy was adopted by the authority or Trust (see notes to s.124(4), above, *i.e.* the landlord became so during the period of an existing introductory tenancy by taking over the previous landlord's interest, or by the surrender of the previous landlord's interest), one year from the date of adoption.

    (c) In each case, however, the period may be shorter if there has been a prior introductory tenancy or more than one prior introductory tenancy, *i.e.* in another property from the same landlord, or from another landlord, which (by definition) excludes an introductory tenancy which has run its full course (see s.124(2), above), *or* if there has been an assured shorthold tenancy from a registered social landlord, *i.e.* a registered assured landlord using assured shorthold as its method of granting what is in spirit an introductory tenancy (see notes to s.124(2), above), *and* (in each case) the introductory tenancy or assured shorthold (or if more than one, the most recent of them) ended immediately before the date specified in subs. (2) (see notes (a) and (b), above): subs. (3).

The period by which the introductory tenancy is shortened is the period of the previous tenancy (subs. (2)). If there was more than one such previous introductory tenancy or assured shorthold, then they will all be taken into account if each succeeded the other without interruption: subs. (3). If the introductory tenancy is held by joint tenants, then it lasts for the *minimum* time that any one of the joint tenants would be subject to it, *i.e.* the maximum previous time is deducted: subs. (4).

Subs. (5)

A tenancy will not be introductory unless it would otherwise have been a secure tenancy: see s.124(2), above. The circumstances may change during the life of the introductory tenancy, so that it would not (if secure) have continued to be secure (*e.g.* change of landlord, cessation of occupation of the premises "as an only or principal home" by the tenant or at least one of joint tenants—Housing Act 1985, s.81, impermissible assignment—*ibid.*, ss.105–106, but *cf.* below, s.134, piecemeal subletting in parts until the whole has been sublet—see Housing Act 1985, s.93): in such circumstances the introductory tenancy ceases to so qualify, although the tenancy itself will not come to an end (see subs. (6)).

This will be the position even if the change of landlord would not necessarily cause the loss of security, *i.e.* where a new town corporation, urban development corporation, the Development Board for Rural Wales, or a housing co-operative within Housing Act 1985, s.27B (as to which, see notes to s.2(1), above) becomes the landlord. It will also be the case if the provisions of s.133(3), below, cause the introductory tenancy to cease to so qualify.

Subject thereto, if the decision to maintain an introductory tenancy regime is revoked, the tenant will become secure.

Only or Principal Home. In *Crawley B.C. v. Sawyer* (1987) 20 H.L.R. 98, C.A., it was held that there was no material difference between this phrase and occupation as a residence under the Rent Acts, as that phrase had been interpreted, although this must be treated with some caution as many of the cases under the Rent Acts were concerned with people who had two homes, and the substantive issue was whether—in the light of the second home—the first was still in use as "a" home: see *Bevington v. Crawford* (1974) 232 E.G. 191, C.A., *Gofor Investment v. Roberts* (1975) 119 Sol. Jo. 320, C.A.; see also *Langford Property Co. Ltd. v. Tureman* [1949] 1 K.B. 29, C.A., and *Beck v. Scholtz* [1953] 1 Q.B. 570, C.A., for two cases usefully illustrating where the line is drawn.

Under the Housing Act 1985, it is clear that occupation must be as an "only or principal home", but subject to this *caveat* occupation—as a home or as a residence—under the two codes of security has the same general meaning ("a substantial degree of regular personal occupation … of an essentially residential nature": *Herbert v. Byrne* [1964] 1 W.L.R. 519, C.A.).

Accordingly, it is not necessary to show actual or continuous physical occupation of the home, so long as the property is still in use as a home, to demonstrate which it will usually be necessary to show some physical or tangible signs of continued such use, coupled with an intention to resume physical occupation (see *Brown v. Brash* [1948] 2 K.B. 247, C.A.): see, *e.g.*, *Roland House Gardens v. Cravitz* (1974) 29 P. & C.R. 432, C.A., *Hampstead Way Investments v. Lewis-Weare* [1985] 1 W.L.R. 164, 17 H.L.R. 152, H.L., *Brickfield Properties v. Hughes* (1987) 20 H.L.R. 108, C.A. Absence in hospital will not affect residence: *Tompkins v. Rowley* [1949] E.G.D. 314, C.A.

In *Sawyer* (above), the tenant left his secure tenancy to live with his girlfriend. The gas and electricity to the premises the subject of the secure tenancy were subsequently cut off and the following year he informed the local authority that he was living with his girlfriend and that they intended to purchase her home. The authority instituted possession proceedings but by the time of the hearing, the tenant and his girlfriend had separated and he was again living at the premises. He gave evidence that he had not abandoned the premises and had every intention of returning to them and the judge found that they were at all times his principal home, a decision upheld by the Court of Appeal.

See also *Regalian Securities Ltd. v. Scheuer* (1982) 5 H.L.R. 48, C.A., and *Richards v. Green* (1984) 11 H.L.R. 1, C.A. A tenancy may go in and out of security, depending on whether the occupation requirement is fulfilled (see, *e.g. Hussey v. L.B. Camden* (1994) 27 H.L.R. 5, C.A.). If the reason for the finding of non-occupation is subletting or parting with possession of the whole of the premises, however, then under Housing Act 1985, s.93 security will be lost and cannot be recovered. A distinction must be drawn, however, between subletting and a mere sharing arrangement where one of the occupiers alone holds the tenancy, and another lives or shares the property with him, from which the normal or natural inference will be that the sharer is no more than a lodger or licensee of the tenant: see *Monmouth B.C. v. Marlog* (1995) 27 H.L.R. 30, C.A.

Under the Leasehold Reform Act 1967, s.1(2) ("only or main residence"), it has been held that a tenant who occupies part but sublets the remainder of his home qualifies: *Harris v. Swick Securities* [1969] 1 W.L.R. 1604, C.A. In *Poland v. Cadogan* [1980] 3 All E.R. 544, C.A. it was held that while long absence may not prevent residential occupation, a long absence abroad with the premises sublet may indicate a lack of intention to occupy, sufficient to defeat the meaning in that Act. In *Powell v. Radford* (1970) 21 P. & C.R. 99, C.A., a claim under the 1967 Act by a husband and wife each to be occupying a different house as the main home was upheld, although considered unusual. Because of the different nature of the rights, these decisions, too, must be treated with caution, and can be distinguished by the statutory context.

Subs. (7)

If a tenancy ceases to be an introductory tenancy, it does not cease in itself, and will therefore have to be determined in the usual way, *i.e.* by notice to quit. If it ceases to be introductory, it cannot resume being an introductory tenancy. Determination need not be by the landlord alone; it could be by a tenant's notice to quit, even a notice to quit by one of a number of joint tenants (even without the assent of the other or others): see General Note to s.127 below.

Licences

126.—(1) The provisions of this Chapter apply in relation to a licence to occupy a dwelling-house (whether or not granted for a consideration) as they apply in relation to a tenancy.

(2) Subsection (1) does not apply to a licence granted as a temporary expedient to a person who entered the dwelling-house or any other land as a trespasser (whether or not, before the grant of that licence, another licence to occupy that or another dwelling-house had been granted to him).

DEFINITIONS

"dwelling house": s.139.
"tenancy": s.29.

GENERAL NOTE

The Housing Act 1980 brought to housing law two conceptual innovations: first, it applied its security code not merely to tenants but also to licensees; secondly, it replaced the former distinction between contractual and statutory periods of security with a single tenancy, not determinable other than by order of the court. The latter is represented in this Act in s.127, below. The former is represented in this section.

Subs. (1)

As to the distinction between tenancy and licence, see generally *Street v. Mountford* [1985] A.C. 809, 17 H.L.R. 402, H.L., *Eastleigh B.C. v. Walsh* [1985] 1 W.L.R. 525, 17 H.L.R. 392, H.L., *A.G. Securities v. Vaughan* [1990] 1 A.C. 417, (1989) 21 H.L.R. 79, H.L. In short, where residential accommodation is granted for a term at a rent with exclusive possession, the grantor providing neither attendance nor services, the legal consequence will normally be the creation of a tenancy.

For a licence to qualify as an introductory tenancy, however, it would have to be such a licence as would (otherwise) qualify as a secure tenancy under Housing Act 1985, Pt. IV, which means that it has to be a licence which confers exclusive possession, which in turns means that the *genuine* reservation of rights inconsistent with tenancy, such as sharing rights, by, *e.g.* a special purposes hostel, will not qualify: *City of Westminster v. Clarke* [1992] A.C. 288, 24 H.L.R. 360, H.L. See also *L.B. Camden v. Shortlife Community House* (1992) 25 H.L.R. 330, C.A., where exclusive possession was held not to have been granted to occupiers of short-life accommodation, having regard to the purpose of the arrangements and to the plaintiffs' need to retain rights of access to in view of the imminence of demolition or redevelopment.

Camden also concerned the want of interest on the part of the landlord out of which to grant a tenancy: see further *Redbank Schools v. Abdullahzadeh* (1995) 28 H.L.R. 431, C.A.

Even if there is exclusive possession, the test of "letting as a separate dwelling" has to be fulfilled (see above, notes to s.16, above): see also *Central Y.M.C.A. v. Saunders* (1990) 23 H.L.R. 212, C.A., *Central Y.M.C.A. v. Goodman* (1991) 24 H.L.R. 109, C.A., in each of which there were lettings of rooms without cooking facilities. In *Tyler v. R.B. Kensington & Chelsea* (1990) 23 H.L.R. 380, C.A., a right to occupy a first floor flat while works were carried out to a ground floor flat, which was let to the occupier on a secure tenancy, was held to be a licence to occupy, *in conjunction with* the ground floor flat and, as such, not let as a separate dwelling.

In *Burrows v. L.B. Brent* (1995) 27 H.L.R. 748, C.A., a *post*-possession order agreement for the tenant to remain on terms (including payment off the arrears) was held to have created a new agreement, which was either tenancy or licence. However, in *Greenwich L.B.C. v. Regan* (1996) 28 H.L.R. 469, C.A., the court, distinguishing *Burrows*, held that it was a question of fact in every case whether what had taken place was the variation of an existing relationship, or the creation of a new tenancy or licence; where a change in payments of arrears had been agreed, this was likely to refer to the court's power to modify a possession order (and, as such, to constitute a variation in the existing arrangement rather than the creation of one that was new).

The mere acceptance of use and occupation charges does not create a licence (nor even if a rent rebate is awarded): *Westminster C.C. v. Basson* (1990) 23 H.L.R. 225, C.A. However, a distinction must be drawn between a case where an occupier seeks to take advantage of bureaucratic incompetence in order to build up an argument in favour of authorised occupation amounting to a licence, and a case such as *L.B. Tower Hamlets v. Ayinde* (1994) 26 H.L.R. 631, C.A., where the occupation was wholly above board, numerous requests were made for the transfer of a tenancy into the occupier's name, and payment was being made, which could only lead to one conclusion, that a tenancy had been created. See also *Vaughan-Armatrading v. Sarsah* (1995) 27 H.L.R. 631, C.A.

Subs. (2)

Excluded from the general extension to licensees are cases where a person entered the land in question, or some other land, as a trespasser, *i.e.* squatter, and has been granted a licence as a temporary expedient, whether the licence was of the land entered as a trespasser or some other land instead. (It is doubtful that it was necessary expressly to include this subsection here. If only those arrangements which could otherwise have been secure can be introductory, such temporary licences already prevented a licence from achieving security under Housing Act 1985, s.79(4), or, thus, introductory status.)

Proceedings for possession

Proceedings for possession

127.—(1) The landlord may only bring an introductory tenancy to an end by obtaining an order of the court for the possession of the dwelling-house.

(2) The court shall make such an order unless the provisions of section 128 apply.

(3) Where the court makes such an order, the tenancy comes to an end on the date on which the tenant is to give up possession in pursuance of the order.

DEFINITIONS

"dwelling-house": s.139.

"tenancy": s.230.

GENERAL NOTE

The second of the new approaches to housing law brought in with the Housing Act 1980 (see Introduction to Pt. V, above) was the abolition of the distinction between a tenant whose tenancy had not yet been determined contractually, and one whose tenancy had been determined contractually but who could still remain in occupation pursuant to a statutory code of security, *i.e.* the statutory tenant. Instead, landlords could not bring tenancies (within security) to an end other than by obtaining an order for possession, which order would only be obtainable on specified grounds, and the tenancy itself would continue until a date was set for possession to be given up (so that a tenant under a suspended order would remain a tenant, instead of entering the conceptual netherland which gave rise to doubts and to litigation under the Rent Acts).

The same approach was taken to assured tenancies under Housing Act 1988 and is, now, taken to introductory tenancies under this Act.

There are, however, two qualifications which have to be entered to this attractive simplicity. First, in *City of London Corporation v. Bown* (1989) 22 H.L.R. 32, C.A., it was held—for the purposes of (then) insolvency law—that a secure periodic tenancy was a mere personal right of occupation rather than a property asset, which seems to run counter to the general thrust of the new approach. (The particular problem in issue was in any event overtaken by Housing Act 1988, s.117, amending the Insolvency Act 1986, so far as it concerned specified residential lettings including secure tenancies.)

Secondly, where a court makes an order for possession which is suspended on terms, and those terms are broken by the tenant, the tenancy—as thus continued—is considered automatically to have terminated, so that, *e.g.*, the landlord can seek a warrant for possession: see *Thompson v. Elmbridge B.C.* (1987) 19 H.L.R. 526, C.A.; see also *Burrows v. L.B. Brent* (1995) 27 H.L.R. 748, C.A., and *Hackney L.B.C. v. Porter* (1996) 28 H.L.R. forthcoming, C.A. This means that a degree of uncertainty as to status can creep into the picture, unless and until it is determined whether or not, and if so when, there has been such a breach. If there is a breach, and yet no (eviction) action is taken, the question will remain whether the arrangements fall on the *Burrows'* side of the line—wholly new tenancy or licence—or whether, as in *Greenwich L.B.C. v. Regan* (1996) 28 H.L.R. 469, C.A., it is a mere modification of the existing tenancy.

The prohibition serves only to restrict the landlord's right to terminate, and does not interfere with that of the tenant. Accordingly, abandonment was in one case held sufficient to amount to termination by the tenant (*R. v. L.B. Croydon, ex p. Toth* (1986) 18 H.L.R. 493, C.A.), although abandonment is not in itself an act of termination but possible evidence of surrender (*City of Westminster v. Peart* (1991) 24 H.L.R. 389, C.A.): see *L.B. Brent v. Sharma & Vyas* (1992) 25 H.L.R. 257, C.A. The termination must, therefore, be a valid termination at law, *e.g.* good notice to quit: *L.B. Hounslow v. Pilling* (1993) 25 H.L.R. 305, C.A. Delivery up of keys or their acceptance by a landlord does not necessarily amount to a surrender, especially if explicable on other grounds, although coupled with other acts it could evidence an intention to yield up and to an intention to take possession: *Proudreed Ltd. v. Microgen Holdings Ltd., The Times,* July 17, 1995, C.A.

Of particular relevance here is the proposition that one of two or more joint tenants may give notice to quit, without the assent of the other (or others): *Hammersmith & Fulham L.B.C. v. Monk* [1992] 1 A.C. 478, 24 H.L.R. 206, H.L., *Crawley B.C. v. Ure* (1995) 27 H.L.R. 524, C.A., *cf. Harrow L.B.C. v. Johnstone* (1995) 28 H.L.R. 83, C.A.

Shall make an order. The court has no discretion: subject to compliance with the requirements of the next two sections, the court must make the order sought, *i.e.* without proof of reasonableness, nor of provision of alternative accommodation.

Notice of proceedings for possession

128.—(1) The court shall not entertain proceedings for the possession of a dwelling-house let under an introductory tenancy unless the landlord has served on the tenant a notice of proceedings complying with this section.

(2) The notice shall state that the court will be asked to make an order for the possession of the dwelling-house.

(3) The notice shall set out the reasons for the landlord's decision to apply for such an order.

(4) The notice shall specify a date after which proceedings for the possession of the dwelling-house may be begun.

The date so specified must not be earlier than the date on which the tenancy could, apart from this Chapter, be brought to an end by notice to quit given by the landlord on the same date as the notice of proceedings.

(5) The court shall not entertain any proceedings for possession of the dwelling-house unless they are begun after the date specified in the notice of proceedings.

(6) The notice shall inform the tenant of his right to request a review of the landlord's decision to seek an order for possession and of the time within which such a request must be made.

(7) The notice shall also inform the tenant that if he needs help or advice about the notice, and what to do about it, he should take it immediately to a Citizens' Advice Bureau, a housing aid centre, a law centre or a solicitor.

DEFINITIONS
"dwelling-house": s.139.
"tenancy": s.230.

GENERAL NOTE
This section is modelled on Housing Act 1985, s.83 (see now, below, s.147). It is a precondition to proceedings for possession of a property subject to an introductory tenancy that notice has been served which complies with the requirements of the section. Subject thereto, the order is mandatory, *i.e.* "the court shall make an order" (see s.127(1), above).

As proceedings have to be begun while a tenancy is still introductory for the provisions of s.130, below, to come into play (tenancies ceasing to be introductory after issue of proceedings), there are no difficulties arising from the shift into a tenancy that is secure, at the least *pro tem* under s.130(4).

Unlike under 1985 Act, s.83, either as was or as is, the form of notice is not prescribed. It merely has to comply with the requirements of the section:

(a) It must state that the court will be asked to make an order for possession;

(b) It must state the reasons for the decision to apply for the order;

(c) It must identify a date after which proceedings may be begun, which must not be earlier than the date on which the tenancy could—but for these provisions—have been brought to an end by notice to quit;

(d) It must inform the tenant of the right to request a review of the decision by serving notice on the landlord within fourteen days after service of the notice (s.124(1), below); and

(e) It must inform the tenant that he can obtain help or advice from a C.A.B., housing aid or law centre, or a solicitor.

There is a one-year window of opportunity in which the proceedings may be commenced, from the date specified in the notice.

Notice to quit. Apart from this Chapter, a notice to quit must be served at least four weeks before it is intended to take effect—Protection from Eviction Act 1977, s.5 (which also requires that the notice be in writing and—in certain cases—that it contains prescribed information, similar to that now required by subs. (6)). The four weeks need not be four clear weeks: *Schnabel v. Allard* [1967] 1 Q.B. 627, C.A. If the periods of tenancy are longer than four weeks, *e.g.* monthly or even quarterly, the notice to quit must *also* be not less than one period of the tenancy (although if the period is yearly, a minimum period of six months is substituted): *doe d. Peacock v. Raffan* (1806) 6 Esp. 4. The notice must expire on the first or the last day of a period: *Crate v. Miller* [1947] K.B. 946.

Reasons. Where a statutory duty to give reasons has been imposed, the courts have held that "the reasons that are set out must be reasons which will not only be intelligible, but which deal with the substantial points that have been raised": *per* Megaw J. in *Re Poyser and Mills Arbitration* [1964] 2 Q.B. 467, approved by the House of Lords in *Westminster City Council v. Great Portland Estates plc* [1985] A.C. 661, H.L. In *Save Britain's Heritage v. Secretary of State for the Environment* [1991] 1 W.L.R. 153, H.L. Lord Bridge of Harwich adopted the same approach: "The three criteria suggested in the dictum of Megaw J. are that the reasons should be proper, intelligible and adequate."

Comparison may be drawn between the duty to give reasons under this section and the duty to give reasons under Housing Act 1965, s.64 (now repealed, and replaced within the provisions of Pt. VII, below), as to why no full assistance would be provided to a homeless person under 1985, Pt. III: see notes to s.184, below.

Forum for Challenge. See General Note to s.124, above.

Review of decision to seek possession

129.—(1) A request for review of the landlord's decision to seek an order for possession of a dwelling-house let under an introductory tenancy must be made before the end of the period of 14 days beginning with the day on which the notice of proceedings is served.

(2) On a request being duly made to it, the landlord shall review its decision.

(3) The Secretary of State may make provision by regulations as to the procedure to be followed in connection with a review under this section.

Nothing in the following provisions affects the generality of this power.

(4) Provision may be made by regulations—

(a) requiring the decision on review to be made by a person of appropriate seniority who was not involved in the original decision, and

(b) as to the circumstances in which the person concerned is entitled to an oral hearing, and whether and by whom he may be represented at such a hearing.

(5) The landlord shall notify the person concerned of the decision on the review.

If the decision is to confirm the original decision, the landlord shall also notify him of the reasons for the decision.

(6) The review shall be carried out and the tenant notified before the date specified in the notice of proceedings as the date after which proceedings for the possession of the dwelling-house may be begun.

DEFINITIONS
    "dwelling-house": s.139.

"landlord": s.229.
"tenant": s.230.

GENERAL NOTE
It is a requirement of the notice seeking possession that the landlord inform the tenant of his opportunity to seek an internal review (s.128(6)) within no more than 14 days of service of the notice on him. This was an Opposition Amendment, accepted by the government—"Under the Bill, the period is seven days. The amendment would increase it to 14 days. It strikes a balance. My guess is that it would be reasonable to allow a period of 28 days for such information, but, because introductory tenancies are designed to provide a means of action against people who behave anti-socially, relatively swift action is necessary..." (Mr Raynsford, Tenth Sitting, col. 366).

The provisions permitting the Secretary of State to prescribe the procedure—including as to seniority, etc.—are substantively the same as those found in relation to review of a homelessness decision under s.202 below, and are considered in the notes thereto, as that section is likely to attract more litigation than this. Note, however, that under this section, the review must be completed and the tenant notified before the date specified in the notice of proceedings under s.128(4) as that after which proceedings may be begun.

Reasons. See notes to previous section.

Effect of beginning proceedings for possession

130.—(1) This section applies where the landlord has begun proceedings for the possession of a dwelling-house let under an introductory tenancy and—
(a) the trial period ends, or
(b) any of the events specified in section 125(5) occurs (events on which a tenancy ceases to be an introductory tenancy).

(2) Subject to the following provisions, the tenancy remains an introductory tenancy until—
(a) the tenancy comes to an end in pursuance of section 127(3) (that is, on the date on which the tenant is to give up possession in pursuance of an order of the court), or
(b) the proceedings are otherwise finally determined.

(3) If any of the events specified in section 125(5)(b) to (d) occurs, the tenancy shall thereupon cease to be an introductory tenancy but—
(a) the landlord (or, as the case may be, the new landlord) may continue the proceedings, and
(b) if he does so, section 127(2) and (3) (termination by landlord) apply as if the tenancy had remained an introductory tenancy.

(4) Where in accordance with subsection (3) a tenancy ceases to be an introductory tenancy and becomes a secure tenancy, the tenant is not entitled to exercise the right to buy under Part V of the Housing Act 1985 unless and until the proceedings are finally determined on terms such that he is not required to give up possession of the dwelling-house.

(5) For the purposes of this section proceedings shall be treated as finally determined if they are withdrawn or any appeal is abandoned or the time for appealing expires without an appeal being brought.

DEFINITIONS
"dwelling-house": s.139.
"introductory tenancy": s.124.
"secure tenancy": s.230.
"tenancy": s.229.
"trial period": s.125.

GENERAL NOTE
Under s.125, an introductory tenancy may come to an end of its trial period (s.125(2)) or otherwise cease to be an introductory tenancy (s.125(6)) with the tenant still in occupation, in which case it will *prima facie* become secure (subject to exceptions: see notes to s.125(6), (7), above). Or, possession may be granted while the tenancy is still introductory: see ss.127–129, below. This section governs what is to happen if possession is sought, but the proceedings are not

yet complete when the tenancy ceases to be introductory.

Its provisions are relatively straightforward: if the reason the introductory tenancy would have ceased to be introductory is expiry of the trial period, the introductory quality of the tenancy continues until the tenant is ordered to give up possession, or the proceedings are otherwise finally determined, *i.e.* the proceedings are dismissed (in which case the tenancy will become secure); if the reason is one of those events specified in s.125(6), which bring the introductory quality of the tenancy to an end regardless of time, then the tenancy either becomes secure (if it would otherwise do so) or merely contractual (non-secure).

If secure, then the right to buy cannot be "exercised" unless and until the possession proceedings are finally determined on terms that allow the tenant to remain in possession. This means that the tenant can commence right to buy procedure, but cannot finally exercise it, *i.e.* require it to be taken to completion—*cf.* Housing Act 1985, ss.119, 120 and 121 (distinguishing between cases where the right does not arise, where it is excepted, and where it cannot be exercised).

Although it is attractive to seek to argue that in this context, exercise could be given a wider meaning (*cf. ibid.*, s.122, referring to claiming to exercise the right to buy), so as to avoid the not inconsiderable work involved in responding to a claim, assessing values, future works and their costs, terms of transaction and so on, it cannot be said that it is absurd in a legal sense for the tenant to be able to make the claim while it is still unknown whether or not he will ever be able finally to complete it, as the date of claim fixes the value of the property (see *ibid.*, ss.122, 127).

Rather more sensible would have been to suspend the later stages—starting with the landlord's response notice under *ibid.*, s.139 and notice of price, terms, etc., under *ibid.*, s.140—so that time did not begin to run until it is ascertained whether or not the tenant is secure. (The circumstances are not analogous to those with which there is only a bar on exercise of the right to buy, so that the landlord may likewise have to engage in ultimately fruitless effort [as, of course, can be the case where the applicant simply changes his mind, or his financial circumstances change] under *ibid.*, s.136, as these are flexible circumstances—supervening possession orders, categories of insolvency—which may or may not arise, and if arising may again change; whether or not an introductory tenant becomes a secure tenant under these provisions is an absolute.)

If the introductory tenancy becomes secure as a result of s.125(5), yet possession proceedings have been commenced, it will be the provisions of Housing Act 1985, Pt. IV, which will govern such matters as succession, rights to consultation and repair, exchange and so on, rather than those in ss.131–137, below, as it is *only* right to buy which is excluded. If the proceedings are finally determined without an order for possession, then security will continue, and secure occupation—whether for right to buy or any other purpose—will date back to the relevant s.125(5) event.

The court retains power, however, both in this case and in a case where the trial period has expired through time, to make an order under s.128, below, as it would if the tenancy remained secure.

Subs. (5)

Leave is needed to appeal the making or refusal of an order for possession: R.S.C. Ord. 59, r.1B. If leave is given by the court which granted or refused possession, there will be four weeks in which to serve notice of appeal: *ibid.*, r.4. If leave is refused by the court below, and is sought from the Court of Appeal, the application must be made within the same period, but the time for service of the notice of appeal is extended to a period of seven days from when leave is granted: *ibid.* If time to appeal, or to seek leave, is extended, on application, then it would seem that—if no order has been made in the interim—the proceedings will not be treated as having finally determined.

In such a case, the tenant will need a stay (unless it is agreed by consent) to prevent eviction, for he will have—at that point—no tenancy. In the case of a tenancy which would have ceased to be introductory by reason of the effluxion of time, a stay (by order or consent) will likewise be needed even if the application for leave is made in time, or an appeal served in time, as there is no automatic stay pending appeal and if the court has set a time for possession to be given up under s.125, below, so also will the tenancy have come to an end and with it any restraint on the eviction. In the case of a tenancy which has ceased to be introductory and has become—even if potentially only *pro tem*—secure, however, the tenancy would seem to continue until final determination.

Succession on death of tenant

Persons qualified to succeed tenant

131. A person is qualified to succeed the tenant under an introductory tenancy if he occupies the dwelling-house as his only or principal home at the time of the tenant's death and either—

(a) he is the tenant's spouse, or

(b) he is another member of the tenant's family and has resided with the tenant throughout the period of twelve months ending with the tenant's death;

unless, in either case, the tenant was himself a successor, as defined in section 132.

DEFINITIONS

"dwelling-house": s.139.
"introductory tenancy": s.124.
"member of the tenant's family": s.140.
"successor": s.132.

GENERAL NOTE

This is the first of a series of sections which details the rights of introductory tenants, modelled on the provisions of Pt. IV Housing Act 1985, governing the rights of secure tenants.

There is a right of statutory succession to the introductory tenancy, available to a qualifying person. This section defines the qualifying person as being the tenant's spouse, absent whom another member of the deceased tenant's family. There is no right to succeed, however, if the deceased tenant was himself a successor, as defined in s.132, below. Operation of the right is governed by s.133, below.

Only or principal home. These rules mean that a spouse does not have to show residence *with* the other party (see *Peabody Donation Fund Governors v. Grant* (1982) 6 H.L.R. 41, C.A.). But residence with the other party does not necessarily connote residence at the subject property: *L.B. Waltham Forest v. Thomas* [1992] A.C. 198, 24 H.L.R. 622, H.L.

Whether or not one person has been residing with another is a question of fact: *Middleton v. Bull* (1951) 2 T.L.R. 1010, C.A. One member of the family *could* live at the same address as another as a tenant or sub-tenant, in which case he will not qualify as they will not have been residing together (*Edmund v. Jones* [1957] 1 W.L.R. 118n, *Collier v. Stoneman* [1957] 1 W.L.R. 1108, C.A.); this would, *in practice*, probably require quite convincing evidence, *either* that such an arrangement had been long-standing, *or* (possibly) that it had been undertaken in order to take advantage of these provisions (see also *Foreman v. Beagley* [1969] 1 W.L.R. 1387, C.A.).

The fact that the vendor or transferor was in hospital at the time of disposal would not, however, prevent residence "with" him, because residence does not necessarily import immediate presence: see *Tompkins v. Rowley* [1949] E.G.D. 314, C.A., *Hedgedale Ltd. v. Hards* (1990) 23 H.L.R. 158, C.A. (grandson residing with grandmother even though for part of the period she was staying at her daughter's following an accident).

In *Camden L.B.C. v. Goldenberg* (1996) 28 H.L.R. forthcoming, C.A., a grandson married and left his grandmother's flat, to "house-sit" for friends, together with his wife, intending to move to their own accommodation if found; when it was not, the grandson returned to his grandmother's, and his wife went to live elsewhere; six months later, the grandmother moved into a nursing home, assigning the flat to her grandson (see s.134).

On the question whether the grandson had lived with her for 12 months, before the assignment, it was held that the combination of the house-sitting arrangement, and no more than a conditional intention to move elsewhere, if such accommodation was found, was insufficient to interrupt the period of residence. A period of absence did not necessarily break the continuity of residence. The grandson had kept his postal address at his grandmother's, and most of his possessions were at her flat. The intention to move elsewhere was not an expectation, but a mere hope, in reality a distant prospect sufficient to qualify, but not to displace, the intention to return.

Cases where the tenant is a successor

132.—(1) The tenant is himself a successor if—

(a) the tenancy vested in him by virtue of section 133 (succession to introductory tenancy),

(b) he was a joint tenant and has become the sole tenant,

(c) he became the tenant on the tenancy being assigned to him (but subject to subsections (2) and (3)), or

(d) he became the tenant on the tenancy being vested in him on the death of the previous tenant.

(2) A tenant to whom the tenancy was assigned in pursuance of an order

under section 24 of the Matrimonial Causes Act 1973 (property adjustment orders in connection with matrimonial proceedings) or section 17(1) of the Matrimonial and Family Proceedings Act 1984 (property adjustment orders after overseas divorce, &c.) is a successor only if the other party to the marriage was a successor.

(3) Where within six months of the coming to an end of an introductory tenancy ("the former tenancy") the tenant becomes a tenant under another introductory tenancy, and—

(a) the tenant was a successor in relation to the former tenancy, and

(b) under the other tenancy either the dwelling-house or the landlord, or both, are the same as under the former tenancy,

the tenant is also a successor in relation to the other tenancy unless the agreement creating that tenancy otherwise provides.

DEFINITIONS

"dwelling-house": s.139.
"introductory tenancy": s.124.

GENERAL NOTE

Modelled on Housing Act 1985, s.88, these provisions govern whether or not a deceased tenant was himself a successor, for the purpose of determining whether or not there is any right to succeed (under the next section). There can only be one statutory succession: subs. (1)(a). If there are joint tenants, and one of them survives the other, he will be a successor (subs. (1)(b)), but only if it is the same tenancy, as distinct from the grant of a new (sole or joint) tenancy: *Bassetlaw D.C. v. Renshaw* (1991) 23 H.L.R. 603, C.A. An assignment under s.134, below, comprises a succession for these purposes (subs. (1)(c)), *i.e.* so that the assignee qualifies as a successor and his spouse or members of the family cannot further succeed. Finally, a vesting on death amounts to a first succession (subs. (1)(d)).

In *Epping Forest D.C. v. Pomphrett* (1990) 22 H.L.R. 475, C.A., an intestate death before the introduction of Housing Act 1980 led to the vesting of the tenancy in the President of the Family Division; as letters of administration were not taken out, it so remained; the grant to the widow of a new tenancy by the authority was accordingly just that—a new tenancy, not a vesting on death.

Subs. (2)

An assignment under s.24, Matrimonial Causes Act 1973 (c. 18) or s.17, Matrimonial and Family Proceedings Act 1984 (c. 42), is not a first succession, so that the tenant taking over the tenancy will only be a successor if the party from whom the tenancy is taken over was himself a successor.

Subs. (3)

Where the tenant becomes the tenant under another introductory tenancy from the same landlord, or of the same property, within six months of the determination of the previous introductory tenancy, he will be a successor under the new introductory tenancy if he was under the old (unless the agreement otherwise provides). This allows a landlord to offer a second chance to someone who has "dropped out" of an introductory tenancy regime without affording him a preferential status in terms of succession. This is to be distinguished from a case where a tenant is moved about during the introductory period without a break, *e.g.* for housing management reasons, in which case—while this provision will have the like effect of preventing an improvement in status—the earlier period will be discounted from the trial period in the new property (see s.125(1), (2), above).

Succession to introductory tenancy

133.—(1) This section applies where a tenant under an introductory tenancy dies.

(2) Where there is a person qualified to succeed the tenant, the tenancy vests by virtue of this section in that person, or if there is more than one such person in the one to be preferred in accordance with the following rules—

(a) the tenant's spouse is to be preferred to another member of the tenant's family;

(b) of two or more other members of the tenant's family such of them is to be preferred as may be agreed between them or as may, where there is no such agreement, be selected by the landlord.

(3) Where there is no person qualified to succeed the tenant, the tenancy ceases to be an introductory tenancy—

(a) when it is vested or otherwise disposed of in the course of the administration of the tenant's estate, unless the vesting or other disposal is in pursuance of an order made under—

(i) section 24 of the Matrimonial Causes Act 1973 (property adjustment orders made in connection with matrimonial proceedings),

(ii) section 17(1) of the Matrimonial and Family Proceedings Act 1984 (property adjustment orders after overseas divorce, &c.), or

(iii) paragraph 1 of Schedule 1 to the Children Act 1989 (orders for financial relief against parents); or

(b) when it is known that when the tenancy is so vested or disposed of it will not be in pursuance of such an order.

DEFINITION
"introductory tenancy": s.124.

GENERAL NOTE
This section is modelled on Housing Act 1985, s.89, and contains the provisions governing succession (a) to a qualifying successor (as to which, see s.131, above), provided (b) the deceased was not himself already a successor (as to which, see s.132, above). The vesting is automatic; the tenant's spouse is to be preferred to any other member of the family; if there is more than one member of the family qualified to succeed, they may agree between themselves who is to succeed or otherwise the landlord may choose. (The agreement will still be valid, and preferred to the landlord's choice, even if it has not been communicated to the landlord: see *General Management Ltd. v. Locke* (1980) 255 E.G. 155, C.A.)

If an order for possession has been made, but time has not yet run out (or, perhaps, it is subject to appeal)—see s.130, above—then the successor will take subject to it: *Sherrin v. Brand* [1956] 1 Q.B. 403, C.A., *American Economic Laundry v. Little* [1951] 1 K.B. 400, C.A.

Subs. (3)
If there is no one qualified to succeed, the introductory tenancy ceases so to qualify, *i.e.* it becomes an ordinary, contractual tenancy capable of termination (by landlord or tenant) as such, unless it was or becomes subject to proceedings under the matrimonial or domestic legislation referred to, which leads to an order, in which case this subsection preserves the right to succeed as an introductory tenant.

In this respect, the provision is different from 1985, s.89 as it has hitherto read, pursuant to which a tenancy remains secure until a vesting occurs, at which point the security is lost unless an order is made under matrimonial legislation (*n.b.* only Matrimonial Causes Act 1973, s.24), in other words the presumptions are reversed. Housing Act 1985, s.89 is, however, now amended, to bring it into line with this section, by Sched. 18, para. 10, below.

Assignment

Assignment in general prohibited

134.—(1) An introductory tenancy is not capable of being assigned except in the cases mentioned in subsection (2).

(2) The exceptions are—

(a) an assignment in pursuance of an order made under—

(i) section 24 of the Matrimonial Causes Act 1973 (property adjustment orders in connection with matrimonial proceedings),

(ii) section 17(1) of the Matrimonial and Family Proceedings Act 1984 (property adjustment orders after overseas divorce, &c.), or

(iii) paragraph 1 of Schedule 1 to the Children Act 1989 (orders for financial relief against parents);

(b) an assignment to a person who would be qualified to succeed the tenant if the tenant died immediately before the assignment.

(3) Subsection (1) also applies to a tenancy which is not an introductory tenancy but would be if the tenant, or where the tenancy is a joint tenancy, at least one of the tenants, were occupying or continuing to occupy the dwelling-house as his only or principal home.

DEFINITION
"introductory tenancy": s.124.

GENERAL NOTE
Modelled on Housing Act 1985, s.91, an introductory tenancy is *per se* incapable of assignment, *save* in the two cases noted, *i.e.* pursuant to an order under the matrimonial and domestic legislation specified, or to a qualifying successor. Note the exclusion in the case of an introductory tenancy of the right to assignment by way of exchange.

Assignment to Potential Successor. This permits a tenant to pre-empt a dispute between one of two potential successors, or else to retire to another town or even country without loss of the asset—see *Peabody Donation Fund v. Higgins* [1983] 1 W.L.R. 1091, 10 H.L.R. 82, C.A. In *Higgins*, there was an express, contractual prohibition on assignment: the assignment was accordingly effective, even though unlawful and giving rise to a ground for possession for breach of term of the tenancy. Under an introductory tenancy, there would be nothing to stop a landlord terminating a tenancy on the basis of the assignment—lawful or unlawful. The exclusion of such assignments from the absolute incapacity to assign does not amount to a statutory consent to assign.
To be effective, however, the assignment must be by deed, even if the tenancy under assignment did not itself require to be in writing: see Law of Property Act 1925, s.52; *Botting v. Martin* (1808) 1 Camp. 317; *Crago v. Julian* [1992] 1 W.L.R. 372, 24 H.L.R. 306, C.A. In some circumstances, evidence in writing may be sufficient, in which case the assignment may take effect as an enforceable contract for the assignment—see Law of Property (Miscellaneous Provisions) Act 1989, s.2. In *Westminster C.C. v. Peart* (1991) 24 H.L.R. 389, C.A., Sir Christopher Slade expressed the view, albeit *obiter*, that it was improbable that the legislature would have intended that parties to a tenancy who wished to take advantage of Housing Act 1985, s.91, would have to undertake the formality and expense of executing a deed.
See also *L.B. Croydon v. Buston & Triance* (1991) 24 H.L.R. 36, C.A., where the putative successor was unable to prove an oral assignment on the facts.

Subs. (3)
This subsection corresponds substantively to s.95, 1985 Act, and is designed to pre-empt the argument that the prohibition on assignment is not circumvented by the argument that as the tenant was not in occupation as an only or principal home, the tenancy is not introductory (see notes to s.125(5), above) and, therefore, the prohibition is simply inapplicable.

Repairs

Right to carry out repairs

135. The Secretary of State may by regulations under section 96 of the Housing Act 1985 (secure tenants: right to carry out repairs) apply to introductory tenants any provision made under that section in relation to secure tenants.

DEFINITIONS
"introductory tenant": s.124.
"secure tenancy": s.230.

GENERAL NOTE
One of the aspects of the Tenants' Charter is the "right to repair" which gives secure tenants rights to require a landlord to appoint a second contractor, when a first contractor has failed to carry out repairs which the landlords are under an obligation to do, failing which the tenant may enjoy a right to compensation—see Secure Tenants of Local Housing Authorities (Right to

Repair) Regulations 1994, (S.I. 1994 No. 133). This section permits the Secretary of State to extend the right to repair to introductory tenants. It is likely that he will decide whether or not to use the power when he sees how widespread the introductory régime becomes, and how commonly tenants who first come into local authority or H.A.T. stock remain in it.

Provision of information and consultation

Provision of information about tenancies

136.—(1) Every local housing authority or housing action trust which lets dwelling-houses under introductory tenancies shall from time to time publish information about its introductory tenancies, in such form as it considers best suited to explain in simple terms, and, so far as it considers it appropriate, the effect of—

(a) the express terms of its introductory tenancies,

(b) the provisions of this Chapter, and

(c) the provisions of sections 11 to 16 of the Landlord and Tenant Act 1985 (landlord's repairing obligations),

and shall ensure that so far as is reasonably practicable the information so published is kept up to date.

(2) The landlord under an introductory tenancy shall supply the tenant with—

(a) a copy of the information for introductory tenants published by it under subsection (1), and

(b) a written statement of the terms of the tenancy, so far as they are neither expressed in the lease or written tenancy agreement (if any) nor implied by law;

and the statement required by paragraph (b) shall be supplied on the grant of the tenancy or as soon as practicable afterwards.

DEFINITIONS

"housing action trust": s.230.
"introductory tenancy": s.124.
"local housing authority": s.230.
"registered social landlord": s.1.
"secure tenancy": s.230.
"tenancy": s.229.

GENERAL NOTE

Modelled on Housing Act 1985, s.104, this section requires landlords under introductory tenancies periodically to produce (and keep up to date) information, in simple terms, to explain the effects of the express terms of its introductory tenancies, the provisions of this Chapter (governing the rights and susceptibilities of introductory tenants), and the provisions of ss.11–16, Landlord and Tenant Act 1985 (the principal repairing obligation imposed on landlords, to keep in repair the structure and exterior of the property—or of the building in which the dwelling-house is situated—including its drains, gutters and external pipes, and to keep in repair and proper working order its installations—and those of a building in which the dwelling-house is situated—for water-supply, gas-supply, electricity-supply, and for sanitation, and to keep in repair and proper working order its installations for water and space heating).

Subs. (2)

On the grant of the tenancy, or as soon as practicable thereafter, the landlord has to give the tenant a copy of the subs. (1) information, *and* a written statement of the terms of the tenancy save so far as they are contained in a written tenancy agreement or lease (in which case the tenant will already have the terms in writing), and save so far as they are implied by law (which in the case of ss.11–16, Landlord and Tenant Act 1985, will be in the subs. (1) information). This means that tenants will have written evidence of all the terms of their tenancies, in one form or another.

Consultation on matters of housing management

137.—(1) This section applies in relation to every local housing authority and housing action trust which lets dwelling-houses under introductory tenancies and which is a landlord authority for the purposes of Part IV of the Housing Act 1985 (secure tenancies).

(2) The authority or trust shall maintain such arrangements as it considers appropriate to enable those of its introductory tenants who are likely to be substantially affected by a relevant matter of housing management—

(a) to be informed of the proposals of the authority or trust in respect of the matter, and

(b) to make their views known to the authority or trust within a specified period;

and the authority or trust shall, before making a decision on the matter, consider any representations made to it in accordance with those arrangements.

(3) A matter is one of housing management if, in the opinion of the authority or trust concerned, it relates to—

(a) the management, improvement, maintenance or demolition of dwelling-houses let by the authority or trust under introductory or secure tenancies, or

(b) the provision of services or amenities in connection with such dwelling-houses;

but not so far as it relates to the rent payable under an introductory or secure tenancy or to charges for services or facilities provided by the authority or trust.

(4) A matter is relevant if, in the opinion of the authority or trust concerned, it represents—

(a) a new programme of maintenance, improvement or demolition, or

(b) a change in the practice or policy of the authority or trust,

and is likely substantially to affect either its introductory tenants as a whole or a group of them who form a distinct social group or occupy dwelling-houses which constitute a distinct class (whether by reference to the kind of dwelling-house, or the housing estate or other larger area in which they are situated).

(5) In the case of a local housing authority, the reference in subsection (3) to the provision of services or amenities is a reference only to the provision of services or amenities by the authority acting in its capacity as landlord of the dwelling-houses concerned.

(6) The authority or trust shall publish details of the arrangements which it makes under this section, and a copy of the documents published under this subsection shall—

(a) be made available at its principal office for inspection at all reasonable hours, without charge, by members of the public, and

(b) be given, on payment of a reasonable fee, to any member of the public who asks for one.

DEFINITIONS
   "dwelling-houses": s.139.
   "housing action trust": s.230.
   "introductory tenancies": s.124.
   "local housing authority": s.230.
   "secure tenancy": s.230.

GENERAL NOTE
   This section is modelled on Housing Act 1985, s.105. The introduction of the concept of the "landlord authority for the purposes of Part IV" reflects *ibid.* s.114, pursuant to which an exception certificate may be issued to a housing action trust if the Secretary of State is satisfied that it has transferred or otherwise disposed of at least three-quarters of the dwellings which have at any time been vested in it.
   Landlords bound by this section are obliged to make and maintain arrangements to secure a degree of consultation with their introductory tenants on matters of housing management, as defined in subs. (3) so as to exclude payments by way of rent or other charges (whether for introductory or secure tenants, bearing in mind that the former may—and most should—

become the latter). The provision of services or amenities is, however, within the obligation, although only *qua* landlord (subs. (5)).

There is a substantial amount of discretion—or subjective judgment—left to the landlord, *e.g.* in terms of the appropriateness of arrangements (but they must be "to enable those of its introductory tenants who are likely to be substantially affected" to be informed and to make their views known—see subs. (2)), in terms of the consideration they give tenants' responses, in terms of whether the tenants are likely to be affected, and whether substantially so, in terms of whether the matter "relates to" the practices specified, in terms of whether there is a new programme of maintenance, improvement or demolition, or whether there is a change in the practice or policy of the authority (subs. (4)). It is, accordingly, not surprising that this provision (as it has existed since 1980) has not given rise to much litigation. Most recently a challenge to consultation arrangements failed in *R. v. Brent L.B.C., ex p. Morris* [1996] E.G.C.S. 20, 28 H.L.R. forthcoming, Q.B.D., where the court held that the duty was not to provide ideal arrangements, but arrangements appropriate to enable an exchange of information and views on specified matters to take place. The court could only interfere if it was satisfied that no authority could reasonably have thought that the arrangements in question would enable tenants to make known their views about matters covered by s.105.

Subss. (3), (4)

A matter is one of housing management if, in the opinion of the authority, it fulfils three conditions: (i) it relates to management, maintenance, improvement or demolition, or the provision of services or amenities, (ii) it represents a new programme or a change in practice or policy, and (iii) it is likely substantially to affect its introductory tenants as a whole or a group of them—*Short v. L.B. Tower Hamlets* (1985) 18 H.L.R. 171, C.A. The requirement that the matter is likely substantially to affect tenants must be understood and applied as if it read "is likely *if implemented* to affect..."—*R. v. L.B. Hammersmith & Fulham L.B.C., ex p. Beddowes* [1987] Q.B. 1050, 18 H.L.R. 458, C.A.

Supplementary

Jurisdiction of county court

138.—(1) A county court has jurisdiction to determine questions arising under this Chapter and to entertain proceedings brought under this Chapter and claims, for whatever amount, in connection with an introductory tenancy.

(2) That jurisdiction includes jurisdiction to entertain proceedings as to whether a statement supplied in pursuance of section 136(2)(b) (written statement of certain terms of tenancy) is accurate notwithstanding that no other relief is sought than a declaration.

(3) If a person takes proceedings in the High Court which, by virtue of this section, he could have taken in the county court, he is not entitled to recover any costs.

(4) The Lord Chancellor may make such rules and give such directions as he thinks fit for the purpose of giving effect to this section.

(5) The rules and directions may provide—

(a) for the exercise by a district judge of a county court of any jurisdiction exercisable under this section, and

(b) for the conduct of proceedings in private.

(6) The power to make rules is exercisable by statutory instrument which shall be subject to annulment in pursuance of a resolution of either House of Parliament.

GENERAL NOTE

This section is analogous to s.110, Housing Act 1985, conferring a broad general jurisdiction on the county court, wider than, and additional to, its jurisdiction under the County Courts Act 1984 (c. 28). In particular, any claim brought in connection with an introductory tenancy may be brought in the county court, regardless of amount: *cf.* the general monetary limits imposed by the Courts and Legal Services Act 1990 (c. 41), s.1, as set by the High Court and County Courts Jurisdiction Order 1991, at £25,000, for most proceedings. It is clear that a declaration may be sought, even if no other relief within the jurisdiction is claimed, on any question arising under this Chapter and on the other questions specified.

Any question within this Chapter will normally be capable of being referred to the county court in any event, and notwithstanding that no relief, other than a declaration—or injunction—is sought, under the County Courts Act 1984, s.38 (as substituted).

Subs. (2)
One cannot help wondering how many introductory tenants will be keen to test the accuracy of the landlord's written statement, presumably when no proceedings are threatened, or other action being taken against the tenant; while retaliatory proceedings would be quite improper, the tenant may yet be taking the risk of failure to "graduate" to security.

Meaning of "dwelling-house"

139.—(1) For the purposes of this Chapter a dwelling-house may be a house or a part of a house.

(2) Land let together with a dwelling-house shall be treated for the purposes of this Chapter as part of the dwelling-house unless the land is agricultural land which would not be treated as part of a dwelling-house for the purposes of Part IV of the Housing Act 1985 (see section 112(2) of that Act).

GENERAL NOTE
This definition is modelled on Housing Act 1985, s.112, but adapted to eliminate the explicit reference to acres, "to meet the requirements of the European directives on the use of imperial measurements ...": Parliamentary Under-Secretary of State for the Environment (Mr Clappison), *Hansard* (H.C.), Standing Committee G, Tenth Sitting, February 27, 1996, col. 380.

Dwelling-house. A dwelling-house may be a house or a part of a house: it may, therefore, be a flat, whether self-contained or not; as, however, introductory tenancies are those which would be secure but for these provisions, the dwelling-house will have to be (and to be capable of being) let as a separate dwelling—see notes to ss.16(2), 126(1), above.

As to whether it is a house at all, see also notes to s.63(1), above. Under the Rent Acts, a purpose-built hotel has been held to be a house (*Luganda v. Services Hotels* [1969] 2 Ch. 209, C.A.), although a room with its own bathroom and W.C., but without its own cooking facilities, was "no more a dwelling-house than a hotel" within the Housing Act 1985 (*Central Y.M.C.A. Housing Association v. Goodman* (1991) 24 H.L.R. 109, C.A. [nor was it let as a separate dwelling—see notes to s.126(1), above]). It is a question of fact whether or not something is a house: *Horford Investments v. Lambert* [1976] Ch. 39, C.A.

What is structurally a mobile home *may* be a house: a caravan with raised wheels and permanent services was so held for tax purposes in *Makins v. Elson* [1977] 1 W.L.R. 221, C.A. See also *R. v. Rent Officer of Nottingham Registration Area, ex p. Allen* (1985) 17 H.L.R. 481, Q.B.D., where it was held that just because something is a caravan does not mean that it cannot be within the Rent Acts, but it will depend on the terms of the letting: if let as a moveable chattel, it cannot be a house; if rendered completely immobile, *e.g.* by removal of wheels or being permanently blocked in, it may be regarded as a house much as a prefabricated house or bungalow would be. See also *Norton v. Knowles* [1969] 1 Q.B. 572 (though there the issue was "any premises" rather than a house).

Land let with house. Housing Act 1985, s.112, treats as part of the house, land let together with it, unless it is agricultural land (as defined in General Rate Act 1967 (c. 9), s.26(3)(a)) exceeding two acres (*cf.* note above). A field of more than two acres not *used* only as a meadow or pasture within *ibid.*, s.26(3)(a) was held not to be excluded in *Bradshaw v. Smith* (1980) 255 E.G. 699, C.A., because it was used mainly or exclusively for recreational purposes.

The letting does not have to be under the one agreement: *Mann v. Merrill* [1945] 1 All E.R. 705, C.A.; see also *Wimbush v. Cibulia* [1949] 2 K.B. 564, C.A. Nor need the land and dwelling be contiguous, provided they are within the same vicinity: *Langford Property Co. v. Batten* [1951] A.C. 223, H.L. Nor even need the landlord be the same, or the payments comprise a single rent: *Jelley v. Buckman* [1974] 2 Q.B. 488, C.A., but *cf. Cumbes v. Robinson* [1951] 2 K.B. 83, C.A., and *Lewis v. Purvis* (1947) 177 L.T. 267, C.A. Of course there must be a dwelling-house for any land to be let together with it: *Ellis & Sons Amalgamated Properties v. Sisman* [1948] 1 K.B. 653, C.A. The question is to be decided at the date when it arises, not the date of the letting: *Mann v. Merrill* (above).

Members of a person's family: Chapter I

140.—(1) A person is a member of another's family within the meaning of this Chapter if—

(a) he is the spouse of that person, or he and that person live together as husband and wife, or

(b) he is that person's parent, grandparent, child, grandchild, brother, sister, uncle, aunt, nephew or niece.

(2) For the purpose of subsection (1)(b)—

(a) a relationship by marriage shall be treated as a relationship by blood,

(b) a relationship of the half-blood shall be treated as a relationship of the whole blood, and

(c) the stepchild of a person shall be treated as his child.

GENERAL NOTE
See notes to s.62, above.

Consequential amendments: introductory tenancies

141.—(1) The enactments mentioned in Schedule 14 have effect with the amendments specified there which are consequential on the provisions of this Chapter.

(2) The Secretary of State may by order make such other amendments or repeals of any enactment as appear to him necessary or expedient in consequence of the provisions of this Chapter.

(3) Without prejudice to the generality of subsection (2), an order under that subsection may make such provision in relation to an enactment as the Secretary of State considers appropriate as regards its application (with or without modifications) or non-application in relation to introductory tenants or introductory tenancies.

GENERAL NOTE
Attention may be drawn to the following amendments:

Succession. Someone is a successor for the purposes of succession under Pt. IV, Housing Act 1985, if he was a successor for the introductory tenancy purposes of this Chapter.

Security. Introductory tenancies are also included in the category of tenancies which are not secure (*cf.* above, notes to s.124(1)), as are tenancies which cease to be introductory because there is no one qualified to succeed (under s.133(3), above), or because the residential requirement (above, s.125(5)) ceases to be fulfilled.

Regulations and orders

142. Any regulations or order under this Part—

(a) may contain such incidental, supplementary or transitional provisions, or savings, as the Secretary of State thinks fit, and

(b) shall be made by statutory instrument which shall be subject to annulment in pursuance of a resolution of either House of Parliament.

Index of defined expressions: introductory tenancies

143. The following Table shows provisions defining or otherwise explaining provisions used in this Chapter (other than provisions defining or explaining an expression in the same section)—

adopt (in relation to periodic tenancy)	section 124(4)
assured tenancy and assured shorthold tenancy	section 230
dwelling-house	section 139
housing action trust	section 230
introductory tenancy and introductory tenant	section 124
local housing authority	section 230

member of family　　　　　　　　　　section 140
registered social landlord　　　　　　section 2
secure tenancy and secure tenant　　section 230

CHAPTER II

REPOSSESSION, &C.: SECURE AND ASSURED TENANCIES

Secure tenancies

Extension of ground of nuisance or annoyance to neighbours, &c

144. For Ground 2 in Schedule 2 to the Housing Act 1985 (nuisance or annoyance to neighbours, &c.) substitute—

"*Ground 2*

The tenant or a person residing in or visiting the dwelling-house—
(a) has been guilty of conduct causing or likely to cause a nuisance or annoyance to a person residing, visiting or otherwise engaging in a lawful activity in the locality, or
(b) has been convicted of—
　　(i) using the dwelling-house or allowing it to be used for immoral or illegal purposes, or
　　(ii) an arrestable offence committed in, or in the locality of, the dwelling-house.".

GENERAL NOTE

This is the first in a series of amendments to existing security law—both in the public sector and in the private sector—intended to address the problem of anti-social conduct by tenants and their families, which led many local authorities during the 1990s to look for novel ways of protecting and preserving the safety and social environment of their estates, including by the use of injunctive proceedings now dealt with specifically in Chap. III of this Part.

This amendment substitutes a discretionary ground for possession, *i.e.* one in relation to which the landlord must also prove not only the facts of the Ground, but also that it is reasonable to make the order sought (Housing Act 1985, s.84(2)(a), Grounds 1–8. Those Grounds which leave the court no discretion, but which mean that the court must make an order once the elements of the Ground have been made out, are known as the mandatory grounds: see 1985 Act, s.84(2)(b), Grounds 9–11. Under the Housing Act 1985, these all require the provision of suitable alternative accommodation in addition to proof that the conditions of Grounds 9–11 have been made out. A third group of grounds requires *both* the provision of suitable alternative accommodation, *and* that it is reasonable to make the order: see 1985 Act, s.84(2)(c), Grounds 12–16).

Hitherto, Ground 2 has read:
"The tenant or a person residing in the dwelling-house has been guilty of conduct which is a nuisance or annoyance to neighbours, or has been convicted of using the dwelling-house or allowing it to be used for immoral or illegal purposes."

Visitors. Both limbs are extended to include *visitors* to property in question.

Nuisance and annoyance. The first limb of this ground is now widened in the following respects:
(a) The nuisance can be caused by a mere visitor to the property, so that the ground will be applicable where, *e.g.*, a family or members of it act as a gathering-point, or catalyst, for others who actually cause the nuisance (but who do not live with them);
(b) It will not be necessary to prove actual nuisance, which is continuing—past conduct which caused a nuisance, or which was likely to cause a nuisance will suffice, which "will enable a third party rather than the victim of the behaviour to give evidence against the perpetrator... The Government's aim is that landlords should be able to obtain possession in some cases on evidence from third parties who are not victims... We have already rehearsed in Committee the extent to which the fear of intimidation of potential witnesses is a problem"—*Hansard* (H.C.), Standing Committee G, Tenth Sitting, February 27, 1996, cols. 382–3, Minister for Local Government, Housing and Urban Regeneration (Mr Curry);
(c) The nuisance need not be to someone who actually lives in the relevant area, but can be to a person living, visiting or merely engaged in a lawful activity, *e.g.* a person carrying out repairs;

and,

(d) The area of the nuisance is no longer confined to someone who lives where he can properly be described as a neighbour, *i.e.* in the neighbourhood, but is extended to the "locality", "to cover as wide an area as possible, while maintaining the link between the tenant's behaviour and the fact that he lives in the area. 'Locality' is our preferred replacement for that, and is designed to catch such behaviour over that larger area", *e.g.* "behaviour ... on a large estate towards tenants on a further part of the estate... Our amendments, by not attempting to give a specific definition to the area that we want to cover, give us ... flexibility... I assure Opposition Members that our amendments are intended to cover all the areas set out in their amendments—the common parts of blocks of flats, other parts of the estate and even parts of the locality that may not have the same landlord ... We want an all-embracing term that common sense people understand..."—*ibid.,* cols. 384–387.

In *Cobstone Investments Ltd. v. Maxim* [1985] 1 Q.B. 140, 15 H.L.R. 113, C.A., the term "adjoining occupiers" under the Rent Act 1977 was wider than contiguous, as one meaning of the word "adjoining" was neighbouring (which means that the case is as applicable under Housing Act 1985), and that all that the context requires is that the premises should be near enough to be affected by the conduct.

Nuisance and annoyance have been held to include racial and sexual harassment (*Woking B.C. v. Bistram* (1993) 27 H.L.R. 1, C.A., and *Kensington & Chelsea R.B.C. v. Simmonds, The Times,* July 15, 1996, 28 H.L.R. forthcoming, C.A.), as has use of premises for prostitution (*Frederick Platts Co. Ltd. v. Grigor* (1950) 66 T.L.R. 859, *Yates v. Morris* [1950] 2 All E.R. 577, C.A.), and indeed private immorality (*Benton v. Chapman* [1953] C.L.Y. 3099, Cty. Ct.), although cohabitation would today not be regarded as immoral for this purpose (*Heglibiston Establishment v. Heyman* (1977) 76 P. & C.R. 351, C.A.

In *Simmonds,* a suspended order against a single mother was upheld, where the conduct was on the part of her son: it would offend common sense and the terms of Ground 2 to suggest that a degree of positive fault had to be shown on the part of the tenant, as distinct from inability to control unruly children; the tenant was entitled to justice, but so were the neighbours.

Nuisance does not necessarily mean nuisance in a technical legal sense, but in a natural sense, and annoyance is in any event a term with a wider meaning, although it must be such as would annoy an ordinary occupier, not an ultra-sensitive one: *Tod-Heatly v. Benham* (1888) 40 Ch.D. 80; see also *National Schizophrenic Fellowship v. Ribble Estates S.A.* (1993) 25 H.L.R. 476, Ch.D. It may be the result of something physical, *e.g.* excessive noise, making a lot of dust, allowing water to overflow onto the premises of another (*Chapman v. Hughes* (1923) 129 L.T. 223, *Parker v. Elvin* (1944) 143 E.G. 129, C.A.) or it may be the result of conduct: *Whitbread v. Ward* (1952) 159 E.G. 494, C.A., *Frederick Platts Co. Ltd. v. Grigor* (above).

The decision in *Ottway v. Jones* [1955] 1 W.L.R. 706, C.A., in which the court refused to make an order where the last act complained of was some nine months before the hearing (although awarded the costs against the defendant), would not seem to be relevant authority under this Ground as redrafted.

Illegal and immoral user. Conviction for "illegal and immoral user" has been held to include use for drugs. It is not necessary that the user be a part of the offence, but use of the premises must be more than incidental, as where the offence is mere possession which happens to be at the premises—compare *S. Schneiders & Sons Ltd. v. Abrahams* [1925] 1 K.B. 301, C.A., *Abrahams v. Wilson* [1971] 2 Q.B. 88, C.A.). Single acts *may* constitute user, but it will be that much harder to establish: *Abrahams v. Wilson.*

In addition, the ground has been widened—in response to opposition amendments to strengthen local authorities' powers to deal with drug dealers (*Hansard* (H.C.), April 30, 1996, Report Stage, Minister for Local Government, Housing and Urban Regeneration [Mr Curry], col. 1009)—to include where either the tenant, or a person residing in, or a person visiting, the dwelling-house has been convicted of an arrestable offence, committed in, or in the locality of, the property. This was explicitly considered to provide "a particularly useful measure to deal with drug dealing cases where the traffic may well take place in the common parts of the estate rather than in a person's home" (*ibid.*), although it applies to much more than drug dealing as "arrestable offence" means (Police and Criminal Evidence Act 1984 (c. 60), s.24):

(i) Any offence which bears a fixed penalty (*e.g.* murder);

(ii) Any offence for which a first offender of 21 or more could be sent to prison for five or more years; and,

(iii) Any offence specifically identified as such.

It would seem, therefore, that the Ground could now be used in the difficult case—regrettably not as uncommon as it ought to be—where violent offences (including murders) are carried out on council estates, where there can be extreme disquiet or distress on the part of the victim, and the victim's family and friends, if the family of the guilty person is allowed to remain in the vicinity. While its use in such cases cannot be in doubt, it is submitted that in lesser cases, not involving drugs (the purpose of the extension), the "reasonableness" override should mean that eviction is far from automatic (at least, on a first offence).

New ground of domestic violence: secure tenancies

145. After Ground 2 in Schedule 2 to the Housing Act 1985 (as substituted by section 144) insert—

"*Ground 2A*

The dwelling-house was occupied (whether alone or with others) by a married couple or a couple living together as husband and wife and—

(a) one or both of the partners is a tenant of the dwelling-house,

(b) one partner has left because of violence or threats of violence by the other towards—

(i) that partner, or

(ii) a member of the family of that partner who was residing with that partner immediately before the partner left, and

(c) the court is satisfied that the partner who has left is unlikely to return.".

GENERAL NOTE

Another major problem which came to the fore in the 1990s was that of domestic breakdown and continued occupation of family-sized accommodation. This was a problem which arose from the grant of joint tenancies to couples who were married or living together as husband and wife, when one member left the home—commonly on account of domestic violence—but the other, as a remaining joint tenant, could continue to claim security: see Housing Act 1985, s.81, defining the tenant condition to include "… where the tenancy is a joint tenancy, that each of the joint tenants is an individual and at least one of them occupies the dwelling-house as his only or principal home").

Where the partner who quit took the children with (usually) her, the further problem was the perceived obligation to rehouse her under what became Pt. III, Housing Act 1985, *i.e.* as a homeless person, in priority need, who could not be considered homeless intentionally (*pace* issues about taking proceedings to exclude the man and/or have the tenancy transferred into her own name): see now, Pt. VII, below. In short, the net effect was all too commonly—at a time of dramatic reductions in public housing stock—the need to provide two family-sized units for one family.

Attention was first paid to this difficulty in an article in (1981) 131 New L.J. 165, where the suggestion was made that the departing joint tenant could, at common law, serve notice to quit which would bring the tenancy to an end (and with it, security of tenure), notwithstanding the want of consent of the other, remaining joint tenant. This approach was tested and upheld by the Court of Appeal in *L.B. Greenwich v. McGrady* (1982) 6 H.L.R. 36, C.A. Following a critical article in [1983] Conv. 194, the question finally found its way to the House of Lords in *L.B. Hammersmith & Fulham v. Monk* [1992] 1 A.C. 478, 24 H.L.R. 206, where it was (again) upheld.

An attempt in *Crawley B.C. v. Ure* (1995) 27 H.L.R. 524, C.A., to invoke the (limited) protection of Law of Property Act 1925, s.26, to introduce a consultation requirement (of the remaining, by the departing joint tenant) failed, on the basis—following *Monk* that, although positive in form, the act of giving notice to quit is no more than an indication of a negative decision not to continue with the periodic tenancy. In *Harrow L.B.C. v. Johnstone* (1995) 28 H.L.R. 83, C.A., however, in somewhat unusual circumstances in which a man had obtained an order against his wife, preventing her from excluding him from the property, the authority were held (by a majority) to have been in contempt of court, by interfering with the administration of justice, when seeking an order for possession on the basis of her notice to quit, and/or knowing of the injunction. (Appeal to the House of Lords is currently scheduled for November, 1996).

To the *Monk* approach has now been added a more direct route to the same end on the part of authorities, not contingent on willingness to co-operate by serving notice to quit, but conversely contingent on the court's view of reasonableness. Under the new Ground 2A (which, therefore, becomes a discretionary ground for possession—see General Note to s.144, above), possession of a dwelling-house may be sought where it was occupied whether alone or with others, by a married couple or a couple living together as husband and wife (see General Note to s.62, above), where three conditions are fulfilled:

(a) One or both of the partners is a tenant—this extends the statutory solution to the problem beyond joint tenants to apply to, and allow the eviction of, a sole tenant, *e.g.* one who has been excluded under the provisions of the Domestic Violence and Matrimonial Proceedings Act

1976, s.1 (ouster orders), on a temporary or fairly short-term basis, but which cannot be used to transfer a tenancy from one partner to another on a permanent basis (although such is available to *married* partners under s.24, Matrimonial Causes Act 1973, s.17, Matrimonial and Family Proceedings Act 1984, and under Matrimonial Homes Act 1983, s.7 and Sched. 1, and even between unmarried partners—who are both parents of the same child—under Children Act 1989, s.15 and Sched. 1).

(b) One partner has left because of the violence or threats of violence of the other towards her or him, or towards her or any member of the family (whether or not also a member of the family of the violent partner), being someone who was residing with her or him immediately before she or he left;

(c) The court is satisfied that the departing party is unlikely to return—this may be evidenced by proceedings, but need not be.

The provision is clearly attractive, insofar as it transfers to the authority a burden that has, under the *Monk* approach, been shouldered at least in part by the departing party, and which may have served to exacerbate bad relations between the parties even to the point of putting her (usually) at increased risk. There has also been some criticism that it makes her (usually) more vulnerable to the accusation by children of the relationship that she has made the father homeless, though it is unlikely that the use of this Ground by the authority would achieve any real difference in this respect.

Herein lies the rub. There is no doubt that, even though there is no obligation to provide alternative accommodation (*cf.* under-occupation by a member of the family—other than a spouse—who has succeeded to a tenancy and who is vulnerable to Ground 16, but only on the provision of suitable alternative accommodation), the availability of somewhere else to live will certainly be a major factor in reasonableness. It is not hard to see that a powerful case can be made by a man—say—that he will be homeless without accommodation, and without accommodation enough to house the children some of the time that there will be adverse effects on his relationship with them and in turn upon them.

One solution may be for "voluntary" alternative accommodation to be secured by the landlord—so far as is consistent with the allocation provisions of Pt. VI, below; even if this is likely to be smaller than the man might claim to need in such circumstances, *i.e.* to provide a part-time home for his children, given the evident intention of the provisions it may well be enough to tilt the balance. Such an offer can be made in relation to reasonableness.

The difficulty of these considerations, and the length of time that it can (still) take to bring final proceedings on for possession (not to mention the possibility that the issue of proceedings causes the remaining tenant to take legal advice, in turn leading to an awareness of rights which results in a counter-claim which might otherwise never have been pursued as a claim in its own right, and which becomes a bargaining chip within the proceedings), does suggest that there is mileage yet in *Monk*. (Nor can it be argued that it is improper in a public law sense to continue to use *Monk* merely because of the introduction of this Ground. What would be thus improper would be to fail to *consider* this Ground as an alternative; but Parliament has—with clear knowledge of the problem and [presumably] the common law solution—permitted the *Monk* principle to survive, rather than deciding to remove it).

Furthermore, the new Ground does not address the decision of the Court of Appeal in *Johnston*, above, if and so far as that decision rested not on the wife's service of the notice to quit (in contravention of the order against her), but on knowledge of the husband's injunction restraining his wife from ousting him.

Extension of ground that grant of tenancy induced by false statement

146. In Ground 5 in Schedule 2 to the Housing Act 1985 (grant of tenancy induced by false statement) for "by the tenant" substitute "by—
    (a) the tenant, or
    (b) a person acting at the tenant's instigation".

GENERAL NOTE

Housing Act 1985, Sched. 2, Ground 5, contains a ground for possession based on obtaining a tenancy by a knowingly or recklessly false statement made by a tenant (whether the only tenant or one of a number of joint tenants); this amendment extends the ground to include such a statement made by someone else on behalf of the tenant. Under Ground 5, the landlord must be *induced* to grant the tenancy by the statement, so that a statement which is patently false, or which any rational landlord would have disregarded, may not suffice. An attempt to recover possession on this ground involves a serious allegation, and will call for a correspondingly high burden of proof on the landlord's part. As to the reasonableness of an order under this Ground, see *Rushcliffe B.C. v. Watson* (1991) 24 H.L.R. 124, C.A.

The requirement is "instigation" of the tenant, so that a deceit advanced by, *e.g.* a family member (for example, as to a tenant's particular needs or problems), *without* the participation of the tenant, will not suffice. It remains to be seen whether a tenant who *knows* that the person intends to lie, and remains silent, but who has not asked that person to do so, will fall within the ground, but—it is suggested—it is more likely than not that it will do so.

Proceedings for possession or termination

147.—(1) For section 83 of the Housing Act 1985 (notice of proceedings for possession or termination) substitute—

"Proceedings for possession or termination: notice requirements

83.—(1) The court shall not entertain proceedings for the possession of a dwelling-house let under a secure tenancy or proceedings for the termination of a secure tenancy unless—
  (a) the landlord has served a notice on the tenant complying with the provisions of this section, or
  (b) the court considers it just and equitable to dispense with the requirement of such a notice.
(2) A notice under this section shall—
  (a) be in a form prescribed by regulations made by the Secretary of State,
  (b) specify the ground on which the court will be asked to make an order for the possession of the dwelling-house or for the termination of the tenancy, and
  (c) give particulars of that ground.
(3) Where the tenancy is a periodic tenancy and the ground or one of the grounds specified in the notice is Ground 2 in Schedule 2 (nuisance or other anti-social behaviour), the notice—
  (a) shall also—
      (i) state that proceedings for the possession of the dwelling-house may be begun immediately, and
      (ii) specify the date sought by the landlord as the date on which the tenant is to give up possession of the dwelling-house, and
  (b) ceases to be in force twelve months after the date so specified.
(4) Where the tenancy is a periodic tenancy and Ground 2 in Schedule 2 is not specified in the notice, the notice—
  (a) shall also specify the date after which proceedings for the possession of the dwelling-house may be begun, and
  (b) ceases to be in force twelve months after the date so specified.
(5) The date specified in accordance with subsection (3) or (4) must not be earlier than the date on which the tenancy could, apart from this Part, be brought to an end by notice to quit given by the landlord on the same date as the notice under this section.
(6) Where a notice under this section is served with respect to a secure tenancy for a term certain, it has effect also with respect to any periodic tenancy arising on the termination of that tenancy by virtue of section 86; and subsections (3) to (5) of this section do not apply to the notice.
(7) Regulations under this section shall be made by statutory instrument and may make different provision with respect to different cases or descriptions of case, including different provision for different areas.

Additional requirements in relation to certain proceedings for possession

83A.—(1) Where a notice under section 83 has been served on a tenant containing the information mentioned in subsection (3)(a) of that section, the court shall not entertain proceedings for the possession of the dwelling-house unless they are begun at a time when the notice is still in force.

(2) Where—

(a) a notice under section 83 has been served on a tenant, and

(b) a date after which proceedings may be begun has been specified in the notice in accordance with subsection (4)(a) of that section,

the court shall not entertain proceedings for the possession of the dwelling-house unless they are begun after the date so specified and at a time when the notice is still in force.

(3) Where—

(a) the ground or one of the grounds specified in a notice under section 83 is Ground 2A in Schedule 2 (domestic violence), and

(b) the partner who has left the dwelling-house as mentioned in that ground is not a tenant of the dwelling-house,

the court shall not entertain proceedings for the possession of the dwelling-house unless it is satisfied that the landlord has served a copy of the notice on the partner who has left or has taken all reasonable steps to serve a copy of the notice on that partner.

This subsection has effect subject to subsection (5).

(4) Where—

(a) Ground 2A in Schedule 2 is added to a notice under section 83 with the leave of the court after proceedings for possession are begun, and

(b) the partner who has left the dwelling-house as mentioned in that ground is not a party to the proceedings,

the court shall not continue to entertain the proceedings unless it is satisfied that the landlord has served a notice under subsection (6) on the partner who has left or has taken all reasonable steps to serve such a notice on that partner.

This subsection has effect subject to subsection (5).

(5) Where subsection (3) or (4) applies and Ground 2 in Schedule 2 (nuisance or other anti-social behaviour) is also specified in the notice under section 83, the court may dispense with the requirements as to service in relation to the partner who has left the dwelling-house if it considers it just and equitable to do so.

(6) A notice under this subsection shall—

(a) state that proceedings for the possession of the dwelling-house have begun,

(b) specify the ground or grounds on which possession is being sought, and

(c) give particulars of the ground or grounds.".

(2) In section 84 of that Act (grounds and orders for possession), for subsection (3) substitute—

"(3) Where a notice under section 83 has been served on the tenant, the court shall not make such an order on any of those grounds above unless the ground is specified in the notice; but the grounds so specified may be altered or added to with the leave of the court.

(4) Where a date is specified in a notice under section 83 in accordance with subsection (3) of that section, the court shall not make an order which requires the tenant to give up possession of the dwelling-house in question before the date so specified.".

(3) In Schedule 2 to that Act, in Ground 16, after "notice of the proceedings for possession was served under section 83" insert "(or, where no such notice was served, the proceedings for possession were begun)".

GENERAL NOTE

This section amends the provisions governing notice of seeking possession against a secure tenant under Housing Act 1985, by the substitution of a new s.83 and the addition of s.83A.

Background

The essential framework for proceedings against a secure tenant—periodic or fixed term (with power for the landlord to determine it, *e.g.* forfeiture clause, break clause)—starts with the proposition that the tenancy cannot be brought to an end by the landlord except by obtaining an order for possession from the court (Housing Act 1985, s.84): *cf.*, above, s.127. The tenancy ends on the date the court orders that possession must be given up: *ibid.*

In the case of a fixed-term secure tenancy, the position is slightly different: when the term expires, a periodic secure tenancy automatically arises, by Housing Act 1985, s.86. If forfeiture proceedings are brought during the term, then if the court would otherwise have ordered possession, it instead orders termination *of the fixed term* (*ibid.*, s.82(3)), in which case a periodic tenancy likewise arises (*ibid.*, ss.82(3), 86(1)).

First stage of proceedings—the notice of seeking possession. Before proceedings are brought either for possession of a dwelling-house let under, or for the termination of, a secure tenancy, prior notice—a notice of seeking possession, as it is known—must be served (*ibid.*, s.83): *cf.*, above, s.128. The notice has to be in a form prescribed by the Secretary of State, specify the ground on which possession or termination will be sought, and give particulars of it: Housing Act 1985, s.83(2).

The purpose is to give the tenant a "warning shot across the bows", so as to tell the tenant what the case is against him and enable him to meet it or to put matters right before proceedings are commenced: *Torridge D.C. v. Jones* (1985) 18 H.L.R. 107, C.A. In *Dudley M.B.C. v. Bailey* (1990) 22 H.L.R. 424, C.A., however, it was said that the requirement may be satisfied by a summary statement of the facts on which the landlord intends to rely; see also *Marath v. MacGillivray* (1996) 28 H.L.R. 484, C.A. A notice served without any belief in the truth of the allegations, to put pressure on a tenant to leave, *might* be considered wholly invalid: *Earl of Stradbroke v. Mitchell* [1991] 1 W.L.R. 469, C.A., under Agricultural Holdings Act 1986 (c. 5). (The court does, however, have power to allow the grounds to be altered or added to under Housing Act 1985, s.84(3): see further below.)

Where the tenancy is periodic, then the notice has to provide a date after which the proceedings can be begun, which must not be earlier than the tenancy could have been brought to an end by notice to quit, and the proceedings themselves must be begun within 12 months of that date: *ibid.*, s.82(3),(4), and see notes to s.127(4),(5), above, as to what these requirements import.

If the secure tenancy is periodic, so that the proceedings are initially for termination, then the notice—which will not have complied with the requirements of Housing Act 1985, s.82(3),(4) (and cannot comply with all of them)—none the less is a functional notice of seeking possession referable to the periodic tenancy that will arise on the termination, *i.e.* the court has the options of terminating the fixed term and allowing a periodic tenancy to arise and subsist (thus penalising the tenant by the loss of the fixed term), or the court can make an order not merely terminating the fixed term tenancy, but also ordering possession under (and thus terminating) the follow-on periodic tenancy.

Second stage of proceedings—possession proceedings. In the proceedings, the landlord has to prove one (or more) of the grounds for possession, discretionary or mandatory—see above, notes to s.144. The court may not make an order on any such grounds, however, unless the ground is specified in the notice seeking possession, but those grounds may be altered or added to with the leave of the court (Housing Act 1985, s.84(3)). This *ipso facto* includes power to alter or add to the particulars: *Camden L.B.C. v. Oppong* (1996) 28 H.L.R. 701, C.A.

New Provisions

The new provisions vary the previous position in the following ways:

(a) *Just and equitable waiver of notice seeking possession.* They introduce a general discretion to dispense with service of the notice of seeking possession if "the court considers it just and equitable" to do so—new s.83(1)(a). A similar discretion has existed under Housing Act 1988, s.8 (see further below, ss.150, 151).

It is wrong to approach the question with any preconceived idea of what is just and equitable. The position as stated in Megarry's The Rent Acts, 11th ed, Vol. 3—"Assured Tenancies", was approved by the Court of Appeal in *Kelsey Housing Association Ltd. v. King* (1995) 28 H.L.R. 270, (*i.e.* that the discretion was "... unlikely to be exercised unless the tenant has in some way become aware of the intended proceedings for possession, unless, perhaps, his misconduct has been so grave as to invite proceedings for possession, in the sense of making such proceedings so likely that he may be taken to have expected them").

(b) *Differentiation between Ground 2 and other grounds.* Where the new nuisance Ground 2 is specified in the notice of seeking possession, against a periodic tenant, then the notice has to specify a date by which the landlord wants the tenant to give up possession, which may be no earlier than the date on which the tenancy could be brought to an end by notice to quit (see notes to s.127(4),(5), above), and ceases to be in force a year after that date, rather than identifying a date after which proceedings may be commenced: new s.83(3). (The details are unchanged for other grounds—new s.83(4),(5); the position is unchanged for fixed-term tenants against whom termination is sought—new s.83(6)).

The purpose of this differentiation between Ground 2 and the other Grounds is to ensure that the provisions of s.83 cannot be used to block the new procedures available under Chap. III, below, aimed at anti-social tenants, against whom possession is likely to be sought under Ground 2. Under new s.83A(1), accordingly, while proceedings for possession on grounds other than Ground 2 cannot be entertained until after the date specified in the notice seeking possessions those on Ground 2, however, may need to be the subject of expedited proceedings, and injunctive relief, and this provision therefore cannot be used to impede them. Instead, no *order* for possession can be made requiring the tenant to give up possession before the date specified in the notice under new s.83(3), *i.e.* the date by which the landlord wants the tenant to give up possession.

(c) *Domestic violence ground.* If Ground 2A (domestic violence ground against remaining partner—see notes to s.145, above) is the ground or one of the grounds in the notice of seeking possession, and the departed partner was *not* a tenant (for if a tenant she—as it will usually be—will usually be a party, and served, in any event), the court is not to entertain the proceedings for possession unless satisfied that the landlord has served a copy of the notice on her, or has taken all reasonable steps to do so. This seems to reflect the element of Ground 2A that refers to her likelihood to return.

The like provisions apply if Ground 2A is added to the notice seeking possession with the leave of the court, under Housing Act 1985, s.84(3) (see note above): new s.83A(3).

Where Ground 2A is sought to be relied on—either originally or by addition—*and* Ground 2 is also to be relied on, however, the requirements for service on the departed partner may be dispensed with by the court if it considers it just and equitable to do so (as to which, see note above): new s.83A(4).

Subs. (2)

This substitutes a new subs. (3) and adds subs. (4) to s.83, Housing Act 1985, the effect of which is to prevent an order for possession being made before the date which the landlord identified in a case under Ground 2 as when it wanted the tenant to leave.

Subs. (3)

This amendment envisages use of the discretion in s.83(1)(b) in connection with Ground 16, Sched. 2, Housing Act 1985, *i.e.* under-occupation.

Assured tenancies

Extension of ground of nuisance or annoyance to adjoining occupiers &c

148. For Ground 14 in Schedule 2 to the Housing Act 1988 (nuisance or annoyance to adjoining occupiers etc.) substitute—

"*Ground 14*

The tenant or a person residing in or visiting the dwelling-house—
  (a)   has been guilty of conduct causing or likely to cause a nuisance or annoyance to a person residing, visiting or otherwise engaging in a lawful activity in the locality, or
  (b)   has been convicted of—
      (i)   using the dwelling-house or allowing it to be used for immoral or illegal purposes, or
     (ii)   an arrestable offence committed in, or in the locality of, the dwelling-house.".

GENERAL NOTE

See notes to s.144, above. This section makes the identical provision for assured tenancies generally (*cf.* following section).

New ground of domestic violence: assured tenancies

149. After Ground 14 in Schedule 2 to the Housing Act 1988 (as substituted by section 148) insert—

"Ground 14A

The dwelling-house was occupied (whether alone or with others) by a married couple or a couple living together as husband and wife and—
  (a) one or both of the partners is a tenant of the dwelling-house,
  (b) the landlord who is seeking possession is a registered social landlord or a charitable housing trust,
  (c) one partner has left the dwelling-house because of violence or threats of violence by the other towards—
      (i) that partner, or
      (ii) a member of the family of that partner who was residing with that partner immediately before the partner left, and
  (d) the court is satisfied that the partner who has left is unlikely to return.

For the purposes of this ground "registered social landlord" and "member of the family" have the same meaning as in Part I of the Housing Act 1996 and "charitable housing trust" means a housing trust, within the meaning of the Housing Associations Act 1985, which is a charity within the meaning of the Charities Act 1993.".

GENERAL NOTE
  See notes to s.145, above. This section makes similar provision for assured tenancies, but only for those who are registered social landlords (see s.1, above) or charitable housing trusts (defined to mean a housing trust within the meaning of the Housing Associations Act 1985 (c. 69) which is also a charity within the meaning of the Charities Act 1993 (c. 10): see notes to s.2(1), above).

Additional notice requirements: domestic violence

150. After section 8 of the Housing Act 1988 insert—

"Additional notice requirements: ground of domestic violence
  8A.—(1) Where the ground specified in a notice under section 8 (whether with or without other grounds) is Ground 14A in Schedule 2 to this Act and the partner who has left the dwelling-house as mentioned in that ground is not a tenant of the dwelling-house, the court shall not entertain proceedings for possession of the dwelling-house unless—
  (a) the landlord or, in the case of joint landlords, at least one of them has served on the partner who has left a copy of the notice or has taken all reasonable steps to serve a copy of the notice on that partner, or
  (b) the court considers it just and equitable to dispense with such requirements as to service.
  (2) Where Ground 14A in Schedule 2 to this Act is added to a notice under section 8 with the leave of the court after proceedings for possession are begun and the partner who has left the dwelling-house as mentioned in that ground is not a party to the proceedings, the court shall not continue to entertain the proceedings unless—
  (a) the landlord or, in the case of joint landlords, at least one of them has served a notice under subsection (3) below on the partner who has left or has taken all reasonable steps to serve such a notice on that partner, or
  (b) the court considers it just and equitable to dispense with the requirement of such a notice.
  (3) A notice under this subsection shall—

(a) state that proceedings for the possession of the dwelling-house have begun,

(b) specify the ground or grounds on which possession is being sought, and

(c) give particulars of the ground or grounds.".

GENERAL NOTE

The approach to the recovery of possession under assured tenancies (Housing Act 1988) is modelled on and similar to those described in the General Note to s.147, above, for secure tenancies. This section makes similar provision to that which is made for secure tenancies, requiring service of a copy of the notice seeking possession on a non-tenant partner who has left as a result of domestic violence (see also s.149, above), whether the ground is initially specified or added: see General Note to s.147, New Provisions (c).

There is no added "just and equitable" waiver of this additional requirement, where the nuisance and annoyance ground is also relied on, as applies to a secure tenancy under new s.83A(4). This is not because of the general power to waive the requirement for notice under Housing Act 1988, s.8(1), as whether or not to waive the notice altogether is an entirely different question from whether or not to waive the requirement to serve a copy of it on the non-tenant, departed partner, but is *either* because the 1988 Act is applicable *both* to registered social landlords (who can avail themselves of the new powers in Chap. III, below) *and* other, conventionally termed "private" landlords, *or* oversight (given that s.8, Housing Act 1988, is itself amended to accommodate Chap. III).

Early commencement of certain proceedings for possession

151.—(1) Section 8 of the Housing Act 1988 (notice of proceedings for possession) is amended as follows.

(2) In subsection (1)(a) for the words "subsections (3) and (4)" substitute "subsections (3) to (4B)".

(3) In subsection (3)(b) for the words from "which," to "of the notice" substitute "in accordance with subsections (4) to (4B) below".

(4) For subsection (4) substitute—

"(4) If a notice under this section specifies in accordance with subsection (3)(a) above Ground 14 in Schedule 2 to this Act (whether with or without other grounds), the date specified in the notice as mentioned in subsection (3)(b) above shall not be earlier than the date of the service of the notice.

(4A) If a notice under this section specifies in accordance with subsection (3)(a) above, any of Grounds 1, 2, 5 to 7, 9 and 16 in Schedule 2 to this Act (whether without other grounds or with any ground other than Ground 14), the date specified in the notice as mentioned in subsection (3)(b) above shall not be earlier than—

(a) two months from the date of service of the notice; and

(b) if the tenancy is a periodic tenancy, the earliest date on which, apart from section 5(1) above, the tenancy could be brought to an end by a notice to quit given by the landlord on the same date as the date of service of the notice under this section.

(4B) In any other case, the date specified in the notice as mentioned in subsection (3)(b) above shall not be earlier than the expiry of the period of two weeks from the date of the service of the notice.".

GENERAL NOTE

This section amends the Housing Act 1988 requirement for notice seeking possession, which is similar to that applicable under Housing Act 1985, s.83 (although contains a two-month minimum period between service of the notice and the commencement of proceedings when those proceedings are on certain, specified grounds), so as to accord with the changes to that section to reflect the added powers in Chap. III, below, *i.e.* increased powers against anti-social tenants, using Ground 14 under the 1988 Act (see s.140, above): see above, s.147, General Note, New Provisions (b).

CHAPTER III

INJUNCTIONS AGAINST ANTI-SOCIAL BEHAVIOUR

Power to grant injunctions against anti-social behaviour

152.—(1) The High Court or a county court may, on an application by a local authority, grant an injunction prohibiting a person from—

(a) engaging in or threatening to engage in conduct causing or likely to cause a nuisance or annoyance to a person residing in, visiting or otherwise engaging in a lawful activity in residential premises to which this section applies or in the locality of such premises,

(b) using or threatening to use residential premises to which this section applies for immoral or illegal purposes, or

(c) entering residential premises to which this section applies or being found in the locality of any such premises.

(2) This section applies to residential premises of the following descriptions—

(a) dwelling-houses held under secure or introductory tenancies from the local authority;

(b) accommodation provided by that authority under Part VII of this Act or Part III of the Housing Act 1985 (homelessness).

(3) The court shall not grant an injunction under this section unless it is of the opinion that—

(a) the respondent has used or threatened to use violence against any person of a description mentioned in subsection (1)(a), and

(b) there is a significant risk of harm to that person or a person of a similar description if the injunction is not granted.

(4) An injunction under this section may—

(a) in the case of an injunction under subsection (1)(a) or (b), relate to particular acts or to conduct, or types of conduct, in general or to both, and

(b) in the case of an injunction under subsection (1)(c), relate to particular premises or a particular locality;

and may be made for a specified period or until varied or discharged.

(5) An injunction under this section may be varied or discharged by the court on an application by—

(a) the respondent, or

(b) the local authority which made the original application.

(6) The court may attach a power of arrest to one or more of the provisions of an injunction which it intends to grant under this section.

(7) The court may, in any case where it considers that it is just and convenient to do so, grant an injunction under this section, or vary such an injunction, even though the respondent has not been given such notice of the proceedings as would otherwise be required by rules of court.

If the court does so, it must afford the respondent an opportunity to make representations relating to the injunction or variation as soon as just and convenient at a hearing of which notice has been given to all the parties in accordance with rules of court.

(8) In this section "local authority" has the same meaning as in the Housing Act 1985.

DEFINITIONS
  "harm": s.157.
  "introductory tenancy": s.230.
  "local authority": subs. (8).
  "secure tenancy": s.230.
  "tenancy": s.229.

GENERAL NOTE

This is the third limb of the attack on anti-social conduct, and follows a move that gained popularity amongst local authorities from about 1994, to combat nuisance and other activity, particularly amongst young people, often in gangs, on local authority estates, by means of injunctions sought—usually—under a variety of provisions, including tenancy agreements, s.222, Local Government Act 1972 (c. 70), actions for trespass as landowner, nuisance, duties under the Race Relations Act 1976 (c. 74), s.71, and the fall-back powers of s.111, Local Government Act 1972 related to the management of land held under Housing Act 1985, Pt. II.

This section is designed to provide an express power which obviates the need to rely on other powers—such as those cited—which were not originally intended for this use, and in relation to which it has been considered possible that some difficulties of application might arise: (*Hansard* (H.L.), July 10, 1996, Report Stage, Lord Lucas (Government Whip), col. 429). Only a local authority can apply for such an injunction, not, *e.g.* a registered social landlord (who may, none the less, be able to apply for an order as landlord—see following section), but any local authority may do so (therefore, including a county council with some housing of their own).

Orders. The orders available—referable to specific acts, or general conduct or types of conduct, and to either specific premises or a locality (subs. (4))—are (subss. (1), (2)):

(a) To prevent a person from engaging in conduct causing, or likely to cause, a nuisance or annoyance to a person residing in, visiting, or otherwise engaging in a lawful activity in residential premises held under secure or introductory tenants from the local authority (*i.e.* the local authority seeking the order), or other accommodation provided by that authority under Pt. VII (or the predecessor, homelessness provisions of Pt. III, Housing Act 1985), *i.e.* the same sort of conduct that is covered by the new Ground 2, see s.144, above—see notes thereto; or

(b) Using or threatening to use the same category of residential premises (held under secure or introductory tenancies granted by the authority seeking the order, or provided by that authority under homelessness powers), for immoral or illegal purposes (also see notes to s.144, above); or

(c) Entering the same category of residential premises or being found in their locality.

It was considered and intended that causing damage to property would be comprised within the term "causing a nuisance": (*Hansard* (H.L.), July 10, 1996, Report Stage, Lord Lucas (Government Whip), col. 430).

Preconditions. The preconditions are (subs. (3)):

(1) The respondent either has used or has threatened to use violence against a person residing in, visiting or otherwise engaging in a lawful activity in residential premises within the section; and,

(2) That there is a significant risk of harm to that person, *or to a person of a similar description* (*e.g.* other tenants, children on an estate, persons of a particular ethnic origin, landlords' employees, postmen, milkmen, etc.) if the injunction is not granted: "harm" here means (s.158) ill-treatment, or the impairment of the physical or mental health of a person of 18 or more, and the ill-treatment (including sexual abuse and non-physical forms of ill-treatment), or impairment of the physical or mental health or development, of a child.

Principles. See *American Cyanamid Co. v. Ethicon* [1975] A.C. 396, H.L. Generally, the central issue is balance of convenience, to which a number of other considerations will be relevant, including whether damages would be a sufficient remedy, whether more harm will be done by withholding than granting the remedy, and whether there is a serious issue to be tried; see also *Love v. Herrity* (1990) 23 H.L.R. 217, C.A.). The prevention of irreparable damage will clearly justify use of the power (*Kent C.C. v. Batchelor* (1976) 75 L.G.R. 151, under Local Government Act 1972, s.222), as will the need for emergency action (*A.G. v. Chaudry* [1971] 1 W.L.R. 1614, under *ibid.*).

Undertaking in damages. In general, an authority will not be required to give an undertaking in damages (*i.e.* should entitlement to the injunction not be established, or should it cause harm beyond its purview), although there is a discretion to do so if there are special circumstances to justify such an order (and even so, it will remain in the discretion of the court, to which whether or not such an undertaking has been asked for may be relevant): *Coventry C.C. v. Finnie, The Times,* May 2, 1996, 29 H.L.R. forthcoming.

Ancillary provisions. The order can subsequently be varied or discharged on the application of either party: subs. (5). The order can be in whole or part subject to a power of arrest (see following sections): subs. (6). The order may be granted *ex parte*, where just and convenient to do so (*e.g.* where to give notice might provoke the very harm it is sought to avert), although the respondent must then have an opportunity to make representations at an *inter partes* hearing as soon as just and convenient: subs. (7). (This does not mean that there must *be* such an *inter partes* hearing; accordingly, the common practice of making an *ex parte* order with liberty to apply—usually on specific notice—will suffice, and will avoid the problem of costly and unnecessary hearings where, simply, there is nothing needed to be done.)

See also s.154, below, specifying criteria for the award of an *ex parte* order.

Review. In all cases, the decision of the authority to seek an injunction is likely to be reviewable on conventional principles of public law (as to which, notes to s.1, above, s.204, below): see *Stoke-on-Trent C.C. v. B. & Q. (Retail) Ltd.* [1984] 1 A.C. 754, H.L. On such an issue, the propriety of the conduct will be tested as at the date of issue of the writ, rather than the relevant resolution to issue the proceedings: *Waverley B.C. v. Hilden* [1988] 1 W.L.R. 246.

Power of arrest for breach of other injunctions against anti-social behaviour

153.—(1) In the circumstances set out in this section, the High Court or a county court may attach a power of arrest to one or more of the provisions of an injunction which it intends to grant in relation to a breach or anticipated breach of the terms of a tenancy.

(2) The applicant is—
(a) a local housing authority,
(b) a housing action trust,
(c) a registered social landlord, or
(d) a charitable housing trust,
acting in its capacity as landlord of the premises which are subject to the tenancy.

(3) The respondent is the tenant or a joint tenant under the tenancy agreement.

(4) The tenancy is one by virtue of which—
(a) a dwelling-house is held under an introductory, secure or assured tenancy, or
(b) accommodation is provided under Part VII of this Act or Part III of the Housing Act 1985 (homelessness).

(5) The breach or anticipated breach of the terms of the tenancy consists of the respondent—
(a) engaging in or threatening to engage in conduct causing or likely to cause a nuisance or annoyance to a person residing, visiting or otherwise engaging in a lawful activity in the locality,
(b) using or threatening to use the premises for immoral or illegal purposes, or
(c) allowing any sub-tenant or lodger of his or any other person residing (whether temporarily or otherwise) on the premises or visiting them to act as mentioned in paragraph (a) or (b).

(6) The court is of the opinion that—
(a) the respondent or any person mentioned in subsection (5)(c) has used or threatened violence against a person residing, visiting or otherwise engaging in a lawful activity in the locality, and
(b) there is a significant risk of harm to that person or a person of a similar description if the power of arrest is not attached to one or more provisions of the injunction immediately.

(7) Nothing in this section prevents the grant of an injunction relating to other matters, in addition to those mentioned above, in relation to which no power of arrest is attached.

DEFINITIONS
"assured tenancy": s.230.
"charitable housing trust": s.157.
"harm": s.157.
"housing action trust": s.230.
"introductory tenancy": s.230.
"local housing authority": s.230.
"registered social landlord": s.1.

"secure tenancy": s.230.
"tenancy": s.229.

GENERAL NOTE
Without prejudice to the power to grant an injunction to which no power of arrest attaches
(subs. (7)), the power is to attach a power of arrest to an injunction which falls within the section:
as to the powers of arrest (and otherwise) that flow from this, see ss.155, 156, below. If no power
of arrest is attached when the order is first made, it may be applied for later: see s.155(3). The
power of arrest may be for a shorter period than the injunction itself: s.157.

A power of arrest should not be regarded as a routine remedy; it is for exceptional situations,
useful where there is persistent disobedience to orders, but not routinely to be added to an order
or injunction: see *Lewis v. Lewis* [1978] Fam. 60, C.A. Another way of putting the point is that it
is additional to the protection of the order itself. A court will be unlikely to attach a power of
arrest if the incidents justifying it are some time ago: *Horner v. Horner* [1982] Fam. 90, C.A. (nine
months since last actual violence). Where an undertaking is accepted in lieu of an injunction, no
power of arrest will be available. If, however, the undertaking is broken, the court will still have
its inherent powers, including in an appropriate case to commit for contempt.

Subss. (2), (4)
This section applies only to injunctions which it is intended to grant in relation to a breach or
anticipated breach of the terms of a tenancy. It is clearly wide enough to include *ex parte* and
other interlocutory injunctions (see notes to s.152, above).

Unless a landlord covenants with other tenants of an estate or block to enforce the terms of a
tenancy, there is no *obligation* on the part of a landlord to take injunctive (or other, *e.g.* possession) proceedings: see *O'Leary v. L.B. Islington* (1983) 9 H.L.R. 81, C.A.

Under this section, the injunctive proceedings must be those brought by one of the stated
landlords, "acting in its capacity as landlord of the premises which are subject to the tenancy", so
excluding other grounds, such as nuisance to neighbouring land in the landlord's ownership. The
proceedings must be against the tenant, or a joint tenant, which is an introductory, secure or
assured tenancy, or else of accommodation provided pursuant to Pt. VII, below (or the predecessor provisions governing homelessness, Pt. III, Housing Act 1985). Tenancy includes licence:
s.158.

It merits comment that a power of arrest is not available in relation to a requirement
attached—commonly, as a condition of occupation in a schedule—to a long lease, or indeed
attached as a covenant to a freehold sale: accordingly, if miscreants are or include persons who
have exercised the right to buy, they—or their children—would appear to be exempt; while of
course owner-occupation (under long lease or freehold) is intended to enjoy additional benefits,
this is a somewhat surprising incidental accrual to its value.

Subs. (5)
There are two categories of conduct which comprise the breach or anticipated breach, which
fall within the ambit of the discretionary grounds for possession available against secure tenants
and assured tenants, as amended by this Act:
(a) *Causing or likely to cause a nuisance or annoyance.* See notes to s.144, above; or,
(b) *Using or threatening to use the premises for immoral or illegal purposes*—also see notes to
s.144, above.
(c) *Allowing nuisance, annoyance or immoral or illegal purposes.* In addition, the conduct may
be comprised of the tenant, or a joint tenant, "allowing" any sub-tenant, lodger or other person residing on the premises, or visiting them, to act in either way: "allowing" includes both
the positive act of giving permission, and the omission to take steps to prevent an act which the
tenant could have taken to prevent the conduct in question—*Commercial General Administration Ltd. v. Thomsett* (1979) 250 E.G. 547, C.A.; see also *Kensington & Chelsea R.B.C. v.
Simmonds, The Times,* July 15, 1996, 29 H.L.R. forthcoming, C.A. (see notes to s.144, above).
In substance, this brings the grounds for an injunction into line with the new Ground 2: see
s.144, above.
The inclusion of sub-tenants, lodgers, or others—and of persons residing temporarily or
otherwise—and of person merely visiting them—should take most technical issues out of the
case: the one obvious, and likely to be common, defence will be that of the absentee tenant
who has been wholly ignorant of the conduct in question.

Subs. (6)
The court cannot attach a power of arrest unless satisfied *both* that the tenant, joint tenant, or
other person who has committed the act in question, has used or threatened violence against a
person residing, visiting or engaged in a lawful activity in the vicinity, *and* that there is a significant risk of harm to that person "or a person of a similar description" (*e.g.* other tenants, the

children of an estate or area, elderly people, people from particular ethnic groups, service-providers, landlord's employees, etc.), unless the power of arrest is attached.

Powers of arrest: ex-parte applications for injunctions

154.—(1) In determining whether to exercise its power under section 152(6) or section 153 to attach a power of arrest to an injunction which it intends to grant on an ex-parte application, the High Court or a county court shall have regard to all the circumstances including—

    (a) whether it is likely that the applicant will be deterred or prevented from seeking the exercise of the power if the power is not exercised immediately, and

    (b) whether there is reason to believe that the respondent is aware of the proceedings for the injunction but is deliberately evading service and that the applicant or any person of a description mentioned in 152(1)(a) or section 153(5)(a) (as the case may be) will be seriously prejudiced if the decision as to whether to exercise the power were delayed until substituted service is effected.

(2) Where the court exercises its power as mentioned in subsection (1), it shall afford the respondent an opportunity to make representations relating to the exercise of the power as soon as just and convenient at a hearing of which notice has been given to all the parties in accordance with rules of court.

GENERAL NOTE

"*Ex parte* injunctions should, in general, only be made where there are strong grounds to justify such an application, where there is real urgency and impossibility of giving notice. It will often be preferable to abridge time and the respondent may attend on short notice…": *per* Butler-Sloss L.J., *Wookey v. Wookey, Re. S (a minor)* [1991] Fam. 121, C.A., at p.131/B–D.

This section codifies the underlying principle that a court will always have regard to all the circumstances, but emphasises (notwithstanding the wording "including") the two stated criteria, whether the applicant will be "deterred or prevented" from seeking an order (*e.g.* because witnesses will be intimidated, or will leave an area in fear) or whether the respondent is aware of the proceedings but is evading service, with serious prejudice to any of those living in, visiting or otherwise engaged in a lawful activity in or in the vicinity of premises held under an introductory, secure or assured tenancy, or accommodation provided to the homeless, *i.e.* the principal victims intended to be protected by these provisions.

Subs. (2)
See note on Ancillary Provisions in notes to s.152, above.

Arrest and remand

155.—(1) If a power of arrest is attached to certain provisions of an injunction by virtue of section 152(6) or section 153, a constable may arrest without warrant a person whom he has reasonable cause for suspecting to be in breach of any such provision or otherwise in contempt of court in relation to a breach of any such provision.

A constable shall after making any such arrest forthwith inform the person on whose application the injunction was granted.

(2) Where a person is arrested under subsection (1)—

    (a) he shall be brought before the relevant judge within the period of 24 hours beginning at the time of his arrest, and

    (b) if the matter is not then disposed of forthwith, the judge may remand him.

In reckoning for the purposes of this subsection any period of 24 hours no account shall be taken of Christmas Day, Good Friday or any Sunday.

(3) If the court has granted an injunction in circumstances such that a power of arrest could have been attached under section 152(6) or section 153 but—

    (a) has not attached a power of arrest under the section in question to any

provisions of the injunction, or
(b) has attached that power only to certain provisions of the injunction,
then, if at any time the applicant considers that the respondent has failed to
comply with the injunction, he may apply to the relevant judge for the issue of
a warrant for the arrest of the respondent.

(4) The relevant judge shall not issue a warrant on an application under
subsection (3) unless—
(a) the application is substantiated on oath, and
(b) he has reasonable grounds for believing that the respondent has failed
to comply with the injunction.

(5) If a person is brought before a court by virtue of a warrant issued under
subsection (4) and the court does not dispose of the matter forthwith, the
court may remand him.

(6) Schedule 15 (which makes provision corresponding to that applying in
magistrates' courts in civil cases under sections 128 and 129 of the Magistrates' Courts Act 1980) applies in relation to the powers of the High Court
and a county court to remand a person under this section.

(7) If a person remanded under this section is granted bail by virtue of
subsection (6), he may be required by the relevant judge to comply, before
release on bail or later, with such requirements as appear to the judge to be
necessary to secure that he does not interfere with witnesses or otherwise
obstruct the course of justice.

DEFINITION
"relevant judge": s.158.

GENERAL NOTE
Where there is a breach of an order backed by a power of arrest under ss.152 or 153, the person
responsible may be arrested without warrant: the same is true of anyone else who is in contempt
of the order, even though the order was not directed at him (see *A.G. v. Leveller Magazine Ltd.*
[1979] A.C. 440, H.L.), *e.g.* a person aiding the breach or facilitating it or even who in some way
relies upon it, a concept that can be extremely widely applied: see (for an extreme example,
where a local authority was described as being in contempt in relation to an order against a wife
not to exclude her husband from the matrimonial home, by seeking possession on the basis of
her subsequent notice to quit their joint tenancy) *Harrow L.B.C. v. Johnstone* (1995) 28 H.L.R.
83, C.A.
    See, generally, *A.G. v. Butterworth* [1963] 1 Q.B. 696, C.A. at p.723, *per* Donovan L.J.:
    "The question to be decided here, as in all cases of alleged contempt, is whether the action
complained of is calculated to interfere with the proper administration of justice. There is
more than one way of so interfering. The authority of a court may be lowered by scurrilous
abuse. Its effectiveness to do justice may be diminished or destroyed in a pending case by
frightening intending witnesses from the witness box. After giving evidence a witness may be
punished for having done so, thereby deterring potential witnesses in future cases from risking
a like vengeance. I see no such difference between any of these three methods as makes the
first two contempt of court, and the third not. Each is calculated to do the same thing, namely,
to interfere with the proper administration of the law in courts of justice".
    Once an arrest has been effected, the applicant for the injunction must be informed.
    The person arrested must be brought before another judge of the High Court if that is where
the order was made, or a judge or district judge of the county court if that is where the order was
made (see s.160) within 24 hours (excluding Christmas Day, Good Friday or any Sunday). If at
that point the matter is not "disposed of", *i.e.* by imprisonment, sequestration or fine, the judge
can remand him, either in custody (to appear before the court at a later date) or on bail (on own
recognisance or with sureties—with provision for remand in custody until sureties can be taken):
Sched. 15, para. 2, below. These powers are exercisable on every occasion when the person
arrested is brought back for further remand: *ibid.*, para. 3.
    Remand in custody cannot be for more than eight days (unless adjourned for a medical report,
in which case it can be for up to three weeks at a time: s.149, below), and if for not more than
three days can be in police custody: *ibid.*, para. 4. If the person remanded cannot be brought back
by reason of illness or accident, then he can be further remanded (without express limit of time):
ibid., para. 5. If remanded on bail, the remand can be subject to additional conditions to secure
non-interference with witnesses or obstruction of the course of justice: subs. (7).
    Where the judge considers that a medical report will be needed, his powers of remand may be

exercised in order to enable a medical examination and report to be made: see s.156.

Constable. Any and every police officer holds the office of constable (*Lewis v. Cattle* [1938] 2 K.B. 454).

Subss. (3)–(5)
The applicant has power to apply for an arrest warrant at any time, even if the order was (or provisions of it were) not backed with a power of arrest when initially granted (or backed with a power arising in limited circumstances only), if the circumstances are such that a power of arrest could have been attached in the first place (to the injunction, or to those parts hitherto unaffected by the power of arrest), and the respondent has failed to comply with the order. Such an application must be supported by sworn evidence, whether oral or affidavit, that gives rise to a reasonable belief of non-compliance, and if the court does not dispose of the matter when the respondent is brought before it, it enjoys the same powers of remand in custody or on bail as in a case where the order (or relevant provision) was initially so backed.

Remand for medical examination and report

156.—(1) If the relevant judge has reason to consider that a medical report will be required, any power to remand a person under section 155 may be exercised for the purpose of enabling a medical examination and report to be made.

(2) If such a power is so exercised the adjournment shall not be for more than 4 weeks at a time unless the judge remands the accused in custody.

(3) If the judge so remands the accused, the adjournment shall not be for more than 3 weeks at a time.

(4) If there is reason to suspect that a person who has been arrested—
(a) under section 155(1), or
(b) under a warrant issued under section 155(4),
is suffering from mental illness or severe mental impairment, the relevant judge shall have the same power to make an order under section 35 of the Mental Health Act 1983 (remand for report on accused's mental condition) as the Crown Court has under section 35 of that Act in the case of an accused person within the meaning of that section.

DEFINITION
"relevant judge": s.158.

GENERAL NOTE
If the judge has reason to believe that a medical report is required, he can exercise the power of remand so as to allow examination and report, for no more than four weeks at a time, or three weeks if the remand is in custody. If, however, there is reason to suspect that a person brought back under either a power of arrest, or a warrant for breach, under s.155, above, is suffering from mental illness or severe mental impairment, then the judge may also make an order under s.35, Mental Health Act 1983, *i.e.* remand to hospital for a report (but only if satisfied that it would be impracticable to make such a report if the respondent was remanded on bail: *ibid.*, s.35(3)).

Such an order cannot be made unless the court is satisfied on the evidence of the registered medical practitioner who will make the report, or some other person representing managers of a hospital, that arrangements have been made for his admission to that hospital (within seven days of the order): *ibid.*, s.35(4). There can be more than one such remand (even without the respondent present, provided he is represented by solicitor or counsel: *ibid.* s.35(6)), if satisfied on the evidence of the medical practitioner that it is necessary to complete the assessment of the respondent's condition: *ibid.*, s.35(5). Remands can only be for 28 days at a time, and for a maximum of 12 weeks: *ibid.*, s.35(7). The respondent can, if he can afford to do so, obtain his own independent medical report, and apply for the remand to be terminated on the basis of it: *ibid.*, s.35(8).

Powers of arrest: supplementary provisions

157.—(1) If in exercise of its power under section 152(6) or section 153 the High Court or a county court attaches a power of arrest to any provisions of an injunction, it may provide that the power of arrest is to have effect for a shorter period than the other provisions of the injunction.

(2) Any period specified for the purposes of subsection (1) may be extended by the court (on one or more occasions) on an application to vary or discharge the injunction.

(3) If a power of arrest has been attached to certain provisions of an injunction by virtue of section 152(6) or section 153, the court may vary or discharge the injunction in so far as it confers a power of arrest (whether or not any application has been made to vary or discharge any other provision of the injunction).

(4) An injunction may be varied or discharged under subsection (3) on an application by the respondent or the person on whose application the injunction was made.

GENERAL NOTE

A power of arrest may be attached for a shorter period than the injunction itself, *e.g.* if the fear is of an immediate reaction rather than conduct in the longer term: subs. (1). The period of a power of arrest may be extended by the court, on an application either to vary the order (by the applicant for it), or to discharge it (by the respondent): subs. (2). Likewise, the power may be attached to other provisions of an order, or removed from some: subs. (3).

Interpretation: Chapter III

158.—(1) For the purposes of this Chapter—

"charitable housing trust" means a housing trust, within the meaning of the Housing Associations Act 1985, which is a charity within the meaning of the Charities Act 1993;

"child" means a person under the age of 18 years;

"harm"—

(a) in relation to a person who has reached the age of 18 years, means ill-treatment or the impairment of health, and

(b) in relation to a child, means ill-treatment or the impairment of health or development;

"health" includes physical or mental health;

"ill-treatment", in relation to a child, includes sexual abuse and forms of ill-treatment which are not physical;

"relevant judge", in relation to an injunction, means—

(a) where the injunction was granted by the High Court, a judge of that court,

(b) where the injunction was granted by a county court, a judge or district judge of that or any other county court;

"tenancy" includes a licence, and "tenant" and "landlord" shall be construed accordingly.

(2) Where the question of whether harm suffered by a child is significant turns on the child's health or development, his health or development shall be compared with that which could reasonably be expected of a similar child.

GENERAL NOTE

Tenancy. The extension to licence is of particular relevance (i) to introductory and secure tenancies—see notes to s.126, above, and (ii) to accommodation provided under Pt. VII below or Pt. III, Housing Act 1985 (homeless persons).

PART VI

ALLOCATION OF HOUSING ACCOMMODATION

Introductory

INTRODUCTION

So far as their own stock is concerned, local authorities have, since Housing Act 1935, s.51, been under an obligation to "secure that in the selection of their tenants a reasonable preference is given to persons who are occupying insanitary or overcrowded houses, have large families or are living under unsatisfactory housing conditions" (as consolidated in Housing Act 1936 (c. 51), s.85(2); see also Housing Act 1957 (c. 56), s.113(2)). These "physical conditions" were supplemented by the "social criteria" of persons towards whom duties were owed under the homelessness legislation (*Hansard* (H.C.), Standing Committee G, Fifteenth Sitting, March 12, 1996, Minister for Local Government, Housing and Urban Regeneration [Mr Curry], col. 587), by amendment to Housing Act 1957, s.113, by Housing (Homeless Persons) Act 1977 (c. 48), s.6— see Housing Act 1985 (c. 68), s.22. Greater attention to social need had been forcefully advocated from 1969, in the Cullingworth Report, Council Housing—Purposes, Procedures and Priorities (9th report of Housing Management Sub-Committee of the Central Housing Advisory Committee), paras. 117, 118.

What the government seeks to achieve under this Part is to "create a single route into social housing" (*Hansard* (H.C.), Standing Committee G, Sixteenth Sitting, March 12, 1996, Minister for Local Government, Housing and Urban Regeneration [Mr Curry], col. 614), in accordance with the policy (*Our Future Homes*, White Paper, June 1995, Chap. 6) of putting "*all*" those with long term housing needs on the same footing, while providing a safety net for emergency and pressing needs". It will be "the only route into social housing allocated by local authorities; it will be dynamic, and will focus on basic underlying need rather than immediate emergency" (*Hansard* (H.C.), Standing Committee G, Fifteenth Sitting, March 12, 1996, Minister for Local Government, Housing and Urban Regeneration [Mr Curry], col. 588).

The purpose is to remove what has been perceived as an automatic priority for all those accepted as homeless under Pt. III, Housing Act 1985, and this Part is an introduction and companion to Pt. VII, below, which replaces Pt. III, 1985 Act, with a new—and much reduced—framework of duties: "We shall not go back to pre-1977 days. We shall keep the 1977 Act concepts of entitlement, homelessness, priority need, intentionality and local connection. Essentially, what we are changing is the way in which the duty is to be discharged" (*ibid.,* col. 587). "We believe it reasonable to examine whether there is a real need for permanent, subsidised accommodation—in other words a lifelong tenancy of a local authority or housing association property" (*ibid.*, col. 588).

"All hon. Members must have heard constituents argue that suitable houses were available but that 'someone else always seems to get it'..." (*ibid.*, col. 600). Particularly in mind were the "homeless at home", those who live with parents while already starting their own families, and—separately—those who postponed having children until they had accommodation (which they were significantly less likely to get without children).

According to the White Paper, over 40% of local authority new tenancies—over 80% in some London authorities—and over a quarter of allocations of housing association tenancies were going to those accepted under the homelessness legislation: "We are committed to maintaining an immediate safety net, but this should be separate from a fair system of allocating long-term accommodation... Allocation schemes should reflect the underlying values of our society. They should balance specific housing needs against the need to support married couples who take a responsible approach to family life, so that tomorrow's generation grows up in a stable home environment" (White Paper, Chap. 6 at p.36).

See also the D.O.E. Consultation Paper, Access to Local Authority and Housing Association Tenancies, January 1994, in which the principal limbs of both this Part and the next were first canvassed.

Allocation of housing accommodation

159.—(1) A local housing authority shall comply with the provisions of this Part in allocating housing accommodation.

(2) For the purposes of this Part a local housing authority allocate housing accommodation when they—

(a) select a person to be a secure or introductory tenant of housing accommodation held by them,

(b) nominate a person to be a secure or introductory tenant of housing accommodation held by another person, or

(c) nominate a person to be an assured tenant of housing accommodation held by a registered social landlord.

(3) The reference in subsection (2)(a) to selecting a person to be a secure tenant includes deciding to exercise any power to notify an existing tenant or licensee that his tenancy or licence is to be a secure tenancy.

(4) The references in subsection (2)(b) and (c) to nominating a person include nominating a person in pursuance of any arrangements (whether legally enforceable or not) to require that housing accommodation, or a

specified amount of housing accommodation, is made available to a person or one of a number of persons nominated by the authority.

(5) The provisions of this Part do not apply to the allocation of housing accommodation by a local housing authority to a person who is already—

(a) a secure or introductory tenant,

(b) an assured tenant (otherwise than under an assured shorthold tenancy) of housing accommodation held by a registered social landlord, or

(c) an assured tenant of housing accommodation allocated to him by a local housing authority.

(6) The provisions of this Part do not apply to the allocation of housing accommodation by a local housing authority to two or more persons jointly if—

(a) one or more of them is a person within subsection (5)(a), (b) or (c), and

(b) none of the others is excluded from being a qualifying person by section 161(2) or regulations under section 161(3).

(7) Subject to the provisions of this Part, a local housing authority may allocate housing accommodation in such manner as they consider appropriate.

DEFINITIONS
"assured shorthold tenant": s.230.
"assured tenant": s.230.
"introductory tenant": s.124.
"local housing authority": s.230.
"secure tenant": s.230.

GENERAL NOTE
This section imposes the fundamental obligation, which is that local housing authorities must comply with this Part when allocating housing accommodation.

Subs. (2)
This subsection contains the central definition of to what activities the requirements of this Part apply:
(a) Selecting a person to be a secure or introductory (*cf.* above, s.124) tenant, whether or not of property held under Pt. II, Housing Act 1985, but, *n.b. not* including the grant of a tenancy which is exempt from security (and, therefore, introductory status) by 1985 Act, Sched. 1 (see notes to s.124(2),(3), above).
Tenancy here includes licence—*cf.* notes to s.126, above; selection includes notifying a tenant or licensee who is not currently secure that he is to become so, *i.e.* under those provisions of Housing Act 1985 which so provide (including the new Sched. 1, para. 4, added by Sched. 14, para. 3, below, accommodation granted under Pt. VII below; see further amendments in Sched. 14, below, providing that accommodation which would automatically become secure under certain provisions of the Housing Act 1985, Sched. 1, will not—if the landlord is a local housing authority—become secure unless and until so notified, so as to bring the provisions of this Part into play: see General Note to s.173, below);
(b) Nomination (whether or not pursuant to an agreement) of a person to be the secure or introductory tenant (or licensee) of another, *e.g.* housing action trust;
(c) Nomination of a person to be an assured tenant of a registered social landlord (again, therefore, not including nomination to a tenancy that will not be assured under Housing Act 1988, Sched. 1, *e.g.* high rateable value tenancies, tenancies at a low rent, agricultural land, lettings to students, but *including* an assured shorthold—see notes to s.10(1), above, *cf.* below, subs. (5)).

Subs. (4)
These provisions reflect long-standing arrangements with housing associations, whereby funding under what has become s.58, Housing Associations Act 1985 (c. 69) (see above, General Note to s.22) has been conditional on the right to nominate a proportion (or even all) of the tenants to a particular property, or to the stock of an association. The exercise of such a nomination arrangement—whether or not legally binding, *i.e.* whether or not pursuant to contract or under deed—constitutes allocation for the purposes of this Part, but because the definition is inclusive, so also will be a nomination pursuant to a voluntary arrangement.

Subs. (5)

This provision exempts from the allocation provisions of this Part allocation to anyone who is *already* a secure or introductory tenant (of whomever), or an assured tenant (not including an assured shorthold tenant) held from a registered social landlord, or an assured tenant of accommodation allocated by a local housing authority, *e.g.* under a nomination arrangement with a body which is not a registered social landlord, or perhaps pursuant to arrangements under Pt. VII, below. The purpose is to provide for "transfers between authorities outside the framework of the housing register": (*Hansard* (H.C.), Standing Committee G, Sixteenth Sitting, March 12, 1996, Minister for Local Government, Housing and Urban Regeneration [Mr Curry], col. 603) (see Sched. 18, para. 2, below).

Subs. (6)

This provision "allow[s] existing tenants to become joint tenants without having to go through the housing register and the allocation process": (*Hansard* (H.C.), April 30, 1996, Report Stage, (Minister for Local Government, Housing and Urban Regeneration [Mr Curry], col. 1026). It only applies, however, provided that at least one of the tenants would be protected by subs. (5), and none of the tenants is excluded by s.161(2) (persons subject to immigration control, see notes below), or s.161(3) (disqualification pursuant to regulations).

Cases where provisions about allocation do not apply

160.—(1) The provisions of this Part about the allocation of housing accommodation do not apply in the following cases.

(2) They do not apply where a secure tenancy—

(a) vests under section 89 of the Housing Act 1985 (succession to periodic secure tenancy on death of tenant),

(b) remains a secure tenancy by virtue of section 90 of that Act (devolution of term certain of secure tenancy on death of tenant),

(c) is assigned under section 92 of that Act (assignment of secure tenancy by way of exchange),

(d) is assigned to a person who would be qualified to succeed the secure tenant if the secure tenant died immediately before the assignment, or

(e) vests or is otherwise disposed of in pursuance of an order made under—

(i) section 24 of the Matrimonial Causes Act 1973 (property adjustment orders in connection with matrimonial proceedings),

(ii) section 17(1) of the Matrimonial and Family Proceedings Act 1984 (property adjustment orders after overseas divorce, &c.), or

(iii) paragraph 1 of Schedule 1 to the Children Act 1989 (orders for financial relief against parents).

(3) They do not apply where an introductory tenancy—

(a) becomes a secure tenancy on ceasing to be an introductory tenancy,

(b) vests under section 133(2) (succession to introductory tenancy on death of tenant),

(c) is assigned to a person who would be qualified to succeed the introductory tenant if the introductory tenant died immediately before the assignment, or

(d) vests or is otherwise disposed of in pursuance of an order made under—

(i) section 24 of the Matrimonial Causes Act 1973 (property adjustment orders in connection with matrimonial proceedings),

(ii) section 17(1) of the Matrimonial and Family Proceedings Act 1984 (property adjustment orders after overseas divorce, &c.), or

(iii) paragraph 1 of Schedule 1 to the Children Act 1989 (orders for financial relief against parents).

(4) They do not apply in such other cases as the Secretary of State may prescribe by regulations.

(5) The regulations may be framed so as to make the exclusion of the provisions of this Part about the allocation of housing accommodation subject to

such restrictions or conditions as may be specified.

In particular, those provisions may be excluded—

    (a) in relation to specified descriptions of persons, or

    (b) in relation to housing accommodation of a specified description or a specified proportion of housing accommodation of any specified description.

DEFINITIONS

"assured tenant": s.230.

"introductory tenant": s.124.

"local housing authority": s.230.

"secure tenant": s.230.

GENERAL NOTE

This section dis-applies this Part in a number of cases, additional to those governed by s.159(5), *i.e.* transfers between authorities. The categories of case to which the allocation restrictions are irrelevant are as follows:

(a) Succession to secure tenancy on death, or devolution of a fixed term in such circumstances that the tenancy remains secure, *cf.* notes to s.129, above;

(b) Assignment by way of exchange of secure tenancy or to a person who could have succeeded to the tenancy, *cf.* notes to s.134, above;

(c) Transfers of secure or introductory tenancies under the provisions of matrimonial and related domestic legislation, *cf.* notes to s.145, above;

(d) Becoming a secure tenant after an introductory tenancy, *cf.* notes to s.125, above;

(e) Succession to introductory tenancy, *cf.* s.133, above;

(f) Assignment of introductory tenancy to a person who could have succeeded to it, *cf.* s.134, above.

Subss. (4), (5)

The Secretary of State has power to prescribe other categories of allocation which will fall outside this Part, subject to restrictions or conditions, including by reference to a specific category or proportion of housing.

The housing register

Allocation only to qualifying persons

161.—(1) A local housing authority shall allocate housing accommodation only to persons ("qualifying persons") who are qualified to be allocated housing accommodation by that authority.

(2) A person subject to immigration control within the meaning of the Asylum and Immigration Act 1996 is not qualified to be allocated housing accommodation by any authority in England and Wales unless he is of a class prescribed by regulations made by the Secretary of State.

(3) The Secretary of State may by regulations prescribe other classes of persons who are, or are not, qualifying persons in relation to local housing authorities generally or any particular local housing authority.

(4) Subject to subsection (2) and any regulations under subsection (3) a local housing authority may decide what classes of persons are, or are not, qualifying persons.

(5) The prohibition in subsection (1) extends to the allocation of housing accommodation to two or more persons jointly if any of them is excluded from being a qualifying person by subsection (2) or regulations under subsection (3).

(6) The prohibition does not otherwise extend to the allocation of housing accommodation to two or more persons jointly if one or more of them are qualifying persons.

DEFINITION

"local housing authority": s.230.

GENERAL NOTE

This section governs who are qualifying persons to whom housing may be allocated: for the principles on which priority between them will be determined, see s.169, below. Subject to the singular statutory disqualification of persons subject to immigration control, which may itself be overridden by regulations, who is entitled to be treated as a qualifying person, or is debarred from being so treated, is something which may be the subject of regulation by the Secretary of State: subs. (2). Subject thereto, however, the authority enjoy freedom to award or withhold qualification for themselves.

There is, accordingly, no general principle that *anyone* is entitled to register (*cf. R. v. Wolverhampton M.B.C., ex p. Watters, The Times,* June 11, 1996, 28 H.L.R. forthcoming, Q.B.D., and *R. v. Canterbury City Council, ex p. Gillespie* (1986) 19 H.L.R. 7), although there was an "instinctive" view on the part of the government that concurred with the intention that "every individual will have a right to be on some housing register somewhere" (*Hansard* (H.C.), Standing Committee G, Sixteenth Sitting, March 12, 1996, col. 623, *per* Mr Betts for the Opposition, and the Minister for Local Government, Housing and Urban Regeneration [Mr Curry]).

Subs. (2)

It was throughout, the intention that "certain categories of persons from abroad should not be allowed to appear on housing registers. These will cover persons excluded from entitlement to housing benefit... Asylum seekers will also be excluded...": *ibid.*, paras. 12, 13. As originally drafted, the Bill did not include subs. (2), and this intention was to be reflected in regulations. The decision in *R. v. Secretary of State for Social Security, ex p. Re B & Joint Council for the Welfare of Immigrants* (1996) *The Times,* July 10, 1996, 29 H.L.R. forthcoming, C.A., however, meant that exclusions had to be effected by primary legislation, which is now to be found in this subsection: see notes to s.185, below.

Subs. (3)

"The Government is clear that households accepted as statutorily homeless and accommodated by an authority outside that authority's area must be entitled to appear on the register of the authority which has rehoused them... There is a case for giving everyone accommodated under the new homelessness duty the right to appear on the register of the authority that accepts the duty towards them": D.O.E. Consultation Paper linked to the Housing Bill, Allocation of Housing Accommodation by Local Authorities, January 1996, para. 10.

Subs. (4)

This section provides for discretionary qualification and disqualification: see Consultation Paper, para. 9—"The Government is aware that some authorities may wish to set their own conditions... Some authorities currently set conditions that apply to the applicant's age, marital status, ownership of other property, local connection with or length of residence in the area, absence of a record of rent arrears or of evidence of causing a nuisance...".

Subss. (5), (6)

If a person is *disqualified*, then the authority are not permitted to allocate a tenancy to him, even jointly with someone else who *is* qualified; but if only one person is qualified, and the other, while not qualified is not disqualified either, then the grant can be to both jointly.

The housing register

162.—(1) Every local housing authority shall establish and maintain a register of qualifying persons (their "housing register").

(2) An authority's housing register may be kept in such form as the authority think fit.

(3) It may, in particular, be kept as part of a register maintained for other housing purposes or maintained in common by the authority and one or more other landlords, provided the entries constituting the authority's housing register can be distinguished.

(4) An authority's housing register shall contain such information about the persons on it and other relevant matters as the Secretary of State may prescribe by regulations.

(5) Subject to any such regulations, the authority may decide what information is to be contained in the register.

DEFINITIONS
   "local housing authority": s.230.
   "qualifying person": s.161.

GENERAL NOTE

Each local housing authority must establish and maintain a housing register, which they may keep in such form as they think fit, including as part of a broader register, kept for other purposes, *e.g.* local taxation or electoral, provided that the elements constituting the housing register can be distinguished; it may also be kept as part of a register held in common between the authority and another landlord or other landlords, *e.g.* local registered social landlords, or even a single such landlord to whom it may be that the bulk or all of the authority's stock has been transferred.

The register must, however, record those details which may be prescribed by regulations, "not only about the applicant but also about members of his household and the circumstances in which he lives" (*Hansard* (H.L.), July 17, 1996, col. 916, Minister of State, Department of the Environment [Earl Ferrers]). "The kind of detail that would be on the register would be whether the person is married; whether he or she has children; and whether he or she may be unwell and need somebody to look after them. Those are the sorts of matters which will be held on the housing register. A prison sentence does not come into it, as far as I know" (*ibid.*, cols. 916–917).

The duty to keep the register is independent of whether or not the authority have any stock of their own.

The idea of registers in common was considered in the White Paper, *Our Future Homes*, Chap. 6, where it was recognised that "Now that housing associations are the main providers of new social housing, there is a clear case for bringing the allocation of local authority and housing association tenancies together on the same footing. The Government, therefore, welcomes the emerging interest in common housing registers being shown by local authorities and housing associations. It is clear, however, that these should be voluntary enterprises, established by mutual agreement...".

Operation of housing register

163.—(1) A person shall be put on a local housing authority's housing register if he applies to be put on and it appears to the authority that he is a qualifying person.

(2) A local housing authority may put a person on their housing register without any application, if it appears to them that he is a qualifying person.

(3) When a local housing authority put a person on their housing register (on his application or otherwise), they shall notify him that they have done so.

(4) A local housing authority may amend an entry on their housing register in such circumstances as they think fit.

If they do so, they shall notify the person concerned of the amendment.

(5) A local housing authority may remove a person from their housing register in such circumstances as they think fit.

(6) They shall do so—

  (a) if it appears to them that he has never been a qualifying person or is no longer such a person, or

  (b) if he requests them to do so and he is not owed any duty under section 193 or 195(2) (main housing duties owed to persons who are homeless or threatened with homelessness).

(7) Before removing a person from the register, a local housing authority shall comply with such requirements, as to notification or otherwise, as the Secretary of State may prescribe by regulations.

DEFINITIONS

"housing register": s.162.
"local housing authority": s.230.
"qualifying person": s.161.

GENERAL NOTE

This section governs the entitlement of a person to be put on the register: to enjoy registration as of right, the person must apply to be registered, and it must appear to the authority that he is a qualifying person, *i.e.* as prescribed by the Secretary of State under s.161(2), above, or—but subject thereto—of a category so defined by the authority themselves under s.161(3). The local housing authority may, however, put someone on the register without waiting for an application. Either way, they must notify the applicant, who has the right to require them to remove his name, under subs. (6)(b)), *unless* he is a homeless person towards whom duties are owed under ss.193, 195.

Accordingly, a homeless person towards whom such a duty is owed cannot remove himself from the register so as, *e.g.*, to pre-empt an offer under this Part which he does *not* want (perhaps because his Pt. VII accommodation is *better* than the permanent offer he will be made), and—in turn—prevent the temporary duty coming to an end under s.193(5).

The authority must also remove a person from the list if they learn that he never was a qualifying person, or if they learn that he is no longer a qualifying person: subs. (6)(a). They may also amend the register (subs. (4)) or remove a person "in such other circumstances as they think fit", subject in each case to notification (subss. (4), (7)). In any case of removal, the Secretary of State may impose requirements, as to notification or otherwise: subs. (8).

Notification is additionally required under the following section, and includes a requirement to inform the person of his right to request a review thereunder. This would be available to cover such requirements as an annual or other periodic confirmation of continued interest in an allocation, or where allocation is means-tested by an authority (if and so far as the regulations permit under s.161(2), above) that qualification continues.

Notification of adverse decision and right to review

164.—(1) If a local housing authority decide—
　(a)　not to put a person on their housing register who has applied to be put on, or
　(b)　to remove a person from their housing register otherwise than at his request,
they shall notify him of their decision and of the reasons for it.

(2) The notice shall also inform him of his right to request a review of the decision and of the time within which such a request must be made.

(3) A request for review must be made before the end of the period of 21 days beginning with the day on which he is notified of the authority's decision and reasons, or such longer period as the authority may in writing allow.

(4) There is no right to request a review of the decision reached on an earlier review.

(5) On a request being duly made to them, the authority shall review their decision.

(6) Notice required to be given to a person under this section shall be given in writing and, if not received by him, shall be treated as having been given if it is made available at the authority's office for a reasonable period for collection by him.

DEFINITIONS
　"housing register": s.162.
　"local housing authority": s.230.

GENERAL NOTE
　This section introduces a right to notification of a decision (and reasons for it) either not to put someone on the waiting list, or else to remove him from it (in the latter case potentially additional to a requirement pursuant to regulations under s.163(7)), and a right to a review: so far as the latter is concerned, it is in substantively identical terms to the provisions of s.202, below, granting a right of review of (in effect) an adverse decision on an application as homeless, see notes thereto (as that is likely to be the section subject to the greater interest and volume of litigation). So far as concerns the formal requirements of subs. (6), governing the notice itself, see also notes to s.202, below. Procedure on a review is governed by the following section, which is substantively considered in the notes to s.203, below.
　As to what is imported by the requirement for reasons, see notes to s.184, below.

Subs. (4)
　This subsection pre-empts the argument that a decision on a review is itself reviewable. In the case of challenge to a decision under these provisions, there would be no alternative but to seek judicial review, as there is no right to appeal to the county court on a point of law as there is under Pt. VII (see s.204, below). See further notes to s.204, as to grounds for review, and for A Note on Judicial Review procedure.

Procedure on a review

165.—(1) The Secretary of State may make provision by regulations as to the procedure to be followed in connection with a review under section 164. Nothing in the following provisions affects the generality of this power.

(2) Provision may be made by regulations—

(a) requiring the decision on review to be made by a person of appropriate seniority who was not involved in the original decision, and

(b) as to the circumstances in which the person concerned is entitled to an oral hearing, and whether and by whom he may be represented at such a hearing.

(3) The authority shall notify the person concerned of the decision on the review.

(4) If the decision is to confirm the original decision, they shall also notify him of the reasons for the decision.

(5) Provision may be made by regulations as to the period within which the review must be carried out and notice given of the decision.

(6) Notice required to be given to a person under this section shall be given in writing and, if not received by him, shall be treated as having been given if it is made available at the authority's office for a reasonable period for collection by him.

GENERAL NOTE

This section is—so far as rights overlap—in substantively the same terms as s.203, below, and is considered in the notes thereto.

Information about housing register

166.—(1) A person on the housing register of a local housing authority is entitled—

(a) to see the entry relating to himself and to receive a copy of it free of charge, and

(b) to be given such general information as will enable him to assess how long it is likely to be before housing accommodation appropriate to his needs becomes available for allocation to him.

(2) The fact that a person is on an authority's housing register, and the information about him included in the register, shall not be divulged to any other member of the public.

DEFINITIONS

"housing register": s.162.
"local housing authority": s.230.

GENERAL NOTE

This section provides two basic entitlements to someone who has been registered as a qualifying person under s.161, above. First, to see the entry relating to himself, and to receive a copy of it, free of charge; secondly, to be given enough information in general terms to assess how long it is likely to be before appropriate housing is allocated to him.

Subs. (1)

This subsection is modelled on Housing Act 1985, s.106(5), and entitles a person to see his own entry, presumably so as to check that the details are correct. No express provision is made for rectification of the register in consequence of an error thus disclosed, but the authority have *power* to rectify the register (see s.162(4), above) and if the error is clear (as opposed to a difference of opinion as to how his circumstances translate into priority) it is difficult to imagine that any authority would decline to amend and not difficult to perceive an entitlement to relief by way of judicial review.

Subs. (2)

As to duties of confidentiality in general, see General Note to s.32, above. This provision deals expressly with disclosure to other members of the public.

The allocation scheme

Allocation in accordance with allocation scheme

167.—(1) Every local housing authority shall have a scheme (their "allocation scheme") for determining priorities, and as to the procedure to be followed, in allocating housing accommodation.

For this purpose "procedure" includes all aspects of the allocation process, including the persons or descriptions of persons by whom decisions are to be taken.

(2) As regards priorities, the scheme shall be framed so as to secure that reasonable preference is given to—

(a) people occupying insanitary or overcrowded housing or otherwise living in unsatisfactory housing conditions,

(b) people occupying housing accommodation which is temporary or occupied on insecure terms,

(c) families with dependent children,

(d) households consisting of or including someone who is expecting a child,

(e) households consisting of or including someone with a particular need for settled accommodation on medical or welfare grounds, and

(f) households whose social or economic circumstances are such that they have difficulty in securing settled accommodation.

The scheme shall also be framed so as to secure that additional preference is given to households within paragraph (e) consisting of someone with a particular need for settled accommodation on medical or welfare grounds who cannot reasonably be expected to find settled accommodation for themselves in the foreseeable future.

(3) The Secretary of State may by regulations—

(a) specify further descriptions of people to whom preference is to be given as mentioned in subsection (2), or

(b) amend or repeal any part of subsection (2).

(4) The Secretary of State may by regulations specify factors which a local housing authority shall not take into account in allocating housing accommodation.

(5) As regards the procedure to be followed, the scheme shall be framed in accordance with such principles as the Secretary of State may prescribe by regulations.

(6) Subject to the above provisions, and to any regulations made under them, the authority may decide on what principles the scheme is to be framed.

(7) Before adopting an allocation scheme, or making an alteration to their scheme reflecting a major change of policy, a local housing authority shall—

(a) send a copy of the draft scheme, or proposed alteration, to every registered social landlord with which they have nomination arrangements (see section 159(4)), and

(b) afford those persons a reasonable opportunity to comment on the proposals.

(8) A local housing authority shall not allocate housing accommodation except in accordance with their allocation scheme.

DEFINITION

"local housing authority": s.230.

GENERAL NOTE

This is a core section, for pursuant to subs. (8), notwithstanding the apparent discretion to allocate housing accommodation "in such manner as they consider appropriate" (above, s.159(7)), it prohibits allocation of housing accommodation (which means by way of grant of tenancy or licence of their own stock, or nomination to the stock of another landlord—see Introduction to Pt. VI, above) other than in accordance with the allocation scheme they are bound to have, which scheme may be subject to the Secretary of State's power to specify matters not to be taken into account when allocation housing (subs. (4)), and the procedure to be followed when allocating housing must be framed in accordance with such principles as the Secretary of State may prescribe (subs. (5)), with "procedure" defined in subs. (1) to mean all aspects of allocation process. Of course, all allocations must in any event be to qualifying persons under s.161, above.

In substance, s.161 says *who* may (or may not) be housed; this section is how priority *between them* is determined and applied.

Subs. (1)

The obligation to describe who may take decisions on allocations is something which may be subject to regulation by the Secretary of State (*e.g.* to eliminate member involvement, as in "a number of well-publicised cases" in Wales where "the published allocation system of the council was found to be a sham and, for all practical purposes, the allocation was in the personal gift of the ward member... I worry about claims of so-called local knowledge, which are used to justify active member involvement in individual allocation decisions... Such practices can be a cover for prejudice and unfairness... *Hansard* (H.C.), Standing Committee G, Seventeenth Sitting, March 14, 1996, col. 648, Parliamentary Under-Secretary of State for Wales [Mr Gwilym Jones]). "Systems for allocating housing should be transparent and operated consistently": *ibid.*

As long ago as 1969, the Cullingworth Report, Council Housing—Purposes, Procedures and Priorities (9th report of Housing Management Sub-Committee of the Central Housing Advisory Committee) had likewise recommended that selection should be by officers not members, and that the function of members should be confined to the policy framework within which selection would take place, which policy should be clearly set out, and published: paras. 119, 122. However, Cullingworth had also rejected increased central control over policies: para. 64.

Subs. (2)

The principles were first discussed in the D.O.E. Consultation Paper linked to the Housing Bill, Allocation of Housing Accommodation by Local Authorities, January 1996. The then intention was to require local authorities to continue to give a reasonable preference to prescribed categories, following the model in s.22, Housing Act 1985 (see Introduction to Pt. VI, above). Two of those in 1985, s.22 are intended to be retained: those in insanitary or overcrowded housing, and those in unsatisfactory housing conditions. Added are: those in conditions of temporary or insecure tenure; families with dependent children or who are expecting a child; households containing someone with an identified need for settled accommodation; and, households with limited opportunities to secure settled accommodation.

Subs. (4)

If and so far as the Secretary of State maintains the current intention to replicate the s.22, Housing Act 1985, *approach*, albeit with different categories of person to whom a preference must be given, then it will remain the case that authorities cannot adopt their policies so rigidly as to fetter their discretion in considering the individual circumstances of particular applicants for housing: *R. v. Canterbury City Council, ex p. Gillespie* (1986) 19 H.L.R. 7, *R. v. Bristol City Council, ex p. Johns* (1992) 25 H.L.R. 249, Q.B.D., *R. v. London Borough of Newham, ex p. Campbell* (1993) 26 H.L.R. 183, Q.B.D., *R. v. London Borough of Newham, ex p. Watkins* (1994) 26 H.L.R. 434, Q.B.D. and *R. v. London Borough of Newham, ex p. Dawson* (1994) 26 H.L.R. 747, Q.B.D. (It is intended that authorities should be able to weigh individual circumstances against the need to make the best use of the housing stock reflected in the principles: Consultation Paper, para. 23.)

There is no reason why an authority's own principles of allocation should not include reference to arrears of rent (*R. v. London Borough of Newham, ex p. Miah* (1995) 28 H.L.R. 279, Q.B.D., *R. v. L.B. Lambeth, ex p. Njomo*, (1996) 28 H.L.R. 737, *R. v. L.B. Islington, ex p. Aldabbagh* (1995) 27 H.L.R. 271, Q.B.D.), but not other categories of arrears, such as local taxation (*R. v. Forest Heath District Council, ex p. West and Lucas* (1991) 24 H.L.R. 85, C.A.: all local taxpayers are to be treated the same way, regardless of their need for housing). Indeed, an authority can determine to give so much weight to the issue of rent arrears that they can decline to register an applicant: *R. v. Wolverhampton M.B.C., ex p. Watters, The Times*, June 11, 1996, 28 H.L.R. forthcoming, Q.B.D.

Alternatively, rent arrears may go to discretionary qualification under s.161(4), above: see Consultation Paper, para. 9, notes to s.161(4), above. The authority cannot exercise such discretion as is left to them for irrelevant reasons: *R. v. Port Talbot Borough Council, ex p. Jones* (1988) 20 H.L.R. 265, C.A. (allocation to a councillor outside policy).

Subs. (7)

This provision requires the authority to afford registered social landlords the opportunity to comment on an allocation scheme before it is adopted or altered in any way that reflects "a major change of policy": see notes to s.5, above, on "consultation"; though that word is not used, the duty is substantively the same, and is likely to be approached in the same way.

The expression "major change of policy" is left undefined and while there may be fine arguments over whether or not it is for the authority or the court to determine as a matter of fact whether or not there is such a change (*cf.* the provisions of Housing Act 1985, s.103, requiring consultation on housing management, when "in the opinion of the authority or trust" there is a new programme or change in practice or policy, which "in the opinion of the authority or trust" relates to management, improvement, maintenance, etc.), it is unlikely to be the sort of issue which will be worth anyone's while taking to litigation.

Information about allocation scheme

168.—(1) A local housing authority shall publish a summary of their allocation scheme and provide a copy of the summary free of charge to any member of the public who asks for one.

(2) The authority shall make the scheme available for inspection at their principal office and shall provide a copy of the scheme, on payment of a reasonable fee, to any member of the public who asks for one.

(3) When the authority make an alteration to their scheme reflecting a major change of policy, they shall within a reasonable period of time notify everyone on their housing register, explaining in general terms the effect of the change.

DEFINITIONS

"allocation scheme": s.167.
"housing register": s.162.
"local housing authority": s.230.

GENERAL NOTE

Authorities have been obliged to publish details of their allocation provisions since Housing Act 1980: see Housing Act 1985, s.106—it was a part of the Tenants' Charter, in its own right, designed to enhance transparency and accountability. This section is modelled on that section, although much scaled down as the balance of that section has been expanded to make up the body of this Part.

Lack of publication does not, however, make a policy *ultra vires*: *R. v. London Borough of Newham, ex p. Miah* (1995) 28 H.L.R. 279.

Only a summary of the allocation scheme which the authority are bound to maintain pursuant to s.167, above, has to be made available free of charge to any member of the public who asks for it (*n.b.* not a member of the public within any particular area). The authority must keep the full scheme available for inspection at their principal office, but a reasonable fee may be charged for a copy of the (full) scheme, to any member of the public who asks for one.

Subs. (3)

The requirement to notify everyone on the housing register of a change arises only if there is an alteration amounting to a "major change in policy", in which case the obligation is to explain the effect of the change in general terms.

Supplementary

Guidance to authorities by the Secretary of State

169.—(1) In the exercise of their functions under this Part, local housing authorities shall have regard to such guidance as may from time to time be given by the Secretary of State.

(2) The Secretary of State may give guidance generally or to specified descriptions of authorities.

DEFINITION
"local housing authority": s.230.

GENERAL NOTE
This section is modelled on s.71, Housing Act 1985 (Code of Guidance for homelessness): see now, notes to s.182, below.

Co-operation between registered social landlords and local housing authorities

170. Where a local housing authority so request, a registered social landlord shall co-operate to such extent as is reasonable in the circumstances in offering accommodation to people with priority on the authority's housing register.

DEFINITIONS
"local housing authority": s.230.
"registered social landlord": s.230.

GENERAL NOTE
This section is modelled on Housing Act 1985, s.72. It empowers the authority to ask for co-operation (*cf. R. v. Wirrall, ex p. Bell* (1994) 27 H.L.R. 24, Q.B.D.—it is a matter for the authority whether or not to use such powers)—and *prima facie* obliges a registered social landlord to co-operate, in the task of offering accommodation to people with priority (see s.166, above) on the authority's register: however, the duty is only to co-operate "to such extent as is reasonable in the circumstances", which must mean reasonable in the eyes or view of the registered social landlord, not the authority (see also *Smith v. Northavon D.C.* (1994) 26 H.L.R. 659, H.L.). See, further, notes to s.213, below.

False statements and withholding information

171.—(1) A person commits an offence if, in connection with the exercise by a local housing authority of their functions under this Part—
  (a) he knowingly or recklessly makes a statement which is false in a material particular, or
  (b) he knowingly withholds information which the authority have reasonably required him to give in connection with the exercise of those functions.
(2) A person guilty of an offence under this section is liable on summary conviction to a fine not exceeding level 5 on the standard scale.

DEFINITION
"local housing authority": s.230.

GENERAL NOTE
It is an offence knowingly or recklessly to make a statement which is false in a material particular, or knowingly to withhold information which the authority have reasonably required, in connection with the authority's exercise of their functions under this Part (punishable by a fine not exceeding level 5 on the standard scale). The offence is committed by anyone, not merely an applicant for accommodation, *e.g.* a family member, whether or not it is someone with whom an applicant has been residing, or a former landlord. Nor is the offence only comprised of false statement (knowingly or recklessly made): the authority also has power to demand information *from anyone* (provided it is information reasonably required, in connection with the exercise of their functions under Pt. VI), and *anyone* can be convicted of an offence of withholding, even an applicants' adviser, (perhaps even—on the face of it—a legal adviser, *cf* s.30(5), above).
The section is modelled on Housing Act 1985, s.74 (see now below, s.214), governing applications as homeless, and to that extent, it may be said not to stretch the existing law: however, in the case of withholding, the offence could only be committed if it was "with intent to induce a local housing authority to believe ... that he or another person—is homeless", etc.

Recklessly. "As a general rule every crime requires a mental element, the nature of which will depend upon the definition of the particular crime in question... The meaning of each [expression] must be determined in the context in which it appears, and the same expression may bear a different meaning in different contexts" (Halsbury's Laws, Vol. 11(1), para. 10).

Regulations

172.—(1) Regulations under this Part shall be made by statutory instrument.

(2) No regulations shall be made under section 167(3) (regulations amending provisions about priorities in allocating housing accommodation) unless a draft of the regulations has been laid before and approved by a resolution of each House of Parliament.

(3) Any other regulations under this Part shall be subject to annulment in pursuance of a resolution of either House of Parliament.

(4) Regulations under this Part may contain such incidental, supplementary and transitional provisions as appear to the Secretary of State appropriate, and may make different provision for different cases including different provision for different areas.

GENERAL NOTE
It is by regulations that the Secretary of State will determine what actual priorities are to be applied in the allocation of social housing held by local authorities, and so far as it may come to be applied by others: see Introduction to Pt. VI, above. Note the requirement for an affirmative resolution where allocation priorities are the subject of regulation (subs. (2)).

Consequential amendments: Part VI

173. The enactments mentioned in Schedule 16 have effect with the amendments specified there which are consequential on the provisions of this Part.

GENERAL NOTE
Attention may be drawn to the following amendments:

Housing Act 1985, s.106. See notes to s.168, above; the requirements of 1985 Act, s.106 will no longer apply so far as what it covers is governed now by this Part.

Tied Accommodation. Under Housing Act 1985, Sched. 1, para. 2, certain categories of letting of accommodation occupied in connection with employment are not secure; these provisions are amended to prevent the occupier becoming automatically secure at the end of specified periods if the landlord is a local housing authority (see *Berkshire C.C. v. Greenfield* (1996) 28 H.L.R. 691, C.A., *cf. South Glamorganshire C.C. v. Griffiths* (1992) 24 H.L.R. 334, C.A.) but provide instead for notification—thus engaging the allocation provisions of this Part.

Employment Arrangements. Similar amendment is made to Housing Act 1985, Sched. 1, para. 5, governing arrangements designed to encourage job mobility, which can become secure after a period of time, to achieve the same effect that, if the landlord is a local housing authority it will only become secure if so notified.

Student Lettings. Again, amendment is made to the same effect to Housing Act 1985, Sched. 1, para. 10, where student lettings can become secure at the end of a period of time but, now, if the tenant of a local housing authority, will only become secure if so notified by that authority.

Index of defined expressions: Part VI

174. The following Table shows provisions defining or otherwise explaining expressions used in this Part (other than provisions defining or explaining an expression used in the same section)—

allocation (of housing)	section 159(2)
allocation scheme	section 167
assured tenancy	section 230
housing register	section 162
introductory tenancy and introductory tenant	sections 230 and 124
local housing authority	section 230
qualifying person (in relation to housing register)	section 161
registered social landlord	sections 230 and 2
secure tenancy and secure tenant	section 230

PART VII

HOMELESSNESS

Homelessness and threatened homelessness

INTRODUCTION

Under the provisions of Pt. III, Housing Act 1985 (a consolidation of provisions first introduced by the Housing (Homeless Persons) Act 1977 (c. 48), local housing authorities have been obliged to secure that accommodation is made available (whether from their own stock, or by securing that it is provided by someone else) for the homeless, in priority need of accommodation, who did not become homeless intentionally. The local connection provisions of Pt. III permitted an authority with which an applicant had no local connection to shift responsibility to another with which he did.

Homelessness. The 1985 Act (s.58) defined "homelessness" by reference to legal rights of occupation: a person was homeless if there was no accommodation which he could occupy by virtue of an interest or estate, or contract, together with anyone else who normally resided with him either as a member of the family, or in circumstances in which it was reasonable for that person to reside with him. In addition, a person was not to be regarded as homeless if he was in occupation in circumstances in which a court order was required for eviction, for example, tenants whose tenancies had been determined. A person was also homeless if he had been locked out of accommodation, had to leave the accommodation because of domestic violence, or, in the case of mobile homes and caravans, there was nowhere to park/moor accommodation and to live in it.

In a series of cases, the courts started to develop their own gloss on the principal definition, importing into the term "accommodation" criteria such as "appropriate" or "suitable" (*Parr v. Wyre B.C.* (1982) 2 H.L.R. 71, C.A., *R. v. Ryedale D.C., ex p. Smith* (1983) 16 H.L.R. 66, Q.B.D.); in other cases, they were developing an equation between being homeless and living in conditions so bad that accommodation could be quit without a finding of intentionality (*R. v. South Herefordshire D.C. ex p. Miles* (1983) 17 H.L.R. 82, Q.B.D., *R. v. Preseli D.C., ex p. Fisher* (1984) 17 H.L.R. 147, Q.B.D., *R. v. Dinefwr B.C.. ex p. Marshall* (1984) 17 H.L.R. 310, Q.B.D., see also the judgment of Ackner L.J. in *In Re Puhlhofer* at the Court of Appeal—(1985) 17 H.L.R. 558. In *City of Gloucester v. Miles* (1985) 17 H.L.R. 292, C.A., it was held that accommodation within the definition of homelessness meant "habitable").

In *In Re Puhlhofer* [1986] A.C. 484, 18 H.L.R. 158, however, the House of Lords rejected these developments (with the possible exception of *City of Gloucester*), and held that a person was not homeless within s.58 if he occupied accommodation that was in some sense capable of being described as accommodation, however poor. (Likewise, an authority's duty towards the homeless under 1985 Act, s.65 was to provide no more than accommodation, unqualified by any such term as "appropriate" or "suitable".) In direct response, Parliament amended s.58 to define as homeless those who, although enjoying the benefit of one of the qualifying rights of occupation, occupied accommodation so bad that it would not be reasonable for them to remain in occupation of it (although, when determining this question, an authority were entitled to have regard to the general housing circumstances of their area, *i.e.* in effect whether or not others may be occupying accommodation just as bad): Housing and Planning Act 1986, s.14.

This amendment drew an exact parallel between homelessness and the conditions under which a person could quit accommodation without a finding of intentionality. In substance, therefore, it seemed that a person would now be homeless if he enjoyed no settled accommodation. By "settled accommodation" (a phrase coined by Ackner L.J. in *Din v. L.B. Wandsworth* at the Court of Appeal: [1983] 1 A.C. 657, C.A. and H.L., 1 H.L.R. 73, C.A.; see also *Dyson v. Kerrier D.C.* [1980] 1 W.L.R. 1205, C.A.) was meant that class of accommodation departure from which could not constitute intentionality, *e.g.* because of its condition, terms of occupation or temporary quality, but acquisition of which would in normal circumstances be the only means of breaking a period of intentional homelessness (thus entitling the applicant to reapply).

Priority need. This meant (1985 Act, s.59): those with children who were residing, or who might reasonably be expected to reside with either the applicant, or with anyone with whom the applicant might be expected to reside; those who were, or who might reasonably be expected to reside with someone who had become, homeless as a result of an emergency; those who were, or who might reasonably be expected to reside with someone who was, vulnerable on account of age, handicap or other special reason; and, a person who was, or who might reasonably be expected to reside with someone who was, a pregnant woman.

Intentional homelessness. Under the 1985 Act (s.60), intentional homelessness was defined by reference to four preconditions. The applicant:

(a) had to have ceased to occupy accommodation—so that those who had never had accommodation or last had it so long ago that it could not properly be taken into account could not be homeless intentionally; and,

(b) had to have ceased to occupy accommodation in consequence of a deliberate act or omission—an act of omission in good faith, in ignorance of a material fact, for example, security of tenure, financial assistance towards housing costs, was not to be considered deliberate; and,

(c) the accommodation had to have been such that it was reasonable to continue to occupy it—although those who optimistically left bad physical conditions were faced with the qualification that in determining whether or not it was reasonable to remain in occupation, a housing authority could take into account housing conditions in their area generally; and,

(d) the accommodation which had been quit had to have been "available for the occupation" of the applicant (meaning available not only for the homeless person but, again, for him and for anyone who might reasonably be expected to reside with him: 1985 Act, s.75, see now below, s.176).

Discharge. The right which applicants acquired was not, however, and as a matter of law, the right to council housing itself. Rather, the authority came under a duty to secure that accommodation was made available for the applicant (and those who might reasonably be expected to reside with him), which duty they might discharge (1985 Act, s.69, as amended by Housing and Planning Act 1986, s.14, also in response to *In Re Puhlhofer*, above):

(a) by making available suitable accommodation held by them under Pt. II, 1985 Act (*i.e.* the principal Part of that Act under which council housing is held) or under any other enactment (*e.g.* housing acquired in the exercise of other functions, such as education, highways, etc.); or

(b) by securing that the applicant obtained suitable accommodation from some other person; or

(c) by giving such advice and assistance as would secure that suitable accommodation was obtained from some other person.

Policy of Pt. VII. The essential purpose and policy of this Part is to effect radical changes to the *discharge* of duties which authorities owe to the homeless, although it has also included a number of amendments to the key question of qualification for assistance. This Part is closely related to Pt. VI, above, insofar as it is a principal purpose of this Part to ensure that the assistance provided to the homeless does *not* comprise the allocation of a secure tenancy, *unless and until* the applicant qualifies from the waiting list maintained under that Part. There is a number of other changes, however, including the statutory disqualification of "persons from abroad": see s.185.

Some of the changes might have been considered superfluous in light of the decision of the House of Lords in *R. v. L.B. Brent, ex p. Awua* [1996] 1 A.C. 55, 27 H.L.R. 453. The decision was one which "caught most people in the housing world somewhat by surprise. It said that a housing authority's duty (under 1985 Act, s.65) could be discharged in as little as 28 days. The legal landscape ... has, therefore, changed", was how the Minister for Local Government, Housing and Urban Regeneration (Mr Curry) described the case, emphasising that the 1996 Act was neither introduced because of the case, nor a response to it (*Hansard* (H.C.), Standing Committee G, Eighteenth Sitting, March 19, 1996, col. 691).

In *Awua*, it was held that "accommodation" in both s.58(1) (definition of homelessness) and s.60(1) (definition of intentionality) of the 1985 Act meant a place which could fairly be described as accommodation and which it would be reasonable, having regard to the general housing conditions in the local housing authority's district, for the person in question to continue to occupy. There was, however, and notwithstanding the *post-Puhlhofer* amendments in the Housing and Planning Act 1986 (c. 63) which had seemed to intend precisely this effect, no additional requirement that it should be settled or permanent. The same was held to be true of the accommodation which the local housing authority were under a duty to make available to an unintentionally homeless person under 1985 Act, s.65(2); the accommodation had to be "suitable", but this did not import any requirement of permanence.

There was, it was held, no reason why temporary accommodation should *ipso facto* be unsuitable. If the tenure was so precarious that the person was likely to have to leave within 28 days without any alternative accommodation being available, then he remained threatened with homelessness (see now s.195, below) and the authority would not have discharged their duty; otherwise the term for which the accommodation was provided was a matter for the authority to decide.

This decision, at a stroke, swept away the concept of settled accommodation (expressly *save* for the purpose of defining that class of accommodation which an intentionally homeless applicant would need to secure for himself before being entitled to reapply), either as it had been used to identify (as unsettled) that accommodation which a person could quit without being found intentionally homeless, or as it was in practice used to refer to the class of accommodation to which a qualifying applicant was entitled.

The 1996 Act is not—as noted—a response to *Awua*, although *Awua* was described by the

Minister for Local Government, Housing and Urban Regeneration (Mr Curry) as removing in statutory terms the safety net of immediate help that the government wished (still) to provide (*Hansard* (H.C.), Standing Committee G, Twentieth Sitting, March 21, 1996, col. 776): see further notes to s.175, below. It is, rather, a response to the allocation of an increasing proportion of (a decreasing stock of available) local authority accommodation to the homeless. It was foreshadowed by a Consultation Paper, *Access to Local Authority and Housing Association Tenancies* (January 1994), which described "two main methods of acquiring a local authority or housing association tenancy—by making a direct application to the landlord concerned (and usually going on the relevant waiting list until a suitable property becomes available), or by being accepted as statutorily 'homeless' by a local authority ..." (para. 2.5).

Research (Routes into Local Authority Housing, D.O.E. Housing Research Summary, No. 16, 1994) published contemporaneously, "shows that people rehoused from the waiting list are in many important respects (such as income, employment status and previous tenure) similar to households through the homelessness route... But statutorily homeless households receive automatic priority over others... As a result, in some areas—particularly in parts of London—it is almost impossible for any applicant ever to be re-housed from the waiting list......Of those who did manage to get re-housed, people using the waiting list route had to wait nearly twice as long ... as people housed under the homelessness legislation..." (Consultation Paper, para. 2.6).

"By giving the local authority a greater responsibility towards those who can demonstrate 'homelessness' than towards anyone else in housing need, the current legislation creates a perverse incentive for people to have themselves accepted by a local authority as homeless... In the great majority of cases, someone accepted as homeless is in fact occupying accommodation of some sort at the time he or she approached the authority. Indeed, the largest single category of households accepted as statutorily homeless are people living as licensees of parents, relatives or friends who are no longer willing or able to accommodate them... There is a growing belief that the homelessness provisions are frequently used as a quick route into a separate home..." (*ibid.*, para. 2.8).

"Against this background, the Government is proposing measures to ensure fairer access to all parts of the rented housing sector. These include measures to prevent homelessness, to remove the distorting effect that the present provisions have on the allocation of housing, and to ensure that subsidised housing is equally available to all who genuinely need it, particularly couples seeking to establish a good home in which to start and raise a family." (*ibid.*, para. 3.1). The proposals were threefold:

    (a) To limit authorities' duties to securing accommodation for the homeless;
    (b) To limit authorities' rights of allocation to allocation from the waiting-list; and,
    (c) To encourage more advisory activity to help people find other accommodation (*ibid.*, para. 3.2).

The effect would be to continue to provide "a safety net" in the interim, while considering longer term allocation to the homeless alongside others seeking council housing (*ibid.*, para. 3.4), which it would achieve by means of the new constraint on allocation from the waiting list, which would itself be subject to "broad principles" established by the government, and control of the conditions which authorities could establish for appearance on waiting lists, which it would encourage authorities to maintain jointly with housing associations operating in their areas: see now Pt. VI, above.

In the White Paper on which the Act was based, *Our Future Homes* (June 1995, Cm. 2901), Chap. 6 pursued the theme that homeless was "usually a short term crisis... We are committed to maintaining an immediate safety net, but this should be separate from a fair system of allocating long term accommodation in a house or flat owned by a local authority or housing association..." (*ibid.*, p.36).

"Local authorities will continue to have an immediate duty to secure accommodation for families and vulnerable individuals who have nowhere to go. Where such people are found to have no alternative available accommodation, the local housing authority will have to secure suitable accommodation for not less than twelve months." (This was subsequently changed to two years: see below, s.193). The authority may continue to secure accommodation for longer than that, although before the two-year period expires, they must check—in substance—that the household's entitlement has not changed (below, s.194). "These arrangements are intended to tide people over the immediate crisis of homelessness, and to give them time to find longer term accommodation..." (White Paper, p. 37).

The White Paper was followed by a linked Consultation Paper, *Allocation of Housing Accommodation by Local Authorities* (January 1996), which Pt. VI of the 1996 Act reflects.

Changes to the law. The proposals represented by Pt. VII take effect by altering the law as it stood under Housing Act 1985 (and as they had stood since 1977) in the following, principal respects (other than as already referred to, *i.e.* the disqualification of persons from abroad, under s.185):

(a) The definition of homelessness is narrowed to exclude not just those who have accommodation in England, Wales or Scotland (1985 Act, s.58(1)) but those who have accommodation whether in the U.K. or elsewhere (s.175); it is extended to broaden the class of person to or from whom the actuality or a threat of domestic violence means that it is not reasonable to remain in occupation of accommodation (s.177; see also s.178); in addition, it now incorporates the criterion of availability of accommodation for occupation, substantively in the same terms as it formerly appeared (1985 Act, s.75), so that a person is homeless not only if he has no accommodation for himself and persons normally residing with him (whether as a member of his family or in circumstances in which it is reasonable for that person to do so), but also if he has no accommodation for himself and members of his family normally residing with him, and for anyone else who might reasonably be expected to reside with, *i.e.* even if not normally so residing;

(b) In all cases in which a substantive housing duty is owed, other than the interim duties (to accommodate a person in priority need pending inquiries under s.188), for the homeless intentionally under s.190, and pending a local connection dispute under s.200), if the authority are satisfied that there is other suitable accommodation available in their area for an applicant, their duty is limited to giving advice and assistance such as they consider is reasonably required to enable the applicant to secure such accommodation for himself (s.197).

(c) The definition of intentional homelessness is extended to include

(i) those who enter into finite arrangements, for the purpose of securing assistance under Pt. VII, and

(ii) those who are assisted by way of advice to secure other suitable accommodation under s.197, but who fail to do so "in circumstances in which it was reasonably to be expected that he would do so" (s.191).

(d) However, the definition is also narrowed to a limited extent, albeit without express alteration, in so far as it imports a broader class of person to or from whom the actuality or threat of violence means that it would not be reasonable to continue to occupy accommodation.

(e) Without prejudice to the right to make a further application, authorities' duties to provide assistance—if not avoided by the application of s.197—are limited to a period of two years, or a shorter time if

(i) the applicant is offered other suitable accommodation—whether further accommodation under Part VII or an offer of a tenancy under Part VI—and the authority, having warned the applicant of this possible consequence, decide that they have discharged their duty,

(ii) the applicant ceases to be eligible for assistance under Part VII, because of the provisions governing persons from abroad or those governing asylum seekers, or

(iii) the applicant becomes homeless intentionally from the Part VII accommodation or otherwise voluntarily leaves it (s.193).

(f) While the authority have power to continue to provide accommodation beyond this period (ss.193, 194), they are under a duty to review its provision towards the end of the two-year period, and terminate their *duty* to provide accommodation accordingly if the qualifying conditions for assistance have ceased (s.194): the effect of these provisions taken together (*i.e.* ss.193, 194) is to prevent *automatic* continuation beyond the initial two-year period, without continued qualification for assistance, but to permit continued occupation where the qualification continues.

(g) The local connection provisions incorporate the broader category of persons, domestic violence towards or from whom will prevent their use (s.198(3)). The conditions permitting referral to another authority are deemed to be fulfilled if that other authority placed the applicant in the area of the authority to which a new application has been made, in discharge of their own Pt. VII functions, within such period as the Secretary of State may prescribe, regardless of such other issues as employment or family connections, or even fear of domestic violence in the area of that other authority (s.198(4)).

(h) Accommodation provided must be suitable, and may still be provided by securing that it is provided by someone other than the authority; however, authorities are under a duty—so far as reasonably practicable—to secure accommodation in their own area (s.208), and if the authority discharge their duty by arrangement with a private landlord, any tenancy granted will not be assured for the first twelve months (unless the landlord chooses to notify the tenant to the contrary), and if the landlord is a registered social landlord (see Pt. I, above), the tenancy cannot even then become a fully assured tenancy unless and until it has been allocated in accordance with Pt. VI (see also Pt. III, Chap. II, above): s.209.

(i) Subject to a power to apply to the Secretary of State for an extension, authorities are also prohibited from providing their own accommodation in discharge of functions under Pt. VI—which does not prevent an offer pursuant to a waiting list qualification under Pt. VI—for more than two years out of any three (whether continuously or in aggregate), unless it is by means of hostel accommodation or accommodation privately leased by the authority from a private (or housing association) landlord (ss.206, 207). Accordingly, even if the duty is extended, there will normally come a time when the applicant has to move home.

(j) There is a corresponding amendment to Housing Act 1985, Pt. IV, which ensures that accommodation thus provided to a homeless person is not secure (see Sched. 17, below; see also s.209, below, in relation to assured tenancies);

(k) Of considerable *procedural* importance, there is not only a right to an internal review of decisions which, in substance, are adverse to the applicant's interests or wishes (s.202), which may become subject to procedural requirements prescribed by the Secretary of State (s.203), but a right of appeal to the county court has been introduced; the right of appeal is on a point of law, which in substance means that it will no longer be necessary (nor, in practice, usually possible) *for an applicant* to challenge an authority's decision by judicial review (s.204), although there may remain other cases when judicial review will remain the only or appropriate course of action.

Note

Although there is much that is familiar, if not identical, to earlier homelessness law, and although as such it is certain that some (if not many) of the earlier subordinate instruments giving details of how this Part will operate in practice will be restated under this Part, the temptation to use such materials—and guidance under the previous law—in explanation or elaboration of this Part has been resisted, as these notes would quickly be not merely out of date in that respect, but may actively tend to mislead (and, in the *interregnum*, may subsequently prove guilty of having raised false expectations). With very few exceptions (where earlier guidance or instrument is the only practicable way to explain an otherwise elliptical statutory expression), these notes (as those under Pt. I, above, and those in the Housing Grants, Construction and Regeneration Act 1996 (c. 53)) are accordingly confined to the policy statements or publications already available, and the statutory provisions themselves.

Homelessness and threatened homelessness

175.—(1) A person is homeless if he has no accommodation available for his occupation, in the United Kingdom or elsewhere, which he—

> (a) is entitled to occupy by virtue of an interest in it or by virtue of an order of a court,
>
> (b) has an express or implied licence to occupy, or
>
> (c) occupies as a residence by virtue of any enactment or rule of law giving him the right to remain in occupation or restricting the right of another person to recover possession.

(2) A person is also homeless if he has accommodation but—

> (a) he cannot secure entry to it, or
>
> (b) it consists of a moveable structure, vehicle or vessel designed or adapted for human habitation and there is no place where he is entitled or permitted both to place it and to reside in it.

(3) A person shall not be treated as having accommodation unless it is accommodation which it would be reasonable for him to continue to occupy.

(4) A person is threatened with homelessness if it is likely that he will become homeless within 28 days.

DEFINITIONS

"available for his occupation": s.176.
"reasonable to continue to occupy": s.177.

GENERAL NOTE

This section is concerned with the crucial issue of what comprises homelessness giving rise to the rights and duties contained in this Part. Homelessness has been defined, since Housing (Homeless Persons) Act 1977 (c. 48) (hereinafter, "1977 Act"), later consolidated into Pt. III, Housing Act 1985 (hereinafter, "1985 Act"), in terms of (a) accommodation, (b) available for the applicant's occupation, to which (c) there are rights of occupation, (d) entry or use to which is not restricted, and which (e) it is reasonable for the applicant to continue to occupy. The section is also concerned (f) with what is meant by being threatened with homelessness.

Accommodation

Location. Under the Housing Act 1985, s.58(1) it was only accommodation in England, Wales or Scotland which was to be taken into account. This had not been stated specifically in the original legislation—the 1977 Act—but was accepted albeit *obiter,* in *R. v. Hillingdon Borough Council, ex p. Streeting* [1980] 1 W.L.R. 1425, D.C., and expressly enacted in the 1985 Act. However, as departure from accommodation abroad could qualify as intentional homelessness (*de Falco, Silvestri v. Crawley Borough Council* [1980] Q.B. 460, C.A., and other cases considered both under the heading Reasonable to Continue to Occupy, below, and in the notes to s.191, below), this did not commonly lead to any benefit.

The change to include accommodation in the U.K. *or elsewhere* now means that authorities will not have to consider applicants with overseas accommodation, beyond reaching the decision that they are not homeless, and accordingly will not have to go on to consider issues of the priority need and intentionality of such applicants.

The meaning of accommodation. The meaning of the term accommodation has proved one of the most controversial under the homelessness legislation, not so much as between applicant and authority (for whom the war that has raged largest and longest has been over intentionality), but between (a) the lower courts and the House of Lords, and (b) the House of Lords and Parliament. Thus, between 1977 and 1986, there was a growing tendency on the part of the courts—High Court and Court of Appeal—to equate a want of accommodation, and accommodation of such poor quality that it could be quit without a finding of intentionality, or a distinction for both purposes (and probably for the purpose of defining the duties owed by authorities) in terms of "settled" and "unsettled" accommodation. This met with firm contradiction by the House of Lords. It led, in turn, to further legislation, first in the Housing and Planning Act 1986 and—to an extent—under this Act too. See the Introduction to Pt. VII, above.

That Introduction, and these notes, are written on the basis that the decision in *R. v. L.B. Brent, ex p. Awua* [1996] 1 A.C. 55, 27 H.L.R. 453, H.L., is correctly decided and that the only gloss on the word "accommodation" which can be imported, other than as the statute imports reference to availability and, thence, to reasonableness to continue in occupation (see next two headings), is that it must mean "a place which can fairly be described as accommodation" (*per* Lord Hoffman at p.461). "As an example of shelter which would have failed this test," [Lord Brightman in *Puhlhofer* [1986] A.C. 484, 18 H.L.R. 158] instanced Diogenes' tub. The modern equivalent would be the night shelter in *R. v. Waveney District Council, ex p. Bowers, The Times,* May 25, 1982, Q.B.D., [not cross-appealed on this point—*cf.* [1983] Q.B. 238, 4 H.L.R. 118, C.A.], in which the applicant "could have a bed if one was available but had to walk the streets of Lowestoft by day" (*Awua*), p. 459).

In *City of Gloucester v. Miles* (1985) 17 H.L.R. 292, C.A., it was held that accommodation within the definition of homelessness means "habitable". This decision was followed by the majority in the Court of Appeal in *Puhlhofer* (see 17 H.L.R. 588), who were upheld by the House of Lords without reference to *City of Gloucester,* nor was the case mentioned in *Awua.*

A diversionary debate. Awua was, however, reached without citation to the Committee of the Asylum and Immigration Appeals Act 1993 (c. 23), in which a distinction was explicitly drawn between "accommodation" in Pt. III of the 1985 Act, and the "temporary accommodation" (reasonable to continue to occupy) without which asylum-seekers would not enjoy any rights under Pt. III. The structure, and the distinction, are the same as is now to be found in s.186, below.

Of course, it may well be said that the later legislation (1993 Act) was no basis for interpreting the earlier legislation (1985 Act) and the meaning of an earlier statute is not altered merely because Parliament proceeds on a mistaken view of the law. Where, however, there is doubt or ambiguity in earlier legislation, later legislation may be used to interpret it, and if in such circumstances there is a choice between two interpretations, one of which would render the later legislation unnecessary and the other would not, the other should be considered correct; further, if Parliament may be considered to have indicated that it has adopted sub-rules to legislation produced by the courts, such sub-rules take on the same force as statute law. Finally, it is of course the case that failure to cite a relevant Act (which begs the question whether or not the Act is relevant) is a basis for considering a decision to be *per incuriam*: see, generally, *Statutory Interpretation,* Bennion, 2nd ed, ss.234–5.

As the 1993 Act was not cited in *Awua, prima facie* the decision was *per incuriam,* although of course this does not mean—or seek to imply—that a different result would necessarily have followed if it had been or were to be cited: the Committee could have decided or could still decide that the apparent conflict between the two Acts reflects a mistaken view of the law.

Added force might have been considered to attach to this question when it is appreciated how relevant *Awua* is to this Act, where precisely the same contradistinction between temporary and other accommodation is expressly perpetuated *post-Awua*, especially in the light of the comment by the Minister of Local Government, Housing and Urban Regeneration (Mr Curry), that the case had removed in statutory terms the safety net of immediate help that the government wished to provide (*Hansard* (H.C.), Standing Committee G, Twentieth Sitting, March 21, 1996, col. 776). Furthermore, the Minister was aware of the implications of *Pepper v. Hart* [1993] A.C. 625, H.L., even if none too accurately, when he had remarked, at *ibid.*, col. 769: "The hon. Gentleman should also know that what Ministers say during the passage of a Bill is taken into consideration in legal proceedings".

Even if, therefore, and contrary to the argument that *Awua* was *per incuriam* in relation to the 1985 Act—so that the case should be treated as one of Parliament having proceeded in the 1993 Act on the basis of a mistaken view of the law under the 1986 Act—it remains to be asked what is to be made of the position today, when Parliament has repeated the distinction between temporary and "other" accommodation (see s.186, below). It cannot be a case of oversight or confusion: *Awua* dominated much of the debate in Committee. The implication of adoption (of the sub-rule distinguishing settled and unsettled accommodation) might be considered strong indeed in such circumstances, see Bennion, *op. cit.*, s.235. In effect, it might have been said either that *Awua* was indeed *per incuriam* all along, or that it was at least arguable that it may be taken to have been rejected by Parliament under Pt. VII, especially in the light of the "safety net" comment of the Minister.

These arguments would seem none the less not to enjoy much chance of success—and may be thought to attract none at all below the House of Lords itself—in the light of *R. v. L.B. Wandsworth, ex p. Wingrove*, and *R. v. L.B. Wandsworth, ex p. Mansoor* [1996] 3 All E.R. 913, C.A., in which the Court of Appeal considered the application of *Awua* to discharge of duty under s.65, 1985 Act, and concluded that there was no conflict between the 1993 Act and *Awua*. (The Court of Appeal was referred to the Bill that has become this Act. The clause number given—cl. 161—was incorrect; it should have been a reference to cl. 167, in the Bill as amended in Committee in the House of Commons, *i.e.* what is now s.193, below: letter from counsel [July 20, 1996]. There is no reference in the judgment to an argument to the effect that *Awua* was *per incuriam*, merely that it had been inconsistent with the 1993 Act). The term "accommodation", it was held, involves no element of permanence; it is to be understood in its ordinary meaning of "somewhere to live", subject to the qualification that "it must be somewhere reasonably tolerable" (*per* Sir Thomas Bingham, M.R.).

Old law. Notwithstanding *Awua* and *Wingrove and Mansoor*, the first three cases on the meaning of accommodation in the context of the definition of homelessness *may* yet retain their value, in the light of Lord Hoffman's approval of *Bowers* (above).

These were *Williams v. Cynon Valley Council*, January (1980) L.A.G. Bulletin 16, C.C., *R. v. London Borough of Ealing, ex p. Sidhu* (1982) 2 H.L.R. 45, Q.B.D., and *R. v. Waveney District Council, ex p. Bowers*, The Times, May 25, 1982, Q.B.D., (see further notes to s.189, below). In each of these cases, the authority claimed that it was under no duty to applicants living in temporary accommodation. In *Cynon Valley*, and *Sidhu*, women were living in refuges. In *Bowers*, a man was staying in a night shelter, on a night by night basis, and he could be turned away if the hostel was full. Each of the occupiers was, of course, no more than a licensee, but occupation under licence is *prima facie* a sufficient right of occupation for the purposes of the definition (see subs. (1)(b), see below under Rights of Occupation).

The courts in each case held that there was no necessary inconsistency between being homeless, and having some temporary accommodation or shelter, even if it was occupied under what amounted to a licence. This proposition had first been mooted in relation to the question of breaks in periods of intentional homelessness: *Din v. London Borough of Wandsworth* [1983] 1 A.C. 657, 1 H.L.R. 73, H.L. In *Sidhu*, the court adopted the words reported to have been spoken by the county court judge in *Cynon Valley*:

"It was important that refuges be seen as temporary crisis accommodation, and that women living in refuges were still homeless under the terms of the Act. If it was suggested that they were not homeless it would be necessary for voluntary organisations to issue immediate 28 days notice when women came in so that they would be under threat of homelessness. This would be totally undesirable and would simply add stress to stress. If living in crisis accommodation took women out of the 'homelessness' category then the Act was being watered down and its protection would be removed from a whole class of persons that it was set up to help and for whom it was extremely important."

The judge in *Sidhu* continued:

"... I myself would be perfectly prepared to speak those words and I adopt them without hesitation. Did I need further support for what I think is plain beyond peradventure the correct construction of this Act, I find it in the speech of Lord Lowry in *Din v. Wandsworth London Borough Council*. I think all I need read are two short sentences from Lord Lowry's speech: 'I consider that to be homeless and to have found some temporary accommodation are not mutually inconsistent concepts. Nor does a person cease to be homeless merely by having a roof over his head or a lodging, however precarious.' "

The other cases to consider the meaning of accommodation within the definition of homelessness, prior to *Puhlhofer* and *Awua*, were those cited in the Introduction to Pt. VII, above: *Parr v. Wyre B.C.* (1982) 2 H.L.R. 71, C.A., *R. v. South Herefordshire D.C., ex p. Miles* (1983) 17 H.L.R. 82, *R. v. Preseli D.C., ex p. Fisher* (1984) 17 H.L.R. 147, Q.B.D., and *R. v. Dinefwr B.C., ex p. Marshall* (1984) 17 H.L.R. 310, Q.B.D.

Other cases have considered "settled accommodation" not in the context of whether or not someone was homeless, but whether or not (a) accommodation that had been lost was sufficiently settled to give rise to a finding of intentional homelessness, or (b) there had been a break in a period of intentional homelessness, such that the applicant could make a new application (which latter use alone was approved in *Awua*, at p.461), or (c) in the context of whether or not an authority's duty had been discharged.

The first two of these approaches are considered under the headings Accommodation Available for Occupation, and Reasonable to Continue to Occupy, in the notes below; the second is also considered in relation to intentionality in the notes to s.191, below). The third is considered, so far as still relevant, in the notes to s.206, below.

Accommodation Available for Occupation

The importation into the definition of homelessness of the term "accommodation available for occupation", as defined by s.176, below, represents a minor advance for the homeless. It was formerly the case, under Housing Act 1985, s.58(2), that a person was homeless if there was no "accommodation which he, together with any other person who normally resides with him as a member of his family or in circumstances in which it is reasonable for that person to reside with him". "Accommodation available for occupation" was an expression which governed (a) whether or not accommodation had been quit intentionally, and (b) the accommodation to be provided, which cast the slightly wider net to include the applicant "and any other person who might reasonably be expected to reside with him".

The difference was between a definition which only included persons *already* (reasonably) residing with an applicant, and all persons who it could be asserted were reasonably to reside with the applicant, whether or not yet doing so. In practice, the effect was that a person might not be viewed as homeless, even though he could quit the accommodation without a finding of intentionality: that, however, though a small proposition of law, required a large investment in action, which might lead to the loss of accommodation: it deferred the authority's decision until the accommodation had been quit, instead of entitling the applicant to a decision while still in occupation.

The current formulation, for all purposes, is the wider formulation: persons who normally reside with the applicant as a member of the family, together with persons who might reasonably be expected to do so, including, *e.g.* a carer: (*Hansard* (H.L.), Report, July 8, 1996, Earl Ferrers, Minister of State, Department of the Environment, col. 64).

In *In Re Islam* [1983] 1 A.C. 688, C.A. and H.L., 1 H.L.R. 107, H.L., the applicant had lost his right to a shared room when his wife and four children flew from Bangladesh to join him in this country. The finding of intentionality was quashed by the House of Lords, on the basis that what had been lost was not accommodation "available for his occupation", meaning that of the applicant and his family. (Furthermore, an argument in the Court of Appeal, that Mr Islam had made the accommodation unavailable by bringing his family over, was dismissed as "a circular argument because that lack is the very circumstance which section 16 [of the 1977 Act, subsequently s.75, 1985 Act, now s.176] and the Act are designed to relieve".)

Accordingly, a family which has never enjoyed accommodation in which there were rights of occupation for all of its members, will at all times have been homeless, *e.g.* a couple without a home of their own, each still living with his or her parents, once a priority need is acquired, will be able to claim a right to assistance under this Part. The only—theoretical—recourse would be to intentional homelessness based on the pregnancy itself, but this would seem to have been caught by *Islam* (In *R. v. Eastleigh B.C., ex p. Beattie (No. 1)* (1983) 10 H.L.R. 134, Q.B.D., the court rejected out of hand a suggestion that pregnancy causing accommodation to cease to be reasonable to occupy could amount to intentionality, but in substance reached the same result as *Islam* had reached, referable to availability for accommodation). Note, however, that while still *en ventre sa mére*, an unborn child will not be a person with whom the applicant would be expected to reside, although when born would give rise to the priority need: see *R. v. L.B. Newham, ex p. Dada* (1995) 27 H.L.R. 502, C.A.

The question of who may reasonably be expected to reside with an applicant is a matter for the authority challengeable only on conventional grounds of public law (see below, notes to s.204), rather than a question of fact which a court can decide for itself: see *R. v. London Borough of*

Lambeth, ex parte Ly (1986) 19 H.L.R. 51, Q.B.D., in which it was held that a son and daughter-in-law, and their eight children, need not all be treated as reasonably expected to reside with the applicant. The applicant was a 74-year-old Vietnamese refugee, who had been separated from her family for over six years and the accommodation offered excluded the four eldest grand-children, who had said that they would be willing to be housed separately from the rest of the family.

The tests are alternative: a member of the family who normally resides with the applicant need not also be shown to do so reasonably: *cf. R. v. Hillingdon Homeless Persons Panel, ex p. Islam, The Times*, February 24, 1981, Q.B.D., not cross-appealed on the proposition, as it relates to priority need: see further notes to s.189, below. In *R. v. London Borough of Lambeth, ex p. Bodunrin* (1992) 24 H.L.R. 647, Q.B.D., the applicant lived in a hostel. He alleged that his two young children had come to live with him from Nigeria and applied to the authority for assistance on the basis that they could not live with him in the hostel accommodation. Lambeth accepted that he was homeless for that reason, but did not accept that he was in priority need. The decision was quashed since in order to qualify as homeless at all, the applicant must necessarily have been in priority need under what is now s.189(1)(b).

In *R. v. Peterborough City Council, ex parte Carr* (1990) 22 H.L.R. 207, C.A., it was held that the authority had erred in law in failing to consider whether the applicant's boyfriend and father of her child was a person with whom she might reasonably be expected to reside; the authority had wrongly reached their decision solely on the basis that they had not lived together at the applicant's last settled accommodation. In *R. v. Southwark L.B.C., ex p. Ryder* (1995) 28 H.L.R. 56, Q.B.D., it was considered unnecessary to determine separately whether persons—not normally residing with the applicant—were reasonably to be expected to reside with her on the basis of her need for care, and on an alternative basis that they were members of her family.

The issue in *Ryder* was also approached improperly, insofar as the authority rejected the applicant's need for larger accommodation so as to be able to have live-in support, on the basis that she did not qualify for a Disability Living Allowance; as the test for the latter is more stringent than—and, it may be said, different from—the question of whether one person is reasonably to be expected to reside with another, it could not be determined by reference to it (although if the claim for Disability Living Allowance had succeeded, it would have been strong evidence of the need for someone to live with the applicant).

In *R. v. L.B. Barking & Dagenham, ex p. Okuneye* (1995) 28 H.L.R. 174, Q.B.D., however, the fact that two people were intending or expecting to reside together did not mean that, when each departed from his and her separate accommodation, they were necessarily reasonably to be expected to reside together *at that time*, so that the authority were entitled to conclude that each had become homeless intentionally for ceasing to occupy available accommodation.

In *R. v. Tower Hamlets L.B.C., ex p. Rouf* (1989) 21 H.L.R. 294, Q.B.D., it was held that an authority could not jump to the conclusion that accommodation would continue to be available to an applicant with an increasing family. See also *R. v. Westminster C.C., ex p. Ali* (1983) 11 H.L.R. 83, Q.B.D., for a case in which the court found the proposition that a single, small room was "available" for a large family (applicant, wife and five children) "quite extraordinary". In other cases, hopelessly inadequate accommodation had been held not to be accommodation it was reasonable to continue to occupy: see below. It is on this proposition that reliance must now be placed—if they can do so at all—by those who seek assistance and new accommodation because what they currently have does not cope for those with whom they are reasonably to be expected to reside, but with whom they do not normally reside.

In *R. v. Wimborne District Council, ex parte Curtis* (1985) 18 H.L.R. 79, Q.B.D., the applicant was occupying her former matrimonial home under a separation agreement which contained a cohabitation clause to the effect that if she cohabited or remarried, the property would be sold. The applicant did start to cohabit, and her husband enforced the power of sale. The authority found her homeless intentionally, a decision quashed by the court because they had not considered availability in the statutory sense, *i.e.* if it was reasonable for her and her cohabitant to live together, whether the property was (as it was not) available to both of them.

Rights of Occupation
There are three categories of occupational right which the applicant must enjoy in relation to accommodation if he is not to be considered homeless:
    (i) Occupation Under Interest or Order;
    (ii) Occupation under Express or Implied Licence; and,
    (iii) Occupation by Enactment or Restriction.

Occupation under interest or order. The right of occupation may be by virtue of an "interest" in the accommodation: this would seem to mean a legal or equitable interest. Those with a legal interest will include owner-occupiers, and tenants, whether under long leases or on short, periodic tenancies, and whether during an initially agreed contractual period or as the contract may have been statutorily extended under the Housing Acts 1985 and 1988, in relation to secure tenants and assured tenants (*cf.* above, s.127). Those with an equitable interest commonly include the spouse of an owner-occupier. Spouses, whether of owner-occupiers or tenants, may also be given a right to occupy under an "order of the court" *i.e.* under matrimonial legislation.

Occupation under express or implied licence. Lodgers will usually be classed as licensees rather than tenants, flatsharers may be only licensees rather than joint tenants, and a child in the home of his parents will almost certainly be a licensee rather than a tenant or sub-tenant: on the distinction between tenant and licensee, see notes to s.126, above.

Where the applicant's licence is as service occupier, and contingent on the contract of employment, there cannot be said to be a licence to occupy once the contract of employment has been terminated. Thus even where the employer of a live-in housekeeper, having terminated the contract of employment, said that the applicant could return to occupy her room, the local authority had made an error of law in concluding that she had a licence to occupy, for the licence was dependent on the contract for employment which no longer existed: *R. v. Royal Borough of Kensington and Chelsea, ex p. Minton* (1988) 20 H.L.R. 648, Q.B.D., and *Norris v. Checksfield* (1991) 23 H.L.R. 425, C.A.

Occupation by enactment or restriction. The final category of "right of occupation" is that of occupation as a residence by virtue of any enactment or rule of law giving the applicant the right to remain in occupation, or restricting the right of any other person to recover possession of it. The section does, however, refer to accommodation which is being so occupied, as distinct from the right to occupy. Thus, a person who walks out of accommodation only occupied under this heading will accordingly be homeless, albeit, possibly, intentionally (but *cf.*, below, in discussion of Reasonable to Continue in Occupation), while a person who walks out of a house in which he has an interest will, presuming it is available for his occupation (see next heading) not be homeless at all, until such time as he divests himself of that interest, *e.g.* by release or sale.

The definition itself closely follows the wording of the Protection from Eviction Act 1977 (c. 43), s.1(1). A tenant within the protection of the Rent Act 1977 (c. 42) will occupy by virtue of an interest until the determination of the tenancy: thereafter, he is a statutory tenant. A statutory tenancy is not an interest in land: *Keeves v. Dean* [1924] 1 K.B. 685, C.A. However, it is a right of occupation by virtue of an enactment or rule of law, and, indeed, one which gives the tenant the right to remain in occupation and which restricts the right of another to recover possession. (This distinction was abolished for the purposes of secure and assured tenants, under the Housing Acts 1985 and 1988, by the device of preventing the landlord determining the tenancy save by obtaining an order of the court, with the tenancy itself continuing until the court orders possession to be given up.)

An agricultural worker in tied accommodation, enjoying the benefit of the Rent (Agriculture) Act 1976 (c. 80), will normally occupy by virtue of a licence before its determination, and thereafter in the same way as a Rent Act statutory tenant, while those who do not enjoy the benefit of that Act derive some temporary benefits under the Protection from Eviction Act 1977 (see s.8(2) applying provisions of that Act to "a person who, under the terms of his employment, had exclusive possession of any premises other than as a tenant..."). Long leaseholders normally continue to occupy beyond what would otherwise contractually be the termination of their interests by virtue of a statutorily extended tenancy, and thus still an interest, and will subsequently become either statutory tenants under the Rent Act 1977 or assured tenants under Housing Act 1988 (c. 50): Landlord and Tenant Act 1954 (c. 56), Pt. I.

The Protection from Eviction Act 1977 itself prohibits the eviction otherwise than by court proceedings of former unprotected tenants and licensees (other than excluded tenants and licensees), those who have had licences granted on or after November 28, 1980 which qualify as restricted contracts within s.19, Rent Act 1977, as well as certain service occupiers, so that all these people will occupy by virtue of an interest or a licence until determination, and subsequently by virtue of an enactment restricting the right of another to recover possession. Matrimonial legislation will commonly protect spouses and sometimes cohabitants by giving them a right to remain in occupation, or restricting the right of another to recover possession.

Those who are left outside the definition altogether are (a) those who have been trespassers from the outset and remain so, and (b) those who have had excluded tenancies and licences which have been brought to an end. It follows that "squatters" properly so-called, as distinct from those to whom a licence to occupy has been granted, are statutorily homeless even although no possession order may yet have been made against them, for, even though they may have the benefit of a roof over their heads, they have no accommodation within any of the classes specified.

Restriction on Entry or Use

Entry prevented. A person is also homeless if he "cannot secure entry to it": subs. (2)(a). This provision is intended principally to benefit the illegally evicted tenant or occupier, but covers anyone else who for some reason cannot immediately be restored to occupation of a home to which he has a legal entitlement. This provision has not proved to be of as much practical use as was intended, because authorities have tended to consider that unless the applicant has used available legal remedies to re-enter, an applicant will be considered intentionally homeless, albeit possibly with temporary assistance until it is obtained. (The legal mechanism for effecting this was never the subject of a decision of the court, but the definition of intentionality was considered wide enough in the case of domestic violence—see further below—and the threat of such a finding sufficient to procure co-operation.)

Authorities should have no policy to this effect, for there must be circumstances in which, although legal redress exists, both the benefits to be gained from using it, and the circumstances generally, suggest that it would be inappropriate, *e.g.* illegal eviction by a resident landlord who will shortly recover possession in any event, and where tensions are such that it is impracticable for the tenant to remain in the property: see, *e.g. British Oxygen Co. Ltd. v. Board of Trade* [1969] 2 Ch. 174, *In Re Betts* [1983] 2 A.C. 613, 10 H.L.R. 97, H.L., *Att.-Gen., ex rel. Tilley v. London Borough of Wandsworth* [1981] 1 W.L.R. 854, C.A.

Moveable structures. A person is also homeless if his accommodation consists of a movable structure, vehicle or vessel designed or adapted for human habitation, and there is no place where the applicant is entitled or permitted both to place it and to reside in it, *e.g.* a mobile home, caravan, houseboat: subs. (2)(b).

In *R. v. Chiltern D.C., ex p. Roberts* (1990) 23 H.L.R. 387, Q.B.D., travelling showmen were considered to be neither homeless nor threatened with homelessness whilst moving between fairgrounds during the fairground season, residing at each in caravans on a temporary basis. Reside does not require permanence: it means "live" or "occupy".

See also *Smith v. Wokingham District Council*, April 1980 L.A.G. Bulletin 92, C.C., in which a county court considered that a caravan, parked on land belonging to a county council, without express permission but in which the applicant and his family had lived for two-and-a-half years, had been the subject of an acquiescence sufficient to constitute permission for the purpose of what is now subs. (2)(b).

Reasonable to Continue to Occupy

A person is homeless if his accommodation is such that it is not reasonable to continue to occupy it: subs. (3). This expression is governed by s.177, below, as to both the issues of domestic violence (s.177(1)), and the general housing circumstances of the area (ss.177(2)). The Secretary of State has power to specify other circumstances in which it is or is not to be regarded as reasonable to continue to occupy accommodation, and matters (other than the general housing circumstances of the area) which are to be taken into account when determining whether or not it is reasonable to continue in occupation: s.177(3).

These additional considerations are not exhaustive of the matters to be taken into account in determining whether or not it is reasonable to continue in occupation: *R. v. London Borough of Hammersmith & Fulham, ex p. Duro-Rama* (1983) 9 H.L.R. 71, Q.B.D. The question is not confined to the accommodation itself, but can extend to its location: *R. v. Wycombe D.C., ex p. Homes* (1988) 22 H.L.R. 150, Q.B.D.

Domestic violence (s.177(1)). It is not reasonable to continue to occupy accommodation if, even though there may be a legal entitlement to occupy it, it is "probable" that occupation of it will lead to violence or threats of violence which are likely to be carried out:

(a) Against the applicant, or

(b) Against any person who normally resides with the applicant (*n.b. not* necessarily as a member of his family, so that *e.g.* a carer would be included here), or against any person who might reasonably be expected to reside with the applicant, from

(c) A person with whom the applicant, or any such other person, is associated.

Violence. It is not necessary to show an actual history of violence, for the test may be satisfied by the lower standard, *i.e.* threats by someone likely to carry them out. Many authorities fail to observe this important distinction, and require a high standard of proof of actual violence in the past, as evidence of both probability and likelihood. As this section draws a careful distinction, so also must authorities. The remarks made in connection with entry prevented about legal redress, and failure to use it, apply with possibly even greater force in this context. It is not, however, possible to say that a reasonable authority could never require a woman to use her domestic remedies, for want of which she may be considered homeless intentionally: see *R. v. Eastleigh B.C., ex p. Evans* (1984) 17 H.L.R. 515, Q.B.D.; see also *R. v. London Borough of Wandsworth, ex p. Nimako-Boateng* (1983) 11 H.L.R. 95, Q.B.D.

Under the 1985 Act, it had been held that an authority had to take into account violence or threats of violence from outside the home, even though not relevant under *ibid.*, s.58(3)(b): *Hammell v. Royal Borough of Kensington & Chelsea* [1989] Q.B. 518, (1988) 20 H.L.R. 666,

C.A., *R. v. Broxbourne B.C., ex p. Willmoth* (1990) 22 H.L.R. 118, C.A., *R. v. Swansea C.C., ex p. Evans* (1990) 22 H.L.R. 467, C.A., and *R. v. Tynedale D.C., ex p. McCabe* (1991) 24 H.L.R. 384, Q.B.D.

In the light of the drafting of this section, little reliance need be placed on those cases, as it seems clear—from the breadth of the definition of person associated (see below), and from the inclusion of persons not living with the applicant (yet who might reasonably be expected to do so)—that they are covered by what was an intention to extend the coverage of the domestic violence basis for not reasonably being able to remain in occupation (*Hansard* (H.L.), Report, July 8, 1996, Earl Ferrers, Minister of State, Department of the Environment, cols. 70–73).

It appears to have been agreed and accepted in *R. v. Kensington and Chelsea R.B.C., Hammersmith & Fulham L.B.C., Westminster C.C., and Islington L.B.C., ex p. Kihara* (1996) 29 H.L.R. forthcoming, C.A. that the victims of domestic violence are intended to be treated as in priority need, by reason of being vulnerable, within s.189(1)(c), below.

Likely to be carried out. See *R. v. Purbeck District Council, ex parte Cadney* (1985) 17 H.L.R. 534, Q.B.D., where the authority's finding on this point was upheld, in the absence of any evidence to show any attempt to occupy, and only the most indirect evidence that if the applicant did attempt to occupy, violence would result.

Residing with applicant. See under Accommodation Available for Occupation, above.

Person associated. While this provision is not an alternative head for illegal eviction or harassment by a resident landlord occupying another unit of accommodation within the same building, it is not, however, confined to domestic violence between spouses or persons living together as husband and wife, or other kinds of partnership. "Person associated" is defined in s.178, by reference to:

(1) Married or formerly married persons;

(2) Cohabitants and former cohabitants (defined in s.178(3), below to mean a man and a woman—and, therefore, not same sex cohabitants [see *Harrogate B.C. v. Simpson* (1984) 17 H.L.R. 206, C.A.]—who, though not married to one another, are living together as husband and wife [as to the meaning of which, see notes to s.62, above]);

(3) Persons who live or have lived in the same household, this would be wide enough to cover same sex partners, and indeed flatsharers, or a carer sharing the same house;

(4) Relatives (defined in s.178(3), below to include parents and step-parents, children and step-children, siblings and step-siblings, grandparents and grandchildren, uncles, aunts, nephews and nieces, whether of the person in question or that person's spouse or former spouse [or persons living or formerly living together as husband and wife], and whether by full-blood, half blood or affinity, [i.e. by marriage]);

(5) Those who have agreed to marry (or had done so); and,

(6) Persons are associated if each of them is a parent of a child, or has or has had parental responsibility for that child (within the meaning of the Children Act 1989, under which in addition to parents, guardians appointed under s.5 of the 1989 Act and those who have a residence order under s.8 may have parental responsibility, see ss.5 and 12—see s.178(3), below).

(7) Detailed provision is also made by s.178(2), below, governing association arising out of adoptions.

General housing circumstances of area (s.177(2)). This is one of the central concepts of previous homelessness law, albeit that most of it was developed in relation to intentionality. Initially, indeed, it bore not at all on the definition of homelessness itself, but it was in practice being applied by the courts at the point in the evolution of the law—considered above, in relation to Accommodation—at which an equation was being drawn between being homeless and the occupation of accommodation so poor that it could be quit without a finding of intentionality.

Notwithstanding *Awua* [1996] 1 A.C. 55, 27 H.L.R. 453, H.L. (above), it is impossible to argue that Parliament intended anything other than the importation of the identical criteria when—by s.14, Housing and Planning Act 1986—it adopted the exact same phraseology (reasonable to continue to occupy, subject to the general housing conditions of the area) for use in the definition (s.58, 1985 Act) of homelessness as already existed in the definition of intentionality (*ibid.*, s.60). See also *R. v. L.B. Wandsworth, ex p. Wingrove*, and *R. v. L.B. Wandsworth, ex p. Mansoor* [1996] 3 All E.R. 913, C.A.

The comparison is between current accommodation, wherever situated, and conditions in the area of the authority to which application is made. Section 177(2) requires the authority to carry out a balancing act between the housing conditions in the authority's area and the accommodation quit, but whether or not it is reasonable to continue to occupy accommodation involves other questions, such as the pattern of life followed by the applicant: *R. v. London Borough of Tower Hamlets, ex p. Monaf* (1988) 20 H.L.R. 529, C.A.

See also *R. v. Newham L.B.C., ex p. Ajayi* (1994) 28 H.L.R. 25, Q.B.D., referring to matters "of social history and national status" such as where children were born, and how long a person has lived somewhere. (In that case, on intentionality, the issue was how long the applicant had formerly lived in the U.K., prior to a period abroad, departure from which accommodation gave rise to the finding: that precise position cannot arise when considering homelessness, because it is only accommodation in the U.K. which is in contemplation—see subs. (1); the principle, however, would seem capable of application to different parts of the U.K.) Such comparisons should only be made, however, where relevant to a case, since they are permissive and not mandatory: *R. v. London Borough of Newham, ex p. London Borough of Tower Hamlets* (1990) 23 H.L.R. 62, C.A.

Subject to the provisions of s.177(2), the question whether it is reasonable to continue to occupy is subjective and is not susceptible to a generalised or objective standard: *R. v. London Borough of Brent, ex p. McManus* (1993) 25 H.L.R. 643, Q.B.D. The question, however, is not whether it is reasonable to *leave* accommodation, but whether or not it is reasonable to *continue* to occupy it: see *R. v. Royal Borough of Kensington and Chelsea, ex p. Bayani* (1990) 22 H.L.R. 406, C.A. The distinction is significant: it will commonly be reasonable (in the sense of not unreasonable) to leave somewhere; what has to be sustained is the proposition that it is positively *not* reasonable to continue in occupation.

Whether or not it is reasonable to continue to occupy accommodation relates not only to the applicant but also to any other person who might reasonably be expected to reside with him: *R. v. Westminster City Council, ex p. Bishop* (1993) 25 H.L.R. 459, C.A., which must also be true of a person residing with the applicant as a member of the family, for it cannot be correct that *non*-family members are in a better position than members of the family.

Section 175(3) does not create a presumption that an applicant's current accommodation is *un*suitable, so as to impose a burden on the authority to rebut it: *R. v. Sedgemoor D.C., ex p. McCarthy* (1996) 28 H.L.R. 608, Q.B.D.

There is a number of different categories under which reasonableness to continue to occupy has been considered:

(i) Physical Conditions. This refers to that to which the consideration in s.177(2) is relevant: physical conditions may produce circumstances in which it is not reasonable to continue to occupy accommodation. This "one ray of hope for the authorities" (*per* Lord Denning M.R. in *de Falco, Silvestri v. Crawley Borough Council* [1980] Q.B. 460, C.A.) allows an authority to say "You ought to have stayed where you were before. You ought not to have landed yourself on us when it would have been reasonable for you to stay where you were."

The decision in *Tickner v. Mole Valley District Council*, August 1980 L.A.G. Bulletin, C.A., in which the applicants were evicted from a caravan site because they refused to pay increased rents which they thought excessive in view of the conditions on the site, turned on what is now s.177(2):

"That is what influenced this authority here. They had long waiting lists for housing. On those lists there were young couples waiting to be married: or young married couples sometimes staying with their in-laws: or people in poor accommodation. All those people were on the housing waiting lists—people who had been waiting for housing for years. The council thought it would be extremely unfair to all those on the waiting lists if these caravan dwellers—by coming in in this way—jumped the queue, when they were well able to pay the rent for the caravans and stay on. Those were perfectly legitimate considerations for the local authority to consider" (*per* Lord Denning M.R.).

In order to rely upon this provision, the authority need not consider in great detail all the information on housing conditions in their area, but may have regard to "the generally prevailing standard of accommodation in their area, with which people have to be satisfied" (*per* Lord Denning M.R. in *Tickner*).

It is clear that—before an applicant can claim with confidence that it would not be reasonable to continue to occupy accommodation on the ground of its physical condition—it will have to be very poor quality indeed. In *R. v. South Herefordshire District Council, ex p. Miles* (1983) 17 H.L.R. 82, Q.B.D., a hut approximately 20 feet by 10 feet, with two rooms, infested by rats, and with no mains services (although services were available in a nearby caravan occupied by relatives), was held to constitute accommodation an authority could consider it reasonable to continue in occupation of, at a time when there were two adults and two children living in it, albeit on the "borderline" of what was reasonable, but as crossing the borderline into what no authority could consider reasonable on the birth of a third child.

In *R. v. Preseli District Council, ex p. Fisher* (1984) 17 H.L.R. 147, Q.B.D., the applicant, and her children, had been living in temporary accommodation. For a period they lived in a caravan. Immediately before her application, they lived on a boat, without bath, shower, W.C., electricity, hot water system or kitchen with a sink. There was one cabin, which was kitchen, living room and bedroom combined, and she occupied it with her children and two friends. This was held not to amount to accommodation which it was reasonable to continue in occupation of.

In *R. v. Gravesham Borough Council, ex p. Winchester* (1986) 18 H.L.R. 208, Q.B.D., the applicant and his family had left accommodation in Alderney. Amongst the reasons for leaving were the fact that the accommodation was in an appalling state of disrepair, suffering from damp and a dangerous outside staircase and balcony. The family were found to be intentionally homeless. In reviewing this decision, the court stated that the main question to which the authority should apply themselves was whether it would have been reasonable for the applicant to stay where he was. It was not sufficient for the applicant's purpose that the authority should conclude merely that it was reasonable for him to leave; if on the facts it would have been reasonable for him to depart or to remain then his application would fail. The decision of the local authority that it would have been reasonable for him to remain was not unreasonable or perverse.

In *R. v. Medina Borough Council, ex p. Dee* (1992) 24 H.L.R. 562, Q.B.D., a decision that it would have been reasonable for a young woman and her new baby to occupy a prefabricated beach bungalow which suffered severe damp problems was quashed on the basis that the authority had given too much weight to the fact that the property was not considered to be unfit for human habitation and too little weight to the medical advice given to the applicant. See also *R. v. London Borough of Kensington and Chelsea, ex p. Youssef Ben-El-Mabrouk* (1995) 27 H.L.R. 564, C.A., where the want of adequate means of escape from fire did not necessarily mean that it was not reasonable for a couple with a small baby to stay in occupation of a fifth floor flat in an H.M.O., although a delay in rehousing the family under the provisions of the Land Compensation Act 1973 (c. 26) might itself (absent explanation from the authority) have been challengeable.

In *Puhlhofer* [1986] A.C. 484, 18 H.L.R. 158, H.L., at the Court of Appeal, Ackner L.J.'s view as to whether or not the applicants had any accommodation (within the meaning of the legislation) at all (see above, Accommodation) was based in part on the question whether or not it would have been reasonable to continue to occupy it, and considered that accommodation for the applicant, his wife and two children in one room in a guest house with no cooking or laundry facilities was not such that it would not have been reasonable to continue to occupy, in the light of the authority's evidence that there were no fewer than 44 families on the council's waiting list for two-bedroomed accommodation considered to be of higher priority under their points system.

In *R. v. Eastleigh Borough Council, ex p. Beattie (No. 1)* (1983) 10 H.L.R. 134, Q.B.D., overcrowding was relevant to the question whether or not it was reasonable for a family to remain in occupation of its accommodation. However, after the case was returned to the authority for reconsideration, the authority were held to be entitled to take into account that the property was not statutorily overcrowded, within 1985, Pt. X, when reaching the conclusion that it would have been reasonable for the family to remain: *R. v. Eastleigh Borough Council, ex p. Beattie (No. 2)* (1984) 17 H.L.R. 168, Q.B.D. See also, on overcrowding, *Krishnan v. London Borough of Hillingdon*, January 1981, L.A.G. Bulletin 137, Q.B.D., *R. v. London Borough of Tower Hamlets, ex p. Ojo* (1991) 23 H.L.R. 488, Q.B.D., and *R. v. London Borough of Tower Hamlets, ex p. Bibi* (1991) 23 H.L.R. 500, Q.B.D.

In *R. v. Westminster City Council, ex p. Ali* (1984) 11 H.L.R. 83, Q.B.D., (above), even if accommodation had been "available", it was said "that anyone should regard it as reasonable that a family of that size should live in one room 10ft × 12ft in size, or thereabouts, is something which I find astonishing. However, the matter has to be seen in the light of s.17(4) of the Housing (Homeless Persons) Act 1977 [now, s.177(2)] which requires that reasonableness must take account of the general circumstances prevailing in relation to housing in the area. No evidence has been placed before me that accommodation in the area of the Westminster City Council is so desperately short that it is reasonable to accept overcrowding of this degree. In the absence of such evidence I am driven to the conclusion that this question could not properly have been determined against the applicant."

If an applicant is claiming to be homeless because it is unreasonable to continue to occupy their accommodation due to overcrowding, an authority cannot refuse to consider the application simply because the accommodation is not statutorily overcrowded: *R. v. Westminster C.C., ex p. Alouat* (1989) 21 H.L.R. 477, Q.B.D.

(ii) Legal Conditions. The fact that the accommodation in *R. v. Exeter City Council, ex p. Gliddon* (1984) 14 H.L.R. 103, Q.B.D., (above), had been obtained by deception meant that it would not have been reasonable to remain in occupation of it. In *R. v. Portsmouth City Council, ex p. Knight* (1984) 10 H.L.R. 115, Q.B.D., and in *R. v. Surrey Heath Borough Council, ex p. Li* (1984) 16 H.L.R. 79, Q.B.D., once service occupancies had been determined and there could accordingly be no defence to an action for possession, the authorities could not consider that the occupiers should reasonably have remained in occupation pending proceedings. (These decisions have, however, always been difficult to reconcile with the definition of rights of occupation—extended to the right to remain in occupation under an enactment, see above, Rights of

Occupation).

None the less, the Code of Guidance issued under s.71, 1985 Act, discouraged authorities from requiring possession orders where there would be no defence, and in *R. v. London Borough of Newham, ex p. Ugbo* (1993) 26 H.L.R. 263, Q.B.D., the authority's failure to consider such guidance—and the implications of the applicant being only an assured shorthold rather than fully assured tenant—invalidated their decision on this issue. This must be compared with *R. v. London Borough of Croydon, ex p. Jarvis* (1993) 26 H.L.R. 194, Q.B.D., where the authority considered the guidance, but still reached the conclusion that it was reasonable to continue to occupy pending a court order following termination of an assured shorthold tenancy. In *R. v. Mole Valley District Council, ex p. Minnett* (1983) 12 H.L.R. 49, Q.B.D., the authority should have disregarded a departure one day before the date specified in a consent order for possession.

(iii) Employment and Financial Conditions. In *R. v. London Borough of Hammersmith & Fulham, ex p. Duro-Rama* (1983) 9 H.L.R. 71, Q.B.D., (above), issues of employment, and the availability of benefits, were held relevant considerations which the authority had ignored by confining itself to the matters set out in s.60(4) (now, s.177(2)).

The first of these considerations reflects the comment of Lord Lowry in *In Re Islam* [1983] 1 A.C. 688, 1 H.L.R. 107, H.L., that:

"There will, of course, and in the interests of mobility of labour ought to be, cases where the housing authority will ... accept that it would not have been reasonable in the circumstances for the applicant to continue to occupy the accommodation which he has left."

To the same effect, in *R. v. Winchester City Council, ex p. Ashton* (1991) 24 H.L.R. 520, C.A., it was held that no reasonable authority would have allowed the provisions of what is now s.177(2) to have governed a decision on intentionality where a middle-aged woman who had been unemployed for six years and had chronic active hepatitis left settled accommodation to take up work in another area.

The second of the considerations raises the question of "affordability": see *R. v. L.B. Wandsworth, ex p. Hawthorne* (1994) 27 H.L.R. 59, C.A., emphasising the need for the authority to consider whether the applicant's failure to pay rent, caused by the inadequacy of her financial resources) entitled her to succeed in her application to have a finding of intentionality quashed, under the general heading of reasonableness to remain in occupation; see also *R. v. Shrewsbury B.C., ex p. Griffiths* (1993) 25 H.L.R. 613, Q.B.D., in which it was said that it cannot be assumed that income support is sufficient to meet housing costs. See further *R. v. L.B. Hillingdon, ex p. Tinn* (1988) 20 H.L.R. 206, Q.B.D., *R. v. L.B. Brent, ex p. Baruwa* (1995) 28 H.L.R. 361, Q.B.D. and *R. v. Camden L.B.C., ex p. Aranda* (1996) 28 H.L.R. 672. Inadequacy of financial resources goes not merely to ability to pay the rent, but also to funding the necessities of life, including food: *R. v. Islington L.B.C., ex p. Bibi, The Times*, July 10, 1996, Q.B.D., 29 H.L.R. forthcoming, following *Tinn*. It is, however, for the authority not the court on a challenge to assess whether or not accommodation is affordable: *R. v. Brent L.B.C., ex p. Grossett* (1994) 28 H.L.R. 9, C.A.

(iv) Other Considerations. In *R. v. Basingstoke & Deane Borough Council, ex p. Bassett* (1983) 10 H.L.R. 125, Q.B.D., the court held that a woman who followed her husband (in that case, to Canada), notwithstanding the uncertainties of their prospects there, could not reasonably have remained in occupation of their secure council accommodation, where going to join him was her only chance of saving their marriage. It would be wrong, however, to view this as anything other than an illustration of the proposition that it is the particular circumstances of applicant and household which are relevant: *cf.* above, *R. v. London Borough of Brent, ex p. McManus* (1993) 25 H.L.R. 643, Q.B.D., and *R. v. Shrewsbury B.C., ex p. Griffiths* (1993) 25 H.L.R. 613, Q.B.D.

See also *R. v. Swansea City Council, ex p. Hearn* (1990) 23 H.L.R. 372, Q.B.D., in which the applicant's sense of isolation was held to be a factor relevant to deciding whether it was reasonable for her to continue to occupy premises. In *R. v. M.B. Sefton, ex p. Healiss* (1994) 27 H.L.R. 34, Q.B.D., the authority failed to consider the applicant's reasons for concluding that it was not reasonable for her to continue in occupation of the accommodation of which she was a secure tenant. Such reasons including repeated break-ins to the empty two (out of four) flats in her block, two burglaries in her own flat, harassment involving strangers knocking at door, stones thrown at windows, and shouting up to her windows at all hours of the day and night; further, gangs of youths congregated on the stairway smoking what was assumed to be drugs, the first floor landing was used as a latrine and smelled as such, and the applicant was too frightened to allow her child to play in the block and gardens.

In *R. v. London Borough of Wandsworth, ex p. Nimako-Boateng* (1983) 11 H.L.R. 95, Q.B.D., however, the court upheld the decision of the authority that a woman could reasonably have remained in occupation of the matrimonial home in Ghana, even though her relationship with her husband had broken down. (The court noted that it had been given no information about

Ghanaian domestic law, and assumed that the woman's rights would have been the same as under English law.) There was no complaint of domestic violence. *Nimako-Boateng* was followed in *R. v. Eastleigh Borough Council, ex p. Evans* (1984) 17 H.L.R. 515, Q.B.D.

An authority, in considering the question of whether it is reasonable to continue to occupy, may not disregard harassment, simply because it is not domestic: *R. v. London Borough of Hillingdon, ex p. H* (1988) 20 H.L.R. 559, Q.B.D.; see also *R. v. Northampton Borough Council, ex p. Clarkson* (1992) 24 H.L.R. 529, Q.B.D., where the issue was whether the applicant had been subjected to sexual harassment by her brother-in-law; see further *R. v. London Borough of Croydon, ex p. Toth* (1987) 20 H.L.R. 576, C.A., where the authority's decision was upheld despite threats of violence from men claiming that her husband owed them money.

Similarly, in *R. v. London Borough of Newham, ex p. McIlroy* (1991) 23 H.L.R. 570, Q.B.D., it would not have been unreasonable to have continued in occupation where Catholic applicants left accommodation in Northern Ireland after being subjected to several years of harassment by Protestant factions, culminating with a shooting incident, on the basis that they had failed to wait to see whether they would be rehoused by their landlords, the Northern Ireland Housing Executive.

Subs. (2)

Threatened with Homelessness
A person is threatened with homelessness for the purposes of Pt. VI, if it is likely that he will become homeless within 28 days. This period of 28 days was originally referable to the "normal" period granted by a court before a possession order would take effect. From October 3, 1980, however, courts have been under an obligation to make orders take effect within 14 days, save where exceptional hardship would be caused: see Housing Act 1980, s.89, although this is applicable only where the court has no other discretion to suspend, for example under the Rent Act 1977, the Housing Act 1985 or the Housing Act 1988.

There is no reason for drawing any distinction in principle between the definitions of homelessness and threatened with homelessness, other than the 28 day criterion: *Dyson v. Kerrier D.C.* [1980] 1 W.L.R. 1206 at p.1212, C.A. This seems to be based on a concession by counsel, but must surely be correct. If inquiries are made before the 28 days (see below, s.184), they will be non-statutory: *R. v. Rugby B.C., ex p. Hunt* (1992) 26 H.L.R. 1, Q.B.D.

Meaning of accommodation available for occupation

176. Accommodation shall be regarded as available for a person's occupation only if it is available for occupation by him together with—

    (a) any other person who normally resides with him as a member of his family, or

    (b) any other person who might reasonably be expected to reside with him.

References in this Part to securing that accommodation is available for a person's occupation shall be construed accordingly.

GENERAL NOTE
See notes to s.175, above.

Whether it is reasonable to continue to occupy accommodation

177.—(1) It is not reasonable for a person to continue to occupy accommodation if it is probable that this will lead to domestic violence against him, or against—

    (a) a person who normally resides with him as a member of his family, or

    (b) any other person who might reasonably be expected to reside with him.

For this purpose "domestic violence", in relation to a person, means violence from a person with whom he is associated, or threats of violence from such a person which are likely to be carried out.

(2) In determining whether it would be, or would have been, reasonable for a person to continue to occupy accommodation, regard may be had to the general circumstances prevailing in relation to housing in the district of the

local housing authority to whom he has applied for accommodation or for assistance in obtaining accommodation.

(3) The Secretary of State may by order specify—

(a) other circumstances in which it is to be regarded as reasonable or not reasonable for a person to continue to occupy accommodation, and

(b) other matters to be taken into account or disregarded in determining whether it would be, or would have been, reasonable for a person to continue to occupy accommodation.

GENERAL NOTE
See notes to s.175, above.

Meaning of associated person

178.—(1) For the purposes of this Part, a person is associated with another person if—

(a) they are or have been married to each other;

(b) they are cohabitants or former cohabitants;

(c) they live or have lived in the same household;

(d) they are relatives;

(e) they have agreed to marry one another (whether or not that agreement has been terminated);

(f) in relation to a child, each of them is a parent of the child or has, or has had, parental responsibility for the child.

(2) If a child has been adopted or has been freed for adoption by virtue of any of the enactments mentioned in section 16(1) of the Adoption Act 1976, two persons are also associated with each other for the purposes of this Part if—

(a) one is a natural parent of the child or a parent of such a natural parent, and

(b) the other is the child or a person—

(i) who has become a parent of the child by virtue of an adoption order or who has applied for an adoption order, or

(ii) with whom the child has at any time been placed for adoption.

(3) In this section—

"adoption order" has the meaning given by section 72(1) of the Adoption Act 1976;

"child" means a person under the age of 18 years;

"cohabitants" means a man and a woman who, although not married to each other, are living together as husband and wife, and "former cohabitants" shall be construed accordingly;

"parental responsibility" has the same meaning as in the Children Act 1989; and

"relative", in relation to a person, means—

(a) the father, mother, stepfather, stepmother, son, daughter, stepson, stepdaughter, grandmother, grandfather, grandson or granddaughter of that person or of that person's spouse or former spouse, or

(b) the brother, sister, uncle, aunt, niece or nephew (whether of the full blood or of the half blood or by affinity) of that person or of that person's spouse or former spouse,

and includes, in relation to a person who is living or has lived with another person as husband and wife, a person who would fall within paragraph (a) or (b) if the parties were married to each other.

GENERAL NOTE
See notes to s.175, above.

General functions in relation to homelessness or threatened homelessness

Duty of local housing authority to provide advisory services

179.—(1) Every local housing authority shall secure that advice and information about homelessness, and the prevention of homelessness, is available free of charge to any person in their district.

(2) The authority may give to any person by whom such advice and information is provided on behalf of the authority assistance by way of grant or loan.

(3) A local housing authority may also assist any such person—

(a) by permitting him to use premises belonging to the authority,

(b) by making available furniture or other goods, whether by way of gift, loan or otherwise, and

(c) by making available the services of staff employed by the authority.

DEFINITION
"local housing authority": ss.217, 218.

GENERAL NOTE
This is a new provision. Under the following section, the Secretary of State for the Environment has, and local authorities have, power to assist voluntary organisations concerned with homelessness, which replicates a power to be found in s.73, 1985 Act; under this section, however, local housing authorities (a) have a duty to secure that advice and information about homelessness and its prevention is available—free of charge—to anyone in their area, and (b) have a power to assist anyone who discharges that duty on their behalf, by way of grant, loan, use of premises, furniture or other goods, and even the services of staff.

The terms of assistance under this section are to be found in s.181, below.

The duty to provide advice and information to person in the area is applicable even to those who are disqualified from assistance under ss.185, 186, below: see also s.183(3).

Assistance for voluntary organisations

180.—(1) The Secretary of State or a local housing authority may give assistance by way of grant or loan to voluntary organisations concerned with homelessness or matters relating to homelessness.

(2) local housing authority may also assist any such organisation—

(a) by permitting them to use premises belonging to the authority,

(b) by making available furniture or other goods, whether by way of gift, loan or otherwise, and

(c) by making available the services of staff employed by the authority.

(3) A "voluntary organisation" means a body (other than a public or local authority) whose activities are not carried on for profit.

DEFINITION
"local housing authority": ss.217, 218.

GENERAL NOTE
Voluntary organisations have long played an important role in assisting the homeless. Bodies such as housing associations have provided significant assistance to local authorities in the discharge of their obligations towards the homeless, especially the homeless in "special categories".

A voluntary organisation is, for the purposes of Pt. VII, a body whose activities are carried on otherwise than for profit, but not including a public or local authority. This definition is clearly wide enough to include housing associations and other non-profit making social landlords: *Goodman v. Dolphin Square Trust Ltd* (1979) 38 P. & C.R. 257, C.A. The powers permit the Secretary of State and a local authority to give money by way of grant or loan, to such voluntary organisations: subs. (1). Local authorities may also assist by letting such organisations use premises belonging to them, on such terms and conditions as may be agreed, and by making available furniture or other goods and the services of staff employed by them: subs. (2).

The terms of assistance under this section are to be found in s.181, below.

Terms and conditions of assistance

181.—(1) This section has effect as to the terms and conditions on which assistance is given under section 179 or 180.

(2) Assistance shall be on such terms, and subject to such conditions, as the person giving the assistance may determine.

(3) No assistance shall be given unless the person to whom it is given undertakes—

(a) to use the money, furniture or other goods or premises for a specified purpose, and

(b) to provide such information as may reasonably be required as to the manner in which the assistance is being used.

The person giving the assistance may require such information by notice in writing, which shall be complied with within 21 days beginning with the date on which the notice is served.

(4) The conditions subject to which assistance is given shall in all cases include conditions requiring the person to whom the assistance is given—

(a) to keep proper books of account and have them audited in such manner as may be specified,

(b) to keep records indicating how he has used the money, furniture or other goods or premises, and

(c) to submit the books of account and records for inspection by the person giving the assistance.

(5) If it appears to the person giving the assistance that the person to whom it was given has failed to carry out his undertaking as to the purpose for which the assistance was to be used, he shall take all reasonable steps to recover from that person an amount equal to the amount of the assistance.

(6) He must first serve on the person to whom the assistance was given a notice specifying the amount which in his opinion is recoverable and the basis on which that amount has been calculated.

GENERAL NOTE

This section governs the terms on which assistance may be provided either to a person discharging on their behalf an authority's duty to afford advice and information to people in their area under s.179, above, or to a voluntary organisation concerned with homelessness under s.180, above.

No assistance of any kind is to be given unless the voluntary organisation first gives an undertaking (a) to use the money, furniture or other goods or premises made available to them, for a specified purpose, and (b) that if required to do so by the body providing such assistance, they will, within 21 days of notice served upon them, certify such information as to the manner in which assistance given to them is being used, as may reasonably be required by the notice: subs. (3).

In every case in which assistance is provided, the conditions must include a requirement that the voluntary organisation keep proper books of account and have them audited in a specified manner, keep records indicating how the assistance has been used and submit accounts and records for inspection by the body providing the assistance: subs. (4).

If it appears to the body providing the assistance that the voluntary organisation is not using it for the purposes specified in the undertaking, the assisting body must take all reasonable steps to recover from the organisation an amount equal to the amount of the assistance, although no such amount is recoverable unless there has first been served on the voluntary organisation a notice specifying the amount alleged to be recoverable, and the basis upon which it has been calculated: subss. (5), (6).

Guidance by the Secretary of State

182.—(1) In the exercise of their functions relating to homelessness and the prevention of homelessness, a local housing authority or social services authority shall have regard to such guidance as may from time to time be given by the Secretary of State.

(2) The Secretary of State may give guidance either generally or to specified descriptions of authorities.

DEFINITIONS
"local housing authority": ss.217, 218.
"social services authority": ss.217.

GENERAL NOTE
This section is the equivalent of s.71, 1985 Act: see also above, s.169.

It is clear that authorities are not bound to follow the Code blindly; they may depart from its provisions so long as they have first had regard to them—*de Falco, Silvestri v. Crawley B.C.* [1980] Q.B. 460, C.A., *Miller v. L.B. Wandsworth, The Times*, March 19, 1980, Q.B.D., *Lambert v. L.B. Ealing* [1981] 1 W.L.R. 550, 2 H.L.R. 58, C.A. As Parliament has required authorities to have regard to it, deviation from its provisions may amount to a *prima facie* case that it has not been take into account, sufficient at least (in practice) to call for an explanation from the authority: *cf. Padfield v. Minister of Agriculture, Fisheries & Food* [1968] A.C. 997, H.L. The Act is, of course, the governing instrument and if there is a conflict between a provision of the Act and of the Code, the Act takes precedence: *R. v. Waveney D.C., ex p. Bowers* [1983] Q.B. 238, 4 H.L.R. 118, C.A.

The Code may none the less remain a useful illustration of policy (*Parr v. Wyre B.C.* (1982) 2 H.L.R. 71, C.A.) and otherwise in terms of interpretation, or correct approach (*R. v. West Dorset D.C., ex p. Phillips* (1985) 17 H.L.R. 336, Q.B.D. In *R. v. L.B. Newham, ex p. Bones* (1992) 25 H.L.R. 357, Q.B.D., regard to the wrong Code under Pt. III, 1985 Act was (combined with inadequate inquiries) sufficient to vitiate the decision, given an intervening change of emphasis. The Code itself would be reviewable at the instigation of an authority: *R. v. Secretary of State for the Environment, ex p. L.B. Tower Hamlets* (1993) 25 H.L.R. 524, C.A. In *R. v. London Borough of Newham, ex p. Bones* (1992) 25 H.L.R. 357, Q.B.D., the authority had regard to the second edition of the Code rather than the third. Since there had been some change of emphasis between the two, this error, combined with a failure to complete the necessary inquiries, led to the quashing of the decision on intentionality.

Application for assistance in case of homelessness or threatened homelessness

Application for assistance

183.—(1) The following provisions of this Part apply where a person applies to a local housing authority for accommodation, or for assistance in obtaining accommodation, and the authority have reason to believe that he is or may be homeless or threatened with homelessness.

(2) In this Part—
"applicant" means a person making such an application,
"assistance under this Part" means the benefit of any function under the following provisions of this Part relating to accommodation or assistance in obtaining accommodation, and
"eligible for assistance" means not excluded from such assistance by section 185 (persons from abroad not eligible for housing assistance) or section 186 (asylum seekers and their dependents).

(3) Nothing in this section or the following provisions of this Part affects a person's entitlement to advice and information under section 179 (duty to provide advisory services).

DEFINITIONS
"homeless": s.175.
"local housing authority": ss.217, 218.
"threatened with homelessness": s.175.

GENERAL NOTE
This is a further definition section. Attention may be drawn to:
(i) The use of the word "assistance" to mean the benefit of a function—therefore, duty or power—under Pt. VII, relating to accommodation or assistance in obtaining it; and,
(ii) The use of the expression "eligible for assistance" to mean someone who is *not* excluded

from such assistance, *either* because he is wholly excluded as a person from abroad under s.185, *or* because he is conditionally excluded, as an asylum seeker, under s.186, if he has "accommodation in the United Kingdom, however temporary, available for his occupation" (see the discussions in the Introduction to Pt. VII, and in the General Note to s.175, above).

Applicants. Any person lawfully in the country may seek to avail himself of the provisions of this Part, save so far as those provisions expressly affect his entitlement (as under ss.185, 186, below): for this purpose, "lawfully" would seem to mean "not unlawfully", *i.e.* not someone who is an offender under s.14, Immigration Act 1971 (c. 77)—see *R. v. Westminster C.C., ex p. Castelli and Tristran-Garcia* (1996) 28 H.L.R. 617, C.A., *R. v. Secretary of State for the Environment, ex p. L.B. Tower Hamlets* [1993] Q.B. 632, 25 H.L.R. 524, C.A., *R. v. Hillingdon L.B.C., ex p. Streeting* [1980] 1 W.L.R. 1425, C.A.

The authority are entitled to reach their own decision as to whether or not an applicant for assistance is so disqualified, albeit (a) only for their own purposes, and (b) subject to a contrary decision by the Home Secretary: see *Castelli and Tristran-Garcia,* and see *ex p. L.B. Tower Hamlets.*

The latter case decided—apparently by concession—that the authority were not only entitled to make inquiries of the immigration authorities, and entitled to provide information to the immigration authorities, but were under a positive duty to report suspected illegal immigrants. If the immigration authorities later determine the matter in the applicant's favour, or else decide not to take immigration action against him, he will cease to be an illegal immigrant for the purposes of Pt. VII, and will be entitled to housing on the same basis as any other. If the applicant secures leave to challenge the authority's decision, the court held that the authority should not evict him pending the determination of that application.

If a person has already been granted accommodation by the authority, questions of status do not serve to deprive him of his rights pursuant to the agreement: see *Akinbolu v. Hackney L.B.C.* (1996) *The Times,* May 13, 1996, 29 H.L.R. forthcoming, C.A.

Streeting held that an application could be made even by a person with no local connection (below, s.199) with anywhere in the U.K.

A dependent child cannot apply in his own right, and otherwise a person must be capable of accepting or rejecting an offer of accommodation or assistance in order to qualify as an applicant: see *R. v. Oldham M.B.C., ex p. Garlick, R. v. Bexley L.B.C., ex p. Bentum, R. v. Tower Hamlets L.B.C., ex p. Begum* [1993] A.C. 509, 25 H.L.R. 319, H.L., in which it was held that dependent children were expected to be provided for by those on whom they were dependent (*i.e.* with assistance where appropriate, *e.g.* under this Part), and in which it was also held that there was only a duty to offer accommodation to those applicants in priority need who could decide whether or not to accept, not including persons so disabled that they have neither the capacity themselves to apply nor to authorise an agent on their behalf. There must be the capacity to understand and respond to the offer, and to undertake its responsibilities; whether or not a person so qualifies is a matter for the authority.

An application for housing by an existing tenant of the authority, is normally to be presumed to be an application for transfer, rather than for assistance under this Part (*R. v. Lambeth L.B.C., ex p. Pattinson* (1985) 28 H.L.R. 214, Q.B.D.), although there may be cases where the information provided shows that the applicant is already homeless or threatened with homelessness (in which case it will need to be treated under this Part notwithstanding the existing accommodation).

Applications. Authorities have to make provision to receive applications; in heavily populated areas, reasonable provision would be expected to require some form of 24-hour cover in respect of homeless persons: *R. v. London Borough of Camden, ex p. Gillan* (1988) 21 H.L.R. 114, Q.B.D. There is no requirement that the application be in writing, or in any particular form: *R. v. Chiltern D.C., ex p. Roberts* (1990) 23 H.L.R. 387, Q.B.D.

An applicant who has been housed pursuant to s.193—the principal duty to the unintentionally homeless in priority need—for the initial two-year period for which that duty lasts—can reapply at the end of it, and if still homeless, in priority need, and not homeless intentionally, will be entitled to rehousing: see General Note to s.193, below. Likewise, a person who has become homeless intentionally from accommodation provided under s.193 or who loses its benefits for some other reason is entitled to re-apply: *ibid.* What is under consideration in these notes is reapplication by a person who is, on application, refused assistance *under s.193,* and offered assistance only under one of the lesser powers (ss.190, 192), or who is offered but declines accommodation under s.193.

"The Act does not place any express limitation on ... who can make an application or as to how many applications can be made ... " (*R. v. North Devon D.C., ex p. Lewis* [1981] 1 W.L.R. 328, Q.B.D.). On the other hand, it is clear that an applicant cannot simply make application after application, to the effect that, for example, even if homeless intentionally, as soon as one period of temporary accommodation (below, s.190(2)) comes to an end, he is entitled to another: *Delahaye v. Oswestry B.C., The Times,* July 29, 1980, Q.B.D.

There is a number of questions:

(a) is the right to reapply dependent on a change in circumstances, or does it require an intervening period of settled accommodation, as where there has been intentionality?

(b) if the authority are exempt from a duty on account of an earlier application, does this mean that they do not have to entertain the new application, or does it mean that while they have to entertain the application, and accordingly engage in inquiries, etc., they can avoid the consequential duty by reference to their earlier discharge?

(c) if reliance is sought to be placed on "separate treatment", *i.e.* that although one member of a household is, or may be treated as, having become homeless intentionally, the other is not (see note on Whose Conduct, under s.191, below), does there have to be a separate application by this "innocent" party, or does a duty to consider this issue arise whoever makes the application?

(d) does the position change when there are applications to different authorities?

Change of Circumstances or Intervening Accommodation? In *Wyness v. Poole B.C.,* July 1979, L.A.G. Bulletin 166, C.C., it was held on an earlier application to the authority that the family had no local connection with Poole, but did have a local connection with Hart, in Hampshire. The family declined to accept a reference back to Hart, but "made do" in Poole until one of its members had acquired employment and thence a local connection with Poole. Poole was held obliged to reconsider the application on the basis of change of circumstances, and the authority's argument that the one discharge (by reference back to Hart) was sufficient was rejected. (The position on acquisition of a local connection was specifically considered in *R. v. London Borough of Tower Hamlets, ex p. Ali; R. v. London Borough of Tower Hamlets, ex p. Bibi* (1992) 25 H.L.R. 158, C.A., and the effect of *Wyness* upheld.)

In *R. v. Westminster C.C., ex p. Chambers* (1982) 6 H.L.R. 15, Q.B.D., the applicants rejected an earlier offer of accommodation and returned, each to live with her and his parents. After a period of time, they reapplied, and the authority held that they had become homeless intentionally, because they had refused the earlier offer. This was clearly unsustainable, on the wording of what is now s.191(1), with its reference to cessation of occupation. The court nonetheless refused relief, on the grounds that the authority had, by their earlier offer, discharged their duties (note now the provisions of s.191(4) and s.196(4), governing failure to take up accommodation in certain circumstances):

"The consequence is not to put housing authorities under an obligation to keep making offers of accommodation to a homeless person who unreasonably refuses to accept an appropriate offer. One such offer is enough. This is so even although the applicant's original state of unintentional homelessness subsists for a protracted period. If, in reality, he is experiencing one incidence of unintentional homelessness, one offer suffices. It will be otherwise with the person who experiences what can realistically be regarded as two separate incidences of unintentional homelessness. The second incidence will put the council under a fresh duty."

There had, however, been no change of circumstances in *Chambers,* so that the *Wyness* argument was not advanced. In *R. v. London Borough of Ealing, ex p. McBain* [1985] 1 W.L.R. 1351; 18 H.L.R. 59, C.A., a woman refused what she considered an inappropriate offer. She was still challenging this offer in the county court (as at that time was considered possible, and as is now again possible: see notes to ss.202, 204, below), when she found she was pregnant again and reapplied. The authority held that they had discharged their duty, because there had been no change by way of intervening settled accommodation.

Necessarily assuming, in the absence of a decision from the county court on the first offer, that the first offer had been adequate, the Court of Appeal nonetheless rejected the "intervening settled accommodation" requirement and its equation of refusal with intentionality, holding instead that reapplication could be made when there had been a "material change of circumstances". This meant such a change that the earlier offer would no longer be suitable or that it would be an inadequate response to current need (*e.g.* because of more children).

In *Ortiz v. City of Westminster* (1993) 27 H.L.R. 364, C.A., a decision on "vulnerability" (see notes to s.189, below), it was said that if—contrary to the authority's view and the evidence (that the applicant would not suffer particular difficulty finding accommodation)—it did prove particularly difficult, the applicant could re-apply. It is unclear on what basis this is said: that it would establish, in substance, a material change of circumstances (from those envisaged by the authority), or perhaps that as it disproved the authority's factual foundation for their decision, that decision would itself be unable to stand. (The doubt cast on his own decision in *Ortiz* by Simon Brown L.J., in *R. v. Kensington and Chelsea R.B.C., Hammersmith & Fulham L.B.C., Westminster C.C., and Islington L.B.C., ex p. Kihara* (1996) *The Times,* July 10, 1996, 28 H.L.R. forthcoming, C.A. must also put the authority of this observation into some doubt.)

In *R. v. L.B. Tower Hamlets, ex p. Saber* (1992) 24 H.L.R. 611, it was held that a request to reconsider a decision was not a reapplication, with the attendant formalities that would follow, unless there had been a material change of circumstances in the *McBain* sense.

No Need to Consider Application, or Reliance on Prior Discharge? Most of the cases have not expressly dealt with the question whether no new duty means that the authority do not even have to entertain a new application, as distinct from whether it means that having received a new application, and decided that there has been no material change, the authority can discharge their duty by reference to the earlier offer, *i.e.* do the authority have to entertain a new application at all, or do they make inquiries, and then rely on the earlier finding?

This is, to some extent, a chicken-and-egg issue, for if the authority do not even inquire, how can they establish that there has been no material change or intervening accommodation? It seems that the point is answered by *Delahaye v. Oswestry Borough Council, The Times,* July 29, 1980, Q.B.D. (above): for the purposes of reapplication after a finding of intentionality there can be no new application, for otherwise the applicant could continue to enjoy new periods not only in s.190(2)(a) accommodation (for the homeless intentionally) but also in s.188 accommodation (pending inquiries); if so of the intentionally homeless, it is hard to see that it could be otherwise for other reapplicants.

In *R. v. London Borough of Tower Hamlets, ex p. Ali; R. v. London Borough of Tower Hamlets, ex p. Bibi* (1992) 25 H.L.R. 158, C.A., it was held that when an authority refer an application to another authority under what is now s.198, there is no discharge of duty under what is now s.193; accordingly, no question of prior discharge arises on a reapplication (once a local connection has been acquired).

Whose Application? It is now well-settled that a further application may be made by a member of the same household, even although another member has been or could be found to have become homeless intentionally: see notes to s.191, below. In *R. v. North Devon District Council, ex p. Lewis* [1981] 1 W.L.R. 328, the application was by the woman whose husband had earlier been found homeless intentionally.

In *R. v. London Borough of Ealing, ex p. Sidhu* (1982) 2 H.L.R. 45, Q.B.D., *R. v. Cardiff City Council, ex p. John* (1982) 9 H.L.R. 56, Q.B.D., *R. v. Eastleigh Borough Council, ex p. Beattie (No. 2)* (1984) 17 H.L.R. 168, Q.B.D., *R. v. West Dorset District Council, ex p. Phillips* (1985) 17 H.L.R. 336, Q.B.D., *R. v. Thanet D.C. ex p. Groves* (1990) 22 H.L.R. 223, Q.B.D., and *R. v. London Borough of Barnet, ex p. O'Connor* (1990) 22 H.L.R. 486, Q.B.D., the new application was also by the putatively "unintentionally homeless" party.

In *R. v. Penwith District Council, ex p. Trevena* (1985) 17 H.L.R. 526, Q.B.D., the application was joint. However, the point of "whose application" was not expressly taken, and in any event it is unclear that the court accepted the intentionality of the "other" party. In *R. v. London Borough of Ealing, ex p. Salmons* (1990) 23 H.L.R. 272, Q.B.D., the application was likewise joint, and the court held that the authority had complied with their duty by considering the position of the husband, who alleged he was unaware of arrears, from that of his wife.

The section itself refers to "a person making ... an application", and inquiries under s.184, below, are whether "he is" eligible for assistance, or whether "he has a local connection" with another authority. The wording, then, suggests that it is "the applicant" who is to be considered. On the other hand, inquiries into the local connection of the applicant alone would not suffice, for the local connections of a person reasonably to be expected to reside with the applicant are relevant (see s.198(2)), and priority need may arise by reference to non-applicants (see s.189). Similarly, if acquiescence to, or participation in, the act of another causing loss of accommodation may result in a finding of intentionality on the part of the applicant, the authority are at least entitled to inquire into matters relating to that other person.

It would introduce a surprising—and inconsistent—degree of legality or formality into Pt. VII if anything turned on who actually signs an application form. It is suggested, therefore, that any person whose circumstances will under Pt. VII necessarily be taken into consideration in determining eligibility for assistance, or the level of assistance, who is intended to fall within the ambit of an application and who could as a matter of law himself qualify as an applicant (*cf.*, above, last heading, Applicants), is someone who has indeed made an application, and is an applicant (albeit possibly through the agency of another).

Application to different authority. In *R. v. Slough Borough Council, ex p. L.B. Ealing* [1981] Q.B. 801, C.A., two applicants had been found homeless intentionally in Slough. One applicant then moved to Ealing, the other to Hillingdon, and both authorities concluded that the applicants were not homeless intentionally. In each case, however, the local connection provisions entitled Ealing and Hillingdon to refer the applicants back to Slough. While this approach may seem anomalous, it serves to illustrate how different authorities can reach different conclusions on the same question.

In the event, it was held that Slough were bound by the decisions of Ealing and Hillingdon. There is therefore nothing to stop an applicant moving around until he finds an authority who concludes that he is not homeless intentionally, and—provided that decision is not one which no reasonable authority could reach or that does not otherwise reflect a misdirection of law—there is no way in which the authority fixed with final responsibility for the applicants can defeat the decision, even although it conflicts with their own original decision.

The *Slough* decision was applied in *R. v. London Borough of Tower Hamlets, ex p. London Borough of Camden* (1989) 21 H.L.R. 197, Q.B.D. However, in its discretion, the court refused judicial review to quash the refusal of the first authority (Tower Hamlets) to accept the referral, as the referring authority (Camden) had failed to make adequate inquiries either of the applicant or of Tower Hamlets in order to resolve factual discrepancies in the applicant's statements to the two authorities. Authorities should examine with care, applications by persons declared homeless intentionally elsewhere; if there has been no intervening change of circumstances; they should afford the first authority to which application was made, and who will bear the burden if a second application is successful, an opportunity to comment on any discrepancies in the accounts given.

In *R. v. Newham London Borough Council, ex p. London Borough of Tower Hamlets* (1990) 23 H.L.R. 62, Q.B.D., the Court of Appeal went further than in the *Camden* case, holding that where an application to a second authority was made, that authority's inquiries should extend to examining the reasons for the refusal of the first authority to assist, and should take into account the general housing circumstances prevailing in the first authority's district. (See further, notes to s.198, below.)

There is, however, one anomaly. While the foregoing represents the position in cases of intentionality, it does not apply in cases where the first authority has made a "prior offer": *R. v. London Borough of Hammersmith & Fulham, ex p. O'Brian* (1985) 17 H.L.R. 471, Q.B.D. If Slough had not found intentionality, but had instead offered accommodation which the applicants had not accepted, and the applicants had similarly applied to Ealing and Hillingdon who had referred them back, Slough could have relied on the prior offer as a discharge under what is now s.193 (*cf.* the converse position when the first authority has merely referred the applicant to another authority, and the applicant later reapplies on the basis of change of circumstance, in which case there has been no prior discharge: *R. v. London Borough of Tower Hamlets, ex p. Ali; R. v. London Borough of Tower Hamlets, ex p. Bibi* (1992) 25 H.L.R. 158, C.A.).

Inquiry into cases of homelessness or threatened homelessness

184.—(1) If the local housing authority have reason to believe that an applicant may be homeless or threatened with homelessness, they shall make such inquiries as are necessary to satisfy themselves—

    (a) whether he is eligible for assistance, and

    (b) if so, whether any duty, and if so what duty, is owed to him under the following provisions of this Part.

(2) They may also make inquiries whether he has a local connection with the district of another local housing authority in England, Wales or Scotland.

(3) On completing their inquiries the authority shall notify the applicant of their decision and, so far as any issue is decided against his interests, inform him of the reasons for their decision.

(4) If the authority have notified or intend to notify another local housing authority under section 198 (referral of cases), they shall at the same time notify the applicant of that decision and inform him of the reasons for it.

(5) A notice under subsection (3) or (4) shall also inform the applicant of his right to request a review of the decision and of the time within which such a request must be made (see section 202).

(6) Notice required to be given to a person under this section shall be given in writing and, if not received by him, shall be treated as having been given to him if it is made available at the authority's office for a reasonable period for collection by him or on his behalf.

DEFINITIONS

    "applicant": s.183.

    "eligible for assistance": s.183.

    "homeless": s.175.

    "local connection": s.199.

    "local housing authority": ss.217, 218.

"threatened with homelessness": s.175.

GENERAL NOTE

This section contains the duty to make inquiries, such as are necessary to satisfy the authority whether or not the applicant is eligible for assistance (meaning, the benefit of any duty under Pt. VII relating to accommodation or assistance in obtaining accommodation), and—if so— whether any duty, and what duty, is owed to him: subs. (1). The duty only arises if the authority "have reason to believe" that the applicant may be homeless or threatened with homelessness, which sets a relatively low threshold before the inquiries have to be engaged in (*cf.* ss.190, 193, 195, 197—"are satisfied", s.211—"have reason to believe", and s.198—"consider"). While the duty arises irrespective of local connection elsewhere, the authority also have power to inquire into local connection: subs. (2).

This section also contains the duty to notify applicants of decisions, and—so far as adverse to his interests—to give reasons for them: subs. (3). Notices have to inform the applicant of the right to request a review: subs. (5).

A Note on Kihara. If the decision in *R. v. Kensington & Chelsea R.B.C., Hammersmith & Fulham L.B.C., Westminster C.C., and Islington L.B.C., ex p. Kihara* (1996) *The Times,* July 10, 1996, 29 H.L.R. forthcoming, C.A. (see further, notes to s.189, below, Vulnerability) is upheld on appeal, then duties under this section may come to impose much greater demands on authorities than hitherto, and may accordingly generate a greater volume of dispute and litigation. In that case, it was held—referable to asylum-seekers—that the phrase "other special reason" within the "vulnerable" category of priority need ("vulnerable as a result of old age, mental illness or handicap or physical disability or other special reason. . .") was not to be approached on an *ejusdem generis* basis, and rejected the argument that, therefore, it was limited to the mental or physical or other personal—or bodily—characteristics of an applicant.

It was held that the category was free-standing, unrestricted by any notion of physical or mental weakness other than that inherent in the word "vulnerable". It could be comprised of a combination of circumstances. The word "special" imported a requirement that the housing difficulties faced by an applicant are of an unusual degree of gravity, enough to differentiate him from other homeless persons, and did not include financial impecuniosity *by itself,* as an absence of means alone did not mark out one case from the generality of cases to a sufficient degree to render it "special", *i.e.* someone peculiarly in need of housing because of the risk of physical harm run from continuing homelessness.

Although asylum seekers excluded from benefit of the same class being considered in *Kihara* will now be excluded by s.185 below, this definition—in its qualitatively negative terms—*is capable of* extending to a very large number of single persons (hitherto believed to be outside the definition), not merely those who the "care in the community" policy have taken out of residential care (most of whom would probably have been accepted in any event), but also those who have never been in residential care but who can describe their conditions and circumstances with reference to something more than mere impecuniosity; put like that, it is hard to think that many single, homeless people—young or otherwise—would not be entitled to attribute their homelessness to a combination of circumstances. *At the lowest,* it will not be difficult—without the first shadow of dishonesty—to give rise to the question that their homelessness *may* have so been caused. (The subjective impressions of many are likely so to accord.)

What does this mean in practice? Given the disapplication of the local connection provisions under this section, it is difficult to see why single, homeless people—who so view their circumstances—should not apply to a number of authorities, in turn, for *consideration as* in priority need; that application will entitle them to housing under s.188 pending a determination (and will empower the authority to continue to house them through review and appeal, sometimes giving rise to circumstances when it would be difficult to refuse to exercise the power, *e.g.* in the case of the somewhat stronger claims).

Where applications are made late in the day (perhaps after the earlier hours have been spent seeking private accommodation), it is very hard indeed to see why there should not be an entitlement to a night's or a weekend's accommodation; not uncommonly, it will mean more. In the capital, the number of individual authorities in geographical proximity will make this a particular problem (and, again, the authority will have to make their own inquiries, and cannot rely on the inquiries of others—see notes to s.184, above—so that, *e.g.* even a central register would do no more than *reduce* the problem, or facilitate the inquiry: it cannot eliminate it).

While there are few who would argue with the social desirability of providing accommodation to all the homeless, it must be said that this prospect cuts across what appears to have been the intention of Parliament under the legislation since 1977 (for it would otherwise have seemed more logical to render temporary accommodation pending inquiries contingent merely on the appearance of homelessness alone), and indeed under the preceding Joint Circular (D.O.E. 18/74, D.H.S.S. 4/74, under National Assistance Act 1948 (c. 29)) from which the wording of the definition of priority need was derived.

Inquiries

The duty to inquire may not be delegated to another organisation. In *R. v. West Dorset D.C., West Dorset H.A., ex p. Gerrard* (1994) 27 H.L.R. 150, Q.B.D., the authority had transferred all of their housing stock to a housing association, and had reached an agreement whereby the association was to carry out the inquiries under what is now this section upon which the authority would base their decisions. Quashing West Dorset's decision that the applicant was not homeless, it was decided that, although the authority were entitled under what is now s.213 to enlist assistance from third parties in making inquiries, they must none the less take an active and dominant part in the investigative process.

On the other hand, in *R. v. Hertsmere B.C., ex p. Woolgar* (1995) 27 H.L.R. 703, Q.B.D., it was held that it was only the decision-making function which was exclusive to the authority, so that the investigative function of making inquiries could properly be delegated to an outside body (in any event, one recognised by statute, such as a registered housing association, which under the 1985 Act fell within the co-operation purview of what is now s.213, below, no longer including associations, or other registered social landlords).

In cases where vulnerability is claimed for medical reasons, it will be both proper and a necessary part of an authority's inquiries to consider a medical opinion. However, the authority must still decide the question of *vulnerability* for themselves: *R. v. London Borough of Lambeth, ex p. Carroll* (1987) 20 H.L.R. 142, Q.B.D.

Where an application is made by an occupier of property owned by the respondent authority, the duty to make inquiries imposes no fetter on any decision to recover possession. In *R. v. London Borough of Barnet, ex p. Grumbridge* (1992) 24 H.L.R. 433, Q.B.D., a trespasser sought judicial review of the authority's decision to evict him before determining his application for housing. It was held that there is no requirement or statutory obligation on a housing authority to determine whether a person is either homeless or in priority need or, indeed, on any of the other matters under (then) Pt. III of the 1985 Act, now this Part, before they decide whether to obtain possession of property occupied by an admitted trespasser.

Where there is no reason to believe that an applicant may be threatened with homelessness, the duty to make inquiries is not triggered, and the authority accordingly cannot make a decision whether or not an applicant is threatened with homelessness intentionally: *R. v. Rugby B.C., ex p. Hunt* (1992) 26 H.L.R. 1, Q.B.D. In *R. v. London Borough of Croydon, ex p. Jarvis* (1993) 26 H.L.R. 194, Q.B.D., the fact that notice had been given that possession would be required of premises let on an assured shorthold tenancy was not of itself sufficient to trigger a duty under this section.

Inquiries extend to making inquiries of other departments of the authority themselves, *e.g.* the housing department (referable to an earlier tenancy): *R. v. Camden L.B.C., ex p. Adair* (1996) *The Times,* April 30, 1996, 29 H.L.R. forthcoming, Q.B.D.

Breach of duty under this section does not *per se* give rise to an action in damages: *R. v. Northavon D.C., ex p. Palmer* (1995) 27 H.L.R. 576, C.A.

Subs. (1)

Manner of inquiry. In *R. v. West Dorset D.C., ex p. Phillips* (1985) 17 H.L.R. 336, Q.B.D., the authority were criticised for failing to make their inquiries in the caring and sympathetic way required by the then Code of Guidance under Pt. III, 1985 Act, but it would probably have been the view of the court that inquiries should be so conducted in any event (see also comments in the decision in *R. v. London Borough of Camden, ex p. Gillan* (1988) 21 H.L.R. 114, Q.B.D. (notes to s.183, above)).

Inconsistencies will frequently be found when someone's native language is not English: *R. v. Surrey Heath B.C., ex p. Li* (1984) 16 H.L.R. 79, Q.B.D. Where there is doubt as to the competence of an interpreter, the test is whether it has been shown that the interpreter is not—to the knowledge of the authority—competent to conduct the interview: *R. v. London Borough of Tower Hamlets, ex p. Jalika Begum* (1990) 24 H.L.R. 188, Q.B.D.

It is for the authority and not the courts to determine how the necessary inquiries are made, including who should conduct interviews and what questions should be asked. In *R. v. London Borough of Tower Hamlets, ex p. Khatun* (1995) 27 H.L.R. 465, C.A., the Court of Appeal overturned the first instance decision that interviews with an applicant (without own independent advisor or counsellor) were inherently flawed because they had been conducted by an employee of the council who would be inclined to protect the employer's limited resources.

Ambit of inquiries. Inquiries must cover all the factors relevant to questions of eligibility, *e.g.* priority need (*R. v. Ryedale D.C., ex p. Smith* (1983) 16 H.L.R. 66, Q.B.D.), risk of domestic violence in another area (*Patterson v. L.B. Greenwich* (1993) 26 H.L.R. 159, C.A.). Inquiries need not be so extensive as to amount to "CID-type" inquiries: *Lally v. Royal Borough of*

Kensington & Chelsea, The Times, March 27, 1980, Q.B.D. However, the burden of making inquiries is clearly and squarely on the authority: *R. v. Woodspring D.C., ex p. Walters* (1984) 16 H.L.R. 73, Q.B.D.; *R. v. Reigate & Banstead D.C., ex p. Paris* (1984) 17 H.L.R. 103, Q.B.D.; *R. v. L.B. Barnet, ex p. Babalola* (1995) 28 H.L.R. 196, Q.B.D. See also *R. v. L.B. Brent, ex p. Baruwa* (1995) 28 H.L.R. 361, Q.B.D., where the authority failed to inquire into the reasonableness of certain items of expenditure in the course of deciding whether or not the applicant could have afforded her rent for the purpose of determining intentionality (below, s.191).

In *Walters*, the applicant's solicitor gave the authority information which, if confirmed, would have led to a finding that the applicant was homeless. The authority wrongly approached the matter on the basis that the burden was on the applicant to prove her homelessness. In *Paris*, it was held that inquiries into matters relevant to a finding of intentionality have to be made, whether or not the applicant provides information which suggests there may be something to follow up, *e.g.* whether or not the last accommodation occupied was available and accommodation reasonable to continue in occupation.

In *R. v. Preseli D.C., ex p. Fisher* (1985) 17 H.L.R. 147, Q.B.D., it was held that such inquiries may have to go back over several years, to the last accommodation occupied by the applicant (if any) which was available and reasonable. See also *R. v. Westminster C.C., ex p. Iqbal* (1990) 22 H.L.R. 215, Q.B.D., where insufficient inquiries were made as to the applicant's claim that he was a political refugee.

The suggestion that an authority should inquire into local employment conditions in Brazil was rejected in *R. v. Royal Borough of Kensington & Chelsea, ex p. Cunha* (1988) 21 H.L.R. 16, Q.B.D. In *R. v. Nottingham C.C., ex p. Costello* (1989) 21 H.L.R. 301, Q.B.D., it was said that inquiries could only be attacked as inadequate if they were inquiries that no reasonable council could have failed to make. See also *R. v. Kensington & Chelsea (Royal) London B.C., ex p. Bayani* (1990), 22 H.L.R. 406, C.A., where the failure of the local authority to make full inquiries into the applicant's employment situation in the Philippines was not fatal to their finding of intentionality.

See further *R. v. Royal Borough of Kensington & Chelsea, ex p. Kassam* (1993) 26 H.L.R. 455, Q.B.D., where it was said that the court should not intervene merely because further inquiries would be sensible or desirable, but only if no reasonable authority could be satisfied that they were sufficient, which would depend on the facts of each case. In *R. v. Westminster C.C., ex p. Augustin* (1993) 25 H.L.R. 281, C.A., it could not be said that on the material before them, the authority could not have been satisfied that the applicant was homeless intentionally, therefore—in the circumstances—it could not be said that they had not made necessary inquiries.

See further *R. v. Newham L.B.C., ex p. Ajayi* (1994) 28 H.L.R. 25, Q.B.D., where it was held to be necessary to inquire for how long the applicant had been away from U.K., and where her children were born—important matters of social history and national status, it was said: the error had been in treating the case as an immigrant's application, rather than an indigenous applicant who had been abroad for a period—which emphasises how carefully and particularly inquiries must be conducted.

In *R. v. Bath C.C., ex p. Sangermano* (1984) 17 H.L.R. 94, Q.B.D., it was held that the authority ought either to have accepted medical evidence which was sent in by advisers, or to have made their own further inquiries. In *R. v. Eastleigh B.C., ex p. Beattie (No. 2)* (1984) 17 H.L.R. 168, Q.B.D., affidavit evidence in earlier proceedings was material which the authority ought to have taken into account, even though not expressly referred to during the course of a further application.

If an application arises through job loss, the authority have to inquire into why the job was lost: *R. v. Thurrock D.C., ex p. Williams* (1981) 1 H.L.R. 128, Q.B.D., see notes to s.191, below. In *Krishnan v. London Borough of Hillingdon*, June 1981 L.A.G. Bulletin 137, Q.B.D., the authority were held to have made inadequate inquiries when they failed to chase up an unanswered letter from themselves to another authority, or to follow up the applicant's own description of pressure on him to leave his earlier accommodation because of overcrowding.

In *Tickner v. Mole Valley D.C.*, August 1980 L.A.G. Bulletin 187, C.A., Lord Denning M.R. criticised the inquiries made as to whether or not the applicants were actually homeless. The applicants, while living in mobile homes, had given permanent addresses to the site manager, on which the authority based their conclusion that they were not homeless:

"They made that finding because each couple gave their permanent address elsewhere. One gave a mother-in-law's address. Another gave a divorced husband's address. I think that was not sufficient. Enquiries should have been made at the addresses given as permanent addresses. If the mother-in-law was asked—or if the divorced husband was asked—the answer would have been: 'We are not going to have that person back'. So Mole Council should have found these couples were homeless."

The cases must all be seen in context. *Tickner* concerned mobile homes. When people are living in mobile homes (in that case under allegedly phony holiday lettings), it is to be expected (a) that they will be asked by the site owner to state a permanent address elsewhere, and (b) that the fact that they give one such permanent address is barely evidence that they have a home elsewhere. All that Lord Denning M.R. was saying is that *in that case* the circumstances were such that the authority should not have drawn the inference of accommodation elsewhere with such ease.

In *de Falco, Silvestri v. Crawley B.C.* [1980] Q.B. 460, C.A., the applicants gave unemployment as their reason for leaving Italy, and did not put forward any material from which it might have been inferred that the accommodation that they had left was not accommodation which had been suitable for their occupation. Accordingly, the authority did not err in drawing the inference that what they had left was suitable accommodation, even though they made no express inquiry to this effect. *De Falco*, however, was an interlocutory application, and treated as such in *R. v. Reigate and Banstead B.C., ex p. Paris* (1984) 17 H.L.R. 103, Q.B.D., where express inquiry was held to be called for.

In *R. v. London Borough of Harrow, ex p. Holland* (1982) 4 H.L.R. 108, C.A., a couple applied as being homeless. They had been living at a series of temporary addresses since leaving a caravan site, which the authority were satisfied had been left in circumstances which amounted to intentional homelessness. At the Court of Appeal, the couple sought to rely on a suggestion that the man had enjoyed an intervening period of what would have been permanent accommodation in a boarding house but for reasons beyond his control, and for this reason could not be treated as being intentionally homeless. The basis for this (not uncomplicated) argument was that (a) the couple had at the relevant point in time separated following a quarrel, and (b) the room in which the man had been living (which was not available to the woman) would have remained available to him, had the boarding house not shut down.

It was found that the authority had been given no reason for suspecting either that one of the addresses might be permanent, or that, even if it was, it would have been acceptable to the man. The separation between the couple had never been mentioned. Accordingly, they had not failed to make appropriate inquiries. The court, however, seems to have accepted that the case must be approached on the basis of what the authority knew or ought to have known, even though in the particular case there was no basis for saying that they ought to have known this particular additional information.

In *R. v. Leeds C.C., ex p. Adamiec* (1991) 24 H.L.R. 138, Q.B.D., where the applicant alleged that he had been constrained to sell his home because of financial circumstances, the court refused to quash the decision that he was intentionally homeless either on the basis that a reasonable authority would have tested the material before them further or that a reasonable authority would have made further inquiries, but *cf. R. v. London Borough of Tower Hamlets, ex p. Ullah* (1992) 24 H.L.R. 680, Q.B.D., for a case where on the facts further (similar) inquiries were held to have been called for.

If someone is homeless, he has normally left other accommodation. The authority must ask why, and whether it was available or reasonable. If someone has been evicted for arrears, it may well be that there is an explanation. In *R. v. West Dorset D.C., ex p. Phillips* (1985) 17 H.L.R. 336, Q.B.D., at interview, the applicant burst out at her husband that she had always told him his drinking would get them into trouble. This was held not to be capable of being construed as acquiescence (see notes to s.191, below), even by the most hard-hearted of officers. It was astonishing that the officer had not made further inquiries. If he had, for example of social services, it would inevitably have led to the conclusion that she could not be blamed.

On the other hand, if reliance is sought to be placed on some eventuality which is not to be taken for granted, such as some peculiar circumstance which would alter the decision, and not even a suspicion of it has come to the authority's attention, it is that much harder to complain of the failure to ask a relevant question. Advisers in particular should be careful to put all relevant matters before an authority. An authority will not be criticised for failing to make inquiries of someone they have no reason to believe will provide relevant information, for example a doctor or a school where health or education were not apparently in issue.

In *R. v. London Borough of Wandsworth, ex p. Henderson* (1986) 18 H.L.R. 522, Q.B.D., the applicants contended that they were unaware of material facts when they agreed to an order for possession being made against them. The authority could not be faulted for failing to make appropriate inquiries when, on the facts available to them including what they had been told by the applicants, they had no reason to be aware of the circumstances. See also *R. v. Wycombe District Council, ex p. Mahsood* (1988) 20 H.L.R. 683, Q.B.D., where it was held that the authority had no reason to be aware of the applicant's ignorance of housing benefit entitlement during a period of absence and *R. v. Royal Borough of Kensington & Chelsea, ex p. Cunha* (1988) 21 H.L.R. 16, Q.B.D., where there had been little or no reference to the illness of the applicant's child as a reason for her return from Brazil and the sufficiency of inquiries was accordingly upheld. See further, *R. v. Sedgemoor D.C., ex p. McCarthy* (1996) 28 H.L.R. 608, Q.B.D., restating that the duty to make inquiries means inquiries appropriate to the facts known to the authority, or of which they ought reasonably to have been aware.

A decision reached without proper inquiries will be invalid. For example, a decision reached pursuant to a policy to treat all those evicted for arrears will be void as a failure to exercise properly the duty to reach an individual decision: *Williams v. Cynon Valley Council,* January 1980 L.A.G. Bulletin 16, C.C. Nor can the authority treat as homeless intentionally all those who have been evicted from premises on grounds which reflect tenant default, for example nuisance and annoyance: *Devenport v. Salford City Council* (1983) 8 H.L.R. 54, C.A.; *R. v. Cardiff City Council, ex p. John* (1982) 9 H.L.R. 56, Q.B.D. An eviction will be relevant material for the authority to take into account, but they must look at the circumstances giving rise to the order: *ibid.*

An authority must bear in mind that possession orders are within the discretion of the county court judge, who may have taken into account matters for which the applicant has no responsibility. Thus in *Stubbs v. Slough Borough Council,* January 1980 L.A.G. Bulletin, C.C., a court ordered the authority to reconsider their decision on intentionality because one element in the decision to order possession on the ground of nuisance had been the proximity of landlord and tenant, and their relationship, over which the tenant had no control.

Fairness. Basic issues have to be put to an applicant. In *R. v. Wyre B.C., ex p. Joyce* (1983) 11 H.L.R. 73, Q.B.D., the authority did not even ask why the applicant had fallen into mortgage arrears, which led them to leave something relevant out of account in their decision-making process, *i.e.* the answer that she might have given. In *R. v. L.B. Brent, ex p. Baruwa* (1995) 28 H.L.R. 361, Q.B.D., the authority did not put to the applicant their view that certain items of expenditure were not reasonably incurred, on the issue of whether or not she could have afforded her rent in the context of their decision on intentionality.

In *R. v. Wandsworth L.B.C., ex p. Rose* (1984) 11 H.L.R. 105, Q.B.D., the authority should have inquired into the applicant's state of mind when she quit her previous accommodation, *i.e.* what she had believed about the accommodation that she was coming to, which turned out to be less than settled. In *R. v. Dacorum B.C., ex p. Brown* (1989) 21 H.L.R. 405, Q.B.D., the authority conducted a brief interview with the applicant's father about why he had asked her and her partner to leave the family home. No record of the interview was made nor was any explanation of the father's comments sought from the applicant. In these circumstances, the inquiries were held to be inadequate.

In *R. v. Tower Hamlets L.B.C., ex p. Rouf* (1989) 21 H.L.R. 294, Q.B.D., the decision of the authority was quashed where they had failed to put to the applicant matters that were ultimately decided against him, and in *R. v. London Borough of Tower Hamlets, ex p. Nadia Saber* (1992) 24 H.L.R. 611, Q.B.D., decisive issues were put to the applicant's husband but not to the applicant herself. On the other hand, see *R. v. Sevenoaks D.C., ex p. Reynolds* (1989) 22 H.L.R. 250, C.A. where a finding of intentionality was upheld, despite important but ultimately not decisive issues not having been put directly to the applicant, who had refused both a home visit and an interview and requested that all communication be made through her solicitors.

In *R. v. Shrewsbury and Atcham B.C., ex p. Griffiths* (1993) 25 H.L.R. 613, Q.B.D., the failure of the authority to put information received from a bank, relating to mortgage arrears, invalidated the decision on intentionality. See also *R. v. London Borough of Brent, ex p. McManus* (1993) 25 H.L.R. 643, Q.B.D., and *R. v. London Borough of Hackney, ex p. Decordova* (1994) 27 H.L.R. 108, Q.B.D.

In *R. v. Poole B.C., ex p. Cooper* (1995) 27 H.L.R. 605, Q.B.D., the council had failed to put matters to the applicant which they believed had been provided to them on a "confidential" basis and which had led them to make an adverse finding against her. The court rejected their argument that the information should be withheld; fairness demanded that the applicant should be entitled to refute the allegations if she could.

The questions of whether the inquiry duty has properly been discharged, and whether a decision has properly been reached will commonly overlap. Thus, lack of natural justice or fairness will usually found a challenge both to the inquiry process, and to the final decision. Indeed, it is unlikely that any attack will be made on the inquiry process alone, for no one will complain of the inquiry process if they do not also object to the decision to which it has led.

When conducting inquiries fairly, authorities are not, however, bound to treat the issue as if in a court of law: *R. v. Southampton City Council, ex p. Ward* (1984) 14 H.L.R. 114, Q.B.D. They act reasonably if they act on responsible material, from responsible people who might reasonably be expected to provide a reliable account. An authority can rely on hearsay, in the sense that they are not obliged to confine themselves to direct evidence, for example where an authority relied on evidence from a social worker's supervisor, rather than the social worker herself: *Ward*; see also *R. v. Nottingham City Council, ex p. Costello* (1989) 21 H.L.R. 301, Q.B.D.

Nor, indeed, are the authority obliged to put everything to the applicant (*Ward*), although quite clearly the applicant must have an opportunity to deal at least with the generality of material which will adversely affect him, and this will normally mean matters of factual detail. In *Goddard v. Torridge District Council,* January 1982 L.A.G. Bulletin 9, High Court, the authority discussed with the applicant's former employers the circumstances in which he had quit his job and, accordingly, had lost his tied accommodation, and went into these matters fully with the applicant on three separate occasions, amounting to a sufficient investigation for these purposes.

In the Divisional Court hearing in *R. v. Hillingdon Homeless Persons Panel, ex p. Islam, The Times,* February 10, 1981, Q.B.D. (not forming part of the subsequent appeals—see [1983] 1 A.C. 688, C.A. and H.L., 1 H.L.R. 107, H.L.), an allegation of want of natural justice failed as—by the time of the decision—the authority had given the applicant the benefit of no less than six interviews. Nonetheless, the judgment seems to assume that a want of natural justice will be fatal to an authority's decision. In *Jennings v. Northavon District Council,* July 17, 1981, High Court, unreported, a want of natural justice was disclaimed by counsel for the applicant, but, again, it seems to be implied that had such an allegation been made and sustained, it would be an appropriate basis for setting the decision of the authority aside.

Summary. For a summary of the proper approach of an authority see *R. v. Gravesham B.C., ex p. Winchester* (1986) 18 H.L.R. 208, Q.B.D., at pp.214–215:

"The burden lies upon the local authority to make appropriate inquiries ... in a caring and sympathetic way ... These enquiries should be pursued rigorously and fairly albeit the authority are not under a duty to conduct detailed C.I.D.-type enquiries ... The applicant must be given an opportunity to explain matters which the local authority is minded to regard as weighing substantially against him ...".

Doubt. If the inquiries suggest that the applicant may have become homeless intentionally, but any doubt or uncertainty remains, then the issue is to be resolved in favour of the applicant: *R. v. North Devon District Council, ex p. Lewis* [1981] 1 W.L.R. 328, Q.B.D.; see also *R. v. Thurrock Borough Council, ex p. Williams* (1982) 1 H.L.R. 71, Q.B.D., and *R. v. Gravesham B.C., ex p. Winchester* (1986) 18 H.L.R. 208, Q.B.D.

Further inquiries. Once a decision has been made, there is no statutory power to make further inquiries in the absence of a new application: *R. v. L.B. Lambeth, ex p. Miah* (1995) 27 H.L.R. 21, Q.B.D. In *R. v. Dacorum B.C., ex p. Walsh* (1991) 24 H.L.R. 401, Q.B.D., however, further inquiries led the authority to the conclusion that an earlier account of being locked out of accommodation was entirely false; it was held that while there was no right to make a new decision on the same facts, the authority could do so if there was a change of circumstances, including new facts (which of definition includes the falsity of former facts). In *R. v. L.B. Southwark, ex p. Dagou* (1995) 28 H.L.R. 72, Q.B.D., it was held that only fraud and deception entitled the authority to re-open inquiries having reached their decision, although new information might still be relevant to the accommodation which was to be provided.

If a decision has been *adverse* to an applicant, however, it may be that if the authority receive new information, they can re-open their inquiries, of their own motion: consider *R. v. Hambleton D.C., ex p. Geoghan* [1985] J.P.L. 394, Q.B.D. This would also serve to cure any defects in their earlier procedure, *e.g.* failure to consider relevant matters. If the authority have power to do so, then it is hard to see that any reasonable authority could refuse to exercise it, *i.e.* at the request of a disappointed applicant, provided at least that the new information could (if accepted) affect the decision.

Subs. (2)

Even if, at an early stage, the authority consider that there may be a local connection, they are still under a duty to make the preliminary inquiries as to eligibility: *Delahaye v. Oswestry B.C., The Times,* July 29, 1980, Q.B.D. Indeed, such inquiries are exclusively in the province of the authority to which application has been made: *R. v. Slough B.C., ex p. London Borough of Ealing* [1981] Q.B. 801, C.A. (see notes to s.184).

If local connection inquiries are made, the first such inquiry is whether the applicant has a local connection with the area of another authority. This is because, if there is no such local connection, it will be irrelevant to consider whether or not there is one with the authority to which application has been made, as persons without a connection elsewhere will remain the responsibility of that authority: *R. v. London Borough of Hillingdon, ex p. Streeting* [1980] 1 W.L.R. 1425, D.C. and C.A.; see also *Betts v. Eastleigh B.C.* [1983] 1 W.L.R. 774, 8 H.L.R. 28, C.A., not overruled on this point by the House of Lords ([1983] 2 A.C. 613, 10 H.L.R. 97). See further, notes to s.198, below.

The authority can inquire into local connection as at the date of application, rather than leaving the matter until the end of their inquiries, and the decision: *R. v. Newham L.B.C., ex p. Smith* (1996), *The Times,* April 11, 29 H.L.R. forthcoming, Q.B.D.

Subs. (3)

Notification
When the authority have completed their inquiries, they must notify their decision to the applicant. If they decide any issue relating to eligibility or level of duty adversely to the applicant, they are also bound to notify him of their reasons for this decision.

Duties to notify and to give reasons for decisions arise independently of the substantive duties to which they refer: *R. v. Beverley Borough Council, ex p. McPhee, The Times*, October 27, 1978, Q.B.D. It is not open to an authority to claim that they have no duty under, for example, s.193 or s.200, on the ground that they have not yet given notice under this section. To hold otherwise would, of course, be to permit an authority to rely upon their own wrong, *i.e.* failure to provide notice "on completion" of inquiries.

Notification, and reasons, must be given in writing, and if not received by the applicant will only be treated as having been given in writing if they were made available at the authority's office for a reasonable time for collection by him or on his behalf: subs. (6). This appears to be so even if a copy of the notice is sent by registered post, or to one of the authority's own hostels, or other property. The express requirement for writing was originally added to the 1985 Act pursuant to Law Commission Recommendations (Cmnd. 9515), No. 5.

Reasons
The purpose of the requirement to give reasons is to enable the recipient to see whether they might be challengeable in law: see (originally) *Thornton v. Kirklees M.B.C.* [1979] Q.B. 626, C.A. (a judicial summary of counsel's submission, rather than a judicial observation in its own right), see also *R. v. Tynedale D.C., ex p. Shield* (1987) 22 H.L.R. 144, Q.B.D., and *R. v. Northampton B.C., ex p. Carpenter* (1993) 25 H.L.R. 349, Q.B.D., in which the decision letter was said to be "manifestly defective" because it failed to address the reasons the applicant had left his previous accommodation and accordingly defeated the purpose of the section which was "to enable someone who is entitled to a decision to see what the reasons are for that decision and to challenge those reasons if they are apparently inadequate.".

In *R. v. L.B. Croydon, ex p. Graham* (1993) 26 H.L.R. 286, C.A., Sir Thomas Bingham M.R. said:
"I readily accept that these difficult decisions are decisions for the housing authority and certainly a pedantic exegesis of letters of this kind would be inappropriate. There is, nonetheless, an obligation under the Act to give reasons and that must impose on the council a duty to given reasons which are intelligible and which convey to the applicant the reasons why the application has been rejected in such a way that if they disclose an error of reasoning the applicant may take such steps as may be indicated."

This quotation was cited with approval in *R. v. Islington L.B.C., ex p. Hinds* (1995) 28 H.L.R. 302, C.A., where the duty to give reasons was found to be complied with as the reasons stated in the decision letter were intelligible and conveyed clearly to the applicant the reason why his application had been rejected.

Save in exceptional circumstances, the courts will not permit the reasons given in the notification to be supplemented by affidavit on a challenge: see *Graham* and *R. v. City of Westminster, ex p. Ermakov* [1995] 8 Admin.L.R. 389, 28 H.L.R. forthcoming, C.A.; see also *R. v. L.B. Southwark, ex p. Dagou* (1995) 28 H.L.R. 72, Q.B.D.; *cf. R. v. Cardiff C.C., ex p. John* (1982) 9 H.L.R. 56, Q.B.D., where the court had held that the fact that the decision letter did not itself disclose the proper reasons for the decision did not prevent the authority from relying on proper reasons and justifying their decision accordingly, and *Hobbs v. Sutton L.B.C.* (1993) 26 H.L.R. 286, C.A., where the Court of Appeal accepted affidavit evidence amplifying and explaining earlier evidence as to reasons).

In *R. v. Westminster C.C., ex p. Augustin* (1993) 25 H.L.R. 281, C.A., however, it was held that a later letter could serve to rectify the shortcomings of an earlier notification (which, however, was not considered defective albeit "sparse"—*per* Auld J. in the court below—or "cryptic" [and brief]—*per* Glidewell L.J. in the Court of Appeal: it was considered to give the applicant the information she needed).

Furthermore, the courts have not always held authorities to the words of their reasons when decisions are challenged. The wording of the decision in *de Falco, Silvestri v. Crawley B.C.* [1980] Q.B. 460, C.A., was, so far as relevant, that "the council is of the opinion that you became homeless intentionally because you came to this country without having ensured that you had permanent accommodation to come to". This was clearly, and has since been expressly held to be, wrong: see notes to s.191, below. It was only upheld because the court was willing to go behind the wording used by the authority, and find that the applicants had left accommodation (in Italy) before coming to this country.

In *R. v. London Borough of Hillingdon, ex p. Islam* [1983] 1 A.C. 688, 1 H.L.R. 107, H.L., at the Court of Appeal, the court was similarly willing to disregard the express words used by the authority, and consider whether—in substance—there had been what could properly be called intentional homelessness. In *R. v. City of Westminster, ex p. Chambers* (1982) 6 H.L.R. 15, Q.B.D., the decision that the applicants had become homeless intentionally could not be sustained (see notes to s.191, below), but relief was withheld as the court considered that the authority had discharged their duties to the applicants by an earlier offer.

It has been held that authorities are entitled to give their reasons quite simply: "their decision and their reasons are not to be analysed in minute detail. They are not to be gone through as it were with a toothcomb. They are not to be criticised by saying: 'They have not mentioned this or that' ": *Tickner v. Mole Valley D.C.* [1980] 2 April, C.A. Transcript. In *Kelly v. Monklands D.C.*, July 12, 1985, Ct. of Session (O.H.), a mere recital of the words of the Act was even held sufficient on this point.

The nature and extent of reasons must, however, relate to the substantive issues raised by an applicant or, perhaps, by an applicant's adviser: see, *Re Poyser & Mills Arbitration* [1964] 2 Q.B. 467, approved by the House of Lords in *Westminster C.C. v. Great Portland Estates Plc* [1985] A.C. 661, and again in *Save Britain's Heritage v. Secretary of State for the Environment* [1991] 1 W.L.R. 153: "the reasons that are set out must be reasons which will not only be intelligible, but which deal with the substation points that have been raised", *per* Megaw J. in *Poyser*, and "The three criteria suggested in the *dictum* of Megaw J. are that the reasons should be proper, intelligible and adequate", *per* Lord Bridge in *Save Britain's Heritage*. See also *Givaudan v. Minister of Housing and Local Government* [1967] 1 W.L.R. 250, *Mountview Court Properties Ltd. v. Devlin* (1970) 21 P. & C.R. 689. In *Edwin H. Bradley & Sons Ltd. v. Secretary of State for the Environment* (1982) 264 E.G. 926, Glidewell J. added to the *dictum* of Megaw J. that reasons can be briefly stated (also approved in *Great Portland Street*).

Thus, in *City of Gloucester v. Miles* (1985) 17 H.L.R. 292, C.A., the Court of Appeal held that in order to comply with the requirement to state reasons, a notification of intentional homelessness (see below, s.191) ought to have stated: (a) that the authority are satisfied that the applicant for accommodation became homeless intentionally; (b) when he or she is considered to have become homeless; (c) why he or she is said to have become homeless at that time, *i.e.* what is the deliberate act or omission in consequence of which it is concluded that at that time he or she ceased to occupy accommodation which was available for his or her occupation; and, (d) that it would have been reasonable for him or her to continue to occupy it.

In *R. v. London Borough of Hillingdon, ex p. H.* (1988) 20 H.L.R. 559, Q.B.D., it was held that while the authority were entitled to express themselves quite simply, and could not be criticised for not having gone into great detail, it was none the less incumbent on them to say what was the deliberate act or omission in consequence of which it had been concluded that the applicant had ceased to occupy accommodation available for his occupation and which it would have been reasonable for him to continue to occupy. In the context of the case, this had required more than a statement that he could have continued to occupy his council tenancy in Northern Ireland. See also *R. v. London Borough of Southwark, ex p. Davies* (1993) 26 H.L.R. 677, Q.B.D.

In *R. v. London Borough of Tower Hamlets, ex p. Monaf* (1988) 20 H.L.R. 529, C.A., the court quashed the decision of the authority on the basis that the letters they had sent to the applicants did not disclose that they had carried out the proper balancing act called for in order to determine whether or not it would have been reasonable for applicants to remain in accommodation in Bangladesh, or to come back to the U.K.

In *R. v. Slough B.C., ex p. Khan* (1995) 27 H.L.R. 492, Q.B.D., a decision letter which addressed only one of a number of grounds on which a local connection was claimed was held to be defective. In *R. v. L.B. Brent, ex p. Baruwa* (1995) 28 H.L.R. 361, Q.B.D., it was impossible to work out from the decision letter any reasoning process, or the primary underlying reasoning, which had led the authority to conclude that the applicant was deliberately declining to pay rent which she could afford. In *R. v. Sedgemoor D.C., ex p. McCarthy* (1996) 28 H.L.R. 608, Q.B.D., however, the decision-letter was upheld, even though it had not dealt with the suitability of the applicant's current accommodation, as that issue had not been raised with the authority.

See also the cases on reasons for the decisions of Housing Benefit Review Boards: *R. v. Housing Benefit Review Board, ex p. Thomas* (1991) 25 H.L.R. 1, Q.B.D.; *R. v. Housing Benefit Review Board for East Devon D.C., ex p. Gibson* (1993) 25 H.L.R. 487, C.A.; *R. v. Sefton M.B.C., ex p. Cunningham* (1991) 23 H.L.R. 534, Q.B.D.; *R. v. Solihull M.B.C. Housing Benefit Review Board, ex p. Simpson* (1994) 27 H.L.R. 41, C.A.; *R. v. London Borough of Sutton, ex p. Partridge* (1994) 28 H.L.R. 315, Q.B.D.

Decisions

Although the obligation to reach a decision is not spelled out in the section, it is implicit: *R. v. London Borough of Ealing, ex p. Sidhu* (1982) 2 H.L.R. 45, Q.B.D. An authority may not defer the obligation in the hope or expectation of a change in circumstances such as might reduce their duties, for example by loss of priority need (*ibid.*), although it may be that in an appropriate case, a "*de minimis*" deferral, of perhaps just a few days, may be permissible where there is solid reason for the authority to anticipate a material change. As, however, the principal housing duty under this Part ends once an applicant ceases to be eligible for assistance (below, s.193(6)(a)), it should not be necessary to defer.

Otherwise, once the authority have completed their inquiries, they must make their decision. The decision must be taken on the basis of the information known to the authority at the time it is made. Thus, an applicant could not complain of a decision which failed to take into account a matter which only came to the knowledge of the authority after they had made their decision: *R. v. Hillingdon Homeless Persons Panel, ex p. Islam, The Times*, February 24, 1981, Q.B.D. (not forming part of the subsequent appeals—[1983] 1 A.C. 688, 1 H.L.R. 107, H.L.). The proper course in such circumstances would appear to be to put the further information before the authority in order for them to re-open their inquiries, and to consider review of a refusal to do so: see note on Further Inquiries, notes to subs. (1), above.

But an authority also must take into account all that is relevant up to the date of their decision. It is clear that it is the date of the decision, not the date of application, because the applicant is under a positive duty to inform the authority of material changes which occur before notification, under criminal sanction for failure to do so (s.214(2)).

The authority must reach their own decision. Even although other authorities must co-operate if they request assistance (s.213, below), one authority cannot simply "rubber-stamp" the decision of another: *R. v. South Herefordshire District Council, ex p. Miles* (1983) 17 H.L.R. 82, Q.B.D. There may, for example be information as to what has occurred between the two applications, for example a separation which means that intervening accommodation was "settled" for the purposes of the separated parts of a family: see notes to s.191, below. See also, above, General Note, under the heading Inquiries, *R. v. West Dorset D.C., West Dorset H.A., ex p. Gerrard* (1995) 27 H.L.R. 150, Q.B.D., *R. v. Hertsmere B.C., ex p. Woolgar* (1995) 27 H.L.R. 703, Q.B.D.

Challenge

Challenge to an adverse decision will normally mean—in the first instance—seeking a review under s.202, below; there is now a right of appeal to the county court on a point of law, under s.204, below, which will obviate—the need of an applicant to—and in the normal case probably prevent the right of an applicant to—seek judicial review: challenge is considered in the notes to s.204.

Eligibility for assistance

Persons from abroad not eligible for housing assistance

185.—(1) A person is not eligible for assistance under this Part if he is a person from abroad who is ineligible for housing assistance.

(2) A person who is subject to immigration control within the meaning of the Asylum and Immigration Act 1996 is not eligible for housing assistance unless he is of a class prescribed by regulations made by the Secretary of State.

(3) The Secretary of State may make provision by regulations as to other descriptions of persons who are to be treated for the purposes of this Part as persons from abroad who are ineligible for housing assistance.

(4) A person from abroad who is not eligible for housing assistance shall be disregarded in determining for the purposes of this Part whether another person—

(a) is homeless or threatened with homelessness, or

(b) has a priority need for accommodation.

DEFINITIONS

"assistance": s.183.
"eligible for assistance": s.183.

GENERAL NOTE

This is the first of two sections which limit or exclude the entitlement to assistance under this Part of immigrants, although unlike s.186, below, which repeats the provisions of the Asylum and Immigration Appeals Act 1993, this is entirely new. Further, while the 1993 Act only excludes entitlement where there is *some* accommodation available—"however temporary" (s.186(1))—this section excludes entitlement to housing assistance altogether (subs. (1)). There are two categories of person from abroad:

(a) Subs. (2): Those who are subject to immigration control within the meaning of the Asylum and Immigration Act 1996 (c. 49), *unless* within regulations made by the Secretary of State, *i.e.* unless "re-qualified" by regulations—see also s.161, above.

(b) Subs. (3): Others—not qualifying as subject to immigration control within the meaning of the Asylum and Immigration Act 1996—who are prescribed by regulations.

The breadth of the powers is striking, and other rules of law which may impact on their exercise will have to be borne in mind, *e.g.* E.C. provisions governing freedom of movement for the purposes of employment, and Race Relations Act 1976. The former was the subject of consideration in *R. v. Westminster C.C., ex p. Castelli and Tristran-Garcia* (1996) 28 H.L.R. 617, C.A.

Given the exclusion from assistance of illegal immigrants (*ibid.*, see also *R. v. Secretary of State for the Environment, ex p. L.B. Tower Hamlets* [1993] Q.B. 632, 25 H.L.R. 524, C.A.), the "targets" are immigrants who enter with leave, issued on the basis that they will not be dependent on "public funds", so defined to include homelessness assistance. (As it has been defined hitherto, housing provided under *Pt. III*, 1985 Act. This was at all times a nonsense, as Pt. III was not a power under which housing was provided, but a power—and duty—to secure that accommodation was made available, which in terms of public housing meant housing provided under *Pt. II*, 1985 Act; there will doubtless now be reference to this Part): Statement of Changes in Immigration Rules, HC 251.

Such an assurance, however genuine and however well-founded, did not exclude assistance for immigrants whose circumstances unexpectedly changed (*e.g.* destruction of owner-occupied accommodation): they would not thus become illegal. Accordingly, they would—just like anyone else legally in the country, unintentionally homeless, in priority need and without the resources to provide their own accommodation—be entitled to help.

As originally drafted, the clause was confined to subs. (3), and therefore did not *per se* disqualify persons from abroad. It was the regulations thereunder which were intended to do so. They were to be framed by reference to analogous provisions governing entitlement to housing benefit, *i.e.* the Housing Benefit (General) Regulations 1987 (S.I. 1987 No. 1971), Reg. 7A, added by the Housing Benefit and Council Tax Benefit (Amendment) Regulations 1994 (S.I. 1994 No. 470), as amended by the Income-Related Benefits Schemes (Miscellaneous Amendments) (No.3) Regulations 1994 (S.I. 1994 No. 1807) and the Social Security (Persons From Abroad) (Miscellaneous Amendments) Regulations 1996 (S.I. 1996 No. 30), which treat persons from abroad, as defined, as not liable to make payments in respect of a dwelling and, thus, take them out of housing benefit entitlement. Those so treated are those with limited leave to enter and remain in the U.K., given in accordance with immigration rules relating to there being, or to there needing to be, no recourse to public funds, or no charge on public funds. Those with a right of abode are unaffected.

Certain categories are excluded from that definition: E.C. nationals, nationals of states which are signatories to the European Convention on Social and Medical Assistance or to the Council of Europe Social Charter, nationals of the Channel Islands and the Isle of Man; also, those who have entered with limited leave (as above), who have during a period of limited leave (or a period as extended) supported themselves without recourse to public funds save for a period of not more than 42 days in which they have been temporarily without funds because remittances from abroad have been disrupted (provided there is a reasonable expectation that the supply of funds will be resumed).

Illegal immigrants or over-stayers, including E.C. nationals required to leave the U.K., and those not habitually resident in the U.K. are also excluded from benefit, although this is defined so as to leave E.C. workers, *refugees*, those with exceptional leave, and those whose deportation has been deferred or who the Secretary of State has allowed to remain, within entitlement.

By the Social Security (Persons from Abroad) (Miscellaneous Amendments) Regulations 1996 (S.I. 1996 No. 30), two further groups were to be excluded from housing benefit, being groups of refugees: (a) those whose applications for asylum had been refused, even though still pursuing an appeal (and even though removal is deferred); and, (b) those refugees who applied for asylum *after* entry, rather than at the point of entry. These two groups were also intended to have been excluded from assistance under this Part by the regulations that would have been made under this clause as drafted.

During the passage of the Bill, however, the Court of Appeal considered these last Regulations and held them to be *ultra vires* their governing legislation (Social Security Contributions and Benefits Act 1992 (c. 4)), on the grounds that they were in conflict with (and rendered nugatory) the rights of refugees necessarily implicit in the provisions of the Asylum and Immigration Appeals Act 1993 (c. 23) (and, if not, that the Regulations contemplated for some a life so destitute that no civilised society could tolerate it): *R. v. Secretary of State for Social Security, ex p. Re B. & Joint Council for the Welfare of Immigrants* (1996) *The Times,* June 27, 29 H.L.R. forthcoming, C.A.

Accordingly, exclusions that were intended to be effected by secondary legislation had to be effected by primary legislation, which led to the redrafting of this provision (and of what is now s.161, above). As with s.161, the subsection goes wider than the two categories under consideration in *ex p. B.*, for under the Asylum and Immigration Act 1996 (c. 43), s.13, a person is subject to immigration control if he requires leave to enter or remain in the U.K. (whether or not such leave has been given), and it accordingly covers *all* those who have entered other than as of right; regulations should, however, re-qualify them, *e.g.* those who are currently outside the housing benefit disqualification (as it would have stood at its widest, *but for* the decision in *B.*).

The Asylum and Immigration Act 1996 (c. 49), s.9, makes equivalent provision for Part III, 1985 Act, and came into effect on August 19, 1996. In *R. v. Secretary of State for the Environment, ex p. Shelter* (1996) 29 H.L.R. forthcoming, it was held that for those asylum-seekers who applied before the Act came into force their position will have to be reconsidered. Where inquiries had not been completed there would be no continuing duty, but the applicant should be given a reasonable period before being evicted from any temporary accommodation. Where applicants had acquired some form of security of tenure then they could only be evicted in accordance with their rights and would have to be reconsidered in the light of the new Act when and if they reapplied as homeless.

Subs. (4)

Persons from abroad thus ineligible are to be disregarded when deciding what duty is owed to someone else who *is* eligible for assistance and with whom the person from abroad resides or is reasonably to be expected to reside. This tends in two directions. On the one hand, a person without priority need would be unable to acquire priority need, or a person without a local connection would be unable to acquire a local connection, by reference to residing with a person from abroad, and the needs of a person from abroad to reside with an eligible applicant would not be taken into account when deciding on the accommodation to be provided. On the other hand, the fact that a person from abroad resides or might reasonably be expected to reside with an eligible person will not deprive that person of his eligibility.

Asylum-seekers and their dependants

186.—(1) An asylum-seeker, or a dependant of an asylum-seeker who is not by virtue of section 185 a person from abroad who is ineligible for housing assistance, is not eligible for assistance under this Part if he has any accommodation in the United Kingdom, however temporary, available for his occupation.

(2) For the purposes of this section a person who makes a claim for asylum—

(a) becomes an asylum-seeker at the time when his claim is recorded by the Secretary of State as having been made, and

(b) ceases to be an asylum-seeker at the time when his claim is recorded by the Secretary of State as having been finally determined or abandoned.

(3) For the purposes of this section a person—

(a) becomes a dependant of an asylum-seeker at the time when he is recorded by the Secretary of State as being a dependant of the asylum-seeker, and

(b) ceases to be a dependant of an asylum-seeker at the time when the person whose dependant he is ceases to be an asylum-seeker or, if it is earlier, at the time when he is recorded by the Secretary of State as ceasing to be a dependant of the asylum-seeker.

(4) In relation to an asylum-seeker, "dependant" means a person—

(a) who is his spouse or a child of his under the age of eighteen, and

(b) who has neither a right of abode in the United Kingdom nor indefinite leave under the Immigration Act 1971 to enter or remain in the United Kingdom.

(5) In this section a "claim for asylum" means a claim made by a person that it would be contrary to the United Kingdom's obligations under the Convention relating to the Status of Refugees done at Geneva on 28th July 1951 and the Protocol to that Convention for him to be removed from, or required to leave, the United Kingdom.

GENERAL NOTE
   This is the second of two sections dealing with immigrants. A person from abroad may be an asylum seeker, and may or may not be disqualified by s.185, above, *i.e.* depending (as current intentions stand) on whether or not application for asylum was made after entry, rather than at the point of entry, and whether or not the application for asylum has been refused, even if still pursuing an appeal. Unless not so disqualified, an asylum seeker's entitlement to assistance may still be limited by reference to this section. The same applies to their dependants (as to the meaning of which, see subss. (3), (4)).
   This section repeats the provisions of the Asylum and Immigration Appeals Act 1993. An asylum seeker—or dependant—will be deprived of assistance if he has accommodation in the U.K. "however temporary". (See, generally, Introduction to Pt. VII, and General Note to s.175, under the heading Accommodation, above, for the difficult relationship between this section—so far as relevant to this point, re-enacting the 1993 Act—and the decision of the House of Lords in *R. v. L.B. Brent, ex p. Awua* [1996] 1 A.C. 55, 27 H.L.R. 453, H.L., and that of the Court of Appeal in *R. v. L.B. Wandsworth, ex p. Wingrove*, and *R. v. L.B. Wandsworth, ex p. Mansoor* [1996] 3 All E.R. 913, C.A.)
   According to the Minister for Local Government, Housing and Urban Regeneration (Mr Curry), only about 5 per cent of claims to asylum are accepted: *Hansard* (H.C.), Standing Committee G, Nineteenth Sitting, March 19, 1996, col. 742.

Subss. (3), (4)
   These provisions define when a person is a dependant of an asylum seeker, who is subject, by subs. (1), to the same limitation on (and, ultimately, pursuant to s.185, disqualification from) Pt. VII assistance as the asylum seeker himself. According to the Minister, 80 per cent of asylum seekers do not have children: *ibid.* (However, in *R. v. Secretary of State for Social Security, ex p. Re B. & Joint Council for the Welfare of Immigrants* (1996) *The Times,* June 27, 29 H.L.R. forthcoming, C.A., the court refers to "roughly a third" of asylum-seekers having dependent children.)
   A spouse with his own right of abode, or limited leave (and not excluded by s.185, above) may still secure assistance in his own right, but without consideration of the asylum seeking partner: see s.185(4).

Subs. (5)
   The Convention Relating to the Status of Refugees, 1951, replaces earlier Arrangements and Conventions, and Protocols thereto (and conditionally retains the status for those so treated), and otherwise (subject to exceptions) applies to persons who have a "well-founded fear of being persecuted for reasons of race, religion, nationality, membership of a particular social group or political opinion", and who "is outside the country of his nationality and is unable or, owing to such fear, is unwilling to avail himself of the protection of that country ..." (Art. 1. The limitation referrable to events occurring before January 1, 1951, was removed by the Protocol adopted by the United Nations on December 16, 1966).
   By Art. 21, "As regards housing, the Contracting States, in so far as the matter is regulated by laws or regulations or is subject to the control of public authorities, shall accord to refugees lawfully staying in their territory treatment as favourable as possible and, in any event, not less favorable than that accorded to aliens generally in the same circumstances". Given the provisions of s.185, this section would appear to comply with this requirement.

Provision of information by Secretary of State

   187.—(1) The Secretary of State shall, at the request of a local housing authority, provide the authority with such information as they may require—
   (a) as to whether a person is or has become an asylum-seeker, or a dependant of an asylum-seeker, and
   (b) to enable them to determine whether such a person is eligible for assistance under this Part under section 185 (persons from abroad not eligible for housing assistance).
   (2) Where that information is given otherwise than in writing, the Secretary of State shall confirm it in writing if a written request is made to him by the authority.
   (3) If it appears to the Secretary of State that any application, decision or other change of circumstances has affected the status of a person about

whom information was previously provided by him to a local housing authority under this section, he shall inform the authority in writing of that fact, the reason for it and the date on which the previous information became inaccurate.

DEFINITIONS
"eligible for assistance": s.183.
"local housing authority": ss.217, 218.

GENERAL NOTE
In *L.B. Tower Hamlets v. Secretary of State for the Environment* (1993) 25 H.L.R. 524, C.A., it was decided—apparently by concession—that authorities were not only entitled to make inquiries of the immigration authorities, and entitled to provide information to the immigration authorities, but were under a positive duty to report suspected illegal immigrants (See General Note to s.183, above). The Secretary of State was under no corresponding duty to provide information to authorities, save under this section so far as concerns asylum seekers (and, formerly, under the 1993 Act): that omission, however, is rectified by this section.

For the background principles of confidentiality, see notes to s.32, above. Only inquiries related to the two categories of information will be protected: use of the section in order to secure information for another purpose, *e.g.* in connection with education, health, social work or employment functions, would not be protected (unless it can be said that the *Tower Hamlets* case sets down a principle of wider application than at first appears from it).

Subs. (3)
The point here is that if admitted on terms that there will be no recourse to public funds (see notes to s.185, above), the very application for assistance may lead the Secretary of State to revoke leave, or alternatively may imply evidence of leave sought on a false basis.

Interim duty to accommodate

Interim duty to accommodate in case of apparent priority need

188.—(1) If the local housing authority have reason to believe that an applicant may be homeless, eligible for assistance and have a priority need, they shall secure that accommodation is available for his occupation pending a decision as to the duty (if any) owed to him under the following provisions of this Part.

(2) The duty under this section arises irrespective of any possibility of the referral of the applicant's case to another local housing authority (see sections 198 to 200).

(3) The duty ceases when the authority's decision is notified to the applicant, even if the applicant requests a review of the decision (see section 202).

The authority may continue to secure that accommodation is available for the applicant's occupation pending a decision on a review.

DEFINITIONS
"available for his occupation": s.176.
"eligible for assistance": s.183.
"homeless": s.175.
"local housing authority": ss.217, 218.
"priority need": s.189.

GENERAL NOTE
This is the first of the housing obligations which comprises assistance under this Part. It is a duty to secure that accommodation is made available for the applicant (and household) pending inquiries under s.184: as to accommodation, and household, see General Note to s.175, above.

The duty arises irrespective of any opportunity the authority may have to refer the matter to another authority under the local connection provisions of ss.198–201 below (subs. (2)), and— unlike most other housing duties—it is not excluded on the grounds that the authority are satisfied that other suitable accommodation is available for the applicant's occupation in their area (s.197(1)).

The duty ceases when the applicant is notified of the authority's decision under s.184(3) above, even if the applicant requests a review under s.202 below, although the authority still have power under this section to continue to house pending the review (subs. (3)), and pending any appeal to the county court against the outcome of that review (see s.204(4), below).

Subs. (1)

The duty arises if "the local housing authority have reason to believe that an applicant may be homeless, eligible for assistance and have a priority need". This suggests a low threshold of belief in contrast to the other terminology in this Part, *i.e.* "are satisfied" (*e.g.* ss.182, 193, 195, 197), "have reason to believe" (s.211), and "consider" (s.198) that a state of affairs exists.

In discharging this duty, the authority are entitled to call for co-operation from other bodies, including another housing authority or a social services or social work department: s.213, see notes thereto, below.

The duty calls for some action on the part of the authority. In *R. v. London Borough of Ealing, ex p. Sidhu* (1982) 2 H.L.R. 45, Q.B.D., a women's refuge, not even in the authority's own area, had provided accommodation, which mere fact did not amount to a discharge of the duty. The fact that the accommodation was in another area was not itself fundamental to the result, but it may not be without relevance. Many such refuges are funded by local authorities. In such circumstances, there are two reasons why accommodation provided voluntarily and other than at the arrangement of the authority may be less susceptible to challenge: (a) because as a matter of practice, the refuge is not entirely independent of the authority; and (b) because the provision of funds for the refuge may be held to denote active participation or assistance by the authority.

The authority may require a person housed under this provision to pay such reasonable charges as they may determine, or to pay an amount towards the payment made by the authority to a third party for accommodation, for example a contribution towards the cost of private sector accommodation: s.206(2).

In *R. v. Tower Hamlets L.B.C., ex p. Thrasyvoulou* (1990) 23 H.L.R. 38, Q.B.D., a hotelier tried unsuccessfully to challenge a decision of the respondent authority to stop using low-grade hotels, including his own, for the purpose of discharging their duty under the analogous provisions of the 1985 Act. Such a claim by the hotelier was held to have no foundation in public law, since it was for the authority to decide which hotels they used in discharging their duty and the applicant had no interest in the issue.

Security of tenure. In *Family Housing Association v. Miah* (1982) 5 H.L.R. 94, C.A., *Restormel District Council v. Buscombe* (1982) 14 H.L.R. 91, C.A., and in *Royal Borough of Kensington and Chelsea v. Haydon* (1984) 17 H.L.R. 114, C.A., some doubt was cast on whether accommodation provided under the 1977 Act amounted to a tenancy or licence within the security provisions of what is now Pt. IV of the 1985 Act. This doubt, however, must be considered to have been resolved by *Eastleigh Borough Council v. Walsh* [1985] 1 W.L.R. 525; 17 H.L.R. 392, H.L., where accommodation provided under the temporary duty was held to amount to tenancy, notwithstanding the authority's attempt—successful at the Court of Appeal—to argue that any temporary accommodation so provided had to be by way of licence. See also *Street v. Mountford* [1985] A.C. 809; 17 H.L.R. 402, H.L. See further, notes to s.126, above.

The importance of this issue is considerably diminished by the removal of security of tenure under the 1985 Act and the Housing Act 1988, by Sched. 17 and s.209 below, although it may still bear on the means of determination of the right of occupation at common law.

Quality. Unlike the position under the 1985 Act, where the statutory requirements for suitability were not applicable to temporary accommodation pending inquiries, the suitability requirements of s.193, below, are applicable to every requirement to secure that accommodation is available, accordingly including under this section: see ss.206(1), 210(1) below.

None the less, earlier decisions on the quality of temporary accommodation under the 1977 Act (at which time there was also no "suitability" criterion applicable to *any* accommodation obligation under the legislation, therefore including that temporarily provided pending inquiries) are likely still to have some relevance, even though both related to temporary accommodation duty for the intentionally homeless (see s.190, below). In *R. v. Exeter City Council, ex p. Gliddon* (1984) 14 H.L.R. 103, Q.B.D., the authority were alleged to have been in breach of their temporary duty because the accommodation provided was in substantial disrepair, requiring works to prevent it becoming statutorily unfit for human habitation.

It was held that the authority were entitled to have regard to the time for which accommodation was likely to be occupied when determining what quality of accommodation is appropriate. The court accepted that some quality of accommodation would fall below the line of acceptable discharge of even a temporary duty, but accommodation needing works to pre-empt statutorily unfitness did not necessarily do so. Accommodation which is so unfit that it is not even reparable might well be inadequate even for a temporary purpose.

In *R. v. Southampton City Council, ex p. Ward* (1984) 14 H.L.R. 114, Q.B.D., accommodation on a caravan site that was described by a social worker as in appalling conditions was nonetheless upheld as an adequate discharge of the temporary duty, having regard to the family's expressed wish to live on a site, rather than in a permanent structure.

The decision in *R. v. Ryedale District Council, ex p. Smith* (1983) 16 H.L.R. 66, Q.B.D. (above, notes to s.184(1)), is also at first sight one under this duty. The applicants were placed in the accommodation—also a mobile home—immediately after application. However, as the court's ruling was that accommodation provided must be governed by what is learned during the inquiries under what is now s.184, it seems that it must be treated as a case on the obligation under what is now s.206, even though it is not clear that the authority had decided that it should be the applicants' permanent offer.

Termination of accommodation. On occasion, in particular when inquiries have taken some time (*e.g.* into accommodation abroad), a local authority will wish themselves to take action, or will have to deal with the position which arises if another landlord providing accommodation on behalf of the authority under this duty has taken or wants to take action, in respect of some default on the part of the occupier, *e.g.* non-payment of charges, nuisance and annoyance, damage to property. In such cases, it is not open to an authority to conclude that the applicant became homeless intentionally for loss of the accommodation provided under this section, as this was not the accommodation lost relative to which an application has been made which requires a decision: see *Din v. London Borough of Wandsworth* [1983] 1 A.C. 657, 1 H.L.R. 73, H.L.

This would appear to be the case notwithstanding the decision in *R. v. L.B. Brent, ex p. Awua* [1996] 1 A.C. 55, 27 H.L.R. 453, H.L., where what had been lost, although interim in quality, was accommodation provided to the applicant (by a previous authority), which had been withdrawn when that other authority had offered, and the applicant had refused, an offer of permanent accommodation (see also *R. v. East Hertfordshire D.C., ex p. Hunt* (1985) 18 H.L.R. 51, Q.B.D., the reasoning in which was criticised in *Awua* as "heroic", but the result of which was not doubted). See also s.193(5), (6) below. Until a decision is reached, what is in issue is the loss of the accommodation that gave rise to the (undetermined) application: intervening accommodation under this section does not create a new period of homelessness.

The position would therefore seem to be that, in such a case, the authority may none the less conclude that they have discharged their duty *under this section*, and decline to provide further accommodation pursuant to it, by parity of reasoning with the decision under what is now s.193 in *R. v. Westminster C.C., ex p. Chambers* (1982) 6 H.L.R. 15, Q.B.D. (see notes to ss.191, 193, below), albeit that they will still be bound to consider (and perhaps discharge) the duty under s.184, relative to the accommodation lost which led to the homelessness which gave rise to the application.

In reaching their decision on whether or not *that* loss amounted to intentionality, the loss of the intervening accommodation will not be relevant (*R. v. London Borough of Islington, ex p. Bashir Hassan* (1995) 27 H.L.R. 485, Q.B.D.), *save* if the conduct involved is of some evidential value in reaching a view on the earlier loss of accommodation, *e.g.* identical or analogous conduct (see *R. v. London Borough of Newham, ex p. Campbell* (1993) 26 H.L.R. 183, Q.B.D.).

Priority need for accommodation

189.—(1) The following have a priority need for accommodation—

    (a) a pregnant woman or a person with whom she resides or might reasonably be expected to reside;

    (b) a person with whom dependent children reside or might reasonably be expected to reside;

    (c) a person who is vulnerable as a result of old age, mental illness or handicap or physical disability or other special reason, or with whom such a person resides or might reasonably be expected to reside;

    (d) a person who is homeless or threatened with homelessness as a result of an emergency such as flood, fire or other disaster.

(2) The Secretary of State may by order—

    (a) specify further descriptions of persons as having a priority need for accommodation, and

    (b) amend or repeal any part of subsection (1).

(3) Before making such an order the Secretary of State shall consult such associations representing relevant authorities, and such other persons, as he considers appropriate.

(4) No such order shall be made unless a draft of it has been approved by resolution of each House of Parliament.

GENERAL NOTE

    This section contains the key definition of priority need, without which there will be no entitlement to substantive housing assistance at any stage, but merely access to advice and information under s.179, above, and to advice and such assistance in any attempts to secure his own accommodation as the authority consider appropriate in the circumstances, under s.190(3), below.

The section repeats 1985 Act, s.59, without change.

Dependent Children

Dependent children do not qualify in priority need in their own right; nor will they qualify as vulnerable either because of their youth or because of any disability: *R. v. Oldham B.C., ex p. G, R. v. London Borough of Bexley, ex p. B., R. v. Tower Hamlets L.B.C., ex p. Begum* [1993] A.C. 509, (1993) 25 H.L.R. 319, H.L. and see notes to s.183, above. Dependent children are expected to be provided for by those on whom they were dependent (*i.e.* with assistance where appropriate, *e.g.* under this Part); there is only a duty to offer accommodation to those applicants who can decide whether or not to accept it. There must be capacity to understand and respond to the offer, and to undertake its responsibilities; whether or not a person so qualifies is a matter for the authority.

In *R. v. Hillingdon Homeless Persons Panel, ex p. Islam, The Times,* February 24, 1981, Q.B.D., not cross-appealed by the authority on this point (*cf. Re Islam* [1983] 1 A.C. 688, C.A. and H.L., 1 H.L.R. 107, H.L.), the authority's unsuccessful contention was that if reliance was placed by an applicant on dependent children living with him, it was also necessary to show that such children might reasonably be expected to reside with him. The court held that the tests were alternative. If there were dependent children living with the applicant at the date of the authority's decision, it was not relevant to consider whether or not they might reasonably be expected to do so. See also *R. v. London Borough of Lewisham, ex p. Creppy* (1991) 24 H.L.R. 121, C.A. and *R. v. London Borough of Lambeth, ex p. Bodunrin* (1992) 24 H.L.R. 647, Q.B.D.

In *R. v. Ealing L.B.C., ex p. Sidhu* (1982) 2 H.L.R. 45, Q.B.D., the applicant was living in a women's refuge. She had an interim custody order from the county court, but the authority argued that they were entitled not to consider her in priority need until a full custody order was granted. The court held that a custody order was irrelevant to the question of priority need, nor indeed could the authority defer their decision in order to have time to assure themselves that no change would take place in the future, *i.e.* in this case, the remote prospect of the applicant losing custody at full hearing.

Although the court held that a custody order is irrelevant, this would not, of course, be so where an applicant's children are not currently residing with him, but might reasonably be expected to do so, *e.g.* where the applicant has won custody but cannot in practice take care of the children, for want of accommodation.

"Dependent" is not defined. *R. v. Royal Borough of Kensington and Chelsea, ex p. Amarfio* (1995) 27 H.L.R. 543, C.A., considered the Code of Guidance under Pt. III, 1985 Act, which referred to children under the age of 16 as dependent, together with those under the age of 19 either receiving full-time education or training or otherwise unable to support themselves, it was held that once a child has gone into full-time employment, he could not be dependent, and that a young person on a youth training scheme was in gainful employment by way of training and ought to be regarded as being in full-time employment. The court recognised, however, that it may be possible to conceive of circumstances where a 16 or 17 year old, although not financially dependent on his parents, is sufficiently dependent on them in other ways to bring him within the subsection.

The test of being "wholly and exclusively dependent" on the applicant and "wholly and exclusively residing with him" is wrong: *R. v. London Borough of Lambeth, ex p. Vagliviello* (1990) 22 H.L.R. 392, C.A. It is possible for a child to reside with and be dependent on more than one person, only one of whom may be applying for assistance. In *R. v. Port Talbot B.C., ex p. McCarthy* (1990) 23 H.L.R. 208, C.A., however, the parents were divorced and although there was a joint custody order, care and control had been given to the mother. Although it had been agreed that the children should spend three days a week with the father, they did not reside with him, as staying access did not equate to residence. Further, it was open to the council to take the view that the children should reasonably be expected to reside with the parent who had care and control. It would only be in very exceptional circumstances that a child might reside with both parents.

In *R. v. Kingswood B.C., ex p. Smith-Morse The Times,* December 8, 1994, the authority were held to have erred in applying the criterion "main" to residence, and in failing to consider the future as well as present arrangements for the child.

Pregnancy

Any length of pregnancy qualifies as priority need. One of the objects of the 1977 Act was to eliminate the practice of some authorities, who refused to consider a woman's pregnancy as a factor until a given length of time into pregnancy. Once the pregnancy is established, the priority need exists.

Vulnerability

Customarily, men and women at or past retirement age are considered vulnerable on account of old age. It was formerly considered that the correct approach was to ask first whether there is vulnerability at all, and second whether the vulnerability is attributable to any of the factors set out in this section, whether to one of them singly or to a combination of them: *R. v. Waveney D.C., ex p. Bowers* [1983] Q.B. 238, 4 H.L.R. 118, C.A. (see also *R. v. London Borough of Lambeth, ex p. Carroll* (1987) 20 H.L.R. 142, Q.B.D.). In *R. v. Kensington and Chelsea R.B.C., Hammersmith & Fulham L.B.C., Westminster C.C., and Islington L.B.C., ex p. Kihara* (1996) *The Times,* July 10, 1996, 29 H.L.R. forthcoming, C.A., however, it was suggested that this two-stage approach was capable of causing confusion, on the basis that the question is composite (without necessarily overruling it).

For this purpose, vulnerability means "less able to fend for oneself so that injury or detriment will result where a less vulnerable man will be able to cope without harmful effects" (*Bowers*) or "less able to fend for oneself when homeless or in finding and keeping accommodation" (*Carroll*), or vulnerability "loosely in terms of housing" or in the context of housing (*R. v. Bath C.C., ex p. Sangermano* (1984) 17 H.L.R. 94, Q.B.D.) or "a need for housing accommodation", *ex p. Kihara,* above).

In *R. v. Nithsdale D.C., ex p. Wilson* (1992) May Scolag 74, S.C., L.A.G., September 1992, p. 21, a young single woman had been excluded from her parental home, since when she had been in transient accommodation and had been subject to a sexual assault which left her anxious and unable to cope on the streets. The authority determined that she was not in priority need. The applicant asserted that she was "vulnerable" for some "other special reason". The court held that vulnerability was to be measured by comparing the position of the applicant in the housing market with other "assumed average or normal or run-of-the-mill homeless person(s)". The authority's decision was quashed since they had failed to make the enquiries necessary to apply the test.

See also *Kelly v. Monklands D.C.* July 12, 1985 Ct. of Session (O.H.): "I am not persuaded that every 16 year old is vulnerable within the meaning of the Act. However, when you find a girl of 16 who has no assets, no income and nowhere to go and who has apparently left home because of violence, I am of opinion that no reasonable authority could fail to conclude that she was vulnerable. A girl of that age and with that background is bound to be less able to fend for herself than a less vulnerable girl; being less able to cope, such a person is liable to injury or harm".

In *Ortiz v. Westminster City Council* (1993) 27 H.L.R. 364, C.A., which was a renewed application for leave, it was held that to establish vulnerability, an applicant must be able to show both (i) that to some material extent he is less able to obtain suitable accommodation than the ordinary person, and (ii) that if he fails to obtain it, he will suffer more than most. Accordingly, an applicant who had suffered from drug addiction and alcoholism, could be said not to be vulnerable because the authority were able to demonstrate that suitable accommodation would be available to her, including private lettings, bed and breakfast and supervised hostel accommodation.

Simon Brown L.J. cast doubt on his own analysis (although not the outcome on the facts) in *Ortiz* in *R. v. Kensington and Chelsea R.B.C., Hammersmith & Fulham L.B.C., Westminster C.C., and Islington L.B.C., ex p. Kihara* (1996) *The Times,* July 10, 1996, 29 H.L.R. forthcoming, C.A., and affirmed that he had not been seeking to establish any new principle of law (especially not so in a short, renewed leave hearing). In his later view, he considered that the first limb might more properly relate to whether or not the applicant is homeless than with priority need. (See further below, under *Other Special Reason.*)

Domestic violence. It appears to have been agreed and accepted in *R. v. Kensington and Chelsea R.B.C., Hammersmith & Fulham L.B.C., Westminster C.C., and Islington L.B.C., ex p. Kihara* (1996) *The Times,* July 10, 1996, 29 H.L.R. forthcoming, C.A., that "battered wives" were intended to be included within this subsection.

Handicap and disability. Grand mal epilepsy may render a person vulnerable if the attacks are taking place with intense regularity: *R. v. Wandsworth B.C., ex p. Banbury* (1987) 19 H.L.R. 76, Q.B.D. In that case, however, the facts before the authority did not disclose or deal with the effect of the disability on the applicant's ability to obtain and maintain accommodation, and accordingly it was held that their decision that the applicant was not vulnerable was not unreasonable. See also *R. v. Reigate and Banstead B.C., ex p. Di Domenico* (1988) 20 H.L.R. 153, Q.B.D., where the decision that a grand mal epileptic was not vulnerable was upheld on the grounds that, in the absence of evidence that the applicant had difficulty in finding or maintaining accommodation or special accommodation, the decision of the authority was not absurd.

On the other hand, in *R. v. Sheffield C.C., ex p. Leek* (1993) 26 H.L.R. 669, C.A., a decision on the vulnerability of an epileptic, which comprised a refusal to reconsider an earlier decision, was quashed on the ground that—as the question of the vulnerability of an epileptic was one of fact and degree—the position of any particular sufferer may need to be re-assessed from time to time.

Where vulnerability is claimed to be based on medical reasons, it is both proper and a necessary part of an authority's enquiries to consider medical opinion, but it remains for the authority to decide the question of vulnerability itself. It is their duty to make all the necessary enquiries, and to satisfy themselves whether the medical opinion is sufficient for them to determine the question of the applicant's vulnerability: *Carroll.*

In *Sangermano,* the court drew attention to the distinction between mental illness that is psychotic, and mental handicap. The latter is not concerned with illness, but with subnormality or severe subnormality. Not all subnormality will necessarily amount to vulnerability. Where medical evidence of subnormality had been put before the authority, however, the authority ought either to have accepted it, or made their own further enquiries. When determining priority need, the applicant's earlier rent arrears were a wholly irrelevant consideration. The court also noted, with reference to one of the features of the case, that language difficulties on their own would not amount to a "special reason" within subs. (1)(c).

Children Act 1989. Parallel provision for the housing of children and young people is to be found in the Children Act 1989 (c. 41). Section 20 provides:

"(1) Every local authority shall provide accommodation for any child in need within their area who appears to them to require accommodation as a result of—

(a) there being no person who has parental responsibility for him;

(b) his being lost or having been abandoned; or

(c) the person who has been caring for him being prevented (whether or not permanently, and for whatever reason) from providing him with suitable accommodation or care."

"(3) Every local authority shall provide accommodation for any child in need within their area who has reached the age of 16 and whose welfare the authority consider is likely to be seriously prejudiced if they do not provide him with accommodation."

The effect of the section is to impose a duty on social services authorities to house children in the circumstances set out in subs. (1) and to house young people in the circumstances set out in subs. (3). Additionally, the social services authority has power to provide accommodation for children and young people if they consider that to do so would safeguard or promote their welfare (s.20(4) and (5)). The specific duties contained in s.20 are supplementary to the general duty imposed by s.17 of the 1989 Act which requires authorities to:

"safeguard and promote the welfare of children within their area who are in need and so far as is consistent with that duty to promote the upbringing of such children by their families."

Just as housing authorities can seek the co-operation of social services authorities under s.213, below, social service authorities can ask housing authorities to assist, in which event, the housing authority must:

"comply with the request if it is compatible with their own statutory or other duties and obligations and does not unduly prejudice the discharge of any of their functions."

In *R. v. London Borough of Tower Hamlets, ex p. Byas* (1992) 25 H.L.R. 105, C.A. it was held that s.27 of the 1989 Act did not apply where one department of a local authority sought help from another department within the same authority.

In *R. v. Northavon D.C, ex p. Smith* [1994] 2 A.C. 402, 26 H.L.R. 659, H.L., Northavon refused Avon's request for assistance in housing a family with children whom Northavon had previously found to be intentionally homeless. In the Court of Appeal, the refusal by the High Court to grant judicial review was overturned on the basis that a previous finding of intentionality could not be decisive of the matters for consideration under s.27. The House of Lords, however, reversed the decision. Although housing and social services authorities were expected to co-operate, if no solution was forthcoming which did not unduly prejudice the discharge of the housing authority's function, in the final analysis the children remained the responsibility of social services.

Other Special Reason. In *R. v. Kensington and Chelsea R.B.C., Hammersmith & Fulham L.B.C., Westminster C.C., and Islington L.B.C., ex p. Kihara* (1996) *The Times,* July 10, 1996, 29 H.L.R. forthcoming, C.A., (understood to be subject to appeal), the court rejected an *ejusdem generis* approach to this phrase, and the argument that, therefore, it was limited to the mental or physical or other personal—or bodily—characteristics of an applicant. The category is free-standing, unrestricted by any notion of physical or mental weakness other than that inherent in the word "vulnerable". It can be comprised of a combination of circumstances. The word "special" imports a requirement that the housing difficulties faced by an applicant are of an unusual degree of gravity, enough to differentiate him from other homeless persons, and does not include financial impecuniosity *by itself,* as an absence of means alone does not mark out one case from the generality of cases to a sufficient degree to render it "special", *i.e.* someone peculiarly in need of housing because of the risk of physical harm run from continuing homelessness.

See the Note on *Kihara,* in the General Note to s.184, above, for the implications of the decision on accommodation pending inquiries.

The words "other special reason" require examination of all the personal circumstances of an applicant, including physical or mental characteristics or disabilities, but not so limited; accordingly, financial impecuniosity will be relevant as will be opportunities to raise money (*e.g.* persons prohibited from employment), whether or not an applicant has family and friends, and familiarity with the language, or—put another way—"utter poverty and resourcelessness".

Emergency
The event which causes the homelessness and the priority need must be both an emergency and a disaster. Fire and flood are not, of course, the only qualifying disasters. In *Noble v. South Herefordshire D.C.* (1983) 17 H.L.R. 80, C.A., it was held that the words "or any other disaster" which appeared in Housing (Homeless Persons) Act 1977, s.2(1)(b), meant another disaster similar to flood or fire. The omission of the word "any" in the 1985 Act, s.59 and in subs. (1)(d) of this section would not seem to affect this.

Noble was concerned with a demolition order under Housing Act 1985, Pt. IX. A demolition order was held not to qualify as a disaster similar to flood or fire, although on the facts of the case the occupiers had moved in after the demolition order had been made and it may be distinguishable in the case of a dangerous structure notice under the Public Health Act 1936 (c. 49), s.58, or analogous powers, imposed without any real forewarning, *cf.* the provisions of Greater London Council (General Powers) Act 1984, s.39 (below).

Where a demolition order under the Housing Act 1985 is imposed, however, the prior procedural steps suggest that it would not qualify as an emergency, and an occupier will in any event normally be entitled to rehousing under s.39, Land Compensation Act 1973 (c. 26). (See also *R. v. R.B. Kensington & Chelsea, ex p. Ben-El-Mabrouk* (1995) 27 H.L.R. 564, C.A., notes to s.175, Reasonable to Continue to Occupy, Physical Conditions, above, in which, accommodation subject to action for want of means of escape from fire could reasonably continue to be occupied pending rehousing under the 1973 Act). The perceived need for s.39, General Powers Act 1984 tends to support this.

A person who had been unlawfully evicted from his home is not in priority need within the subsection; if not actually flood or fire, the emergency must be of a similar nature, and must be construed *ejusdem generis: R. v. Bristol C.C., ex p. Bradic* (1995) 27 H.L.R. 584, C.A. (following *Noble*). The subsection is not confined to emergencies amounting to *"force majeure"*, but embraces all emergencies consisting of physical damage: *Bradic.*

The following persons are deemed to have become homeless or threatened with homelessness as a result of emergency such as flood, fire or other disaster (Greater London Council (General Powers) Act 1984, s.39, as amended by Sched. 17, below):

(i) A person who resides in a building in outer London in respect of which an order has been made by a magistrates' court under Greater London Council (General Powers) Act 1984, s.37, that the occupants are to be removed because of its dangerous state;

(ii) A person who resides in a building in inner or outer London whose occupants are in danger by reason of its proximity to a dangerous structure or building, within subs. (1) of *ibid.,* s.38, in respect an order has been made by the magistrates' court under *ibid.* s.38(2).

Subs. (2)
An analogous power was to be found in 1985 Act, s.59(2).

Subs. (3)

Consultation. See notes to s.5, above.

Duties to persons found to be homeless or threatened with homelessness

Duties to persons becoming homeless intentionally

190.—(1) This section applies where the local housing authority are satisfied that an applicant is homeless and is eligible for assistance but are also satisfied that he became homeless intentionally.

(2) If the authority are satisfied that the applicant has a priority need, they shall—

   (a) secure that accommodation is available for his occupation for such period as they consider will give him a reasonable opportunity of securing accommodation for his occupation, and

   (b) provide him with advice and such assistance as they consider appropriate in the circumstances in any attempts he may make to secure that accommodation becomes available for his occupation.

(3) If they are not satisfied that he has a priority need, they shall provide him with advice and such assistance as they consider appropriate in the circumstances in any attempts he may make to secure that accommodation becomes available for his occupation.

DEFINITIONS
"available for his occupation": s.176.
"eligible for assistance": s.183.
"homeless": s.175.
"homeless intentionally": s.191.
"local housing authority": ss.217, 218.
"priority need": s.189.

GENERAL NOTE

This is the second (*cf.*, above, s.188) substantive duty, governing the obligations of the authority towards those who they are satisfied are homeless intentionally (defined in the following section). See the notes to s.184 above, as to the proper approach to inquiries and decisions in relation to this issue: note that the authority must be satisfied of the intentionality, not merely "have reason to believe" (*cf.* ss.184, 211), or "consider" (s.198).

Although it does not expressly so state (*cf.* s.188(2), above) this duty likewise arises irrespective of any opportunity the authority may have to refer the matter to another authority under the local connection provisions of ss.198–201 below: decision-making on intentionality is exclusively within the province of the authority to which application has been made, who accordingly carry the relatively minor duties which follow such a finding—see General Note to s.184, above, Application to Different Authority. Nor is the section excluded on the grounds that the authority are satisfied that other suitable accommodation is available for the applicant's occupation in their area (s.197(1)).

Subs. (1)

This class of applicant is the homeless intentionally, but in priority need. The principal duty with which it is concerned is that contained in sub-para. (a), *i.e.* the duty imposed on the authority, to secure that accommodation is made available for the applicant's occupation—therefore, for applicant and household (see General Note to s.175, above)—"for such period as they consider will give him a reasonable opportunity of himself securing accommodation for his occupation".

An authority may discharge their duties under this provision not only by providing their own accommodation, but also by arranging for it to be provided by someone else, or by giving advice such as will secure that it is provided by someone else: s.206. Their own accommodation will not be secure under 1985 Act, Pt. IV: see Sched. 17, below. Nor will that of a private landlord be fully assured: see s.209, below. The question of quality of accommodation—which is governed by ss.206(1) and 210, below, and therefore requires to be "suitable", has been considered in the notes to s.188, above.

The duty has given rise to a number of problems. The first question is: from when does the time run? In *Dyson v. Kerrier D.C.* [1980] 1 W.L.R. 120, C.A., the applicant was told on May 21 that she would be provided with one month's accommodation from May 25 (the date when her homelessness would actually occur). This decision appears to have been taken by an official, and appears to have required ratification by a committee. In the event, the time was subsequently extended, to July 6, but it was not until July 3 that the committee's ratification was communicated to the applicant. It was held that time could run from the earlier notification, by the official, as the letter of July 3 was merely confirmation of that decision.

In *de Falco, Silvestri v. Crawley Borough Council* [1980] Q.B. 460, C.A., only four days had been allowed between notification of decision, and the expiry of what is now s.188 accommodation. The Master of the Rolls thought that this period was probably adequate, having regard to the several weeks in accommodation provided by the authority, prior to their decision. He was, however, also influenced by the time during which the applicants had been accommodated between the issue of proceedings and the hearing before the Court of Appeal. As *de Falco* was the hearing of an interlocutory appeal, for an interlocutory injunction to house until trial, that matter was conclusive on the exercise of judicial discretion.

The same point influenced Bridge L.J., although he was of the view that time prior to communication of the local authority's decision was wholly irrelevant, and that only time since that decision had been communicated could be of relevance. As the purpose of the provisions is to give the applicant time to find somewhere else to live once it has been decided that the authority need not provide permanent assistance, this view seems preferable. (Sir David Cairns thought that the decision was unreviewable.)

The courts may, however, be less generous towards an applicant who lives with another person who has previously been found homeless intentionally, and who has already enjoyed a period of subs. (2)(a) accommodation, although it seems to be an irresistible inference from *R. v. North Devon District Council, ex p. Lewis* [1981] 1 W.L.R. 328, Q.B.D., and other cases on this point (see General Note to s.191, below), that such a person may, indeed, re-apply, and will be entitled to new periods of s.193 and this section, subs. (2)(a) accommodation even if himself found homeless intentionally, and *prima facie* could and should benefit from the reasoning of Bridge L.J. in *de Falco*. Some reconciliation of merits and principle will probably be found in the extent of acquiescence or participation in the act which results in the finding of intentionality, and the corresponding extent to which such finding should, accordingly, have been anticipated.

In *Smith v. Bristol City Council*, January 20, 1981, C.C., a county court judge held that even where a substantial period of warning had been given to the applicant, the authority were still obliged to give some period of accommodation because the finding of intentionality preceded the homelessness, itself deferred by legal challenge:

"I cannot accept that 'no time' can in any circumstances be a reasonable period. . . . I find that a reasonable time must be given to the applicant after she actually becomes homeless . . . ."

The case went on appeal ((1981) L.A.G. Bulletin 287, C.A.) but there was no cross-appeal on this point by the authority.

A further problem is posed by "policies". In particular, the frequency with which all kinds of applicants receive identical offers of 28 days' accommodation suggests that many authorities operate a policy under this provision. If an inflexible policy can be demonstrated, it can be set aside: see, *e.g. British Oxygen Co. Ltd. v. Board of Trade* [1969] 2 Ch. 174, *In Re Betts* [1983] 2 A.C. 613, 10 H.L.R. 97, H.L., *Att.-Gen., ex rel. Tilley v. L.B. Wandsworth* [1981] 1 W.L.R. 854, C.A. See notes to s.204, below. However, if the 28-day rule is merely a guideline, which is reconsidered in each case, it may not be possible to set it aside as *ultra vires*.

This much is clear: an applicant's circumstances must be individually considered, and if it can be shown that time allowed has been reached without regard to his circumstances or was such a short period that no authority could have considered that it gave the applicant a reasonable opportunity to find somewhere for himself, the courts will order sufficient time: *Lally v. Royal Borough of Kensington and Chelsea, The Times*, March 27, 1980, Ch.D.

It may be that, in determining time under this section, an authority with both housing and social service functions should have regard to the duties that will arise under Children Act 1989 (see notes to s.189, above) on its expiry: see *R. v. L.B. Tower Hamlets, ex p. Monaf* (1988) 20 H.L.R. 529, C.A.

Subs. (3)

In *Ephraim v. London Borough of Newham* (1992) 25 H.L.R. 208, C.A., the plaintiff had been directed to a guest house by Newham as part of their advice and assistance. As a result, she took up occupation in a bed-sitting room in a house in multiple occupation. Subsequently, there was a fire in the property and the plaintiff suffered severe injuries. The H.M.O. lacked proper fire precautions. The plaintiff sued Newham, alleging that they were under a duty of care to satisfy themselves that the premises they advised her to go to were reasonably safe, particularly in relation to fire. This argument was rejected since the imposition of such a duty would put the authority in the dilemma of having either to inspect a particular property, or else to not advise people to seek accommodation which was there. It was more desirable that the authority should give advice which enables homeless people to obtain accommodation, even though some of the properties where they obtain it may prove not to be properly equipped in every respect, including in relation to fire resistance, than to restrict the range of advice and thus make it more difficult for the homeless to find housing.

Becoming homeless intentionally

191.—(1) A person becomes homeless intentionally if he deliberately does or fails to do anything in consequence of which he ceases to occupy accommodation which is available for his occupation and which it would have been reasonable for him to continue to occupy.

(2) For the purposes of subsection (1) an act or omission in good faith on the part of a person who was unaware of any relevant fact shall not be treated as deliberate.

(3) A person shall be treated as becoming homeless intentionally if—

(a) he enters into an arrangement under which he is required to cease to occupy accommodation which it would have been reasonable for him

to continue to occupy, and
  (b) the purpose of the arrangement is to enable him to become entitled to assistance under this Part,
and there is no other good reason why he is homeless.
  (4) A person who is given advice or assistance under section 197 (duty where other suitable alternative accommodation available), but fails to secure suitable accommodation in circumstances in which it was reasonably to be expected that he would do so, shall, if he makes a further application under this Part, be treated as having become homeless intentionally.

DEFINITION
"available for his occupation": s.176.

GENERAL NOTE
This section defines intentionality, the major area for contention under the 1977 and 1985 Acts. In substance, it repeats the definition formerly to be found in 1985 Act, s.60, with the following changes:
  (i) The definition is extended to include arrangements under which an applicant is required to cease to occupy accommodation which it would have been reasonable for him to continue to occupy, which arrangement had been entered into for the purpose of enabling him to become entitled to assistance under Pt. VII, and there is no other good reason why the applicant is homeless (subs. (3)): this category absorbs some classes of accommodation which would not be considered "settled" and so would not break a period of intentionality so as to entitle an applicant to re-apply (see further below, Intervening Accommodation), and comprises in part the related proposition that failure to take up occupation is not, and could not be, intentionality under the principal (subss. (1), (2)) definition—see *R. v. Westminster C.C., ex p. Chambers* (1982) 6 H.L.R. 24, Q.B.D., and other cases under the heading Cessation of Occupation, notes to subss. (1), (2), below.
  (ii) The definition is likewise extended to include persons to whom advice and assistance has been given under s.197, below, where the authority are satisfied that other suitable accommodation is available for the applicant's occupation in their area (see notes thereto, below) and the circumstances are such that it was reasonably to be expected that he would take it up. This likewise comprises in part the related proposition over failure to take up occupation.

Subss. (1), (2)
  The elements of the principal definition—all of which must be fulfilled before there can be a finding of intentionality on this ground—are:
  (a) the applicant must deliberately have done something or failed to do something;
  (b) the loss of accommodation must be in consequence of the act or omission;
  (c) there must be a cessation of occupation as distinct from a failure to take up accommodation;
  (d) the accommodation must have been available for the occupation of the homeless person; and
  (e) it must have been reasonable for the homeless person to continue to occupy the accommodation.
  Before considering these elements of intentionality, there is one other preliminary question to address, that of whose conduct it is to be taken into account.

Whose Conduct?
  The question has now arisen in a number of cases as to how an authority should treat an application where one of the applicants, or a member of the applicant's household, has either already been adjudged homeless intentionally, or is at least susceptible to a finding of intentionality.
  The question was first (and still most authoritatively) considered in *R. v. North Devon D.C., ex p. Lewis* [1981] 1 W.L.R. 328, Q.B.D., where a man quit his employment and lost his tied accommodation. He applied to the authority, which held that he had become homeless intentionally. Thereupon, the woman with whom he lived applied in her own name. The court rejected the authority's argument that they need only consider one application for the family unit as a whole. Each applicant was entitled to individual consideration. The court did, however, uphold the authority's alternative argument that, in considering whether or not she had become homeless intentionally, they could take into account conduct to which she had been a party, or in which she had acquiesced:
  "In my view, the fact that the Act requires consideration of the family unit as a whole indicates

that it would be perfectly proper in the ordinary case for the housing authority to look at the family as a whole and assume, in the absence of material which indicates to the contrary, where the conduct of one member of the family was such that he should be regarded as having become homeless intentionally, that was conduct to which the other members of the family were a party ...

"If, however, at the end of the day because of material put before the housing authority by the wife, the housing authority are not satisfied that she was a party to the decision, they would have to regard her as not having become homeless intentionally. In argument the housing authority drew my attention to the difficulties which could arise in cases where the husband spent the rent on drink. If the wife acquiesced to his doing this then it seems to me it would be proper to regard her, as well as him, as having become homeless intentionally. If, on the other hand, she had done what she could to prevent the husband spending his money on drink instead of rent then she had not failed to do anything (the likely result of which would be that she would be forced to leave the accommodation) and it would not be right to regard her as having become homeless intentionally ..."

This creates a degree of shift in the normal burden that lies on the authority to make the inquiries, and imposes on an applicant seeking to avail himself of the principle a positive obligation to show why acquiescence should not be presumed: see notes to s.184, above, Inquiries— *R. v. Woodspring D.C., ex p. Walters* (1984) 16 H.L.R. 73, Q.B.D.; *R. v. Reigate & Banstead D.C., ex p. Paris* (1984) 17 H.L.R. 103, Q.B.D. See also *R. v. Nottingham C.C., ex p. Caine* (1995) 28 H.L.R. 374, C.A., in which the Court of Appeal held that a committee was entitled to look at the family as a whole and to infer that the applicant was aware that her partner was withholding rent; the committee was entitled to infer that the couple would have discussed the matter, even in the absence of any direct evidence that they had done so; the committee could not be criticised for proceeding on the basis that what was under consideration was a normal family and a normal couple.

Lewis was applied to the benefit of the applicant in *R. v. London Borough of Ealing, ex p. Sidhu* (1982) 2 H.L.R. 45, Q.B.D., where the authority additionally (*cf.* notes to s.189(1), above) sought to rely on an earlier finding of intentionality on account of rent arrears which had occurred while the applicant was still living with her husband, now that the couple had separated. It was also applied to the benefit of the applicant in *R. v. Eastleigh B.C., ex p. Beattie (No. 2)* (1984) 17 H.L.R. 168, Q.B.D., a case of non-payment of mortgage arrears, even though the couple were still living together, and in *R. v. West Dorset D.C., ex p. Phillips* (1985) 17 H.L.R. 336, Q.B.D., also a case of rent arrears, caused by the husband's drinking, again even though the couple were still living together. The law is usefully restated in *R. v. Mole Valley D.C., ex p. Burton* (1988) 20 H.L.R. 479, Q.B.D., where it was accepted that the wife had acquiesced but the authority had failed properly to consider whether she was unaware of a relevant fact.

It was applied again in *R. v. Penwith D.C., ex p. Trevena* (1984) 17 H.L.R. 526, Q.B.D., where a wife who was the sole tenant of a flat surrendered the tenancy in order to move in with another man in another town, leaving her husband in (unlawful) occupation: possession proceedings had to be taken for his eviction. Subsequently, the couple were reconciled, and he was able to rely on his lack of his acquiescence in (indeed, clear opposition to) the surrender, and notwithstanding the reconciliation. It was implicit in the *Lewis* decision that one partner may seek the benefit of the principle, even though continued cohabitation is intended.

In *R. v. Cardiff C.C., ex p. Thomas* (1983) 9 H.L.R. 64, Q.B.D., however, Woolf J., who had decided *Lewis*, although restating the principle, found "acquiescence" on the part of a male joint tenant, whose cohabitant had caused the loss of their council tenancy, by nuisance and annoyance, even though the man had been in prison both at the time of the conduct, and at the time of the proceedings for possession. The factors which influenced the court were (a) that the man had been offered, but had declined, an opportunity to attend the hearing, and (b) that there was no evidence of attempts by him to persuade her to desist in the conduct, which had persisted up until the hearing.

There may come a point though, particularly in arrears cases, where the spouse finds out too late to be able to do anything about the conduct. So, for example, the arrears may be so substantial when she discovers them that it cannot be said that simple awareness of the debt before homelessness amounts to acquiescence: *R. v. East Northamptonshire D.C., ex p. Spruce* (1988) 20 H.L.R. 508, Q.B.D., but see *R. v. London Borough of Barnet, ex p. O'Connor* (1990) 22 H.L.R. 486, Q.B.D., where it was held that the authority were entitled to conclude that there had been acquiescence, and *R. v. London Borough of Ealing, ex p. Salmons* (1990) 23 H.L.R. 272, Q.B.D., where the authority had confronted the critical question whether they were entitled to conclude that the applicant must have known about, or at least turned a blind eye to, the arrears, and were entitled to reach their view that the applicant had either not been honest about his knowledge of the arrears, or at least that he had been reckless about the true situation.

The point is not confined to cohabitants. In *Smith v. Bristol C.C.,* December 1981 L.A.G. Bulletin 287, C.A., a woman was held responsible for acts of nuisance caused by her son and lodgers, which resulted in her eviction. Similarly, the basis for the order for possession which resulted in a finding of intentionality in *R. v. Salford C.C., ex p. Devenport* (1983) 8 H.L.R. 54, C.A., was conduct by the children of the family, and conduct by children was included in the reasons for the finding of intentionality in *R. v. Southampton C.C., ex p. Ward* (1984) 14 H.L.R. 114, Q.B.D.

In *R. v. East Hertfordshire D.C., ex p. Bannon* (1986) 18 H.L.R. 515, Q.B.D., the conduct of the family as a whole had resulted in the grant of a possession order against the applicant's husband from whom she was subsequently estranged. It was held that the authority were entitled to take into account the fact that the applicant was the mother of the family and to consider her acquiescence as such. In *R. v. Cardiff C.C., ex p. John* (1982) 9 H.L.R. 56, Q.B.D., nuisance and annoyance by a lodger caused the eviction of the tenant, even though it occurred only when she was out of the flat, and he was both younger and considerably stronger than she, and she was unable to control his behaviour. Her "acquiescence" was the failure to evict him.

An attempt to raise a finding of intentionality against a wife, dating from before she met her husband, in relation to their subsequent joint application, was, unsurprisingly, rejected out of hand by the court in *R. v. London Borough of Hillingdon, ex p. Puhlhofer* (1985) 17 H.L.R. 278, not appealed on this point—see (1985) 17 H.L.R. 588, C.A.

In *R. v. London Borough of Tower Hamlets, ex p. Khatun* (1995) 27 H.L.R. 344, C.A., it was unsuccessfully argued on behalf of a Bangladeshi wife that she had not acquiesced in her husband's conduct in leaving accommodation which it would have been reasonable to continue to occupy, because as a matter of culture and practice she had no choice but to abide by her husband's decision. Dismissing the appeal, the court held that since the wife had been content to leave making decisions to her spouse, and to co-operate in implementing those decisions, she could properly be regarded as having acquiesced.

An attempt to use the principle of non-acquiescence on behalf of child applicants failed on the basis that the children were not in priority need in their own right: *R. v. Metropolitan Borough of Oldham, ex p. G.; R. v. London Borough of Bexley, ex p. B.* (1993) 25 H.L.R. 319, H.L. (see notes to ss.183 and 189, above).

Deliberate Act or Omission

The provisions of subs. (2) have given rise to a number of cases, most (but not all) of which have concerned rent/mortgage arrears. It is this provision which introduces a subjective element into the analysis of intentionality: *R. v. Exeter C.C., ex p. Tranckle* (1993) 26 H.L.R. 244, C.A.

Ignorance of Facts. It is ignorance of a relevant fact which is not deliberate, not ignorance of the legal consequences: *R. v. Eastleigh B.C., ex p. Beattie (No. 2)* (1984) 17 H.L.R. 168, Q.B.D., *R. v. London Borough of Croydon, ex p. Toth* (1988) 20 H.L.R. 576, C.A.; *cf. R. v. Mole Valley D.C., ex p. Burton* (1988) 20 H.L.R. 479, Q.B.D., where the applicant's belief in assurances by her husband that they would be rehoused under a union agreement was held to be a belief of fact, not of law.

Where an applicant temporarily went to live with her mother while at college but was warned by her father that she would not be allowed to return, it was held that the authority had misdirected themselves in disregarding the applicant's genuine belief that he did not mean it and that therefore she would be able to come back. The father's state of mind was a relevant fact so that the daughter's action taken in genuine ignorance of her father's true intent could not be classed as deliberate: *Wincentzen v. Monklands D.C.* (1988) S.L.T. (Court of Session) 259, September 1988 L.A.G. Bulletin, p. 13.

Where a person had been misled as to business prospects, which led him to move abroad, it was held to be a case of unawareness of a relevant fact in *R. v. London Borough of Hammersmith and Fulham, ex p. Lusi* (1991) 23 H.L.R. 460, Q.B.D.

Good faith. In deciding whether the ignorance is in good faith, an authority must distinguish between honest blundering and carelessness on the one hand, where a person can still act in good faith, and dishonesty, where there can be no question of good faith: *Lusi; R. v. City of Westminster, ex p. Ali and Bibi* (1992) 25 H.L.R. 109, Q.B.D. The question is whether an action is taken in good faith, not whether conduct is reasonable. In *R. v. London Borough of Tower Hamlets, ex p. Rouf* (1991) 23 H.L.R. 460, Q.B.D., a finding of intentionality was quashed in respect of an applicant who returned to a flat that had been repossessed after an absence of three years, who had none the less believed that it would still be available. The authority had failed to consider whether the belief was genuine, deciding instead that the applicant's conduct was unreasonable.

In *R. v. London Borough of Ealing, ex p. Sukhija* (1994) 26 H.L.R. 726, Q.B.D., a distinction was drawn between a mistake of fact (which could be within the good faith defence) and a mere unfulfilled hope (which was not). The decision that the applicant, who had come to England in the mistaken belief that she would find employment and a home, was intentionally homeless was accordingly upheld. See also *R. v. London Borough of Tower Hamlets, ex p. Khatun* (1994) 27 H.L.R. 465, C.A., in which the applicant was described as having no more than a reasonable expectation of being able to live temporarily with her parents-in-law on her return to the U.K., which was not a fact to which the good faith defence could be applied.

In *R. v. London Borough of Wandsworth, ex p. Onwudiwe* (1994) 26 H.L.R. 302, C.A., the applicant's conduct in taking on large mortgage commitments while unemployed, for a business for which there had been no market-testing, took the case beyond the stage of honest incompetence and provided material upon which it could be said that he was deliberately putting his house at risk.

In *R. v. Winchester C.C., ex p. Ashton* (1991) 24 H.L.R. 48, Q.B.D., a middle-aged woman moved from her home in Tunbridge Wells to take up a temporary job in Winchester where the authority provided her with a tenancy subject to the exception contained in Sched. 1, para. 5 of the Housing Act 1985 (temporary accommodation for persons taking up employment: see also Sched. 14, below). After a year, the authority obtained possession of the premises. At first instance, a decision that the accommodation was not settled was upheld but a finding that the applicant was intentionally homeless was quashed on the basis, *inter alia*, that in leaving Tunbridge Wells the applicant had acted in good faith, being unaware that she would be unable to find either housing or employment after the initial year; accordingly her action in surrendering the tenancy at Tunbridge Wells should not have been taken to be deliberate. The decision of Kennedy J. was upheld by the Court of Appeal (see 24 H.L.R. 520) on the additional basis that the respondents had given too much weight to the factors in what is now s.177(1) when reaching their conclusion.

In *R. v. Westminster C.C., ex p. Obeid, The Times,* July 16, 1996, 29 H.L.R. forthcoming, Q.B.D., the applicant had taken private sector accommodation in the belief that her rent would be covered by housing benefit, in ignorance of (and without making inquiries about) the provisions of the Housing Benefit Regulations 1987 which could limit benefit to a proportion of her rent. This was held to be capable of constituting ignorance of a relevant fact.

See also the illustrations below, in particular under the sub-heading Accommodation Arrangements but also generally.

Act causing loss of accommodation. The act of good faith referred to in subs. (2) is the same act which is considered under subs. (1). Therefore, where the cause of homelessness was an applicant's inability to meet mortgage repayments as a result of a severe downturn in business, the homelessness was intentional because the mortgage had been obtained as a result of the applicant's fraudulent misrepresentation of her annual income: *R. v. London Borough of Barnet, ex p. Rughooputh* (1993) 25 H.L.R. 607, C.A., but see also *R. v. Exeter C.C., ex p. Tranckle* (1993) 26 H.L.R. 244, C.A. where the applicant entered into an imprudent financial arrangement, but in good faith because he was unaware of the (un)reality of the prospects of success for a public house which she was purchasing, which had been concealed from her by the brewery.

Ironically, a person who takes the trouble to find out relevant facts, and reaches a decision on them, may be vulnerable to a finding of intentionality, where a person who has omitted to make any such inquiries at all may not be: see *R. v. Westminster C.C., ex p. Obeid, The Times,* July 16, 1996, 29 H.L.R. forthcoming, Q.B.D., above.

Bad faith. Where bad faith is suspected, it is not invariably necessary to put the matter to the applicant: *Hobbs v. London Borough of Sutton* (1993) 26 H.L.R. 132, C.A., but see *R. v. City of Westminster, ex p. Moozary-Oraky* (1993) 26 H.L.R. 214, Q.B.D., where the want of good faith relative to awareness of housing benefit was considered one of jurisdictional fact, without which no reasonable authority could reach a conclusion on intentionality, into which the authority were required to make explicit inquiry of the applicant as to whether or not she had seen a letter informing her that her benefit had been stopped.

Illustrations. There is a large number of cases, which can be considered in different categories, but must be remembered that they are all illustrative, and that each case requires individual consideration.

(i) Rent/Mortgage Arrears. The Code of Guidance issued under Pt. III, 1985 Act, recognised the difference between those who lose their homes because of real financial difficulties, and those who have chosen to sell or who have lost their homes because of wilful and persistent refusal to pay rent or mortgage (See *R. v. L.B. Wandsworth, ex p. Hawthorne* (1994) 27 H.L.R. 59, C.A., where it was held that the Code did not in this respect mis-state the law.)

A similar view was expressed by the Master of the Rolls, in *R. v. Slough B.C., ex p. L.B. Ealing* [1981] Q.B. 801, C.A., although the case concerned intentional homelessness only indirectly: "They had a council house ... but fell into arrears with their rent. In 1972 the council got an order for possession and payments of arrears ... They did not keep up the instalments. So the order for possession was executed ... They were housed by the Slough Council for a month. They were then granted a fresh tenancy of another council house ... at a low rent of £2.89 a week. They did not pay this rent either. So another eviction order was made. It was executed on 12th April 1977 ... The Slough Council found that the Lynch family was homeless intentionally ... I should think their finding was debatable. Their non-payment of rent was deplorable, but it may not have been 'deliberate' in the sense required by s.17(1) [now, this section]. The family did not do it deliberately so as to get turned out ... "

In *Robinson v. Torbay B.C.* [1982] 1 All E.R. 726, the High Court declined to follow Lord Denning's dictum, and, instead, adopted the view that the word "deliberate" governed only the act or omission. A person can be deemed homeless intentionally, if he "deliberately does an act the reasonable result of which is his eviction, and the act is in fact the cause of his eviction ... even though he did not appreciate that it would be the cause. Similarly, if a person deliberately does an act and eviction is the likely result of what he deliberately does, then he becomes threatened with homelessness intentionally, even though he may not have appreciated that it would be the likely result."

Robinson was approved by the Court of Appeal in *R. v. Salford C.C., ex p. Devenport* (1983) 8 H.L.R. 54, C.A., and Lord Denning's *dictum* not followed:

"It is not necessary to show that the tenant deliberately did something intending to get himself turned out. That seems to me contrary to the language of s.17(1) [now, this section]. The word 'deliberately,' in my opinion, governs only the act or omission ... "

In *R. v. Eastleigh B.C., ex p. Beattie (No. 2)* (1984) 17 H.L.R. 168, Q.B.D., persistent failure to pay mortgage arrears was upheld as deliberate, notwithstanding that the male applicant had been advised to the contrary by his solicitors. See also *R. v. Westminster C.C., ex p. Reid* (1994) 26 H.L.R. 677, Q.B.D., in which a decision on intentionality was quashed because of the authority's failure to consider whether eviction was the reasonable result of the applicant's assault on his son.

In *White v. Exeter C.C.*, December 1981 L.A.G. Bulletin 287, High Court, the applicant had occupied a freehold property, purchased with a mortgage from the authority. There were arrears, which increased during periods of sickness and unemployment. In October 1980, the applicant became unemployed through no fault of his own. As from January 1981, he believed that the Department of Health and Social Security were, or ought to be, paying the whole of the interest element on the mortgage instalments, by direct deduction from his benefit. In fact, his Supplementary Benefit entitlement was so low that the D.H.S.S. could not pay the full amount of the interest, so that arrears continued to mount.

In June 1981, when the arrears totalled approximately £600, the authority, as mortgagees, obtained possession of the house. The applicant was held to have become homeless intentionally, because of non-payment of mortgage. In oral evidence, it emerged that the effective reason for the decision was non-payment of interest due under the mortgage, between November 1980 and June 1981, rather than arrears generally. The court found that for most of this period the applicant was under a genuine misapprehension as to the relevant fact—namely whether or not the D.H.S.S. were paying the whole of the interest payments—and that he had acted in good faith in failing himself to make the payments. There was accordingly no deliberate omission and, in consequence, no intentional homelessness: knowing of the applicant's belief, at the time of its decision, the authority had acted unreasonably in reaching a decision of intentional homelessness at all.

In *R. v. Wyre B.C., ex p. Joyce* (1983) 11 H.L.R. 73, Q.B.D., the authority did not even ask the applicant why mortgage arrears had arisen, and this failure was accordingly fatal to its decision for it had omitted to take something relevant into account, *i.e.* her explanation or answer. Similarly, in *R. v. L.B. Brent, ex p. Baruwa* (1995) 28 H.L.R. 361, Q.B.D., the authority failed to inquire into the reasonableness of the applicant's expenditure (on a car, and on a telephone) before reaching their decision that she had become homeless intentionally. Their decision was quashed because it was impossible to come to a satisfactory conclusion as to what the applicant's financial position was, either from the authority's decision letter, or from the figures before the court.

In *R. v. Hillingdon L.B.C., ex p. Tinn* (1988) 20 H.L.R. 305, Q.B.D., Kennedy J. expressed the view that, as a matter of common sense, it cannot be reasonable for a person to continue to occupy accommodation when they can no longer discharge their financial obligations in relation to that accommodation, *i.e.* pay the rent and make the mortgage payments, without so straining their resources as to deprive themselves of the ordinary necessities of life, such as food, clothing, heat, transport and so forth.

In *R. v. London Borough of Wandsworth, ex p. Hawthorne* (1994) 27 H.L.R. 59, C.A. the failure of the respondents to consider whether the applicant's failure to pay rent was caused by the inadequacy of her financial resources entitled her to succeed in her application to have a finding of intentionality quashed: it was a question the authority were *bound* to ask. See also *R. v. Shrewsbury and Atcham, B.C., ex p. Griffiths* (1993) 25 H.L.R. 613, Q.B.D., in which the authority were held to have failed to have regard to the family's particular circumstances, and *R. v. Islington L.B.C., ex p. Bibi, The Times*, July 10, 1996, Q.B.D., 29 H.L.R. forthcoming, where the authority had failed to make a finding as to whether the applicant could reasonably have continued to occupy accommodation, in the light of her stated financial inability to feed her family. On the other hand, in *R. v. City of Westminster, ex p. Khan* (1991) 23 H.L.R. 230, Q.B.D., the authority were entitled to reach the view that the applicant had not been forced to sell by reason of financial pressure (see also *R. v. Leeds City Council, ex p. Adamiec* (1991) 24 H.L.R. 138, Q.B.D.).

(ii) Nuisance and Annoyance. Nuisance and annoyance can clearly be considered "deliberate" for this purpose: *R. v. Salford C.C., ex p. Devenport* (1983) 8 H.L.R. 54, C.A., *R. v. Cardiff C.C., ex p. John* (1982) 9 H.L.R. 56, Q.B.D. See also *R. v. Hammersmith & Fulham L.B.C., ex p. P.* (1989) 22 H.L.R. 21, Q.B.D., where a finding of intentionality was upheld, where alleged criminal and anti-social behaviour (confirmed by the authority's own enquiries) had led to death threats from I.R.A.

In *R. v. Wirral M.B.C., ex p. Bell* (1994) 27 H.L.R. 234, Q.B.D., a possession order was obtained against the applicant on the grounds of nuisance and annoyance. She was accepted by Wirral as having a priority need because of the state of her mental health. Applying a test to be found in the Code of Guidance under Pt. III, 1985 Act, which referred to capacity to manage her affairs, the authority, none the less, found that she had become homeless intentionally. Her application for judicial review was dismissed; it was said to be one thing to be less able to fend for oneself (for the purpose of establishing vulnerability)—see notes to s.189(1), above—and another to be incapable of managing one's own affairs (for the purpose of being intentionally homeless); there was accordingly no inconsistency between the findings of the authority on the two issues.

(iii) Accommodation Arrangements. It will be seen below that leaving settled accommodation to move into unsettled accommodation can amount to intentional homelessness. Ignorance about the unsettled nature of intended accommodation, however, can amount to ignorance of a relevant fact, and as such may mean that the prior departure was not "deliberate", within subs. (1): *R. v. Wandsworth L.B.C., ex p. Rose* (1984) 11 H.L.R. 105, Q.B.D., and *R. v. London Borough of Hammersmith & Fulham, ex p. Lusi* (1991) 23 H.L.R. 460, Q.B.D. Such a move would not be capable of being caught by the first of the new definitions of intentionality (subs. (3)), as "the purpose of the arrangement" must include a degree of intention on the applicant's part ("to enable him to become entitled to assistance"), which would not in any event have qualified as a non-deliberate move.

In *R. v. Christchurch B.C., ex p. Conway* (1987) 19 H.L.R. 238, Q.B.D., a woman erroneously, but genuinely, believed that she had a further period of a year in which to decide whether to extend her existing protected shorthold tenancy: this error vitiated the finding of intentionality, because it constituted ignorance of a material fact, *i.e.* the time remaining in which to make her decision.

(iv) Pregnancy. A person does not become homeless intentionally by becoming pregnant, for example, because accommodation is lost, whether on account of its size (*R. v. Eastleigh B.C., ex p. Beattie (No. 1)* (1983) 10 H.L.R. 134, Q.B.D.), or for other reasons, such as terms of accommodation, or because it is in the family home and the family rejects the pregnant woman. There is an alternative approach to the same point: in some cases, becoming pregnant will not so much have caused the loss of accommodation, as have rendered the accommodation unavailable for the applicant's occupation under s.176. To render accommodation unavailable in the statutory sense is not to commit an act which can be treated as intentional homelessness: *In Re Islam* [1983] 1 A.C. 688, 1 H.L.R. 107, H.L.

(v) Failure to Use Other Remedies. It is not, however, possible to say that a reasonable authority could never require a woman to use her domestic remedies, for want of which she may be considered homeless intentionally: see *R. v. Eastleigh B.C., ex p. Evans* (1984) 17 H.L.R. 515, Q.B.D.; see also *R. v. London Borough of Wandsworth, ex p. Nimako-Boateng* (1983) 11 H.L.R. 95, Q.B.D.

(vi) Loss of Tied Accommodation. It was not merely accepted in *R. v. North Devon D.C., ex p. Lewis* [1981] 1 W.L.R. 328, Q.B.D. (above), that the man's departure from his job, and consequent loss of accommodation, qualified as intentional, but notes that an earlier (and otherwise unreported) challenge to that decision had been, albeit reluctantly, dismissed. Loss of tied accommodation also amounted to intentionality in *Goddard v. Torridge D.C.*, December 1981 L.A.G. Bulletin 287, High Court, and *Jennings v. Northavon D.C.*, December 1981 L.A.G. Bulletin 287, High Court, although the cases were fought on the meaning of "in consequence" and are as such, considered below.

In *R. v. Thurrock B.C., ex p. Williams* (1982) 1 H.L.R. 129, Q.B.D., the manager of a public house was dismissed for stock and profit irregularities, which he denied. In the course of an appeals procedure, which he pursued with the assistance of his union representative, his employers offered him the choice of resigning or dismissal. He resigned and, while threatened with homelessness, applied to the local authority for accommodation. It was accepted that if an employee occupying tied accommodation lost it through his own wilful neglect or wrong-doing, he could be held homeless intentionally. The issue of wrong-doing was, however, in contention, and while the authority made their own inquiries, their conclusion in substance was that either the applicant resigned (intentional homelessness) or he would have been dismissed (intentional homelessness), and they ignored the "grey area" of dispute, which had led to the compromise. On their failure to resolve the conflict, they had not acquired any information on the basis of which they could properly be satisfied that the applicant had become homeless intentionally.

R. v. Thanet D.C., ex p. Reeve (1981) 6 H.L.R. 31, Q.B.D., was also a case on loss of tied accommodation, although it may be considered a case as much on the meaning of "in consequence" as "deliberate." A woman worked as a receptionist for a car hire firm, and lived above the office. She was living with a man. She told her employers that he was not disqualified from driving. In fact, he was, and when the employers found out they dismissed her. The authority found that she lost her accommodation, because of the misconduct leading to loss of employment, which misconduct was the statement made to the employers. The allegation was, at the time of dismissal and indeed at the time of local authority decision and of hearing at the High Court, disputed. Nonetheless, the authority had investigated, and concluded that the dismissal was "for that deliberate act of misconduct". It is this express finding which distinguishes the case from *Williams*.

In Consequence

The homelessness must be "in consequence of" the deliberate act or omission. This is a question of "cause and effect" (*Dyson v. Kerrier D.C.* [1980] 1 W.L.R. 1206, C.A., *Din v. London Borough of Wandsworth* [1983] 1 A.C. 657, 1 H.L.R. 73, H.L.) and the principal issue which has arisen is the attribution of present homelessness to past act or omission. That is to say, there is commonly an act which has been the subject of a finding of intentionality, or which is susceptible to such a finding, and the argument becomes whether or not it (that act or omission) is the cause of this homelessness. See also *R. v. London Borough of Islington, ex p. Bashir Hassan* (1995) 27 H.L.R. 485, where the authority wrongly sought to rely on events which *post*-dated the onset of homelessness, but *cf. R. v. London Borough of Newham, ex p. Campbell* (1993) 26 H.L.R. 183, Q.B.D., where subsequent conduct was held relevant to earlier conduct, so far as it served to test the intentionality.

(i) Intervening Accommodation. A causal link may continue to subsist following an act of intentionality, even although the applicant in the interim ceases to be homeless, *e.g.* because he finds some temporary accommodation from which he is subsequently evicted: *R. v. Brent L.B.C., ex p. Awua* [1996] 1 A.C. 55, 27 H.L.R. 453, H.L. The authority must look back to the original cause of the homelessness and ask if the intentionality still persists (*Din v. Wandsworth L.B.C.*, above). This is based on the wording of the provisions, and the distinction to be found between tenses within, *inter alia*, what is now s.190(1) ("is" homeless, but "became" homeless intentionally; see also s.189(2), "has a priority need", and s.191 "is homeless … and has a priority need, and did not become homeless intentionally").

The question, then, becomes one of whether the applicant has enjoyed a period of accommodation between act of intentionality and application: the phrase used is "settled accommodation", (*Din*, per Lord Wilberforce, adopting Ackner L.J. in the Court of Appeal) or "other than temporary accommodation" (*Din*, per Lord Lowry). Nothing in *Awua* was to be taken to cast doubt on this use of the concept of settled accommodation (although Lord Hoffman left open whether only the acquisition of intervening settled accommodation could break the period of intentional homelessness) see Introduction to Pt. VII and General Note to s.175, above:

"The distinction between a settled residence and temporary accommodation is thus being used to identify what will break the causal link between departure from accommodation which it would have been reasonable to continue to occupy and homelessness separated from that departure by a period or periods of accommodation elsewhere." (per Lord Hoffmann).

In *de Falco, Silvestri v. Crawley B.C.* [1980] Q.B. 460, C.A., the Court of Appeal held that it was permissible to look beyond a period of some months spent with relatives, to an earlier time when the families involved in the cases had quit their last permanent accommodation, in Italy.

In *Smith* v. *Wokingham D.C.*, 1980 L.A.G. Bulletin 92, C.C., a family spent some years in a caravan, parked on land belonging to another local authority. Though they had no formal right of occupation, sufficient to break their homelessness, the case was decided on the basis that a new period of not being homeless within what is now s.175(2)(b) was necessarily sufficient to break the period.

As an early, and county court, decision, this is not a decision of much authority, and that it may not necessarily follow was demonstrated in *Dyson* v. *Kerrier D.C.* [1980] 1 W.L.R. 1206, C.A., in which a woman took an out-of-season, or winter, let, in order to be near her sister, and, after taking the winter let, surrendered her previous, local authority tenancy. At the termination of the winter let, she was held to have become threatened with homelessness intentionally, on account of the surrender of her previous accommodation. The principal point was that the new, and temporary, accommodation was secured before yielding up the earlier, and secure or permanent accommodation. Thus, the period in the winter let was a part of the act which had caused the loss of the earlier accommodation. (In *Din*, however, Lord Lowry doubted this basis for the decision, inclining rather to the view that because the winter let was temporary, the woman never ceased to be homeless.)

In *Davis* v. *Kingston-upon-Thames Royal London Borough*, *The Times*, March 27, 1981, C.A., a family who came from a travelling background, gave up secure council accommodation, "to go back on the road". The caravan they acquired for this purpose subsequently became unusable. A replacement was found, but this, too, lasted for only a temporary period. The family were found by the authority to have become intentionally homeless when they left the earlier accommodation. It would appear that their first caravan had been purchased before quitting their council accommodation, which would put the case on the same basis as *Dyson*. The Court of Appeal held that the date when intentional homelessness was caused was primarily a matter for the local authority, and the authority had not erred in treating it as at the date when they left their council accommodation, rather than either when their first or when their second caravan came to the end of its useful life:

"The evidence was such that the council could properly conclude that any accommodation which the Davises had, or might obtain, on leaving their council flat would only be precarious. Their decision was therefore reasonable in the circumstances of the case ..."

In *Lambert* v. *London Borough of Ealing* [1981] 1 W.L.R. 550, 2 H.L.R. 41, C.A., a family gave up accommodation in Lyons, France, in circumstances which the authority could construe as intentional homelessness. They bought a caravan, in which they lived in this country for a while before they sold it. Then they took two holiday lettings, and on the expiry of the second applied to the authority. The Court of Appeal, following *Dyson* and *de Falco*, held that the authority were entitled to link the family's present homelessness to the departure from accommodation in Lyons. In *R.* v. *London Borough of Harrow, ex p. Holland* (1980) 4 H.L.R. 108, C.A., a couple was similarly held to be intentionally homeless because they left a caravan site on which the authority decided they could have continued to live, despite a series of intervening accommodation arrangements, all of which were temporary.

The question to be asked is whether the intervening accommodation is settled (as contrasted with that which is precarious, temporary or transient), so that an arrangement whereby a family moved in with a single man to look after him, which was intended to be a lasting one but which in fact lasted only four and a half months could properly be found not to be settled. It does not matter if the intervening accommodation was such that the applicants could be said not to be homeless under s.175 while living there: *R.* v. *London Borough of Merton, ex p. Ruffle* (1988) 21 H.L.R. 361, Q.B.D. An attempt by the couple to rely on an "intervening separation", so that intervening accommodation might be considered "settled", or adequate, for the purposes of their separate needs, was rejected on the basis that the separation had never been mentioned to the authority.

This aspect of the case may be contrasted with the decision in *R.* v. *South Herefordshire D.C., ex p. Miles* (1983) 17 H.L.R. 82, Q.B.D., in which the authority wrongly "rubber-stamped" an earlier finding of intentionality by another authority, and thus failed to consider whether or not intervening accommodation might have been settled for the same reason, *i.e.* because it was adequate for the needs of the "two halves" of the family.

In *Goddard* v. *Torridge D.C.*, December 1981 L.A.G. Bulletin 287, High Court, a family quit tied accommodation in Hastings, in circumstances which had placed them under considerable pressure, and returned to Devon, where they had formerly lived. As in *Dyson*, the accommodation in Devon was an out-of-season, or a winter letting, and, again, it had been arranged before the departure from Hastings. The decision of the authority that the applicant was homeless intentionally was upheld.

In *Jennings* v. *Northavon D.C.*, December 1981 L.A.G. Bulletin 187, High Court, a family quit secure council accommodation in order to move into a cottage belonging to the man's employers, to whom he subsequently gave notice determining his employment. Notwithstanding his belief that, regardless of how his employment ended, they would enjoy a further nine months' rights of occupation, the authority decided that he had exchanged secure for insecure accommodation: in this case, though, the intentional homelessness was made up, as it were, of two elements—departing the earlier accommodation, and quitting the employment.

In *R. v. Purbeck D.C., ex p. Cadney* (1985) 17 H.L.R. 534, Q.B.D., a woman sought to rely on a period of three months during which she had moved out of the matrimonial home and into the home of another man; their relationship was not successful, and she left. She claimed that this should be treated as a period of intervening accommodation, because she had intended to stay with him permanently. The court held that this was too subjective an approach, and that the authority were entitled to take the view that it was a transient or precarious arrangement, *i.e.* that an objective test could be applied.

In *R. v. Swansea C.C., ex p. Evans* (1990) 22 H.L.R. 467, C.A., however, the applicants left secure council accommodation for larger premises in the private sector. Although their agreement for the new premises purported to be on a bed and breakfast basis, there was a strong argument that they had full Rent Act protection. Following serious threats of and actual violence from their landlord, the applicants left the accommodation. The respondent's decision that the applicants were intentionally homeless for leaving their council accommodation was quashed, *inter alia*, on the basis of failure to consider whether the privately rented accommodation had been "settled".

In *R. v. Winchester C.C., ex p. Ashton* (1991) 24 H.L.R. 520, C.A., a decision by the local authority that occupation of premises under a tenancy falling within the exception contained in Sched. 1, para. 5 of the Housing Act 1985 (temporary accommodation for persons taking up employment—see also below, Sched. 14) was not occupation of settled accommodation, was upheld.

In *R. v. London Borough of Croydon, ex p. Easom* (1992) 25 H.L.R. 262, Q.B.D., it was held that, although the applicants had lived in secure accommodation in Australia for six years, it was still not settled accommodation as they had been in the country illegally and accordingly could have been deported at any time.

In *R. v. Rochester-upon-Medway C.C., ex p. Williams* (1994) 26 H.L.R. 588, Q.B.D., an assured shorthold tenancy was held to constitute settled accommodation. (This finds support in *R. v. Wandsworth L.B.C., ex p. Crooks* (1995) 27 H.L.R. 660, Q.B.D., in which it was held that an assured shorthold letting could comprise an adequate discharge of duty, a decision that was not referred to in, but that evidently is consistent with *R. v. Brent L.B.C., ex p. Awua* [1996] 1 A.C. 55, 27 H.L.R. 453, H.L., and a proposition that was explicitly upheld in *R. v. L.B. Wandsworth, ex p. Wingrove*, and *R. v. L.B. Wandsworth, ex p. Mansoor* [1996] 3 All E.R. 913, C.A. [cases heard at first instance together with *Crooks*; see also *R. v. L.B. Newham, ex p. Miah* (1995) 28 H.L.R. 279, Q.B.D.]).

(ii) Cause and Effect. There is no requirement for the accommodation which has been lost to be "settled", the requirement is that it was available and reasonable to continue to occupy (*R. v. Brent L.B.C., ex p. Awua* [1996] 1 A.C. 55, 27 H.L.R. 453, H.L.; see also *R. v. L.B. Wandsworth, ex p. Wingrove*, and *R. v. L.B. Wandsworth, ex p. Mansoor*, above). The question whether occupation of a settled residence is the sole and exclusive method by which the causal link can be broken was expressly reserved. In *R. v. Harrow L.B.C., ex p. Fahia* (1996) 29 H.L.R. forthcoming, the decision of the authority was quashed for failing to consider whether the chain of causation could have been broken by another means.

Awua concerned an applicant who had been accepted as unintentionally homeless but who was evicted from temporary accommodation provided to her in the course of discharging the authority's duty towards her, following the refusal of an offer of permanent accommodation. She then applied to a second authority (where as she also had a local connection they would be unable to refer her case under the provisions now to be found in ss.198–201, below). The second authority found that she was intentionally homeless, as her eviction from the temporary accommodation was the result of her decision not to accept the permanent offer. At first instance and in the Court of Appeal, the argument turned on whether the temporary accommodation was "settled". The House of Lords rejected this analysis and it may accordingly be treated as illustrative of the "cause and effect" aspect of the expression "in consequence".

The following cases would all seem liable to have been decided in the same way *post-Awua* as beforehand, on the basis that the loss of the intervening accommodation was not the cause of the homelessness.

The authority must act reasonably in regarding present homelessness as being caused by a departure from earlier accommodation. In *Krishnan v. London Borough of Hillingdon*, January 1981 L.A.G. Bulletin 137, High Court, a family moved out of accommodation shared with relatives in Birmingham because the local authority in Birmingham had been putting pressure to reduce overcrowding in the premises. There was also a possibility of promotion if the family could move to London. Another relative offered accommodation in his home in Uxbridge, until such time as the family could afford to buy its own house.

Subsequently, the Uxbridge relative decided to sell his house and move to Canada, and it was then that the family's homelessness arose. The authority considered that the family could reasonably have gone on occupying the Birmingham property, on which point their decision was not upheld, and took the view that the Uxbridge arrangement was only temporary. On this, too, their decision was set aside by the court, on the basis of insufficient enquiry as to knowledge and expectations of the applicant at the time when he moved:

"As I have already indicated, the Plaintiff's expectation at the time when he moved ... was that the accommodation there would be available for him for at least a year. It follows as it seems to me that if the Council's officers had been aware of that fact they might well have taken the view that the Plaintiff became homeless not because he moved to [Uxbridge] from ... Birmingham, but because the Plaintiff's cousin changed his mind about the length of time for which he was willing to accommodate the Plaintiff and his family .... "

Similarly, in *R. v. London Borough of Wandsworth, ex p. Rose* (1983) 11 H.L.R. 105, Q.B.D., although decided on the meaning of the word "deliberate" (above), the point may as easily be made that the earlier departure did not cause the homelessness: what had caused the homelessness was the loss of the intervening, temporary accommodation, which the applicant had not appreciated was—or was likely to be—temporary.

In *R. v. Basingstoke & Deane B.C., ex p. Bassett* (1983) 10 H.L.R. 125, Q.B.D., temporary accommodation was lost not because of its temporary quality, but because it was accommodation with the applicant's sister-in-law, and the applicant separated from her husband. This decision, however, has been considered inconsistent with the decision in *Awua* at the Court of Appeal ((1994) 26 H.L.R. 539): *R. v. L.B. Ealing, ex p. Sukhija* (1994) 26 H.L.R. 726, C.A.

In *R. v. Exeter C.C., ex p. Gliddon* (1984) 14 H.L.R. 103, Q.B.D., the applicants became homeless when they quit private sector accommodation of which they had originally been granted a tenancy. The landlord alleged that they had obtained it by deception and compelled them to enter into a licence agreement in substitution, which was subsequently terminated and which was the immediate cause of the homelessness. At first, the authority advised the applicants to await court proceedings for determination of their status: this was a valid approach, the court held (see further below—Advice from the Authority).

On their failure to follow this advice, however, the authority reached a new decision, that the accommodation had been obtained by deception. Accordingly, it had been lost by the applicants' own fault. In the light of this finding of fact by the authority, however, it was no longer possible for them to conclude that the applicants could reasonably have remained in occupation, and the accommodation obtained by deception ought accordingly to have been ignored, so that the authority were obliged to look back instead to the applicants' previous accommodation.

In *R. v. Thanet D.C., ex p. Reeve* (1981) 6 H.L.R. 672, Q.B.D., the facts of which are set out above, the court said:

"It seems to me that the answer to the question of whether or not the council were entitled to take the view which they did of the applicant's conduct depends on the proper interpretation of s.17(1) [now this section]. It appears to me that the use of the words 'in consequence' in that subsection does raise problems of causation. Really, what is involved in deciding whether or not the applicant is right is a decision as to remoteness .... "

See also the comments of Schiemann J. in *R. v. Hammersmith & Fulham L.B.C., ex p. P.* (1989) 22 H.L.R. 21, Q.B.D., where he described causation as a notorious minefield in jurisprudence and philosophy. He upheld a finding of intentionality against a number of related applicants living in Belfast who had been considered guilty of anti-social and criminal behaviour. This behaviour had led to death threats from the I.R.A., in consequence of which the families had fled. The authority—who carried out their own enquiries into the conduct of the relatives—were entitled to conclude that the misbehaviour was something "in consequence of which" the applicants ceased to occupy accommodation. In *R. v. L.B. Islington, ex p. Hinds* (1995) 28 H.L.R. 302, C.A., the applicant undertook to leave the matrimonial home, to avoid an ouster order; this led to termination of the secure tenancy. The authority's decision that it was his violence towards his wife which had caused the loss of accommodation was upheld.

In *R. v. Camden L.B.C., ex p. Aranda* (1996) 28 H.L.R. 672, the judge applied a "but for" test, where the applicant had given up a secure tenancy to live in Columbia, having received a grant of £20,000 from the authority so to do. The matters relied upon by the authority were not matters but for which the applicant would have continued in occupation of the property in Columbia, instead they were matters but for which she might never have gone to Columbia at all; as such they were not deliberate acts which could be said to have caused the applicants loss of accommodation.

The decision in *City of Gloucester v. Miles* (1985) 17 H.L.R. 292, C.A., referred to in the Court of Appeal in *Puhlhofer* ((1985) 17 H.L.R. 558, C.A.) but not criticised either in that case at the House of Lords ([1986] A.C. 484, 18 H.L.R. 158, H.L.), or in *Awua*, may also be considered a question of cause and effect. The applicant had left her home for a period, but had not clearly or certainly quit it; during her absence her estranged husband returned and caused damage rendering the property entirely uninhabitable. As she was not a party to the vandalisation, she had done nothing that could be classed as intentional, even if she might subsequently have lost the property, either through failing to resume residence, or because arrears had accrued and there was a threat of proceedings.

(iii) Hypothetical Circumstances. The question posed in *Din* (above), was whether any circumstance other than a new period of housing or "settled residence" could break the chain of causation, a point expressly reserved in *R. v. L.B. Brent, ex p. Awua* [1996] 1 A.C. 55, 27 H.L.R. 453, H.L. (above). Can an act which at its inception was one causing intentional homelessness cease to qualify as such?

In *Din*, a family left accommodation under extremely trying circumstances, but they had been given advice from the local authority to remain in occupation until a court order was made against them. It was common ground, at least on appeal, that if an application had been made immediately after their departure, the authority could have found them intentionally homeless, because at that date it would have been reasonable to remain in occupation. But on application at a later date, it was conceded by the authority that the family would by then almost certainly have become homeless in any event, and not intentionally. There was no defence to the landlord's proposed proceedings for possession and the order would have already taken effect.

During the interim period, the family had stayed with relatives, and it was not argued that there had, on that account, been a break in their homelessness. Rather, it was argued that the original cause of homelessness had ceased to be effective, for the family would not be unintentionally homeless regardless of their premature departure. The argument was upheld in the county court, but dismissed on appeal (by a majority). The House of Lords similarly failed to reach a unanimous decision: the majority upheld the result in the Court of Appeal: the question was whether the present period of homelessness had, at its inception, been intentional, so that the fact that the applicants would have become unintentionally homeless by the date of application was irrelevant, and hypothetical.

Cessation of Occupation
The accommodation which has been lost can be accommodation abroad, and the act causing its loss an act abroad: *de Falco, Silvestri v. Crawley B.C.* [1980] Q.B. 460, C.A. In that case, the reasons given by the authority for finding intentional homelessness were that the families concerned had come to this country without arranging permanent accommodation. This reason was patently bad on its face. It was upheld by the Court of Appeal only by expanding it, against the factual background, to refer to the departure from accommodation in Italy. This point was made clear in *R. v. Reigate & Banstead B.C., ex p. Paris* (1984) 17 H.L.R. 103, Q.B.D., where the authority used the same wording as originally used in *de Falco*, and were held to have erred in failing to look at the accommodation which had been quit, and the circumstances of departure from it. See also *R. v. London Borough of Tower Hamlets, ex p. Monaf* (1987) 19 H.L.R. 577, C.A.

While it would seem probable that the accommodation lost must itself be such as to qualify as "settled", where the authority are providing temporary housing pending a permanent allocation, the loss of one such "stage" may lead to a finding of intentionality: *R. v. East Hertfordshire D.C., ex p. Hunt* (1985) 18 H.L.R. 51, Q.B.D. The basis for the decision was criticised (described as "heroic") in *R. v. L.B. Brent, ex p. Awua* [1996] 1 A.C. 55, 27 H.L.R. 453, H.L. (above), but the outcome itself remains correct: see, in particular, s.193(6)(b), below.

In *R. v. Christchurch B.C., ex p. Conway* (1987) 19 H.L.R. 238, Q.B.D., the applicant failed to take up the renewal of a protected shorthold tenancy. It was held that this failure to take up the extension could amount to a deliberate omission, although on the facts it was held that the omission was not deliberate as it had occurred in ignorance of a relevant fact (see above).

In *In Re Islam*, at the Court of Appeal, one of the grounds for upholding the decision in the court below, once it was argued that the accommodation lost had not been available for the occupation of the applicant and his family (who had recently arrived from Bangladesh)—see above, General Note to s.175—was that the applicant had been in notional occupation, through his wife and children, of the family home in Bangladesh; another was that the accommodation occupied and available was made up of both the family home in Bangladesh and the shared room the applicant was occupying in Uxbridge. The House of Lords ([1983] 1 A.C. 688, 1 H.L.R. 107) rejected both of these approaches:
"The Master of the Rolls was ... using the word occupation in an artificial sense which ... is quite inconsistent with its ordinary meaning and with the probably narrower sense in which it is used in the Act. When it speaks of occupying accommodation, the Act has in contemplation people who are residing in that accommodation ..."
An applicant may, however, be held to be in occupation of accommodation even though not

physically residing there. In *R. v. City of Westminster, ex p. Khan* (1991) 23 H.L.R. 230, Q.B.D., applicants had represented to immigration authorities that they would be living in a house, which the first applicant subsequently sold. It was held that, even although the second applicant had never lived in the house, the first applicant could be said to be occupying it, though in fact it was his parents and brothers who were in actual occupation of the house, while he had been living in tied accommodation elsewhere at the time. The applicants were accordingly occupying the house for the purpose of intentionality, and on its sale could be considered to have ceased to occupy it.

See also *R. v. Westminster C.C., ex p. Chambers* (1982) 6 H.L.R. 24, Q.B.D., where the authority had sought to find as intentionally homeless a person towards whom they had formerly acknowledged a full housing duty, but who had failed to take up an offer of accommodation under that duty. This was not a proper finding, because "ceasing to occupy" does not mean "failing to take up occupation". However, the authority could still, in appropriate circumstances (as to which, see notes to s.193, below) maintain that they have discharged their duties by making the offer. See also notes to s.183, above, on Prior Discharge, and to subs. (4), below, on failure to take up accommodation considered available within s.197, below. This decision is now embodied in s.193(5), below.

Available for Occupation
See General Note to s.175, above.

Reasonable to Continue to Occupy
Although this proposition is to be found both in subs. (1) of this section, and in s.177—see notes to s.175, above, as already noted (above, General Note), there are circumstances in which the phrase may have an effect in relation to intentionality that would not arise when considering homelessness itself.

Thus, in *Miller v. Borough of Wandsworth, The Times*, March 19, 1980, High Court, a couple were advised to reoccupy fire-damaged premises once repairs had been carried out. Their failure to comply with this advice led to a finding of intentional homelessness. In *R. v. Penwith District Council, ex p. Hughes*, August 1980 L.A.G. Bulletin 187, Q.B.D., it appeared that an alleged winter letting might not fall within the provisions of Rent Act 1977, Sched. 15, Case 13, so that there would be no mandatory ground for possession. The occupier was advised to await the outcome of proceedings but did not do so:

"The important point which this application raises ... is the question as to what extent an authority exercising its powers under (the) Act is entitled to say to a person .... 'You should remain in accommodation which you at present occupy and not leave that accommodation until there is a court order made against you requiring you to vacate ...'

"Under section 3 [now, s.184] ... it is the authority's task to make the appropriate enquiries. The authority are not entitled to say merely because they find the case is a difficult one that the court should make the enquiries and not the authority. However, where there is a situation which is doubtful or difficult it is reasonable for the authority to give advice to a person who is a prospective candidate for assistance under the ... Act ... that they should not vacate the accommodation which they are at present occupying without the order of the court because otherwise they may be regarded as persons intentionally homeless.

"If after having given that advice and notwithstanding that advice the person concerned chooses not to follow the advice and leaves the accommodation, then the duty under the Act remains and there is the obligation upon the authority to do their best to decide the matter making the enquiries which they are required to make under the Act. If after having made those enquiries the authority comes to the conclusion that the person indeed was intentionally homeless, then an applicant cannot come before this court and say if this court were to investigate the matter they would come to a different conclusion and because of that the authority must have been in breach of their duty ,..."

In *R. v. Leeds City Council, ex p. Adamiec* (1991) 24 H.L.R. 138, Q.B.D., the failure of an applicant to heed advice not to sell his home resulted in an upheld finding of intentionality, as he had not yet reached the state where he was obliged to sell, although it might have arisen if his financial circumstances had not improved.

Whether it is reasonable for an applicant to continue to occupy the accommodation is to be judged at the time that the behaviour in consequence of which the accommodation was lost took place, not at the later date when the applicant actually left the accommodation: *R. v. Hammersmith & Fulham L.B.C., ex p. P.* (1989) 22 H.L.R. 21, Q.B.D. Whether it is reasonable to continue to occupy may be affected by the question whether alternative accommodation is available, if the applicants remain in their present accommodation in the short term: *ibid.*, and see *R. v. London Borough of Newham, ex p. McIlory* (1991) 23 H.L.R. 570, Q.B.D., in which a finding of intentionality was upheld where the Catholic applicants left accommodation in Northern

Ireland after being subjected to several years of harassment by Protestant factions, culminating with a shooting incident, on the ground that they failed to wait and see whether they would be rehoused by their landlords, the Northern Ireland Housing Executive.

In *R. v. London Borough of Hillingdon, ex p. Wilson* (1983) 12 H.L.R. 61, Q.B.D., the court, with some hesitation, held that it was not reasonable for a woman to remain in accommodation in Australia, because (a) she had no legal permission to remain, and (b) she was pregnant and would shortly have reached the stage of pregnancy when airlines would not permit her to fly.

Subs. (3)

This provision is aimed at collusive arrangements, designed to give the impression of intervening accommodation which the authority should not look past, on the basis that it would have been reasonable to continue to occupy it (although, *n.b.* it does not also have to have been "available for his occupation"), so as to create an apparent right to assistance under Pt. VII. If it would not even have been accommodation reasonable to remain in occupation of, it will not qualify and should be disregarded (and will not qualify as accommodation the loss of which could constitute intentionality under subs. (1)), although this would not prevent the authority looking past it to the loss of previous accommodation, and concluding that *its* loss was the cause of present homelessness (provided *it* was both available, and reasonable to continue in occupation of, *i.e.* provided it qualified within subs. (1)).

Even if the subsection is applicable, there must also be no other "good reason" for the homelessness.

Subs. (4)

If the duty to assist is comprised of advice and assistance under s.186(2), such as the authority consider appropriate to assist the applicant to obtain alternative suitable accommodation which they are satisfied is available in their area, there may have been no accommodation taken up, and accordingly no loss of it: it seems probable that in any event such a circumstance could be met with the plea of "discharge" (see notes to s.183, above, on Prior Discharge), but, for the avoidance of doubt, this provision will also entitle the authority to deem the applicant to have become homeless intentionally, notwithstanding the lack of accommodation which he has ceased to occupy (which prevents subs. (1) applying to the application).

While the issue is not whether or not it was reasonable for the applicant to fail to secure the alternative accommodation, but whether or not the circumstances were such that he was reasonably to be expected to do so, the difference is slight and must be considered a likely area for contention under the new provisions.

Duty to persons not in priority need who are not homeless intentionally

192.—(1) This section applies where the local housing authority—

(a) are satisfied that an applicant is homeless and eligible for assistance, and

(b) are not satisfied that he became homeless intentionally,

but are not satisfied that he has a priority need.

(2) The authority shall provide the applicant with advice and such assistance as they consider appropriate in the circumstances in any attempts he may make to secure that accommodation becomes available for his occupation.

DEFINITIONS

"available for his occupation": s.176.
"eligible for assistance": s.183.
"homeless": s.175.
"homeless intentionally": s.191.
"local housing authority": ss.217, 218.
"priority need": s.189.

GENERAL NOTE

This section seeks to reinstate the provisions of 1985, s.65(4), but there is a new element that is difficult to identify in terms of policy or practice: under s.65(4), the advice and assistance to be proffered was available to all those in priority need; there was no requirement that the applicant should also not be homeless intentionally. This was unsurprising, because if a person did not appear to have a priority need, an authority will not normally inquire into intentionality—there is simply no purpose. Because, at the end of the day, advice and assistance envisaged by this section has so little practical value, it is unlikely that the change will attract contention, but it is none the less an oddity.

Those who are in priority need, but who are also homeless intentionally, will still be able to avail themselves of the right to free advice and assistance under s.179, above.

Duty to persons with priority need who are not homeless intentionally

193.—(1) This section applies where the local housing authority are satisfied that an applicant is homeless, eligible for assistance and has a priority need, and are not satisfied that he became homeless intentionally.

This section has effect subject to section 197 (duty where other suitable accommodation available).

(2) Unless the authority refer the application to another local housing authority (see section 198), they shall secure that accommodation is available for occupation by the applicant.

(3) The authority are subject to the duty under this section for a period of two years ("the minimum period"), subject to the following provisions of this section.

After the end of that period the authority may continue to secure that accommodation is available for occupation by the applicant, but are not obliged to do so (see section 194).

(4) The minimum period begins with—

(a) if the applicant was occupying accommodation made available under section 188 (interim duty to accommodate), the day on which he was notified of the authority's decision that the duty under this section was owed to him;

(b) if the applicant was occupying accommodation made available to him under section 200(3) (interim duty where case considered for referral but not referred), the date on which he was notified under subsection (2) of that section of the decision that the conditions for referral were not met;

(c) in any other case, the day on which accommodation was first made available to him in pursuance of the duty under this section.

(5) The local housing authority shall cease to be subject to the duty under this section if the applicant, having been informed by the authority of the possible consequence of refusal, refuses an offer of accommodation which the authority are satisfied is suitable for him and the authority notify him that they regard themselves as having discharged their duty under this section.

(6) The local housing authority shall cease to be subject to the duty under this section if the applicant—

(a) ceases to be eligible for assistance,

(b) becomes homeless intentionally from the accommodation made available for his occupation,

(c) accepts an offer of accommodation under Part VI (allocation of housing), or

(d) otherwise voluntarily ceases to occupy as his only or principal home the accommodation made available for his occupation.

(7) The local housing authority shall also cease to be subject to the duty under this section if—

(a) the applicant, having been informed of the possible consequence of refusal, refuses an offer of accommodation under Part VI, and

(b) the authority are satisfied that the accommodation was suitable for him and that it was reasonable for him to accept it and notify him accordingly within 21 days of the refusal.

(8) For the purposes of subsection (7) an applicant may reasonably be expected to accept an offer of accommodation under Part VI even though he is under contractual or other obligations in respect of his existing accommodation, provided he is able to bring those obligations to an end before he is required to take up the offer.

(9) A person who ceases to be owed the duty under this section may make a

fresh application to the authority for accommodation or assistance in obtaining accommodation.

DEFINITIONS
"available for his occupation": s.176.
"eligible for assistance": s.183.
"homeless": s.175.
"homeless intentionally": s.191.
"local housing authority": ss.217, 218.
"priority need": s.189.

GENERAL NOTE
This section identifies the duties towards the unintentionally homeless in priority need under Pt. VII. For the duties towards those intentionally homeless, see s.190 above; for the duties towards those not in priority need and not homeless intentionally, see s.192 above.

This section contains one of the principal policy changes, for the duty which it imposes is initially limited in time to a period of two years, as defined, after which—without prejudice to a new application (subs. (9))—the authority, although empowered to continue to assist have no obligation to do so.

The section may be seen—and in policy terms was undoubtedly designed—as a reduction in the rights of the homeless; conversely, and ironically, however, it may now also be seen to be something of an advance, for in *R. v. London Borough of Brent, ex p. Awua* [1996] 1 A.C. 55, 27 H.L.R. 453, the House of Lords held that—while the accommodation must be "suitable"—there is no requirement for any degree of permanence, suggesting that the authority may wish to use temporary accommodation and "wait and see" whether long-term accommodation is required, *e.g.* whether a pregnant woman keeps her child. (See *Hansard* (H.L.), May 16, 1996, Minister of State, Department of Social Security [Lord Mackay of Ardbrecknish], col. 565, describing the provisions as "a more certain guarantee of assistance than the present legislation provides following the recent *Awua* judgment").

In *R. v. L.B. Wandsworth, ex p. Wingrove*, and *R. v. L.B. Wandsworth, ex p. Mansoor* [1996] 3 All E.R. 913, C.A., the Court of Appeal considered the application of *Awua* to discharge of duty under s.65, 1985 Act, and rejected an argument that it was *obiter*. The term "accommodation", it was held, involves no element of permanence; it is to be understood in its ordinary meaning of "somewhere to live", subject to the qualification that "it must be somewhere reasonably tolerable" (*per* Sir Thomas Bingham, M.R.). A challenge to an offer of accommodation on temporal grounds could only be mounted on the basis of *Wednesbury* unreasonableness (see below, notes to s.191).

Evans L.J., agreeing, was none the less somewhat more cautious about the want of temporal requirement, and suggested that the authority's decision on the point "must be proportionate to the relevant circumstances of the case," a decision with an undertone similar to that which gave rise to the decision in *R. v. L.B. Ealing, ex p. McBain* [1985] 1 W.L.R. 1351, 18 H.L.R. 59, C.A., *i.e.* that there could be re-application when former offer would not be an adequate response to the current circumstances of the applicant (see above, notes to s.183). The needs of the applicant, as well as to the situation in the local housing market, would both form part of the relevant circumstances, he held, illustrating a young family with dependent children of school age who could reasonably expect to remain in the same area, even if not the same home, for a number of years.

As a matter of statutory construction, he considered that an offer must at least be capable of being distinguished from that to be provided to the homeless intentionally (see now, s.189(2), above). Finally, he considered that in some cases, the provision of short-term or interim accommodation would not necessarily amount to a full discharge of duty, so that the applicant would have to re-apply, but that in certain circumstances the duty may revive (if the accommodation ceases to be available, and the applicant remains both unintentionally homeless and in priority need), so that in this sense the duty would be indefinite (quoting Lord Hoffman at [1996] 1 A.C. p.71/B).

Ward L.J., however, while expressing some sympathy for these views, expressly agreed with the Master of the Rolls and did not consider that the questions arose in that case.

The issues will not be relevant to decisions arising *wholly* under Pt. VII, though may be relevant where accommodation was provided under Pt. III, 1985 Act before this Part came into force, and it is sought to rely on the greater duties under that Part than under this. In substance, this section overtakes and replaces both *Awua* and *Wingrove and Mansoor* (and was intended to do so: see Introduction to Pt. VII, and General Note to s.175, above). It refers to a "minimum period". That period may be reduced by "cessation" under subss. (4)–(8), but—to pursue the same example—loss of priority need is not one of the grounds for such cessation. It follows that the *Awua* method of averting responsibility is no longer available, and that this statutory structure is substituted.

The section must be read together with s.206, below, which confines the use of the authority's own, principal housing stock to a maximum period of two years out of any three. The two-year period is intended to ensure that the majority of people will have secured permanent accommodation by the time it expires: *Hansard* (H.C.), Standing Committee G, Twentieth Sitting, March 21, 1996, col. 777, Minister for Local Government, Housing and Urban Regeneration (Mr Curry).

The applicant, may, however, re-apply where the duty is terminated or the authority cease to be subject to it: subs. (9). This accords with the policy: "What happens when the full duty is to accommodate for two years unless the applicant moves out or is offered permanent accommodation? ... A household can reapply before eviction from a previous property and be reassessed. If the tests are passed, a fresh two-year period of duty starts. If a household is still in priority need and still has no suitable accommodation, the local authority can continue to sponsor accommodation for any period up to two more years ...": *per* Minister for Local Government, Housing and Urban Regeneration (Mr Curry), *Hansard* (H.C.), Standing Committee G, Eighteenth Sitting, March 19, 1996, col. 692.

Even if not under a new *duty* after the two year period, the authority retain *power* to provide accommodation for the homeless, *e.g.* where priority need has been lost because a child has ceased to be dependent, or where a claim to asylum is refused but it is decided not to require the applicant to leave: subs. (3).

Subs. (1)

The duty is subject to the provisions of s.197, below, under which authorities who are satisfied that other suitable accommodation is available for the applicant's occupation in their area (s.197(1)), are under no more duty that to furnish advice and such assistance as they consider appropriate in the applicant's circumstances in his own attempts to secure such accommodation (s.197(2)): see General Note to s.197, below.

Subss. (2), (3)

The duty also has effect subject to the provisions of ss.198–201, below, pursuant to which the authority may, if the applicant has no local connection with their area, be able to refer the application to the authority for an area with which he does have such a local connection (subject to the risk of domestic violence in that other area): see notes, below.

The obligation is to secure that accommodation becomes available for the applicant's occupation, which by definition means for all those reasonably to be expected to reside with the applicant: see General Note to s.175, above. Accommodation may be secured by making available the authority's own accommodation, by securing that the applicant obtains accommodation from some other person, or by giving such advice and assistance that secures that accommodation is obtained from some other person: s.206(2); the provision of the authority's own accommodation is, however, for limited periods only (see s.207(1)). Reasonable charges may be made for accommodation, or a contribution sought towards payments the authority make to another: s.206(2). The accommodation secured must also be suitable: s.206(1), in determining which criteria are to be found in s.210.

Subs. (4)

Subject to the provisions of s.200 (housing of persons subject to a local connection referral), this subsection defines the minimum period of two years as beginning on the day when notification was first given under s.184, above, to a person already accommodated pending inquiries under s.188, on the day when notification was given under s.199(2) that conditions for referral are not met, and in any other case on the date when the accommodation is first made available to the applicant.

Subss. (5)–(8)

These subsections define circumstances when the authority cease to be subject to the duty, other than by expiry of time (see also the duty to review, under s.194, below).

Offer under this section. First, the duty ceases if the applicant is made an offer of suitable accommodation under this section which he refuses, having been warned that the authority will regard themselves as having discharged their duty if he does so: this embodies the effect of *R. v. Westminster C.C., ex p. Chambers* (1982) 6 H.L.R. 24, Q.B.D., see notes to s.191 above.

Such an offer not only will not be of permanent accommodation by means of allocation under

Pt. VI, above, but cannot be: see s.207 below. An offer by way of shorthold tenancy—whether from a registered social landlord or in the wholly private sector—will clearly be suitable for this purpose: see *R. v. L.B. Wandsworth, ex p. Wingrove* and *R. v. L.B. Wandsworth, ex p. Mansoor* [1996] 3 All E.R. 913, C.A., *R. v. Rochester-upon-Medway C.C., ex p. Williams* (1994) 26 H.L.R. 588, Q.B.D. and *R. v. L.B. Newham, ex p. Miah* (1995) 28 H.L.R. 279, Q.B.D.

Permanent allocation. Secondly, the authority cease to be subject to the duty if the applicant refuses an offer of permanent rehousing under Pt. VI, having been warned that if he does so the authority's duty will so cease, provided that the authority are satisfied that the accommodation offered was suitable (see s.210, below), and that it was reasonable for him to accept the offer, and so notify him within 21 days of the refusal. This likewise embodies the effect of *Chambers.* It is a reasonable basis for refusal that the applicant is occupying accommodation in respect of which he is under contractual or other obligations which cannot be terminated by the time he is obliged to take up the offer (subs. (8)).

An offer may not be deferred for any extraneous reason: see *R. v. London Borough of Tower Hamlets, ex p. Khalique* (1994) 26 H.L.R. 517, Q.B.D., where the authority sought to postpone making an offer of permanent accommodation pending a reduction in arrears of rent owed by the applicant, although such a consideration may be relevant to the type of accommodation offered: *R. v. L.B. Newham, ex p. Miah* (1995) 28 H.L.R. 279, Q.B.D.

A conditional offer would not, however, qualify as an offer an applicant can reasonably be expected to accept, unless there is positive evidence of ability to perform the condition, *e.g.* pay the sum involved.

It seems likely that the offer must remain open during the 21-day period of notification, for the limitation does not appear to have any other good purpose. It has been held that in any event an offer should remain open for consideration by the applicant for a reasonable time: *R. v. London Borough of Wandsworth, ex p. Lindsay* (1986) 18 H.L.R. 502, Q.B.D. The same had been held in *Parr v. Wyre B.C.* (1982) 2 H.L.R. 71, C.A., which was disapproved in *R. v. London Borough of Hillingdon, ex p. Puhlhofer* [1986] A.C. 484, 18 H.L.R. 158, H.L., so far as it was based on the introduction of the word "appropriate:" see General Note to s.175, above. This would not seem to alter the need for time for acceptance.

An offer must, at the time that it falls to be accepted or rejected, be one which takes account of all the relevant circumstances known to the authority: *R. v. Wycombe D.C., ex p. Hazeltine* (1993) 25 H.L.R. 313, C.A., in which the authority sought to maintain that they had properly discharged their duty to house, by means of an offer which was only open to be accepted by the applicant for a limited period, prior to the receipt and evaluation of the medical reports requested from her, on the basis of which its suitability would retrospectively be determined. If the property was accepted, the allegation of non-suitability had to be abandoned. If rejected and determined to be unsuitable, the applicant would be made another offer; but if rejected and determined to be suitable, no new offer would be made; this procedure could not be regarded as fair.

In *R. v. London Borough of Ealing, ex p. Denny* (1995) 27 H.L.R. 424, Q.B.D., however, an offer made at a time when the property was occupied by squatters and could only be viewed from outside, was upheld as valid as it had been made clear to the applicant that she could later withdraw her acceptance for good reason.

In *R. v. London Borough of Newham, ex p. Gentle* (1993) 26 H.L.R. 466, Q.B.D., the authority's policy of requiring applicants to move into offered property before an appeal in respect of suitability would be considered, was held to be irrational on the basis that it was too rigidly applied (see also *R. v. L.B. Brent, ex p. Baruwa* (1995) 28 H.L.R. 361, Q.B.D.). In *R. v. London Borough of Newham, ex p. Laronde* (1994) 27 H.L.R. 215, Q.B.D., the same authority's refusal of a right of appeal against an offer, without taking up the tenancy, again led to the offer being quashed; the offer itself had been made at a time when material matters (medical condition, state of repair and related financial and practical problems) had been raised by the applicant but not considered by the authority. By the time of *R. v. London Borough of Newham, ex p. Dada* (1995) 27 H.L.R. 502, C.A., however, a sufficient degree of discretion had been built in to the requirement, to overcome the rigidity which had caused the authority to lose the previous two cases. See also *R. v. London Borough of Newham, ex p. Begum* (1996) 28 H.L.R. 646, Q.B.D.

So far as the "appeal procedure"—not rigidly applied—has accordingly been upheld, the approach is distinguishable from *Hazeltine*, because the applicant is allowed to accept the property *and* challenge suitability, and if the appeal fails, still has the property.

Subs. (9)

A person towards whom the authority are under a duty under this section which is terminated, or ceases, may re-apply.

Power exercisable after minimum period of duty under s.193

194.—(1) Where a local housing authority have been subject to the duty under section 193 in relation to a person until the end of the minimum period, they may continue to secure that accommodation is available for his occupation.

(2) They shall not do so unless they are satisfied on a review under this section that—

(a) he has a priority need,

(b) there is no other suitable accommodation available for occupation by him in their district, and

(c) he wishes the authority to continue securing that accommodation is available for his occupation;

and they shall not continue to do so for more than two years at a time unless they are satisfied on a further review under this section as to those matters.

The review shall be carried out towards the end of the minimum period, or subsequent two year period, with a view to enabling the authority to make an assessment of the likely situation at the end of that period.

(3) They shall cease to do so if events occur such that, by virtue of section 193(6) or (7), they would cease to be subject to any duty under that section.

(4) Where an authority carry out a review under this section they shall make such inquiries as they consider appropriate to determine—

(a) whether they are satisfied as to the matters mentioned in subsection (2)(a) to (c), and

(b) whether any of the events referred to in subsection (3) has occurred;

and on completing the review they shall notify the applicant of their determination and of whether they propose to exercise, or continue to exercise, their power under this section.

(5) The authority may at any time, whether in consequence of a review or otherwise, give notice to the person concerned that they propose to cease exercising their power under this section in his case.

(6) The notice must specify—

(a) the day on which they will cease exercising their power under this section, and

(b) any action that they intend to take as a result,

and must be given not less than the prescribed period before the day so specified.

DEFINITIONS
"available for his occupation": s.176.
"local housing authority": ss.217, 218.

GENERAL NOTE
Under this section, where an authority have been under a *duty* to secure accommodation (under s.193, above), they may continue to secure accommodation after the end of the period. They may *not* do so, however, in certain circumstances. The first of these circumstances is that that they have conducted a review and as a result of it they have failed to satisfy themselves that the applicant is still in priority need, and that there is no other suitable accommodation for him in their district, and that he still wants the authority to continue to secure that accommodation is available: subs. (2).

Furthermore, if they do provide further accommodation under this power, they may not do so for more than two years at a time: *ibid.* If they decline to assist under this power, but the applicant qualifies within s.193, above, the applicant may make a further application, *i.e.* for *de novo* consideration: s.193(9), above. This structure accords with the overriding policy aim, that accommodation should not be provided for more than two years at a time without review: see Introduction to Pt. VII, above; General Note to s.193, above.

The time for the review is "towards the end" of the two-year, minimum period, in time to make an assessment at the end of that period: subs. (2). If, as a result of any of the conditions set out in s.193(6) (cessation of eligibility, becoming homeless from the accommodation provided under s.193, accepting an offer under Pt. VI, above, or otherwise voluntarily ceasing to occupy the property made available for him as an only or principal home—see notes to s.193(6), above), or s.193(7) (refusal of an offer under Pt. VI which it was reasonable for him to accept—see notes to s.193(7), above), he would have ceased to qualify for assistance under s.193, so also are the authority prohibited from exercising the power to assist under this section: subs. (3).

The review requires the authority to make inquiries (subs. (4)). The inquiries are into the conditions in subs. (2) (priority need, no other accommodation, applicant wishes authority to continue to secure accommodation) and disqualification under subs. (3) (*i.e.* under s.193(6), (7) above). There is no reason to think that this duty (which will lead to a decision whether or not the housing duty under this section will continue) is to be conducted any the less thoroughly, or fairly, than the initial duty to inquire—see notes to s.184, above.

Subs. (4)

Though the authority have to give notice of the outcome of a review, and whether or not they propose to exercise their power to continue to secure that accommodation is made available under this section, their decision is not *per se* reviewable under s.202, below, and, therefore, cannot be challenged on appeal to the county court (see notes to s.204 below), but only by way of judicial review; however, constituent *elements* of the decision may be so reviewable (under s.202)—*cf.* below s.202(1).

Subs. (5)

The authority can at any time give notice of their intention to cease exercising their powers under this section, but that will not stop the applicant making a new application under s.193(9) above.

Duties in case of threatened homelessness

195.—(1) This section applies where the local housing authority are satisfied that an applicant is threatened with homelessness and is eligible for assistance.

(2) If the authority—

(a) are satisfied that he has a priority need, and

(b) are not satisfied that he became threatened with homelessness intentionally,

they shall take reasonable steps to secure that accommodation does not cease to be available for his occupation.

This subsection has effect subject to section 197 (duty where other suitable accommodation available).

(3) Subsection (2) does not affect any right of the authority, whether by virtue of a contract, enactment or rule of law, to secure vacant possession of any accommodation.

(4) Where in pursuance of the duty under subsection (2) the authority secure that accommodation other than that occupied by the applicant when he made his application is available for occupation by him, the provisions of section 193(3) to (9) (period for which duty owed) and section 194 (power exercisable after minimum period of duty) apply, with any necessary modifications, in relation to the duty under this section as they apply in relation to the duty under section 193.

(5) If the authority—

(a) are not satisfied that the applicant has a priority need, or

(b) are satisfied that he has a priority need but are also satisfied that he became threatened with homelessness intentionally,

they shall furnish him with advice and such assistance as they consider appropriate in the circumstances in any attempts he may make to secure that accommodation does not cease to be available for his occupation.

DEFINITIONS

"available for his occupation": s.176.

"eligible for assistance": s.183.

"local housing authority": ss.217, 218.

"priority need": s.189.

GENERAL NOTE

This section is the source of assistance available to those who are (a) threatened with homelessness (meaning those likely to become homeless within 28 days—see s.175(4), above), who are (b) eligible for assistance, *i.e.* not disqualified from assistance by reference to ss.185, 186 above. The substantive duty is qualified by s.197 below, so that if the authority are satisfied that there is other suitable accommodation available for the applicant, their duties will arise under that section instead of under this.

Without prejudice to the authority's right to recover possession of any accommodation—so that this section cannot be used as a defence to proceedings brought for possession of an authority's own housing—the authority's duty is to take reasonable steps to secure that accommodation does not cease to be available for the applicant's accommodation. The provision does not make an authority's refusal to withdraw "stop notices", under planning legislation, which would render the applicants, who were a group of travelling showmen, perverse: *R. v. Chiltern D.C., ex p. Roberts* (1990) 23 H.L.R. 387, Q.B.D.

Subs. (5)

When the applicant is only threatened with homelessness when a finding of intentionality is made, the authority's duty is to "furnish him with advice and such assistance as they consider appropriate in any attempts he may make to secure that accommodation does not cease to be available for his occupation" which may obviously include financial advice, or advice on the powers of the court to suspend an order. It would seem that when homelessness itself occurs, the applicant is still entitled to a period of temporary accommodation under s.189(2)(a), although the point cannot be entirely free from doubt.

The duties in this section apply even although an issue of local connection may apply: It is only s.193 which is subject to s.198, not this section. It has been held in the county court that the local connection provisions are not applicable when the authority's duty arises because of threatened homelessness under this section. In *Williams v. Exeter City Council*, September 1981 L.A.G. Bulletin 211, C.C., a woman was occupying army property let to her husband, a serviceman, in the Exeter area. As such, she had no connection with Exeter on the basis of residence of choice, nor on any other ground (*cf.* notes to s.199 below). The Ministry of Defence secured an order for possession against her, and before it was executed she applied to the authority.

The authority agreed that she was threatened with homelessness but referred her case to East Devon D.C. As Ms Williams did not wish to leave the area, she challenged the decision and it was held that the local connection provisions applied only when the duty arose under s.193. It is unclear from the short report, however, whether the authority could have used the local connection provisions once actual homelessness occurred, or whether what was held is that the structure of the provisions implies that if a decision is made while the applicant is still only threatened with homelessness, the local connection provisions will remain irrelevant once actual homelessness occurs: the former seems the more likely interpretation.

If inquiries are made before the 28 days, they will be non-statutory: *R. v. Rugby B.C., ex p. Hunt* (1992) 26 H.L.R. 1, Q.B.D. A discharge of duty which means that an applicant is already threatened with homelessness anew will not constitute an adequate discharge: *R. v. L.B. Brent, ex p. Awua* [1996] 1 A.C. 55, 27 H.L.R. 453, H.L.

Becoming threatened with homelessness intentionally

196.—(1) A person becomes threatened with homelessness intentionally if he deliberately does or fails to do anything the likely result of which is that he will be forced to leave accommodation which is available for his occupation and which it would have been reasonable for him to continue to occupy.

(2) For the purposes of subsection (1) an act or omission in good faith on the part of a person who was unaware of any relevant fact shall not be treated as deliberate.

(3) A person shall be treated as becoming threatened with homelessness intentionally if—

(a) he enters into an arrangement under which he is required to cease to occupy accommodation which it would have been reasonable for him to continue to occupy, and

(b) the purpose of the arrangement is to enable him to become entitled to assistance under this Part,

and there is no other good reason why he is threatened with homelessness.

(4) A person who is given advice or assistance under section 197 (duty where, other suitable alternative accommodation available), but fails to secure suitable accommodation in circumstances in which it was reasonably to be expected that he would do so, shall, if he makes a further application

under this Part, be treated as having become threatened with homelessness intentionally.

"available for his occupation": s.176.
"threatened with homelessness intentionally": s.195.

GENERAL NOTE
See notes to s.191 above: there is no distinction in principle between the definitions of intentional homelessness and threatened with homelessness intentionally, other than the 28 day criterion: *Dyson v. Kerrier D.C.* [1980] 1 W.L.R. 1206, at p.1213, C.A. This seems to be based on a concession by counsel, but must surely be correct.

Duty where other suitable accommodation available

Duty where other suitable accommodation available

197.—(1) This section applies if the local housing authority would be under a duty under this Part—
  (a) to secure that accommodation is available for occupation by an applicant, or
  (b) to secure that accommodation does not cease to be available for his occupation,
but are satisfied that other suitable accommodation is available for occupation by him in their district.
  (2) In that case, their duty is to provide the applicant with such advice and assistance as the authority consider is reasonably required to enable him to secure such accommodation.
  (3) The duty ceases if the applicant fails to take reasonable steps to secure such accommodation.
  (4) In deciding what advice and assistance to provide under this section, and whether the applicant has taken reasonable steps, the authority shall have regard to all the circumstances including—
  (a) the characteristics and personal circumstances of the applicant, and
  (b) the state of the local housing market and the type of accommodation available.
  (5) For the purposes of this section accommodation shall not be regarded as available for occupation by the applicant if it is available only with assistance beyond what the authority consider is reasonable in the circumstances.
  (6) Subsection (1) does not apply to the duty of a local housing authority under—
    section 188 (interim duty to accommodate in case of apparent priority need),
    section 190(2)(a) (limited duty to person becoming homeless intentionally), or
    section 200(1), (3) or (4) (interim duties where case is considered for referral or referred).

DEFINITIONS
"available for his occupation": s.176.
"local housing authority": ss.217, 218.

GENERAL NOTE
Although there is not currently a great deal that can be said about this section, it will undoubtedly prove one of the most contentious of the changes, if not the most, for it is an over-reaching provision entitling authorities entirely to side-step duties to secure accommodation for the unintentionally homeless in priority need.
To enjoy the benefit of this effective exemption from Pt. VII, the authority must, however, be satisfied (*n.b.* a higher rather than lower standard, *cf.* "have reason to believe" in ss.183, 184, 188 and 211, and "consider" in s.198) "that other suitable accommodation is available for occupation by him in their district". If so satisfied, their only duty is to advise and provide such assistance as

they consider is reasonably required in his own attempts to secure such accommodation.

The important points to draw out are that they must be satisfied:

(i) that such other accommodation is "suitable" (see ss.206, 210, below, and notes thereto), and

(ii) that such other accommodation is available for his occupation in the statutory sense (see General Note to s.175, above), and

(iii) that it is available "for occupation by him" which means in practice so available, and

(iv) that it is so available in their district.

Assuming these conditions are fulfilled, the duty to assist:

(v) Must be such as they consider is "reasonably required" to "enable him to secure such accommodation".

Whether other accommodation is available under this section was said during the passage of the Bill to be reviewable under s.202, below (*per* Minister for Local Government, Housing and Urban Regeneration, *Hansard* (H.C.), Standing Committee G, Twenty-first Sitting, March 26, col. 815).

Other suitable accommodation. A number of decisions have been reported under the provisions of the Housing Benefit Regulations, now the Housing Benefit (General) Regulations 1987 (S.I. 1987 No. 1971), as amended, Reg. 11(2) of which empowers an authority to restrict benefit on the basis that the claimant's rent is unreasonably high, in comparison to rent payable "in respect of suitable alternative accommodation" elsewhere, although in certain cases no such restriction is to apply "unless suitable cheaper alternative accommodation is available" (Reg. 11(3)).

In *R. v. Housing Benefit Review Board of South Herefordshire D.C., ex p. Smith* (1987) 19 H.L.R. 218, Q.B.D., under analogous provisions of the Housing Benefit Regulations 1985, it was held that it was not necessary for an authority to be able to identify specific alternative accommodation for what is now Reg. 11(3) purposes, so long as the authority were satisfied that there was some such accommodation to which the claimant could have gone: in that case, there was not simply a want of ability to identify a specific alternative, but no evidence that there was anywhere to which she could have gone.

In *R. v. Sefton M.B.C., ex p. Cunningham* (1991) 23 H.L.R. 534, Q.B.D., under Reg. 11(3), it was held that while there was evidence of accommodation generally available, there was no evidence of its suitability for the particular claimant's needs: it would have been sufficient if the authority could have pointed to the existence of a class of properties in an area, of a sort which could have been seen to be appropriate to the needs of the applicant, but not sufficient merely to say that there were a lot of properties available, and at cheaper rents.

In *R. v. Housing Benefit Review Board of East Devon D.C., ex p. Gibson* (1993) 25 H.L.R. 487, Q.B.D., also under Reg. 11(3), it was held that it was sufficient to point to a range of properties as being available, without pointing to specific properties, and that there was sufficient such evidence, on which the authority were entitled to rely, but that there was a lack of any explanation in the Review Board's decision letter which explained how it had felt able to conclude that these properties would be suitable.

In *R. v. Manchester C.C., ex p. Harcup* (1993) 26 H.L.R. 402, Q.B.D., the authority's decision—again under Reg. 11(3)—was upheld on the basis of a sufficient range rather than a specific property (*R. v. East Yorkshire Borough of Beverley Housing Benefits Review Board, ex p. Hare* (1995) 27 H.L.R. 637, Q.B.D., under Reg. 11(2), does not bear upon the point raised by this section).

It is the Reg. 11(3) cases which are of relevance, as it is clear that it is the particular applicant for whom (and for whose household) the property must be both suitable and available: see subs. (4)(a), with the reference to the "characteristics and personal circumstances of the applicant". Given the context, and the extent to which this section comprises an outright alternative to the authority themselves taking on responsibility for finding somewhere for the applicant (which could in any event mean privately rented accommodation—see s.206(1)(b) below—or advice and assistance such that other accommodation is obtained by the applicant—see s.206(1)(c) below), it is submitted that quite a lot more is called for in terms of "satisfaction" than mere general knowledge of accommodation being available, or even being available to persons of particular characteristics (including those of the applicant): see also subs. (4)(b), with the reference to the state of the local market and type of accommodation available.

In so saying, there may be borne in mind not merely the general requirements of suitability discussed in the notes to s.210, below, but the specific requirement of subs. (5), that accommodation is not to be regarded as available if it is only available with assistance beyond that which the authority consider reasonable in the circumstances: this prevents an authority concluding on the one hand that there is suitable accommodation available, but proffering assistance insufficient to enable the applicant to secure it (arguing that their decision on level of assistance is, none the less, within the ambit of what a, or any reasonable authority could decide was reasonable, on principles of administrative law—see notes to s.204, below).

It had in any event been held under Pt. III, 1985 Act, s.69 (the equivalent of s.206 below), that accommodation must be affordable if it is to be suitable—see *R. v. Tower Hamlets L.B.C., ex p. Kaur* (1994) 26 H.L.R. 597, Q.B.D., where accommodation secured for the applicant in the private sector was not suitable because the contractual rent exceeded the amount which would be met in housing benefit and the applicant could not afford to meet the shortfall from his own resources. In *R. v. London Borough of Brent, ex p. Awua* [1996] 1 A.C. 55, 27 H.L.R. 453, H.L., it was said that while what is now s.210 points to suitability being primarily a matter of space and arrangement, other matters such as whether the applicant can afford the rent may also be material.

Subss. (2), (4)
The requirement to provide such advice and assistance as the authority consider is reasonably required to enable the applicant to secure other suitable accommodation—and the criteria to be taken into account in reaching that decision (subs. (4))—serve to colour the need for the authority to be satisfied that such accommodation is actually or practically available, and to the applicant, rather than theoretically or generally available (see notes above), and suggests active assistance, or assistance in relation to activity by the applicant, in relation to which it is not likely to be enough to provide applicants with lists of, *e.g.* accommodation agencies or local landlords, without the authority also satisfying themselves that such bodies have accommodation available, for occupiers of the same characteristics as the applicant, at the relevant time.

Subss. (3), (4)
If the duty is discharged, and the accommodation refused, then re-application will be governed by the considerations discussed in the notes to s.183, above.

Subs. (6)
This exemption from the duty to secure accommodation does not apply to the temporary duties—pending inquiries (s.188), to the homeless intentionally (s.190), or to those the subject of a possible local connection referral (s.199).

Referral to another local housing authority

Referral of case to another local housing authority

198.—(1) If the local housing authority would be subject to the duty under section 193 (accommodation for those with priority need who are not homeless intentionally) but consider that the conditions are met for referral of the case to another local housing authority, they may notify that other authority of their opinion.

The authority need not consider under section 197 whether other suitable accommodation is available before proceeding under this section.

(2) The conditions for referral of the case to another authority are met if—

(a) neither the applicant nor any person who might reasonably be expected to reside with him has a local connection with the district of the authority to whom his application was made,

(b) the applicant or a person who might reasonably be expected to reside with him has a local connection with the district of that other authority, and

(c) neither the applicant nor any person who might reasonably be expected to reside with him will run the risk of domestic violence in that other district.

(3) For this purpose a person runs the risk of domestic violence—

(a) if he runs the risk of violence from a person with whom he is associated, or

(b) if he runs the risk of threats of violence from such a person which are likely to be carried out.

(4) The conditions for referral of the case to another authority are also met if—

(a) the applicant was on a previous application made to that other authority placed (in pursuance of their functions under this Part) in accommodation in the district of the authority to whom his application is now made, and

(b) the previous application was within such period as may be prescribed of the present application.

(5) The question whether the conditions for referral of a case are satisfied shall be decided by agreement between the notifying authority and the notified authority or, in default of agreement, in accordance with such arrangements as the Secretary of State may direct by order.

(6) An order may direct that the arrangements shall be—

(a) those agreed by any relevant authorities or associations of relevant authorities, or

(b) in default of such agreement, such arrangements as appear to the Secretary of State to be suitable, after consultation with such associations representing relevant authorities, and such other persons, as he thinks appropriate.

(7) No such order shall be made unless a draft of the order has been approved by a resolution of each House of Parliament.

DEFINITIONS
"district": s.217.
"local housing authority": ss.217, 218.

GENERAL NOTE
This section governs the circumstances in which a local authority may refer an applicant to another authority. The principal questions—as to eligibility for assistance, priority need and intentionality—fall to the authority to which the application is made, even where an earlier decision on intentionality has been made by another authority: see notes to s.183, above, under Application to Different Authority, and the cases of *R. v. Slough Borough Council, ex p. L.B. Ealing* [1981] Q.B. 801, C.A., *R. v. London Borough of Tower Hamlets, ex p. London Borough of Camden* (1989) 21 H.L.R. 197, Q.B.D., *R. v. Newham London Borough Council, ex p. London Borough of Tower Hamlets* (1990) 23 H.L.R. 62, C.A., *R. v. London Borough of Hammersmith & Fulham, ex p. O'Brian* (1985) 17 H.L.R. 471, Q.B.D., and *R. v. London Borough of Tower Hamlets, ex p. Ali; R. v. London Borough of Tower Hamlets, ex p. Bibi* (1992) 25 H.L.R. 158, C.A. This is so even if it becomes apparent that the local connection provisions may apply: *Delahaye v. Oswestry Borough Council, The Times,* July 29, 1980, Q.B.D.

The local connection provisions exempt an authority from duties under s.193. They do not affect the provision of temporary accommodation provided for a person who is homeless, and in priority need, but who the authority to which application has been made have determined is homeless intentionally, which arises under s.195. It has been held in the county court that the local connection provisions are not applicable when the authority's duty arises because of threatened homelessness: *Williams v. Exeter City Council,* September 1981 L.A.G. Bulletin 211, C.C., see notes to s.195, above.

Subs. (2)
An authority will be entitled to rely on the local connection provisions when they are satisfied that the applicant is homeless and in priority need, not satisfied that the applicant became homeless intentionally, and are of the opinion that the conditions for referral apply. The conditions are:

(a) neither the applicant nor any person who might reasonably be expected to reside with him has a local connection with their area; and

(b) the applicant or a person who might reasonably be expected to reside with him does have a local connection with the area of another housing authority; and

(c) neither the applicant nor any person who might reasonably be expected to reside with him will run the risk of domestic violence in that other authority's area.

The local connection of a person from abroad who is residing with the applicant must be disregarded: see s.185(4), above.

It is clear that all three factors must be present: there must (i) be no local connection with the one area; and (ii) be a local connection with the other area; and (iii) be no risk of domestic violence: *R. v. Hillingdon Borough Council, ex p. Streeting* [1980] 1 W.L.R. 1425, C.A. The procedure does not arise if there is a local connection with the area to which application has been made, but that authority are of the opinion that the applicant has a greater or closer local connection elsewhere: *Betts v. Eastleigh Borough Council* [1983] 1 W.L.R. 774, 8 H.L.R. 28, C.A., not overruled on this point in the House of Lords (see [1983] 2 A.C. 613, 10 H.L.R. 97, H.L.): this was one of the mischiefs the 1977 Act was intended to end.

The decision to refer is discretionary and as such may be vulnerable to challenge if exercised unreasonably, see *R. v. London Borough of Newham, ex p. London Borough of Tower Hamlets* (1990) 23 H.L.R. 62, C.A., where it was held that the referring authority must be satisfied as to homelessness and priority need, and also not be satisfied that the homelessness was intentional; whilst their decision on intentionality could not be appealed, it could not found a referral if flawed to the extent that in appropriate judicial review proceedings it would have been quashed. Newham's decision in the case was so flawed, *inter alia*, in that it failed to take account of the general circumstances prevailing in relation to housing in Tower Hamlets.

The circumstances in which a person runs the risk of domestic violence are the same as those considered in relation to whether or not it would have been reasonable (on this ground) to continue to occupy accommodation, pursuant to s.177: see notes to s.175, above—see subs. (3). The authority are under a positive duty to inquire whether the applicant is subject to such a risk: *Patterson v. L.B. Greenwich* (1993) 26 H.L.R. 159, C.A.

One point which may be made relates to the interaction of this part of the provisions with intentional homelessness. It is not uncommon for women not merely to leave home on account of domestic violence, but to leave or try to leave the area. Some authorities who find that a person in these circumstances is not homeless intentionally, will none the less seek to refer her back. It is true that there is no necessary conflict between finding that a woman is homeless (perhaps on account of the domestic violence) and not finding that she will run the risk of domestic violence in the area from which she has fled. An authority can take the view that while domestic violence drove her out, the risk is no longer present. None the less, it is a relatively sophisticated distinction, for which there ought to be material reasons, and clear that automatically to refer her back without considering this distinction will be a bad decision in law.

In this connection, it may be noted that in *R. v. Bristol City Council, ex p. Browne* [1979] 1 W.L.R. 1437, D.C., which for these purposes and on this issue may be treated as if a local connection case (see notes to s.206 below), the authority had not found intentional homelessness, but appeared to have addressed themselves expressly to the point made in the last paragraph. In *R. v. London Borough of Islington, ex p. Adigun* (1986) 20 H.L.R. 600, Q.B.D., it was stressed that the task of determining whether or not there was a risk of domestic violence is one for the local authority; so long as there was material on which they could base their decision, the court would not intervene.

Although it is lawful for an authority to have a policy about how they may exercise their discretion, they cannot decide in advance that in all cases in which there is a local connection elsewhere, the unintentionally homeless applicant should be referred: *R. v. London Borough of Harrow, ex p. Carter* (1992) 26 H.L.R. 32, Q.B.D. In *Wyness v. Poole B.C.* (1979) July L.A.G. Bulletin 166, C.C., it was held that to attempt to discharge the authority's duty towards a family which had acquired a local connection with their area by reason of employment, by arrangement with another authority (to which, without the connection, the family might have been referred, but which was too far away to keep up the employment), was impermissible, as it would defeat the purpose of the *limits* on the power to refer.

Subs. (4)

A new provision, added by this Act, deems the conditions for referral to be fulfilled—therefore, regardless of local connection with authority to which the application was made, and regardless of risk of domestic violence—if the applicant was placed by another authority, within such period as may be prescribed, in accommodation in the area of the authority to which the application has been made, in discharge of their functions under this Part (see ss.193, 206): *n.b.* such placement in discharge of functions under Pt. III, 1985 Act, will not have this over-reaching effect.

Subss. (5)–(7)

The first step is for authorities to seek to agree who has responsibility. If they cannot agree, the matter is to be resolved in accordance with arrangements made by the Secretary of State. Those arrangements are to be those agreed by the authorities, or associations of authorities, or in default of agreement such as appear to the Secretary of State to be suitable, after consultation with the local authority associations, and such other persons as he thinks appropriate.

In *R. v. Mr. Referee McCall, ex p. Eastbourne B.C.,* April 29, 1981, Q.B.D. but cited in *Betts v. Eastleigh B.C.* (1981) 8 H.L.R. 48, under the equivalent provisions of the 1977 Act, it was held that although an arbitrator will not normally be entitled to apply criteria set out in a Local Authority Agreement, without the consent of the authorities, it is proper for him to have regard to the wishes of the applicant where issues are evenly balanced; indeed, where all other considerations give no indication one way or another, the court described it as "perfectly reasonable and perfectly sensible, and within the spirit of the statutory provisions", to have regard to the wishes of the family.

Local connection

199.—(1) A person has a local connection with the district of a local housing authority if he has a connection with it—
- (a) because he is, or in the past was, normally resident there, and that residence is or was of his own choice,
- (b) because he is employed there,
- (c) because of family associations, or
- (d) because of special circumstances.

(2) A person is not employed in a district if he is serving in the regular armed forces of the Crown.

(3) Residence in a district is not of a person's own choice if—
- (a) he becomes resident there because he, or a person who might reasonably be expected to reside with him, is serving in the regular armed forces of the Crown, or
- (b) he, or a person who might reasonably be expected to reside with him, becomes resident there because he is detained under the authority of an Act of Parliament.

(4) In subsections (2) and (3) "regular armed forces of the Crown" means the Royal Navy, the regular forces as defined by section 225 of the Army Act 1955, the regular air force as defined by section 223 of the Air Force Act 1955 and Queen Alexandra's Royal Naval Nursing Service.

(5) The Secretary of State may by order specify other circumstances in which—
- (a) a person is not to be treated as employed in a district, or
- (b) residence in a district is not to be treated as of a person's own choice.

DEFINITIONS
"district": s.217.
"local housing authority": ss.217, 218.

GENERAL NOTE
The local connection provisions allow one authority to pass on to another the burden of securing that permanent accommodation is made available to an applicant: ss.198, 200. The provisions operate only in specified circumstances: it was one of the principal aims of the 1977 Act to end "shuttling" homeless persons between different local authorities, each alleging there was "greater" connection with the other.

Subs. (1)
The four stated circumstances in which a local connection arises are but "grounds" of "local connection" and the latter remains the overriding consideration: see *In Re Betts* [1983] 2 A.C. 613, 10 H.L.R. 97, H.L. The applicant was living with his family in the district of Blaby D.C. between 1978 and 1980. In August 1980, he obtained a job in Southampton, and moved into a houseboat in the area, where he was joined by his family. In October 1980, he was given a house by Eastleigh B.C. Soon after, however, he lost his job through no fault of his own, fell into arrears with his rent, and was evicted. In February 1981, shortly before the order for possession expired, he applied under the 1977 Act. Eastleigh referred the application to Blaby. The reason given for the decision was that the family had lived in Eastleigh's district for less than six months, and was not, accordingly, normally resident in their area. The applicant challenged this decision.

The Court of Appeal allowed this challenge on the basis that the only reason given for the finding that the family was not normally resident in its area was that it had lived in the area for less than six months, and that this decision had been reached by rigid application of the Local Authority Agreement (see s.198(6)). Normal residence was where a person intended to settle, not necessarily permanently or indefinitely (*R. v. Barnet London Borough Council, ex p. Shah* [1983] 2 A.C. 309, H.L.), and a person may have more than one normal residence at different times. It required consideration of many features of residence, not merely the application of a six month, or any other arbitrary, period.

Allowing the appeal, the House of Lords said that the fundamental question was whether or not the applicant had a local connection with the area. This meant more than "normal residence"; normal residence, or any of the other specified grounds of local connection, was only a subsidiary component of the formula to be applied. It is governed by the proposition that residence of any sort will be irrelevant unless and until it is such as to establish a local connection. This approach was followed in *R. v. London Borough of Islington, ex p. Adigun* (1986) 20 H.L.R. 600, Q.B.D. It was also followed in *R. v. Westminster C.C., ex p. Benniche, The Times*, April 15, 1996, 29 H.L.R. forthcoming, C.A., in which daily attendance at a mosque did not prevent referral to another authority, from which such attendance would only be possible infrequently.

The House of Lords did not dissent from the proposition that a rigid application of the Local Authority Agreement would constitute a fetter on the authority's discretion: see also, *British Oxygen Co. Ltd. v. Board of Trade* [1969] 2 Ch. 174, *Att.-Gen., ex rel. Tilley v. London Borough of Wandsworth* [1981] 1 W.L.R. 854, C.A. The Agreement could be taken into account, and applied as a guideline, provided the authority do not shut out the particular facts of the individual case, *i.e.* its application is given individual consideration. In the present case, however, the House of Lords found that the authority had not misdirected themselves in this respect.

Residence

Residence has to be "of choice". There is no residence of choice if the applicant, or a person who might reasonably be expected to reside with him, is serving in the regular armed forces (*i.e.* the Royal Navy, the regular armed forces as defined by the Army Act 1955 (c. 18), s.225, the regular air force as defined by the Air Force Act 1955 (c. 19), s.227, Queen Alexandra's Royal Nursing Service and the Women's Royal Naval Service: subs. (4)).

Nor is there residence of choice if the applicant or anyone who might reasonably be expected to reside with him is detained under the authority of any Act of Parliament. Thus, prisoners (whether or not convicted) and those detained under the Mental Health Act 1983 (c. 20) will not acquire a local connection with the area in which prison or hospital is situated. The Secretary of State has power to specify further circumstances in which residence is not to be considered "of choice" (subs. (5)).

Residence resulting from service in the armed forces was considered in *R. v. Vale of White Horse District Council, ex p. Smith and Hay* (1984) 17 H.L.R. 160, in which applicants had been allowed (in accordance with armed forces' practice) a period of time after the termination of service, before recovering possession of married quarters. It was held that the exclusion of residence as a result of service in the armed forces refers to the time residence commences. A fresh residence after leaving the armed forces can be established, even in the same premises, but it will not normally be established merely by holding over in married quarters after service has come to an end.

In *Smith and Hay*, a period of a few months some ten years before application, during which one of the spouses had been employed, and therefore resident, in an area was considered to be both short, and as not necessarily establishing a local connection.

Employment

A person is not regarded as being employed in an area if he is serving in the regular armed forces, or in such other circumstances as the Secretary of State may by order specify (subs. (5)). Given that employment is a subsidiary consideration, and merely one of the grounds for establishing a local connection, it is clearly open to an authority to exclude casual work, but not, it is submitted, the self-employed. In *R. v. Vale of White Horse D.C., ex p. Smith and Hay* (1984) 17 H.L.R. 160, Q.B.D., the same few months' employment (above), some 10 years before the application, was described as limited and of short duration and the authority did not err in finding that it did not give rise to a local connection.

Family Associations

There is no statutory definition of this phrase. An applicant who objects to being referred to an area on account of family associations should not be so referred. (However, *cf. R. v. Mr Referee McCall, ex p. Eastbourne B.C.*, April 29, 1981, Q.B.D. but cited in *Betts v. Eastleigh B.C.* (1981) 8 H.L.R. 48, notes to s.198, above, in which it was observed that though the applicant's wishes are relevant where other factors are equally balanced, they cannot override the words of the statute.)

Once a family association has been raised by the applicant, the authority should address the issue, and a decision letter which failed to do so (after the issue had been raised) was held defective in *R. v. Slough B.C., ex p. Khan* (1995) 27 H.L.R. 492, Q.B.D. (because it appeared from the letter that no more than the issue of residence had been addressed).

In *R. v. Hammersmith & Fulham L.B.C., ex p. Avdic, The Times*, June 11, 1996, Q.B.D., it was held that family associations did not extend beyond parents, adult children or siblings, so that a claim based on a first cousin once removed was insufficient. This seems somewhat rigid, for people may have close associations or relations—within the intention of the definition—with a wider range of family members. See also the note below, on Other Special Circumstances.

Other Special Circumstances

This is likewise left undefined. In *R. v. Vale of White Horse D.C., ex p. Smith and Hay* (1984) 17 H.L.R. 160, Q.B.D., one of the families attempted to place some reliance on their membership of an evangelical church, around the life of which their own lives revolved. Following *In Re Betts* [1983] 2 A.C. 613, 10 H.L.R. 97, H.L., to the effect that the fundamental test is whether or not there is a local connection, it was held that the authority had not erred in concluding as a matter of fact that this association did not amount to a special circumstance giving rise to a local connection in their case. Nor does a mere desire not to return to an area with which the applicant has a local connection amount to a special circumstance giving rise to a local connection with a different area: *R. v. London Borough of Islington, ex p. Adigun* (1986) 20 H.L.R. 600, Q.B.D.

It has been said that family associations too weak to qualify under subs. (1)(c) cannot amount to a special circumstance under this subsection: see *R. v. Slough B.C., ex p. Khan* (1995) 27 H.L.R. 492, Q.B.D.; *R. v. Hammersmith & Fulham L.B.C., ex p. Avdic, The Times*, June 11, 1996, Q.B.D. This does seem, however, a little too rigid: if a connection of special importance exists, which could be based on what amounts to a weak family association, it should not automatically rule out qualification as a special circumstance. Indeed, it would seem that if the exclusion of a range of family members from qualification as family association is correct (see note above), this category ought to catch it. That is not to say that a mere distant relation should automatically qualify as a connection under this head, but if the connection with the distant relation is of special significance, nor should it automatically be disqualified.

Duties to applicant whose case is considered for referral or referred

200.—(1) Where a local housing authority notify an applicant that they intend to notify or have notified another local housing authority of their opinion that the conditions are met for the referral of his case to that other authority—

(a) they cease to be subject to any duty under section 188 (interim duty to accommodate in case of apparent priority need), and

(b) they are not subject to any duty under section 193 (the main housing duty),

but they shall secure that accommodation is available for occupation by the applicant until he is notified of the decision whether the conditions for referral of his case are met.

(2) When it has been decided whether the conditions for referral are met, the notifying authority shall notify the applicant of the decision and inform him of the reasons for it.

The notice shall also inform the applicant of his right to request a review of the decision and of the time within which such a request must be made.

(3) If it is decided that the conditions for referral are not met, the notifying authority shall secure that accommodation is available for occupation by the applicant until they have considered whether other suitable accommodation is available for his occupation in their district.

If they are satisfied that other suitable accommodation is available for his occupation in their district, section 197(2) applies; and if they are not so satisfied, they are subject to the duty under section 193 (the main housing duty).

(4) If it is decided that the conditions for referral are met, the notified authority shall secure that accommodation is available for occupation by the applicant until they have considered whether other suitable accommodation is available for his occupation in their district.

If they are satisfied that other suitable accommodation is available for his occupation in their district, section 197(2) applies; and if they are not so satisfied, they are subject to the duty under section 193 (the main housing duty).

(5) The duty under subsection (1), (3) or (4) ceases as provided in that subsection even if the applicant requests a review of the authority's decision (see section 202).

The authority may continue to secure that accommodation is available for the applicant's occupation pending the decision on a review.

(6) Notice required to be given to an applicant under this section shall be

given in writing and, if not received by him, shall be treated as having been given to him if it is made available at the authority's office for a reasonable period for collection by him or on his behalf.

DEFINITIONS
   "district": s.217.
   "local housing authority": ss.217, 218.
   "other suitable accommodation": s.197.

GENERAL NOTE
   Pending resolution of a local connection issue, it is the authority to which application was made which must provide accommodation: subs. (1). This is temporary accommodation, and the observations as to security, and its quality, which were made in relation to temporary accommodation under ss.188, 190, will apply here too. If the authority conclude that the applicant is homeless, in priority need, and has not become homeless intentionally, but they intend to notify another authority of his application, they must notify the applicant of this and of their reasons for the decision: s.184(4), (5).
   The duty to make all preliminary enquiries into (a) homelessness, (b) priority need and (c) intentional homelessness lies upon the authority to which application is made: see General Note to s.189, above. A referral under s.187 creates a different duty to that imposed by s.183: *R. v. London Borough of Tower Hamlets, ex p. Ali; R. v. London Borough of Tower Hamlets, ex p. Bibi* (1992) 25 H.L.R. 158, C.A. (overruling *R. v. London Borough of Hammersmith and Fulham, ex p. O'Brian* (1985) 17 H.L.R. 471, Q.B.D. on this point). Therefore, where an authority chose to refer an application to another authority under s.198, they will not have discharged a s.193 duty and may at a later stage be required to provide accommodation to the same applicant, if he has in the meantime acquired a local connection and subsequently re-applied to them.
   An authority who find an applicant homeless intentionally but wrongly refer the applicant to another authority, are not bound by their error, and the erroneous reference may simply be ignored, *i.e.* because the local connection provisions are inapplicable if there is intentionality; it does not necessarily follow that the erroneous subsequent referral "eradicates" or "eliminates" the intentionality decision: *Delahaye*. Conversely, the mere fact that an authority have unsuccessfully sought to shift the burden onto another authority is not, of itself, any basis on which to alter the original decision that the applicant has not become homeless intentionally: *R. v. Beverley Borough Council, ex p. McPhee, The Times*, October 27, 1978, D.C.

Subss. (2)–(4)
   The obligation to house passes to the notified authority when the conditions for referral are fulfilled, but even when the resolution of the dispute results in the burden lying upon the notified authority, it is still the duty of the notifying authority to provide notification of the result of the reasons for it, to the applicant. If the burden of providing housing does not shift to the notified authority, it will remain with the notifying authority, in which case the first matter to consider is whether s.197, above, applies, *i.e.* whether the duty can be discharged by advice and assistance to secure other suitable accommodation (see notes thereto, above); if not, the principal housing duty under s.193 will apply. Likewise, if the duty does pass, s.197 applies to the duty of the notified authority, but if no other suitable accommodation, they will also be under the s.193 duty.

Subs. (5)
   Duties cease even if the applicant seeks a review, although the duties are replaced by a power to house: see also notes to s.204(4), below.

Application of referral provisions to cases arising in Scotland

   201. Sections 198 and 200 (referral of application to another local housing authority and duties to applicant whose case is considered for referral or referred) apply—
   (a) to applications referred by a local authority in Scotland in pursuance of sections 33 and 34 of the Housing (Scotland) Act 1987, and
   (b) to persons whose applications are so transferred,
as they apply to cases arising under this Part (the reference in section 198 to this Part being construed as a reference to Part II of that Act).

Right to request review of decision

Right to request review of decision

202.—(1) An applicant has the right to request a review of—

(a) any decision of a local housing authority as to his eligibility for assistance,

(b) any decision of a local housing authority as to what duty (if any) is owed to him under sections 190 to 193 and 195 to 197 (duties to persons found to be homeless or threatened with homelessness),

(c) any decision of a local housing authority to notify another authority under section 198(1) (referral of cases),

(d) any decision under section 198(5) whether the conditions are met for the referral of his case,

(e) any decision under section 200(3) or (4) (decision as to duty owed to applicant whose case is considered for referral or referred), or

(f) any decision of a local housing authority as to the suitability of accommodation offered to him in discharge of their duty under any of the provisions mentioned in paragraph (b) or (e).

(2) There is no right to request a review of the decision reached on an earlier review.

(3) A request for review must be made before the end of the period of 21 days beginning with the day on which he is notified of the authority's decision or such longer period as the authority may in writing allow.

(4) On a request being duly made to them, the authority or authorities concerned shall review their decision.

DEFINITIONS

"available for his occupation": s.176.
"conditions for referral": s.198.
"eligibility for assistance": ss.183, 185, 186.
"homeless": s.175.
"threatened with homelessness": s.175.
"threatened with homelessness intentionally": s.195.

GENERAL NOTE

This is a new provision, entitling an applicant to request a review of any of the following decisions, as a prerequisite to the (new) right to appeal to the county court, under s.204 below:

(i) Decision on eligibility, which means whether or not he is a person from abroad, or whether as an asylum-seeker he is disqualified because he has temporary accommodation—see ss.183, 185, 186, above;

(ii) Decision on what if any duty is owed to the applicant under ss.190, and 184 to 186, which means whether or not the applicant is in priority need (s.190(3)), whether intentionally homeless (s.190(1)), whether a duty has ceased under s.193(6), whether the authority can rely on s.197, and corresponding questions concerning those threatened with homelessness under s.195;

(iii) Decision to refer the case to another authority, or to agree the outcome with the other authority, or as to the duties owed by the notified authority: see ss.198–201;

(iv) Decision of the authority as to suitability of accommodation offered in discharge: see s.210, below.

Whether other accommodation is available under s.197 was said during the passage of the Bill to be reviewable under this section (Minister for Local Government, Housing and Urban Regeneration, *Hansard* (H.C.), Standing Committee G, Twenty-first Sitting, March 26, col. 815). The wording—"offered"—in subs. (1)(f) might on its own suggest that s.197 was not within the right to a review, but this would not seem sufficient to override the clear wording of subs. (1)(b).

The local connection "review" decisions are aimed at the housing duties, hence the inclusion of s.200(6) which mirrors s.197 when discharge is by the authority to which application is made. It is surprising to find review of the decision that the conditions for referral are met when it is statutorily a matter for agreement or arbitration (with agreement within review), but far from absurd: both agreement and arbitration can involve lengthy periods of delay and uncertainty. It is, however, only a decision to agree under s.198(5), as an outcome by way of arbitration would not seem to fall within use of the word "decision".

The notion of internal review is similar to the right of a person affected to seek review of a housing benefit decision under Housing Benefit (General) Regulations 1987 (S.I. 1987 No. 1971), as amended, Reg. 79. The formal requirements are those yet to be laid down under the following section, *e.g.* to make sure that the review is carried out by a person of appropriate seniority not involved in the original decision, and whether or not the applicant can have an oral hearing.

Subs. (2)

This is a provision "for the avoidance of doubt", as it is highly likely that the courts would so have construed the entitlement in any event.

Subs. (3)

A request for a review should be made within 21 days of notification of decision under s.184: the right to request a review must be notified in the decision notification (see s.184(5)) and if it is not, clearly time cannot be considered to have begun. If the notification did inform the applicant of the right to review, then *prima facie* the applicant who fails to exercise this right will lose it. This is only *prima facie*, however, for the authority have power to extend time, and the authority which declined to review their own decision, if the reason no request was made in time is a good reason, may well find that refusal *judicially* reviewable, even though not *appealable* under the provisions of s.204, below (which is only available to an applicant who has sought a review under this section).

Procedure on a review

203.—(1) The Secretary of State may make provision by regulations as to the procedure to be followed in connection with a review under section 202. Nothing in the following provisions affects the generality of this power.

(2) Provision may be made by regulations—

(a) requiring the decision on review to be made by a person of appropriate seniority who was not involved in the original decision, and

(b) as to the circumstances in which the applicant is entitled to an oral hearing, and whether and by whom he may be represented at such a hearing.

(3) The authority, or as the case may be either of the authorities, concerned shall notify the applicant of the decision on the review.

(4) If the decision is—

(a) to confirm the original decision on any issue against the interests of the applicant, or

(b) to confirm a previous decision—

(i) to notify another authority under section 198 (referral of cases), or

(ii) that the conditions are met for the referral of his case,

they shall also notify him of the reasons for the decision.

(5) In any case they shall inform the applicant of his right to appeal to a county court on a point of law, and of the period within which such an appeal must be made (see section 204).

(6) Notice of the decision shall not be treated as given unless and until subsection (5), and where applicable subsection (4), is complied with.

(7) Provision may be made by regulations as to the period within which the review must be carried out and notice given of the decision.

(8) Notice required to be given to a person under this section shall be given in writing and, if not received by him, shall be treated as having been given if it is made available at the authority's office for a reasonable period for collection by him or on his behalf.

GENERAL NOTE

This provision is analogous to that to be found in s.165, above.

Even without the express power to ensure that the review is carried out by someone other than, and senior to, the original decision-maker, it would not have been surprising if the courts had so implied such a requirement: the courts are willing to supplement statutory procedures, where it is necessary to do so in order to ensure the achievement of fairness (*Wiseman v. Borne-man* [1971] A.C. 297, H.L., *R. v. Hull Prison Visitors, ex p. St. Germain* [1979] 1 W.L.R. 1401, *Lloyd v. McMahon* [1987] A.C. 625, see also most recently *R. v. R.B. Kensington & Chelsea, ex p. Grillo* (1995) 28 H.L.R. 94, C.A., on the duty—or want of duty—to give reasons, which is itself imported by the requirement of fairness (see, *e.g.*, *R. v. Higher Education Funding Council, ex p. Institute of Dental Surgery* [1994] 1 W.L.R. 242). If the powers to make regulations remain unexercised, or do not appear to the courts to go far enough, these cases may yet be relied on.

In this case, there is no need to consider importation of a duty to give reasons, as such is spelled out in subs. (4) so far as the decision is against the interests of the applicant (identifying decisions to refer to another authority as such *ex abundantia cautelli* as the applicant may be presumed so to have considered it when he elected to seek a review under s.203). As to the extent to which reasons have to be spelled out, see notes to s.184, above.

Right of appeal to county court on point of law

204.—(1) If an applicant who has requested a review under section 202—
  (a) is dissatisfied with the decision on the review, or
  (b) is not notified of the decision on the review within the time prescribed under section 203,
he may appeal to the county court on any point of law arising from the decision or, as the case may be, the original decision.

(2) An appeal must be brought within 21 days of his being notified of the decision or, as the case may be, of the date on which he should have been notified of a decision on review.

(3) On appeal the court may make such order confirming, quashing or varying the decision as it thinks fit.

(4) Where the authority were under a duty under section 188, 190 or 200 to secure that accommodation is available for the applicant's occupation, they may continue to secure that accommodation is so available—
  (a) during the period for appealing under this section against the authority's decision, and
  (b) if an appeal is brought, until the appeal (and any further appeal) is finally determined.

GENERAL NOTE

Hitherto, and except in a small number of circumstances, any challenge to a local authority's decision under Pt. III, Housing Act 1985, would have to have been by way of judicial review under Supreme Court Act 1981 (c. 54), s.31, and R.S.C. Ord. 53: see, in particular, *Cocks v. Thanet D.C.* [1983] A.C. 286, 6 H.L.R. 15, H.L.; see further the discussion below, under Final Relief—Damages.

With relatively little debate, and less fanfare, a significant change to the enforcement of home-lessness rights is introduced by this section, conferring a right to appeal on a point of law on an applicant who has requested a review under s.203, but whether arising from the decision on review or from the original decision, in two circumstances: where dissatisfied with the decision on review; or, where not notified of the decision on review within any time prescribed by the Secretary of State.

A number of preliminary points may be made:
  (a) Application for review under s.202 is an essential precondition to the right of appeal;
  (b) Under subs. (3), the court's powers are to make an order which confirms, quashes or varies the decision, which seems to imply that appeal against a failure to conform to the time require-ment will secure no more than an order to render a decision, as distinct from opening up a jurisdiction on the part of the court to reach the decision for itself;
  (c) The power to vary the decision—as well as to confirm or quash it—is somewhat wider than is usually available on judicial review, insofar as under R.S.C. Ord. 53, the court will usually do no more than quash a decision (although on occasion its declaration as to the law and any findings of fact may mean that there is only one lawful decision left to the authority—see also *Barty-King v. Ministry of Defence* [1979] 2 All E.R. 80, Ch.D.;
  (d) The appeal is only on a point of law, as distinct from a rehearing.

Appeal v. Judicial Review. The right of appeal is on a point of law, which includes issues of jurisdiction or *vires* (see, *e.g.*, *R. v. I.R.C., ex p. Preston* [1985] A.C. 835, H.L., *Pearlman v. Keep-ers & Governors of Harrow School* [1979] Q.B. 56, C.A.).

The distinction between a point of law and a question of fact is not always straightforward, insofar as a conclusion of fact for which there is no, or insufficient, evidence may in itself comprise an error of law: see further below, particularly *Secretary of State for Education and Science v. Tameside M.B.C.* [1977] A.C. 1014, H.L. Furthermore, even a straightforward error or mistake of fact may itself serve to vitiate a decision as a matter of law: see, *e.g., Avon C.C. v. Howlett* [1983] 1 W.L.R. 605, C.A., *Mason v. Secretary of State for the Environment* (1984) J.P.L. 332, Q.B.D., *Jagendorff & Trott v. Secretary of State for the Environment* (1987) J.P.L. 771, Q.B.D., *R. v. London Residuary Body, ex p. I.L.E.A., The Times,* July 3, 1987, C.A., *Simplex G.E. (Holdings) Ltd. v. Secretary of State for the Environment* [1988] 3 P.L.R. 25, C.A., *R. v. Legal Aid Area No. 10 (East Midlands), ex p. McKenna* (1990) 2 Admin.L.R. 585.

Primarily what will be in issue on an appeal on a point of law are the same grounds as traditionally give rise to judicial review: see also notes to s.1, above. Judicial review, and the corresponding principles of administrative law, comprise a growth area of legal activity and have generated both a substantial body of case-law, and of legal literature. New editions of the two leading textbooks in the area have both recently been issued: *Administrative Law,* Wade & Forsyth, 7th. ed. (1994), and *Judicial Review of Administrative Action,* de Smith, Woolf & Jowell, 5th. ed. (1995). Recourse may also usefully be had to *Judicial Remedies in Public Law,* Lewis (1992), and, for the increasing reliance on E.C. law, its companion volume, *Remedies and the Enforcement of European Community Law,* Lewis (1996). Introductory texts are to be found in *Judicial Review Proceedings,* Manning (1995), and *Judicial Review: Law and Procedure,* Gordon, 2nd ed. (1996). Fordham's *Judicial Review Handbook* (1994, and accompanying loose-leaf update) contains a near-exhaustive record of cases, catalogued and classified in a highly practical manner.

When Parliament provides an appeal procedure, it will not be easy to secure leave to pursue judicial review, unless the case can be distinguished from the category for which the appeal procedure is provided (*R. v. Secretary of State for the Home Department, ex p. Swati* [1986] 1 W.L.R. 4772, C.A.), *e.g.* where it is not the individual decision that is in issue but the underlying legality of the decision of which the individual decision is the result of its application (*R. v. Paddington Valuation Officer, ex p. Peachey Property Corporation Ltd.* [1966] 1 Q.B. 380, C.A.), or where the decision was made without jurisdiction or contained an error of law (*R. v. Hillingdon L.B.C., ex p. Royco Homes Ltd.* [1974] 1 Q.B. 720, D.C.). Thus, in *East Yorkshire Borough of Beverley Housing Benefits Review Board, ex p. Hare* (1995) 27 H.L.R. 637, the court declined to refuse relief on the basis of alternative remedy (Housing Benefit Review Board), where the point raised was in part a point of statutory interpretation of general importance which it was therefore appropriate for the court to rule on.

Even these circumstances are, however, unlikely to lead to the grant of leave to a homeless person aggrieved by a decision on his application to seek judicial review under this Part, as the appeal procedure—on a point of law—in substance embraces precisely the same grounds as those on which judicial review would be available (as distinct from an appeal on the facts). It would seem that the *intention* could not be much clearer, to transfer that work from the Crown Office to the county court, at least where the appeal process is available.

It would be wrong, however, to think that (once it has cleared the backlog under the 1985 Act), the Crown Office list of the High Court will have no more to do with homelessness. There remains a number of circumstance in which it is likely that judicial review will continue to be available for example:

(i) Where what is under challenge is a policy rather than a decision; such a challenge could be sought by a person prospectively aggrieved or affected by it, but not yet (although equally the court *could* take the view that the proper course was to go through the individual application process, and appeal, on the basis that it was a concealed method of obtaining a ruling in advance of application, *cf.* below, *R. v. Hillingdon L.B.C., ex p. Tinn* (1988) 20 H.L.R. 305, Q.B.D.).

Alternatively, and with no alternative route by way of appeal, judicial review might be available at the instigation of a special interest, campaigning or "lobby group"—see *R. v. Inland Revenue Commissioners, ex p. National Federation of Self-Employed and Small Business Ltd.* [1982] A.C. 617, H.L., *R. v. Secretary of State for Social Services, ex p. Child Poverty Action Group* [1990] 2 Q.B. 540, C.A., and *R. v. Secretary of State for Foreign and Commonwealth Affairs, ex p. World Development Movement Ltd.* [1995] 1 W.L.R. 386, Q.B.D.

(ii) If an authority unreasonably refuse to extend time to apply for a review under s.202(3), which would not seem to qualify as a decision permitting appeal under this section, there would not seem to be any alternative but to try to quash the refusal and thus procure an extension.

(iii) Where two authorities are at odds (whether under the local connection provisions of ss.200–201, below, or the co-operation provisions of s.213, below, to which, again, the county court appeal procedure does not apply).

(iv) Where the authority refuse to exercise the power to continue housing under s.194, above, without the applicant re-qualifying for mandatory assistance under s.193, above.

(v) Where what is in issue is discharge of the property provisions, which are not subject to review or, therefore, to appeal (see ss.211, 212, below).

(vi) Where the authority simply fail to make any decision on an application, so that there is no decision on which to seek an internal review, in such a case it is likely that the grant of leave for judicial review, would be sufficient to provoke action from the authority.

(vii) Where an applicant seeks an internal review on the facts alone, i.e. without reference to a point of law, but the authority do not conduct the review (or notify the applicant of the outcome) within the prescribed time, there may need to be application for judicial review rather than appeal to the county court (see further below, on Powers of the Courts).

Leave to pursue an application under Ord. 53 for a declaration in advance of any homelessness or threatened homelessness that the applicant should not be considered intentionally homeless, which—not being a decision clearly also cannot be within s.202 nor, therefore, appeal under this section—would also seem likely to be refused: see *R. v. Hillingdon L.B.C., ex p. Tinn* (1988) 20 H.L.R. 305, Q.B.D.

Point of Law

Limits of appeal on a point of law. What confinement to "point of law" will import is that a straightforward difference of opinion or judgment between the authority and the applicant as to what decision should have been reached will not suffice to justify an appeal. It is not sufficient merely to know what rights and duties are set out in Pt. VII, or of knowing what the Code of Guidance under s.182 may suggest is appropriate in a particular case. Where Pt. VII imposes a duty on an authority, the duty arises only when the authority have "reason to believe", "consider", or are "satisfied" that a certain state of affairs exists: see ss.183, 184, 188, 190, 193, 195, 197, 198, 211. A homeless person's rights therefore only arise and can only be enforced—and, therefore, the court can only use its power in subs. (3) to quash or vary the decision—once the authority's satisfaction, belief or view has been established (*Cocks v. Thanet D.C.* [1983] A.C. 286, 6 H.L.R. 15, H.L.).

At first glance, one might think that this subjective assessment of rights and duties would mean that an authority's decision could never be challenged at all: "The section is framed in a 'subjective' form ... This form of section is quite well-known and at first sight might seem to exclude judicial review..." *per* Lord Wilberforce, *Secretary of State for Education and Science v. Metropolitan Borough of Tameside* [1977] A.C. 1014, at H.L. 1047. It is here, however, that the principles evolved—primarily on judicial review, but not infrequently in other procedures (see most recently *Crédit Suisse v. Allerdale M.B.C., Crédit Suisse v. Waltham Forest L.B.C., The Times,* May 20, 1996, C.A.—come into play.

Illustration not rule. It is difficult, if not impossible, to seek to encapsulate the relevant principles—or indeed adequately to describe the relevant procedures—in notes of this order. The extensive case law in the notes to substantive homelessness provisions is, in itself, a full body of illustration of the operation of the principles (and, on occasion, of the procedures). The overwhelming bulk of homelessness case law is of this order: illustration of the operation of the principles of administrative law, in relation to the statutes governing the rights of the homeless. For that reason, while of course of binding effect (depending on level of decision) as to statutory interpretation, and in some cases of considerable persuasive effect where facts are too near to those of decided cases to justify different treatment, the cases are no more than illustration, they do not comprise rules, and they should always be approached with this caution in mind.

Role of courts. A small number of homelessness cases have made a wider contribution to administrative law, and will be referred to in the notes below. In the main, even (non-homelessness) cases cited below are also no more than illustration of principles (and, as such, are highly selective): at the heart of them all is the proposition that Parliament intends that bodies such as local authorities should always act properly, in the sense of reasonably and lawfully. That is not to say that they would always arrive at "the" reasonable decision: one person's view of what is reasonable will often quite properly differ from that of another. If Parliament has entrusted a decision to a local authority, it is that authority's view of what is reasonable which must prevail, rather than that of a court: *Associated Provincial Picture Houses Ltd. v. Wednesbury Corporation* [1948] 1 K.B. 223, C.A.

The House of Lords in *R. v. London Borough of Hillingdon, ex p. Puhlhofer* (1986) 18 H.L.R. 158 likewise stressed the point, that in cases where the wording of an obligation is subjectively qualified (in the *Tameside* sense), Parliament intended the local authority and not the court to be the judge of fact. Although the action or inaction of a local authority is clearly susceptible to judicial review where the authority have misconstrued the Act (in that case the Housing (Homeless Persons) Act 1977, now this Part), or abused their powers, or otherwise acted perversely or unreasonably, so as to be verging on an absurdity, it should not be made use of to monitor the actions of local authorities under the Act save in exceptional cases.

Ultra Vires. What the principles invariably involve is that authorities should always approach their decisions in a lawful manner. If it can be shown that a public body such as a local authority have approached their decision unlawfully, the decision will be void and the courts will not give effect to it. A decision improperly reached is *ultra vires, i.e.* outside the authority's powers, and without effect in law, whether it is because on the face of the statute there was no authority to engage in the action at all, or because the statute has been misconstrued, or because the authority have misapplied the statute in another sense, *e.g.* by failing to use the powers to implement the purpose of the statute, or by reaching a decision under the statute by reference to something which is irrelevant, or in ignorance of something which is relevant, to the way the power under the statute is intended to be operated (see, most recently, *Crédit Suisse v. Allerdale M.B.C., Crédit Suisse v. Waltham Forest L.B.C., The Times,* May 20, 1996, C.A.).

Wednesbury. In all of these cases, however, it is important to bear in mind that the court does not act as an appeal tribunal from the authority's decision; instead, it is undertaking an investigation into the way in which the decision has been reached: *Associated Provincial Picture Houses Ltd. v. Wednesbury Corporation* [1948] 1 K.B. 223, C.A. Lord Greene M.R. said:

"What, then, is the power of the courts? They can only interfere with an act of executive authority if it be shown that the authority has contravened the law. It is for those who assert that the local authority has contravened the law to establish that proposition ... It is not to be assumed *prima facie* that responsible bodies like the local authority in this case will exceed their powers; but the court, whenever it is alleged that the local authority have contravened the law, must not substitute itself for that authority ... When an executive discretion is entrusted by Parliament to a body such as the local authority in this case, what appears to be an exercise of that discretion can only be challenged in the courts in a strictly limited class of case. ... When discretion of this kind is granted the law recognises certain principles upon which that discretion must be exercised, but within the four corners of those principles the discretion ... is an absolute one and cannot be questioned in any court of law. What then are those principles? They are well understood. They are principles which the court looks to in considering any question of discretion of this kind. The exercise of such a discretion must be a real exercise of the discretion. If, in the statute conferring the discretion, there is to be found expressly or by implication matters which the authority exercising the discretion ought to have regard to, then in exercising the discretion it must have regard to those matters. Conversely, if the nature of the subject-matter and the general interpretation of the Act make it clear that certain matters would not be germane to the matter in question, the authority must disregard those irrelevant collateral matters" (p.228).

"There have been in the cases expressions used relating to the sort of things that authorities must not do ... I am not sure myself whether the permissible grounds of attack cannot be defined under a single head. ... Bad faith, dishonesty—those of course, stand by themselves— unreasonableness, attention given to extraneous circumstances, disregard of public policy and things like that have all been referred to, according to the facts of individual cases, as being matters which are relevant to the question. If they cannot all be confined under one head, they at any rate ... overlap to a very great extent. For instance, we have heard in this case a great deal about the meaning of the word 'unreasonable'.

"It is true the discretion must be exercised reasonably. Now what does that mean? ... It has frequently been used and is frequently used as a general description of the things that must not be done. ... A person entrusted with a discretion must ... direct himself properly in law. He must call his own attention to the matters which he is bound to consider. He must exclude from his consideration matters which are irrelevant to what he has to consider. If he does not obey those rules, he may truly be said, and often is said, to be acting 'unreasonably'. Similarly, there may be something so absurd that no sensible person could ever dream that it lay within the powers of the authority. Warrington L.J. in *Short v. Poole Corporation* [1926] Ch. 66 gave the example of the red-haired teacher, dismissed because she had red hair. That is unreasonable in one sense. In another sense it is taking into consideration extraneous matters. It is so unreasonable that it might almost be described as being done in bad faith; and, in fact, all these things run into one another ... " (p.229).

"It is true to say that, if a decision on a competent matter is so unreasonable that no reasonable authority could ever have come to it, then the courts can interfere ... But to prove a case of that kind would require something overwhelming ... [The] proposition that the decision of the local authority can be upset if it is proved to be unreasonable, really meant that it must be proved to be unreasonable in the sense that the court considers it to be a decision that no reasonable body could have come to. It is not what the court considers unreasonable, a different thing altogether ... The effect of the legislation is not to set up the court as an arbiter of the correctness of one view over another. It is the local authority that are set in that position and, provided they act, as they have acted, within the four corners of their jurisdiction, this court ... cannot interfere ..." (pp.230–231).

"The court is entitled to investigate the action of the local authority with a view to seeing whether they have taken into account matters which they ought not to take into account, or, conversely, have refused to take into account or neglected to take into account matters which they ought to take into account. Once that question is answered in favour of the local authority, it may still be possible to say that, although the local authority have kept within the four corners of the matters which they ought to consider, they have nevertheless come to a conclusion so unreasonable that no reasonable authority could ever have come to it. In such a case, again, I think the court can interfere. The power of the court to interfere in each case is not as an appellate authority to override a decision of the local authority, but as a judicial authority which is concerned, and concerned only, to see whether the local authority have contravened the law by acting in excess of the powers which Parliament has confided in them" (pp.233–234).

Modern Re-classification. The principles of administrative law may be expressed, and classified, in a number of different ways. In *Council of Civil Service Unions v. Minister for the Civil Service* [1985] 1 A.C. 374, H.L., Lord Diplock re-classified them under three headings: "illegality", "irrationality" and "procedural impropriety":

"By 'illegality' as a ground of judicial review I mean that the decision-maker must understand correctly the law that regulates his decision-making power and must give effect to it. Whether he has or not is par excellence a justiciable question to be decided, in the event of dispute, by those persons, the judges, by whom the judicial power of the state is exercisable.

"By 'irrationality' I mean what can by now be succinctly referred to as 'Wednesbury unreasonableness'... It applies to a decision which is so outrageous in its defiance of logic or of accepted moral standards that no sensible person who had applied his mind to the question to be decided could have arrived at it. Whether a decision falls within this category is a question that judges by their training and experience should be well equipped to answer, or else there would be something badly wrong with our judicial system... 'Irrationality' by now can stand upon its own feet as an accepted ground on which a decision may be attacked by judicial review. I have described the third head as 'procedural impropriety' rather than failure to observe basic rules of natural justice or failure to act with procedural fairness towards the person who will be affected by the decision. This is because susceptibility to judicial review under this head covers also failure by an administrative tribunal to observe procedural rules that are expressly laid down in the legislative instrument by which its jurisdiction is conferred, even where such failure does not involve any denial of natural justice ..."

This statement has been described as "a valuable, and already 'classical' " statement (though "certainly not exhaustive" (*per* Lord Scarman in *Nottinghamshire County Council v. Secretary of State for the Environment* [1986] 1 A.C. 240, H.L. at p.249). In *R. v. Secretary of State for the Environment, ex p. Hammersmith & Fulham L.B.C.* [1991] 1 A.C. 521, H.L., Lord Bridge explained that a challenge on the grounds that something irrelevant has been taken into account, or something relevant has not been taken into account, falls within the "illegality" category, while a challenge on the basis of bad faith, absurdity or improper motive falls within "irrationality" (pp. 596–597).

It may be noted that in *C.C.S.U.* Lord Diplock raised—but did not answer—the question whether or not the principle of "proportionality" might yet be imported into domestic administrative law from Europe (at p.410), although it is considered (see *R. v. Secretary of State for the Home Department, ex p. Brind* [1991] 1 A.C. 696, H.L.) that it does not enjoy any standing independently of conventional unreasonableness. Proportionality is the doctrine that there has to be a reasonable relationship between the governmental (including local) action under review, and its purpose in a given context.

Practical classification. In practice, the principles tend to overlap with one another. They may be considered under one or more of the following sub-headings:

(i) A statutory authority must take into account all the relevant factors before making their decision, and must disregard the irrelevant: *Wednesbury.* See also *Bristol District Council v. Clark* [1975] 1 W.L.R. 1443, C.A. It is sufficient to void a decision for illegality on the basis that an irrelevant factor has been taken into account if the factor is significant, or potentially of influence, meaning that if it had not been taken into account, the decision may have been different: see also *Hanks v. Ministry of Housing and Local Government* [1963] 1 Q.B. 999, *R. v. Lewisham L.B.C., ex p. Shell (UK) Ltd.* [1988] 1 All E.R. 938, C.A.

(ii) The decision must be based on the facts; a decision totally at variance with the facts or for which there is no factual basis cannot be sustained:

"If a judgment requires, before it can be made, the existence of some facts, then although the evaluation of those facts is for the Secretary of State alone, the courts must enquire whether those facts exist, and have been taken into account, whether the judgment has been made on a proper self-direction as to those facts, whether the judgment has not been made on other facts which ought not to have been taken into account ..."

(*Per* Lord Wilberforce, *Secretary of State for Education and Science v. Metropolitan Borough of Tameside* [1977] A.C. 1014, H.L., at p.1047). (See also the cases cited above, under the sub-heading Law and Fact).

(iii) The authority must not act in bad faith or dishonestly: *Wednesbury.*

(iv) The authority must direct themselves properly in law, so that a decision based on a misunderstanding or misapplication of the law will not have been reached properly: *ibid.* This is the point in *Wednesbury* that is restated as "illegality" in *C.C.S.U.* See also *Anisminic Ltd. v. Foreign Compensation Commission* [1969] 2 A.C. 147, H.L.

(v) The authority must act so as to promote, and not to defeat, the objects or policy of the Act in question: *Padfield v. Minister of Agriculture, Fisheries & Food* [1968] A.C. 997, H.L.; see also *Meade v. Haringey L.B.C.* [1979] 1 W.L.R. 1, C.A. Powers conferred for public purposes must be used in a way that Parliament can be presumed to have intended: *R. v. Tower Hamlets L.B.C., ex p. Chetnik Developments Ltd.*, [1988] A.C. 858, H.L. A challenge on this basis is likewise a challenge to the legality of the decision: *R. v. Secretary of State for the Environment, ex p. Hammersmith & Fulham L.B.C.* [1991] 1 A.C. 521, H.L. (see above).

(vi) The decision must not be one to which no reasonable authority could have come: this is conclusive evidence that the decision is improper (or void as irrational)—*Wednesbury;* see also *C.C.S.U.* and *Nottinghamshire.*

(vii) The authority must reach their own decision on each individual case; they must not fetter their discretion by approaching a decision with a predetermined policy as to how they will deal with any case falling within a particular class. The leading case on this is now probably *British Oxygen Co. Ltd. v. Minister of Technology* [1969] 2 Ch. 174. See also *R. v. Secretary of State for the Environment, ex p. L.B. Brent* [1982] Q.B. 593.

While a public authority can adopt a policy or limiting rule in order to guide the future exercise of their discretion if they think good administration requires it, they must consider its application individually in every case where it is sought to make an exception: *Stringer v. Minister of Housing and Local Government* [1970] 1 W.L.R. 1281, C.A., *Cumings v. Birkenhead Corporation* [1972] Ch. 12, C.A., *Elliott v. Brighton B.C.* (1981) 79 L.G.R. 506, C.A. *British Oxygen* was adopted and applied by the House of Lords in *In re Betts* [1983] 2 A.C. 613, 10 H.L.R. 97, H.L. Even the "guideline" approach was disapproved by Templeman L.J. in *Att.-Gen., ex rel. Tilley v. London Borough of Wandsworth* [1981] 1 W.L.R. 854, C.A., but the other two judges expressly reserved their positions on this and, of course, *British Oxygen* is the superior authority.

(viii) It is the authority who are entrusted with the decision-making power and must make the decision. The authority cannot avoid their duties by adopting the decision of another body: *Lavender & Sons v. Minister of Housing and Local Government* [1970] 1 W.L.R. 1231. See also *R. v. Bolsover District Council and the Rent Officer for the Derbyshire Registration Area, ex p. East Midlands Development Ltd., and Denis Rye Ltd.* (1995) 28 H.L.R. 329, Q.B.D., where the authority could not lawfully delegate to a rent officer their function of determining a notional increase in rental value (for grant aid purposes), even though statutorily entitled to take his advice into account. (However, in the absence of any evidence to contradict the basis on which a rent officer had proceeded, it was considered unrealistic to expect them to adopt any other figure.)

Note that there is power in s.70, Deregulation and Contracting Out Act 1994 (c. 40), for functions to be designated as capable of being exercised by others, not being members or employees of the authority, which would override these propositions. No order relevant to homelessness has, however, been made.

(ix) As the full authority are *prima facie* entrusted with the decision-making power, the full authority must reach the decision unless they have, as they are empowered to do under Local Government Act 1972, s.101, delegated this power to a sub-committee or to an officer. It is the authority who must execute the function: it cannot be transferred to another (even by the court), see *Gardner v. London Chatham and Dover Railway Co. (No. 1)* (1867) L.R. 2 Ch. App. 201, *Marshall v. South Staffordshire Tramways Co.* [1895] 2 Ch. 36 and, most recently, *Parker v. L.B. Camden* [1986] 1 Ch. 162, C.A.

There can be no delegation to a single member, as there cannot be a committee or sub-committee of one: *R. v. Secretary of State for the Environment, ex p. Hillingdon L.B.C.* [1986] 1 W.L.R. 807, C.A. (However, there can be delegation to an officer, to be exercised in consultation with a member, so long as the member does not play the dominant role to the extent that the officer cannot be said to have reached the decision himself: *R. v. Port Talbot B.C., ex p. Jones* [1988] 2 All E.R. 208, Q.B.D.). There can be no delegation to a person or body outside the authority, even a company formed by the authority: *Crédit Suisse v. Allerdale M.B.C., Crédit Suisse v. Waltham Forest L.B.C., The Times,* May 20, 1996, C.A.

(x) In all cases, an authority must act fairly, or in accordance with natural justice: *Ridge v. Baldwin* [1964] A.C. 40; Re *HK* [1967] 2 Q.B. 617, C.A. The extent of this duty will depend upon circumstances, and the nature of the decision. It is important to bear in mind that even if a statute or other instrument contains its own procedural requirements to ensure fairness, including to give reasons for decisions, the courts may—if they consider that the circumstances of an individual case (or, presumably, class of case) call for it—impose yet further requirements to ensure that a matter has been decided fairly and/or give reasons: see *Wiseman v. Borneman* [1971] A.C. 297, H.L., *R. v. Hull Prison Visitors, ex p. St. Germain* [1979] 1 W.L.R. 1401, *Lloyd v. McMahon* [1987] A.C. 625, *R. v. Civil Service Appeal Board, ex p. Cunningham* [1991] 4 All E.R. 310, *R. v. Secretary of State for the Home Department, ex p. Doody* [1994] 1 A.C. 531, H.L., *R. v. Higher Education Funding Council, ex p. Institute of Dental Surgery* [1994] 1 W.L.R. 242, and *R. v. R.B. Kensington & Chelsea, ex p. Grillo* (1995) 28 H.L.R. 94, C.A. (see also notes to s.203, above). It will always mean that, if relevant to the decision, an applicant must know what is being said against him: *Board of Education v. Rice* [1911] A.C. 179, H.L.; *Kanda v. Governor of Malaya* [1962] A.C. 362, P.C.

Variations on a theme. These propositions or principles are all, by and large, variations upon a theme. In *R. v. Greater London Council, ex p. Bromley L.B.C.* [1983] 1 A.C. 768, H.L., the arguments in the House of Lords were described as different ways of saying the same thing. Lack of natural justice or administrative fairness will usually mean that a public body have also failed to take something relevant into account, *i.e.* the views of the person affected, and what they might have told the authority. Similarly, the policy of an Act is a relevant consideration, and so also are the correct meaning of the law, and the correct facts. Bad faith or dishonesty would indicate consideration of irrelevant matters. Improper delegation, and the application of policy where an individual decision is required, both amount to a failure to consider the question (in the particular case) at all, which necessarily means that there has been a failure to take all that is relevant into account (see also *Wednesbury*, above).

Burden of proof. Whenever the decision of a public body is challenged on these principles, the burden of proof lies upon the person seeking to show that the decision is void: *Wednesbury, Cannock Chase D.C. v. Kelly* [1978] 1 W.L.R. 1, C.A. The allegations must be both substantiated, and particularised: *ibid.* For example, it is never enough to say simply that the applicant is a homeless person and in priority need, because this would not be enough to raise the inference of a duty: The duty arises only when the authority are satisfied, or have reason to believe, or consider that the fact or state of affairs is as it is claimed to be. It must be alleged that they have refused or failed to reach a decision, or that such decision as has been reached must be treated by the courts as void, for want of compliance with specified principles, and the factual basis for this allegation must be set out.

Procedure. The appeal must be brought within 21 days of being notified of the decision, or when the applicant should have been so notified: subs. (2). In practice, this will often mean issuing the proceedings without legal aid, although presumably time could be extended by the court (if not agreed by the authority and embodied into a consent order) under C.C.R. Ord. 13, r.4. Delay in obtaining legal aid may constitute an acceptable reason for extending time: *R. v. Stratford-upon-Avon D.C., ex p. Jackson* [1985] 1 W.L.R. 1319, C.A., *R. v. Dairy Produce Quota, ex p. Caswell* [1990] 2 A.C. 738, H.L.

Costs. In relation to judicial review proceedings it has been held that before launching an appeal, the applicant's legal advisors should write a letter before action setting out the case, or risk a wasted costs order: *R. v. Horsham D.C., ex p. Wenman* [1995] 1 W.L.R. 680; *R. v. Home Secretary, ex p. Shahina Begum* [1995] C.O.D. 177. It is not uneccessary to write such a letter because it is believed that it is inevitable that the claim will be denied: *Wenman.* Thus, although the matter will already have been considered by the authority under s.203, it is generally adviseable to set out the points of law on which reliance is to be placed in order that the authority should have the opportunity to accept or reject them. In general, once proceedings have been issued, the question of costs is a matter for the discretion of the court: see Supreme Court Act 1981, s.51 and C.C.R. Ord. 38, r. 1.

It does not seem that costs can be awarded if a letter before action brings the desired result (*cf.* on judicial review, *R. v. Royal Borough of Kensington & Chelsea, ex p. Ghebregiogis* (1994) 27 H.L.R. 602, Q.B.D., in which a comprehensive letter before action had been sent by the applicant's solicitors to the authority explaining the applicant's position and dealing with the authority's adverse contentions. The applicant commenced judicial review proceedings. Just before the matter came on for hearing the authority changed their mind. The applicant successfully sought his costs as the authority should have properly considered the case when they received the letter).

It has recently been held that non-legal officers of an authority could be ordered personally to pay costs, in substance for causing unnecessary legal expenditure by failing to respond to litigation: *R. v. L.B. Lambeth, ex p. Wilson* (1996) 8 Admin.L.R. 376, Q.B.D., following a suggestion in *R. v. L.B. Lambeth, ex p. Mahmood, The Times,* February 23, 1994 (*Wilson* is currently under appeal). Lawyers are subject to such jurisdiction under s.51, Supreme Court Act 1981 (c. 54), inserted by s.4, Courts and Legal Services Act 1990 (c. 41), see C.C.R. Ord. 38, r.1(3): as to the exercise of this power, see *Ridehalgh v. Horsefield* [1994] Ch. 206, C.A.; see also *In Re A Barrister (Wasted Costs Order)* [1993] Q.B. 293, C.A.

Relief. The real relief sought will be housing. The legal issues arising are: confidentiality of proceedings; interlocutory relief; powers of the county court; damages; and, appeal.

(i) Confidentiality. The court has inherent jurisdiction (see *Norman v. Mathews* (1916) 85 L.J.K.B. 857, affd. (1916) 23 T.L.R. 369, C.A.) to make an order granting anonymity to an applicant, and to support it with an order under s.11, Contempt of Court Act 1981, preventing publication of an applicant's name, address and photograph: *R. v. Westminster C.C., ex p. Castelli, R. v. Same, ex p. Tristran-Garcia* (1995) 28 H.L.R. 125. Such an order should only be made, however, where it could be shown that a failure to do so would render the attainment of justice doubtful, or in effect impracticable. If no order is sought and obtained before proceeding, then (a) no subsequent order could relate back, with the result that (b) it might become inappropriate to make an order in relation to the substantive proceedings themselves simply by reason of any publicity derived from preliminary proceedings.

The proper course, therefore, is to apply the court *ex parte* under s.11, 1981 Act, at the same time as proceedings are to be issued, if appropriate asking for a hearing to be *in camera*; if there is power to make an order, because the preconditions are satisfied, the court can grant it for a short time, for notice to be given to the press: *ibid.* In some cases, it may be necessary for papers not to be lodged until the application can be dealt with immediately, so as to prevent disclosure by way of inspection of office documents: *ibid.*

(ii) Interlocutory Relief. Interlocutory relief will not be needed if the authority agree to use their power under subs. (4) to house pending the appeal (and any subsequent appeal). Interlocutory relief is in any event available in the course of county court proceedings: County Courts Act 1984 (c. 28), s.38. The normal position is that an interlocutory order will be granted if it can be shown that the balance of convenience is in favour of the order: *American Cyanamid v. Ethicon* [1975] A.C. 396, H.L., *Fellowes v. Fisher* [1976] Q.B. 122, C.A. In *de Falco, Silvestri v. Crawley Borough Council* [1980] Q.B. 460, C.A., however, Lord Denning M.R. said that in homeless persons' actions it was necessary to show that there was a strong *prima facie* case of breach by the authority.

The justification for adopting a different approach was that, almost invariably, the applicant would be unable to give a worthwhile undertaking in damages should he eventually lose, although the House of Lords had in *Cyanamid* already included ability to give a meaningful undertaking in damages as just one of the factors to be weighed up in determining the balance of convenience. Furthermore, the *de Falco* approach would seem to conflict with Lord Denning M.R.'s own approach in *Allen v. Jambo Holdings Ltd.* [1980] 1 W.L.R. 1252, C.A., a case in which the owners of an aircraft sought discharge of a Mareva injunction on the grounds that the plaintiff, who was legally aided, could not give a valuable cross undertaking in damages. Lord Denning commented:

"It is said that whenever a Mareva injunction is granted the plaintiff has to give the cross-undertaking in damages. Suppose the widow should lose this case altogether. She is legally aided. Her undertaking is worth nothing. I would not assent to that argument ... A legally aided plaintiff is by our statutes not to be in any worse position by reason of being legally aided than any other plaintiff would be. I do not see why a poor plaintiff should be denied a Mareva injunction just because he is poor, whereas a rich plaintiff would get it ..."

In *R. v. Royal Borough of Kensington and Chelsea, ex p. Hammell* [1989] Q.B. 518; (1988) 20 H.L.R. 666, C.A., it was argued that, following *R. v. London Borough of Hillingdon, ex p. Puhlhofer* [1986] A.C. 484, 18 H.L.R. 158, H.L., it was necessary to show something akin to "exceptional circumstances" before an interlocutory injunction would be granted. This argument was rejected: interlocutory relief is discretionary, although the discretion is one that must be exercised in accordance with principles of law, not whimsically; in a clear case of breach there is likely to be no issue on whether or not such relief should be granted. In *R. v. Cardiff City Council, ex p. Barry* (1989) 22 H.L.R. 261, C.A., it was held that where a court grants leave to move for judicial review of an authority's decision, a strong *prima facie* case will have been made out, but this is unlikely to help in the county court, where appeal is as of right, save by way of illustration of circumstances when an interlocutory order should be made.

(iii) Powers of the court. Under its appeal powers, the county court has wide powers: it can confirm a decision, or quash it, and it can also vary the decision as it thinks fit (subs. (3)). The power arises if the applicant is dissatisfied with the decision on review, or is not notified of the decision on review within the prescribed time (subs. (1)). The appeal is on "any point of law arising from the decision or, as the case may be, the original decision" (*ibid.*). A point of law arising from the original decision will only arise if there is no decision on review, as the point will either have been rectified or adopted on the review (or, perhaps, been subject to substitution with an alternative error of law); there would not be an appeal on a point of law arising on the original decision which had been corrected, *i.e.* for its own sake.

There does not seem to be any provision for appealing to the county court in respect of a review which has been sought by the applicant purely on the facts, and that does not rely on any error of law in the original decision. In such a case, there is no point of law arising from any decision, nor indeed would the county court have any decision to confirm, quash or vary. *Ancillary* relief may well be available (County Courts Act 1984, s.38), but not, it is submitted, if there is no *final* relief available. Nor can the county court make an order of mandamus to require the authority to carry out the review (*ibid.*, s.38(3)).

The difficulty does, however, premise that the powers of the court are related to the grounds of appeal, *i.e.* confirmation, quashing and variation of decision. The latter is a somewhat wider power than is available on judicial review (see A Note on Judicial Review, below). One argument may be that the power to vary implies a much wider meaning to the term "point of law" than it has been given so far in these notes, and that it extends to findings of fact: yet this renders the limitation meaningless; if Parliament had intended an appeal on the facts, it could have omitted the reference to point of law.

Another argument, somewhat stronger, is that—while the appeal is confined to a point of law—if the applicant is successful on the appeal, it "opens the door" to the county court's substitution of its own views (even on matters of judgment or evaluation of facts) for that of the authority. It is not an answer to this to say that—just because the appeal is on a point of law—there will not be the evidential material before the court on which to do so, for (a) that will not be true in all cases (and would therefore merely limit the occasions when the power could be used), and (b) it is, in any event, a chicken-and-egg point, for if the court *has* the wider powers, then material can be put before it even if only relevant to the exercise of its powers.

The strongest argument would appear to remain, therefore, that the power to vary imports nothing more than an alternative to quashing a decision, where the variation relates to, reflects or rectifies the error of law itself, *e.g.* where the decision can be identified in the light of the authority's factual findings and/or evaluation, so that remission to the authority would be unnecessary. (It is not suggested that this is the only circumstance when the power might be used; merely that the power does not go wide enough to permit variation of factual findings *other than* as a result of a corrected approach of law.)

(iv) Damages. Hitherto, there has been no possibility of action in the county court for damages—for breach of statutory duty—unless the "preconditions" to the existence of a duty had been established, which has meant by way of judicial review (*Cocks v. Thanet D.C.* [1983] A.C. 286, 6 H.L.R. 15, H.L.). It was at one time thought that if the applicant was content with the nature of the decision and wished only to challenge the manner of its discharge, or if the authority simply declined to carry out their duty, then action might so proceed: *Thornton v. Kirklees M.B.C.* [1979] Q.B. 626, C.A. Action for breach of statutory duty was expressly approved in *Cocks*, subject to completion of the public law decision-making stage which was essential to identify what duties were owed.

In *Mohram Ali v. London Borough of Tower Hamlets* [1993] Q.B. 407, (1992) 24 H.L.R. 474, C.A., however, the plaintiff had been notified by the defendants that they owed him a full housing duty. Subsequently he was made an offer of accommodation which he declined to accept, as he considered it to be unsuitable. He then sought an injunction in the county court requiring the defendants to fulfil their duties under 1985 Act, ss.65 and 69 (now, ss.193, 206, 210). At first instance, the plaintiff succeeded on a preliminary issue as to jurisdiction. The Court of Appeal reversed the decision. In his judgment, Nolan L.J. stated that:

(1) The critical distinction between public law and private law duties is one between the decision-making functions of the local authority and their executive functions, *i.e.* the administrative acts to be performed in giving effect to the relevant decision; having regard to the terms of 1985 Act, s.69(1) (now, s.206), the duty which it imposes upon the local authority is on the decision-making, as distinct from the executive, side of the line; the closing words of the subsection (now, represented by the wording of s.210(1)) call for the exercise by the local authority of a subjective judgment as to what constitutes suitable accommodation; this judgment has to be made before the executive act of securing the suitable accommodation for the applicant can be performed; and,

(2) The public law duties of the defendants were not discharged until they had completed the process of deciding upon the suitable accommodation which they were obliged to secure for the plaintiff; if this process was properly carried out as a matter of public law, then the conse-

quential private law right of the plaintiff was simply a right to the accommodation which the defendants had decided to be suitable.

In *London Borough of Tower Hamlets v. Abdi* (1992) 25 H.L.R. 80, C.A. the defendant contested possession proceedings in respect of her temporary accommodation on the basis that the offer of permanent accommodation made by Tower Hamlets was unsuitable. In rejecting the defendant's argument, the Court of Appeal considered itself bound by *Mohram Ali*. The case was not assisted by *London Borough of Wandsworth v. Winder* [1985] 1 A.C. 461, H.L., in which the alleged illegality of a rent increase could be raised in (and as a defence to) an action for possession, since the only private law right acquired by the defendant in *Abdi* was to the permanent accommodation which she had rejected, while in *Winder* the private law right being asserted was to the accommodation the subject of the proceedings.

In *London Borough of Hackney v. Lambourne* (1992) 25 H.L.R. 172, C.A., a further attempt to defend possession proceedings in respect of temporary accommodation on the basis that decisions to serve a notice to quit and commence possession proceedings in respect of temporary accommodation were flawed likewise failed. It was argued that a challenge to the propriety of those decisions could form the basis of a defence to the proceedings to evict. The Court of Appeal rejected the argument: "to permit the validity of the plaintiff's decision to be raised in the County Court action under the guise of considering the validity of the notice to quit would be to circumvent the reasoning and the policy of the decisions in *Ali* and *Abdi* ...".

The circumstances in which breach of action for statutory duty were considered to be available were accordingly limited. In *R. v. London Borough of Lambeth, ex p. Barnes* (1992) 25 H.L.R. 140, Q.B.D., the failure of the authority to secure permanent accommodation for the applicant within a reasonable time was held to amount to a breach of statutory duty and negligence for which the applicant was entitled to damages. By contrast, however, in *R. v. Northavon D.C., ex p. Palmer* (1995) 27 H.L.R. 576, C.A., it was held that breach of the duty to undertake inquiries under what is now s.184 would not sound in damages.

It seems more probable than not that the same principles will remain applicable to a claim for damages on—or related to, or arising out of—an appeal, and that the right of appeal does not open up a greater scope for claiming damages. Accordingly, it will not be possible to claim damages merely because of a successful appeal, and unless, therefore, there has been a decision on what accommodation it would be suitable to offer, or a concession, the authority will not have completed their public law decision-making functions and there is no basis for a claim: *ibid.* See also *R. v. Ealing L.B.C., ex p. Parkinson* [1995] 8 Admin.L.R. 281. (*Cf. R. v. L.B. Lambeth, ex p. Campbell* (1994) 26 H.L.R. 618, where such a concession was made on the premise that an unsuitable offer was no offer, and that damages for breach of statutory duty would accordingly be available, which must be in doubt in the light of *Palmer*.)

In *Parkinson*, it was said that the law recognises no right of compensation for breach of duty arising only in public law (unless the case "slips into the realm of misfeasance in public office"); and, public law functions do not end until the authority have identified a property; a complaint that goes to the authority's "composite duty" (*per* Nolan L.J. in *Mohran Ali*) of securing suitable accommodation within a reasonable time does not sound in damages. Nor was there a free-standing, common law duty of care on which a claim could proceed, for [surprising as the court recognised that it might seem] a decision on what accommodation to provide was in substance a policy decision within the meaning of *X. v. Bedfordshire C.C.* [1995] 2 A.C. 663, H.L.

In *O'Rourke v. Camden L.B.C.* (1996) 28 H.L.R. 601, C.A., it was held that a claim for damages could be pursued where accommodation pending inquiries had been provided under what is now s.188, above, and—it was alleged—wrongly withdrawn.

(v) Appeal. Appeal lies to the Court of Appeal, under the County Courts Act 1984, s.77. It is unclear whether leave will be needed. Under the County Court Appeals Order 1991 (S.I. 1991 No. 1877), Ord. 2(1)(b) leave is needed from either the judge or the Court of Appeal when the judge "is acting in an appellate capacity". The White Book (para. 59/1/34) suggests that where an appeal against an administrative decision or order, *e.g.* a statutory appeal against a closing order under the Housing Act 1985 is made by a local authority, the judge is not acting in an appellate capacity. The reasoning for this is that a statutory appeal is simply the mechanism for having the matter adjudicated upon for the first time and the judge could not properly be regarded therefore as sitting in an appellate capacity. The position regarding homeless appeals is less clear cut. The appeal is on a point of law only, and in that sense is not clearly a first adjudication on the matter, on the other hand the decision by the local authority under s.202 is still an administrative one, rather than a judicial one. Given that leave is needed to appeal a judicial review decision (see R.S.C. Ord. 59, r.1B), it may well be that the County Court Rules will be amended to clarify the position and require leave. Where it is an interlocutory matter which is being appealed, leave is required: R.S.C. Ord. 59, r.1B.

Notice of appeal must be served within four weeks of the judgment or order: R.S.C. Ord. 59, r.4(1). Where leave is required this should normally be sought from the judge at the time that judgment is given. If it is not forthcoming, then application should be made to the Court of Appeal within four weeks. In such a case time for bringing the appeal is extended to seven days after the application for leave is granted: *ibid.* r.4(3).

A Note on Judicial Review

A number of circumstances were referred to above as illustrations of when judicial review may still be an appropriate proceeding:

(a) challenge to a *policy* rather than a decision (by a person likely to be aggrieved, or by a campaigning organisation) or,

(b) unreasonable refusal to extend time to apply for a review under s.202(3); or,

(c) two authorities at odds; or,

(d) discharge of a s.194 power;

(e) failure to make any decision by the authority; or,

(f) where the authority do not conduct a review which the applicant seeks, but which is only on the facts and includes no point of law.

There may well be other cases where the High Court is willing to accept jurisdiction, because of the importance of the point. In addition, of course, judicial review is the only recourse following an unsatisfactory outcome of an allocation decision under ss.164, 165, above.

The forum for challenging a local authority's decision by judicial review is in the Divisional Court of the Q.B.D., by application under R.S.C. Ord. 53 (see also Supreme Court Act, s.31). Such proceedings can only be pursued with leave, and leave must always be sought promptly (and in any event within three months from the date when the grounds for the application arise, unless there is good reason for extending that period—R.S.C. Ord. 53, r.4(1)). If there has been undue delay, the court may refuse to grant leave, on the grounds of substantial hardship to or prejudice to the rights of any person, or of detriment to good administration: Supreme Court Act 1981, s.31(6).

There is a high duty of care on the part of applicants to make full and frank disclosure on an application for leave (even if unhelpful to the applicant): see, *e.g.*, *R. v. Wirral M.B.C., ex p. Bell* (1994) 27 H.L.R. 234, Q.B.D. (although non-disclosure will not *necessarily* be fatal, if it causes no advantage to the applicant and no prejudice to the respondents): even if not leading to the refusal of leave, it could still affect relief: *ibid.*

Leave should invariably be sought without delay: the fact that application has been made within three months does not necessarily mean that it has been made promptly: *R. v. Stratford-upon-Avon D.C., ex p. Jackson* [1985] 1 W.L.R. 1319, C.A. If no application is made promptly, or within three months, there is undue delay, which means that it will then be a matter of discretion whether to extend time, or to refuse leave; even if time is extended, the issue of undue delay may be decided at full hearing. However, delay in obtaining legal aid may constitute an acceptable reason for granting leave belatedly: *ibid.* See also *R. v. Dairy Produce Quota, ex p. Caswell* [1990] 2 A.C. 738, H.L.

When what is under challenge is a policy, however, time only begins to run when it affects the individual applicant: *R. v. L.B. Tower Hamlets, ex p. Mohib Ali* (1993) 25 H.L.R. 218, D.C. In *R. v. L.B. Newham, ex p. Ajayi* (1994) 28 H.L.R. 25, the applicant's advisers had written to the authority setting out their case; it was held that, in the absence of a response from the authority, they might reasonably have been induced to believe that the authority were revising their decision, and that relief should not be refused because no application had been made within three months—the same could be true of a request to review and alter a policy.

Note the discussion on costs, above, and the wider powers of the court to order costs even though no leave is granted: *R. v. Royal Borough of Kensington & Chelsea, ex p. Ghebregiogis* (1994) 27 H.L.R. 602, Q.B.D. The discussion of relief (interlocutory and final) in relation to appeal to the county court is largely based on cases of judicial review and, so far as judicial review remains applicable to individual cases, will accordingly apply in the same way. Damages are only available on judicial review if and to the extent that they would be recoverable for breach of a private law duty—*R. v. Northavon D.C., ex p. Palmer* (1995) 27 H.L.R. 576, C.A. (See further, the discussion above.) If confidentiality is needed, then the need to secure an order of the court *ex parte* applies as at the time leave is sought.

Powers of the court

The powers of the High Court on judicial review are somewhat easier to describe. Where a decision is *ultra vires,* a court on judicial review can adopt one of two courses of action. First, it may quash the decision and compel the authority to approach it afresh. Second, although the court will not usually substitute its own decision for that of the authority, the findings of fact or law made by the court may on occasion be such that there is only one decision that the authority can lawfully make, *i.e.* with which they are left. In such cases, either directly or indirectly, the court will (in effect) order the authority to come to that decision: m*Barty-King v. Ministry of Defence* [1979] 2 All E.R. 80, Ch.D.

Subs. (4)
　　See notes on Interlocutory Relief, above.
　　Subsection (4)(b), see notes on "Appeal" above.

Supplementary provisions

Discharge of functions: introductory

205.—(1) The following sections have effect in relation to the discharge by a local housing authority of their functions under this Part to secure that accommodation is available for the occupation of a person—
　　section 206 (general provisions),
　　section 207 (provision of accommodation by authority),
　　section 208 (out-of-area placements),
　　section 209 (arrangements with private landlord).
　　(2) In those sections those functions are referred to as the authority's "housing functions under this Part".

GENERAL NOTE
　　This section has no greater purpose than to introduce the following sections, and the expression "housing functions under this Part", meaning those ways in which an authority can discharge their functions (except for under s.197, above, *i.e.* other suitable accommodation).

Discharge of functions by local housing authorities

206.—(1) A local housing authority may discharge their housing functions under this Part only in the following ways—
　　(a) by securing that suitable accommodation provided by them is available,
　　(b) by securing that he obtains suitable accommodation from some other person, or
　　(c) by giving him such advice and assistance as will secure that suitable accommodation is available from some other person.
　　(2) A local housing authority may require a person in relation to whom they are discharging such functions—
　　(a) to pay such reasonable charges as they may determine in respect of accommodation which they secure for his occupation (either by making it available themselves or otherwise), or
　　(b) to pay such reasonable amount as they may determine in respect of sums payable by them for accommodation made available by another person.

DEFINITION
　　"local housing authority": ss.217, 218.

GENERAL NOTE
　　This section governs how the authority may—and how they may not—discharge their duties under s.193 (limited as it is in time: see notes thereto, above). Accommodation to be secured must be available for the occupation of the applicant (see notes to s.175, above): see s.193(2). The accommodation to be provided must be suitable: see also s.210, below. The accommodation to be provided can be the authority's own accommodation or that secured from someone else: subs. (1). Where the accommodation secured belongs to the authority, it is subject to the constraints in s.207, below; so far as practicable accommodation is to be in the authority's own area—see s.208; where the accommodation secured belongs to a registered social landlord, it cannot be an assured tenancy (*i.e.* the normal form of letting for such a landlord), but must be an assured shorthold: see s.108, below (see also above, Pt. III, Chap. II).
　　As a matter of language, and construction, this section is exhaustive of the means of providing accommodation, so that it cannot be used—even in conjunction with s.111, Local Government Act 1972 (c. 70)—to guarantee the acquisition of accommodation by another even if the purpose is to let it to the homeless, or to let it to the authority for re-let to the homeless: *Crédit Suisse v.*

L.B. Waltham Forest, The Times, May 20, 1996, C.A. (The acquisition of such accommodation by a registered social landlord *could*, however, be guaranteed under s.22, above.)

Suitable Accommodation

Suitability is governed (in part) by s.210, below, identifying considerations which must be taken into account—the law governing unfitness, overcrowding, and houses in multiple occupation. In *R. v. London Borough of Brent, ex p. Awua* [1996] 1 A.C. 55, (1995) 27 H.L.R. 453, H.L., it was said that those considerations point to suitability being *primarily* a matter of space and arrangement, but other matters such as whether the applicant can afford the rent may also be material. They are not, accordingly, exhaustive. See also *R. v. Tower Hamlets L.B.C., ex p. Kaur* (1994) 26 H.L.R. 597, Q.B.D., where accommodation secured for the applicant in the private sector was not suitable because the contractual rent exceeded the amount which would be met in housing benefit and the applicant could not afford to meet the shortfall from his own resources.

In *R. v. L.B. Wandsworth, ex p. Wingrove* and *R. v. L.B. Wandsworth, ex p. Mansoor* [1996] 3 All E.R. 913, C.A., Evans L.J. thought that the tenure, or time element, of suitability had to be proportionate to the circumstances of the case, including the needs of the applicant (see notes to s.193, above).

In *R. v. London Borough of Brent, ex p. Omar* (1991) 23 H.L.R. 446, Q.B.D., a political refugee was offered accommodation in a basement flat in an estate. The condition of the premises and the layout of the estate strongly reminded the applicant of the prisons in which she had been held and abused, to such an extent that she maintained that she would rather commit suicide than live there. In quashing the authority's decision that the offer was suitable, the court held that the accommodation must be suitable for the person to whom the duty was owed and in determining suitability the authority should have regard to the relevant circumstances of the applicant as well as to the matters set out in s.210, below.

Omar was considered in *R. v. London Borough of Lewisham, ex p. Dolan* (1992) 25 H.L.R. 68, Q.B.D., where Lewisham's decision to offer accommodation was held to have been flawed since they had separated out the medical and social considerations and had not taken an overall view of the applicant's needs: it was said that "the ultimate decision as to suitability must be the result of a composite assessment".

Issues of racial harassment and risk of violence have also been held to be relevant. In *R. v. London Borough of Tower Hamlets, ex p. Abdul Subhan* (1992) 24 H.L.R. 541, Q.B.D., Tower Hamlets offered a Bangladeshi applicant accommodation in a block of flats in which there was active racial harassment. The authority had themselves set up a Racial Incidents Panel, had been provided with details of incidents of racial harassment by the local Law Centre, and had also received reports from a research project set up by the Home Office Crime Prevention Unit. The decision to make the offer was quashed since the authority had failed to take into account the material on harassment which was before them.

See also *R. v. Southwark L.B.C., ex p. Solomon* (1994) 26 H.L.R. 693, Q.B.D., in which it was held that the authority should have considered the applicant's risk of violence from her former partner, who was accustomed to shop and visit friends in the area where they proposed to house her. In *R. v. L.B. Lambeth, ex p. Campbell* (1994) 26 H.L.R. 618, Q.B.D., a cockroach-infested property was considered not to be suitable for the applicant, on account of its condition, a decision which, on its facts, would probably still stand post-*Awua*.

A more unusual challenge to offers of accommodation was mounted in *R. v. London Borough of Tower Hamlets, ex p. Mohib Ali, Uddin, Wahb, Miah & Miah* (1993) 25 H.L.R. 218, Q.B.D., in the context of Tower Hamlets' allocation policy. Although the court found that it was acceptable for an authority to apply different allocation standards to the homeless, where that policy was based on seeking to reduce the time homeless families spent in temporary accommodation, the application of the policy was quashed in the particular, because the authority had been unfair and irrational in the way that safeguards of a right of appeal against the offer, and the right to go on the transfer list, had been removed, and because of the arbitrary and random way in which the policy was operated in different neighbourhoods. (The court held, however, that the policy did not discriminate directly or indirectly under the Race Relations Act 1976.) See also the cases on "offers" in the notes to s.193, above.

The mode of challenge to the suitability of an offer is by review under s.202 and appeal under s.204. There is no obligation to give reasons why an offer is considered to be suitable, on the original decision (*R. v. R.B. Kensington & Chelsea, ex p. Grillo* (1995) 28 H.L.R. 94, C.A.), but such will now be imported by s.203(4).

Whose Accommodation

Advice and assistance such that the applicant secures accommodation from another under subs. (1) seems wide enough to cover advice and assistance leading to house purchase by an applicant who is financially able to undertake such a step. Some other person, in the context of subs. (1), may be a person—or authority—abroad. In *R. v. Bristol C.C., ex p. Browne* [1979] 1 W.L.R. 1437, D.C., a woman with no local connection with Bristol, and no local connection with the area of any other housing authority in England, Wales or Scotland, was offered assistance to return to her home town of Tralee, Eire, where the authorities were prepared to ensure that she was housed.

It may be noted that, in order to sustain this decision, Bristol did not need to know the exact details of the accommodation which was to be made available to her. The arrangement was, however, only appropriate once it was established by Bristol that, in their opinion, the woman ran no risk of domestic violence in Tralee: it would seem from the report that had there been a risk of domestic violence, the arrangement would not have been acceptable, for otherwise Bristol would have managed to circumvent the local connection provisions: see s.198, above.

In *Wyness v. Poole B.C.*, July 1979 L.A.G. Bulletin 166, C.C., a county court rejected an attempt to house an applicant in the area of another authority, when the local connection provisions were inapplicable because of an employment connection, as living in the area of the other authority would have meant that the employment would have to be given up: the court held that no reasonable authority could thus discharge the duty. (See also, now, s.208, below.)

In *Parr v. Wyre B.C.* (1982) 2 H.L.R. 71, C.A., an authority sought to discharge their duty by securing an offer of accommodation in Birmingham, an area with which the applicants had no connection at all. There were no details available of the accommodation to be provided, and the applicants had a limited time in which to accept. While it was common ground that discharge could be in another area (but, again, see now s.208, below), the Court of Appeal did not uphold this offer. The court distinguished *Browne*. It held that the offer had to be of "appropriate accommodation", in terms of size of family and area.

In *R. v. London Borough of Hillingdon, ex p. Puhlhofer* [1986] A.C. 484, 18 H.L.R. 158, the House of Lords considered *Parr*, and overruled the introduction of the word "appropriate": see General Note to s.175, above. None the less, the result itself might yet be the same, so far as it related to relocation in another, altogether distant, area.

Charges

If the authority provide their own accommodation, they can in any event make a reasonable charge under 1985 Act, s.24. They may also call for a contribution towards costs paid by the authority to someone else, *e.g.* private sector accommodation.

The provision of assistance under this Part is not contingent on ability to pay: *R. v. Secretary of State for Social Security, ex p. B. & Joint Council for the Welfare of Immigrants* (1996) *The Times*, June 27, 29 H.L.R. forthcoming, C.A. However, there is no reason why—even if unable to *make* a payment—an authority should not reserve the *right to* payment, and a number of reasons why they should do so, and keep *enforcement* of it under review, both during occupancy and for a period afterwards (*e.g.* future change of fortunes on the part of an applicant. It should also be said that access to the precise cost to the authority of the provision of free accommodation represents good accounting practice).

Discharge of functions: provision of accommodation by the authority

207.—(1) A local housing authority shall not under section 206(1)(a) discharge their housing functions under this Part by providing accommodation other than—

(a) accommodation in a hostel within the meaning of section 622 of the Housing Act 1985, or

(b) accommodation leased to the authority as mentioned in subsection (2) below,

for more than two years (continuously or in aggregate) in any period of three years.

This applies irrespective of the number of applications for accommodation or assistance in obtaining accommodation made by the person concerned.

(2) The accommodation referred to in subsection (1)(b) is accommodation—

(a) leased to the authority with vacant possession for use as temporary housing accommodation on terms which include provision for the lessor to obtain vacant possession from the authority on the expiry of a specified period or when required by the lessor,

(b) the lessor of which is not an authority or body within section 80(1) of the Housing Act 1985 (the landlord condition for secure tenancies),

and
(c) in which the authority have no interest other than under the lease in question or as a mortgagee.

(3) The authority shall not discharge such functions in relation to a person who—

(a) normally resides with another person as a member of his family, or
(b) might reasonably be expected to reside with another person,

in such a way that subsection (1) would be contravened if the functions were discharged in relation to that other person.

(4) The Secretary of State may, on the application of a local housing authority, by direction exclude or modify the operation of subsection (1) in relation to that authority if it appears to him that the authority will not otherwise be able reasonably to discharge their housing functions under this Part.

(5) Any such direction shall have effect only—

(a) with respect to applicants of a description specified in the direction, and
(b) for a period specified in the direction, which shall not exceed one year,

and may be expressed to have effect subject to any conditions specified in the direction.

(6) Where the Secretary of State gives or has given a direction under subsection (4), he may give the authority such directions as he considers appropriate as to the discharge of their housing functions under this Part in cases affected by the direction having or ceasing to have effect.

DEFINITIONS
"local housing authority": ss.217, 218.

GENERAL NOTE
This section contains one of the principal objectives of the changes contained in Pt. VII, that an authority's own accommodation should not be allocated permanently to the homeless, other than in accordance with their normal allocation criteria: see now, Pt. VI, above. To achieve this effect, there is a prohibition on the use of an authority's own stock (whether held under Pt. II, 1985 Act, *i.e.* the principal powers under which authorities hold a housing stock, or not, *e.g.* housing acquired incidental to other powers, such as education, social services, roads, compulsory purchase, etc.) for more than two years out of any three, whether continuously or in aggregate: subs. (1).

If an authority choose to use the power to continue to secure accommodation beyond the two-year period of s.193, *e.g.* following a review under s.194 under which the applicant's qualifications do not mean that he would be successful on a new application, yet the authority none the less permit the applicant to remain (see s.193(3)), they are likewise caught by the prohibition. Similarly, repeat applications lead to a single period in terms of the prohibition. Nor can the prohibition be avoided by making an application in the name of one person, for the benefit of another (*e.g.* one whose permissible period had been or is about to be used up): subs. (3). (As to persons who are reasonably to be expected to reside with one another, see General Note to s.175, above.)

In substance, if no offer is made under Pt. VI, above, after two years the applicant will have to be moved out of the authority's accommodation for a year, so as "to preserve the principle of a single route into long-term social housing" (*Hansard* (H.L.), Report Stage, July 8, 1996, Earl Ferrers, Minister of State, Department of the Environment, col. 133 (see also Introduction to Pt. VI, above).

The sole exceptions to the prohibition are (a) hostel accommodation, and (b) privately leased accommodation.

Hostel accommodation. Under 1985 Act, s.622, a hostel
"means a building in which is provided, for persons generally or for a class or classes of persons—
(a) residential accommodation otherwise than in separate and self-contained sets of premises, and
(b) either board or facilities for the preparation of food adequate to the needs of those persons, or both".

Privately leased accommodation. This exception is modelled on 1985 Act, Sched. 1, para. 6 and, as such, refers not merely to accommodation of which the authority are the tenant strictly so-called, but includes that of which they are themselves mere licensees: see *L.B. Tower Hamlets v. Sabru Miah* (1991) 24 H.L.R. 199, C.A. A mere power to give notice is sufficient to qualify the agreement within subs. (2)(a): *L.B. Tower Hamlets v. Abdi* (1992) 25 H.L.R. 80, C.A. The accommodation must be leased—with vacant possession, in the sense that it would serve no function for the homeless unless available for their occupation (*cf. Abdi*)—from a landlord whose tenants are not themselves secure tenants under 1985 Act, s.80 (see notes to s.16, above); nor can the authority have an interest other than under the lease, unless it is as mortgagee. The purpose of the letting must be for use as temporary housing accommodation.

Subss. (4), (5), (6)
An authority who are in difficulties complying with the limitations in this section may, however, apply to the Secretary of State for an extension, which the terms of the final two subsections suggest is likely only to be granted subject to limitations.

Discharge of functions: out-of-area placements

208.—(1) So far as reasonably practicable a local housing authority shall in discharging their housing functions under this Part secure that accommodation is available for the occupation of the applicant in their district.

(2) If they secure that accommodation is available for the occupation of the applicant outside their district, they shall give notice to the local housing authority in whose district the accommodation is situated.

(3) The notice shall state—
(a) the name of the applicant,
(b) the number and description of other persons who normally reside with him as a member of his family or might reasonably be expected to reside with him,
(c) the address of the accommodation,
(d) the date on which the accommodation was made available to him, and
(e) which function under this Part the authority was discharging in securing that the accommodation is available for his occupation.

(4) The notice must be in writing, and must be given before the end of the period of 14 days beginning with the day on which the accommodation was made available to the applicant.

DEFINITIONS
"available for occupation": s.176.
"district": s.217.
"local housing authority": ss.217, 218.

GENERAL NOTE
"So far as practicable" the authority must secure accommodation in their own area: this is a condition which may come to be affected by the exercise of the Secretary of State's discretion to extend time in the authority's own accommodation, under s.207(4)–(6), above. Under subss. (2)–(4), if they accommodate someone in another area, they must give the required notice, which, *inter alia*, relates back to the condition for referral in s.198(4), although *could* in an appropriate case give the authority in whose area the applicant has been accommodated the grounds for seeking judicial review of the placing authority's decision (*cf.* General Note to s.204, above).

Discharge of functions: arrangements with private landlord

209.—(1) This section applies where in pursuance of any of their housing functions under this Part a local housing authority make the arrangements with a private landlord to provide accommodation.

For this purpose a "private landlord" means a landlord who is not within section 80(1) of the Housing Act 1985 (the landlord condition for secure tenancies).

(2) If the housing function arises under section 188, 190, 200, or 204(4) (interim duties), a tenancy granted in pursuance of the arrangements to a person specified by the authority cannot be an assured tenancy before the end of the period of twelve months beginning with—
(a) the date on which the applicant was notified of the authority's decision

under section 184(3) or 198(5), or

(b) if there is a review of that decision under section 202 or an appeal to the court under section 204, the date on which he is notified of the decision on review or the appeal is finally determined,

unless, before or during that period, the tenant is notified by the landlord (or, in the cases of joint landlords, at least one of them) that the tenancy is to be regarded as an assured shorthold tenancy or an assured tenancy other than an assured shorthold tenancy. A registered social landlord cannot serve such a notice making such a tenancy an assured tenancy other than an assured shorthold tenancy.

(3) Where in any other case a tenancy is granted in pursuance of the arrangements by a registered social landlord to a person specified by the authority—

(a) the tenancy cannot be an assured tenancy unless it is an assured shorthold tenancy, and

(b) the landlord cannot convert the tenancy to an assured tenancy unless the accommodation is allocated to the tenant under Part VI.

DEFINITIONS
"assured tenancy": s.230.
"local housing authority": ss.217, 218.
"private landlord": subs. (1).
"registered social landlord": s.1.

GENERAL NOTE
This section corresponds in its effect to the exemption from security of the tenure under Housing Act 1985, of those housed under this Part (see Sched. 17, para. 3, substituting a new para. 4 to 1985 Act, Sched. 1, as it now has effect subject to the prohibition on the allocation to the homeless of the authority's own accommodation on a long-term basis (other than when an allocation is made in accordance with Pt. VI)—see s.207, above. There are in essence two provisions:

(a) If the accommodation provided is by a private landlord—which means any landlord whose tenants are not secure—through whom accommodation has been secured pursuant to the temporary housing duties (pending inquiries under s.188, to the intentionally homeless under s.190, or pursuant to a local connection referral under s.200), a tenancy is not assured for the first year, unless the landlord notifies to the contrary, in which case he may notify the tenant that it is to be either a fully assured tenancy or an assured shorthold (see above, Pt. III, Chap. II); *and*

(b) If the landlord is not merely a private landlord but a registered social landlord, the notice can *only* be one that the tenancy is to be an assured shorthold, *and so it must remain* unless it is allocated under Pt. VI, above.

Private landlord—i.e. landlords who cannot grant secure tenancies and accordingly are not authorities and bodies listed by Housing Act 1985, s.80(1) which are:
—local authorities,
—new town corporations,
—housing action trusts,
—urban development corporations,
—the Development Board for Rural Wales or
—housing co-operatives within the meaning of the Housing Act 1985, s.27B.

Suitability of accommodation

210.—(1) In determining for the purposes of this Part whether accommodation is suitable for a person, the local housing authority shall have regard to Parts IX, X and XI of the Housing Act 1985 (slum clearance; overcrowding; houses in multiple occupation).

(2) The Secretary of State may by order specify—

(a) circumstances in which accommodation is or is not to be regarded as suitable for a person, and

(b) matters to be taken into account or disregarded in determining whether accommodation is suitable for a person.

DEFINITION
"local housing authority": ss.217, 218.

GENERAL NOTE
The requirements of this section (first introduced by s.14, Housing and Planning Act 1986, into s.69, 1985 Act) suggest that what is *predominantly* (but *not* exclusively) in mind when securing that accommodation is made available are matters of space and arrangement: see *R. v. L.B. Brent, ex p. Awua* [1996] 1 A.C. 55, 27 H.L.R. 453, H.L.; see also *R. v. L.B. Wandsworth, ex p. Wingrove* and *R. v. L.B. Wandsworth, ex p. Mansoor* [1996] 3 All E.R. 913, C.A., in which Evans L.J. thought that the tenure, or time element, of suitability had to be proportionate to the circumstances of the case, including the needs of the applicant and *R. v. Tower Hamlets L.B.C., ex p. Kaur* (1994) 26 H.L.R. 597, Q.B.D., notes to s.206, above.

The obligation is to "have regard to" these provisions of the Housing Act 1985, an obligation introduced by Housing and Planning Act 1986, s.14, in direct response to the decision of the House of Lords in *In Re Puhlhofer* [1986] A.C. 484, 18 H.L.R. 158, in which both the Court of Appeal and the House of Lords rejected the decision at first instance that, *inter alia*, accommodation which was statutorily overcrowded could not be accommodation for the purposes of what is now s.175 (nor would it prevent such accommodation being provided in discharge, under what is now s.206): see, generally, the discussion in the General Note to s.175, above.

Even now, the wording is not strong enough to amount to a prohibition on housing someone in overcrowded or unfit property, although it *is* strong enough to vitiate a decision in which the authority had ignored the issue—wilfully or even because they were unaware of the relevant conditions—and *may* be strong enough to require the authority to justify their decision so to accommodate (consider *Padfield v. Minister of Agriculture, Fisheries & Food* [1968] A.C. 997, H.L., see notes to s.191, above).

Subs. (2)
This is a new power, to specify circumstances in which accommodation is (or is not) to be regarded as suitable (which is a more dominant test than have regard to matters or circumstances), and to specify other matters to be taken into account or disregarded when determining suitability.

Protection of property of homeless persons and persons threatened with homelessness

211.—(1) This section applies where a local housing authority have reason to believe that—
  (a) there is danger of loss of, or damage to, any personal property of an applicant by reason of his inability to protect it or deal with it, and
  (b) no other suitable arrangements have been or are being made.
  (2) If the authority have become subject to a duty towards the applicant under—
    section 188 (interim duty to accommodate),
    section 190, 193 or 195 (duties to persons found to be homeless or threatened with homelessness), or
    section 200 (duties to applicant whose case is considered for referral or referred),
then, whether or not they are still subject to such a duty, they shall take reasonable steps to prevent the loss of the property or prevent or mitigate damage to it.
  (3) If they have not become subject to such a duty, they may take any steps they consider reasonable for that purpose.
  (4) The authority may decline to take action under this section except upon such conditions as they consider appropriate in the particular case, which may include conditions as to—
    (a) the making and recovery by the authority of reasonable charges for the action taken, or
    (b) the disposal by the authority, in such circumstances as may be specified, of property in relation to which they have taken action.
  (5) References in this section to personal property of the applicant include

personal property of any person who might reasonably be expected to reside with him.

(6) Section 212 contains provisions supplementing this section.

"local housing authority": ss.217, 218.

GENERAL NOTE

These provisions—which appeared in both the 1977 and 1985 Acts—are of considerable practical importance. Those who are homeless or threatened with it are likely to be from amongst the poorer sections of the community and failure to take steps to protect their belongings can only have the effect of prolonging or worsening their economic position. This section contains (a) a duty to protect personal property in some circumstances, and (b) a power to do so in others. The ancillary powers of authorities are to be found in s.212, below. These notes relate to both sections.

The duty is owed in respect of "personal property". In *R. v. Chiltern D.C., ex p. Roberts* (1990) 23 H.L.R. 387, it was thought likely that this would not extend to equipment used by an applicant in his business, at any rate where the business is conducted other than at the accommodation. The property in question is that of the applicant, and anyone who might reasonably be expected to reside with him: subs. (5).

To whom is a duty owed?

The duty is owed to an applicant towards whom the authority has become subject to a housing duty under one of the following provisions: s.188 (accommodation pending enquiries), s.193 (full duty), s.190 (temporary accommodation for the homeless intentionally in priority need), s.195 (accommodation for those threatened with homelessness, in priority need and not so threatened intentionally), and s.200 (accommodation for those who are or have been the subject of a local connection issue).

When is the duty owed?

The duty is owed when the authority have reason to believe (a) that by reason of his inability to protect or deal with it, there is a danger of loss of, or damage to, any personal property of the applicant, or other person to whom the duty is owed, and (b) that no other suitable arrangements have been or are being made: subs. (1).

The duty is owed not only when the authority are subject to one of the prescribed housing duties, but also when they have been so subject: subs. (2). For example, a person may be evicted from accommodation, and subsequently be held to be homeless intentionally. The former landlord may have been willing to hold on to his property for a period of time. That period may be no longer than the period for which accommodation has been provided under s.190(2)(a). If, after the expiry of the s.190(2)(a) accommodation, the property duty has not expired, application may yet be made for assistance under this section and if the relevant conditions are fulfilled, the authority will be obliged to provide that assistance.

Subject to the provisions of s.212(2), the duty continues until the authority are of the opinion that there is no longer any reason to believe that there is a danger of loss of, or damage to, that property by reason of the applicant's inability, or that of another to whom the duty is owed, to protect or deal with it: s.212(3).

Section 212(2) applies if the applicant asks the authority to move his property to a particular location nominated by him; the authority can discharge their duty by doing so (if they consider the request reasonable), and owe no further duty—and have no further power—to take action under this provision. They must, however, warn the applicant of the consequences of his request: *ibid.*

What is the duty?

The duty is to take reasonable steps to prevent loss or prevent or mitigate damage to the property: subs. (2). In order to discharge the duty, the authority have a quite exceptional power of entry onto private property, which serves to underline the importance of these provisions: s.212(1). Such provisions were also to be found in legislation preceding the 1977 Act—see s.48, National Assistance Act 1948 (c. 29). At all reasonable times, they may enter any premises which are "the usual place of residence of the applicant or which were his last usual place of residence", and deal with his property in any way which is reasonably necessary, including by storing or arranging to store the property.

Arranging storage is what the authority generally have to do. They may, however, refuse to exercise the duty, except upon appropriate conditions: subs. (4). This means such conditions as they consider appropriate in a particular case, and can include conditions empowering them (a) to charge for the discharge of the duty, and (b) to dispose of the property in respect of which they discharged the duty, in such circumstances as may be specified (*ibid.*).

Whether or not a charge is made or a duty to store exists the authority must, as bailees of the property, take reasonable care of it, and deliver it up when reasonably requested to do so. Failure to do this will render them liable to damages, even if the failure to deliver up is accidental, albeit negligent accident: *Mitchell v. Ealing London Borough Council* [1979] Q.B. 1. The standard of care is high, and the burden of disproving negligence when damage has resulted from an accident lies upon the authority, as bailees: *Port Swettenham Authority v. T.W. Wu & Co.* [1979] A.C. 580, P.C.

The position under this section may, however, have to be read subject to s.41, Local Government (Miscellaneous Provisions) Act 1982 (c. 30). That section applies wherever property comes into the possession of a local authority, after being found on premises owned or managed by them, or property has been deposited with the local authority and is not collected from them in accordance with the terms on which it was deposited. The section entitles the authority to give the owner or depositor of the property notice in writing that they require him to collect the property by a date specified in the notice, and that if he does not do so the property will vest in the authority as from that date. If the person notified then fails to comply with the notice, the property does vest in the authority on that date.

The date to be specified is to be not less than one month from the date of the notice. When an authority find property, as distinct from when it is deposited with them, and it appears to them that it is impossible to serve a notice, the property simply vests in them one month from the date when they so find it. In any other case, including deposit, when the authority are satisfied after reasonable enquiry that it is impossible to serve notice, the property simply vests in them six months after the property was deposited with them expired, whichever is the later.

Perishable property, and property the continued storage of which would involve the authority in unreasonable expense or inconvenience, may, in any event, be sold or otherwise disposed of by the authority as they think fit. In such a case, the proceeds of sale vest in the authority on the same date as the property itself would have done were it not perishable or inconvenient or too expensive to store. If property is claimed by its owner prior to the date when it vests in the authority, he can only collect it on payment to the authority of their costs in storing the property, and in making enquiries or carrying out any of the other steps referred to in this section.

There is no express reference in the 1982 Act to the provisions of the 1977 Act, nor (by amendment) to the 1985 Act or to this Part. The courts may therefore consider that references in the 1982 Act to "property deposited" with the authority do not include property taken into safe keeping under this section. If so these provisions only will apply. If not, the 1982 Act makes it much easier for authorities to limit the effect of their duties.

The Power to Protect Property

The authority have power to take such steps as they consider reasonable to prevent loss of property, or to prevent or mitigate damage to it, as they are obliged to take when they are under the duty described above, in any case where there is no duty to do so: subs. (3). This power might benefit those not in priority need of accommodation, and those who, though in priority need of accommodation, are only threatened with homelessness, and in respect of whom no decision on intentionality has yet been taken.

They also have power to protect property, subject to s.212(2), when a duty to do so has expired, because the authority have formed the view that there is no further danger of loss of or damage to the property, or that the applicant is no longer unable to protect or deal with it, the authority continue to have power to continue to protect that property: subs. (3). Property may be kept in store, and conditions on which it was taken into store will continue to have effect, with any necessary modifications (s.212(3)).

Where the authority exercise this power, they have the same ancillary powers as in relation to the duty, *i.e.* entry into premises, imposing conditions, etc.

Notification of Cessation of Responsibility

When the authority consider that they no longer have a duty or a power to protect property, they are obliged to notify the person towards whom they were subject to the duty, or in relation to whose property they have exercised the power (a) that they have ceased to be subject to the duty, or to enjoy the power, and (b) why they are of the opinion that the duty or power has come to an end: s.212(4). The notification must be given by delivery to the person to be notified, or by leaving it, or sending it by post to, his last known address: s.212(5).

Protection of property: supplementary provisions

212.—(1) The authority may for the purposes of section 211 (protection of property of homeless persons or persons threatened with homelessness)—

    (a) enter, at all reasonable times, any premises which are the usual place of residence of the applicant or which were his last usual place of residence, and

(b) deal with any personal property of his in any way which is reasonably necessary, in particular by storing it or arranging for its storage.

(2) Where the applicant asks the authority to move his property to a particular location nominated by him, the authority—

(a) may, if it appears to them that his request is reasonable, discharge their responsibilities under section 211 by doing as he asks, and

(b) having done so, have no further duty or power to take action under that section in relation to that property.

If such a request is made, the authority shall before complying with it inform the applicant of the consequence of their doing so.

(3) If no such request is made (or, if made, is not acted upon) the authority cease to have any duty or power to take action under section 211 when, in their opinion, there is no longer any reason to believe that there is a danger of loss of or damage to a person's personal property by reason of his inability to protect it or deal with it.

But property stored by virtue of their having taken such action may be kept in store and any conditions upon which it was taken into store continue to have effect, with any necessary modifications.

(4) Where the authority—

(a) cease to be subject to a duty to take action under section 211 in respect of an applicant's property, or

(b) cease to have power to take such action, having previously taken such action,

they shall notify the applicant of that fact and of the reason for it.

(5) The notification shall be given to the applicant—

(a) by delivering it to him, or

(b) by leaving it, or sending it to him, at his last known address.

(6) References in this section to personal property of the applicant include personal property of any person who might reasonably be expected to reside with him.

GENERAL NOTE
See notes to s.211, above.

Co-operation between relevant housing authorities and bodies

213.—(1) Where a local housing authority—

(a) request another relevant housing authority or body, in England, Wales or Scotland, to assist them in the discharge of their functions under this Part, or

(b) request a social services authority, in England, Wales or Scotland, to exercise any of their functions in relation to a case which the local housing authority are dealing with under this Part,

the authority or body to whom the request is made shall co-operate in rendering such assistance in the discharge of the functions to which the request relates as is reasonable in the circumstances.

(2) In subsection (1)(a) "relevant housing authority or body" means—

(a) in relation to England and Wales, a local housing authority, a new town corporation, a registered social landlord or a housing action trust;

(b) in relation to Scotland, a local authority, a development corporation, a registered housing association or Scottish Homes.

Expressions used in paragraph (a) have the same meaning as in the Housing Act 1985; and expressions used in paragraph (b) have the same meaning as in the Housing (Scotland) Act 1987.

(3) Subsection (1) above applies to a request by a local authority in Scotland under section 38 of the Housing (Scotland) Act 1987 as it applies to a

request by a local housing authority in England and Wales (the references to this Part being construed, in relation to such a request, as references to Part II of that Act).

DEFINITIONS
"local housing authority": ss.217, 218.
"relevant housing authority": s.217.
"social services authority": s.217.

GENERAL NOTE
Where housing duties of any class arise, or when inquiry duties arise, the authority may seek co-operation from one of the specified bodies, or may even request a social services authority to take over their functions, and that authority shall co-operate to the extent "as is reasonable in the circumstances". A decision of the social service authority is one that is reserved to their social service committee: Local Authority Social Services Act 1970 (c. 42), s.1 and Schedule, as amended by Sched. 17, below.

Although an authority may request assistance under this section, they may not delegate their substantive duty to inquire under s.184: *R. v. West Dorset D.C., West Dorset H.A., ex p. Gerrard* (1995) 27 H.L.R. 150, because they had not taken an active and dominant part in the investigative process, but contrast *R. v. Hertsmere B.C., ex p. Woolgar* (1995) 27 H.L.R. 703, where it was held that so long as the decision-making function was preserved by the authority, the inquiries themselves could be carried out by another body on their behalf: see General Note to s.184, above.

Whether an authority seek assistance under this section or not is primarily a matter for them and the court will be slow to interfere with the exercise of such a discretion: *R. v. Wirral M.B.C., ex p. Bell* (1994) 27 H.L.R. 234, Q.B.D. In *R. v. London Borough of Tower Hamlets, ex p. Byas* (1992) 25 H.L.R. 105, C.A. it was held that the equivalent provision of s.27, Children Act 1989, did not apply where one department of a local authority sought help from another department within the same authority. In *R. v. Northavon D.C., ex p. Smith* [1994] 2 A.C. 402, 26 H.L.R. 659, H.L., under the same provisions, the House of Lords held that although housing and social services authorities were expected to co-operate, if no solution was forthcoming, the responsibility would remain with the authority seeking (rather than from which is sought) the co-operation.

General provisions

False statements, withholding information and failure to disclose change of circumstances

214.—(1) It is an offence for a person, with intent to induce a local housing authority to believe in connection with the exercise of their functions under this Part that he or another person is entitled to accommodation or assistance in accordance with the provisions of this Part, or is entitled to accommodation or assistance of a particular description—

(a) knowingly or recklessly to make a statement which is false in a material particular, or

(b) knowingly to withhold information which the authority have reasonably required him to give in connection with the exercise of those functions.

(2) If before an applicant receives notification of the local housing authority's decision on his application there is any change of facts material to his case, he shall notify the authority as soon as possible.

The authority shall explain to every applicant, in ordinary language, the duty imposed on him by this subsection and the effect of subsection (3).

(3) A person who fails to comply with subsection (2) commits an offence unless he shows that he was not given the explanation required by that subsection or that he had some other reasonable excuse for non-compliance.

(4) A person guilty of an offence under this section is liable on summary conviction to a fine not exceeding level 5 on the standard scale.

DEFINITION
"local housing authority": ss.217, 218.

GENERAL NOTE

To prevent abuse of Pt. VII, certain attempts to obtain accommodation are made criminal offences, *cf.*, above, s.171 for the corresponding provisions governing the waiting list.

There are three such offences:

(i) making a false statement;
(ii) withholding information; and
(iii) failing to notify changes.

Offences under these provisions are prosecuted in the magistrates' court, and carry a maximum fine of level 5 on the standard scale, which means the standard scale under the Criminal Justice Act 1982 (c. 48), s.37, as amended by the Criminal Justice Act 1991 (c. 53).

Making a False Statement. This offence is committed by anyone, not just an applicant, who knowingly or recklessly makes a statement which is false in a material particular, with intent to induce an authority, in connection with the exercise of their functions under Pt. VII, to believe that the person making the statement, or any other person, is entitled to accommodation or assistance. For this purpose, assistance means the benefit of any duty under Pt. VII which relates to accommodation or to assistance in obtaining accommodation: s.183(2), above. The offence is sufficiently widely drafted to catch, *e.g.* an adviser who makes representations on behalf of an applicant, but the offence requires proof of intent to induce the authority to believe something which is not true, and the prosecutor must accordingly include proof of such intent as part of the prosecution.

Withholding Information. This offence is committed by anyone, again not just an applicant, who knowingly withholds information which the authority have reasonably required him to give in connection with the exercise of their functions under Pt. VII. This is a surprisingly widely drafted provision, enabling an authority to require information from, for example, a relative or a former landlord. However, an intent must be shown to induce the authority, in connection with the exercise of their Pt. VII functions, to believe that the person making the statement, or any other person, is entitled to accommodation or assistance. For this purpose, assistance means the benefit of any duty under Pt. VII which relates to accommodation or to assistance in obtaining accommodation: s.183(2), above.

Failure to Notify Changes. This offence may be committed only by an applicant. An applicant is under a positive duty to inform the authority as soon as possible of any change of facts material to his application, which occurs before the receipt of notification of their decision on his application. This is less straightforward than the two offences previously considered. Of particular difficulty is the issue of what constitutes a "material change of facts". In accordance with the usual principles of criminal law, the courts should interpret the provisions narrowly, in favour of the accused.

A related duty is imposed upon authorities: to explain to an applicant, in ordinary language, both the nature of his duty to notify them of material changes and the fact that failure to do so is a criminal offence. It is a defence for the applicant to show that he was not given such an explanation, and it is also a defence to show that he had a reasonable excuse for non-compliance.

Regulations and orders

215.—(1) In this Part "prescribed" means prescribed by regulations of the Secretary of State.

(2) Regulations or an order under this Part may make different provision for different purposes, including different provision for different areas.

(3) Regulations or an order under this Part shall be made by statutory instrument.

(4) Unless required to be approved in draft, regulations or an order under this Part shall be subject to annulment in pursuance of a resolution of either House of Parliament.

Transitional and consequential matters

216.—(1) The provisions of this Part have effect in place of the provisions of Part III of the Housing Act 1985 (housing the homeless) and shall be construed as one with that Act.

(2) Subject to any transitional provision contained in an order under section 232(4) (power to include transitional provision in commencement order), the provisions of this Part do not apply in relation to an applicant whose application for accommodation or assistance in obtaining accommo-

dation was made before the commencement of this Part.

(3) The enactments mentioned in Schedule 17 have effect with the amendments specified there which are consequential on the provisions of this Part.

GENERAL NOTE

The provisions of 1985 Act, Pt. III, will continue to govern applications made before the commencement of this Part, unless an order made under s.232(4), below, provides otherwise.

Minor definitions: Part VII

217.—(1) In this Part, subject to subsection (2)—

"relevant authority" means a local housing authority or a social services authority; and

"social services authority" means a local authority for the purposes of the Local Authority Social Services Act 1970, as defined in section 1 of that Act.

(2) In this Part, in relation to Scotland—

(a) "local housing authority" means a local authority within the meaning of the Housing (Scotland) Act 1988, and

(b) "social services authority" means a local authority for the purposes of the Social Work (Scotland) Act 1968.

(3) References in this Part to the district of a local housing authority—

(a) have the same meaning in relation to an authority in England or Wales as in the Housing Act 1985, and

(b) in relation to an authority in Scotland, mean the area of the local authority concerned.

Index of defined expressions: Part VII

218. The following Table shows provisions defining or otherwise explaining expressions used in this Part (other than provisions defining or explaining an expression used in the same section)—

accommodation available for occupation	section 176
applicant	section 183(2)
assistance under this Part	section 183(2)
associated (in relation to a person)	section 178
assured tenancy and assured shorthold tenancy	section 230
district (of local housing authority)	section 217(3)
eligible for assistance	section 183(2)
homeless	section 175(1)
housing functions under this Part (in sections 206 to 209)	section 205(2)
intentionally homeless	section 191
intentionally threatened with homelessness	section 196
local connection	section 199
local housing authority—	
—in England and Wales	section 230
—in Scotland	section 217(2)(a)
minimum period (for purposes of section 193)	section 193(3) and (4)
prescribed	section 215(1)
priority need	section 189
reasonable to continue to occupy accommodation	section 177
registered social landlord	section 230
relevant authority	section 217(1)
social services authority	section 217(1) and (2)(b)
threatened with homelessness	section 175(4)

Part VIII

Miscellaneous and General Provisions

Miscellaneous

Directions as to certain charges by social landlords

219.—(1) The Secretary of State may give directions to social landlords about the making of service charges in respect of works of repair, maintenance or improvement—

(a) requiring or permitting the waiver or reduction of charges where relevant assistance is given by the Secretary of State, and

(b) permitting the waiver or reduction of charges in such other circumstances as may be specified in the directions.

(2) A direction shall not require the waiver or reduction of charges by reference to assistance for which application was made before the date on which the direction was given, but subject to that directions may relate to past charges or works to such extent as appears to the Secretary of State to be appropriate.

(3) Directions which require or permit the waiver or reduction of charges have corresponding effect—

(a) in relation to charges already demanded so as to require or permit the non-enforcement of the charges, and

(b) in relation to charges already paid so as to require or permit a refund.

(4) For the purposes of this section "social landlord" means—

(a) an authority or body within section 80(1) of the Housing Act 1985 (the landlord condition for secure tenancies), other than a housing co-operative, or

(b) a registered social landlord.

(5) In this section "assistance" means grant or other financial assistance of any kind; and directions may specify what assistance is relevant for the purposes of this section, and to what buildings or other land any assistance is to be regarded as relevant.

(6) The provisions of section 220 supplement this section.

DEFINITIONS
"registered social landlord": s.1.
"service charge": s.220.

GENERAL NOTE
In June 1995, the DoE issued a good practice guide on the administration of service charges and improvement contributions of flats purchased under the right to buy. Chapter 10 of the guide concerned special-funded schemes such as City Challenge, Estate Action, and Single Regeneration Budget, and stated that:
"Local authorities will wish to act reasonably towards their leaseholders. It might be reasonable **not** to require leaseholders to contribute towards the costs "incurred" for works to the extent that a proportion of those costs will be reimbursed to the authority by either grant or subsidy on loan charges. This could result in double funding."
A number of authorities were, however, concerned about the legality of foregoing service charge income to which they were entitled. Counsel's advice was sought by one London authority, which confirmed that:
"—it may be reasonable to reduce charges; but an authority can only act where it has a power to do so;
—the terms of most leases will require authorities to recover estate improvement costs which have been incurred, regardless of the extent to which they are being funded by central government;
—an authority would be in breach of its fiduciary duty if it did not recover from the leaseholder the costs incurred; amending the lease could also involve conflict with that duty;
—DoE should consider options for resolving the problem, in particular by introducing legislation".

This advice was accepted by the DoE in a letter to all authorities dated January 23, 1996, and views were sought on the nature of that legislation.

This and the following section are the outcome of that consultation.

Subss. (1), (2), (3)

Power is given to the Secretary of State to issue directions to social landlords (see subs. (4)) about the making of service charges in respect of works of repair, maintenance or improvement. Service charges are defined in s.220. The directions may *permit* waiver or reduction of service charges generally. Waiver or reduction may be *required* where the landlord is receiving financial assistance from the Secretary of State. The directions may relate to past charges or works, permitting the Secretary of State to backdate permission so as to deal with existing problems. The directions may not, however, *require* waiver or reduction unless an application for financial assistance has been made on or after the date of the direction. Directions may differentiate between landlords or descriptions of landlords and by area: s.219(1). They may provide for a specific amount or proportion of reduction, or for other means of determination, and for the criteria which landlords are to take into account in determining whether to reduce and to what extent: s.219(2), (3).

The DoE has issued a consultation paper, *Further Proposals to Reduce Charges for Repairs and Improvements*, dated June 14, 1996, on the Secretary of State's proposals for the use of these powers.

High Cost Projects

Where projects have particularly high costs to the leaseholder, whether funded from central government or otherwise, the landlord would be permitted to reduce bills so that they did not exceed £10,000 *per* property over five years. The amount of the reduction would be a matter for the landlord, but they would need to have regard to any substantial financial benefit which accrued to the leaseholder through the works. Landlords would also have regard to the individual means of leaseholders.

Projects which have received special government assistance

Where government assistance through grant, supplementary credit approvals or clearly identified special enhancements to the Housing Investment Programme allocation in relation to Estate Action Schemes, City Challenge funding or the Single Regeneration Budget (SRB) Challenge Fund has been received, landlords would be permitted to reduce charges for works by any amount up to the proportion of the total project costs met by central government funding. The decision as to whether and how much to reduce would be left to landlord, again taking into account the financial benefit to the leaseholder and individual means. It is also proposed that the direction would allow reduction where assistance is provided through the 1996/97 Estates Renewal Challenge Fund (ERCF) round to estates which transfer to a new landlord, to the extent of the allocation of funding to cover leaseholders' costs.

Future Projects

The Secretary of State is proposing to use his power to require reductions in respect of future awards of SRB Challenge Fund and ERCF. In each case the landlord would not be able to charge more than £10,000 in any five year period for funded works, unless the benefit of those works to the leaseholder exceeded that amount, in which case the higher amount could be charged. Even if less than £10,000, landlords would be able to reduce the charge if the leaseholder would suffer hardship. Each leaseholder would have to be sent a copy of the direction and accompanying guidance notes. Where the final charge to the leaseholder did exceed £10,000, the landlord would have to send to the leaseholder an explanation of the calculation which arrived at the higher amount and give him the opportunity to propose reductions on the grounds of hardship.

Subs. (4)

The authorities and bodies listed by Housing Act 1985, s.80(1) are:

—local authorities,

—new town corporations,

—housing action trusts,

—urban development corporations,

—the Development Board for Rural Wales.

—See notes to s.1, above for registered social landlords.

Directions as to certain charges: supplementary provisions

220.—(1) Directions under section 219 may make different provision for different cases or descriptions of case.

This includes power to make—

(a) different provision for different social landlords or descriptions of social landlords, and

(b) different provision for different areas.

(2) Directions under section 219 requiring the reduction of a service charge may specify the amount (or proportion) of the reduction or provide for its determination in such manner as may be specified.

(3) Directions under section 219 permitting the waiver or reduction of a service charge may specify criteria to which the social landlord is to have regard in deciding whether to do so or to what extent.

(4) The Secretary of State shall publish any direction under section 219 relating to all social landlords or any description of social landlords in such manner as he considers appropriate for bringing it to the notice of the landlords concerned.

(5) For the purposes of section 219 "service charge" means an amount payable by a lessee of a dwelling—

(a) which is payable, directly or indirectly, for repairs, maintenance or improvements, and

(b) the whole or part of which varies or may vary according to the relevant costs.

(6) The relevant costs are the costs or estimated costs incurred or to be incurred by or on behalf of the social landlord, or a superior landlord, in connection with the matters for which the service charge is payable.

For this purpose costs are relevant costs in relation to a service charge whether they are incurred, or to be incurred, in the period for which the service charge is payable or in an earlier or later period.

(7) In this section—

"costs" includes overheads, and

"dwelling" means a building or part of a building occupied or intended to be occupied as a separate dwelling.

DEFINITION

"social landlords": s.219.

GENERAL NOTE

This section makes a number of supplementary provisions in respect of s.219, see notes thereto.

Subs. (4)

The Secretary of State is required to publish the directions.

Subs. (5)

The definition of service charges is taken from the Landlord and Tenant Act 1985 (c. 70), s.18, although in this case limited to costs of repairs, maintenance or improvements. The amount may be payable directly or indirectly. The relevant costs are either the actual costs, or estimated costs incurred by or on behalf of the social landlord or a superior landlord. "Costs" includes overheads. They may be relevant in relation to the service charge for one period even if they have been or are to be incurred during a different period. The charge must be variable, and does not encompass fixed sums: *Coventry City Council v. Cole* (1993) 25 H.L.R. 555, C.A.

Exercise of compulsory purchase powers in relation to Crown land

221.—(1) This section applies to any power to acquire land compulsorily under—

(a) the Housing Act 1985,

(b) the Housing Associations Act 1985,

(c) Part III of the Housing Act 1988 (housing action trust areas), or

(d) Part VII of the Local Government and Housing Act 1989 (renewal areas).

(2) Any power to which this section applies may be exercised in relation to an interest in Crown land which is for the time being held otherwise than by or on behalf of the Crown, but only with the consent of the appropriate authority.

(3) In this section "Crown land" means land in which there is a Crown interest or a Duchy interest.

For this purpose—

"Crown interest" means an interest belonging to Her Majesty in right of the Crown or belonging to a government department or held in trust for Her Majesty for the purposes of a government department; and

"Duchy interest" means an interest belonging to Her Majesty in right of the Duchy of Lancaster or belonging to the Duchy of Cornwall.

(4) For the purposes of this section "the appropriate authority", in relation to Crown land, is—

(a) in the case of land belonging to Her Majesty in right of the Crown and forming part of the Crown Estate, the Crown Estate Commissioners:

(b) in relation to any other land belonging to Her Majesty in right of the Crown, the government department having the management of that land;

(c) in relation to land belonging to Her Majesty in right of the Duchy of Lancaster, the Chancellor of the Duchy;

(d) in relation to land belonging to the Duchy of Cornwall, such person as the Duke of Cornwall, or the possessor for the time being of the Duchy of Cornwall, appoints;

(e) in the case of land belonging to a government department or held in trust for Her Majesty for the purposes of a government department, that department.

(5) If any question arises as to what authority is the appropriate authority in relation to any land, that question shall be referred to the Treasury, whose decision shall be final.

GENERAL NOTE
Crown land is generally excluded from compulsory acquisition, this section provides an exception to that rule. The housing powers set out in subs. (1) may be exercised over interests in Crown land (as defined in subs. (3)) which is not currently held by or on behalf of the Crown, provided the consent of the appropriate authority is obtained: subs. (2).

Miscellaneous minor amendments

222. The enactments mentioned in Schedule 18 have effect with the amendments specified there, which are miscellaneous minor amendments relating to housing.

Part I relates to housing management.

Part II relates to housing finance.

Part III relates to orders in relation to property in family and matrimonial proceedings, etc.

Part IV relates to other housing provisions.

GENERAL NOTE
Of the amendments in Sched. 18, the most significant are as follows:

Para. 1. Repeal of the tenants' choice provisions contained in Housing Act 1988 (c. 50), Pt. IV.

Para. 2. Grants to tenants or licensees of local housing authorities to facilitate transfers or other authorities or registered social landlords.

Pt. III. A number of housing provisions, relating *e.g.* to succession rights or to recovery of grants or discounts paid to occupiers, make exemptions in the case of vesting of the property under matrimonial legislation. Most of the provisions do not include vesting under the Matrimonial and Family Proceedings Act 1984 (c. 42) (relating to overseas divorce) or the Children Act 1989 (c. 41) (used principally by cohabitees with children). Part III accordingly makes provision for amendment of a wide range of provisions to take this into account, and also in some cases to overturn the decision in *R. v. Rushmore B.C., ex p. Barrett* (1988) 20 H.L.R. 366, C.A.

General

Offences by body corporate

223.—(1) Where an offence under this Act committed by a body corporate is proved to have been committed with the consent or connivance of a director, manager, secretary or other similar officer of the body corporate, or a person purporting to act in such a capacity, he as well as the body corporate is guilty of an offence and liable to be proceeded against and punished accordingly.

(2) Where the affairs of a body corporate are managed by its members, subsection (1) applies in relation to the acts and defaults of a member in connection with his functions of management as if he were a director of the body corporate.

The Common Council of the City of London

224.—(1) The Common Council of the City of London may appoint a committee, consisting of so many persons as they think fit, for any purposes of this Act which in their opinion may be better regulated and managed by means of a committee.

(2) A committee so appointed—

(a) shall consist as to a majority of its members of members of the Common Council, and

(b) shall not be authorised to borrow money or to make a rate,

and shall be subject to any regulations and restrictions which may be imposed by the Common Council.

(3) A person is not, by reason only of the fact that he occupies a house at a rental from the Common Council, disqualified from being elected or being a member of that Council or any committee of that Council; but no person shall vote as a member of that Council, or any such committee, on a resolution or question which is proposed or arises in pursuance of this Act and relates to land in which he is beneficially interested.

(4) A person who votes in contravention of subsection (3) commits a summary offence and is liable on conviction to a fine not exceeding level 4 on the standard scale; but the fact of his giving the vote does not invalidate any resolution or proceeding of the authority.

The Isles of Scilly

225.—(1) This Act applies to the Isles of Scilly subject to such exceptions, adaptations and modifications as the Secretary of State may by order direct.

(2) An order shall be made by statutory instrument which shall be subject to annulment in pursuance of a resolution of either House of Parliament.

Corresponding provision for Northern Ireland

226. An Order in Council under paragraph 1(1)(b) of Schedule 1 to the Northern Ireland Act 1974 (legislation for Northern Ireland in the interim period) which states that it is made only for purposes corresponding to those of section 120 (payment of housing benefit to third parties)—

(a) shall not be subject to paragraph 1(4) and (5) of that Schedule (affirmative resolution of both Houses of Parliament), but

(b) shall be subject to annulment in pursuance of a resolution of either House of Parliament.

Repeals

227. The enactments specified in Schedule 19 are repealed to the extent specified.

Financial provisions

228.—(1) There shall be paid out of money provided by Parliament—

(a) any expenses of the Secretary of State incurred in consequence of this Act, and

(b) any increase attributable to this Act in the sums payable out of money so provided under any other enactment.

(2) There shall be paid out of the National Loans Fund any increase attributable to this Act in the sums so payable under any other enactment.

(3) Any sums received by the Secretary of State under this Act shall be paid into the Consolidated Fund.

Meaning of "lease" and "tenancy" and related expressions

229.—(1) In this Act "lease" and "tenancy" have the same meaning.

(2) Both expressions include—

(a) a sub-lease or a sub-tenancy, and

(b) an agreement for a lease or tenancy (or sub-lease or sub-tenancy).

(3) The expressions "lessor" and "lessee" and "landlord" and "tenant", and references to letting, to the grant of a lease or to covenants or terms, shall be construed accordingly.

Minor definitions: general

230. In this Act—

"assured tenancy", "assured shorthold tenancy" and "assured agricultural occupancy" have the same meaning as in Part I of the Housing Act 1988;

"enactment" includes an enactment comprised in subordinate legislation (within the meaning of the Interpretation Act 1978);

"housing action trust" has the same meaning as in the Housing Act 1988;

"housing association" has the same meaning as in the Housing Associations Act 1985;

"introductory tenancy" and "introductory tenant" have the same meaning as in Chapter I of Part V of this Act;

"local housing authority" has the same meaning as in the Housing Act 1985;

"registered social landlord" has the same meaning as in Part I of this Act;

"secure tenancy" and "secure tenant" have the same meaning as in Part IV of the Housing Act 1985.

Final provisions

Extent

231.—(1) The provisions of this Act extend to England and Wales, and only to England and Wales, subject as follows.

(2) The following provisions also extend to Scotland—

Part IV (housing benefit and related matters), and

the provisions of this Part so far as relating to Part IV.

(3) Section 226 (power to make corresponding provision for Northern Ireland) also extends to Northern Ireland.

(4) Any amendment or repeal by this Act of an enactment has the same extent as the enactment amended or repealed, except that—

(a) amendments or repeals of provisions of the Housing Associations Act 1985, other than in consequence of paragraph 1 of Schedule 18 to this Act (repeal of Part IV of the Housing Act 1988), do not extend to

Scotland,
(b) amendments or repeals of provisions of the Housing Act 1988 relating to registered housing associations do not extend to Scotland,
(c) amendments or repeals of provisions of the Asylum and Immigration Appeals Act 1993 or the Asylum and Immigration Act 1996 do not extend to Scotland or Northern Ireland, and
(d) repeals of the following provisions do not extend to Scotland—
    (i) section 24(5)(a) and (c) of the Local Government Act 1988,
    (ii) section 182 of the Local Government and Housing Act 1989,
    (iii) paragraph 21(3) of Schedule 6 to the Charities Act 1993, and
    (iv) provisions in Schedule 26 to the Local Government, Planning and Land Act 1980.

(5) Any power conferred by this Act to make consequential amendments or repeals of enactments may be exercised in relation to enactments as they extend to any part of the United Kingdom.

Commencement

232.—(1) The following provisions of this Act come into force on Royal Assent—
section 110 (new leases: valuation principles),
section 120 (payment of housing benefit to third parties), and
sections 223 to 226 and 228 to 233 (general provisions).

(2) The following provisions of this Act come into force at the end of the period of two months beginning with the date on which this Act is passed—
sections 81 and 82 (restriction on termination of tenancy for failure to pay service charge),
section 85 (appointment of manager by the court),
section 94 (provision of general legal advice about residential tenancies),
section 95 (jurisdiction of county courts),
section 221 (exercise of compulsory purchase powers in relation to Crown land),
paragraph 24 (powers of local housing authorities to acquire land for housing purposes), paragraph 26 (preserved right to buy) and paragraphs 27 to 29 of Schedule 18 (local authority assistance in connection with mortgages), and
sections 222 and 227, and Schedule 19 (consequential repeals), in so far as they relate to those paragraphs.

(3) The other provisions of this Act come into force on a day appointed by order of the Secretary of State, and different days may be appointed for different areas and different purposes.

(4) An order under subsection (3) shall be made by statutory instrument and may contain such transitional provisions and savings as appear to the Secretary of State to be appropriate.

Short title

233. This Act may be cited as the Housing Act 1996.

SCHEDULES

SCHEDULE 1

Registered social landlords: regulation

Part I

Control of payments to members, &c.

Payments by way of gift, dividend or bonus

1.—(1) A registered social landlord shall not make a gift or pay a sum by way of dividend or bonus to—

(a) a person who is or has been a member of the body,

(b) a person who is a member of the family of a person within paragraph (a), or

(c) a company of which a person within paragraph (a) or (b) is a director,

except as permitted by this paragraph.

(2) The following are permitted—

(a) the payment of a sum which, in accordance with the constitution or rules of the body, is paid as interest on capital lent to the body or subscribed by way of shares in the body;

(b) the payment by a fully mutual housing association to a person who has ceased to be a member of the association of a sum which is due to him either under his tenancy agreement with the association or under the terms of the agreement under which he became a member of the association.

(3) Where an industrial and provident society or a company registered under the Companies Act 1985 pays a sum or makes a gift in contravention of this paragraph, the society or company may recover the sum or the value of the gift, and proceedings for its recovery shall be taken if the Corporation so directs.

Payments and benefits to officers and employees, &c.

2.—(1) A registered social landlord which is an industrial and provident society or a company registered under the Companies Act 1985 shall not make a payment or grant a benefit to—

(a) an officer or employee of the society or company,

(b) a person who at any time within the preceding twelve months has been a person within paragraph (a),

(c) a close relative of a person within paragraph (a) or (b), or

(d) a business trading for profit of which a person falling within paragraph (a), (b) or (c) is a principal proprietor or in the management of which such a person is directly concerned,

except as permitted by this paragraph.

(2) The following are permitted—

(a) payments made or benefits granted to an officer or employee of the society or company under his contract of employment with the society or company;

(b) the payment of remuneration or expenses to an officer of the society or company who does not have a contract of employment with the society or company;

(c) any such payment as may be made in accordance with paragraph 1(2) (interest payable in accordance with the rules and certain sums payable by a fully mutual housing association to a person who has ceased to be a member);

(d) the grant or renewal of a tenancy by a co-operative housing association;

(e) where a tenancy of a house has been granted to, or to a close relative of, a person who later became an officer or employee, the grant to that tenant of a new tenancy whether of the same or another house;

(f) payments made or benefits granted in accordance with any determination made by the Corporation.

(3) A determination for the purposes of sub-paragraph (2)(f) may specify the class or classes of case in which a payment may be made or benefit granted and specify the maximum amount.

(4) Where a society or company pays a sum or grants a benefit in contravention of this paragraph, the society or company may recover the sum or value of the benefit; and proceedings for its recovery shall be taken if the Corporation so directs.

Maximum amounts payable by way of fees, expenses, &c.

3.—(1) The Corporation may from time to time specify the maximum amounts which may be paid by a registered social landlord which is an industrial and provident society or a company registered under the Companies Act 1985—

    (a) by way of fees or other remuneration, or by way of expenses, to a member of the society or company who is not an officer or employee of the society or company, or

    (b) by way of remuneration or expenses to an officer of the society or company who does not have a contract of employment with the society or company.

(2) Different amounts may be so specified for different purposes.

(3) Where a society or company makes a payment in excess of the maximum permitted under this paragraph, the society or company may recover the excess, and proceedings for its recovery shall be taken if the Corporation so directs.

GENERAL NOTE

Para. 1.

Registered social landlords are not permitted to make gifts, or pay sums by way of dividend or bonus, to anyone who is or has been a member of the body in question, or to the member of the family of such (as to the meaning of which, see above s.62), or to a company of which either a member, or a family member, is a director. The exceptions are:

    (a) Interest on capital lent or subscribed by way of shares, in accordance with the constitution or rules of the body; and,

    (b) The payment to a former member of a fully mutual housing association (as to the meaning of which, see below, s.63; see also notes to s.2(2), above) of a sum due either under his tenancy agreement or the agreement under which he became a member, *i.e.* payment to the member of an equity share co-operative or co-ownership scheme.

Where an industrial and provident society or a company pays a sum or makes a gift in contravention of these provisions, the sum or value (i) *may* be recovered by the body, and (ii) *must* be so recovered if the Corporation directs it to do so. No analogous provisions are required for registered charities, the members of which are already prohibited by law from benefiting.

Para. 2.

There are also prohibitions on payments or benefits to the officers (see General Note to s.7, above) and employees of companies and industrial and provident societies who are registered social landlords. The provisions are applicable to any officer or employee of the company or society, and to anyone who has been such an officer or employee during the previous year, and to a "close relative" of such an (existing or previous) officer or employee, and to a business trading for profit of which such an (existing or previous) officer or employee, or his close relative is a principal proprietor, or directly concerned in the management.

"Close relative" is not defined, but would seem to be narrower than "member of the family" (see s.62), although Housing Corporation Circular 42/89 defines relative in terms that are almost identical, while stating that whether or not the relative is "close" is a question of fact, to be determined by reference to whether "there is a real risk that the decision of the association to grant him/her a benefit could be influenced by that relationship"—see its para. 3.6. That it is a question of fact must be right; but the criterion may be a little wider than is naturally imported by the word "close", for—however distant—there is always a risk, and at that a real risk, of being influenced by familial relationships.

Excepted payments and benefits are:

    (a) Payments under contracts of employment;

    (b) Remuneration or expenses to those who have no such contract (*e.g.* committee members). This could include loss of earnings: *Hansard* (H.C.), April 29, 1996, Report Stage, Minister for Local Government, Housing and Urban Regeneration (Mr Curry), col. 813;

    (c) The same category as is permitted under para. 1 (above);

    (d) The grant or renewal of a tenancy by a co-operative housing association (as to the meaning of which, see s.63, above; in short, it is a fully mutual housing association which is also a society registered under the Industrial and Provident Societies Act 1965);

    (e) The grant of a new tenancy (of the same or another property) to a tenant who later became, or whose close relative (see note to para. 1, above) later became an officer or employee of the body in question;

    (f) Payments or benefits in accordance with any determination made by the Corporation. (A former requirement for the approval of the Secretary of State was deleted in order to comply with a recommendation of the Nolan Committee, Second Report of the Committee on Standards in Public Life, Local Public Spending Bodies, Cm 3270-1, Recommendation 40).

Again, where an industrial and provident society or a company pays a sum or grants a benefit in contravention of these provisions, the sum or value (i) *may* be recovered by the body, and (ii) *must* be so recovered if the Corporation directs it to do so.

Para. 3.

Maximum fees or other remuneration, or expenses, payable to members of bodies who are not its officers (see General Note to s.7, above) or employees, or expenses payable to an officer without a contract of employment, may be specified by the Corporation in respect of registered social landlords who are industrial and provident societies or companies, payments in excess of which (i) *may* be recovered by the body, and (ii) *must* be so recovered if the Corporation directs it to do so.

PART II

CONSTITUTION, CHANGE OF RULES, AMALGAMATION AND DISSOLUTION

General power to remove director, trustee, &c.

4.—(1) The Corporation may, in accordance with the following provisions, by order remove—

(a) a director or trustee of a registered social landlord which is a registered charity,

(b) a committee member of a registered social landlord which is an industrial and provident society, or

(c) a director of a registered social landlord which is a company registered under the Companies Act 1985.

(2) The Corporation may make an order removing any such person if—

(a) he has been adjudged bankrupt or has made an arrangement with his creditors;

(b) he is subject to a disqualification order under the Company Directors Disqualification Act 1986;

(c) he is subject to an order under section 429(2) of the Insolvency Act 1986 (failure to pay under county court administration order);

(d) he is disqualified under section 72 of the Charities Act 1993 from being a charity trustee;

(e) he is incapable of acting by reason of mental disorder;

(f) he has not acted; or

(g) he cannot be found or does not act and his absence or failure to act is impeding the proper management of the registered social landlord's affairs.

(3) Before making an order the Corporation shall give at least 14 days' notice of its intention to do so to the person whom it intends to remove, and to the registered social landlord.

(4) That notice may be given by post, and if so given to the person whom the Corporation intend to remove may be addressed to his last known address in the United Kingdom.

(5) A person who is ordered to be removed under this paragraph may appeal against the order to the High Court.

Restriction on power of removal in case of registered charity

5.—(1) The Corporation may make an order under paragraph 4 removing a director or trustee of a registered charity only if the charity has, at any time before the power is exercised—

(a) received financial assistance under section 24 of the Local Government Act 1988 (assistance for privately let housing accommodation),

(b) had property transferred to it on a qualifying disposal under section 135 of the Leasehold Reform, Housing and Urban Development Act 1993, or

(c) received a grant or loan under any of the following provisions.

(2) The provisions are—

section 18 of this Act (social housing grants),

section 22 of this Act or section 58 of the Housing Associations Act 1985 (grants or loans by local authorities),

section 50 of the Housing Act 1988, section 41 of the Housing Associations Act 1985 or any enactment replaced by that section (housing association grant),

section 51 of the Housing Act 1988 or section 54 or 55 of the Housing Associations Act 1985 (revenue deficit grant or hostel deficit grant),

section 79 of the Housing Associations Act 1985 (loans by Housing Corporation),

section 31 of the Housing Act 1974 (management grants), or

any enactment mentioned in paragraph 2 or 3 of Schedule 1 to the Housing Associations Act 1985 (pre-1974 grants and certain loans).

Registered charity: power to appoint new director or trustee

6.—(1) The Corporation may by order appoint a person to be a director or trustee of a registered social landlord which is a registered charity—

(a) in place of a person removed by the Corporation,

(b) where there are no directors or no trustees, or

(c) where the Corporation is of the opinion that it is necessary for the proper management of the charity's affairs to have an additional director or trustee.

The power conferred by paragraph (c) may be exercised notwithstanding that it will cause the maximum number of directors or trustees permissible under the charity's constitution to be exceeded.

(2) The Corporation shall only exercise its power under sub-paragraph (1) if—

(a) the charity has, at any time before the power is exercised, received financial assistance, had property transferred to it, or received a grant or loan as mentioned in paragraph 5, and

(b) the Corporation has consulted the Charity Commissioners.

(3) A person may be so appointed notwithstanding any restrictions on appointment in the charity's constitution or rules.

(4) A person appointed under this paragraph shall hold office for such period and on such terms as the Corporation may specify; and on the expiry of the appointment the Corporation may renew the appointment for such period as it may specify.

This does not prevent a person appointed under this paragraph from retiring in accordance with the charity's constitution or rules.

(5) A person appointed under this paragraph as director or trustee of a registered charity is entitled—

(a) to attend, speak and vote at any general meeting of the charity and to receive all notices of and other communications relating to any such meeting which a member is entitled to receive,

(b) to move a resolution at any general meeting of the charity, and

(c) to require a general meeting of the charity to be convened within 21 days of a request to that effect made in writing to the directors or trustees.

Company: power to appoint new director

7.—(1) The Corporation may by order appoint a person to be a director of a registered social landlord which is a company registered under the Companies Act 1985—

(a) in place of a director removed by the Corporation,

(b) where there are no directors, or

(c) where the Corporation is of the opinion that it is necessary for the proper management of the company's affairs to have an additional director.

(2) A person may be so appointed whether or not he is a member of the company and notwithstanding anything in the company's articles of association.

(3) Where a person is appointed under this paragraph—

(a) he shall hold office for such period and on such terms as the Corporation may specify, and

(b) on the expiry of the appointment the Corporation may renew the appointment for such period as it may specify.

This does not prevent a person from retiring in accordance with the company's articles of association.

(4) A person appointed under this paragraph is entitled—

(a) to attend, speak and vote at any general meeting of the company and to receive all notices of and other communications relating to any general meeting which a member of the company is entitled to receive,

(b) to move a resolution at any general meeting of the company, and

(c) to require an extraordinary general meeting of the company to be convened within 21 days of a request to that effect made in writing to the directors of the company.

Industrial and provident society: power to appoint new committee member

8.—(1) The Corporation may by order appoint a person to be a committee member of a registered social landlord which is an industrial and provident society—

(a) in place of a person removed by the Corporation,

(b) where there are no members of the committee, or

(c) where the Corporation is of the opinion that it is necessary for the proper management of the society's affairs to have an additional committee member.

The power conferred by paragraph (c) may be exercised notwithstanding that it will cause the maximum number of committee members permissible under the society's constitution to be exceeded.

(2) A person may be so appointed whether or not he is a member of the society and, if he is not, notwithstanding that the rules of the society restrict appointment to members.

(3) A person appointed under this paragraph shall hold office for such period and on such terms as the Corporation may specify; and on the expiry of the appointment the Corporation may renew the appointment for such period as it may specify.

This does not prevent a person appointed under this paragraph from retiring in accordance with the rules of the society.

(4) A person appointed under this paragraph is entitled—

(a) to attend, speak and vote at any general meeting of the society and to receive all notices of and other communications relating to any general meeting which a member of the society is entitled to receive,

(b) to move a resolution at any general meeting of the society, and

(c) to require a general meeting of the society to be convened within 21 days of a request to that effect made in writing to the committee of the society.

Change of rules, &c. by industrial and provident society

9.—(1) This paragraph applies to an industrial and provident society whose registration as a social landlord has been recorded by the appropriate registrar.

(2) Notice shall be sent to the Corporation of any change of the society's name or of the situation of its registered office.

(3) Any other amendment of the society's rules is not valid without the Corporation's consent given by order under the seal of the Corporation.

(4) A copy of that consent shall be sent with the copies of the amendment required by section 10(1) of the Industrial and Provident Societies Act 1965 to be sent to the appropriate registrar.

(5) The Industrial and Provident Societies Act 1965 applies in relation to the provisions of this paragraph as if they were contained in section 10 of that Act (amendment of registered rules).

Change of objects by certain charities

10.—(1) This paragraph applies to a registered social landlord—

(a) which is a registered charity and is not a company incorporated under the Companies Act 1985, and

(b) whose registration under this Part of this Act has been recorded by the Charity Commissioners in accordance with section 3(3).

(2) No power contained in the provisions establishing the registered social landlord as a charity, or regulating its purposes or administration, to vary or add to its objects may be exercised without the consent of the Charity Commissioners.

Before giving their consent the Charity Commissioners shall consult the Corporation.

Change of memorandum or articles of association of company

11.—(1) This paragraph applies to a company registered under the Companies Act 1985 (including such a company which is also a registered charity) whose registration as a social landlord has been recorded by the registrar of companies.

(2) Notice shall be sent to the Corporation of any change of the company's name or of the address of its registered office.

(3) Any other alteration of the company's memorandum or articles of which notice is required to be given to the registrar of companies is not valid without the Corporation's consent given by order under the seal of the Corporation.

(4) A copy of that consent shall be sent with any copy of the alterations required to be sent to the registrar of companies under the Companies Act 1985.

Amalgamation and dissolution &c. of industrial and provident society

12.—(1) This paragraph applies to an industrial and provident society whose registration as a social landlord has been recorded by the appropriate registrar.

(2) The registrar shall not register a special resolution which is passed for the purposes of—

(a) section 50 of the Industrial and Provident Societies Act 1965 (amalgamation of societies),

(b) section 51 of that Act (transfer of engagements between societies), or

(c) section 52 of that Act (power of a society to convert itself into, amalgamate with or transfer its engagements to a company registered under the Companies Act 1985),

unless, together with the copy of the resolution, there is sent to him a copy of the Corporation's consent to the amalgamation, transfer or conversion.

(3) Any new body created by the amalgamation or conversion or, in the case of a transfer of engagements, the transferee, shall be deemed to be registered as a social landlord forthwith upon the amalgamation, conversion or transfer taking effect.

(4) If the society resolves by special resolution that it be wound up voluntarily under the

Insolvency Act 1986, the resolution has no effect unless—

  (a) before the resolution was passed the Corporation gave its consent to its passing, and

  (b) a copy of the consent is forwarded to the appropriate registrar together with a copy of the resolution required to be so forwarded in accordance with the Companies Act 1985.

(5) If the society is to be dissolved by instrument of dissolution, the appropriate registrar shall not—

  (a) register the instrument in accordance with section 58(5) of the Industrial and Provident Societies Act 1965, or

  (b) cause notice of the dissolution to be advertised in accordance with section 58(6) of that Act,

unless together with the instrument there is sent to him a copy of the Corporation's consent to its making.

(6) The references in this paragraph to the Corporation's consent are to consent given by order under the seal of the Corporation.

Arrangement, reconstruction, &c. of company

13.—(1) This paragraph applies to a company registered under the Companies Act 1985 whose registration as a social landlord has been recorded by the registrar of companies.

(2) An order of the court given for the purposes of section 425 of the Companies Act 1985 (compromise or arrangement with creditors or members) is not effective unless the Corporation has given its consent.

A copy of the consent shall be sent to the registrar of companies along with the office copy of the order delivered to him under that section.

(3) An order of the court given for the purposes of section 427 of the Companies Act 1985 (transfer of undertaking or property for purposes of reconstruction or amalgamation) is not effective unless the Corporation has given its consent.

A copy of the consent shall be sent to the registrar of companies along with the office copy of the order delivered to him under that section.

(4) The registrar of companies shall not register any resolution under section 53 of the Industrial and Provident Societies Act 1965 (conversion of company into industrial and provident society), unless, together with the copy of the resolution, there is sent to him a copy of the Corporation's consent to the conversion.

(5) Where a director, administrator or liquidator of the company proposes to make a voluntary arrangement with the company's creditors under section 1 of the Insolvency Act 1986, the arrangement shall not take effect under section 5 (effect of approval by members and creditors) of that Act unless the Corporation has given its consent to the voluntary arrangement.

(6) If the company resolves by special resolution that it be wound up voluntarily under the Insolvency Act 1986, the resolution has no effect unless—

  (a) before the resolution was passed the Corporation gave its consent to its passing, and

  (b) a copy of the consent is forwarded to the registrar of companies together with a copy of the resolution required to be so forwarded in accordance with section 380 of the Companies Act 1985.

(7) The references in this paragraph to the Corporation's consent are to consent given by order under the seal of the Corporation.

(8) Where sub-paragraph (3) or (4) applies, the transferee or, as the case may be, any new body created by the conversion shall be deemed to be registered as a social landlord forthwith upon the transfer or conversion taking effect.

Corporation's power to petition for winding up

14.—(1) The Corporation may present a petition for the winding up under the Insolvency Act 1986 of a registered social landlord which is—

  (a) a company incorporated under the Companies Act 1985 (including such a company which is also a registered charity), or

  (b) an industrial and provident society (to which the winding up provisions of the Insolvency Act 1986 apply in accordance with section 55(a) of the Industrial and Provident Societies Act 1965),

on either of the following grounds.

(2) The grounds are—

  (a) that the landlord is failing properly to carry out its purposes or objects, or

(b) that the landlord is unable to pay its debts within the meaning of section 123 of the Insolvency Act 1986.

Transfer of net assets on dissolution or winding up

15.—(1) This paragraph applies—

(a) where a registered social landlord which is an industrial and provident society is dissolved as mentioned in section 55(a) or (b) of the Industrial and Provident Societies Act 1965 (winding-up under the Insolvency Act 1986 or by instrument of dissolution), and

(b) where a registered social landlord which is a company registered under the Companies Act 1985 is wound up under the Insolvency Act 1986.

(2) On such a dissolution or winding-up, so much of the property of the society or company as remains after meeting the claims of its creditors and any other liabilities arising on or before the dissolution or winding-up shall be transferred to the Corporation or, if the Corporation so directs, to a specified registered social landlord.

The above provision has effect notwithstanding anything in the Industrial and Provident Societies Act 1965, the Companies Act 1985 or the Insolvency Act 1986, or in the rules of the society or, as the case may be, in the memorandum or articles of association of the company.

(3) In order to avoid the necessity for the sale of land belonging to the registered social landlord and thereby secure the transfer of the land under this paragraph, the Corporation may, if it appears to it appropriate to do so, make payments to discharge such claims or liabilities as are referred to in sub-paragraph (2).

(4) Where the registered social landlord which is dissolved or wound up is a charity, the Corporation may dispose of property transferred to it by virtue of this paragraph only to another registered social landlord—

(a) which is also a charity, and

(b) the objects of which appear to the Corporation to be, as nearly as practicable, akin to those of the body which is dissolved or wound up.

(5) In any other case the Corporation may dispose of property transferred to it by virtue of this paragraph to a registered social landlord or to a subsidiary of the Corporation.

(6) Where property transferred to the Corporation by virtue of this paragraph includes land subject to an existing mortgage or charge (whether in favour of the Corporation or not), the Corporation may, in exercise of its powers under Part III of the Housing Associations Act 1985, dispose of the land either—

(a) subject to that mortgage or charge, or

(b) subject to a new mortgage or charge in favour of the Corporation securing such amount as appears to the Corporation to be appropriate in the circumstances.

GENERAL NOTE

Para. 4.

The Corporation enjoys power—irrespective of those powers it may exercise after an inquiry under Sched. 1, Pt. IV—to remove directors, trustees or committee members, in the following cases:

(a) Bankruptcy, or where an arrangement has been made with creditors;

(b) Disqualification under the Company Directors (Disqualification) Act 1986 (c. 46);

(c) Failure to pay under a county court administration order pursuant to s.429(2), Insolvency Act 1986 (c. 45);

(d) Disqualification under s.72, Charities Act 1993 (c. 10);

(e) Incapacity by reason of mental disorder;

(f) Failure to act;

(g) Cannot be found or does not act, which absence or omission is impeding proper management.

The Corporation must give 14 days' notice of intention to use these powers, which may be given by post and may be sent to the last known address in the U.K. of the person it is intended to remove; there is an appeal to the High Court against the order (see General Note to s.6, above).

Para. 5.

The Corporation can only remove the director or trustee of a registered charity if the charity has received assistance under s.24, Local Government Act 1988, for the provision of privately let accommodation (see notes to s.22), or has taken a qualifying disposal (more than 499 in aggregate) of dwellings from a local authority under s.135, Leasehold Reform, Housing and Urban

Development Act 1993, or received a grant under any one of a schedule of provisions (including under ss.18, 22 of this Act, s.58, Housing Associations Act 1985 [see notes to s.22, above], housing association, revenue deficit, hostel or management grant, loans from the Corporation, etc.).

Para. 6.
In the case of such (*cf.* para. 5, above) a registered charity, and after consultation with the Charity Commissioners, the Corporation can appoint a new director or trustee, in one of three circumstances:
  (a) In place of a director or trustee removed; or
  (b) Where there are no directors or trustees; or
  (c) Where the Corporation considers it necessary to have an additional director or trustee for the proper management of affairs (even if this would mean bringing the number of directors or trustees above any maximum number specified in the charity's constitution).
The period and terms of office are as determined by the Corporation, who may renew the term, and may take effect regardless of any restrictions in the charity's constitution. A person so appointed may attend, speak and vote at any general meeting of the charity, and is entitled to all notices and other communications to which a member is entitled, and is entitled to move resolutions at a general meeting and, in any event, is entitled to require a general meeting of the charity to be convened on 21 days notice in writing to the directors or trustees. The appointment as a director or trustee already empowers them to attend, speak and vote at a directors' or trustees' meeting.
As to consultation, see notes to s.5, above.

Paras. 7, 8.
There are powers analogous to those to be found in para. 6 to appoint a director or committee member of a company or industrial and provident society which is a registered social landlord (but no requirement to consult the appropriate registrar).

Para. 9.
If a registered social landlord which is an industrial and provident society changes its name or registered office, the Corporation must be notified. There can be no registration of an amendment to the rules without the Corporation's consent given under seal.

Para. 10.
A registered charity, not being a company incorporated under the Companies Act 1985, may not vary or add to its objects without the consent of the Charity Commissioners, who must consult the Corporation before giving it.

Para. 11.
Notification of change of name or registered office of a registered social landlord which is a company registered under the Companies Act 1985 must be given to the Corporation. Any other alteration of the company's memorandum or articles, of which notice is required to be given to the registrar of companies, is not valid without the Corporation's consent, given under seal.

Para. 12.
No power to register an amalgamation of two or more industrial and provident societies, or a transfer of engagements between such societies, or of a resolution to convert into, amalgamate with or transfer engagements to, a company, can be exercised by the appropriate registrar unless it is accompanied by a copy of the Corporation's consent thereto. Nor can such a body resolve voluntarily to wind itself up without the consent of the Corporation. In each case, consent has to be under the Corporation's seal.

Para. 13.
A court order under s.425, Companies Act 1985, governing a compromise or arrangement between a company and its creditors or members, or under s.427, transferring an undertaking or property for the purposes of a reconstruction or amalgamation, is ineffective without the consent of the Corporation (the language suggesting that a court could *make* such an order—without Corporation consent—albeit that it would remain ineffective until such consent was available, *i.e.* consent could be given subsequent to the order). A copy of the relevant consent must be given to the registrar along with the office copy of the order. Nor can there be a conversion of the company into an industrial and provident society without such consent. Nor can there be a voluntary arrangement with the company's creditors under s.1, Insolvency Act 1986 without such consent. Nor can there be a voluntary winding up without such consent. In each case, consent has to be under the Corporation's seal.

Para. 14.

The Corporation has power to present a petition for the winding up (under the Insolvency Act 1986) or either a company or an industrial and provident society, either because the registered social landlord is failing to carry out its purposes or objects, or because it is unable to pay its debts (as defined in *ibid.*, s.123).

Para. 15.

Where an industrial and provident society is dissolved or wound up by reason of insolvency, or a company wound up under the Insolvency Act 1986, the Corporation is to take a transfer (or may order the transfer to another registered social landlord) of whatever remains of the property of the society or company after meeting the claims of the creditors and any other pre-dissolution or winding up liabilities, regardless the provisions of the relevant Acts (Industrial and Provident Societies Act 1965, Companies Act 1985, Insolvency Act 1986) or the rules of the society or the memorandum or articles of association of the company.

Where a registered social landlord which is a charity is dissolved, the available assets may be required by the Corporation to be transferred to another charity, the objects of which appear to be akin to those of the dissolved charity, or as nearly as practicable.

PART III

ACCOUNTS AND AUDIT

General requirements as to accounts and audit

16.—(1) The Corporation may from time to time determine accounting requirements for registered social landlords with a view to ensuring that the accounts of every registered social landlord—

(a) are prepared in a proper form, and

(b) give a true and fair view of—

(i) the state of affairs of the landlord, so far as its housing activities are concerned, and

(ii) the disposition of funds and assets which are, or at any time have been, in its hands in connection with those activities.

(2) The Corporation by a determination under sub-paragraph (1) may lay down a method by which a registered charity is to distinguish in its accounts between its housing activities and other activities.

(3) The accounts of every registered social landlord shall comply with the requirements laid down under this paragraph.

(4) The auditor's report shall state, in addition to any other matters which it is required to state, whether in the auditor's opinion the accounts do so comply.

(5) Every registered social landlord shall furnish to the Corporation a copy of its accounts and auditor's report within six months of the end of the period to which they relate.

Appointment of auditors by industrial and provident societies

17. Section 4 of the Friendly and Industrial and Provident Societies Act 1968 (obligation to appoint qualified auditors to audit accounts and balance sheet for each year of account) applies to every industrial and provident society which is a registered social landlord, without regard to the volume of its receipts and payments, the number of its members or the value of its assets.

Accounting and audit requirements for charities

18.—(1) A registered social landlord which is a registered charity shall, in respect of its housing activities (and separately from its other activities, if any), be subject to the following provisions (which impose accounting and audit requirements corresponding to those imposed by the Friendly and Industrial and Provident Societies Act 1968).

This does not affect any obligation of the charity under sections 41 to 45 of the Charities Act 1993 (charity accounts).

(2) The charity shall in respect of its housing activities—

(a) cause to be kept properly books of account showing its transactions and its assets and liabilities, and

(b) establish and maintain a satisfactory system of control of its books of accounts, its cash holdings and all its receipts and remittances.

The books of account must be such as to enable a true and fair view to be given of the state of affairs of the charity in respect of its housing activities, and to explain its transactions in the course of those activities.

(3) The charity shall for each period of account prepare—
(a) a revenue account giving a true and fair view of the charity's income and expenditure in the period, so far as arising in connection with its housing activities, and
(b) a balance sheet giving a true and fair view as at the end of the period of the state of the charity's affairs.

The revenue account and balance sheet must be signed by at least two directors or trustees of the charity.

(4) The charity shall in each period of account appoint a qualified auditor to audit the accounts prepared in accordance with sub-paragraph (3).

A qualified auditor means a person who is eligible for appointment as auditor of the charity under Part II of the Companies Act 1989 or who would be so eligible if the charity were a company registered under the Companies Act 1985.

(5) The auditor shall make a report to the charity on the accounts audited by him, stating whether in his opinion—
(a) the revenue account gives a true and fair view of the state of income and expenditure of the charity in respect of its housing activities and of any other matters to which it relates, and
(b) the balance sheet gives a true and fair view of the state of affairs of the charity as at the end of the period of account.

(6) The auditor in preparing his report shall carry out such investigations as will enable him to form an opinion as to the following matters—
(a) whether the association has kept, in respect of its housing activities, proper books of account in accordance with the requirements of this paragraph,
(b) whether the charity has maintained a satisfactory system of control over its transactions in accordance with those requirements, and
(c) whether the accounts are in agreement with the charity's books;

and if he is of opinion that the charity has failed in any respect to comply with this paragraph, or if the accounts are not in agreement with the books, he shall state that fact in his report.

(7) The auditor—
(a) has a right of access at all times to the books, deeds and accounts of the charity, so far as relating to its housing activities, and to all other documents relating to those activities, and
(b) is entitled to require from officers of the charity such information and explanations as he thinks necessary for the performance of his duties;

and if he fails to obtain all the information and explanations which, to the best of his knowledge and belief, are necessary for the purposes of his audit, he shall state that fact in his report.

(8) A period of account for the purposes of this paragraph is twelve months or such other period not less than six months or more than 18 months as the charity may, with the consent of the Corporation, determine.

Responsibility for securing compliance with accounting requirements

19.—(1) Every responsible person, that is to say, every person who—
(a) is directly concerned with the conduct and management of the affairs of a registered social landlord, and
(b) is in that capacity responsible for the preparation and audit of accounts,

shall ensure that paragraph 16 (general requirements as to accounts and audit) and, where applicable, paragraph 18 (accounting and audit requirements for charities) are complied with by the registered social landlord.

(2) If—
(a) paragraph 16(5) (furnishing of accounts and auditor's report) is not complied with,
(b) the accounts furnished to the Corporation under that provision do not comply with the accounting requirements laid down under paragraph 16(1),
(c) paragraph 18 (accounting and audit requirements for charities), where applicable, is not complied with,
(d) section 55(9) of the Housing Act 1988 (surplus rental income: power to require information) is not complied with, or
(e) any notice under section 26 (information relating to disposal proceeds fund) is not complied with,

every responsible person, and the registered social landlord itself, commits a summary offence and is liable on conviction to a fine not exceeding level 3 on the standard scale.

(3) In proceedings for an offence under this paragraph it is a defence—
(a) for a responsible person to prove that he did everything that could reasonably have been expected of him by way of discharging the relevant duty;
(b) for a registered social landlord to prove that every responsible person did everything that

could reasonably have been expected of him by way of discharging the relevant duty in relation to the registered social landlord.

(4) Proceedings for an offence under this paragraph may be brought only by or with the consent of the Corporation or the Director of Public Prosecutions.

GENERAL NOTE

Para. 16.

The Corporation is empowered to establish accounting requirements to ensure that all registered social landlords prepare their accounts in a proper form which gives a "true and fair view" of the state of affairs of the landlord so far as concerns its housing activities and the disposition of its funds and assets which are or have been in its hands in connection with such activities.

Every registered social landlord has to provide the Corporation with a copy of the accounts, and the auditor's report thereon certifying, *inter alia*, compliance with these requirements, within six months of the end of the period to which they relate.

All registered social landlords will be under some form of obligation to prepare and provide accounts, whether as an industrial and provident society, a charity (but see now, para. 18, below) or a company: the purpose of this provision is to ensure that all social landlords comply with accounting requirements—so far as they concern their housing activities—in a uniform way.

Para. 17.

Industrial and provident societies are obliged to appoint a qualified auditor for each year of account: Friendly and Industrial and Provident Societies Act 1968, s.4. Small societies—as defined—are, however, exempt: *ibid.*, s.4(2). This means where the receipts and payments did not exceed £5,000 in aggregate, there were no more than 500 members in that year, and the value of the assets at the end of the year did not exceed £5,000: *ibid.* This exemption is inapplicable in the case of a registered social landlord, *i.e.* even such a small landlord is bound by s.4.

Para. 18.

Extended accounting requirements—analogous to those applicable to industrial and provident societies—are applicable to registered charities who are registered social landlords, "in respect of its housing activities (and separately from its other activities, if any) ...".

"Housing activities" means all the activities of the registered social landlord in pursuance of the purposes, objects and powers mentioned in (or prescribed under) s.2, see notes thereto, above.

Para. 19.

It is a criminal offence, punishable by a fine not exceeding level 3 on the standard scale, committed by "every responsible person" and the landlord itself, to fail to comply with specified parts of the accounting requirements in paras. 16 and 18. A responsible person is one who is directly concerned with the conduct and management of the affairs of the landlord, and who in that capacity has responsibility for the preparation and audit of accounts (accordingly, an external accountant or auditor would not seem to be brought within the definition). It is a defence to proceedings for a responsible person to prove (*n.b.* burden) that he did everything that could reasonably have been expected of him to discharge the relevant duty, and for a landlord to prove (*n.b.*) that every responsible person did everything that could reasonably have thus been expected.

An offence can only be brought by or with the consent of either the Corporation or the D.P.P.

See also s.223, above, as to the concurrent liability of a director, manager, secretary or other similar officer of a corporate body with whose consent or connivance an offence is proved to have been committed.

PART IV

INQUIRY INTO AFFAIRS OF REGISTERED SOCIAL LANDLORDS

Inquiry

20.—(1) The Corporation may direct an inquiry into the affairs of a registered social landlord if it appears to the Corporation that there may have been misconduct or mismanagement.

For this purpose "misconduct" includes any failure to comply with the requirements of this Part of this Act.

(2) Any such inquiry shall be conducted by one or more persons appointed by the Corporation.

(3) If one person is appointed he must be a person who is not a member or an employee of the Corporation and has not been such a member or employee within the previous five years; and if more than one person is appointed at least one of them must be such a person.

(4) If the Corporation so directs, or if during the course of the inquiry the person or persons conducting the inquiry consider it necessary, the inquiry shall extend to the affairs of any other body which at any material time is or was a subsidiary or associate of the registered social landlord.

(5) The person or persons conducting the inquiry may, if they think fit during the course of the inquiry, make one or more interim reports on such matters as appear to them to be appropriate.

(6) On completion of the inquiry the person or persons conducting the inquiry shall make a final report on such matters as the Corporation may specify.

(7) An interim or final report shall be in such form as the Corporation may specify.

Power of appointed person to obtain information

21.—(1) A person appointed by the Corporation under paragraph 20 to conduct an inquiry (or, if more than one person is so appointed, each of those persons) has, for the purposes of the inquiry, the same powers as are conferred on the Corporation by section 30 (general power to obtain information).

(2) Where by virtue of a notice under that section given by an appointed person any documents are produced to any person, the person to whom they are produced may take copies of or make extracts from them.

(3) Section 31 (enforcement of notice to provide information, &c.) applies in relation to a notice given under this paragraph by an appointed person as it applies in relation to a notice given under section 30 by the Corporation.

Extraordinary audit for purposes of inquiry

22.—(1) For the purposes of an inquiry under paragraph 20 the Corporation may require the accounts and balance sheet of the registered social landlord concerned, or such of them as the Corporation may specify, to be audited by a qualified auditor appointed by the Corporation.

(2) A person is a qualified auditor for this purpose if he would be eligible for appointment as auditor of the ordinary accounts of the registered social landlord.

(3) On completion of the audit the appointed auditor shall make a report to the Corporation on such matters and in such form as the Corporation may specify.

(4) The expenses of the audit, including the remuneration of the auditor, shall be paid by the Corporation.

(5) An audit under this paragraph is additional to, and does not affect, any audit made or to be made under any other enactment.

Powers exercisable on interim basis

23.—(1) The Corporation may make an order under this paragraph—
(a) where an inquiry has been directed under paragraph 20 and the Corporation has reasonable grounds to believe—
    (i) that there has been misconduct or mismanagement in the affairs of the registered social landlord, and
    (ii) that immediate action is needed to protect the interests of the tenants of the registered social landlord or to protect the assets of the landlord; or
(b) where an interim report has been made under paragraph 20(5) as a result of which the Corporation is satisfied that there has been misconduct or mismanagement in the affairs of a registered social landlord.

(2) The orders that may be made under this paragraph are—
(a) an order suspending any officer, employee or agent of the registered social landlord who appears to the Corporation to have been responsible for or privy to the misconduct or mismanagement or by his conduct to have contributed to or facilitated it;
(b) an order directing any bank or other person who holds money or securities on behalf of the registered social landlord not to part with the money or securities without the approval of the Corporation;
(c) an order restricting the transactions which may be entered into, or the nature or amount of the payments which may be made, by the registered social landlord without the approval of the Corporation.

(3) An order under this paragraph, if not previously revoked by the Corporation, shall cease to have effect six months after the making of the final report under paragraph 20(6) unless the Corporation renews it, which it may do for a further period of up to six months.

(4) A person suspended by an order under sub-paragraph (2)(a) may appeal against the order to the High Court.

(5) Where a person is suspended by such an order, the Corporation may give directions with respect to the performance of his functions and otherwise as to matters arising from his suspension.

The Corporation may, in particular, appoint a named person to perform his functions.

(6) A person who contravenes an order under sub-paragraph (2)(b) commits an offence and is liable on summary conviction to a fine not exceeding level 5 on the standard scale or imprisonment for a term not exceeding three months, or both.

Proceedings for such an offence may be brought only by or with the consent of the Corporation or the Director of Public Prosecutions.

Powers exercisable as a result of final report or audit

24.—(1) Where the Corporation is satisfied, as the result of an inquiry under paragraph 20 or an audit under paragraph 22, that there has been misconduct or mismanagement in the affairs of a registered social landlord, it may make an order under this paragraph.

(2) The orders that may be made under this paragraph are—

(a) an order removing any officer, employee or agent of the registered social landlord who appears to the Corporation to have been responsible for or privy to the misconduct or mismanagement or by his conduct to have contributed to or facilitated it;

(b) an order suspending any such person for up to six months, pending determination whether he should be removed;

(c) an order directing any bank or other person who holds money or securities on behalf of the registered social landlord not to part with the money or securities without the approval of the Corporation;

(d) an order restricting the transactions which may be entered into, or the nature or amount of the payments which may be made, by the registered social landlord without the approval of the Corporation.

(3) Before making an order under sub-paragraph (2)(a) the Corporation shall give at least 14 days' notice of its intention to do so—

(a) to the person it intends to remove, and

(b) to the registered social landlord concerned.

Notice under this sub-paragraph may be given by post, and if so given to the person whom the Corporation intends to remove may be addressed to his last known address in the United Kingdom.

(4) A person who is ordered to be removed under sub-paragraph (2)(a) or suspended under sub-paragraph (2)(b) may appeal against the order to the High Court.

(5) Where a person is suspended under sub-paragraph (2)(b), the Corporation may give directions with respect to the performance of his functions and otherwise as to matters arising from the suspension.

The Corporation may, in particular, appoint a named person to perform his functions.

(6) A person who contravenes an order under sub-paragraph (2)(c) commits an offence and is liable on summary conviction to a fine not exceeding level 5 on the standard scale or imprisonment for a term not exceeding three months, or both.

Proceedings for such an offence may be brought only by or with the consent of the Corporation or the Director of Public Prosecutions.

Disqualification as officer of registered social landlord

25.—(1) A person is disqualified from being an officer of a registered social landlord if the Corporation has made an order against him under—

(a) paragraph 24(2)(a) (removal for misconduct or mismanagement), or

(b) section 30(1)(a) of the Housing Associations Act 1985 or section 20(1)(a) of the Housing Act 1974 (corresponding earlier provisions).

(2) The Corporation may, on the application of any such person, waive his disqualification either generally or in relation to a particular registered social landlord or particular class of registered social landlord.

(3) Any waiver shall be notified in writing to the person concerned.

(4) For the purposes of this paragraph the Corporation shall keep, in such manner as it thinks fit, a register of all persons who have been removed from office by the Corporation under the provisions mentioned in sub-paragraph (1).

(5) The register shall be available for public inspection at all reasonable times.

Persons acting as officer while disqualified

26.—(1) A person who acts as an officer of a registered social landlord while he is disqualified under paragraph 25(1) commits an offence.

A person guilty of such an offence is liable—
(a) on summary conviction, to imprisonment for a term not exceeding six months or to a fine not exceeding the statutory maximum, or both;
(b) on conviction on indictment, to imprisonment for a term not exceeding two years or to a fine, or both.

(2) Proceedings for an offence under sub-paragraph (1) may be brought only by or with the consent of the Corporation or the Director of Public Prosecutions.

(3) Acts done as an officer of a registered social landlord by a person who is disqualified under paragraph 25(1) are not invalid by reason only of that disqualification.

(4) Where the Corporation is satisfied—
(a) that a person has acted as an officer of a registered social landlord while disqualified under paragraph 25(1), and
(b) that while so acting he has received from the registered social landlord any payments or benefits in connection with his so acting,

it may by order direct him to repay to the registered social landlord the whole or part of any such sums or, as the case may be, to pay to it the whole or part of the monetary value (as determined by it) of any such benefit.

Power to direct transfer of land

27.—(1) Where as a result of an inquiry under paragraph 20 or an audit under paragraph 22 the Corporation is satisfied as regards a registered social landlord—
(a) that there has been misconduct or mismanagement in its administration, or
(b) that the management of its land would be improved if its land were transferred in accordance with the provisions of this paragraph,

the Corporation may, with the consent of the Secretary of State, direct the registered social landlord to make such a transfer.

(2) Where the registered social landlord concerned is a charity, the Corporation may only direct a transfer to be made to another registered social landlord—
(a) which is also a charity, and
(b) the objects of which appear to the Corporation to be, as nearly as practicable, akin to those of the registered social landlord concerned.

(3) In any other case the Corporation may direct a transfer to be made to the Corporation or to another registered social landlord.

(4) The transfer shall be on such terms as the Corporation may direct on the basis of principles determined by it.

The consent of the Secretary of State is required both for the terms of the transfer and for the determination of the principles on which it is based.

(5) The price shall not be less than the amount certified by the district valuer to be the amount the property would command if sold by a willing seller to another registered social landlord.

(6) The terms shall include provision as to the payment of debts and liabilities (including debts and liabilities secured on the land).

Availability of powers in relation to registered charities

28.—(1) The Corporation may exercise its powers under paragraphs 20 to 26 in relation to a registered charity only if the charity has, at any time before the powers are exercised—
(a) received financial assistance under section 24 of the Local Government Act 1988 (assistance for privately let housing accommodation),
(b) had property transferred to it on a qualifying disposal under section 135 of the Leasehold Reform, Housing and Urban Development Act 1993, or
(c) received a grant or loan under any of the following provisions.

(2) The provisions are—
     section 18 of this Act (social housing grant),
     section 22 of this Act or section 58 of the Housing Associations Act 1985 (grants or loans by local authorities),
     section 50 of the Housing Act 1988, section 41 of the Housing Associations Act 1985 or any enactment replaced by that section (housing association grant),
     section 51 of the Housing Act 1988 or section 54 or 55 of the Housing Associations Act 1985 (revenue deficit grant or hostel deficit grant),
     section 79 of the Housing Associations Act 1985 (loans by Housing Corporation),
     section 31 of the Housing Act 1974 (management grants), or
     any enactment mentioned in paragraph 2 or 3 of Schedule 1 to the Housing Associations Act 1985 (pre-1974 grants and certain loans).

(3) In relation to a registered charity paragraphs 20 to 26 have effect with the following adaptations—

(a) references to its affairs are confined to its housing activities and such other activities (if any) as are incidental to or connected with its housing activities;

(b) references to its accounts do not include revenue accounts which do not relate to its housing activities, except so far as such accounts are necessary for the auditing of revenue accounts which do so relate or of the balance sheet;

(c) a person is a qualified auditor for the purpose of paragraph 22 (extraordinary audit) only if he is an auditor qualified for the purposes of paragraph 18 (accounting and audit requirements for charities).

(4) The Corporation shall notify the Charity Commissioners upon the exercise in relation to a registered charity of its powers under—

(a) paragraph 20(1) (inquiry into affairs of registered social landlord),

(b) paragraph 23(2)(a) (interim suspension of person in connection with misconduct or mismanagement), or

(c) paragraph 24(2)(a) or (b) (removal of person in connection with misconduct or mismanagement or suspension with a view to removal).

29. The Corporation may not exercise its powers under paragraph 27 in relation to a registered charity.

GENERAL NOTE

Para. 20.

The best-known power of the Corporation—and its lurking sanction—was the power to direct an inquiry into the affairs of a housing association, now available in relation to any registered social landlord. It is exercisable "if it appears to the Corporation that there may have been misconduct or mismanagement". For this purpose, misconduct includes any failure to comply with requirements of Sched. 1, Pt. IV, itself (see below).

There are three reasons why the phraseology produces a low threshold for action: first, because it need only "appear to" (*cf.* notes to s.188, above) the Corporation that—secondly— there "may have been" misconduct or mismanagement (*cf.* paras. 23, 24, below), and thirdly because the courts can be expected to resist challenge to mere *investigation* where public monies are involved. The only obvious candidate for challenge would be a case that the Corporation were using their powers not on account of misconduct or mismanagement but for some ulterior—*e.g.* policy—purpose of its own. As the Corporation has additional powers under Chap. IV, above (see generally, General Note to s.7, above), however, such recourse should be unnecessary.

The Corporation can only exercise this power by appointing one or more persons to conduct it, not being—or if more than one, at least one of whom is not—someone who has been a member or employee of the Corporation during the preceding five years. The Corporation may direct that the inquiry can extend to the affairs of a subsidiary or associate of the registered social landlord. As to subsidiary, see notes to s.60, below; as to associate, see notes to s.6. The appointed person may issue one or more interim reports, as seems appropriate, and there must be a final report on such matters as the Corporation specify on completion of the inquiry.

Where there is more than one person appointed jointly to conduct the inquiry, and they do not agree on any matter relating to its conduct, then the view of the majority prevails (*i.e.* presumably if an odd number of persons appointed), but each can make an interim, and each *shall* make a final, report, either jointly or separately, *e.g.* in different factions.

Para. 21.

A person appointed to conduct an inquiry has the same powers to obtain information as does the Corporation under s.31, see notes thereto above. It is a criminal offence for a registered social landlord or other person on whom a notice may be served without reasonable excuse to fail to comply with a notice to provide information (in the form and manner, and at the time and place, as the notice may specify) or to produce documents (at the time and place specified): s.32.

Para. 22.

The Corporation can require the accounts of the registered social landlord audited by a qualified auditor, *i.e.* any auditor eligible to be appointed as an auditor to the ordinary accounts of a registered social landlord (which in turn depends, *inter alia*, on the specific regulatory requirements of the constitutional regime in question), *i.e.* can cause a special audit to be carried out.

Para. 23.

Even if an inquiry is not completed, the Corporation has interim powers exercisable where it "has reasonable grounds to believe (i) that there has been misconduct or mismanagement . . . , and (ii) that immediate action is needed to protect the interests of the tenants . . . or . . . the assets of the landlord . . .". The words "has been misconduct" etc., may be contrasted with the words of para. 20, that "there may have been misconduct", as indeed may the introduction of "reasonable grounds" for the belief.

The Corporation may also act on the basis of an interim report (above, para. 20) as a result of which it "is satisfied that there has been misconduct or mismanagement". In other words, a lower standard may be adopted—albeit higher than is required under para. 20 to justify initiation of an inquiry—provided that there are reasonable grounds for believing that there has been misconduct, etc., *and* for believing that immediate action is necessary (on the grounds stated)—or if the higher standard of satisfaction (on the basis of the interim report) is fulfilled, there is no requirement to consider the need for immediate action.

The interim orders that may be made include suspension of officers (see General Note to s.7, above), employees or agents (responsible for or privy to, or having contributed to or facilitated, the misconduct or mismanagement), directing assets not to be released by bankers or others without the consent of the Corporation (breach of which direction is subject to criminal sanctions), and subjecting to the consent of the Corporation the exercise of powers of the landlord (so far as so restricted). (See also s.223, above, as to the concurrent liability of a director, manager, secretary or other similar officer of a corporate body with whose consent or connivance an offence is proved to have been committed.)

An interim order lasts initially for no more than six months, but may then be renewed for a single further period of six months. The order may be appealed to the High Court: see notes to s.6, above. The Corporation may also appoint a person to perform the functions of a person who has been suspended.

Para. 24.
Where, on the basis of an inquiry under para. 20 or an audit under para. 22, the Corporation is satisfied that there has been misconduct or mismanagement in the affairs of a registered social landlord, it enjoys the same powers, but on a permanent basis. "Satisfaction" is clearly a higher standard than either (under para. 20) "may have been" or (under para. 23) "has reasonable grounds to believe . . . that there has been". The orders that may be made are as follows:
    (a) Removal of officer (see General Note to s.7, above), employee or agent (responsible for or privy to, or having contributed to or facilitated, the misconduct or mismanagement); before using this power the Corporation must give both to the body in question and to the person it intends to remove a minimum of 14 days notice, in the latter case by serving the notice at his last known address in the U.K. See also paras. 25, 26, below, for the long-term consequences of a removal order;
    (b) Suspension of such a person for up to six months, pending a decision on removal;
    (c) Directing assets not to be released by bankers or others without the consent of the Corporation (breach of which direction is subject to criminal sanctions: see also s.223, above, as to the concurrent liability of a director, manager, secretary or other similar officer of a corporate body with whose consent or connivance an offence is proved to have been committed);
    (d) Subjecting to the consent of the Corporation the exercise of powers of the landlord (so far as so restricted).
A removal or a suspending order may be appealed to the High Court: see notes to s.6, above. Where a person has been suspended, the Corporation may give directions regarding his functions and otherwise as to matters arising from the suspension, and may appoint a person to perform his functions.

Para. 25.
The sting in the tail of a removal order is disqualification from being an officer (see General Note to s.7, above) of a registered social landlord if a removal order has been made under either para. 24 or under the corresponding earlier provisions of the Housing Associations Act 1985, s.30 (and its predecessor provision of the Housing Act 1974, s.20). The disqualification may be waived in general or in relation to a particular social landlord, or class of social landlord. The Corporation must keep a register of persons removed from office, which is open to public inspection at all reasonable times. Disqualification is *not* appealable to the High Court and could, therefore, only be challenged (if at all) by judicial review: see notes to s.1, above.

Para. 26.
Acting as an officer (see General Note to s.7, above) of a registered social landlord while disqualified is an offence (carrying not merely a fine, but the possibility of imprisonment), but acts done by an officer while disqualified are not invalid for that reason alone. If the Corporation

is satisfied that a person has received payment or other benefits in connection with acting as an officer while disqualified, it can order repayment of the whole or part of the sums or value of the benefit. Proceedings require the consent of the Corporation, or the Director of Public Prosecutions.

Para. 27.

Where satisfied as a result of an inquiry under para. 20 or an audit under para. 22 *either* that there has been misconduct or mismanagement, *or* (merely) that the management of the social landlord's land would be improved if transferred, the Corporation may order the land to be transferred to the Corporation or another social landlord (save, in the case of a charity, that the transfer must be to another registered charity, the objects of which are—as nearly as practicable—akin to those of the landlord from which the land is being transferred.

These powers can only be exercised with the consent of the Secretary of State not merely for the transfer itself, but also for the terms of the transfer (which must include provision for the payment of debts and liabilities, including those secured on the land) and the principles on which it is based. The price for the transfer is to be not less than the amount certified by the District Valuer as the amount the property would command if sold by a willing seller to another registered social landlord.

Para. 28.

The exercise of powers under paras. 20–26 (inquiry to disqualification) can be exercised in relation to a registered charity only if it has received assistance under the same provisions as under para. 5, above. In such a case, the powers confined to the housing activities of the charity, and only their other activities if they are incidental to or connected with its housing activities, and to the accounts of the charity which relate to its housing activities (save so far as other accounts are necessary to the audit of the housing-related accounts). The Corporation must notify the Charity Commissioners on exercising the powers to conduct an inquiry, or to suspend a person on an interim basis under para. 23, or to remove or suspend under para. 24.

Section 51   SCHEDULE 2

SOCIAL RENTED SECTOR: HOUSING COMPLAINTS

Social landlords required to be member of approved scheme

1.—(1) A social landlord must be a member of an approved scheme covering, or more than one approved scheme which together cover, all his housing activities.

(2) If a social landlord fails to comply with the duty imposed by this paragraph, the Secretary of State may apply to the High Court for an order directing him to comply within a specified period and the High Court may, if it thinks fit, make such an order.

(3) Nothing in this Schedule shall be construed as restricting membership of an approved scheme to social landlords.

Matters for which scheme must provide

2.—(1) A scheme shall not be approved for the purposes of this Schedule unless it makes provision for—

1. The establishment or appointment of an independent person to administer the scheme.
2. The criteria for membership for—
    (a) social landlords under a duty to be members of an approved scheme, and
    (b) other persons.
3. The manner of becoming or ceasing to be a member.
4. The matters about which complaints may be made under the scheme.
5. The grounds on which a matter may be excluded from investigation, including that the matter is the subject of court proceedings or was the subject of court proceedings where judgment on the merits was given.
6. The descriptions of individual who may make a complaint under the scheme.
7. The appointment of an independent individual to be the housing ombudsman under the scheme.
8. The appointment of staff to administer the scheme and to assist the housing ombudsman and the terms upon which they are appointed.
9. A duty of the housing ombudsman to investigate any complaint duly made and not withdrawn, and a power to investigate any complaint duly made but withdrawn, and where he investigates to make a determination.
10. A power of the housing ombudsman to propose alternative methods of resolving a dispute.

11. The powers of the housing ombudsman for the purposes of his investigations, and the procedure to be followed in the conduct of investigations.

12. The powers of the housing ombudsman on making a determination.

13. The making and publication of annual reports by the housing ombudsman on the discharge of his functions.

14. The manner in which determinations are to be—

(a) communicated to the complainant and the person against whom the complaint was made, and

(b) published.

15. The manner in which the expenses of the scheme are to be defrayed by the members.

16. The keeping and auditing of accounts and the submission of accounts to the Secretary of State.

17. The making of annual reports on the administration of the scheme.

18. The manner of amending the scheme.

(2) The Secretary of State may by order amend sub-paragraph (1) by adding to or deleting from it any item or by varying any item for the time being contained in it.

(3) An order under sub-paragraph (2) shall be made by statutory instrument which shall be subject to annulment in pursuance of a resolution of either House of Parliament.

Approval of scheme, or amendment, and withdrawal of approval

3.—(1) An application to the Secretary of State for approval of a scheme shall be made in such manner as the Secretary of State may determine, and shall be accompanied by such information as the Secretary of State may require.

(2) If it appears to the Secretary of State that the scheme—

(a) provides for the matters specified in paragraph 2, and

(b) is a satisfactory scheme for the purposes of this Schedule,

he shall approve the scheme.

(3) An amendment of an approved scheme is not effective unless approved by the Secretary of State.

Sub-paragraph (1) applies in relation to an application for approval of an amendment as it applies to an application for approval of a scheme; and the Secretary of State shall approve the amendment if it appears to him that the scheme as amended meets the conditions in sub-paragraph (2).

(4) The Secretary of State may withdraw his approval of a scheme.

(5) If the Secretary of State proposes to withdraw his approval of a scheme, he shall serve on the person administering the scheme and on the housing ombudsman under the scheme, a notice stating—

(a) that he proposes to withdraw his approval,

(b) the grounds for the proposed withdrawal of his approval, and

(c) that the person receiving the notice may make representations with respect to the proposed withdrawal of approval within such period of not less than 14 days as is specified in the notice;

and he shall, before reaching a decision on whether to withdraw approval, consider any representations duly made to him.

(6) The Secretary of State shall give notice of his decision on a proposal to withdraw approval of a scheme, together with his reasons, to every person on whom he served a notice under sub-paragraph (5).

(7) Withdrawal of approval by the Secretary of State has effect from such date as is specified in the notice of his decision.

(8) Where the person administering a scheme is given notice of a decision to withdraw approval of the scheme, he shall give notice of the decision to every member of the scheme.

Notice to he given of becoming a member of an approved scheme

4.—(1) A social landlord who—

(a) becomes a member of an approved scheme, or

(b) is a member of a scheme which becomes an approved scheme,

shall, within the period of 21 days beginning with the date of becoming a member or, as the case may be, of being informed of the Secretary of State's approval of the scheme, give notice of that fact to the Corporation.

(2) The Corporation, on receiving the notice, shall record his membership of an approved scheme.

(3) A person who fails to comply with sub-paragraph (1) commits an offence and is liable on summary conviction to a fine not exceeding level 4 on the standard scale.

Proceedings for such an offence may be brought only by or with the consent of the Corporation or the Director of Public Prosecutions.

Withdrawal from approved scheme

5.—(1) A social landlord wishing to withdraw from membership of an approved scheme shall send notice of his proposed withdrawal to the Corporation.

(2) The notice shall specify—

(a) the housing activities in relation to which he is subject to investigation under the scheme,

(b) the approved scheme or schemes of which he is also a member or will, on his withdrawal, become a member, and

(c) under which scheme or schemes the housing activities mentioned in paragraph (a) will be subject to investigation after his withdrawal.

(3) If the Corporation is satisfied that withdrawal by the landlord from the scheme will not result in a failure to comply with his duty under paragraph 1, it shall confirm the landlord's withdrawal from the scheme.

(4) If the Corporation is not so satisfied, it shall withhold confirmation of the landlord's withdrawal from the scheme; and the landlord shall continue to be a member of the scheme and bound and entitled under the scheme accordingly.

Register of approved schemes

6.—(1) The Corporation shall maintain a register of schemes approved by the Secretary of State for the purposes of this Schedule and of the social landlords who are members of those schemes.

(2) The Secretary of State shall give notice to the Corporation—

(a) when he grants or withdraws his approval of a scheme, and

(b) when he approves an amendment of a scheme,

and he shall supply the Corporation with copies of any approved scheme or any amendment to a scheme.

(3) A member of the public shall be entitled, upon payment of such fees as the Corporation may determine, to receive a copy of an approved scheme and a list of the social landlords who are members of it.

Determinations by housing ombudsman

7.—(1) A housing ombudsman under an approved scheme shall investigate any complaint duly made to him and not withdrawn, and may investigate any complaint duly made but withdrawn, and where he investigates a complaint he shall determine it by reference to what is, in his opinion, fair in all the circumstances of the case.

(2) He may in his determination—

(a) order the member of a scheme against whom the complaint was made to pay compensation to the complainant, and

(b) order that the member or the complainant shall not exercise or require the performance of any of the contractual or other obligations or rights existing between them.

(3) If the member against whom the complaint was made fails to comply with the determination within a reasonable time, the housing ombudsman may order him to publish in such manner as the ombudsman sees fit that he has failed to comply with the determination.

(4) Where the member is not a social landlord, the housing ombudsman may also order that the member—

(a) be expelled from the scheme, and

(b) publish in such manner as the housing ombudsman sees fit that he has been expelled and the reasons for his expulsion.

(5) If a person fails to comply with an order under sub-paragraph (3) or (4)(b), the housing ombudsman may take such steps as he thinks appropriate to publish what the member ought to have published and recover from the member the costs of doing so.

(6) A member who is ordered by the housing ombudsman to pay compensation or take any other steps has power to do so, except that a member which is also a charity shall not do anything contrary to its trusts.

Publication of determinations, &c.

8.—(1) A housing ombudsman under an approved scheme may publish—

(a) his determination on any complaint, and

(b) such reports as he thinks fit on the discharge of his functions.

(2) He may include in any such determination or report statements, communications, reports, papers or other documentary evidence obtained in the exercise of his functions.

(3) In publishing any determination or report, a housing ombudsman shall have regard to the need for excluding so far as practicable—

(a) any matter which relates to the private affairs of an individual, where publication would seriously and prejudicially affect the interests of that individual, and

(b) any matter which relates specifically to the affairs of a member of an approved scheme, where publication would seriously and prejudicially affect its interests, unless the inclusion of that matter is necessary for the purposes of the determination or report.

Absolute privilege for communications, &c.

9. For the purposes of the law of defamation absolute privilege attaches to—

(a) any communication between a housing ombudsman under an approved scheme and any person by or against whom a complaint is made to him,

(b) any determination by such an ombudsman, and

(c) the publication of such a determination or any report under paragraph 8.

Appointment and status of housing ombudsman

10.—(1) Where an approved scheme provides that it shall be administered by a body corporate, that body shall appoint on such terms as it thinks fit the housing ombudsman for the purposes of the scheme and the appointment and its terms shall be subject to the approval of the Secretary of State.

(2) Where an approved scheme does not so provide—

(a) the housing ombudsman for the purposes of the scheme shall be appointed by the Secretary of State on such terms as the Secretary of State thinks fit,

(b) the Secretary of State may by order provide that the housing ombudsman for the purposes of the scheme shall be a corporation sole, and

(c) the staff to administer the scheme and otherwise assist the ombudsman in the discharge of his functions shall be appointed and employed by him.

(3) The Secretary of State may at any time remove from office a housing ombudsman (whether appointed by him or otherwise).

(4) A housing ombudsman appointed by the Secretary of State or otherwise shall not be regarded as the servant or agent of the Crown or as enjoying any status, privilege or immunity of the Crown or as exempt from any tax, duty, rate, levy or other charge whatsoever, whether general or local, and any property held by him shall not be regarded as property of, or held on behalf of, the Crown.

Subscriptions payable in respect of approved schemes

11.—(1) Members of an approved scheme shall pay a subscription, calculated as set out in the scheme, to the person administering the scheme.

(2) If a social landlord fails to comply with his duty under paragraph 1, the Secretary of State may determine—

(a) which approved scheme or schemes he should have joined, and

(b) what sums by way of subscription he should have paid,

and may require him to pay those amounts to the person administering the scheme or schemes.

(3) The person administering an approved scheme may recover sums payable under subparagraph (1) or (2) as if they were debts due to him.

(4) The Secretary of State or the Corporation may pay grant and provide other financial assistance to—

(a) a body corporate administering an approved scheme, or

(b) in a case where paragraph 10(2) applies, to the housing ombudsman under an approved scheme,

for such purposes and upon such terms as the Secretary of State or, as the case may be, the Corporation thinks fit.

GENERAL NOTE

Para. 1.

Once a landlord qualifies as a "social landlord" and, thence, as an obligatory member of an approved scheme, all of its housing activities must be covered. The social landlord may, however, belong to more than one approved scheme, and if it does so, it is only necessary that all of its housing activities are covered by the schemes taken together, *e.g.* if there is a special scheme for retirement lettings.

The Secretary of State may obtain an order of the High Court to require a social landlord to join an approved scheme.

Para. 2.

To qualify for approval, the scheme has to cover a schedule of matters (which the Secretary of State may add to or delete from):

1. Independent person to administer scheme (see below, 7);

2. Membership criteria (both for social landlords who have to belong to an approved scheme and voluntary members);

3. Joining and quitting membership of the scheme;

4. What matters may be the subject of complaint;

5. The grounds on which matters *prima facie* within the scheme may yet be excluded from investigation, *e.g.* subject matter of court proceedings;

6. Who may complain (which *could* include people who live near a social landlord's property);

7. Independent person to be the scheme's Housing Ombudsman (see above, 1);

8. Appointment of staff and terms;

9. The Housing Ombudsman's duty to investigate and to make a determination, and power to continue to investigate and determine a complaint that has been withdrawn (see also para. 7, below);

10. The Housing Ombudsman's power to propose an alternative method of resolving a dispute;

11. The Housing Ombudsman's investigative powers and procedures;

12. The Housing Ombudsman's powers on reaching a determination;

13. Annual reports by the Housing Ombudsman;

14. Method of communicating and publishing determinations;

15. How the expenses of the scheme are to be met by its members;

16. Accounts and audit, and the submission of accounts to the Secretary of State;

17. Annual reports on administration of the scheme; and,

18. How the scheme may be amended.

Para. 3.

The Secretary of State is to determine how applications for approval of schemes are to be made. A scheme must be approved if it covers the matters in para. 2 *and* "is a satisfactory scheme for the purposes of this Schedule". Again, there is an absence of definition: indeed, there is still no mention of unfairness or maladministration (see *e.g.* Parliamentary Commissioner Act 1967 (c. 13), Commissioner for Complaints Act (Northern Ireland) 1969, Local Government Act 1974 (c. 7), National Health Service Act 1977 (c. 49), Building Societies Act 1986 (c. 53), Pension Schemes Act 1993 (c. 48)).

Any amendment of the scheme must secure the approval of the Secretary of State; and, the Secretary of State's approval of a scheme may be withdrawn (on notice, providing both the scheme's administrator and its Housing Ombudsman with an opportunity to comment). It is the obligation of the scheme's administrator to notify scheme members of withdrawal of approval.

Para. 4.

The Corporation must record membership of schemes by social landlords (whether registered social landlords or not), and social landlords are obliged (under sanction of a fine) to notify the Corporation within 21 days of becoming a member of an approved scheme, or of a scheme to which it belongs becoming approved. Prosecution may be with the consent of the Corporation or of the Director of Public Prosecutions.

Para. 5.

Notice must be given to the Corporation of intention to withdraw from an approved scheme, identifying any housing activities currently being investigated under the scheme, its proposed replacement approved scheme, and which approved scheme will continue the investigation. The Corporation must confirm withdrawal if satisfied that the landlord will not be in breach of its duty to belong to an approved scheme; it must withhold confirmation if not so satisfied.

Para. 6.

The Corporation must maintain a register of approved schemes and social landlords which belong to them, which must be provided to members of the public on payment of a fee determined by the Corporation. The Secretary of State must notify the Corporation of the grant or withdrawal of approval, and the approval of an amendment.

Para. 7.

The Housing Ombudsman has power to order the member of a scheme against whom a complaint was made to pay compensation: this might have been implied in any event (see *Westminster C.C. v. Haywood*, *The Times*, March 12, 1995, although based on the power to direct "steps" to be taken—held to include compensation for distress and inconvenience—in Pension Schemes Act 1993, s.151. The case is subject to appeal). Social landlords are deemed to have power to pay such compensation, save that a charitable social landlord cannot do so if it would be contrary to its trusts.

The Housing Ombudsman also has power to order the member or the complainant not to "exercise or require the performance of any of the contractual or other obligations or rights existing between them". This is a bizarre formulation, and it is difficult to see that an order of the Housing Ombudsman could, *e.g.* limit the provisions of s.11, Landlord and Tenant Act 1985 (principal repairing covenant) which cannot itself be contracted out of without the permission of a county court (see its s.12). For how long will this last? Must a tenant dissatisfied with the order get it quashed by judicial review?

If the member fails to comply with the determination within a reasonable time, the Housing Ombudsman may order him to publish a statement of his failure; if the member is not a social landlord, *i.e.* a mandatory member, it may also be ordered to be expelled and be obliged to publish a statement saying why. To enforce either category of publication order—each of which requires publication "in such manner as the ombudsman sees fit"—the Housing Ombudsman may himself take such steps as he considers appropriate to publish what the member ought to have published, and recover from the members his costs of doing so.

There is no obligation to inform, *e.g.*, other tenants of the failure, *cf.* Building Societies Act 1986, Sched. 12, Pt. III, para. 6, obliging the body to comply with the direction if it accepts the determination, and only permitting the body to decline to do so if it gives notice to its members, and to the public, of its reasons for doing so (see Local Government Act 1974, ss.30–31A; see also, *e.g.* Pensions Schemes Act 1993, s.151, by which a determination of the Pensions Ombudsman is final and binding subject only to appeal on a point of law).

Para. 8.

This empowers the Housing Ombudsman to publish his determination, and such reports as he thinks fit on the discharge of his function, and include in either statements, communications, reports, papers or other documentary evidence, after having regard to the need, so far as is practicable, to exclude matters relating to the private affairs of an individual, where publication would seriously and prejudicially affect his interests, or matters relating to the affairs of a member of an approved scheme, where publication would affect his interests in the same way, *unless* inclusion of that matter is necessary for the purposes of the publication.

Para. 9.

Communications with, and publications by, the Housing Ombudsman attach absolute privilege.

Para. 10.

If the approved scheme is to be administered by a body corporate, it appoints its Housing Ombudsman on such terms as it thinks fit, but subject to the approval of the Secretary of State (as to appointment and terms); if the approved scheme is to be administered by an individual, then the Secretary of State himself appoints and determines the terms of the Housing Ombudsman (and may remove him).

Para. 11.

The schemes are intended to be self-financing, from the subscriptions of their members. A social landlord who fails to join an approved scheme may be subject to a determination by the Secretary of State as to the scheme it should have joined, and the sums it should have paid by way of subscription, and to an order to pay them to the person administering the scheme. Both the Secretary of State and the Corporation enjoy power to make grants in respect of approved schemes, either to a body corporate administering the scheme, or to a Housing Ombudsman appointed by the Secretary of State.

Section 55   SCHEDULE 3

SOCIAL RENTED SECTOR: MINOR AMENDMENTS

Finance Act 1981 (c. 35)

1.—(1) Section 107 of the Finance Act 1981 (stamp duty payable upon sale of houses at a discount) is amended as follows.

(2) After subsection (3)(e) insert—

"(ea) a registered social landlord within the meaning of Part I of the Housing Act 1996;".

(3) In subsection (3)(f) for the words from "registered" to the end substitute "registered—

(i) in Scotland, under the Housing Associations Act 1985, or

(ii) in Northern Ireland, under Part II of the Housing (Northern Ireland) Order 1992;".

(4) In subsection (3A) (exclusion of certain sub-sales), for "subsection (3)(f)" substitute "subsection (3)(ea) or (f)".

(5) After subsection (3B) insert—

"(3C) A grant under section 20 or 21 of the Housing Act 1996 (purchase grants in respect of disposals at a discount by registered social landlords) shall not be treated as part of the consideration for a conveyance or transfer to which this section applies made by a body falling within subsection (3)(ea) above.".

Local Government Finance Act 1982 (c. 32)

2.—(1) In Part III of the Local Government Finance Act 1982 (establishment and functions of Audit Commission), after section 28A insert—

"General functions of Commission in relation to registered social landlords

28B.—(1) The Corporation and the Commission may agree one or more programmes of comparative studies designed to enable the Commission to make recommendations for improving economy, efficiency and effectiveness of registered social landlords.

(2) Where the Corporation and the Commission fail to agree a programme proposed by either of them, either of them may refer the matter to the Secretary of State who may direct that the programme be carried out either without modifications or with modifications specified in the direction.

(3) Where a programme is agreed or is directed to be carried out, the Commission shall ensure that studies giving effect to the programme are carried out by it or on its behalf.

(4) It shall be a term of every such programme that the Corporation make good to the Commission the full costs incurred by the Commission in carrying out the programme.

(5) The Commission shall publish reports on the studies carried out under this section.

(6) Before publishing any such report the Commission shall show a draft of it to the Corporation and shall consider whether to revise the draft in the light of the comments made by the Corporation.

Provisions supplementary to s.28B

28C.—(1) The Commission may, if authorised to do so by the Corporation—

(a) require a registered social landlord, or any officer or member of a registered social landlord, to supply such information as the Commission may require for the purposes of any study under section 28B above; and

(b) require a registered social landlord included in any such study to make available for inspection such documents as are reasonably required for the purposes of the study.

(2) The Commission may require the information to be supplied, or the documents to be made available, to the Commission or to a person authorised by the Commission for the purposes of this section.

(3) A person who without reasonable excuse fails to comply with a requirement under this section commits an offence and is liable on summary conviction to a fine not exceeding level 3 on the standard scale.

(4) Information obtained by the Commission, or by a person acting on behalf of the Commission, in the course of a study under section 28B above may be disclosed by the Commission to the Corporation notwithstanding anything in section 30 below (general restriction on disclosure of information relating to particular bodies or persons).

Functions of Commission in relation to audit of accounts of registered social landlords

28D.—(1) The Commission may provide the Corporation with consultancy services relating to the audit of accounts of registered social landlords.

(2) The Commission may recover from the Corporation such costs incurred in providing the services as may be agreed by the Corporation.

Meaning of "the Corporation" and "registered social landlord"

28E. In sections 28B to 28D above "the Corporation" and "registered social landlord" have the same meaning as in Part I of the Housing Act 1996.".

(2) In paragraph 9 of Schedule 3 to the Local Government Finance Act 1982 (the Audit Commission: duty to balance income and expenditure), in sub-paragraph (2) (functions to be man-

aged separately) after sub-paragraph (a) insert—
    "(aa) its functions under sections 28B and 28C relating to registered social landlords;
    (ab) its functions under section 28D relating to such landlords;".

Housing Associations Act 1985 (c. 69)

3. Section 33 of the Housing Associations Act 1985 (recognition of central association) shall cease to have effect.

4. In section 69(1) of the Housing Associations Act 1985 (power to vary or terminate certain agreements with housing associations: agreements to which the section applies), omit paragraphs (e) and (g).

5. In section 75(1) of the Housing Associations Act 1985 (general functions of the Corporation) for paragraphs (a) to (c) substitute—
    "(a) to facilitate the proper performance of the functions of registered social landlords;
    (b) to maintain a register of social landlords and to exercise supervision and control over such persons;
    (c) to promote and assist the development of self-build societies (other than registered social landlords) and to facilitate the proper performance of the functions, and to publicise the aims and principles, of such societies;".

6. In Part III of the Housing Associations Act 1985 (general provisions relating to the Housing Corporation and Housing for Wales), after section 76 (general power of Secretary of State to give directions to Corporation) insert—

"Realisation of value of Corporation's loans portfolio
    76A.—(1) The Corporation may, and if so directed by the Secretary of State (under section 76) shall, enter into arrangements of a description approved by the Secretary of State for the purpose of realising the value of the whole or part of its loans portfolio.
    (2) The arrangements may provide for—
    (a) the transfer of any estate or interest of the Corporation, or
    (b) the creation or disposal of economic interests not involving a transfer of an estate or interest,
and may extend to such incidental or ancillary matters as the Corporation or the Secretary of State considers appropriate.
    (3) In this section the Corporation's "loans portfolio" means the Corporation's rights and obligations in relation to any loans or related securities.
    (4) Nothing in the terms of any loan or related transaction entered into by the Corporation shall be construed as impliedly prohibiting or restricting the Corporation from dealing with its loans portfolio in accordance with arrangements under this section.".

7. In section 87 of the Housing Associations Act 1985 (financial assistance for formation, management, &c. of housing associations), for subsection (1) substitute—
    "(1) The Corporation may give financial assistance to any person to facilitate the proper performance of the functions of registered social landlords or co-operative housing associations.".

Income and Corporation Taxes Act 1988 (c. 1)

8.—(1) The Income and Corporation Taxes Act 1988 is amended as follows.
    (2) In section 488 (co-operative housing associations), after subsection (7) insert—
    "(7A) The Secretary of State may delegate any of his functions under subsections (6) and (7)—
    (a) to the Housing Corporation, in the case of a body registered as a social landlord in the register maintained by the Housing Corporation under Part I of the Housing Act 1996, and
    (b) to Housing for Wales, in the case of a body registered as a social landlord in the register maintained under that Part by Housing for Wales,
to such extent and subject to such conditions as he may specify.".
    (3) In section 489 (self-build societies), after subsection (5) insert—
    "(5A) The Secretary of State may delegate any of his functions under subsections (4) and (5) to—
    (a) the Housing Corporation, where the society has its registered office in England for the purposes of the Industrial and Provident Societies Act 1965, and
    (b) Housing for Wales, where the society has its registered office in Wales for the purposes of that Act,

to such extent and subject to such conditions as he may specify.".

Housing (Scotland) Act 1988 (c. 43)

9. After section 2 of the Housing (Scotland) Act 1988 (general functions of Scottish Homes) insert—

"Sale of Scottish Homes' loans portfolio
2A.—(1) Subject to subsection (2) below, Scottish Homes may enter into arrangements of a description approved by the Secretary of State for the purpose of realising the value of the whole or part of its loans portfolio.

(2) Without prejudice to the power of the Secretary of State to give directions under section 2(10) above, the Secretary of State may direct Scottish Homes to enter into arrangements under this section and it shall be the duty of Scottish Homes to comply with any such direction.

(3) The arrangements may provide for—
(a) the transfer of any estate or interest of Scottish Homes, or
(b) the creation or disposal of economic interests not involving a transfer of an estate or interest,
and may extend to such incidental or ancillary matters as Scottish Homes or the Secretary of State considers appropriate.

(4) In this section, Scottish Homes' "loans portfolio" means Scottish Homes' rights and obligations in relation to any loans or related securities.

(5) Nothing in the terms of any loan or related transaction entered into by Scottish Homes shall be construed as impliedly prohibiting or restricting it from dealing with its loans portfolio in accordance with arrangements under this section.

(6) A direction given under subsection (2) above may be varied or revoked by a subsequent direction given by the Secretary of State.".

Housing Act 1988 (c. 50)

10. Section 58 of the Housing Act 1988 (application of Housing Acts to certain transactions) shall cease to have effect.

11. In section 79(2) of the Housing Act 1988 (permitted disposals of land by housing action trusts) for paragraph (a) and the word "or" at the end of the paragraph substitute—
"(a) to a registered social landlord (within the meaning of Part I of the Housing Act 1996), or".

GENERAL NOTE
See General Note to s.55, above.

Section 84   SCHEDULE 4

RIGHTS EXERCISABLE BY SURVEYOR APPOINTED BY TENANTS' ASSOCIATION

Introductory

1.—(1) A surveyor appointed for the purposes of section 84 has the rights conferred by this Schedule.

(2) In this Schedule—
(a) "the tenants' association" means the association by whom the surveyor was appointed, and
(b) the surveyor's "functions" are his functions in connection with the matters in respect of which he was appointed.

Appointment of assistants

2.—(1) The surveyor may appoint such persons as he thinks fit to assist him in carrying out his functions.

(2) References in this Schedule to the surveyor in the context of—
(a) being afforded any such facilities as are mentioned in paragraph 3, or
(b) carrying out an inspection under paragraph 4,
include a person so appointed.

Right to inspect documents, &c.

3.—(1) The surveyor has a right to require the landlord or any other relevant person—

   (a) to afford him reasonable facilities for inspecting any documents sight of which is reasonably required by him for the purposes of his functions, and

   (b) to afford him reasonable facilities for taking copies of or extracts from any such documents.

  (2) In sub-paragraph (1) "other relevant person" means a person other than the landlord who is or, in relation to a future service charge, will be—

   (a) responsible for applying the proceeds of the service charge, or

   (b) under an obligation to a tenant who pays the service charge in respect of any matter to which the charge relates.

  (3) The rights conferred on the surveyor by this paragraph are exercisable by him by notice in writing given by him to the landlord or other person concerned.

Where a notice is given to a person other than the landlord, the surveyor shall give a copy of the notice to the landlord.

  (4) The landlord or other person to whom notice is given shall, within the period of one week beginning with the date of the giving of the notice or as soon as reasonably practicable thereafter, either—

   (a) afford the surveyor the facilities required by him for inspecting and taking copies or extracts of the documents to which the notice relates, or

   (b) give the surveyor a notice stating that he objects to doing so for reasons specified in the notice.

  (5) Facilities for the inspection of any documents required under subparagraph (1)(a) shall be made available free of charge.

This does not mean that the landlord cannot treat as part of his costs of management any costs incurred by him in connection with making the facilities available.

  (6) A reasonable charge may be made for facilities for the taking of copies or extracts required under sub-paragraph (1)(b).

  (7) A notice is duly given under this paragraph to the landlord of a tenant if it is given to a person who receives on behalf of the landlord the rent payable by that tenant.

A person to whom such a notice is so given shall forward it as soon as may be to the landlord.

Right to inspect premises

4.—(1) The surveyor also has the right to inspect any common parts comprised in relevant premises or any appurtenant property.

  (2) In sub-paragraph (1)—

"common parts", in relation to a building or part of a building, includes the structure and exterior of the building or part and any common facilities within it;

"relevant premises" means so much of—

     (i) the building or buildings containing the dwellings let to members of the tenants' association, and

     (ii) any other building or buildings,

as constitute premises in relation to which management functions are discharged in respect of the costs of which service charges are payable by members of the association; and

"appurtenant property" means so much of any property not contained in relevant premises as constitutes property in relation to which any such management functions are discharged.

For the purposes of the above definitions "management functions" includes functions with respect to the provision of services, or the repair, maintenance or insurance of property.

  (3) On being requested to do so, the landlord shall afford the surveyor reasonable access for the purposes of carrying out an inspection under this paragraph.

  (4) Such reasonable access shall be afforded to the surveyor free of charge.

This does not mean that the landlord cannot treat as part of his costs of management any costs incurred by him in connection with affording reasonable access to the surveyor.

  (5) A request is duly made under this paragraph to the landlord of a tenant if it is made to a person appointed by the landlord to deal with such requests or, if no such person has been appointed, to a person who receives on behalf of the landlord the rent payable by that tenant.

A person to whom such a request is made shall notify the landlord of the request as soon as may be.

Enforcement of rights by the court

5.—(1) If the landlord or other person to whom notice was given under paragraph 3 has not, by the end of the period of one month beginning with the date on which notice was given, complied with the notice, the court may, on the application of the surveyor, make an order requiring him to do so within such period as is specified in the order.

(2) If the landlord does not, within a reasonable period after the making of a request under paragraph 4, afford the surveyor reasonable access for the purposes of carrying out an inspection under that paragraph, the court may, on the application of the surveyor, make an order requiring the landlord to do so on such date as is specified in the order.

(3) An application for an order under this paragraph must be made before the end of the period of four months beginning with the date on which notice was given under paragraph 3 or the request was made under paragraph 4.

(4) An order under this paragraph may be made in general terms or may require the landlord or other person to do specific things, as the court thinks fit.

Documents held by superior landlord

6.—(1) Where a landlord is required by a notice under paragraph 3 to afford the surveyor facilities for inspection or taking copies or extracts in respect of any document which is in the custody or under the control of a superior landlord—

(a) the landlord shall on receiving the notice inform the surveyor as soon as may be of that fact and of the name and address of the superior landlord, and

(b) the surveyor may then give the superior landlord notice in writing requiring him to afford the facilities in question in respect of the document.

(2) Paragraphs 3 and 5(1) and (3) have effect, with any necessary modifications, in relation to a notice given to a superior landlord under this paragraph.

Effect of disposal by landlord

7.—(1) Where a notice under paragraph 3 has been given or a request under paragraph 4 has been made to a landlord, and at a time when any obligations arising out of the notice or request remain to be discharged by him—

(a) he disposes of the whole or part of his interest as landlord of any member of the tenants' association, and

(b) the person acquiring that interest ("the transferee") is in a position to discharge any of those obligations to any extent,

that person shall be responsible for discharging those obligations to that extent, as if he had been given the notice under paragraph 3 or had received the request under paragraph 4.

(2) If the landlord is, despite the disposal, still in a position to discharge those obligations, he remains responsible for doing so.

Otherwise, the transferee is responsible for discharging them to the exclusion of the landlord.

(3) In connection with the discharge of such obligations by the transferee, paragraphs 3 to 6 apply with the substitution for any reference to the date on which notice was given under paragraph 3 or the request was made under paragraph 4 of a reference to the date of the disposal.

(4) In this paragraph "disposal" means a disposal whether by the creation or transfer of an estate or interest, and includes the surrender of a tenancy; and references to the transferee shall be construed accordingly.

Effect of person ceasing to be a relevant person

8. Where a notice under paragraph 3 has been given to a person other than the landlord and, at a time when any obligations arising out of the notice remain to be discharged by him, he ceases to be such a person as is mentioned in paragraph 3(2), then, if he is still in a position to discharge those obligations to any extent he remains responsible for discharging those obligations, and the provisions of this Schedule continue to apply to him, to that extent.

GENERAL NOTE
  See notes to s.84.

Section 87   SCHEDULE 5

TEXT OF PART II OF THE LANDLORD AND TENANT ACT 1987, AS AMENDED

"PART II

APPOINTMENT OF MANAGERS BY LEASEHOLD VALUATION TRIBUNAL

Tenant's right to apply to tribunal for appointment of manager

21.—(1) The tenant of a flat contained in any premises to which this Part applies may, subject to the following provisions of this Part, apply to a leasehold valuation tribunal for an order under section 24 appointing a manager to act in relation to those premises.

(2) Subject to subsection (3), this Part applies to premises consisting of the whole or part of a building if the building or part contains two or more flats.

(3) This Part does not apply to any such premises at a time when—

(a) the interest of the landlord in the premises is held by an exempt landlord or a resident landlord, or

(b) the premises are included within the functional land of any charity.

(4) An application for an order under section 24 may be made—

(a) jointly by tenants of two or more flats if they are each entitled to make such an application by virtue of this section, and

(b) in respect of two or more premises to which this Part applies;

and, in relation to any such joint application as is mentioned in paragraph (a), references in this Part to a single tenant shall be construed accordingly.

(5) Where the tenancy of a flat contained in any such premises is held by joint tenants, an application for an order under section 24 in respect of those premises may be made by any one or more of those tenants.

(6) An application to the court for it to exercise in relation to any premises any jurisdiction to appoint a receiver or manager shall not be made by a tenant (in his capacity as such) in any circumstances in which an application could be made by him for an order under section 24 appointing a manager to act in relation to those premises.

(7) References in this Part to a tenant do not include references to a tenant under a tenancy to which Part II of the Landlord and Tenant Act 1954 applies.

Preliminary notice by tenant

22.—(1) Before an application for an order under section 24 is made in respect of any premises to which this Part applies by a tenant of a flat contained in those premises, a notice under this section must (subject to subsection (3)) be served on the landlord by the tenant.

(2) A notice under this section must—

(a) specify the tenant's name, the address of his flat and an address in England and Wales (which may be the address of his flat) at which the landlord may serve notices, including notices in proceedings, on him in connection with this Part;

(b) state that the tenant intends to make an application for an order under section 24 to be made by a leasehold valuation tribunal in respect of such premises to which this Part applies as are specified in the notice, but (if paragraph (d) is applicable) that he will not do so if the landlord complies with the requirement specified in pursuance of that paragraph;

(c) specify the grounds on which the tribunal would be asked to make such an order and the matters that would be relied on by the tenant for the purpose of establishing those grounds;

(d) where those matters are capable of being remedied by the landlord, require the landlord, within such reasonable period as is specified in the notice, to take such steps for the purpose of remedying them as are so specified; and

(e) contain such information (if any) as the Secretary of State may by regulations prescribe.

(3) A leasehold valuation tribunal may (whether on the hearing of an application for an order under section 24 or not) by order dispense with the requirement to serve a notice under this section in a case where it is satisfied that it would not be reasonably practicable to serve such a notice on the landlord, but the tribunal may, when doing so, direct that such other notices are served, or such other steps are taken, as it thinks fit.

(4) In a case where—

(a) a notice under this section has been served on the landlord, and

(b) his interest in the premises specified in pursuance of subsection (2)(b) is subject to a mortgage,

the landlord shall, as soon as is reasonably practicable after receiving the notice, serve on the mortgagee a copy of the notice.

Application to tribunal for appointment of manager

23.—(1) No application for an order under section 24 shall be made to a leasehold valuation tribunal unless—

(a) in a case where a notice has been served under section 22, either—

(i) the period specified in pursuance of paragraph (d) of subsection (2) of that section has expired without the landlord having taken the steps that he was required to take in pursuance of that provision, or

(ii) that paragraph was not applicable in the circumstances of the case; or

(b) in a case where the requirement to serve such a notice has been dispensed with by an order under subsection (3) of that section, either—

(i) any notices required to be served, and any other steps required to be taken, by virtue of the order have been served or (as the case may be) taken, or

(ii) no direction was given by the tribunal when making the order.

(2) Procedure regulations shall make provision—

(a) for requiring notice of an application for an order under section 24 in respect of any premises to be served on such descriptions of persons as may be specified in the regulations; and

(b) for enabling persons served with any such notice to be joined as parties to the proceedings.

Appointment of manager by the tribunal

24.—(1) A leasehold valuation tribunal may, on an application for an order under this section, by order (whether interlocutory or final) appoint a manager to carry out in relation to any premises to which this Part applies—

(a) such functions in connection with the management of the premises, or

(b) such functions of a receiver,

or both, as the tribunal thinks fit.

(2) A leasehold valuation tribunal may only make an order under this section in the following circumstances, namely—

(a) where the tribunal is satisfied—

(i) that the landlord either is in breach of any obligation owed by him to the tenant under his tenancy and relating to the management of the premises in question or any part of them or (in the case of an obligation dependent on notice) would be in breach of any such obligation but for the fact that it has not been reasonably practicable for the tenant to give him the appropriate notice, and

(ii) that it is just and convenient to make the order in all the circumstances of the case;

(ab) where the tribunal is satisfied—

(i) that unreasonable service charges have been made, or are proposed or likely to be made, and

(iii) that it is just and convenient to make the order in all the circumstances of the case;

(ac) where the tribunal is satisfied—

(i) that the landlord has failed to comply with any relevant provision of a code of practice approved by the Secretary of State under section 87 of the Leasehold Reform, Housing and Urban Development Act 1993 (codes of management practice), and

(ii) that it is just and convenient to make the order in all the circumstances of the case; or

(b) where the tribunal is satisfied that other circumstances exist which make it just and convenient for the order to be made.

(2A) For the purposes of subsection (2)(ab) a service charge shall be taken to be unreasonable—

(a) if the amount is unreasonable having regard to the items for which it is payable,

(b) if the items for which it is payable are of an unnecessarily high standard, or

(c) if the items for which it is payable are of an insufficient standard with the result that additional service charges are or may be incurred.

In that provision and this subsection "service charge" means a service charge within the meaning of section 18(1) of the Landlord and Tenant Act 1985, other than one excluded from that section by section 27 of that Act (rent of dwelling registered and not entered as variable).

(3) The premises in respect of which an order is made under this section may, if the tribunal thinks fit, be either more or less extensive than the premises specified in the application on which the order is made.

(4) An order under this section may make provision with respect to—

(a) such matters relating to the exercise by the manager of his functions under the order, and

(b) such incidental or ancillary matters,

as the tribunal thinks fit; and, on any subsequent application made for the purpose by the manager, the tribunal may give him directions with respect to any such matters.

(5) Without prejudice to the generality of subsection (4), an order under this section may provide—

(a) for rights and liabilities arising under contracts to which the manager is not a party to become rights and liabilities of the manager;

(b) for the manager to be entitled to prosecute claims in respect of causes of action (whether contractual or tortious) accruing before or after the date of his appointment;

(c) for remuneration to be paid to the manager by the landlord, or by the tenants of the premises in respect of which the order is made or by all or any of those persons;

(d) for the manager's functions to be exercisable by him (subject to subsection (9)) either during a specified period or without limit of time.

(6) Any such order may be granted subject to such conditions as the tribunal thinks fit, and in particular its operation may be suspended on terms fixed by the tribunal.

(7) In a case where an application for an order under this section was preceded by the service of a notice under section 22, the tribunal may, if it thinks fit, make such an order notwithstanding—

(a) that any period specified in the notice in pursuance of subsection (2)(d) of that section was not a reasonable period, or

(b) that the notice failed in any other respect to comply with any requirement contained in subsection (2) of that section or in any regulations applying to the notice under section 54(3).

(8) The Land Charges Act 1972 and the Land Registration Act 1925 shall apply in relation to an order made under this section as they apply in relation to an order appointing a receiver or sequestrator of land.

(9) A leasehold valuation tribunal may, on the application of any person interested, vary or discharge (whether conditionally or unconditionally) an order made under this section; and if the order has been protected by an entry registered under the Land Charges Act 1972 or the Land Registration Act 1925, the tribunal may by order direct that the entry shall be cancelled.

(9A) The court shall not vary or discharge an order under subsection (9) on a landlord's application unless it is satisfied—

(a) that the variation or discharge of the order will not result in a recurrence of the circumstances which led to the order being made, and

(b) that it is just and convenient in all the circumstances of the case to vary or discharge the order.

(10) An order made under this section shall not be discharged by a leasehold valuation tribunal by reason only that, by virtue of section 21(3), the premises in respect of which the order was made have ceased to be premises to which this Part applies.

(11) References in this section to the management of any premises include references to the repair, maintenance or insurance of those premises.

Jurisdiction of leasehold valuation tribunal

24A.—(1) The jurisdiction conferred by this Part on a leasehold valuation tribunal is exercisable by a rent assessment committee constituted in accordance with Schedule 10 to the Rent Act 1977 which when so constituted for the purposes of exercising any such jurisdiction shall be known as a leasehold valuation tribunal.

(2) The power to make regulations under section 74(1)(b) of the Rent Act 1977 (procedure of rent assessment committees) extends to prescribing the procedure to be followed in connection with any proceedings before a leasehold valuation tribunal under this Part.

Such regulations are referred to in this Part as "procedure regulations".

(3) Any order made by a leasehold valuation tribunal under this Part may, with the leave of the court, be enforced in the same way as an order of the county court.

(4) No costs incurred by a party in connection with proceedings under this Part before a leasehold valuation tribunal shall be recoverable by order of any court.

(5) Paragraphs 2, 3 and 7 of Schedule 22 to the Housing Act 1980 (supplementary provisions relating to leasehold valuation tribunals: appeals and provision of information) apply to a leasehold valuation tribunal constituted for the purposes of this section.

(6) No appeal shall lie to the Lands Tribunal from a decision of a leasehold valuation tribunal under this Part without the leave of the leasehold valuation tribunal concerned or the Lands Tribunal.

(7) On an appeal to the Lands Tribunal from a decision of a leasehold valuation tribunal under this Part—

(a) the Lands Tribunal may exercise any power available to the leasehold valuation tribunal in relation to the original matter, and

(b) an order of the Lands Tribunal may be enforced in the same way as an order of the leasehold valuation tribunal.

Leasehold valuation tribunal: applications and fees

24B.—(1) The Secretary of State may make provision by order as to the form of, or the particulars to be contained in, an application made to a leasehold valuation tribunal under this Part.

(2) The Secretary of State may make provision by order—

(a) requiring the payment of fees in respect of any such application, or in respect of any proceedings before, a leasehold valuation tribunal under this Part; and

(b) empowering a leasehold valuation tribunal to require a party to proceedings before it to reimburse any other party the amount of any fees paid by him.

(3) The fees payable shall be such as may be specified in or determined in accordance with the order subject to this limit, that the fees payable in respect of any one application or reference by the court together with any proceedings before the tribunal arising out of that application or reference shall not exceed £500 or such other amount as may be specified by order of the Secretary of State.

(4) An order under this section may make different provision for different cases or classes of case or for different areas.

(5) An order may, in particular, provide for the reduction or waiver of fees by reference to the financial resources of the party by whom they are to be paid or met.

Any such order may apply, subject to such modifications as may be specified in the order, any other statutory means-testing regime as it has effect from time to time.

(6) An order under this section shall be made by statutory instrument.

(7) No order altering the limit under subsection (3) shall be made unless a draft of the order has been laid before and approved by a resolution of each House of Parliament.

(8) Any other order under this section, unless it contains only such provision as is mentioned in subsection (1), shall be subject to annulment in pursuance of a resolution of either House of Parliament.".

Section 92(1)   SCHEDULE 6

AMENDMENTS OF PART I OF THE LANDLORD AND TENANT ACT 1987

PART I

RIGHTS OF FIRST REFUSAL

The following sections are substituted for sections 5 to 10 of the Landlord and Tenant Act 1987—

"Rights of first refusal

Landlord required to serve offer notice on tenants

5.—(1) Where the landlord proposes to make a relevant disposal affecting premises to which this Part applies, he shall serve a notice under this section (an "offer notice") on the qualifying tenants of the flats contained in the premises (the "constituent flats").

(2) An offer notice must comply with the requirements of whichever is applicable of the following sections—

section 5A (requirements in case of contract to be completed by conveyance, &c.),

section 5B (requirements in case of sale at auction),

section 5C (requirements in case of grant of option or right of pre-emption),

section 5D (requirements in case of conveyance not preceded by contract, &c.);

and in the case of a disposal to which section 5E applies (disposal for non-monetary consideration) shall also comply with the requirements of that section.

(3) Where a landlord proposes to effect a transaction involving the disposal of an estate or interest in more than one building (whether or not involving the same estate or interest), he shall, for the purpose of complying with this section, sever the transaction so as to deal with each building separately.

(4) If, as a result of the offer notice being served on different tenants on different dates, the period specified in the notice as the period for accepting the offer would end on different dates, the notice shall have effect in relation to all the qualifying tenants on whom it is served as if it provided for that period to end with the latest of those dates.

(5) A landlord who has not served an offer notice on all of the qualifying tenants on whom it was required to be served shall nevertheless be treated as having complied with this section—

(a) if he has served an offer notice on not less than 90% of the qualifying tenants on whom such a notice was required to be served, or

(b) where the qualifying tenants on whom it was required to be served number less than ten, if he has served such a notice on all but one of them.

Offer notice: requirements in case of contract to be completed by conveyance, &c.

5A.—(1) The following requirements must be met in relation to an offer notice where the disposal consists of entering into a contract to create or transfer an estate or interest in land.

(2) The notice must contain particulars of the principal terms of the disposal proposed by the landlord, including in particular—

(a) the property, and the estate or interest in that property, to which the contract relates,

(b) the principal terms of the contract (including the deposit and consideration required).

(3) The notice must state that the notice constitutes an offer by the landlord to enter into a contract on those terms which may be accepted by the requisite majority of qualifying tenants of the constituent flats.

(4) The notice must specify a period within which that offer may be so accepted, being a period of not less than two months which is to begin with the date of service of the notice.

(5) The notice must specify a further period of not less than two months within which a person or persons may be nominated by the tenants under section 6.

(6) This section does not apply to the grant of an option or right of pre-emption (see section 5C).

Offer notice: requirements in case of sale by auction

5B.—(1) The following requirements must be met in relation to an offer notice where the landlord proposes to make the disposal by means of a sale at a public auction held in England and Wales.

(2) The notice must contain particulars of the principal terms of the disposal proposed by the landlord, including in particular the property to which it relates and the estate or interest in that property proposed to be disposed of.

(3) The notice must state that the disposal is proposed to be made by means of a sale at a public auction.

(4) The notice must state that the notice constitutes an offer by the landlord, which may be accepted by the requisite majority of qualifying tenants of the constituent flats, for the contract (if any) entered into by the landlord at the auction to have effect as if a person or persons nominated by them, and not the purchaser, had entered into it.

(5) The notice must specify a period within which that offer may be so accepted, being a period of not less than two months beginning with the date of service of the notice.

(6) The notice must specify a further period of not less than 28 days within which a person or persons may be nominated by the tenants under section 6.

(7) The notice must be served not less than four months or more than six months before the date of the auction; and

(a) the period specified in the notice as the period within which the offer may be accepted must end not less than two months before the date of the auction, and

(b) the period specified in the notice as the period within which a person may be nominated under section 6 must end not less than 28 days before the date of the auction.

(8) Unless the time and place of the auction and the name of the auctioneers are stated in the notice, the landlord shall, not less than 28 days before the date of the auction, serve on the requisite majority of qualifying tenants of the constituent flats a further notice stating those particulars.

Offer notice: requirements in case of grant or option or right of pre-emption

5C.—(1) The following requirements must be met in relation to an offer notice where the disposal consists of the grant of an option or right of pre-emption.

(2) The notice must contain particulars of the principal terms of the disposal proposed by the landlord, including in particular—

(a) the property, and the estate or interest in that property, to which the option or right of pre-emption relates,

(b) the consideration required by the landlord for granting the option or right of pre-emption, and

(c) the principal terms on which the option or right of pre-emption would be exercisable, including the consideration payable on its exercise.

(3) The notice must state that the notice constitutes an offer by the landlord to grant an option or right of pre-emption on those terms which may be accepted by the requisite majority of qualifying tenants of the constituent flats.

(4) The notice must specify a period within which that offer may be so accepted, being a period of not less than two months which is to begin with the date of service of the notice.

(5) The notice must specify a further period of not less than two months within which a person or persons may be nominated by the tenants under section 6.

Offer notice: requirements in case of conveyance not preceded by contract, &c.

5D.—(1) The following requirements must be met in relation to an offer notice where the disposal is not made in pursuance of a contract, option or right of pre-emption binding on the landlord.

(2) The notice must contain particulars of the principal terms of the disposal proposed by the landlord, including in particular—
  (a) the property to which it relates and the estate or interest in that property proposed to be disposed of, and
  (b) the consideration required by the landlord for making the disposal.

(3) The notice must state that the notice constitutes an offer by the landlord to dispose of the property on those terms which may be accepted by the requisite majority of qualifying tenants of the constituent flats.

(4) The notice must specify a period within which that offer may be so accepted, being a period of not less than two months which is to begin with the date of service of the notice.

(5) The notice must specify a further period of not less than two months within which a person or persons may be nominated by the tenants under section 6.

Offer notice: disposal for non-monetary consideration

5E.—(1) This section applies where, in any case to which section 5 applies, the consideration required by the landlord for making the disposal does not consist, or does not wholly consist, of money.

(2) The offer notice, in addition to complying with whichever is applicable of sections 5A to 5D, must state—
  (a) that an election may made under section 8C (explaining its effect), and
  (b) that, accordingly, the notice also constitutes an offer by the landlord, which may be accepted by the requisite majority of qualifying tenants of the constituent flats, for a person or persons nominated by them to acquire the property in pursuance of sections 11 to 17.

(3) The notice must specify a period within which that offer may be so accepted, being a period of not less than two months which is to begin with the date of service of the notice.

Acceptance of landlord's offer: general provisions

6.—(1) Where a landlord has served an offer notice, he shall not during—
  (a) the period specified in the notice as the period during which the offer may be accepted, or
  (b) such longer period as may be agreed between him and the requisite majority of the qualifying tenants of the constituent flats,
dispose of the protected interest except to a person or persons nominated by the tenants under this section.

(2) Where an acceptance notice is duly served on him, he shall not during the protected period (see subsection (4) below) dispose of the protected interest except to a person duly nominated for the purposes of this section by the requisite majority of qualifying tenants of the constituent flats (a "nominated person").

(3) An "acceptance notice" means a notice served on the landlord by the requisite majority of qualifying tenants of the constituent flats informing him that the persons by whom it is served accept the offer contained in his notice.

An acceptance notice is "duly served" if it is served within—
  (a) the period specified in the offer notice as the period within which the offer may be accepted, or
  (b) such longer period as may be agreed between the landlord and the requisite majority of qualifying tenants of the constituent flats.

(4) The "protected period" is the period beginning with the date of service of the acceptance notice and ending with—
  (a) the end of the period specified in the offer notice as the period for nominating a person under this section, or
  (b) such later date as may be agreed between the landlord and the requisite majority of qualifying tenants of constituent flats.

(5) A person is "duly nominated" for the purposes of this section if he is nominated at the same time as the acceptance notice is served or at any time after that notice is served and before the end of—

(a) the period specified in the offer notice as the period for nomination, or

(b) such longer period as may be agreed between the landlord and the requisite majority of qualifying tenants of the constituent flats.

(6) A person nominated for the purposes of this section by the requisite majority of qualifying tenants of the constituent flats may be replaced by another person so nominated if, and only if, he has (for any reason) ceased to be able to act as a nominated person.

(7) Where two or more persons have been nominated and any of them ceases to act without being replaced, the remaining person or persons so nominated may continue to act.

Failure to accept landlord's offer or to make nomination

7.—(1) Where a landlord has served an offer notice on the qualifying tenants of the constituent flats and—

(a) no acceptance notice is duly served on the landlord, or

(b) no person is nominated for the purposes of section 6 during the protected period,

the landlord may, during the period of 12 months beginning with the end of that period, dispose of the protected interest to such person as he thinks fit, but subject to the following restrictions.

(2) Where the offer notice was one to which section 5B applied (sale by auction), the restrictions are—

(a) that the disposal is made by means of a sale at a public auction, and

(b) that the other terms correspond to those specified in the offer notice.

(3) In any other case the restrictions are—

(a) that the deposit and consideration required are not less than those specified in the offer notice, and

(b) that the other terms correspond to those specified in the offer notice.

(4) The entitlement of a landlord, by virtue of this section or any other corresponding provision of this Part, to dispose of the protected interest during a specified period of 12 months extends only to a disposal of that interest, and accordingly the requirements of section 1(1) must be satisfied with respect to any other disposal by him during that period of 12 months (unless the disposal is not a relevant disposal affecting any premises to which at the time of the disposal this Part applies).

Landlord's obligations in case of acceptance and nomination

8.—(1) This section applies where a landlord serves an offer notice on the qualifying tenants of the constituent flat and—

(a) an acceptance notice is duly served on him, and

(b) a person is duly nominated for the purposes of section 6,

by the requisite majority of qualifying tenants of the constituent flats.

(2) Subject to the following provisions of this Part, the landlord shall not dispose of the protected interest except to the nominated person.

(3) The landlord shall, within the period of one month beginning with the date of service of notice of nomination, either—

(a) serve notice on the nominated person indicating an intention no longer to proceed with the disposal of the protected interest, or

(b) be obliged to proceed in accordance with the following provisions of this Part.

(4) A notice under subsection (3)(a) is a notice of withdrawal for the purposes of section 9B(2) to (4) (consequences of notice of withdrawal by landlord).

(5) Nothing in this section shall be taken as prejudicing the application of the provisions of this Part to any further offer notice served by the landlord on the qualifying tenants of the constituent flats.

Landlord's obligation: general provisions

8A.—(1) This section applies where the landlord is obliged to proceed and the offer notice was not one to which section 5B applied (sale by auction).

(2) The landlord shall, within the period of one month beginning with the date of service of the notice of nomination, send to the nominated person a form of contract for the acquisition of the protected interest on the terms specified in the landlord's offer notice.

(3) If he fails to do so, the following provisions of this Part apply as if he had given notice under section 9B (notice of withdrawal by landlord) at the end of that period.

(4) If the landlord complies with subsection (2), the nominated person shall within the period of two months beginning with the date on which it is sent or such longer period beginning with that date as may be agreed between the landlord and that person, either—

(a) serve notice on the landlord indicating an intention no longer to proceed with the acquisition of the protected interest, or

(b) offer an exchange of contracts, that is to say, sign the contract and send it to the landlord, together with the requisite deposit.

In this subsection "the requisite deposit" means a deposit of an amount determined by or under the contract or an amount equal to 10 per cent. of the consideration, whichever is the less.

(5) If the nominated person—

(a) serves notice in pursuance of paragraph (a) of subsection (4), or

(b) fails to offer an exchange of contracts within the period specified in that subsection,

the following provisions of this Part apply as if he had given notice under section 9A (withdrawal by nominated person) at the same time as that notice or, as the case may be, at the end of that period.

(6) If the nominated person offers an exchange of contracts within the period specified in subsection (4), but the landlord fails to complete the exchange within the period of seven days beginning with the day on which he received that person's contract, the following provisions of this Part apply as if the landlord had given notice under section 9B (withdrawal by landlord) at the end of that period.

Landlord's obligation: election in case of sale at auction

8B.—(1) This section applies where the landlord is obliged to proceed and the offer notice was one to which section 5B applied (sale by auction).

(2) The nominated person may, by notice served on the landlord not less than 28 days before the date of the auction, elect that the provisions of this section shall apply.

(3) If a contract for the disposal is entered into at the auction, the landlord shall, within the period of seven days beginning with the date of the auction, send a copy of the contract to the nominated person.

(4) If, within the period of 28 days beginning with the date on which such a copy is so sent, the nominated person—

(a) serves notice on the landlord accepting the terms of the contract, and

(b) fulfils any conditions falling to be fulfilled by the purchaser on entering into the contract, the contract shall have effect as if the nominated person, and not the purchaser, had entered into the contract.

(5) Unless otherwise agreed, any time limit in the contract as it has effect by virtue of subsection (4) shall start to run again on the service of notice under that subsection; and nothing in the contract as it has effect by virtue of a notice under this section shall require the nominated person to complete the purchase before the end of the period of 28 days beginning with the day on which he is deemed to have entered into the contract.

(6) If the nominated person—

(a) does not serve notice on the landlord under subsection (2) by the time mentioned in that subsection, or

(b) does not satisfy the requirements of subsection (4) within the period mentioned in that subsection,

the following provisions of this Part apply as if he had given notice under section 9A (withdrawal by nominated person) at the end of that period.

Election in case of disposal for non-monetary consideration

8C.—(1) This section applies where an acceptance notice is duly served on the landlord indicating an intention to accept the offer referred to in section 5E (offer notice: disposal for non-monetary consideration).

(2) The requisite majority of qualifying tenants of the constituent flats may, by notice served on the landlord within—

(a) the period specified in the offer notice for nominating a person or persons for the purposes of section 6, or

(b) such longer period as may be agreed between the landlord and the requisite majority of qualifying tenants of the constituent flats,

elect that the following provisions shall apply.

(3) Where such an election is made and the landlord disposes of the protected interest on terms corresponding to those specified in his offer notice in accordance with section 5A, 5B, 5C or 5D, sections 11 to 17 shall have effect as if—

(a) no notice under section 5 had been served;

(b) in section 11A(3) (period for serving notice requiring information, &c.), the reference to four months were a reference to 28 days; and

(c) in section 12A(2) and 12B(3) (period for exercise of tenants' rights against purchaser) each reference to six months were a reference to two months.

(4) For the purposes of sections 11 to 17 as they have effect by virtue of subsection (3) so much of the consideration for the original disposal as did not consist of money shall be treated as such amount in money as was equivalent to its value in the hands of the landlord.

The landlord or the nominated person may apply to have that amount determined by a leasehold valuation tribunal.

Disposal in pursuance of option or right of pre-emption

8D.—(1) Where—

(a) the original disposal was the grant of an option or right of pre-emption, and

(b) in pursuance of the option or right, the landlord makes another disposal affecting the premises ("the later disposal") before the end of the period specified in subsection (2),

sections 11 to 17 shall have effect as if the later disposal, and not the original disposal, were the relevant disposal.

(2) The period referred to in subsection (1)(b) is the period of four months beginning with the date by which—

(a) notices under section 3A of the Landlord and Tenant Act 1985 (duty of new landlord to inform tenants of rights) relating to the original disposal, or

(b) where that section does not apply, documents of any other description—

(i) indicating that the original disposal has taken place, and

(ii) alerting the tenants to the existence of their rights under this Part and the time within which any such rights must be exercised,

have been served on the requisite majority of qualifying tenants of the constituent flats.

Covenant, &c. affecting landlord's power to dispose

8E.—(1) Where the landlord is obliged to proceed but is precluded by a covenant, condition or other obligation from disposing of the protected interest to the nominated person unless the consent of some other person is obtained—

(a) he shall use his best endeavours to secure that the consent of that person to that disposal is given, and

(b) if it appears to him that that person is obliged not to withhold his consent unreasonably but has nevertheless so withheld it, he shall institute proceedings for a declaration to that effect.

(2) Subsection (1) ceases to apply if a notice of withdrawal is served under section 9A or 9B (withdrawal of either party from transaction) or if notice is served under section 10 (lapse of landlord's offer: premises ceasing to be premises to which this Part applies).

(3) Where the landlord has discharged any duty imposed on him by subsection (1) but any such consent as is there mentioned has been withheld, and no such declaration as is there mentioned has been made, the landlord may serve a notice on the nominated person stating that to be the case.

When such a notice has been served, the landlord may, during the period of 12 months beginning with the date of service of the notice, dispose of the protected interest to such person as he thinks fit, but subject to the following restrictions.

(4) Where the offer notice was one to which section 5B applied (sale by auction), the restrictions are—

(a) that the disposal is made by means of a sale at a public auction, and

(b) that the other terms correspond to those specified in the offer notice.

(5) In any other case the restrictions are—

(a) that the deposit and consideration required are not less than those specified in the offer notice or, if higher, those agreed between the landlord and the nominated person (subject to contract), and

(b) that the other terms correspond to those specified in the offer notice.

(6) Where notice is given under subsection (3), the landlord may recover from the nominated party and the qualifying tenants who served the acceptance notice any costs reasonably incurred by him in connection with the disposal between the end of the first four weeks of the nomination period and the time when that notice is served by him.

Any such liability of the nominated person and those tenants is a joint and several liability.

Notice of withdrawal by nominated person

9A.—(1) Where the landlord is obliged to proceed, the nominated person may serve notice on the landlord (a "notice of withdrawal") indicating his intention no longer to proceed with the acquisition of the protected interest.

(2) If at any time the nominated person becomes aware that the number of the qualifying

tenants of the constituent flats desiring to proceed with the acquisition of the protected interest is less than the requisite majority of qualifying tenants of those flats, he shall forthwith serve a notice of withdrawal.

(3) Where notice of withdrawal is given by the nominated person under this section, the landlord may, during the period of 12 months beginning with the date of service of the notice, dispose of the protected interest to such person as he thinks fit, but subject to the following restrictions.

(4) Where the offer notice was one to which section 5B applied (sale by auction), the restrictions are—

(a) that the disposal is made by means of a sale at a public auction, and

(b) that the other terms correspond to those specified in the offer notice.

(5) In any other case the restrictions are—

(a) that the deposit and consideration required are not less than those specified in the offer notice or, if higher, those agreed between the landlord and the nominated person (subject to contract), and

(b) that the other terms correspond to those specified in the offer notice.

(6) If notice of withdrawal is served under this section before the end of the first four weeks of the nomination period specified in the offer notice, the nominated person and the qualifying tenants who served the acceptance notice are not liable for any costs incurred by the landlord in connection with the disposal.

(7) If notice of withdrawal is served under this section after the end of those four weeks, the landlord may recover from the nominated person and the qualifying tenants who served the acceptance notice any costs reasonably incurred by him in connection with the disposal between the end of those four weeks and the time when the notice of withdrawal was served on him.

Any such liability of the nominated person and those tenants is a joint and several liability.

(8) This section does not apply after a binding contract for the disposal of the protected interest—

(a) has been entered into by the landlord and the nominated person, or

(b) has otherwise come into existence between the landlord and the nominated person by virtue of any provision of this Part.

Notice of withdrawal by landlord

9B.—(1) Where the landlord is obliged to proceed, he may serve notice on the nominated person (a "notice of withdrawal") indicating his intention no longer to proceed with the disposal of the protected interest.

(2) Where a notice of withdrawal is given by the landlord, he is not entitled to dispose of the protected interest during the period of 12 months beginning with the date of service of the notice.

(3) If a notice of withdrawal is served before the end of the first four weeks of the nomination period specified in the offer notice, the landlord is not liable for any costs incurred in connection with the disposal by the nominated person and the qualifying tenants who served the acceptance notice.

(4) If a notice of withdrawal is served after the end of those four weeks, the nominated person and the qualifying tenants who served the acceptance notice may recover from the landlord any costs reasonably incurred by them in connection with the disposal between the end of those four weeks and the time when the notice of withdrawal was served.

(5) This section does not apply after a binding contract for the disposal of the protected interest—

(a) has been entered into by the landlord and the nominated person, or

(b) has otherwise come into existence between the landlord and the nominated person by virtue of any provision of this Part.

Lapse of landlord's offer

10.—(1) If after a landlord has served an offer notice the premises concerned cease to be premises to which this Part applies, the landlord may serve a notice on the qualifying tenants of the constituent flats stating—

(a) that the premises have ceased to be premises to which this Part applies, and

(b) that the offer notice, and anything done in pursuance of it, is to be treated as not having been served or done;

and on the service of such a notice the provisions of this Part cease to have effect in relation to that disposal.

(2) A landlord who has not served such a notice on all of the qualifying tenants of the constituent flats shall nevertheless be treated as having duly served a notice under subsection (1)—

(a) if he has served such a notice on not less than 90% of those tenants, or
(b) where those qualifying tenants number less than ten, if he has served such a notice on all but one of them.

(3) Where the landlord is entitled to serve a notice under subsection (1) but does not do so, this Part shall continue to have effect in relation to the disposal in question as if the premises in question were still premises to which this Part applies.

(4) The above provisions of this section do not apply after a binding contract for the disposal of the protected interest—
(a) has been entered into by the landlord and the nominated person, or
(b) has otherwise come into existence between the landlord and the nominated person by virtue of any provision of this Part.

(5) Where a binding contract for the disposal of the protected interest has been entered into between the landlord and the nominated person but it has been lawfully rescinded by the landlord, the landlord may, during the period of 12 months beginning with the date of the rescission of the contract, dispose of that interest to such person (and on such terms) as he thinks fit.".

PART II

ENFORCEMENT BY TENANTS OF RIGHTS AGAINST PURCHASER

The following sections are substituted for sections 11 to 15 of the Landlord and Tenant Act 1987—

"Enforcement by tenants of rights against purchaser

Circumstances in which tenants' rights enforceable against purchaser

11.—(1) The following provisions of this Part apply where a landlord has made a relevant disposal affecting premises to which at the time of the disposal this Part applied ("the original disposal"), and either—
(a) no notice was served by the landlord under section 5 with respect to that disposal, or
(b) the disposal was made in contravention of any provision of sections 6 to 10,
and the premises are still premises to which this Part applies.

(2) In those circumstances the requisite majority of the qualifying tenants of the flats contained in the premises affected by the relevant disposal (the "constituent flats") have the rights conferred by the following provisions—
    section 11A (right to information as to terms of disposal, &c.),
    section 12A (right of qualifying tenants to take benefit of contract),
    section 12B (right of qualifying tenants to compel sale, &c. by purchaser), and
    section 12C (right of qualifying tenants to compel grant of new tenancy by superior landlord).

(3) In those sections the transferee under the original disposal (or, in the case of the surrender of a tenancy, the superior landlord) is referred to as "the purchaser".

This shall not be read as restricting the operation of those provisions to disposals for consideration.

Right to information as to terms of disposal, &c.

11A.—(1) The requisite majority of qualifying tenants of the constituent flats may serve a notice on the purchaser requiring him—
(a) to give particulars of the terms on which the original disposal was made (including the deposit and consideration required) and the date on which it was made, and
(b) where the disposal consisted of entering into a contract, to provide a copy of the contract.

(2) The notice must specify the name and address of the person to whom (on behalf of the tenants) the particulars are to be given, or the copy of the contract provided.

(3) Any notice under this section must be served before the end of the period of four months beginning with the date by which—
(a) notices under section 3A of the Landlord and Tenant Act 1985 (duty of new landlord to inform tenants of rights) relating to the original disposal, or
(b) where that section does not apply, documents of any other description—
    (i) indicating that the original disposal has taken place, and
    (ii) alerting the tenants to the existence of their rights under this Part and the time within which any such rights must be exercised,
have been served on the requisite majority of qualifying tenants of the constituent flats.

(4) A person served with a notice under this section shall comply with it within the period of one month beginning with the date on which it is served on him.

Right of qualifying tenants to take benefit of contract

12A.—(1) Where the original disposal consisted of entering into a contract, the requisite majority of qualifying tenants of the constituent flats may by notice to the landlord elect that the contract shall have effect as if entered into not with the purchaser but with a person or persons nominated for the purposes of this section by the requisite majority of qualifying tenants of the constituent flats.

(2) Any such notice must be served before the end of the period of six months beginning—

(a) if a notice was served on the purchaser under section 11A (right to information as to terms of disposal, &c.), with the date on which the purchaser complied with that notice;

(b) in any other case, with the date by which documents of any description—

(i) indicating that the original disposal has taken place, and

(ii) alerting the tenants to the existence of their rights under this Part and the time within which any such rights must be exercised,

have been served on the requisite majority of qualifying tenants of the constituent flats.

(3) The notice shall not have effect as mentioned in subsection (1) unless the nominated person—

(a) fulfils any requirements as to the deposit required on entering into the contract, and

(b) fulfils any other conditions required to be fulfilled by the purchaser on entering into the contract.

(4) Unless otherwise agreed, any time limit in the contract as it has effect by virtue of a notice under this section shall start to run again on the service of that notice; and nothing in the contract as it has effect by virtue of a notice under this section shall require the nominated person to complete the purchase before the end of the period of 28 days beginning with the day on which he is deemed to have entered into the contract.

(5) Where the original disposal related to other property in addition to premises to which this Part applied at the time of the disposal—

(a) a notice under this section has effect only in relation to the premises to which this Part applied at the time of the original disposal, and

(b) the terms of the contract shall have effect with any necessary modifications.

In such a case the notice under this section may specify the subject-matter of the disposal, and the terms on which the disposal is to be made (whether doing so expressly or by reference to the original disposal), or may provide for that estate or interest, or any such terms, to be determined by a leasehold valuation tribunal.

Right of qualifying tenants to compel sale, &c. by purchaser

12B.—(1) This section applies where—

(a) the original disposal consisted of entering into a contract and no notice has been served under section 12A (right of qualifying tenants to take benefit of contract), or

(b) the original disposal did not consist of entering into a contract.

(2) The requisite majority of qualifying tenants of the constituent flats may serve a notice (a "purchase notice") on the purchaser requiring him to dispose of the estate or interest that was the subject-matter of the original disposal, on the terms on which it was made (including those relating to the consideration payable), to a person or persons nominated for the purposes of this section by any such majority of qualifying tenants of those flats.

(3) Any such notice must be served before the end of the period of six months beginning—

(a) if a notice was served on the purchaser under section 11A (right to information as to terms of disposal, &c.), with the date on which the purchaser complied with that notice;

(b) in any other case, with the date by which—

(i) notices under section 3A of the Landlord and Tenant Act 1985 (duty of new landlord to inform tenants of rights) relating to the original disposal, or

(ii) where that section does not apply, documents of any other description indicating that the original disposal has taken place, and alerting the tenants to the existence of their rights under this Part and the time within which any such rights must be exercised,

have been served on the requisite majority of qualifying tenants of the constituent flats.

(4) A purchase notice shall where the original disposal related to other property in addition to premises to which this Part applied at the time of the disposal—

(a) require the purchaser only to make a disposal relating to those premises, and

(b) require him to do so on the terms referred to in subsection (2) with any necessary modifications.

In such a case the purchase notice may specify the subject-matter of the disposal, and the terms on which the disposal is to be made (whether doing so expressly or by reference to the original disposal), or may provide for those matters to be determined by a leasehold valuation tribunal.

(5) Where the property which the purchaser is required to dispose of in pursuance of the purchase notice has since the original disposal become subject to any charge or other incumbrance, then, unless the court by order directs otherwise—

(a) in the case of a charge to secure the payment of money or the performance of any other obligation by the purchaser or any other person, the instrument by virtue of which the property is disposed of by the purchaser to the person or persons nominated for the purposes of this section shall (subject to the provisions of Part I of Schedule 1) operate to discharge the property from that charge; and

(b) in the case of any other incumbrance, the property shall be so disposed of subject to the incumbrance but with a reduction in the consideration payable to the purchaser corresponding to the amount by which the existence of the incumbrance reduces the value of the property.

(6) Subsection (5)(a) and Part I of Schedule 1 apply, with any necessary modifications, to mortgages and liens as they apply to charges; but nothing in those provisions applies to a rentcharge.

(7) Where the property which the purchaser is required to dispose of in pursuance of the purchase notice has since the original disposal increased in monetary value owing to any change in circumstances (other than a change in the value of money), the amount of the consideration payable to the purchaser for the disposal by him of the property in pursuance of the purchase notice shall be the amount that might reasonably have been obtained on a corresponding disposal made on the open market at the time of the original disposal if the change in circumstances had already taken place.

Right of qualifying tenants to compel grant of new tenancy by superior landlord

12C.—(1) This section applies where the original disposal consisted of the surrender by the landlord of a tenancy held by him ("the relevant tenancy").

(2) The requisite majority of qualifying tenants of the constituent flats may serve a notice on the purchaser requiring him to grant a new tenancy of the premises which were subject to the relevant tenancy, on the same terms as those of the relevant tenancy and so as to expire on the same date as that tenancy would have expired, to a person or persons nominated for the purposes of this section by any such majority of qualifying tenants of those flats.

(3) Any such notice must be served before the end of the period of six months beginning—

(a) if a notice was served on the purchaser under section 11A (right to information as to terms of disposal, &c.), with the date on which the purchaser complied with that notice;

(b) in any other case, with the date by which documents of any description—

    (i) indicating that the original disposal has taken place, and

    (ii) alerting the tenants to the existence of their rights under this Part and the time within which any such rights must be exercised,

have been served on the requisite majority of qualifying tenants of the constituent flats.

(4) If the purchaser paid any amount to the landlord as consideration for the surrender by him of that tenancy, the nominated person shall pay that amount to the purchaser.

(5) Where the premises subject to the relevant tenancy included premises other than premises to which this Part applied at the time of the disposal, a notice under this section shall—

(a) require the purchaser only to grant a new tenancy relating to the premises to which this Part then applied, and

(b) require him to do so on the terms referred to in subsection (2) subject to any necessary modifications.

(6) The purchase notice may specify the subject-matter of the disposal, and the terms on which the disposal is to be made (whether doing so expressly or by reference to the original disposal), or may provide for those matters to be determined by a leasehold valuation tribunal.

Nominated persons: supplementary provisions

12D.—(1) The person or persons initially nominated for the purposes of section 12A, 12B or 12C shall be nominated in the notice under that section.

(2) A person nominated for those purposes by the requisite majority of qualifying tenants of the constituent flats may be replaced by another person so nominated if, and only if, he has (for any reason) ceased to be able to act as a nominated person.

(3) Where two or more persons have been nominated and any of them ceases to act without being replaced, the remaining person or persons so nominated may continue to act.

(4) Where, in the exercise of its power to award costs, the court or the Lands Tribunal makes, in connection with any proceedings arising under or by virtue of this Part, an award of costs against the person or persons so nominated, the liability for those costs is a joint and several liability of that person or those persons together with the qualifying tenants by whom the relevant notice was served.

Determination of questions by leasehold valuation tribunal

13.—(1) A leasehold valuation tribunal has jurisdiction to hear and determine—
  (a) any question arising in relation to any matters specified in a notice under section 12A, 12B or 12C, and
  (b) any question arising for determination as mentioned in section 8C(4), 12A(5) or 12B(4) (matters left for determination by tribunal).

(2) On an application under this section the interests of the persons by whom the notice was served under section 12A, 12B or 12C shall be represented by the nominated person; and accordingly the parties to any such application shall not include those persons.

Withdrawal of nominated person from transaction under s.12B or 12C

14.—(1) Where notice has been duly served on the landlord under—
    section 12B (right of qualifying tenants to compel sale, &c. by purchaser), or
    section 12C (right of qualifying tenants to compel grant of new tenancy by superior landlord),
the nominated person may at any time before a binding contract is entered into in pursuance of the notice, serve notice under this section on the purchaser (a "notice of withdrawal") indicating an intention no longer to proceed with the disposal.

(2) If at any such time the nominated person becomes aware that the number of qualifying tenants of the constituent flats desiring to proceed with the disposal is less than the requisite majority of those tenants, he shall forthwith serve a notice of withdrawal.

(3) If a notice of withdrawal is served under this section the purchaser may recover from the nominated person any costs reasonably incurred by him in connection with the disposal down to the time when the notice is served on him.

(4) If a notice of withdrawal is served at a time when proceedings arising under or by virtue of this Part are pending before the court or the Lands Tribunal, the liability of the nominated person for any costs incurred by the purchaser as mentioned in subsection (3) shall be such as may be determined by the court or (as the case may be) by the Tribunal.

(5) The costs that may be recovered by the purchaser under this section do not include any costs incurred by him in connection with an application to a leasehold valuation tribunal.".

PART III

ENFORCEMENT OF RIGHTS AGAINST SUBSEQUENT PURCHASERS AND TERMINATION OF RIGHTS

The following sections replace sections 16 and 17 of the Landlord and Tenant Act 1987—

"*Enforcement by tenants of rights against subsequent purchasers*

Rights of qualifying tenants against subsequent purchaser

16.—(1) This section applies where, at the time when a notice is served on the purchaser under section 11A, 12A, 12B or 12C, he no longer holds the estate or interest that was the subject-matter of the original disposal.

(2) In the case of a notice under section 11A (right to information as to terms of disposal, &c.) the purchaser shall, within the period for complying with that notice—
  (a) serve notice on the person specified in the notice as the person to whom particulars are to be provided of the name and address of the person to whom he has disposed of that estate or interest ("the subsequent purchaser"), and
  (b) serve on the subsequent purchaser a copy of the notice under section 11A and of the particulars given by him in response to it.

(3) In the case of a notice under section 12A, 12B or 12C the purchaser shall forthwith—
  (a) forward the notice to the subsequent purchaser, and
  (b) serve on the nominated person notice of the name and address of the subsequent purchaser.

(4) Once the purchaser serves a notice in accordance with subsection (2)(a) or (3)(b), sections 12A to 14 shall, instead of applying to the purchaser, apply to the subsequent purchaser as if he

were the transferee under the original disposal.

(5) Subsections (1) to (4) have effect, with any necessary modifications, in a case where, instead of disposing of the whole of the estate or interest referred to in subsection (1) to another person, the purchaser has disposed of it in part or in parts to one or more other persons.

In such a case, sections 12A to 14—

(a) apply to the purchaser in relation to any part of that estate or interest retained by him, and

(b) in relation to any part of that estate or interest disposed of to any other person, apply to that other person instead as if he were (as respects that part) the transferee under the original disposal.

Termination of rights against purchasers or subsequent purchasers

Termination of rights against purchaser or subsequent purchaser

17.—(1) If, at any time after a notice has been served under section 11A, 12A, 12B or 12C, the premises affected by the original disposal cease to be premises to which this Part applies, the purchaser may serve a notice on the qualifying tenants of the constituent flats stating—

(a) that the premises have ceased to be premises to which this Part applies, and

(b) that any such notice served on him, and anything done in pursuance of it, is to be treated as not having been served or done.

(2) A landlord who has not served such a notice on all of the qualifying tenants of the constituent flats shall nevertheless be treated as having duly served a notice under subsection (1)—

(a) if he has served such a notice on not less than 90% of those tenants, or

(b) where those qualifying tenants number less than ten, if he has served such a notice on all but one of them.

(3) Where a period of three months beginning with the date of service of a notice under section 12A, 12B or 12C on the purchaser has expired—

(a) without any binding contract having been entered into between the purchaser and the nominated person, and

(b) without there having been made any application in connection with the notice to the court or to a leasehold valuation tribunal,

the purchaser may serve on the nominated person a notice stating that the notice, and anything done in pursuance of it, is to be treated as not having been served or done.

(4) Where any such application as is mentioned in subsection (3)(b) was made within the period of three months referred to in that subsection, but—

(a) a period of two months beginning with the date of the determination of that application has expired,

(b) no binding contract has been entered into between the purchaser and the nominated person, and

(c) no other such application as is mentioned in subsection (3)(b) is pending,

the purchaser may serve on the nominated person a notice stating that any notice served on him under section 12A, 12B or 12C, and anything done in pursuance of any such notice, is to be treated as not having been served or done.

(5) Where the purchaser serves a notice in accordance with subsection (1), (3) or (4), this Part shall cease to have effect in relation to him in connection with the original disposal.

(6) Where a purchaser is entitled to serve a notice under subsection (1) but does not do so, this Part shall continue to have effect in relation to him in connection with the original disposal as if the premises in question were still premises to which this Part applies.

(7) References in this section to the purchaser include a subsequent purchaser to whom sections 12A to 14 apply by virtue of section 16(4) or (5).".

PART IV

CONSEQUENTIAL AMENDMENTS

1. In section 4(2) of the Landlord and Tenant Act 1987 (relevant disposals: excluded disposals), in paragraph (aa) (disposals by way of security for a loan) omit the words "consisting of the creation of an estate or interest".

2. Before section 19 of the Landlord and Tenant Act 1987, under the heading *"Supplementary provisions"*, insert—

"The requisite majority of qualifying tenants

18A.—(1) In this Part "the requisite majority of qualifying tenants of the constituent flats" means qualifying tenants of constituent flats with more than 50 per cent. of the available votes.

(2) The total number of available votes shall be determined as follows—

(a) where an offer notice has been served under section 5, that number is equal to the total number of constituent flats let to qualifying tenants on the date when the period specified in that notice as the period for accepting the offer expires;

(b) where a notice is served under section 11A without a notice having been previously served under section 5, that number is equal to the total number of constituent flats let to qualifying tenants on the date of service of the notice under section 11A;

(c) where a notice is served under section 12A, 12B or 12C without a notice having been previously served under section 5 or section 11A, that number is equal to the total number of constituent flats let to qualifying tenants on the date of service of the notice under section 12A, 12B or 12C, as the case may be.

(3) There is one available vote in respect of each of the flats so let on the date referred to in the relevant paragraph of subsection (2), which shall be attributed to the qualifying tenant to whom it is let.

(4) The persons constituting the requisite majority of qualifying tenants for one purpose may be different from the persons constituting such a majority for another purpose.".

3.—(1) Section 20(1) of the Landlord and Tenant Act 1987 (interpretation of Part I) is amended as follows.

(2) For the definition of "acceptance notice" substitute—

" "acceptance notice" has the meaning given by section 6(3);".

(3) For the definition of "constituent flat" substitute—

" "constituent flat" shall be construed in accordance with section 5(1) or 11(2), as the case may require;".

(4) Omit the definition of "the new landlord".

(5) After that definition insert—

" "the nominated person" means the person or persons for the time being nominated by the requisite majority of the qualifying tenants of the constituent flats for the purposes of section 6, 12A, 12B or 12C, as the case may require;".

(6) For the definition of "the protected interest" substitute—

" "the protected interest" means the estate, interest or other subject-matter of an offer notice;".

(7) After that definition insert—

" "the protected period" has the meaning given by section 6(4);".

(8) For the definition of "purchase notice" substitute—

" "purchase notice" has the meaning given by section 12B(2);".

(9) After that definition insert—

" "purchaser" has the meaning given by section 11(3);".

(10) In the definition of "the requisite majority" for "section 5(6) and (7)" substitute"section 18A".

4. In section 20(2) of the Landlord and Tenant Act 1987, omit the words "or counter-offer" in each place where they occur.

5. In Part III of the Landlord and Tenant Act 1987 (compulsory acquisition by tenants of their landlord's interest), in section 31 (determination of terms by rent assessment committees)—

(a) for "rent assessment committee", wherever occurring, substitute "leasehold valuation tribunal";

(b) for "such a committee" or "the committee", wherever occurring, substitute "the tribunal"; and

(c) omit subsection (5).

6. In section 52(1) of the Landlord and Tenant Act 1987 (jurisdiction of county courts) for "rent assessment committee" substitute "leasehold valuation tribunal".

7. After section 52 of the Landlord and Tenant Act 1987 insert—

"Jurisdiction of leasehold valuation tribunal under Part I or III

52A.—(1) Any jurisdiction conferred by Part I or III of this Act on a leasehold valuation tribunal is exercisable by a rent assessment committee constituted in accordance with Schedule 10 to the Rent Act 1977 which when so constituted for the purposes of exercising any such jurisdiction shall be known as a leasehold valuation tribunal.

(2) The power to make regulations under section 74(1)(b) of the Rent Act 1977 (procedure of rent assessment committees) extends to prescribing the procedure to be followed in connection with any proceedings before a leasehold valuation tribunal under this Act.

(3) Any application under this Act to a leasehold valuation tribunal must be in such form, and contain such particulars, as the Secretary of State may by regulations prescribe.

(4) Any costs incurred by a party to any such application in connection with the application shall be borne by that party.

(5) Paragraphs 1, 2, 3 and 7 of Schedule 22 to the Housing Act 1980 (supplementary provisions relating to leasehold valuation tribunals: constitution, appeals and provision of information) apply to a leasehold valuation tribunal constituted for the purposes of this section.".

8. In section 53(2)(b) of the Landlord and Tenant Act 1987 (regulations subject to negative resolution), for the words from "section 13(2)" to "section 31)" substitute "section 52A(3)".

9. In section 54(4) of the Landlord and Tenant Act 1987 (saving for power under section 20(4)) for "either of the periods specified in section 5(2)" substitute "any of the periods specified in section 5A(4) or (5), 5B(5) or (6), 5C(4) or (5), 5D(4) or (5) or 5E(3)".

10. In section 60(1) of the Landlord and Tenant Act 1987 (general interpretation), omit the definition of "rent assessment committee".

11.—(1) In Schedule 1 to the Landlord and Tenant Act 1987 (discharge of mortgages, &c), in paragraph 1 (construction of provisions relating to discharge in pursuance of purchase notice)—
(a) for the words "the new landlord" wherever they appear substitute "the purchaser";
(b) in the definition of consideration payable"—
    (i) for the words "section 12(4)" substitute "section 12B(7)", and
    (ii) for the words "section 16(2) or (3)" substitute "section 16(4) or (5)";
(c) in the definition of "nominated person", for the words "section 12(1)" substitute "section 12B(2)".

(2) In paragraphs 2, 4 and 5 of that Schedule (duty of nominated person to redeem mortgages, payments into court and savings)—
(a) for the words "section 12(4)(a)" wherever they appear substitute "section 12B(5)(a)";
(b) for the words "the new landlord" or "the new landlord's" wherever they appear substitute "the purchaser" or "the purchaser's.

GENERAL NOTE
See notes to s.92.

Section 96 SCHEDULE 7

ASSURED TENANCIES: SCHEDULE INSERTED AFTER SCHEDULE 2 TO THE HOUSING ACT 1988

"SCHEDULE 2A

ASSURED TENANCIES: NON-SHORTHOLDS

Tenancies excluded by notice

1.—(1) An assured tenancy in respect of which a notice is served as mentioned in sub-paragraph (2) below.
(2) The notice referred to in sub-paragraph (1) above is one which—
(a) is served before the assured tenancy is entered into,
(b) is served by the person who is to be the landlord under the assured tenancy on the person who is to be the tenant under that tenancy, and
(c) states that the assured tenancy to which it relates is not to be an assured shorthold tenancy.
2.—(1) An assured tenancy in respect of which a notice is served as mentioned in sub-paragraph (2) below.
(2) The notice referred to in sub-paragraph (1) above is one which—
(a) is served after the assured tenancy has been entered into,
(b) is served by the landlord under the assured tenancy on the tenant under that tenancy, and
(c) states that the assured tenancy to which it relates is no longer an assured shorthold tenancy.

Tenancies containing exclusionary provision

3. An assured tenancy which contains a provision to the effect that the tenancy is not an assured shorthold tenancy.

Tenancies under section 39

4. An assured tenancy arising by virtue of section 39 above, other than one to which subsection (7) of that section applies.

Former secure tenancies

5. An assured tenancy which became an assured tenancy on ceasing to be a secure tenancy.

Tenancies under Schedule 10 to the Local Government and Housing Act 1989

6. An assured tenancy arising by virtue of Schedule 10 to the Local Government and Housing Act 1989 (security of tenure on ending of long residential tenancies).

Tenancies replacing non-shortholds

7.—(1) An assured tenancy which—
(a) is granted to a person (alone or jointly with others) who, immediately before the tenancy was granted, was the tenant (or, in the case of joint tenants, one of the tenants) under an assured tenancy other than a shorthold tenancy ("the old tenancy"),
(b) is granted (alone or jointly with others) by a person who was at that time the landlord (or one of the joint landlords) under the old tenancy, and
(c) is not one in respect of which a notice is served as mentioned in sub-paragraph (2) below.
(2) The notice referred to in sub-paragraph (1)(c) above is one which—
(a) is in such form as may be prescribed,
(b) is served before the assured tenancy is entered into,
(c) is served by the person who is to be the tenant under the assured tenancy on the person who is to be the landlord under that tenancy (or, in the case of joint landlords, on at least one of the persons who are to be joint landlords), and
(d) states that the assured tenancy to which it relates is to be a shorthold tenancy.
8. An assured tenancy which comes into being by virtue of section 5 above on the coming to an end of an assured tenancy which is not a shorthold tenancy.

Assured agricultural occupancies

9.—(1) An assured tenancy—
(a) in the case of which the agricultural worker condition is, by virtue of any provision of Schedule 3 to this Act, for the time being fulfilled with respect to the dwelling-house subject to the tenancy, and
(b) which does not fall within sub-paragraph (2) or (4) below.
(2) An assured tenancy falls within this sub-paragraph if—
(a) before it is entered into, a notice—
　　(i) in such form as may be prescribed, and
　　(ii) stating that the tenancy is to be a shorthold tenancy,
is served by the person who is to be the landlord under the tenancy on the person who is to be the tenant under it, and
(b) it is not an excepted tenancy.
(3) For the purposes of sub-paragraph (2)(b) above, an assured tenancy is an excepted tenancy if—
(a) the person to whom it is granted or, as the case may be, at least one of the persons to whom it is granted was, immediately before it is granted, a tenant or licensee under an assured agricultural occupancy, and
(b) the person by whom it is granted or, as the case may be, at least one of the persons by whom it is granted was, immediately before it is granted, a landlord or licensor under the assured agricultural occupancy referred to in paragraph (a) above.
(4) An assured tenancy falls within this sub-paragraph if it comes into being by virtue of section 5 above on the coming to an end of a tenancy falling within sub-paragraph (2) above.".

GENERAL NOTE
　See notes to s.96.

Section 104　　　　　SCHEDULE 8

ASSURED TENANCIES: CONSEQUENTIAL AMENDMENTS

Housing Act 1985 (c. 68)

1. In section 553(2) of the Housing Act 1985, for paragraph (c) there shall be substituted—
　"(c) the tenancy is not by virtue of any provision of Part I of the Housing Act 1988 an assured shorthold tenancy;".

Housing Act 1988 (c. 50)

2.—(1) The Housing Act 1988 shall be amended as follows.
(2) In section 14, there shall be inserted at the end—

"(9) This section shall apply in relation to an assured shorthold tenancy as if in subsection (1) the reference to an assured tenancy were a reference to an assured shorthold tenancy.".

(3) In section 20, for the side-note and subsection (1) there shall be substituted—

"Assured shorthold tenancies: pre-Housing Act 1996 tenancies

20.—(1) Subject to subsection (3) below, an assured tenancy which is not one to which section 19A above applies is an assured shorthold tenancy if—

(a) it is a fixed term tenancy granted for a term certain of not less than six months,

(b) there is no power for the landlord to determine the tenancy at any time earlier than six months from the beginning of the tenancy, and

(c) a notice in respect of it is served as mentioned in subsection (2) below.".

(4) In that section, after subsection (5) there shall be inserted—

"(5A) Subsections (3) and (4) above do not apply where the new tenancy is one to which section 19A above applies.".

(5) In section 22, in subsection (1), the words from "in respect of" to "above" shall be omitted.

(6) In that section, after subsection (5) there shall be inserted—

"(5A) Where—

(a) an assured tenancy ceases to be an assured shorthold tenancy by virtue of falling within paragraph 2 of Schedule 2A to this Act, and

(b) at the time when it so ceases to be an assured shorthold tenancy there is pending before a rent assessment committee an application in relation to it under this section,

the fact that it so ceases to be an assured shorthold tenancy shall, in relation to that application, be disregarded for the purposes of this section.".

(7) In section 34(3), after "whether or not" there shall be inserted ", in the case of a tenancy to which the provision applies,".

(8) In section 39(7), after "whether or not" there shall be inserted ", in the case of a tenancy to which the provision applies,".

Section 106   SCHEDULE 9

LOW RENT TEST: EXTENSION OF RIGHTS

Right to enfranchisement

1. In the Leasehold Reform Act 1967, after section 1A there shall be inserted—

"Additional right to enfranchisement only in case of houses whose rent exceeds applicable limit under section 4

1AA.—(1) Where—

(a) section 1(1) above would apply in the case of the tenant of a house but for the fact that the tenancy is not a tenancy at a low rent, and

(b) the tenancy falls within subsection (2) below and is not an excluded tenancy,

this Part of this Act shall have effect to confer on the tenant the same right to acquire the freehold of the house and premises as would be conferred by section 1(1) above if it were a tenancy at a low rent.

(2) A tenancy falls within this subsection if—

(a) it is granted for a term of years certain exceeding thirty-five years, whether or not it is (or may become) terminable before the end of that term by notice given by or to the tenant or by re-entry, forfeiture or otherwise,

(b) it is for a term fixed by law under a grant with a covenant or obligation for perpetual renewal, unless it is a tenancy by sub-demise from one which is not a tenancy which falls within this subsection,

(c) it is a tenancy taking effect under section 149(6) of the Law of Property Act 1925 (leases terminable after a death or marriage), or

(d) it is a tenancy which—

(i) is or has been granted for a term of years certain not exceeding thirty-five years, but with a covenant or obligation for renewal without payment of a premium (but not for perpetual renewal), and

(ii) is or has been once or more renewed so as to bring to more than thirty-five years the total of the terms granted (including any interval between the end of a tenancy and the grant of a renewal).

(3) A tenancy is an excluded tenancy for the purposes of subsection (1) above if—

(a) the house which the tenant occupies under the tenancy is in an area designated for the purposes of this provision as a rural area by order made by the Secretary of State,

(b) the freehold of that house is owned together with adjoining land which is not occupied for residential purposes and has been owned together with such land since the coming into force of section 106 of the Housing Act 1996, and

(c) the tenancy was granted on or before the day on which that section came into force.

(4) Where this Part of this Act applies as if there were a single tenancy of property comprised in two or more separate tenancies, then, if each of the separate tenancies falls within subsection (2) above, this section shall apply as if the single tenancy did so.

(5) The power to make an order under subsection (3) above shall be exercisable by statutory instrument which shall be subject to annulment in pursuance of a resolution of either House of Parliament.".

2.—(1) In consequence of paragraph 1 above, the Leasehold Reform Act 1967 shall be amended as follows.

(2) In section 1(3A)(b) (extension of rights not to apply to existing lettings by charitable housing trusts), after "1A" there shall be inserted ", 1AA".

(3) In section 3(3) (provision for aggregation of successive tenancies), after "this Part of this Act" there shall be inserted ", except section 1AA,".

(4) In section 9(1C) (price payable by tenant on enfranchisement by virtue of section 1A or 1B), after "1A" there shall be inserted ", 1AA".

(5) In section 9A(1) (compensation payable where right to enfranchisement arises by virtue of section 1A or 1B), after "1A" there shall be inserted ", 1AA".

(6) In section 32A(1)(b) (extensions to right to enfranchisement not to apply in relation to existing tenancies of property transferred for public benefit), at the end there shall be inserted "or if section 1AA above were not in force".

(7) In section 37(4) (treatment for the purposes of Part I of tenancy granted to continue as a periodical tenancy after the expiration of a term of years certain), after "this Part of this Act" there shall be inserted ", except section 1AA,".

(8) In Part II of Schedule 3 (procedural provisions), in paragraph 6 (which makes provision about the contents of a tenant's notice under Part I), after sub-paragraph (1) there shall be inserted—

"(1A) Where the tenant gives the notice by virtue of section 1AA of this Act, sub-paragraph (1) above shall have effect with the substitution for paragraph (b) of—

"(b) such particulars of the tenancy as serve to identify the instrument creating the tenancy and show that the tenancy is one in relation to which section 1AA(1) of this Act has effect to confer a right to acquire the freehold of the house and premises;".".

(9) In that Part of that Schedule, in paragraph 7(4) (admission in landlord's notice of tenant's right to have freehold to be binding on landlord, so far as relating to matters mentioned in section 1(1)(a) and (b)), for "mentioned in section 1(1)(a) and (b) of this Act" there shall be substituted "relevant to the existence of that right".

Right to collective enfranchisement

3.—(1) Chapter I of Part I of the Leasehold Reform, Housing and Urban Development Act 1993 (collective enfranchisement in case of tenants of flats) shall be amended as follows.

(2) Section 5 (qualifying tenants) shall be amended as follows—

(a) in subsection (1) (which defines a qualifying tenant as a tenant of a flat under a long lease at a low rent), for "at a low rent" there shall be substituted "which is at a low rent or for a particularly long term", and

(b) in subsection (2)(c) (which excludes from the definition a tenant under a lease granted in breach of the terms of a superior lease which is not a long lease at a low rent), after "rent" there shall be inserted "or for a particularly long term".

(3) After section 8 there shall be inserted—

"Meaning of "particularly long term"

8A.—(1) For the purposes of this Chapter a long lease is for a particularly long term if—

(a) it is granted for a term of years certain exceeding 35 years, whether or not it is (or may become) terminable before the end of that term by notice given by or to the tenant or by re-entry, forfeiture or otherwise,

(b) it is for a term fixed by law under a grant with a covenant or obligation for perpetual renewal (other than a lease by sub-demise from one which is not for a particularly long term),

(c) it takes effect under section 149(6) of the Law of Property Act 1925 (leases terminable after a death or marriage), or

(d) it is a lease which—

(i) is or has been granted for a term of years certain not exceeding 35 years, but with a covenant or obligation for renewal without payment of a premium (but not

for perpetual renewal), and
(ii) is or has been renewed on one or more occasions so as to bring to more than 35 years the total of the terms granted (including any interval between the end of a lease and the grant of a renewal).

(2) A long lease which does not fall within subsection (1) above shall nonetheless be treated for the purposes of this Chapter as being for a particularly long term if it is a long lease by virtue of paragraph (c) or (d) of section 7(1).

(3) Where this Chapter applies as if there were a single lease of property comprised in two or more separate leases, then, if each of the separate leases is for a particularly long term, this Chapter shall apply as if the single lease were for such a term.".

(4) In section 13(3)(e) (particulars to be included in initial notice which relevant to whether person a qualifying tenant), in sub-paragraph (ii), for "a lease at a low rent" there shall be substituted "at a low rent or for a particularly long term".

Right to new lease

4.—(1) Chapter II of that Part (individual right of tenant of flat to acquire new lease) shall be amended as follows.

(2) In section 39(3) (provisions of Chapter I which apply for the purposes of Chapter II), at the end of paragraph (c) there shall be inserted ", and
(d) section 8A,".

(3) In section 42(3) (particulars to be included in notice by qualifying tenant of claim to exercise right), in paragraph (b)(iii), there shall be inserted at the end "or, in accordance with section 8A (as that section so applies), a lease for a particularly long term".

5.—(1) In Chapter VII of that Part (general), section 94 (Crown land) shall be amended as follows.

(2) In subsection (3) (disapplication of restriction imposed by section 3(2) of the Crown Estate Act 1961 on term for which lease may be granted by Crown Estate Commissioners), in paragraph (a), for "at a low rent" there shall be substituted "which is at a low rent or for a particularly long term".

(3) In subsection (4) (power to shadow statutory rights), for "at a low rent" there shall be substituted "which is at a low rent or for a particularly long term".

(4) For subsection (12) there shall be substituted—
"(12) For the purposes of this section "long lease which is at a low rent or for a particularly long term" shall be construed in accordance with sections 7, 8 and 8A.".

GENERAL NOTE
See notes to s.106, above.

Section 107   SCHEDULE 10

SECTION 107: CONSEQUENTIAL AMENDMENTS

1. Chapter I of Part I of the Leasehold Reform, Housing and Urban Development Act 1993 shall be amended as follows.

2. In section 1(4) (right to acquire additional property satisfied by grant of rights over that property or other property)—
(a) in paragraph (a), for "freeholder" there shall be substituted "person who owns the freehold of that property", and
(b) in paragraph (b), for "freeholder" there shall be substituted "person who owns the freehold of that property".

3.—(1) Section 9 (the reversioner and other relevant landlords) shall be amended as follows.

(2) In subsection (1), after "any premises" there shall be inserted "the freehold of the whole of which is owned by the same person".

(3) In subsection (2)—
(a) after "such claim" there shall be inserted "as is mentioned in subsection (1)", and
(b) in paragraph (b), after "premises," there shall be inserted "every person who owns any freehold interest which it is proposed to acquire by virtue of section 1(2)(a),".

(4) After that subsection there shall be inserted—
"(2A) In the case of any claim to exercise the right to collective enfranchisement in relation to any premises the freehold of the whole of which is not owned by the same person—
(a) the reversioner in respect of the premises shall for the purposes of this Chapter be the person identified as such by Part IA of Schedule I to this Act, and
(b) every person who owns a freehold interest in the premises, every person who owns

any freehold interest which it is proposed to acquire by virtue of section 1(2)(a), and every person who owns any leasehold interest which it is proposed to acquire under or by virtue of section 2(1)(a) or (b), shall be a relevant landlord for those purposes.".

(5) In subsection (3), after "subsection (2)" there shall be inserted "or (2A)".

4.—(1) Section 10 (premises with a resident landlord) shall be amended as follows.

(2) In subsection (1)(b)—

(a) for "the freeholder, or an adult member of the freeholder's" there shall be substituted "a relevant person, or an adult member of a relevant person's", and

(b) in sub-paragraph (i), after "premises" there shall be inserted "which is a qualifying flat".

(3) In subsection (2)—

(a) in paragraph (a)—

(i) for "freeholder" there shall be substituted "relevant person", and

(ii) after "Chapter", where it first occurs, there shall be inserted ", or, as the case may be, the amendments of this Chapter made by the Housing Act 1996,", and

(b) in paragraph (b)—

(i) for "freeholder, or an adult member of the freeholder's" there shall be substituted "relevant person, or an adult member of that person's", and

(ii) in sub-paragraph (i), after "premises" there shall be inserted "which is a qualifying flat".

(4) In subsection (4)—

(a) for "freehold interest" there shall be substituted "interest of a relevant person", and

(b) for "the freeholder" there shall be substituted "a relevant person".

(5) After that subsection there shall be inserted—

"(4A) For the purposes of this section a person is a relevant person, in relation to any premises, if he owns the freehold of the whole or any part of the premises.".

(6) In subsection (6) there shall be inserted at the end—

" "qualifying flat", in relation to a relevant person, or an adult member of a relevant person's family, means a flat the freehold of the whole of which is owned by the relevant person.".

5.—(1) Section 11 (right of qualifying tenant to obtain information about superior interests etc.) shall be amended as follows.

(2) In subsection (1)—

(a) for "his immediate landlord", in both places, there shall be substituted "any immediate landlord of his", and

(b) for "the person who owns the freehold of" there shall be substituted "every person who owns a freehold interest in".

(3) In subsection (2)(b), for "the tenant's immediate landlord" there shall be substituted "any immediate landlord of the tenant".

(4) In subsection (3), for "the person who owns the freehold of" there shall be substituted "any person who owns a freehold interest in".

(5) In subsection (4), for paragraph (a) there shall be substituted—

"(a) to any person who owns a freehold interest in the relevant premises,

(aa) to any person who owns a freehold interest in any such property as is mentioned in subsection (3)(c),".

(6) In subsection (8)(b)(i), after "premises" there shall be inserted "or in any such property as is mentioned in subsection (3)(c)".

(7) In subsection (9), in the definition of "the relevant premises"—

(a) in paragraph (a), after "owns", where it second occurs, there shall be inserted ", or the persons who own the freehold interests in the flat own,", and

(b) in paragraph (b), after "owns" there shall be inserted ", or those persons own,".

6.—(1) Section 13 (notice by qualifying tenants of claim to exercise right to collective enfranchisement) shall be amended as follows.

(2) In subsection (2), in paragraph (a)—

(a) after "must" there shall be inserted—

"(i) in a case to which section 9(2) applies,",

and

(b) after "premises;" there shall be inserted "and

(ii) in a case to which section 9(2A) applies, be given to the person specified in the notice as the recipient;".

(3) After that subsection there shall be inserted—

"(2A) In a case to which section 9(2A) applies, the initial notice must specify—

(a) a person who owns a freehold interest in the premises, or

(b) if every person falling within paragraph (a) is a person who cannot be found or whose

identity cannot be ascertained, a relevant landlord,
    as the recipient of the notice.".

(4) In subsection (3)(d)(i), there shall be inserted at the end "or, if the freehold of the whole of the specified premises is not owned by the same person, each of the freehold interests in those premises".

7.—(1) Section 19 (effect of notice under section 13 on subsequent transactions by freeholder etc) shall be amended as follows.

(2) In subsection (1)(a)—

(a) for "the person who owns the freehold of the specified premises" there shall be substituted "any person who owns the freehold of the whole or any part of the specified premises or the freehold of any property specified in the notice under section 13(3)(a)(ii)", and

(b) in sub-paragraph (i), for the words from "any property" to the end there shall be substituted "that property".

(3) In subsection (2), for paragraph (a) there shall be substituted—

"(a) any person who owns the freehold of the whole or any part of the specified premises or the freehold of any property specified in the notice under section 13(3)(a)(ii) disposes of his interest in those premises or that property,".

(4) In subsection (4), for paragraph (a) there shall be substituted—

"(a) by any person who owns the freehold of the whole or any part of the specified premises or the freehold of any property specified in the notice under section 13(3)(a)(ii),".

8.—(1) Section 21 (reversioner's counter-notice) shall be amended as follows.

(2) In subsection (3)(d), for "the person who owns the freehold of the specified premises, or any other" there shall be substituted "any".

(3) In subsection (4), for "the person who owns the freehold of the specified premises or of any other" there shall be substituted "any".

9.—(1) Section 26 (application to court where relevant landlords cannot be found) shall be amended as follows.

(2) In subsection (1)(b), after "section 9(2)" there shall be inserted "or (2A)".

(3) In subsection (3), after "If" there shall be inserted ", in a case to which section 9(2) applies,".

(4) After that subsection there shall be inserted—

"(3A) Where in a case to which section 9(2A) applies—

(a) not less than two-thirds of the qualifying tenants of flats contained in any premises to which this Chapter applies desire to make a claim to exercise the right to collective enfranchisement in relation to those premises, and

(b) paragraph (b) of subsection (1) does not apply, but

(c) a copy of a notice of that claim cannot be given in accordance with Part II of Schedule 3 to any person to whom it would otherwise be required to be so given because he cannot be found or his identity cannot be ascertained,

the court may, on the application of the qualifying tenants in question, make an order dispensing with the need to give a copy of such a notice to that person.".

(5) In subsection (4), for "or (2)" there shall be substituted ", (2) or (3A)".

(6) In subsection (7), after "(2)" there shall be inserted "or (3A)".

10. In section 30 (effect on acquisition of institution of compulsory acquisition procedures), at the end of subsection (2)(a) there shall be inserted "or, where the freehold of the whole of the premises is not owned by the same person, any person who owns the freehold of part of them".

11.—(1) Section 34 (conveyance to nominee purchaser) shall be amended as follows.

(2) In subsection (1)—

(a) after "specified premises" there shall be inserted ", of a part of those premises", and

(b) after "those premises" there shall be inserted ", that part of those premises".

(3) In subsection (2), after "premises" there shall be inserted ", the part of the specified premises".

12.—(1) Section 36 (nominee purchaser required to grant leases back to former freeholder) shall be amended as follows.

(2) In subsection (1)—

(a) for "the freehold of" there shall be substituted "a freehold interest in", and

(b) for "freehold", where it second occurs, there shall be substituted "interest".

(3) In subsection (2), for "of the specified premises" there shall be substituted "interest concerned".

13. In section 38 (interpretation of Chapter I), in subsection (3), after "section 9(2)(b)" there shall be inserted "or (2A)(b)".

14. In Schedule 1 (conduct of proceedings by reversioner on behalf of other landlords), in Part

I (identification of reversioner in case of premises with relevant landlords), in paragraph 1, after "2 to 4," there shall be inserted "in a case to which section 9(2) applies,".

15. In that Schedule, after Part I there shall be inserted—

"Part IA

The reversioner: premises with multiple freeholders

Initial reversioner

5A. Subject to paragraphs 5B to 5D, in a case to which section 9(2A) applies, the reversioner in respect of any premises is the person specified in the initial notice in accordance with section 13(2A) as the recipient.

Change of reversioner

5B. The court may, on the application of all the relevant landlords of any premises, appoint to be the reversioner in respect of those premises (in place of the person designated by paragraph 5A) such person as may have been determined by agreement between them.

5C. If it appears to the court, on the application of a relevant landlord of any premises—

(a) that the respective interests of the relevant landlords of those premises, the absence or incapacity of the person referred to in paragraph 5A or other special circumstances require that some person other than the person there referred to should act as the reversioner in respect of the premises, or

(b) that the person referred to in that paragraph is unwilling to act as the reversioner,

the court may appoint to be the reversioner in respect of those premises (in place of the person designated by paragraph 5A) such person as it thinks fit.

5D. The court may also, on the application of any of the relevant landlords or of the nominee purchaser, remove the reversioner in respect of any premises and appoint another person in his place, if it appears to the court proper to do so by reason of any delay or default, actual or apprehended, on the part of the reversioner.

5E. A person appointed by the court under any of paragraphs 5B to 5D—

(a) must be a relevant landlord; but

(b) may be so appointed on such terms and conditions as the court thinks fit.".

16. In Schedule 2 (special categories of landlords), in paragraph 1(1), in the definition of "Chapter I landlord", for "the reversioner or any other" there shall be substituted "a".

17.—(1) Part II of Schedule 3 (which makes provision for the giving of copies of the notice under section 13 to relevant landlords) shall be amended as follows.

(2) In paragraph 11, after "section 9(2)" there shall be inserted "or (2A)".

(3) In paragraph 12, in sub-paragraph (1), there shall be inserted at the beginning "In a case to which section 9(2) applies,".

(4) After that paragraph there shall be inserted—

"12A.—(1) In a case to which section 9(2A) applies, the qualifying tenants by whom the initial notice is given shall, in addition to giving the initial notice to the person specified in it as the recipient, give a copy of the notice to every other person known or believed by them to be a relevant landlord of the specified premises.

(2) The initial notice shall state whether copies are being given in accordance with sub-paragraph (1) to anyone other than the person specified in it as the recipient and, if so, to whom.".

(5) In paragraph 13(3)(a), after "12(2)" there shall be inserted "or, as the case may be, 12A(2)".

(6) In paragraph 14(2)(b)—

(a) after "12" there shall be inserted ", 12A", and

(b) for "either" there shall be substituted "any".

18.—(1) Schedule 6 (purchase price payable by nominee purchaser) shall be amended as follows.

(2) In paragraph 1(1) (interpretation)—

(a) the definition of "the freeholder" shall be omitted, and

(b) for the definition of "the valuation date" there shall be substituted—

" "the valuation date" means—

(a) the date when it is determined, either by agreement or by a leasehold valuation tribunal under this Chapter, what freehold interest in the specified premises is to be acquired by the nominee purchaser, or

(b) if there are different determinations relating to different freehold interests in the specified premises, the date when determinations have been made in relation to all the freehold interests in the premises.".

(3) In paragraph 2 (price payable for the freehold of the specified premises), in sub-paragraph (1)—

(a) after "this paragraph," there shall be inserted "where the freehold of the whole of the specified premises is owned by the same person", and

(b) for "the specified" there shall be substituted "those".

(4) In paragraph 3(1A), after paragraph (b) there shall be inserted—

"(ba) an owner of an interest which the nominee purchaser is to acquire in pursuance of section 1(2)(a), or".

(5) After paragraph 5 there shall be inserted—

"Price payable for freehold of part of specified premises

5A.—(1) Where different persons own the freehold of different parts of the specified premises—

(a) a separate price shall be payable by the nominee purchaser for the freehold of each of those parts, and '

(b) sub-paragraph (2) shall apply to determine the price so payable.

(2) Subject to sub-paragraph (3), the price payable by the nominee purchaser for the freehold of part of the specified premises shall be the aggregate of—

(a) the value of the freeholder's interest in the part as determined in accordance with paragraph 3, modified as mentioned in paragraph 5B, and

(b) the freeholder's share of the marriage value as determined in accordance with paragraph 4, modified as mentioned in paragraph 5C, and

(c) any amount of compensation payable to the freeholder under paragraph 5.

(3) Where the amount arrived at in accordance with sub-paragraph (2) is a negative amount, the price payable by the nominee purchaser for the freehold of the part shall be nil.

5B.—(1) In its application in accordance with paragraph 5A(2)(a), paragraph 3 shall have effect with the following modifications.

(2) In sub-paragraph (1)(a)(ii), there shall be inserted at the end "so far as relating to the part of the premises in which the freeholder's interest subsists".

(3) In sub-paragraph (1A), after paragraph (a) there shall be inserted—

"(aa) an owner of a freehold interest in the specified premises, or".

(4) In sub-paragraph (4)—

(a) the words "the whole of" shall be omitted, and

(b) for "2(1)(a)" there shall be substituted "5A(2)(a)".

5C.—(1) In its application in accordance with paragraph 5A(2)(b), paragraph 4 shall have effect with the following modifications.

(2) In sub-paragraph (2)—

(a) after "the specified premises" there shall be inserted "so far as relating to the part of the premises in which the freeholder's interest subsists",

(b) after "participating tenants", where it first occurs, there shall be inserted "in whose flats the freeholder's interest subsists", and

(c) in paragraph (a), for "the", where it second occurs, there shall be substituted "those".

(3) In sub-paragraph (3)—

(a) after "the specified premises" there shall be inserted "so far as relating to the part of the premises in which the freeholder's interest subsists", and

(b) in paragraph (a), for "2(1)(a)" there shall be substituted "5A(2)(a)".

(4) In sub-paragraph (4)(a), after "3(1)", where it first occurs, there shall be inserted "as applied by paragraph 5A(2)(a)".".

(6) For paragraph 8 there shall be substituted—

"8.—(1) Where the owner of the intermediate leasehold interest will suffer any loss or damage to which this paragraph applies, there shall be payable to him such amount as is reasonable to compensate him for that loss or damage.

(2) This paragraph applies to—

(a) any diminution in value of any interest of the owner of the intermediate leasehold interest in other property resulting from the acquisition of his interest in the specified premises; and

(b) any other loss or damage which results therefrom to the extent that it is referable to his ownership of any interest in other property.

(3) Without prejudice to the generality of paragraph (b) of sub-paragraph (2), the kinds of loss falling within that paragraph include loss of development value in relation to the specified premises to the extent that it is referable as mentioned in that paragraph.

(4) In sub-paragraph (3) "development value", in relation to the specified premises, means any increase in the value of the interest in the premises of the owner of the intermedi-

ate leasehold interest which is attributable to the possibility of demolishing, reconstructing or carrying out substantial works of construction on, the whole or a substantial part of the premises.".

(7) In paragraph 9 (owners of intermediate interests entitled to part of marriage value), in sub-paragraph (1), after "where" there shall be inserted "paragraph 2 applies and".

(8) After that paragraph there shall be inserted—

"9A.—(1) This paragraph applies where paragraph 5A applies and—

(a) the price payable for the freehold of a part of the specified premises includes an amount in respect of the freeholder's share of the marriage value, and

(b) the nominee purchaser is to acquire any intermediate leasehold interests which subsist in that part.

(2) The amount payable to the freeholder of the part in respect of his share of the marriage value shall be divided between the freeholder and the owners of the intermediate leasehold interests which subsist in that part in proportion to the value of their respective interests in the part (as determined for the purposes of paragraph 5A(2)(a) or paragraph 6(1)(b)(i), as the case may be).

(3) Where an intermediate leasehold interest subsists not only in the part of the specified premises in which the freeholder's interest subsists ("the relevant part") but also in another part of those premises—

(a) the value of the intermediate leasehold interest as determined for the purposes of paragraph 6(1)(b)(i) shall be apportioned between the relevant part and the other part of the specified premises in which it subsists, and

(b) sub-paragraph (2) shall have effect as if the reference to the value of the intermediate leasehold interest in the relevant part as determined for the purposes of paragraph 6(1)(b)(i) were to the value of that interest as determined on an apportionment in accordance with paragraph (a).

(4) Where the owner of an intermediate leasehold interest is entitled in accordance with sub-paragraph (2) to any part of the amount payable to the freeholder in respect of the freeholder's share of the marriage value, the amount to which he is so entitled shall be payable to him by the freeholder.".

(9) For paragraph 13 there shall be substituted—

"13.—(1) Where the owner of any such freehold or leasehold interest as is mentioned in paragraph 10(1) or (2) ("relevant interest") will suffer any loss or damage to which this paragraph applies, there shall be payable to him such amount as is reasonable to compensate him for that loss or damage.

(2) This paragraph applies to—

(a) any diminution in value of any interest in other property belonging to the owner of a relevant interest, being diminution resulting from the acquisition of the property in which the relevant interest subsists; and

(b) any other loss or damage which results therefrom to the extent that it is referable to his ownership of any interest in other property.

(3) Without prejudice to the generality of paragraph (b) of sub-paragraph (2), the kinds of loss falling within that paragraph include loss of development value in relation to the property in which the relevant interest subsists to the extent that it is referable to his ownership of any interest in other property.

(4) In sub-paragraph (3) "development value", in relation to the property in which the relevant interest subsists, means any increase in the value of the relevant interest which is attributable to the possibility of demolishing, reconstructing or carrying out substantial works of construction on, the whole or a substantial part of the property.".

(10) In paragraph 14 (valuation of freehold and intermediate leasehold interests), in sub-paragraph (1)—

(a) in paragraph (a), for "the", where it second occurs, there shall be substituted "a" and for "in accordance with paragraph 3" there shall be substituted "for the relevant purposes",

(b) in paragraph (b), for "in accordance with paragraph 7" there shall be substituted "for the relevant purposes", and

(c) for "the relevant" there shall be substituted "those".

(11) In that paragraph, after sub-paragraph (3) there shall be inserted—

"(3A) Where sub-paragraph (2) applies—

(a) for the purposes of paragraph 5A(2)(a), and

(b) in relation to an intermediate leasehold interest in relation to which there is more than one immediately superior interest,

any reduction in value made under that sub-paragraph shall be apportioned between the immediately superior interests.".

(12) In that paragraph, in sub-paragraph (5)(a)—

(a) for "the", where it first occurs, there shall be substituted "a", and

(b) after "2(1)(a)" there shall be inserted "or, as the case may be, 5A(2)(a)".

(13) In paragraph 15 (calculation of marriage value), there shall be inserted at the end—

"(4) References in this paragraph to paragraph 4(2), (3) or (4) extend to that provision as it applies in accordance with paragraph 5A(2)(b).".

(14) In paragraph 16 (apportionment of marriage value), in sub-paragraph (2), for "the", where it first occurs, there shall be substituted "a".

(15) In paragraph 17 (adjustment of compensation), in sub-paragraph (4)(a), after "2(1)(c)" there shall be inserted ", 5A(2)(c)".

(16) In that paragraph, there shall be inserted at the end—

"(6) Where any reduction in value under sub-paragraph (2) of paragraph 14 is apportioned in accordance with sub-paragraph (3A) of that paragraph, any amount of compensation payable by virtue of this paragraph shall be similarly apportioned.".

19. In Schedule 7 (conveyance to nominee purchaser on enfranchisement), in paragraph 1—

(a) for sub-paragraphs (a) and (b) there shall be substituted—

"(a) "the relevant premises" means, in relation to the conveyance of any interest, the premises in which the interest subsists;

(b) "the freeholder" means, in relation to the conveyance of a freehold interest, the person whose interest is to be conveyed;",

and

(b) for sub-paragraph (d) there shall be substituted—

"(d) "the appropriate time" means, in relation to the conveyance of a freehold interest, the time when the interest is to be conveyed to the nominee purchaser.".

20.—(1) Schedule 9 (grant of leases back to former freeholder) shall be amended as follows.

(2) In paragraph 1—

(a) for the definition of "the appropriate time" there shall be substituted—

" "the appropriate time", in relation to a flat or other unit contained in the specified premises, means the time when the freehold of the flat or other unit is acquired by the nominee purchaser;", and

(b) for the definition of "the freeholder" there shall be substituted—

" "the freeholder", in relation to a flat or other unit contained in the specified premises, means the person who owns the freehold of the flat or other unit immediately before the appropriate time;".

(3) In paragraph 2, in sub-paragraph (1), for "contained in the specified premises" there shall be substituted "falling within sub-paragraph (1A)", and after that sub-paragraph there shall be inserted—

"(1A) A flat falls within this sub-paragraph if—

(a) the freehold of the whole of it is owned by the same person, and

(b) it is contained in the specified premises.".

(4) In paragraph 3, in sub-paragraph (1), for "contained in the specified premises" there shall be substituted "falling within sub-paragraph (1A)", and after that sub-paragraph there shall be inserted—

"(1A) A flat falls within this sub-paragraph if—

(a) the freehold of the whole of it is owned by the same person, and

(b) it is contained in the specified premises.".

(5) In paragraph 5, in sub-paragraph (1), for "contained in the specified premises" there shall be substituted "falling within sub-paragraph (1A)", and after that sub-paragraph there shall be inserted—

"(1A) A unit falls within this sub-paragraph if—

(a) the freehold of the whole of it is owned by the same person, and

(b) it is contained in the specified premises.".

(6) In paragraph 6, for sub-paragraphs (1) and (2) there shall be substituted—

"(1) Sub-paragraph (2) applies where, immediately before the freehold of a flat or other unit contained in the specified premises is acquired by the nominee purchaser—

(a) those premises are premises with a resident landlord by virtue of the occupation of the flat or other unit by the freeholder of it, and

(b) the freeholder of the flat or other unit is a qualifying tenant of it.

(2) If the freeholder of the flat or other unit ("the relevant unit") by notice requires the nominee purchaser to do so, the nominee purchaser shall grant to the freeholder a lease of the relevant unit in accordance with section 36 and paragraph 7 below; and, on the grant of such a lease to the freeholder, he shall be deemed to have surrendered any lease of the relevant unit held by him immediately before the appropriate time.".

(7) In that paragraph, in sub-paragraph (3), for "(1)(c)" there shall be substituted "(1)(b)".

GENERAL NOTE
See notes to s.107, above.

Section 116   SCHEDULE 11

COMPENSATION FOR POSTPONEMENT OF TERMINATION IN CONNECTION WITH INEFFECTIVE CLAIMS

Claims under Part I of the Leasehold Reform Act 1967

1.—(1) After section 27 of the Leasehold Reform Act 1967 there shall be inserted—

"**Compensation for postponement of termination in connection with ineffective claims**
27A.—(1) This section applies where, on or after 15th January 1999—
(a) a tenant of any property makes a claim to acquire the freehold or an extended lease of it, and
(b) the claim is not made at least two years before the term date of the tenancy in respect of which the claim is made ("the existing tenancy").
(2) The tenant shall be liable to pay compensation if the claim is not effective and—
(a) the making of the claim caused a notice served under paragraph 4(1) of Schedule 10 to the Local Government and Housing Act 1989 to cease to have effect and the date on which the claim ceases to have effect is later than four months before the termination date specified in the notice,
(b) the making of the claim prevented the service of an effective notice under paragraph 4(1) of Schedule 10 to the Local Government and Housing Act 1989 (but did not cause a notice served under that provision to cease to have effect) and the date on which the claim ceases to have effect is a date later than six months before the term date of the tenancy, or
(c) the existing tenancy is continued under paragraph 3(1) of Schedule 3 to this Act by virtue of the claim.
(3) Compensation under subsection (2) above shall become payable at the end of the appropriate period and be the right of the person who is the tenant's immediate landlord at that time.
(4) The amount which the tenant is liable to pay under subsection (2) above shall be equal to the difference between—
(a) the rent for the appropriate period under the existing tenancy, and
(b) the rent which might reasonably be expected to be payable for that period were the property to which the existing tenancy relates let for a term equivalent to that period on the open market by a willing landlord on the following assumptions—
(i) that no premium is payable in connection with the letting,
(ii) that the letting confers no security of tenure, and
(iii) that, except as otherwise provided by this paragraph, the letting is on the same terms as the existing tenancy.
(5) For the purposes of subsection (2) above, a claim to acquire the freehold or an extended lease is not effective if it ceases to have effect for any reason other than—
(a) the acquisition in pursuance of the claim of the interest to which it relates, or
(b) the lapsing of the claim under any provision of this Act excluding the tenant's liability for costs.
(6) For the purposes of subsections (3) and (4) above, the appropriate period is—
(a) in a case falling within paragraph (a) of subsection (2) above, the period—
(i) beginning with the termination date specified in the notice mentioned in that paragraph, and
(ii) ending with the earliest date of termination which could have been specified in a notice under paragraph 4(1) of Schedule 10 to the Local Government and Housing Act 1989 served immediately after the date on which the claim ceases to have effect, or, if the existing tenancy is terminated before then, with the date of its termination;
(b) in a case falling within paragraph (b) of subsection (2) above, the period—
(i) beginning with the later of six months from the date on which the claim is made and the term date of the existing tenancy, and
(ii) ending six months after the date on which the claim ceases to have effect, or, if the existing tenancy is terminated before then, with the date of its termination; and
(c) in a case falling within paragraph (c) of subsection (2) above, the period for which the

existing tenancy is continued under paragraph 3(1) of Schedule 3 to this Act.

(7) For the purposes of this section—

(a) references to a claim to acquire the freehold or an extended lease shall be taken as references to a notice of a person's desire to acquire it under Part I of this Act and as including a claim made by a tenant not entitled to acquire it, and

(b) references to the date on which a claim ceases to have effect shall, in relation to a notice which is not a valid notice, be taken as references to the date on which the notice is set aside by the court or withdrawn or would, if valid, cease to have effect, that date being taken, where the notice is set aside, or would (if valid) cease to have effect, in consequence of a court order, to be the date when the order becomes final.

Modification of section 27A where change in immediate reversion

27B.—(1) Where a tenant's liability to pay compensation under section 27A above relates to a period during which there has been a change in the interest immediately expectant on the determination of his tenancy, that section shall have effect with the following modifications.

(2) For subsections (3) and (4) there shall be substituted—

"(3) Compensation under subsection (2) above shall become payable at the end of the appropriate period and there shall be a separate right to compensation in respect of each of the interests which, during that period, have been immediately expectant on the determination of the existing tenancy.

(4) Compensation under subsection (2) above shall—

(a) in the case of the interest which is immediately expectant on the determination of the existing tenancy at the end of the appropriate period, be the right of the person in whom that interest is vested at that time, and

(b) in the case of an interest which ceases during the appropriate period to be immediately expectant on the determination of the existing tenancy, be the right of the person in whom the interest was vested immediately before it ceased to be so expectant.

(4A) The amount which the tenant is liable to pay under subsection (2) above in respect of any interest shall be equal to the difference between—

(a) the rent under the existing tenancy for the part of the appropriate period during which the interest was immediately expectant on the determination of that tenancy, and

(b) the rent which might reasonably be expected to be payable for that part of that period were the property to which the existing tenancy relates let for a term equivalent to that part of that period on the open market by a willing landlord on the following assumptions—

(i) that no premium is payable in connection with the letting,

(ii) that the letting confers no security of tenure, and

(iii) that, except as otherwise provided by this paragraph, the letting is on the same terms as the existing tenancy."

(3) In subsection (6), for "(3) and (4)" there shall be substituted "(3) to (4A)"."

(2) In section 21(1) of that Act (matters to be determined by leasehold valuation tribunal), after paragraph (c) there shall be inserted—

"(ca) the amount of any compensation payable under section 27A;".

Claims under Chapter I of Part I of the Leasehold Reform, Housing and Urban Development Act 1993

2.—(1) After section 37 of the Leasehold Reform, Housing and Urban Development Act 1993 there shall be inserted—

"Landlord's right to compensation in relation to ineffective claims

Compensation for postponement of termination in connection with ineffective claims

37A.—(1) This section applies where a claim to exercise the right to collective enfranchisement in respect of any premises is made on or after 15th January 1999 by tenants of flats contained in the premises and the claim is not effective.

(2) A person who is a participating tenant immediately before the claim ceases to have effect shall be liable to pay compensation if—

(a) the claim was not made at least two years before the term date of the lease by virtue of which he is a qualifying tenant ("the existing lease"), and

(b) any of the conditions mentioned in subsection (3) is met.

(3) The conditions referred to above are—

(a) that the making of the claim caused a notice served under paragraph 4(1) of Schedule 10 to the Local Government and Housing Act 1989 in respect of the existing lease to cease to have effect and the date on which the claim ceases to have effect is later than four months before the termination date specified in the notice,

(b) that the making of the claim prevented the service of an effective notice under paragraph 4(1) of Schedule 10 to the Local Government and Housing Act 1989 in respect of the existing lease (but did not cause a notice served under that provision in respect of that lease to cease to have effect) and the date on which the claim ceases to have effect is a date later than six months before the term date of the existing lease, and

(c) that the existing lease has been continued under paragraph 6(1) of Schedule 3 by virtue of the claim.

(4) Compensation under subsection (2) shall become payable at the end of the appropriate period and be the right of the person who is the tenant's immediate landlord at that time.

(5) The amount which a tenant is liable to pay under subsection (2) shall be equal to the difference between—

(a) the rent for the appropriate period under the existing lease, and

(b) the rent which might reasonably be expected to be payable for that period were the property to which the existing lease relates let for a term equivalent to that period on the open market by a willing landlord on the following assumptions—

(i) that no premium is payable in connection with the letting,

(ii) that the letting confers no security of tenure, and

(iii) that, except as otherwise provided by this paragraph, the letting is on the same terms as the existing lease.

(6) For the purposes of subsections (4) and (5), the appropriate period is—

(a) in a case falling within paragraph (a) of subsection (3), the period—

(i) beginning with the termination date specified in the notice mentioned in that paragraph, and

(ii) ending with the earliest date of termination which could have been specified in a notice under paragraph 4(1) of Schedule 10 to the Local Government and Housing Act 1989 in respect of the existing lease served immediately after the date on which the claim ceases to have effect, or, if the existing lease is terminated before then, with the date of its termination;

(b) in a case falling within paragraph (b) of subsection (3), the period—

(i) beginning with the later of six months from the date on which the claim is made and the term date of the existing lease, and

(ii) ending six months after the date on which the claim ceases to have effect, or, if the existing lease is terminated before then, with the date of its termination; and

(c) in a case falling within paragraph (c) of subsection (3), the period for which the existing lease is continued under paragraph 6(1) of Schedule 3.

(7) In the case of a person who becomes a participating tenant by virtue of an election under section 14(3), the references in subsections (3)(a) and (b) and (6)(b)(i) to the making of the claim shall be construed as references to the making of the election.

(8) For the purposes of this section—

(a) references to a claim to exercise the right to collective enfranchisement shall be taken as references to a notice given, or purporting to be given (whether by persons who are qualifying tenants or not), under section 13,

(b) references to the date on which a claim ceases to have effect shall, in the case of a claim made by a notice which is not a valid notice under section 13, be taken as references to the date on which the notice is set aside by the court or is withdrawn or would, if valid, cease to have effect or be deemed to have been withdrawn, that date being taken, where the notice is set aside, or would, if valid, cease to have effect, in consequence of a court order, to be the date when the order becomes final, and

(c) a claim to exercise the right to collective enfranchisement is not effective if it ceases to have effect for any reason other than—

(i) the application of section 23(4), 30(4) or 31(4),

(ii) the entry into a binding contract for the acquisition of the freehold and other interests falling to be acquired in pursuance of the claim, or

(iii) the making of an order under section 24(4)(a) or (b) or 25(6)(a) or (b) which provides for the vesting of those interests.

Modification of section 37A where change in immediate reversion

37B.—(1) Where a tenant's liability to pay compensation under section 37A relates to a period during which there has been a change in the interest immediately expectant on the determination of his lease, that section shall have effect with the following modifications.

(2) For subsections (4) and (5) there shall be substituted—

"(4) Compensation under subsection (2) shall become payable at the end of the appropriate period and there shall be a separate right to compensation in respect of each of the interests which, during that period, have been immediately expectant on the determination of the existing lease.

(5) Compensation under subsection (2) above shall—

(a) in the case of the interest which is immediately expectant on the determination of the existing lease at the end of the appropriate period, be the right of the person in whom that interest is vested at that time, and

(b) in the case of an interest which ceases during the appropriate period to be immediately expectant on the determination of the existing lease, be the right of the person in whom the interest was vested immediately before it ceased to be so expectant.

(5A) The amount which the tenant is liable to pay under subsection (2) above in respect of any interest shall be equal to the difference between—

(a) the rent under the existing lease for the part of the appropriate period during which the interest was immediately expectant on the determination of that lease, and

(b) the rent which might reasonably be expected to be payable for that part of that period were the property to which the existing lease relates let for a term equivalent to that part of that period on the open market by a willing landlord on the following assumptions—

(i) that no premium is payable in connection with the letting,

(ii) that the letting confers no security of tenure, and

(iii) that, except as otherwise provided by this paragraph, the letting is on the same terms as the existing lease."

(3) In subsection (6), for "(4) and (5)" there shall be substituted "(4) to (5A)"."

(2) In section 91(2) of that Act (matters to be determined by leasehold valuation tribunal), after paragraph (c) there shall be inserted—

"(ca) the amount of any compensation payable under section 37A;".

Claims under Chapter II of Part I of the Leasehold Reform, Housing and Urban Development Act 1993

3.—(1) After section 61 of the Leasehold Reform, Housing and Urban Development Act 1993 there shall be inserted—

"*Landlord's right to compensation in relation to ineffective claims*

Compensation for postponement of termination in connection with ineffective claims

61A.—(1) This section applies where, on or after 15th January 1999—

(a) a tenant of a flat makes a claim to acquire a new lease of the flat, and

(b) the claim is not made at least two years before the term date of the lease in respect of which the claim is made ("the existing lease").

(2) The tenant shall be liable to pay compensation if the claim is not effective and—

(a) the making of the claim caused a notice served under paragraph 4(1) of Schedule 10 to the Local Government and Housing Act 1989 to cease to have effect and the date on which the claim ceases to have effect is later than four months before the termination date specified in the notice,

(b) the making of the claim prevented the service of an effective notice under paragraph 4(1) of Schedule 10 to the Local Government and Housing Act 1989 (but did not cause a notice served under that provision to cease to have effect) and the date on which the claim ceases to have effect is a date later than six months before the term date of the existing lease, or

(c) the existing lease is continued under paragraph 5(1) of Schedule 12 by virtue of the claim.

(3) Compensation under subsection (2) shall become payable at the end of the appropriate period and be the right of the person who is the tenant's immediate landlord at that time.

(4) The amount which the tenant is liable to pay under subsection (2) shall be equal to the difference between—

(a) the rent for the appropriate period under the existing lease, and

(b) the rent which might reasonably be expected to be payable for that period were the property to which the existing lease relates let for a term equivalent to that period on the open market by a willing landlord on the following assumptions—

(i) that no premium is payable in connection with the letting,

(ii) that the letting confers no security of tenure, and

(iii) that, except as otherwise provided by this paragraph, the letting is on the same terms as the existing lease.

(5) For the purposes of subsections (3) and (4), the appropriate period is—

(a) in a case falling within paragraph (a) of subsection (2), the period—

(i) beginning with the termination date specified in.the notice mentioned in that paragraph, and

(ii) ending with the earliest date of termination which could have been specified in a notice under paragraph 4(1) of Schedule 10 to the Local Government and Housing Act 1989 served immediately after the date on which the claim ceases to have effect, or, if the existing lease is terminated before then, with the date on which it is terminated;

(b) in a case falling within paragraph (b) of subsection (2), the period—

(i) beginning with the later of six months from the date on which the claim is made and the term date of the existing lease, and

(ii) ending six months after the date on which the claim ceases to have effect, or, if the existing lease is terminated before then, with the date of its termination; and

(c) in a case falling within paragraph (c) of subsection (2), the period for which the existing lease is continued under paragraph 5(1) of Schedule 12.

(6) For the purposes of subsection (2), a claim to a new lease is not effective if it ceases to have effect for any reason other than—

(a) the application of section 47(1) or 55(2), or

(b) the acquisition of the new lease in pursuance of the claim.

(7) For the purposes of this section—

(a) references to a claim to acquire a new lease shall be taken as references to a notice given, or purporting to be given (whether by a qualifying tenant or not), under section 42, and

(b) references to the date on which a claim ceases to have effect shall, in the case of a claim made by a notice which is not a valid notice under section 42, be taken as references to the date on which the notice is set aside by the court or is withdrawn or would, if valid, cease to have effect or be deemed to have been withdrawn, that date being taken, where the notice is set aside, or would, if valid, cease to have effect, in consequence of a court order, to be the date when the order becomes final.

Modification of section 61A where change in immediate reversion

61B.—(1) Where a tenant's liability to pay compensation under section 61A relates to a period during which there has been a change in the interest immediately expectant on the determination of his lease, that section shall have effect with the following modifications.

(2) For subsections (3) and (4) there shall be substituted—

"(3) Compensation under subsection (2) shall become payable at the end of the appropriate period and there shall be a separate right to compensation in respect of each of the interests which, during that period, have been immediately expectant on the determination of the existing lease.

(4) Compensation under subsection (2) above shall—

(a) in the case of the interest which is immediately expectant on the determination of the existing lease at the end of the appropriate period, be the right of the person in whom that interest is vested at that time, and

(b) in the case of an interest which ceases during the appropriate period to be immediately expectant on the determination of the existing lease, be the right of the person in whom the interest was vested immediately before it ceased to be so expectant.

(4A) The amount which the tenant is liable to pay under subsection (2) above in respect of any interest shall be equal to the difference between—

(a) the rent under the existing lease for the part of the appropriate period during which the interest was immediately expectant on the determination of that lease, and

(b) the rent which might reasonably be expected to be payable for that part of that period were the property to which the existing lease relates let for a term equivalent to that part of that period on the open market by a willing landlord on the following assumptions—

(i) that no premium is payable in connection with the letting,

(ii) that the letting confers no security of tenure, and

(iii) that, except as otherwise provided by this paragraph, the letting is on the same terms as the existing lease."

(3) In subsection (5), for "(3) and (4)" there shall be substituted "(3) to (4A)".".

(2) In section 91(2) of that Act (matters to be determined by leasehold valuation tribunal), after paragraph (c) there shall be inserted—

"(cb) the amount of any compensation payable under section 61A;".

GENERAL NOTE
See notes to s.116.

Section 121 SCHEDULE 12

ADMINISTRATION OF HOUSING BENEFIT, &C

Administration of housing benefit

1.—(1) Section 134 of the Social Security Administration Act 1992 (arrangements for housing benefit) is amended as follows.

(2) For subsection (1) (administering authority and form of benefit) substitute—

"(1) Housing benefit provided by virtue of a scheme under section 123 of the Social Security Contributions and Benefits Act 1992 (in this Part referred to as "the housing benefit scheme") shall be funded and administered by the appropriate housing authority or local authority.

(1A) Housing benefit in respect of payments which the occupier of a dwelling is liable to make to a housing authority shall take the form of a rent rebate or, in prescribed cases, a rent allowance funded and administered by that authority.

The cases that may be so prescribed do not include any where the payment is in respect of property within the authority's Housing Revenue Account.

(1B) In any other case housing benefit shall take the form of a rent allowance funded and administered by the local authority for the area in which the dwelling is situated or by such other local authority as is specified by an order made by the Secretary of State.".

(3) In subsection (2)(b) omit the words "or rates".

(4) Omit subsections (3), (4), (6) and (7).

(5) For subsection (5) (agreements with other authorities for carrying out of functions) substitute—

"(5) Authorities may—

(a) agree that one shall discharge functions relating to housing benefit on another's behalf; or

(b) discharge any such functions jointly or arrange for their discharge by a joint committee.

(5A) Nothing in this section shall be read as excluding the general provisions of the Local Government Act 1972 or the Local Government (Scotland) Act 1973 from applying in relation to the housing benefit functions of a local authority.".

(6) In subsection (9) for the words from "the rebates or allowances" to the end substitute "the housing benefit which will be paid by the authority in any year will not exceed the permitted total or any subsidiary limit specified by order of the Secretary of State.".

(7) In subsection (11) for the words from "the rebates or allowances" to the end substitute "the housing benefit paid by them during the year exceeds the permitted total or any subsidiary limit specified by order of the Secretary of State.".

(8) For subsection (12) substitute—

"(12) The Secretary of State—

(a) shall by order specify the permitted total of housing benefit payable by any authority in any year; and

(b) may by order specify one or more subsidiary limits on the amount of housing benefit payable by any authority in any year in respect of any matter or matters specified in the order.

The power to specify the permitted total or a subsidiary limit may be exercised by fixing an amount or by providing rules for its calculation.".

Administration of council tax benefit

2. In section 138 of the Social Security Administration Act 1992 (council tax benefit: nature of benefit), at the end of subsection (1) insert—

"References in any enactment or instrument (whenever passed or made) to payment, in relation to council tax benefit, include any of those ways of giving the benefit.".

3.—(1) Section 139 of the Social Security Administration Act 1992 (arrangements for council tax benefit) is amended as follows.

(2) For subsections (4) and (5) (agreements with other authorities for carrying out of functions) substitute—

"(4) Nothing in this section shall be read as excluding the general provisions of the Local Government Act 1972 or the Local Government (Scotland) Act 1973 from applying in relation to the council tax benefit functions of a local authority.".

(3) In subsection (7) for the words from "the benefits which will be allowed" to the end substitute "the amount of benefit which will be paid by them in any year will not exceed the permitted total or any subsidiary limit specified by order of the Secretary of State.".

(4) In subsection (9) for the words from "the benefits allowed by it" to the end substitute "the amount of benefit paid by them in any year exceeds the permitted total or any subsidiary limit specified by order of the Secretary of State.".

(5) For subsection (10) substitute—

"(10) The Secretary of State—
- (a) shall by order specify the permitted total of council tax benefit payable by any authority in any year; and
- (b) may by order specify one or more subsidiary limits on the amount of council tax benefit payable by any authority in any year in respect of any matter or matters specified in the order.

The power to specify the permitted total or a subsidiary limit may be exercised by fixing an amount or by providing rules for its calculation.".

Subsidy

4. After section 140 of the Social Security Administration Act 1992 insert—

"Subsidy

Subsidy

140A.—(1) For each year the Secretary of State shall pay a subsidy to each authority administering housing benefit or council tax benefit.

(2) He shall pay—
- (a) rent rebate subsidy to each housing authority;
- (b) rent allowance subsidy to each local authority; and
- (c) council tax benefit subsidy to each billing authority or levying authority.

(3) In the following provisions of this Part "subsidy", without more, refers to subsidy of any of those descriptions.

Calculation of amount of subsidy

140B.—(1) The amount of subsidy to be paid to an authority shall be calculated in the manner specified by order made by the Secretary of State.

(2) Subject as follows, the amount of subsidy shall be calculated by reference to the amount of relevant benefit paid by the authority during the year, with any additions specified in the order but subject to any deductions so specified.

In the case of a housing authority in England and Wales, any Housing Revenue Account rebates paid by them shall be excluded from the total.

(3) The order may provide that the amount of subsidy in respect of any matter shall be a fixed sum or shall be nil.

(4) The Secretary of State may deduct from the amount which would otherwise be payable by way of subsidy such amount as be considers it unreasonable to pay by way of subsidy.

(5) The Secretary of State may pay to an authority as part of the subsidy an additional amount in respect of the costs of administering the relevant benefit.

Any such additional amount shall be a fixed sum specified by, or shall be calculated in the manner specified by, an order made by the Secretary of State.

(6) In this section "relevant benefit" means housing benefit or council tax benefit, as the case may be.

(7) Nothing in this section shall be taken to imply that any such addition or deduction as is mentioned in subsection (2) or (4) above may not be determined by reference to—
- (a) the amount of relevant benefit paid by the authority during a previous year; or
- (b) the amount of subsidy paid to the authority in respect of a previous year, under this section.

(8) The amount of subsidy payable to an authority shall be calculated to the nearest pound, disregarding an odd amount of 50 pence or less and treating an odd amount exceeding 50 pence as a whole pound.

Payment of subsidy

140C.—(1) Subsidy shall be paid by the Secretary of State in such instalments, at such times, in such manner and subject to such conditions as to claims, records, certificates, audit or otherwise as may be provided by order of the Secretary of State.

(2) The order may provide that if an authority has not, within such period as may be specified in the order, complied with the conditions so specified as to claims, records, certificate, audit or otherwise, the Secretary of State may estimate the amount of subsidy payable to the authority and employ for that purpose such criteria as he considers relevant.

(3) Where subsidy has been paid to an authority and it appears to the Secretary of State—

(a) that subsidy has been overpaid; or

(b) that there has been a breach of any condition specified in an order under this section,

he may recover from the authority the whole or such part of the payment as he may determine.

Without prejudice to other methods of recovery, a sum recoverable under this subsection may be recovered by withholding or reducing subsidy.

(4) An order made by the Secretary of State under this section may be made before, during or after the end of the year or years to which it relates.

Rent rebate subsidy: accounting provisions

140D.—(1) Rent rebate subsidy is payable—

(a) in the case of a local authority in England and Wales, for the credit of a revenue account of theirs other than their Housing Revenue Account or Housing Repairs Account;

(b) in the case of a local authority in Scotland, for the credit of their rent rebate account;

(c) in the case of a development corporation in England and Wales or the Development Board for Rural Wales, for the credit of their housing account; and

(d) in the case of a new town corporation in Scotland or Scottish Homes, for the credit of the account to which rent rebates granted by them, or it, are debited.

(2) Every local housing authority in England and Wales shall for each year carry to the credit of their Housing Revenue Account from some other revenue account of theirs which is not a Housing Repairs Account an amount equal to the aggregate of—

(a) so much of each Housing Revenue Account rebate paid by them during the year as was paid—

(i) in the exercise of a discretion conferred by the housing benefit scheme; or

(ii) in pursuance of any modification of that scheme under section 134(8)(b) above; and

(b) unless the authority otherwise determine, so much of each such rebate as was paid in pursuance of such modifications of that scheme as are mentioned in section 134(8)(a) above.

Supplementary provisions

Financing of joint arrangements

140E.—(1) Where two or more authorities make arrangements for the discharge of any of their functions relating to housing benefit or council tax benefit—

(a) by one authority on behalf of itself and one or more other authorities; or

(b) by a joint committee,

the Secretary of State may make such payments as he thinks fit to the authority or committee in respect of their expenses in carrying out those functions.

(2) The provisions of sections 140B and 140C (subsidy: calculation and supplementary provisions) apply in relation to a payment under this section as in relation to a payment of subsidy.

(3) The Secretary of State may (without prejudice to the generality of his powers in relation to the amount of subsidy) take into account the fact that an amount has been paid under this section in respect of expenses which would otherwise have been met in whole or in part by the participating authorities.

No requirement for annual orders

140F.—(1) Any power under this Part to make provision by order for or in relation to a year does not require the making of a new order each year.

(2) Any order made under the power may be revoked or varied at any time, whether before, during or after the year to which it relates.

Interpretation: Part VIII

140G. In this Part, unless the context otherwise requires—

"Housing Repairs Account" means an account kept under section 77 of the LocalGovernment and Housing Act 1989;

"Housing Revenue Account" means the account kept under section 74 of the Local Government and Housing Act 1989, and—

(a) references to property within that account have the same meaning as in Part VI of that Act, and

(b) "Housing Revenue Account rebate" means a rebate debited to that account in accordance with that Part;

"rent rebate subsidy" and "rent allowance subsidy" shall be construed in accordance with section 134 above;

"year" means a financial year within the meaning of the Local Government Finance Act 1992.".

Transitional provision

5.—(1) The Secretary of State may by order make such transitional provision, and such consequential provision and savings, as appear to him appropriate in connection with the coming into force of the provisions of this Schedule.

(2) Without prejudice to the generality of that power, the order may provide for the recovery by the withholding or reduction of subsidy payable under the provisions inserted by paragraph 4 above of any amount which would have been recoverable under the provisions of Part VIII of the Social Security Administration Act 1992 repealed by this Act.

(3) Section 189(3) to (7) of the Social Security Administration Act 1992 (general provisions as to regulations and orders) apply in relation to the power conferred by sub-paragraph (1) as they apply in relation to a power conferred by that Act to make an order.

(4) A statutory instrument containing an order under this paragraph shall be subject to annulment in pursuance of a resolution of either House of Parliament.

GENERAL NOTE
See notes to s.121.

Section 123   SCHEDULE 13

HOUSING BENEFIT AND RELATED MATTERS: CONSEQUENTIAL AMENDMENTS

Rent Act 1977 (c. 42)

1. In section 63(7) of the Rent Act 1977 (expenditure on rent officers to be met by Secretary of State), in paragraph (a), for "or an order under section 121 of the Housing Act 1988" substitute "or an order under section 122 of the Housing Act 1996".

Housing Act 1985 (c. 68)

2. In section 425(2)(b) of the Housing Act 1985 (housing subsidy: local contribution differential), for "section 135" substitute "section 140A".

Social Security Administration Act 1992 (c. 5)

3.—(1) The Social Security Administration Act 1992 is amended as follows.

(2) In section 5(3) (regulations about benefit: information required by a rent officer), for "section 121 of the Housing Act 1988" substitute "section 122 of the Housing Act 1996".

(3) In section 116(4) (legal proceedings for offences: definition of "appropriate authority")—

(a) omit paragraph (a);

(b) in paragraph (b), for "that subsection" substitute "section 134 below"; and

(c) in paragraph (c), for "that subsection" substitute "that section".

(4) In section 176 (consultation with representative organisations), in subsection (1)(b) for "section 134(12), 135, 139 or 140 above" substitute "any provision of Part VIII above".

(5) In section 189(8) (requirement for consent of the Treasury), for "135, 140" substitute "140B, 140C".

(6) In section 191 (interpretation: general)—

(a) at the appropriate place insert—
" "council tax benefit scheme" shall be construed in accordance with section 139(1) above;";
(b) in the definition of "rate rebate", "rent rebate" and "rent allowance", omit the reference to rate rebate;
(c) omit the definitions of "rates" and "rating authority".

Leasehold Reform, Housing and Urban Development Act 1993 (c. 28)

4. In section 135(8) of the Leasehold Reform, Housing and Urban Development Act 1993 (programmes for disposals of dwelling-houses by local authorities), for "section 135(1) of the Social Security Administration Act 1992 (housing benefit finance)" substitute "section 140A of the Social Security Administration Act 1992 (subsidy)".

Section 141(1) SCHEDULE 14

INTRODUCTORY TENANCIES: CONSEQUENTIAL AMENDMENTS

Housing Act 1985 (c. 68)

1. In section 88(1) of the Housing Act 1985 (cases where the secure tenant is a successor) after paragraph (e) insert "or
(f) the tenancy was previously an introductory tenancy and he was a successor to the introductory tenancy.".
2. In section 104(2) of the Housing Act 1985 (provision of information about secure tenancies) for the words "on the grant of the tenancy" substitute "when the secure tenancy arises".
3. After section 115 of the Housing Act 1985 insert—

"Meaning of "introductory tenancy"
115A. In this Part "introductory tenancy" has the same meaning as in Chapter I of Part V of the Housing Act 1996.".
4. In section 117 of the Housing Act 1985 (index of defined expressions: Part IV) insert at the appropriate place—
"introductory tenancy section 115A".
5. In Schedule 1 to the Housing Act 1985 (tenancies which are not secure tenancies) after paragraph 1 insert—

"Introductory tenancies

1A. A tenancy is not a secure tenancy if it is an introductory tenancy or a tenancy which has ceased to be an introductory tenancy—
(a) by virtue of section 133(3) of the Housing Act 1996 (disposal on death to non-qualifying person), or
(b) by virtue of the tenant, or in the case of a joint tenancy every tenant, ceasing to occupy the dwelling-house as his only or principal home.".

GENERAL NOTE
See General Note to s.141, above.

Section 155(6) SCHEDULE 15

ARREST FOR ANTI-SOCIAL BEHAVIOUR: POWERS OF HIGH COURT AND COUNTY COURT TO REMAND

Introductory

1.—(1) The provisions of this Schedule apply where the court has power to remand a person under section 155(2) or (5) (arrest for breach of injunction, &c.).
(2) In this Schedule "the court" means the High Court or a county court and includes—
(a) in relation to the High Court, a judge of that court, and
(b) in relation to a county court, a judge or district judge of that court.

Remand in custody or on bail

2.—(1) The court may—
(a) remand him in custody, that is, commit him to custody to be brought before the court at the end of the period of remand or at such earlier time as the court may require, or

(b) remand him on bail, in accordance with the following provisions.

(2) The court may remand him on bail—

(a) by taking from him a recognizance, with or without sureties, conditioned as provided in paragraph 3, or

(b) by fixing the amount of the recognizances with a view to their being taken subsequently, and in the meantime committing him to custody as mentioned in sub-paragraph (1)(a).

(3) Where a person is brought before the court after remand, the court may further remand him.

3.—(1) Where a person is remanded on bail, the court may direct that his recognizance be conditioned for his appearance—

(a) before that court at the end of the period of remand, or

(b) at every time and place to which during the course of the proceedings the hearing may from time to time be adjourned.

(2) Where a recognizance is conditioned for a person's appearance as mentioned in sub-paragraph (1)(b), the fixing of any time for him next to appear shall be deemed to be a remand.

(3) Nothing in this paragraph affects the power of the court at any subsequent hearing to remand him afresh.

4.—(1) The court shall not remand a person for a period exceeding 8 clear days, except that—

(a) if the court remands him on bail, it may remand him for a longer period if he and the other party consent, and

(b) if the court adjourns a case under section 156(1) (remand for medical examination and report), the court may remand him for the period of the adjournment.

(2) Where the court has power to remand a person in custody it may, if the remand is for a period not exceeding 3 clear days, commit him to the custody of a constable.

Further remand

5.—(1) If the court is satisfied that a person who has been remanded is unable by reason of illness or accident to appear or be brought before the court at the expiration of the period for which he was remanded, the court may, in his absence, remand him for a further time.

This power may, in the case of a person who was remanded on bail, be exercised by enlarging his recognizance and those of any sureties for him to a later time.

(2) Where a person remanded on bail is bound to appear before the court at any time and the court has no power to remand him under sub-paragraph (1) the court may in his absence enlarge his recognizance and those of any sureties for him to a later time.

The enlargement of his recognizance shall be deemed to be a further remand.

(3) Paragraph 4(1) (limit of period of remand) does not apply to the exercise of the powers conferred by this paragraph.

Postponement of taking of recognizance

6. Where under paragraph 2(2)(b) the court fixes the amount in which the principal and his sureties, if any, are to be bound, the recognizance may afterwards be taken by such person as may be prescribed by rules of court, with the same consequences as if it had been entered into before the court.

GENERAL NOTE

See notes to s.155, above.

Section 173　　　　　　　SCHEDULE 16

ALLOCATION OF HOUSING ACCOMMODATION: CONSEQUENTIAL AMENDMENTS

Housing Act 1985 (c. 68)

1. In section 106 of the Housing Act 1985 (information about allocation of secure tenancies) at the end insert—

"(6) The provisions of this section do not apply to a landlord authority which is a local housing authority so far as they impose requirements corresponding to those to which such an authority is subject under sections 166 and 168 of the Housing Act 1996 (provision of information about housing registers and allocation schemes).".

2.—(1) Schedule 1 to the Housing Act 1985 (tenancies which are not secure tenancies) is amended as follows.

(2) In paragraph 2 (premises occupied in connection with employment) at the beginning of sub-paragraph (1), (2) and (3) insert in each case "Subject to subparagraph (4B)".

(3) In sub–paragraph (4) of that paragraph—

(a) at the beginning insert "Subject to sub-paragraph (4A) and (4B)", and

(b) omit the words from "until" to the end.

(4) After sub-paragraph (4) of that paragraph insert—

"(4A) Except where the landlord is a local housing authority, a tenancy under sub-paragraph (4) shall become a secure tenancy when the periods during which the conditions mentioned in sub-paragraph (1), (2) or (3) are not satisfied with respect to the tenancy amount in aggregate to more than three years.

(4B) Where the landlord is a local housing authority, a tenancy under sub-paragraph (1), (2), (3) or (4) shall become a secure tenancy if the authority notify the tenant that the tenancy is to be regarded as a secure tenancy.".

(5) In paragraph 5 (temporary accommodation for persons taking up employment) in sub-paragraph (1)—

(a) for the words from the beginning to first "grant" substitute "Subject to sub-paragraphs (1A) and (1B), a tenancy is not a secure tenancy", and

(b) omit from "unless" to the end.

(6) After sub-paragraph (1) of that paragraph insert

"(1A) Except where the landlord is a local housing authority, a tenancy under sub-paragraph (1) shall become a secure tenancy on the expiry of one year from the grant or on earlier notification by the landlord to the tenant that the tenancy is to be regarded as a secure tenancy.

(1B) Where the landlord is a local housing authority, a tenancy under sub-paragraph (1) shall become a secure tenancy if at any time the authority notify the tenant that the tenancy is to be regarded as a secure tenancy.".

(7) In paragraph 10 (student lettings) in sub-paragraph (1)—

(a) for the words from the beginning to "sub-paragraph (3)" substitute "Subject to sub-paragraphs (2A) and (2B), a tenancy of a dwelling-house is not a secure tenancy", and

(b) omit from "unless" to the end.

(8) After sub-paragraph (2) of that paragraph insert—

"(2A) Except where the landlord is a local housing authority, a tenancy under sub-paragraph (1) shall become a secure tenancy on the expiry of the period specified in sub-paragraph (3) or on earlier notification by the landlord to the tenant that the tenancy is to be regarded as a secure tenancy.

(2B) Where the landlord is a local housing authority, a tenancy under sub-paragraph (1) shall become a secure tenancy if at any time the authority notify the tenant that the tenancy is to be regarded as a secure tenancy.".

(9) In sub-paragraph (3) of that paragraph for the words "sub-paragraph (1)" substitute "sub-paragraph (2A)".

Asylum and Immigration Act 1996 (c. 49)

3.—(1) Section 9 of the Asylum and Immigration Act 1996 (entitlement to housing accommodation and assistance) is amended as follows.

(2) In subsection (1) (entitlement to housing accommodation)—

(a) for "housing authority" substitute "local housing authority within the meaning of the Housing Act 1985", and

(b) for "the accommodation Part" substitute "Part II of that Act".

(3) After subsection (4) insert—

"(5) This section does not apply in relation to any allocation of housing accommodation to which Part VI of the Housing Act 1996 (allocation of housing accommodation) applies.

GENERAL NOTE

See General Note to s.173, above.

Section 216(3)   SCHEDULE 17

HOMELESSNESS: CONSEQUENTIAL AMENDMENTS

Local Authority Social Services Act 1970 (c. 42)

1. In Schedule 1 to the Local Authority Social Services Act 1970 (enactments conferring functions assigned to Social Services Committee) for the entry relating to the Housing Act 1985 substitute—

"Housing Act 1996
Section 213(1)(b)

Co-operation in relation to homeless
persons and persons threatened with
homelessness.".

Greater London Council (General Powers) Act 1984 (c. xxvii)

2. In section 39 of the Greater London Council (General Powers) Act 1984 (occupants removed from buildings to have priority housing need) for "Part III of the Housing Act 1985 (housing the homeless)" substitute "Part VII of the Housing Act 1996 (homelessness)".

Housing Act 1985 (c. 68)

3. In Schedule 1 to the Housing Act 1985 (tenancies which are not secure tenancies), for paragraph 4 (accommodation for homeless persons) substitute—

Accommodation for homeless persons

4. A tenancy granted in pursuance of any function under Part VII of the Housing Act 1996 (homelessness) is not a secure tenancy unless the local housing authority concerned have notified the tenant that the tenancy is to be regarded as a secure tenancy.".

Housing (Scotland) Act 1987 (c. 26)

4. In section 42 of the Housing (Scotland) Act 1987 (application of Part II to cases arising in England and Wales: request for co-operation)—
    (a) in subsection (1) for "section 67(1) of the Housing Act 1985" substitute "section 198(1) of the Housing Act 1996"; and
    (b) in subsections (2) and (3) for "section 72 of the Housing Act 1985" substitute "section 213 of the Housing Act 1996".

Section 222

SCHEDULE 18

MISCELLANEOUS PROVISIONS

PART I

HOUSING MANAGEMENT

Repeal of Part IV of the Housing Act 1988

1. Part IV of the Housing Act 1988 (change of landlord: secure tenants) is hereby repealed.

Payments to encourage local housing authority tenants to move to other accommodation

2.—(1) A local housing authority may make payments to or for the benefit of a tenant or licensee of a dwelling-house within its Housing Revenue Account with a view to assisting or encouraging that person to move to qualifying accommodation.
(2) In sub-paragraph (1) "qualifying accommodation" means a dwelling-house made available to the person concerned as tenant or licensee by any of the following—
    (a) the local housing authority making the grant or any other local housing authority; or
    (b) a registered social landlord.
(3) The reference in sub-paragraph (1) to a dwelling-house being within the Housing Revenue Account of a local housing authority is to a dwelling-house to which section 74(1) of the Local Government and Housing Act 1989 for the time being applies.
(4) In this paragraph—
"dwelling-house" has the meaning given by section 112 of the Housing Act 1985; and
"tenant" does not include a tenant under a long tenancy as defined in section 115 of that Act.

Consultation with respect to housing management

3.—(1) Part II of the Housing Act 1985 (provision of housing accommodation) is amended as follows.
(2) After section 27B insert—

"Consultation with respect to housing management

Consultation with respect to management
    27BA.—(1) The Secretary of State may make regulations for imposing requirements on

a local housing authority to consult tenants, or to consider representations made to them by tenants, with respect to the exercise of their management functions (including proposals as to the exercise of those functions), in relation to any of the authority's houses or other land held for a related purpose.

(2) The regulations may include provision requiring a local housing authority to consult tenants, or consider representations made by tenants, with respect to—

    (a) the terms of a written specification to be prepared by the authority of functions proposed to be exercised by the authority or another person;

    (b) a proposal of the authority to exercise management functions themselves;

    (c) any person whom the authority propose to invite to submit a bid to exercise any of their management functions;

    (d) the standards of service for the time being achieved by the authority or (as the case may be) the person with whom they have entered into a management agreement;

    (e) a proposal to enforce the standards of service required by a management agreement.

(3) The requirements imposed on a local housing authority by the regulations may include provision with respect to—

    (a) the tenants to be consulted or whose representations are to be considered;

    (b) the means by which consultation is to be effected (including the arrangements to be made for tenants to consider the matters on which they have been consulted);

    (c) the arrangements to be made for tenants to make representations to the authority;

    (d) the action to be taken by the authority where representations are made.

(4) The regulations may include provision requiring a local housing authority to consult representatives of tenants, or to consider representations made to them by such representatives, as well as (or instead of) the tenants themselves; and accordingly, references in subsections (1) to (3) above to tenants include references to such representatives.

(5) The regulations may include provision for particular questions arising under them to be determined by a local housing authority on whom they impose requirements.

(6) Nothing in subsections (2) to (5) above shall be taken as prejudicing the generality of subsection (1).

(7) Regulations under this section—

    (a) may make different provision with respect to different cases or descriptions of case, including different provision for different areas,

    (b) may contain such incidental, supplementary or transitional provisions as appear to the Secretary of State to be necessary or expedient, and

    (c) shall be made by statutory instrument which shall be subject to annulment in pursuance of a resolution of either House of Parliament.

(8) Except as otherwise provided by the regulations, in the case of secure tenants, the provisions of the regulations shall apply in place of the provisions of section 105 (consultation on matters of housing management).

(9) Except as otherwise provided by the regulations, in the case of introductory tenants, the provisions of the regulations shall apply in place of the provisions of section 137 of the Housing Act 1996 (consultation on matters of housing management).

(10) References in this section to the management functions of a local housing authority in relation to houses or land shall be construed in the same way as references to any such functions in section 27.".

(3) In section 20(1) (application of housing management provisions) for "section 27B" substitute "section 27BA".

(4) In section 27 (management agreements), after subsection (5) insert—

"(5A) Nothing in section 6 of the Local Government Act 1988 (restrictions on authority carrying out functional work) shall apply in relation to any management functions which, in pursuance of a management agreement, are carried out by the manager as agent of the local housing authority.".

(5) In section 27AB (management agreements with tenant management organisations), in subsection (7)(b)(i), for the words from "section 27A" to the end substitute "regulations under section 27BA (consultation with respect to management)".

PART II

HOUSING FINANCE

Housing Revenue Account: directions as to certain matters

4.—(1) In Part VI of the Local Government and Housing Act 1989 (housing finance), after section 78 (directions as to proper accounting practices) insert—

"Directions as to treatment of service charges &c

78A.—(1) The Secretary of State may give directions as to what items or amounts are to be regarded as referable to property within a local housing authority's Housing Revenue Account where one or more parts of a building have been disposed of but the common parts remain property within that account.

(2) Any such direction also has effect for the purposes of any Housing Repairs Account kept by the authority.

(3) Directions under this section may give the authority a discretion as to whether items or amounts are accounted for in the Housing Revenue Account or any Housing Repairs Account or in another revenue account.

(4) In this section "common parts" includes the structure and exterior of the building and common facilities provided, whether in the building or elsewhere, for persons who include the occupiers of one or more parts of the building.

Directions as to accounting for work subject to competitive tendering

78B.—(1) This section applies where work is carried out by a local housing authority which has successfully bid for the work on a competitive basis.

(2) The Secretary of State may give directions—

(a) to secure that the amount debited to the Housing Revenue Account or any Housing Repairs Account of the authority in respect of the work reflects the amount of the authority's successful bid for the work rather than expenditure actually incurred;

(b) allowing an authority to credit to its Housing Revenue Account any surpluses reasonably attributable to work undertaken on or in connection with property within that account.

(3) Directions under subsection (2)(a) may make provision for determining the amount to be treated as the amount of the authority's successful bid.

References in this Part to expenditure shall be construed as references to the amount falling to be debited in accordance with the directions.

(4) Directions under subsection (2)(b) may make provision as to the ascertainment of the surpluses referred to and the circumstances in which a surplus is or is not to be taken to be attributable to property within an authority's Housing Revenue Account.".

(2) The above amendment has effect for the financial year beginning on 1st April 1997 and subsequent financial years.

Housing Revenue Account subsidy: final decision on amount

5.—(1) In Part VI of the Local Government and Housing Act 1989 (housing finance), after section 80 (calculation of Housing Revenue Account subsidy) insert—

"Final decision on amount of Housing Revenue Account subsidy

80A.—(1) The Secretary of State shall, as soon as he thinks fit after the end of the year, make a final decision as to the amount (if any) of Housing Revenue Account subsidy payable to a local housing authority for that year and notify the authority in writing of his decision.

(2) Once notified to the authority the decision is conclusive as to the amount (if any) payable by way of subsidy and shall not be questioned in any legal proceedings.

(3) Where the amount of Housing Revenue Account subsidy paid to an authority is less than the amount finally decided, the authority is entitled to be paid the balance.

(4) Where Housing Revenue Account subsidy has been paid to an authority in excess of the amount finally decided, the Secretary of State may recover the excess, with interest from such time and at such rates as he thinks fit.

Without prejudice to other methods of recovery, a sum recoverable under this subsection may be recovered by withholding or reducing subsidy.

(5) Nothing in this section affects any power of the Secretary of State to vary a determination as to the amount of subsidy before the final decision is made.".

(2) The above amendment applies in relation to the amount of subsidy payable—

(a) to authorities in England for the financial year beginning on 1st April 1996 and subsequent years; and

(b) to authorities in Wales for such financial years as the Secretary of State may specify by order made by statutory instrument.

Abolition of exchequer contributions for agricultural housing

6.—(1) No contribution shall be made by the Secretary of State by virtue of Part II of Schedule

15 to the Housing Act 1985 (exchequer contributions for agricultural housing) in respect of any year after the year ending on 31st March 1996.

(2) Part II of Schedule 15 to that Act is amended as follows.

(3) For the heading substitute—

"ANNUAL GRANTS FOR AGRICULTURAL HOUSING"

(4) For paragraph 1 substitute—

"Annual grants by local housing authorities

1.—(1) Annual grants shall, notwithstanding the abolition of exchequer contributions by paragraph 6(1) of Schedule 18 to the Housing Act 1996, continue to be payable by local housing authorities in respect of agricultural housing provided in pursuance of arrangements made under section 46 of the Housing (Financial Provisions) Act 1958.

(2) Subject to the provisions of this Part of this Schedule, such annual grants are payable, in respect of any house as to which the Secretary of State originally undertook to make annual contributions under section 46 of the Housing (Financial Provisions) Act 1958, for the remainder of the 40 year period for which that undertaking was given.

(3) The amount paid by way of annual grant to the owner of a house shall not be less than the amount of the last annual contribution paid by the Secretary of State in respect of the house.".

(5) For paragraph 2(1) substitute—

"Conditions of payment of annual grant

2.—(1) It is a condition of the payment of a grant in respect of a house in any year that throughout the year the house—

(a) is reserved for members of the agricultural population, and

(b) if let, is let at a rent not exceeding the limit applicable in accordance with the following provisions of this paragraph,

and that in the opinion of the local housing authority all reasonable steps have been taken to secure the maintenance of the house in a proper state of repair during the year.".

(6) In paragraph 3(1), for "contribution" substitute "grant".

(7) For paragraph 4 substitute—

"4. A grant shall not be made or shall be reduced, as the local housing authority think fit, if (before the grant is paid) the local housing authority are of the opinion that during the whole or the greater part of the period to which the payment of the grant is referable the house has not been available as a dwelling fit for habitation, unless the authority is satisfied that that could not with reasonable diligence have been achieved.".

(8) In paragraph 5 omit the words "the Secretary of State or".

(9) After paragraph 5 insert—

"Commutation of future annual grant

6.—(1) A local authority may make an offer in writing to the person who is for the time being the owner of a house as respects which annual grant is payable under this Part of this Schedule to pay a lump sum in lieu of—

(a) the annual grant payable for the year in which the offer is accepted; and

(b) any further payments of annual grant that would (apart from this paragraph) be payable for the remainder of the period for which the original arrangements under section 46 of the Housing (Financial Provisions) Act 1958 were made.

(2) An owner may accept an offer made under this paragraph by notice in writing to the local housing authority.

(3) Subject to sub-paragraph (4) below, where such an offer is accepted the local housing authority shall pay to the owner a lump sum calculated in such manner as the authority may determine.

(4) A lump sum shall not be paid as respects a house unless the local housing authority are satisfied that the conditions in this Part of this Schedule have been observed throughout the year preceding the date on which the lump sum would otherwise be paid.

(5) On payment of a lump sum under this paragraph to the owner of a house—

(a) no further annual grants under this Part of this Schedule shall be payable in respect of the house; and

(b) the conditions described in this Part of this Schedule shall cease to apply to the house.".

(10) Nothing in this paragraph affects the operation of Part II of Schedule 15 to the Housing

Act 1985 in respect of any year ending before 1st April 1996.

PART III

ORDERS IN RELATION TO PROPERTY IN FAMILY AND MATRIMONIAL PROCEEDINGS &C.

Housing Act 1980 (c. 51)

7. In section 54(2) of the Housing Act 1980 (prohibition on assignment of protected shorthold tenancy or protected tenancy of dwelling-house), for "except in pursuance of an order under section 24 of the Matrimonial Causes Act 1973" substitute—
"except in pursuance of an order under—
    (a) section 24 of the Matrimonial Causes Act 1973 (property adjustment orders in connection with matrimonial proceedings),
    (b) section 17(1) of the Matrimonial and Family Proceedings Act 1984 (property adjustment orders after overseas divorce, &c.), or
    (c) paragraph 1 of Schedule 1 to the Children Act 1989 (orders for financial relief against parents).".

Housing Act 1985 (c. 68)

8.—(1) Section 39 of the Housing Act 1985 (exempted disposals) is amended as follows.
(2) In subsection (1), for paragraph (c) substitute—
"(c) it is a disposal of the whole of the house in pursuance of any such order as is mentioned in subsection (3);".
(3) After subsection (2) add—
"(3) The orders referred to in subsection (1)(c) are orders under—
    (a) section 24 or 24A of the Matrimonial Causes Act 1973 (property adjustment orders or orders for the sale of property in connection with matrimonial proceedings),
    (b) section 2 of the Inheritance (Provision for Family and Dependants) Act 1975 (orders as to financial provision to be made from estate),
    (c) section 17 of the Matrimonial and Family Proceedings Act 1984 (property adjustment orders or orders for the sale of property after overseas divorce, &c.), or
    (d) paragraph 1 of Schedule 1 to the Children Act 1989 (orders for financial relief against parents).".

9. In section 88(2) of the Housing Act 1985 (cases where secure tenant is a successor) after "proceedings)" insert "or section 17(1) of the Matrimonial and Family Proceedings Act 1984 (property adjustment orders after overseas divorce, &c.)".

10. In section 89 of the Housing Act 1985 (succession to periodic tenancy), for subsection (3) substitute—
"(3) Where there is no person qualified to succeed the tenant, the tenancy ceases to be a secure tenancy—
    (a) when it is vested or otherwise disposed of in the course of the administration of the tenant's estate, unless the vesting or other disposal is in pursuance of an order made under—
        (i) section 24 of the Matrimonial Causes Act 1973 (property adjustment orders made in connection with matrimonial proceedings),
        (ii) section 17(1) of the Matrimonial and Family Proceedings Act 1984 (property adjustment orders after overseas divorce, &c.), or
        (iii) paragraph 1 of Schedule 1 to the Children Act 1989 (orders for financial relief against parents); or
    (b) when it is known that when the tenancy is so vested or disposed of it will not be in pursuance of such an order.".

11. In section 90(3) of the Housing Act 1985 (devolution of secure tenancy), for paragraph (a) and the word "or" at the end of the paragraph substitute—
"(a) the vesting or other disposal is in pursuance of an order made under—
        (i) section 24 of the Matrimonial Causes Act 1973 (property adjustment orders in connection with matrimonial proceedings),
        (ii) section 17(1) of the Matrimonial and Family Proceedings Act 1984 (property adjustment orders after overseas divorce, &c.), or
        (iii) paragraph 1 of Schedule 1 to the Children Act 1989 (orders for financial relief against parents), or".

12. In section 91(3) of the Housing Act 1985 (cases where assignment of secure tenancy permitted), for paragraph (b) substitute—
"(b) an assignment in pursuance of an order made under—

(i) section 24 of the Matrimonial Causes Act 1973 (property adjustment orders in connection with matrimonial proceedings),

(ii) section 17(1) of the Matrimonial and Family Proceedings Act 1984 (property adjustment orders after overseas divorce, &c.), or

(iii) paragraph 1 of Schedule 1 to the Children Act 1989 (orders for financial relief against parents);".

13. In section 99B(2) of the Housing Act 1985 (persons qualifying for compensation for improvements) for paragraph (e) substitute—

"(e) a person to whom the tenancy was assigned by the improving tenant in pursuance of an order made under—

(i) section 24 of the Matrimonial Causes Act 1973 (property adjustment orders in connection with matrimonial proceedings),

(ii) section 17(1) of the Matrimonial and Family Proceedings Act 1984 (property adjustment orders after overseas divorce, &c.), or

(iii) paragraph 1 of Schedule 1 to the Children Act 1989 (orders for financial relief against parents);".

14. In section 101(3) of the Housing Act 1985 (rent not increased on account of tenant's improvements: qualifying persons) for paragraph (c) substitute—

"(c) a person to whom the tenancy was assigned by the tenant in pursuance of an order made under—

(i) section 24 of the Matrimonial Causes Act 1973 (property adjustment orders in connection with matrimonial proceedings),

(ii) section 17(1) of the Matrimonial and Family Proceedings Act 1984 (property adjustment orders after overseas divorce, &c.), or

(iii) paragraph 1 of Schedule 1 to the Children Act 1989 (orders for financial relief against parents);".

15.—(1) Section 160 of the Housing Act 1985 (exempted disposals in relation to right to buy) is amended as follows.

(2) In subsection (1), for paragraph (c) substitute—

"(c) it is a disposal of the whole of the dwelling–house in pursuance of any such order as is mentioned in subsection (3);".

(3) After subsection (2) add—

"(3) The orders referred to in subsection (1)(c) are orders under—

(a) section 24 or 24A of the Matrimonial Causes Act 1973 (property adjustment orders or orders for the sale of property in connection with matrimonial proceedings),

(b) section 2 of the Inheritance (Provision for Family and Dependants) Act 1975 (orders as to financial provision to be made from estate),

(c) section 17 of the Matrimonial and Family Proceedings Act 1984 (property adjustment orders or orders for the sale of property after overseas divorce, &c.), or

(d) paragraph 1 of Schedule 1 to the Children Act 1989 (orders for financial relief against parents).".

16. In section 171B(4)(b) of the Housing Act 1985 (extent of preserved right to buy: qualifying successors of tenant), after sub-paragraph (ii) insert—

"or

(iii) a property adjustment order under section 17(1) of the Matrimonial and Family Proceedings Act 1984 (property adjustment orders after overseas divorce, &c.), or

(iv) an order under paragraph 1 of Schedule 1 to the Children Act 1989 (orders for financial relief against parents),".

17. In paragraph 1(2) of Schedule 6A to the Housing Act 1985 (obligation to redeem landlord's share: excluded disposals), for paragraph (c) substitute—

"(c) it is a disposal in pursuance of an order under—

(i) section 24 or 24A of the Matrimonial Causes Act 1973 (property adjustment orders or orders for the sale of property in connection with matrimonial proceedings),

(ii) section 2 of the Inheritance (Provision for Family and Dependants) Act 1975 (orders as to financial provision to be made from estate),

(iii) section 17 of the Matrimonial and Family Proceedings Act 1984 (property adjustment orders or orders for the sale of property after overseas divorce, &c.), or

(iv) paragraph 1 of Schedule 1 to the Children Act 1989 (orders for financial relief against parents),".

Landlord and Tenant Act 1987 (c. 31)

18. In section 4(2) of the Landlord and Tenant Act 1987 (right of first refusal: excluded disposals), for paragraph (c) substitute—
    "(c) a disposal in pursuance of an order made under—
        (i) section 24 of the Matrimonial Causes Act 1973 (property adjustment orders in connection with matrimonial proceedings),
        (ii) section 24A of the Matrimonial Causes Act 1973 (orders for the sale of property in connection with matrimonial proceedings) where the order includes provision requiring the property concerned to be offered for sale to a person or class of persons specified in the order,
        (iii) section 2 of the Inheritance (Provision for Family and Dependants) Act 1975 (orders as to financial provision to be made from estate),
        (iv) section 17(1) of the Matrimonial and Family Proceedings Act 1984 (property adjustment orders after overseas divorce, &c.),
        (v) section 17(2) of the Matrimonial and Family Proceedings Act 1984 (orders for the sale of property after overseas divorce, &c.) where the order includes provision requiring the property concerned to be offered for sale to a person or class of persons specified in the order, or
        (vi) paragraph 1 of Schedule 1 to the Children Act 1989 (orders for financial relief against parents);".

Housing Act 1988 (c. 50)

19.—(1) Paragraph 4 of Schedule 11 to the Housing Act 1988 (repayment of discount on disposal: exempted disposals) is amended as follows.
    (2) In sub-paragraph (1), for paragraph (c) substitute—
        "(c) it is a disposal of the whole of the house in pursuance of any such order as is mentioned in sub-paragraph (4) below;".
    (3) After sub-paragraph (3) add—
        "(4) The orders referred to in sub-paragraph (1)(c) above are orders under—
        (a) section 24 or 24A of the Matrimonial Causes Act 1973 (property adjustment orders or orders for the sale of property in connection with matrimonial proceedings),
        (b) section 2 of the Inheritance (Provision for Family and Dependants) Act 1975 (orders as to financial provision to be made from estate),
        (c) section 17 of the Matrimonial and Family Proceedings Act 1984 (property adjustment orders or orders for the sale of property after overseas divorce, &c.), or
        (d) paragraph 1 of Schedule 1 to the Children Act 1989 (orders for financial relief against parents).".

PART IV

OTHER HOUSING PROVISIONS

Abolition of consent requirements for exercise of certain housing powers

20. Section 16 of the Housing Act 1985 (consent requirements for exercise of certain housing powers) shall cease to have effect.

Amendments of section 133 of the Housing Act 1988

21.—(1) Section 133 of the Housing Act 1988 (consent required for certain subsequent disposals) is amended as follows.
    (2) After subsection (1) insert—
        "(1A) This section does not apply if the original disposal was made before the date on which this section comes into force.".
    The amendment made by this sub-paragraph shall be deemed always to have had effect.
    (3) After subsection (2) insert—
        "(2A) Consent required for the purposes of this section may be given either generally to all persons who may require such consent or to any particular person or description of person who may require such consent.".
    (4) After subsection (5) insert—
        "(5A) A person seeking any consent required by virtue of this section is not required to consult a tenant of the land or house proposed to be disposed of if—
        (a) consent is sought for the disposal of the land or house to that tenant or to persons including that tenant; or

(b) consent is sought subject to the condition that the land or house is vacant at the time of the disposal;

and, accordingly, subsection (5) does not apply in either case.".

Abolition of requirements for Treasury consent

22.—(1) Any requirement in the following enactments for the consent or approval of the Treasury shall cease to have effect—

(a) in the Rent Act 1977—

section 63(2) (schemes for appointment of rent officers), and

Schedule 10 (rent assessment committees);

(b) Schedule 26 to the Local Government, Planning and Land Act 1980 (urban development corporations);

(c) in the Housing Act 1985—

section 156(4) (liability to repay discount: approved lending institutions), and

section 429A (financial assistance for persons concerned with housing management);

(d) in the Housing Associations Act 1985—

section 85(2) (meaning of "recognised body"), and

paragraphs 5 and 6 of Schedule 6 (remuneration, allowances and pensions);

(e) Schedule 7 to the Housing Act 1988 (constitution of housing action trusts);

(f) Schedule 17 to the Leasehold Reform, Housing and Urban Development Act 1993 (constitution of the Urban Regeneration Agency).

(2) In Schedule 10 to the Rent Act 1977 (rent assessment committees), in paragraph 9(c), for "the Minister for the Civil Service" substitute "the Secretary of State".

(3) The amendments in this paragraph do not extend to Scotland.

Disposal of dwelling-houses subject to secure tenancies: consultation requirements

23. In section 106A of the Housing Act 1985 (consultation before disposal to private sector landlord) at the end insert—

"(3) That Schedule, and this section, do not apply in relation to any disposal of an interest in land by a local authority if—

(a) the interest has been acquired by the authority (whether compulsorily or otherwise) following the making of an order for compulsory purchase under any enactment, other than section 290 (acquisition of land for clearance),

(b) the order provides that the interest is being acquired for the purpose of disposal to a registered social landlord, and

(c) such a disposal is made within one year of the acquisition.

(4) In this section "registered social landlord" has the same meaning as in Part I of the Housing Act 1996.".

Powers of local housing authorities to acquire land for housing purposes

24.—(1) In section 17(2) of the Housing Act 1985 (acquisition of land for housing purposes) at end insert "or facilities which serve a beneficial purpose in connection with the requirements of persons for whom housing accommodation is provided".

(2) In section 74(3)(b) of the Local Government and Housing Act 1989 (land excluded from Housing Revenue Account) at end insert "or facilities which serve a beneficial purpose in connection with the requirements of persons for whom housing accommodation is provided".

Housing action trusts

25.—(1) In section 63 of the Housing Act 1988 (objects etc of housing action trusts)—

(a) in subsection (1)(d) after "conditions" insert "of those living"; and

(b) after subsection (2) insert—

"(2A) For the avoidance of doubt it is hereby declared that it is immaterial for the purposes of this section whether action taken by a housing action trust for achieving its objects or exercising the powers conferred on it by subsection (2) above also—

(a) benefits persons who do not live in the designated area; or

(b) improves the social conditions or general environment of an area outside the designated area.".

(2) In section 64 of that Act (proposals for area of housing action trust) in subsections (1) and (5) after "in" insert "relation to".

Preserved right to buy

26.—(1) In section 171B of the Housing Act 1985 (qualifying persons in relation to preserved right to buy)—

    (a) in subsection (4)(a), at the end insert "or in whom that assured tenancy vested under section 17 of the Housing Act 1988 (statutory succession to assured tenancy)"; and

    (b) in subsection (5)(b), for "subsection (4)(a) or (b)" substitute "subsection (4)".

(2) The amendment made by sub-paragraph (1)(a) does not apply in relation to qualifying disposals (within the meaning of Part V of the Housing Act 1985) made before, or made under a contract entered into before, the day on which this paragraph comes into force.

Local authority assistance in connection with mortgages

27.—(1) Section 442 of the Housing Act 1985 (agreements by local authority to indemnify mortgagees) is amended as follows.

(2) In subsection (1)—

    (a) for the words from the beginning to "house" (in the second place it appears) substitute "A local authority may enter into an agreement with a person or body making an advance on the security of a house (or a building to be converted into a house)";

    (b) for "society or body" (in both places) substitute "mortgagee".

(3) After subsection (1) insert—

    "(1A) The local authority may only enter into the agreement if the advance is for one or more of the purposes specified in subsection (1) of section 435; and subsections (2) to (4) of that section apply in relation to power to enter into such an agreement as they apply to the power to make an advance under that section.".

(4) In subsection (2) for "building society or recognised body" substitute "mortgagee";

(5) Subsections (4) and (5) shall cease to have effect.

28. In section 443 of the Housing Act 1985 (local authority contributions to mortgage costs)—

    (a) in subsection (1), for "a building society or recognised body" substitute "any person or body"; and

    (b) subsections (2) and (3) shall cease to have effect.

29.—(1) For section 444 of the Housing Act 1985 (meaning of "recognised body" and "relevant advance") substitute—

"Relevant advances for the purposes of section 443

    444. The expression "relevant advance" in section 443 (contributions to mortgage costs) means an advance made to a person whose interest in the house (or building to be converted into a house) on the security of which the advance is made is, or was, acquired by virtue of a conveyance of the freehold, or a grant or assignment of a long lease, by a housing authority.".

(2) Any reference in an agreement made under section 442 of the Housing Act 1985 before the date on which this paragraph comes into force which defines the expression "recognised body" by reference to section 444 of that Act shall (notwithstanding the amendment made by sub-paragraph (1) of this paragraph) continue to have the same meaning as it had immediately before that date.

30. In paragraph 21(d) of Schedule 13 to the Local Government (Wales) Act 1994 (Residuary Body a local authority for purposes of section 442 of Housing Act 1985—

    (a) omit the words from "(so" to "subsection (1)(b))", and

    (b) after "local authority" insert "agreement to indemnify mortgagee and".

Section 227   SCHEDULE 19

Repeals

Part I

Social rented sector

Chapter	Short title	Extent of repeal
1985 c. 69.	Housing Associations Act 1985.	Sections 3 to 8. Section 9(1) and (4). Section 11. Sections 13 to 33. Section 36A. Section 67. Section 69(1)(e) and (g). Schedules 2 and 3.

Chapter	Short title	Extent of repeal
1988 c. 9.	Local Government Act 1988.	Section 24(5)(a) and (c).
1988 c. 50.	Housing Act 1988.	Sections 48 and 49. Section 55(1)(a). Section 58. Section 79(6) to (10). In section 92(2), the words from "but" to the end. In Schedule 6, paragraphs 3 to 6 and 9 to 23.
1989 c. 42.	Local Government and Housing Act 1989.	Section 182.
1993 c. 10.	Charities Act 1993.	In Schedule 6, paragraph 21(3).
1993 c. 28.	Leasehold Reform, Housing and Urban Development Act 1993.	Section 134.

PART II

HOUSES IN MULTIPLE OCCUPATION

Chapter	Short title	Extent of repeal
1985 c. 68.	Housing Act 1985.	In section 365(5), the words "and (e)". In section 368(3), the words from "and if" to the end. Part XII. Section 619(1).
1989 c.42.	Local Government and Housing Act 1989.	In Schedule 9— (a) paragraphs 45 to 47 and 53(2). (b) in paragraph 53(3) the words from "after" to "(2A)" and" and the words "of that subsection", (c) paragraphs 55(2), 63, 66 and 68(2). In Schedule 11, paragraphs 75 and 76.

PART III

TENANTS' RIGHTS

Chapter	Short title	Extent of repeal
1985 c. 70.	Landlord and Tenant Act 1985.	In section 19(3), the words "within the meaning of Part I of the Arbitration Act 1996". Section 19(4).
1987 c. 31.	Landlord and Tenant Act 1987.	In section 4(2)(aa), the words "consisting of the creation of an estate or interest". In section 20(1), the definition of "the new landlord". In section 20(2), the words "or counter-offer" in each place where they occur. Section 24(2)(a)(ii). Section 31(5). In section 60(1), the definition of "rent assessment committee".
1996 c. 23.	Arbitration Act 1996.	In Schedule 3, paragraph 43.

PART IV

ASSURED TENANCIES

Chapter	Short title	Extent of repeal
1985 c. 68.	Housing Act 1985.	In section 553(2)(b), the words "or under section 20(1)(c) of that Act (notice served in respect of assured shorthold tenancies)".
1988 c. 50.	Housing Act 1988.	Section 20(7). In section 22, in subsection (1), the words from "in respect of" to "above" and, in subsection (2), the word "or" after paragraph (a). In Schedule 17, paragraph 60(c).

PART V

LEASEHOLD REFORM

Chapter	Short title	Extent of repeal
1993 c. 28.	Leasehold Reform, Housing and Urban Development Act 1993.	In section 1, in subsection (3), the words "the freehold of it is owned by the person who owns the freehold of the relevant premises and" and, in subsection (7), the definition of "the freeholder". In section 3(1)(a), the words "and the freehold of the whole of the building or of that part of the building is owned by the same person". In section 10(6), the definition of "the freeholder". In section 11(4)(i), the words "as is mentioned in subsection (3)(c)". In section 13, in subsection (3)(a)(iii), the words "of the person who owns the freehold of the specified premises" and "by him" and subsections (4), (6) and (7). In section 39, in subsection (3), the word "and" at the end of paragraph (b), and subsection (6). In Schedule 6, in paragraph 1(1), the definition of "the freeholder".

PART VI

HOUSING BENEFIT AND RELATED MATTERS

Chapter	Short title	Extent of repeal
1988 c. 50.	Housing Act 1988.	Section 121.
1988 c. 43.	Housing (Scotland) Act 1988.	Section 70.
1992 c. 4.	Social Security Contributions and Benefits Act 1992.	Section 130(5).
1992 c. 5.	Social Security Administration Act 1992.	Section 116(4)(a). In section 134— (a) in subsection (2)(b), the words "or rates"; (b) subsections (3), (4), (6) and (7).

Chapter	Short title	Extent of repeal
1992 c.5,	Social Security Administration Act 1992.	Sections 135 to 137. Section 140. In section 191— (a) in the definition of "rate rebate", "rent rebate" and "rent allowance", the reference to rate rebate; (b) the definitions of "rates" and "rating authority".
1992 c. 6.	Social Security (Consequential Provisions) Act 1992.	In Schedule 2, paragraph 104.
1992 c. 14.	Local Government Finance Act 1992.	In Schedule 9, paragraph 21.
1994 c. 39.	Local Government etc. (Scotland) Act 1994.	In Schedule 13, in paragraph 175, in sub-paragraph (3) the words "138(1), 139(2), (5) and (6) and 140(1), (2), (4) and (7)" and sub-paragraph (4).

PART VII

ALLOCATION OF HOUSING ACCOMMODATION

Chapter	Short title	Extent of repeal
1985 c. 68.	Housing Act 1985.	Section 22. In Schedule 1, in paragraph 2(4) the words from "until" to the end and in paragraphs 5(1) and 10(1) the words from "unless" to the end.
1996 c. 49.	Asylum and Immigration Act 1996.	In section 9(4), the definitions of "the accommodation Part", "housing authority" and "licence to occupy" and, in the definition of "tenancy" the words ", in relation to England and Wales,".

PART VIII

HOMELESSNESS

Chapter	Short title	Extent of repeal
1985 c. 68.	Housing Act 1985.	Part III.
1985 c. 71.	Housing (Consequential Provisions) Act 1985.	In Schedule 2, paragraphs 19 and 60(3).
1986 c. 63.	Housing and Planning Act 1986.	Section 14.
1987 c. 26.	Housing (Scotland) Act 1987.	In Schedule 23, paragraph 30(1).
1988 c. 50.	Housing Act 1988.	Section 1(6) and (7). Section 70.
1993 c. 23.	Asylum and Immigration Appeals Act 1993.	Sections 4 and 5. Schedule 1.
1994 c. 39.	Local Government etc. (Scotland) Act 1994.	In Schedule 13, paragraph 142(2).
1996 c. 49.	Asylum and Immigration Act 1996.	In section 9, subsection (2), in subsection (3) (a) the words "or assistance" and in subsection (4) the definition of "the homelessness Part".

PART IX

CHANGE OF LANDLORD: SECURE TENANTS

Chapter	Short title	Extent of repeal
1985 c. 68.	Housing Act 1985.	In section 32(1) and 43(1), the words from "and Part IV" to "tenants)".
1985 c. 69.	Housing Associations Act 1985.	In section 9(1), the word ", 105(6)".
1988 c. 50.	Housing Act 1988.	In section 79(2)(a), the words "either" and "or under section 94 below". Sections 93 to 114. In Schedule 2, in Ground 6, the paragraph beginning "For the purposes of this ground, every acquisition under Part IV". Schedule 12. In Schedule 17, paragraphs 38 and 39.
1989 c. 42.	Local Government and Housing Act 1989.	Section 174. In Schedule 11, paragraphs 107 and 109.
S.I. 1990/778.	Local Authorities (Capital Finance) (Consequential Amendments) Order 1990.	In the Schedule, paragraph 2.
1993 c. 28.	Leasehold Reform, Housing and Urban Development Act 1993.	Section 124(4) to (6). In Schedule 10, paragraph 1(2)(d).
1995 c. 8.	Agricultural Tenancies Act 1995.	In the Schedule, paragraph 33.
1995 c. 38.	Civil Evidence Act 1995.	In Schedule 1, paragraph 14.

PART X

CONSULTATION WITH RESPECT TO HOUSING MANAGEMENT

Chapter	Short title	Extent of repeal
1985 c. 68.	Housing Act 1985.	Sections 27A and 27AA.
1993 c. 28.	Leasehold Reform, Housing and Urban Development Act 1993.	Sections 130 and 131.

PART XI

ABOLITION OF EXCHEQUER CONTRIBUTIONS FOR AGRICULTURAL HOUSING

Chapter	Short title	Extent of repeal
1985 c. 68.	Housing Act 1985.	In section 432, the entry for Part II of Schedule 15. In Schedule 15, Part II.

PART XII

ABOLITION OF CERTAIN CONSENT REQUIREMENTS

Chapter	Short title	Extent of repeal
1985 c. 68.	Housing Act 1985.	Section 16.

PART XIII

REMOVAL OF TREASURY CONSENT REQUIREMENTS

Chapter	Short title	Extent of repeal
1977 c. 42.	Rent Act 1977.	In section 63(2)(a), the words "with the consent of the Treasury". In Schedule 10, in paragraphs 7, 7A and 8, the words "with the consent of the Minister for the Civil Service".
1980 c. 65.	Local Government Planning and Land Act 1980.	In Schedule 26, in paragraphs 8, 9 and 10, the words "with the consent of the Minister for the Civil Service" and, in paragraph 12(5), the words "given with the consent of the Minister for the Civil Service".
1985 c. 68.	Housing Act 1985.	In section 156(4), the words "with the consent of the Treasury". In section 429A, in subsections (1) and (3), the words "with the consent of the Treasury" and "with the like consent" and, in subsection (5), the words "with the consent of the Treasury".
1985 c. 69.	Housing Associations Act 1985.	In section 85(2), the words "with the consent of the Treasury". In Schedule 6, in paragraphs 5(1) and 6(1), the words "with the consent of the Treasury".
1988 c. 50.	Housing Act 1988.	In Schedule 7, in paragraph 8, the words "with the approval of the Treasury", in paragraph 9, the words "with the approval of the Treasury" and "with that approval", in paragraphs 10 and 12(2), the words "with the approval of the Treasury" and, in paragraph 12(5), the words "given with the consent of the Treasury".
1993 c. 28.	Leasehold Reform, Housing and Urban Development Act 1993.	In Schedule 17, paragraphs 2(4) and 3(8) and, in paragraph 5(5), the words "with the approval of the Treasury".

PART XIV

LOCAL AUTHORITY ASSISTANCE IN CONNECTION WITH MORTGAGES

Chapter	Short title	Extent of repeal
1974 c. 39.	Consumer Credit Act 1974.	In section 16(1)(ff), "444(1)".
1985 c. 68.	Housing Act 1985.	Section 442(4) and (5). Section 443(2) and (3). In section 459, the entry for "recognised body".
1986 c. 53.	Building Societies Act 1986.	In Schedule 18, paragraph 18(2).
1994 c. 19.	Local Government (Wales) Act 1994.	In Schedule 13, in paragraph 21(d) the words from "(so" to "subsection (1)(b))".

INDEX

Generally, references are to the relevant section or Schedule number of the Act. References to the commentary to the section or Schedule are denoted by the letter 'N'. Thus the reference s.35N is to the General Note to section 35 of the Act.

Index

Index

Index

Index